Rome

WORLD BIBLIOGRAPHICAL SERIES

General Editors:
Robert G. Neville (Executive Editor)
John J. Horton

Robert A. Myers   Hans H. Wellisch
Ian Wallace   Ralph Lee Woodward, Jr.

John J. Horton is Deputy Librarian of the University of Bradford and was formerly Chairman of its Academic Board of Studies in Social Sciences. He has maintained a longstanding interest in the discipline of area studies and its associated bibliographical problems, with special reference to European Studies. In particular he has published in the field of Icelandic and of Yugoslav studies, including the two relevant volumes in the World Bibliographical Series.

Robert A. Myers is Associate Professor of Anthropology in the Division of Social Sciences and Director of Study Abroad Programs at Alfred University, Alfred, New York. He has studied post-colonial island nations of the Caribbean and has spent two years in Nigeria on a Fulbright Lectureship. His interests include international public health, historical anthropology and developing societies. In addition to *Amerindians of the Lesser Antilles: a bibliography* (1981), *A Resource Guide to Dominica, 1493-1986* (1987) and numerous articles, he has compiled the World Bibliographical Series volumes on *Dominica* (1987), *Nigeria* (1989) and *Ghana* (1991).

Ian Wallace is Professor of German at the University of Bath. A graduate of Oxford in French and German, he also studied in Tübingen, Heidelberg and Lausanne before taking teaching posts at universities in the USA, Scotland and England. He specializes in contemporary German affairs, especially literature and culture, on which he has published numerous articles and books. In 1979 he founded the journal *GDR Monitor*, which he continues to edit under its new title *German Monitor*.

Hans H. Wellisch is Professor emeritus at the College of Library and Information Services, University of Maryland. He was President of the American Society of Indexers and was a member of the International Federation for Documentation. He is the author of numerous articles and several books on indexing and abstracting, and has published *The Conversion of Scripts and Indexing and Abstracting: an International Bibliography*, and *Indexing from A to Z*. He also contributes frequently to *Journal of the American Society for Information Science*, *The Indexer* and other professional journals.

Ralph Lee Woodward, Jr. is Director of Graduate Studies at Tulane University, New Orleans. He is the author of *Central America, a Nation Divided*, 2nd ed. (1985), as well as several monographs and more than seventy scholarly articles on modern Latin America. He has also compiled volumes in the World Bibliographical Series on *Belize* (1980), *El Salvador* (1988), *Guatemala* (Rev. Ed.) (1992) and *Nicaragua* (Rev. Ed.) (1994). Dr. Woodward edited the Central American section of the *Research Guide to Central America and the Caribbean* (1985) and is currently associate editor of Scribner's *Encyclopedia of Latin American History*.

VOLUME 222

Rome

Chris Michaelides

Compiler

CLIO PRESS

OXFORD, ENGLAND · SANTA BARBARA, CALIFORNIA
DENVER, COLORADO

© Copyright 2000 by ABC-CLIO Ltd.

British Library Cataloguing in Publication Data

Michaelides, Chris
Rome. – (World bibliographical series; v. 222)
1. Rome (Italy) – Bibliography
I. Title
016.9´45632

ISBN 1–85109–315–X

ABC-CLIO Ltd.,
Old Clarendon Ironworks,
35A Great Clarendon Street,
Oxford OX2 6AT, England.

———————

ABC-CLIO Inc.,
130 Cremona Drive,
Santa Barbara,
CA 93117, USA

Designed by Bernard Crossland.
Typeset by ABC-CLIO Ltd., Oxford, England.
Printed and bound in Great Britain by print in black, Midsomer Norton.

THE WORLD BIBLIOGRAPHICAL SERIES

This series, which is principally designed for the English speaker, will eventually cover every country (and some of the world's principal regions and cities), each in a separate volume comprising annotated entries on works dealing with its history, geography, economy and politics; and with its people, their culture, customs, religion and social organization. Attention will also be paid to current living conditions – housing, education, newspapers, clothing, etc. – that are all too often ignored in standard bibliographies; and to those particular aspects relevant to individual countries. Each volume seeks to achieve, by use of careful selectivity and critical assessment of the literature, an expression of the country and an appreciation of its nature and national aspirations, to guide the reader towards an understanding of its importance. The keynote of the series is to provide, in a uniform format, an interpretation of each country that will express its culture, its place in the world, and the qualities and background that make it unique. The views expressed in individual volumes, however, are not necessarily those of the publisher.

VOLUMES IN THE SERIES

*Dedicated to the memory of
my mother Galatea*

Contents

Contents

Contents

Contents

Introduction

A brief historical background

Rome grew up on the east bank of the Tiber, some 20 kilometres from the Tyrrhenian Sea, where an island, Isola Tiberina (Tiber Island), facilitated the crossing of the river. The proximity to the sea and the river's navigability were advantageous, both militarily and commercially, and greatly contributed to the city's later expansion. Evidence of a cluster of settlements occupying the future site of Rome dates from as early as *c.* 1500 BC, the Palatine, the Capitoline and the neighbouring hills being natural strongholds and offering protection from floods. By the 9th century BC, these settlements had formed themselves into a federation called the *Septimontium*, which was dominated by the Palatine settlement and ruled by an elected king who combined the functions of military commander and high priest. According to legend, Rome was founded on 21 April 753 or 754 BC by Romulus, a descendant of Aeneas, the hero of the Trojan War. Virgil's epic poem, the *Aeneid*, relates how Aeneas fled from Troy and came eventually to Latium, where he married the King's daughter, Lavinia; his son, Ascanius, founded Alba Longa on Lake Albano. According to other legends surrounding the foundation of Rome, there was later a dynastic dispute between Ascanius's heirs, during which Rhea Silvia (or Ilia) was condemned to enforced virginity as a priestess of Vesta, but was then raped by the god Mars and gave birth to twins Romulus and Remus; an attempt to drown the infants in the Tiber resulted in their being washed ashore near the Palatine and nursed by a she-wolf before being adopted by the shepherd Faustulus and his wife. When they grew up, the twins killed Amulius, the usurper, and restored Numitor, their grandfather and legitimate King, to the throne of Alba Longa. They also founded a new city on the site of Rome. Remus, however, was killed by Romulus after he mockingly jumped over the city walls built by his brother.

The origin of the city's name has been disputed – it has been variously explained as deriving from *Romulus*, the founder of the city; *Ruma*, the name of an Etruscan clan; from the Greek word meaning strength; or from *Rumo*, an ancient name of the Tiber and, therefore, meaning 'the city on the river'.

Until 509 BC, the city was ruled by an elected monarchy. Four Latin kings (Romulus, Numa Pompilius, Tullus Hostilius and Ancus Marcius) were succeeded by three Etruscans (Tarquinius Priscus, Servius Tullius and Tarquinius Superbus). The kings were initially controlled by the Senate, a council of 100 members, or *patres*, representing the leading clans. The decline of Etruscan dominance in Rome and the influence of a strong ruling class contributed to the overthrow of the kings and the establishment of an aristocratic Republic (509-27 BC). According to legend, the popular revolt against the Etruscans, led by Lucius Junius Brutus, was caused by the rape of Lucretia by Sextus Tarquinius, the son of Tarquinius Superbus.

Republican Rome was governed by two members of the patrician class elected annually to the civil and military leadership as joint consul. The plebeians, who were excluded from civic and religious office, formed their own state within the state, and eventually succeeded in obtaining representation in the form of the office of Tribune, established in 494 BC; by the end of the 4th century BC, they had won access to all offices of the state. In 390 BC, Rome suffered a major setback when it was sacked by the Gauls and left in ruins. The so-called Servian Wall (previously believed to date from the reign of Servius Tullius in the 6th century BC) is now generally thought to have been erected shortly after this catastrophe. It enclosed most of the Esquiline and Caelian and all of the other five hills (the Capitoline, Palatine, Aventine, Quirinal and Viminal).

The city grew in strength and became the head of a confederacy of all Italians, by 270 BC dominating the peninsula. Rome's policy of welcoming vanquished enemies as friends contributed to this expansion and its various territories were united by a common language and religion and connected by a network of well-constructed roads. After its successful wars against Carthage, the great Phoenician city in North Africa, in the 3rd and 2nd centuries BC, Rome was left in control of the Western Mediterranean. In the first half of the 2nd century BC, it extended its hold to the entire Mediterranean (which then became known as *mare nostrum* – our sea) through the conquest of Greece, Macedonia, and Syria. During the 1st century BC, the population of the city reached one million. The empire of which it was the capital was then at its most prosperous. Great fortunes were made, especially through the sale of slaves, and Greek culture had enormous influence on Roman literature, architecture and the arts. The wars in the Mediterranean also resulted in internal social problems and unrest as they made available for farm labour large numbers of slaves to the detriment of the free peasantry who, unable to compete, migrated to the city, and swelled the ranks of the urban proletariat. Tiberius Sempronius Gracchus and his brother Gaius carried out reforms to reduce urban poverty and exploitation, but their proposed re-distribution of land antagonized the propertied classes and led to their assassinations in 133 BC and 122 BC. Civil strife persisted during the first half of the 1st century BC, erupting into civil war first between Caius Marius and Sulla (88-82 BC) and later between Pompey and Julius Caesar (49-48 BC). Caesar eventually assumed total power as dictator but his attempts to deal with social problems were cut short by his assassination in 44 BC. Caesar embellished Rome with his Forum, near the Forum Romanum, and rebuilt the Curia. After his death, the Empire was divided between Mark Antony, Emilius Lepidus and Caesar Octavian, Julius Caesar's adopted son. Octavian attained absolute power in 31 BC and in 27 BC was proclaimed emperor, with the name of Augustus. During his forty-year rule, a period of relative peace and stability, he reorganized and beautified the city. He claimed that he 'inherited a city in brick and left it in marble'. Monuments built during this period include: the Ara Pacis (the Altar of Peace, with reliefs depicting the family of Augustus and legends of Rome's foundation), a huge sundial with an Egyptian obelisk as its pointer, and the Mausoleum of Augustus (all three in the Campus Martius); the Pantheon (built by Vipsanius Agrippa, as the inscription on its façade testifies, though later reconstructed under Hadrian); and a new forum between the Esquiline and Caesar's Forum. In 7 AD, Augustus reorganized the municipal administration of the city dividing it into fourteen *regiones* (wards, regions), which were sub-divided into *vici* (precincts), each with its own administrative officers reporting to the emperor.

In the following centuries, Rome reached the peak of its power as the capital of an empire that extended from India to Spain, Gaul and Britain. The city was adorned with the spoils of the various conquered countries and its population reached 1,200,000. The great fire of 64 AD, which destroyed about one third of the city, encouraged more systematic urban planning with broad avenues and secondary streets forming a grid over part of the city. It also brought about great changes in the materials used in the construction of buildings, with fire-resistant materials such as concrete, stone and brick now being used instead of timber. The fire also enabled Nero to construct the Domus Aurea (Golden House), an architectural folly which covered twenty-five times the area of the Colosseum (which was built in 80 AD on the site of the palace's ornamental lake).

During the Flavian dynasty (69-96 AD), a number of other works embellished the city. Domitian, the last Flavian emperor, built a huge palace (the Domus Augustana) on the Palatine, which was to remain the residence of the emperors for the next three hundred years. Domitian also built a new circus (whose central area is the present Piazza Navona), and during his reign work started on a new forum, which was completed under Nerva. Other emperors in the 2nd century added temples, baths, fora, and stadiums. The Forum of Trajan, the largest of all the fora, was officially dedicated in 112 AD.

Constantine, the first Christian Emperor, established (with the Edict of Milan in 313) religious toleration for Christianity. In 330, he made Constantinople the capital of the Empire but Rome's loss of political prestige was compensated for by the growing importance of the bishop of Rome as the leader, the prince, of all other bishops. With the development of the cult of the saints in the 4th and 5th centuries, Rome, as the burial place of St Peter and St Paul, became a major pilgrimage centre and the heart of the Christian world. The city's monuments evoking ancient glory also played a major role in shaping Rome's dominant place in the medieval world. The earliest Christian places of worship were unobtrusive and hidden in the urban fabric; burial places were outside the city walls. Constantine founded several important churches in Rome, monumental in size and splendidly decorated, although located far from the pagan centre. The basilicas of S. Giovanni in Laterano and St Peter's were both erected during his reign, the former near the Aurelian Wall in the south east and the latter on the Vatican Hill, outside the city limits. Large funerary basilicas, such as S. Sebastiano and S. Lorenzo fuori le mura, were also built outside the city walls near the shrines of the martyrs. S. Maria Maggiore was added later in the century. The location of these splendid churches influenced the future development of the city.

Over the next five centuries, the city suffered a succession of barbarian invasions, beginning with the Visigoths under Alaric I in 410. They were followed by the Vandals under Genserick (455), the Goths under Totila (546), the Lombards (568), and the Saracens (846). The fear of invasion prompted the construction of a new city wall, called the Aurelian Wall as it was begun during the reign of Aurelian (270-275), although it was completed under Probus (276-282). This covered a much wider area than previous fortifications – indeed, it is almost 12 miles long. During the Middle Ages, when the population of Rome declined drastically, the inhabited part of Rome (the *abitato*) was contained within the bend of the Tiber and large areas within the wall (the *disabitato*) were sparsely populated.

The last Roman Emperor of the West, Romulus Augustulus, was deposed by the German chieftain Odoacer in 476, and by the 6th century Rome was politically just another city of the Byzantine Empire, whose Western capital was Ravenna. In the 8th century, it became the capital of the temporal possessions of the papacy, and after the coronation of Charlemagne in Rome in 800, it became, in theory if not in reality, the capital of the Holy Roman Empire. Its population continued to decline dramatically.

Following the Saracen invasion and the looting of St Peter's in 846, the Leonine Wall, named after Pope Leo IV, was constructed enclosing the basilica of St Peter's, its surrounding buildings, and the area of the Borgo (the *Civitas Leonina*).

A municipal administration, the *Comune*, was established in 1144, with a senatorial palace on the Capitoline Hill, and the struggle between it, the papacy, and the aristocracy was central to the history of the city during the 12th and the 13th centuries, a period of bitter rivalries between noble families such as the Orsini and the Colonna.

In 1300, Pope Boniface VIII proclaimed the first Jubilee, and some 200,000 pilgrims visited the city. In 1302, his claim that papal authority was superior to that of secular rulers brought about a rupture in relations with the French monarchy, which was to have a grave consequence when Clement V, under pressure from Philip IV of France, transferred the papal see to Avignon, thus beginning the so-called 'Babylonian captivity' of the papacy that lasted from 1309 to 1377. The absence of the papal court from Rome impoverished the city, whose population fell to under 20,000. During those years, the *Comune* in Rome achieved the importance it had in other city states on the peninsula, and Cola di Rienzo's revolution in 1347, when he proclaimed himself a tribune of the people, attempted to revive the city's ancient glory. Cola's rule was, however, short-lived. The return of the papacy in 1377 was followed by the Great Schism (during which two lines of rival popes, one based in Rome and the other at Avignon, each claimed authority over the Church), which lasted for some forty years, ending with the election of Pope Martin V Colonna in 1417. Martin V laid the foundations of an authoritarian papacy, and firmly established both the pope's spiritual leadership and his power as the temporal ruler of extensive possessions in central Italy, the latter enduring until 1870. Later in the century, especially during the reigns of Nicholas V (1447-55) and Eugenius IV (1471-84), Rome also became one of the major centres of Italian humanism. Roman humanism was closely related to the functions of the Curia and the administrative needs of the Renaissance papacy.

The next three centuries were the golden age of Rome's art and architecture thanks to the patronage and town-planning schemes of a succession of munificent popes, from Sixtus IV to Alexander VII. Artists from all over Europe came to Rome to study its monuments as well as the great public and private collections of classical antiquities which were constantly being enriched by new discoveries – the collections in the Palazzo dei Conservatori on the Capitoline Hill, the Cortile del Belvedere in the Vatican, the Palazzo Farnese and many others were training grounds for innumerable artists whose drawings and prints disseminated knowledge of Rome's classical past. Their works are also important records of the appearance of the city, and of monuments that have since disappeared. As well as being a period in which antiquity was rediscovered and studied, the Renaissance was also, paradoxically, a period when the destruction of ancient remains was far greater than in any of the preceding centuries, ancient buildings serving as quarries for materials used in new buildings. This tendency was to continue in the 17th century, the most notorious example being the removal, under Pope Urban VIII Barberini, of ancient bronze beams from the portico of the Pantheon for the construction of the Baldacchino in St Peter's, which inspired the famous pasquinade 'Quod non fecerunt barbari, fecerunt Barberini' ('What the barbarians did not do, the Barberini did').

Artists in Rome also copied and made more accessible contemporary art commissioned by popes and other patrons of the arts. Some of the greatest masterpieces of the towering geniuses of Western civilization were created in Rome – Bramante's new St Peter's (begun in 1506), Michelangelo's ceiling of the Sistine Chapel (1508-12) and *The Last Judgement* (1541), and Raphael's Vatican *Stanze* (1509-17).

The Sack of Rome in 1527 by the troops of Emperor Charles V sent shock waves throughout Europe, devastated the city reducing its population from 50,000 to 30,000, and dispersed its artistic community. Rome recovered during the pontificate of Paul III Farnese (1534-49), who reasserted papal authority by convening the Council of Trent, which met intermittently between 1545 and 1563 and provided legislation aimed at reforming the internal life and discipline of the church and replying to the doctrinal challenges of the Protestant Reformation. The second half of the 16th century was also a period of religious conservatism and intolerance. The Roman

Introduction

Ghetto was created in 1555 and the publication of the Index of Forbidden Books in 1559 marked the real beginning of the Counter-Reformation in Rome. New orders of Catholic clergy were founded – among them the Jesuits, Theatines and the Oratorians.

The reassertion of Catholicism was also translated into grandiose town-planning schemes for the capital of the Catholic faith – those of Sixtus V included new thoroughfares radiating from S. Maria Maggiore, the repair of aqueducts, and new churches and palaces. Numerous obelisks were erected and pagan monuments were 'christianized' (the statue of St Peter was placed on top of the Column of Trajan and that of St Paul on top of the Column of Marcus Aurelius).

The city also became the stage for splendid celebrations and festivals, accompanied by spectacular ephemeral decorations, from Charles V's triumphal procession through the city in 1536 (only nine years after his troops' sacking of the city) to the celebrations organized for Queen Christina of Sweden in 1668.

In the 17th century, Rome became the artistic capital of the world, its artistic heritage and lavish commissions from a wide spectrum of patrons attracting artists from all over Italy and Europe (among them Nicolas Poussin and Claude Lorrain, who both spent most of their creative years in Rome, Caravaggio, Rubens, and many others). Huge private collections of antiquities, and Renaissance and contemporary art, were built up by popes and their families (among them the Borghese, Barberini, Colonna, and Doria Pamphilj collections) and private connoisseurs and antiquarians (such as Cassiano Dal Pozzo). With Gianlorenzo Bernini (1598-1680) as its leading genius, Rome was transformed into the Baroque city *par excellence*. Sculptor, architect, draughtsman, stage designer, and painter, Bernini worked for nine popes from Paul V Borghese to Clement IX Rospigliosi and, for over fifty years, he was the controlling influence on most aspects of artistic production in the city. His greatest architectural achievement was the construction of St Peter's Square (1656-67) and its colonnade.

The artistic vitality of Rome continued in the 18th century when it became the centre of a thriving art market generated by foreign visitors on their Grand Tour – a huge number of portraits of noble visitors with the city's monuments in the background, and of paintings and prints depicting the city's ancient ruins or the buildings and public spaces created in the 17th and 18th centuries, were produced. Pompeo Batoni, Gaspar Van Wittel, Giovanni Paolo Pannini, Hubert Robert, and Piranesi are the most prominent among the large number of artists who produced work for this market. The first half of the century also saw a resurgence of public commissions (for example, the completion of the basilica of S. Giovanni in Laterano, the Trevi Fountain, and the Spanish Steps). Rome continued to be a centre of antiquarianism and some of the private collections built up during this period, such as the collection of Cardinal Alessandro Albani, were major attractions for visitors. In the second half of the century it became the centre of Neo-classicism, the movement that was given its impetus by new archaeological excavations in and around Rome and the discovery of Pompeii and Herculaneum. Most of the theorists and practitioners of the movement were active in Rome – Johann Joachim Winckelmann,

Anton Raffael Mengs, Angelika Kauffmann, Jacques-Louis David, Bertel Thorvaldsen and Antonio Canova.

The Napoleonic Wars put a temporary stop to the Grand Tour (though foreign visitors began to return after 1815). In February 1798, Rome was occupied by French troops under general Berthier and the first Roman Republic was proclaimed. Pius VI Braschi was exiled to France, where he died the following year. Papal rule was restored in 1800 with Pius VII Chiaramonti (1800-23). His relations with Napoleon were initially good (in 1801 he signed the Concordat and in 1804 he crowned Napoleon Emperor) but his resistance to Napoleon's attempts to dominate the Catholic Church led to his imprisonment in Savona and France between 1809 and 1814, when Rome came, once more, under French rule. During this period, archaeological excavations (for example Trajan's Forum) and new town-planning projects were carried forward. In 1811, Napoleon requisitioned thousands of works of art (including some of the city's greatest treasures) for the Louvre in Paris. Most of these were returned after 1815.

After the restoration of the papacy, Pius VII rebuilt the Piazza del Popolo (1816-24), Giuseppe Valadier's design unifying various elements (the 15th-century church of S. Maria del Popolo, the 16th-century Porta del Popolo and the 17th-century churches of S. Maria di Montesanto and S. Maria dei Miracoli), and constructed the Pincian Gardens overlooking the piazza. The area between Piazza del Popolo and Piazza di Spagna became, during the first half of the century, the artistic centre of Rome, with colonies of English, French, German, Flemish, and American artists living there and meeting in cafés such as the Caffè Greco (in Via dei Condotti) and Caffè Aragno (in Via del Corso). The French Academy moved to the Villa Medici, on the Pincio, in 1803.

Rome remained unaffected by the revolutions in 1831 but the initial liberal attitude of Pius IX soon after his accession in 1846 proved to be a false dawn, the assassination, on 15 November 1848, of Pellegrino Rossi, his minister of the interior and effective head of government, precipitating the revolution in Rome, the flight of Pius IX to Gaeta in the Kingdom of the two Sicilies, and the proclamation, in 1849, of the second Roman Republic by the Constituent Assembly. The Republic was again short-lived; within a year it had been suppressed by the Catholic countries, which reinstated Pius IX in 1850.

Between 1859 and 1861, most of the temporal domains of the church were seized in the process of the unification of Italy. In the 1860s, attempts to make Rome the capital of the new state either through negotiation (Cavour's method) or by force (Garibaldi's) failed because of the resistance of other Catholic powers, notably France. The right moment presented itself in 1870 when, during the Franco-Prussian War, the French troops protecting the Pope were removed from Rome. Italian troops stormed Rome and, after the breach in the Aurelian Wall near Porta Pia on 20 September 1870, brought temporal papal power to an end. On 1 February 1871, Rome was proclaimed the capital of the Kingdom of Italy. Relations between Italy and the Holy See remained hostile, the Pope rejecting the assurances provided by the

Introduction

Law of Papal Guarantees of May 1871 which stated the prerogatives of the Pope and the Holy See (which included extraterritoriality for the Vatican and defined the relationship between Church and State in Italy) and considering himself a 'prisoner' in the Vatican palace. The Roman Question was finally settled in 1929 with the Lateran Accords, which recognized Roman Catholicism as the religion of the state and acknowledged the sovereignty and independence of a new state, the Vatican City, which was declared to be neutral and inviolable territory.

During its first fifty years as the new capital of Italy, the appearance of Rome underwent enormous change, expanding outward (the 'oilstain' expansion) in order to accommodate the huge influx of people. New residential districts of four- or five-storey houses were created on the Esquiline, and in the Castro Pretorio and Prati districts. Most ministerial offices were initially housed in former convents and papal offices. A new administrative centre was planned along the Via XX Settembre, beginning with the Palazzo delle Finanze (1872-79) and the Palazzo Montecitorio, which was adapted to house the Chamber of Deputies.

New housing for civil servants and administrative buildings were also built in areas previously occupied by the great villas and their huge gardens, the 'green belt' of Rome, most of which were sold by the nobility as building lots for residential development. The central railway station, which had opened in the 1860s and was built on the grounds of Villa Peretti Montalto, was dramatically enlarged, making Rome the centre of a vast railway network, though its expansion was beset with problems because of the unsuitability of the site and the presence of antiquities in the vicinity. New arterial roads were created – the Via Nazionale (with the Piazza delle Terme [now the Piazza della Repubblica] laid out at its end, beside S. Maria degli Angeli), the Corso Vittorio Emanuele II, and the Via XX Settembre. The construction of the Tiber embankment (the *muraglioni*) freed the city from the danger of flooding. The Vittoriano, the monument to Vittorio Emanuele II that dominates Piazza Venezia, the construction of which necessitated the destruction of part of the Capitoline Hill and the medieval quarter of the city, was inaugurated in 1911. The Palazzo delle Esposizioni (on the Via Nazionale), inaugurated in 1883, a building that still remains Rome's centre for major art exhibitions, housed several biennial (later quadrennial) exhibitions. Rome also hosted the International Exhibition of 1911, organized to celebrate the first fifty years of the Italian Kingdom. Its legacy was the development of the area around the Viale delle belle arti into a museum district; it includes the Palazzo delle belle arti – which, since 1915, has housed the Galleria dell'arte moderna e contemporanea, and the British School at Rome (originally the English Pavilion, designed by Sir Edwin Lutyens).

During the Fascist era, Mussolini's town-planning schemes aiming to emulate Ancient Rome's imperial grandeur included the opening of new thoroughfares such as the Via dell'Impero (1932), now called Via dei Fori Imperiali, which cut through the newly excavated Imperial Fora; and the Via della Conciliazione (the construction of which began in 1936, though it opened in 1950), which destroyed the medieval district of the Borgo. Construction also began on the new district to the south of Rome originally intended to house the Universal Exhibition of 1942, hence known as EUR (Esposizione Universale di Roma). The district was to be the first step toward the expansion of Rome along the motorway which opened in 1939, linking the city with Ostia. The plan was abandoned during the Second World War, however, in the 1950s and 1960s EUR was developed into an administrative, cultural, and residential area. New buildings in this area include the Velodromo and the Palazzo dello Sport, constructed on the occasion of the Olympic Games in 1960. A competition for the design of a Congress Centre took place in 1998.

The Cinecittà studios were also created during the Fascist era, Mussolini seeing the great potential of cinema as a propaganda weapon. Inaugurated in 1937, they have been at the centre of Italian film production ever since. Countless films have been made there, from neorealist masterpieces to Hollywood epics, from Italian-style comedies to the avant-garde films of Antonioni, Visconti and Fellini. Today the studios are mostly used for television productions and also for American films.

During the Second World War, Rome was damaged by Allied bombings in 1943 (the basilica of S. Lorenzo fuori le Mura being the most important casualty) and the German occupation. After the proclamation of the Republic in 1946, Rome became the capital both of Italy and of the newly-created region of Lazio.

Today the ancient walled city covers only 4 per cent of the modern municipality's area (1,507 square kilometres) and is the smallest of the city's twelve administrative zones. The walled centre is divided into twenty-one *rioni* (districts), the fourteen historic ones corresponding to the Augustan regions (*regiones*) and eight modern ones created post-1870 to include the areas outside the historic centre of the city (Prati, the twenty-second *rione*, lies outside the Wall). In the 1991 census, the population of Rome was 2,830,569.

The city, which lacks large-scale commerce and industry, is an important administrative centre and one of the great cultural and tourist attractions of the world. A city rich in contrasts, its heritage spans a period of nearly 3,000 years. In recent years an impressive programme of museum refurbishments and new displays of their collections, accompanied by more generous opening hours, has been carried out. The Galleria Borghese reopened, splendidly restored, in 1998 after some fourteen years of total or partial closure. This was followed by the redeployment, between 1998 and 2000, of the collections of the Museo nazionale romano into newly renovated spaces in the Palazzo Altemps, the Palazzo Massimo, the Museo delle Terme di Diocleziano, and the Crypta Balbi. At the time of writing, the refurbishment has recently taken place of the Museo nazionale etrusco di Villa Giulia (with future plans to extend the display of its collections into the nearby Villa Poniatowski) and of the Musei Capitolini. A new temporary exhibition space has also been created in the Scuderie Papali (Papal stables) on the Quirinale. The Millennium Jubilee celebrations have also included the opening of a new and more spacious entrance hall to the Vatican Museums and the completion of restoration work on numerous churches. New cultural spaces planned include the Centro per le arti contemporanee (designed by Zaha Hadid) and the Città della Musica (designed by Renzo Piano).

Introduction

The bibliography

The bibliography, which contains 881 entries, aims to provide a reference guide to Rome for scholars, librarians and anyone with a general interest in the city, its history and culture. The emphasis is on English-language publications which are both up to date and generally available, although foreign language publications, especially those covering subjects not readily available in English, and important earlier works published since the mid-19th century, have also been included. The enormous number of works on Rome (the *Bibliografia romana* lists over 800 items annually) has allowed only a very small number of articles to be included here. Most of the works in the bibliography are available from the British Library, the Library of Congress, and British and American University libraries. A special mention should be made of the library of the Warburg Institute and its rich holdings of classical art and archaeology and Renaissance art.

The checking of bibliographical references and other searches were greatly facilitated by the Public Online Catalogue of URBS (Unione Romana Biblioteche Scientifiche) and SASCAT (School of Advanced Study Catalogue of the University of London).

Entries within each of the chapter headings or sub-headings are arranged by title. Critical and descriptive annotations accompany each item. Several entries also include full bibliographical references to related works.

I have used the original Italian names of people, places, monuments and buildings with only the occasional exception in cases where the English form is so well known that use of the Italian would almost seem pedantic (St Peter's, Raphael). I have used the abbreviation 'S.' to stand for different forms of the word 'Saint' – 'San', 'Sant', 'Santo', and 'Santa'.

Acknowledgements

I am grateful to several colleagues in the British Library for their practical assistance, useful suggestions, and forbearance, in particular Alison Hill, Marcella Leembruggen, Stephen Parkin, Susan Reed, Denis Reidy, Dennis E. Rhodes, Barry Taylor and Geoff West. In Rome my researches were greatly helped by Laura Biancini and Maria Gaia Gajo of the Biblioteca nazionale centrale di Roma, Anna Maria Amadio of the Biblioteca della Fondazione Marco Besso, and Christina Huemer, Librarian of the American Academy in Rome. Thanks are also due to Dr Graham Kent for some useful editorial suggestions and, last but not least, to Dr Robert Neville and Julia Goddard of ABC-CLIO for their infinite patience, and to Daniel Nunn for his editorial skill and efficiency.

Chronology

753 BC	Legendary date of the foundation of Rome by Romulus. In fact, the settlement on the Palatine Hill and in the small nearby villages probably started to appear as early as the 15th century BC. By the 9th century BC, all seven hills of Rome are settled by Latin and Sabine tribes of farmers and shepherds.
753-509 BC	Regal period.
753-616 BC	Latin kings (Romulus, Numa Pompilius, Tullus Hostilius, Ancus Marcius).
616-509 BC	Etruscan kings (Tarquinius Priscus, Servius Tullius [578-535 BC], Tarquinius Superbus).
509-27 BC	Republican era. During this period Rome is ruled by two annually elected Consuls who are army leaders and also legislators. The Consuls choose an advisory council, the Senate, whose members come from the patrician class. Rome becomes supreme as the head of a confederacy of all Italians. After the success of the Punic Wars (3rd-2nd centuries BC), it dominates the Western Mediterranean area. The last years of the Republic are dominated by civil wars, first between Lucius Sulla and Gaius Marius and, later, between Julius Caesar and Pompey.
494 BC	Establishment of the office of Tribune, elected from the ranks of the plebeians.
451 BC	Roman law encoded in the Twelve Tables.
396 BC	Destruction, after a ten-year siege, of the Etruscan fortress-town of Veii, twelve kilometres to the north of Rome. This first conquest is followed by numerous other wars and treaties that, by 276 BC, bring the whole peninsula under Roman control.
390 BC	Rome is burned and pillaged by the Gauls of Brenno.
378-350 BC	Construction of city walls (11 kilometres) enclosing an area of some 426 hectares.

Chronology

264-241 BC	The First Punic War marks the beginning of Rome's overseas expansion and its conflict with Carthage, the great commercial city on the north coast of Africa (near the present Tunis). It erupts when Rome besieges the Carthaginian cities of Sicily. After the destruction of its navy, Carthage loses Sicily and, in 238 BC, Sardinia and Corsica.
218-202 BC	Second Punic War – Hannibal, the formidable commander of the Carthaginian forces in Spain (where Carthage had built a powerful empire in the years following the First Punic War), marches across Europe and, in September 218 BC, crosses the Alps and conquers the whole of Northern Italy. However, he fails to convince Roman allies and subject cities to join him. In 216 BC Rome suffers a humiliating defeat at Cannae in southern Italy, after which the whole of southern Italy and Sicily join Hannibal. In 211 he marches against Rome but fails to lay siege to it. By 206, Roman troops, led by Publius Cornelius Scipio, reconquer Spain and in 204 BC cross into Africa, besieging Carthage. Hannibal is forced to retreat and return to Carthage, where his defeat at the battle of Zama reduces Carthage to a dependent state and leaves Rome in control of the whole of the western Mediterranean and northern Africa.
149-146 BC	Third Punic War and destruction of Carthage which, after its defeat in 202 BC, had recovered its commercial activities and prosperity.
133 BC	Assassination of the tribune Tiberius Sempronius Gracchus, whose attempts at agrarian reform alienated large sections of the Senate. Gaius Sempronius Gracchus, his younger brother, pursues the same policies and meets with the same fate in 122 BC.
90-88 BC	The Social or Italic War – Rome's allies in central and southern Italy take up arms against it. They win citizenship and other concessions.
88-82 BC	Civil War between Gaius Marius and Lucius Sulla.
82-79 BC	Dictatorship of Lucius Sulla, who implements constitutional reforms in order to strengthen the Republic.
60 BC	First triumvirate, composed of Julius Caesar, Crassus and Pompey.
58-52 BC	Caesar's conquest of Gaul.
49-45 BC	Civil war between Pompey and Julius Caesar.
48-44 BC	Dictatorship of Julius Caesar.

44 BC	Julius Caesar is assassinated on the Ides of March. In his will he names Octavian, his great-nephew and adopted son, as his successor.
43 BC	Second triumvirate composed of Octavian (in the West), Lepidus (in Africa) and Mark Antony (in the East).
31 BC	Octavian defeats Mark Antony, his last rival, at the battle of Actium off north-west Greece. He attains absolute power.
27 BC	Octavian restores the Republican constitution and accepts the name Augustus offered to him by the Senate. He reorganizes and embellishes the city.
14 AD	Death of Augustus; he is succeeded by his stepson Tiberius.
61-63	St Paul visits Rome, where he continues his proselytizing.
64	The Great Fire of Rome destroys large areas of the city. It also gives Nero the opportunity to rebuild Rome in the Greek style and to begin his Golden House. Christians, who are blamed for starting the fire, are persecuted.
64 or 67	Death of St Peter in Rome.
70	Capture and destruction of Jerusalem by Titus. The Arch of Titus at the entrance of the Roman Forum commemorates this victory.
79	Titus becomes Emperor.
80	The Colosseum, the construction of which had started some ten years earlier under Vespasian, is officially dedicated. Domitian completes the work in 82 by adding another storey.
81	Titus dies suddenly, his death supposedly hastened by Domitian, his brother who succeeds him as emperor.
98	Trajan becomes Emperor. He rules in exemplary fashion until 117, extending the boundaries of the empire and carrying out an important building programme in Rome which includes the Column of Trajan (112), commemorating the conquest of Dacia (a campaign which Trajan personally commanded), and Trajan's Markets.
117-138	Reign of Hadrian, Trajan's nephew, who consolidates Rome's empire. He rebuilds the Pantheon, which had been destroyed by fire. In 123, he begins to build a mausoleum (the modern Castel S. Angelo), inspired by the Mausoleum of Augustus.
166	German invasion of Rome.
250	Persecution of the Christians.
270-274	Reign of Aurelian.
271-275	Construction of the Aurelian Wall. The work is completed during the reign of Probus.

Chronology

284-305	Reign of Diocletian and institution of the Tetrarchy (the rule of the empire by four).
302	Another outburst of ruthless persecution of the Christians occurs.
306	On Constantius's death, his son Constantine is acclaimed Emperor by the army. A series of civil wars is unleashed as Maxentius rebels in Rome.
312	Fighting under a banner bearing the insignia of the Christian faith, Constantine defeats Maxentius at the Milvian Bridge near Rome and becomes ruler of the Empire in the West, consolidating his rule over the whole Empire. He confirms the status of the Christian Church.
313	Edict of Milan allowing the Christians freedom of worship, restoring their property to them and giving them buildings where they could worship.
330	Emperor Constantine transfers the imperial capital from Rome to Constantinople, his 'second Rome', the newly-founded Christian capital on the Bosphorus strait.
384	In his edict *Cunctos populos*, the emperor Theodosius I abolishes the worship of Rome's ancient gods and establishes Christianity as the official religion of the Empire.
386	Conversion to Christianity of St Augustine.
404	Imperial decree abolishing gladiatorial games.
410	After a three-day siege, Alaric and the Visigoths enter the city on 24 August 410. The event causes consternation throughout the Empire and prompts the writing of St Augustine's *City of God* to counter claims that this was the result of adopting Christianity, with its teaching of meekness and submission, as the official religion.
440-461	Pontificate of Leo I. In 452 he encounters Attila the Hun and persuades him not to attack Rome; likewise, three years later, when the Vandals under Genseric occupy the city, he prevents its sacking.
476	End of the Western Roman Empire after the deposition of Romulus Augustulus by the German warrior Odoacer, who becomes ruler of Italy. He is succeeded by the Ostrogoth Theodoric (d. 526).
527-565	Reign of Justinian I who attempts to re-establish Imperial rule in the West and to drive the Ostrogoths out of the Peninsula. His general Belisarius occupies Rome.
546	The Goths under Totila enter Rome through the Porta Asinaria.

552	Narses, Emperor Justinian's general, defeats Totila and occupies Rome. Rome becomes subject to the Emperor of Byzantium, who is represented in Ravenna by an exarch.
568	The Lombards (a Germanic tribe) lay waste the countryside around Rome.
590-565	Pontificate of Pope Gregory I. A great administrator and diplomat, Gregory is considered to be the creator of medieval papacy. Pilgrims and refugees flood into Rome.
7th century	Rome grows increasingly independent of Byzantium.
609	The Pantheon becomes a Christian church (S. Maria ad martyres), which ensures its survival.
663	Emperor Constans II of Byzantium visits Rome.
753	The Lombards lift their siege of Rome after negotiations with Pope Stephen II. Alliance of Stephen II with Pepin the Short, King of the Franks. Defeat of the Lombards, who are forced to restore to Rome the Patrimony of St Peter, the lands in Central Italy that would become the Papal States.
773	Charlemagne, King of the Franks, is invited by Pope Adrian I to fight the Lombards. His victory at Pavia brings Lombard rule of Northern Italy to an end. On his entry into Rome, in 774, he is greeted as protector and deliverer of the city.
800	Charlemagne is crowned Emperor of the Romans by Pope Leo III. The alliance between the Papacy and the Carolingian dynasty was to disintegrate later in the century.
846	Saracens attack and sack churches outside the Aurelian Wall.
847-854	Construction of the Leonine Wall enclosing the Basilica of S. Peter's and its surrounding buildings, and the area of the Borgo (Civitas Leonina).
962	Otto I is crowned Holy Roman Emperor by Pope John XII. A treaty is also concluded regulating the relationship between the Emperor and the papacy and confirming the temporal power of the latter.
964	First revolt against the German Emperor Otto who had deposed Pope John XII and installed Leo VIII, Otto's nominee. Rivalry between Roman nationalists and imperialists. Succession of popes and antipopes.
1073	Pope Gregory VII asserts the authority of the Church, emphasizing the need for spiritual and ecclesiastical renewal and for a more powerful Church autonomous from both the Emperor and the aristocracy of Rome. He quarrels with Henry IV.

1083	Siege of Rome by Henry IV, who breaks through the Leonine Wall and takes possession of S. Peter's. Gregory VII occupies the Castel S. Angelo.
1084	Henry IV takes possession of the Lateran Palace with his antipope Clement III. Robert Guiscard, the Norman Duke of Apulia and Calabria, comes to Gregory's rescue and his troops pillage the city.
1085	Death of Gregory VII at Salerno. Over the next century Rome becomes a battleground between popes and antipopes, supporters of the Pope and those of the Emperor.
1143	Revolt of the Roman people, who proclaim the establishment of a Republic, the restoration of the senate and the appointment of a head of government called the *Patricius*, who would have the Pope's temporal power.
1167	Frederick Barbarossa, German King and Holy Roman Emperor, challenges papal authority and attempts to establish German predominance in Western Europe. He storms and captures the Leonine City.
1188	Pope Clement III recognizes the city as a commune with rights to declare war and make peace, and to appoint senators and a prefect. In exchange, the Senate recognizes the Pope's temporal powers.
1198-1227	Under Innocent III and Honorius III, the Papacy regains and extends its influence and becomes a dominant force in Western Europe.
1227-1308	Conflict between the Commune and the Pope. Charles of Anjou comes to the protection of the Pope and order is restored. The French dominate the affairs of Rome.
1300	Boniface VIII proclaims the first Holy (or Jubilee) Year. It is attended by an estimated 200,000 pilgrims.
1302	The Bull *Unam Sanctam* (One Holy) declares the supremacy of the Pope's spiritual power over earthly powers. This contributes to a further deterioration in Boniface's already strained relations with Philip IV of France, who has him arrested at Anagni in 1303 in order to summon him before a General Council. Boniface dies later in the same year.
1303	The Studium Urbis (the University of Rome) is founded by Pope Boniface VIII.
1309	Under pressure from Philip IV, Pope Clement V (Bertrand de Got, Archbishop of Bordeaux) moves the papal residence to Avignon, which in 1290 was given to Charles II, King of

	Naples and Count of Provence, a vassal of the Pope (in 1348 it was bought from Queen Joan of Provence and remained papal property until the French Revolution).
1343	A delegation is led by Cola di Rienzo in Avignon to request Clement VI's return to Rome.
1347	In May, Cola di Rienzo announces a series of edicts against the nobles and assumes dictatorial powers, taking the title of Tribune. During his short-lived rule he attempts to re-establish Rome as the capital of a 'sacred Italy' and confers Roman citizenship on all the cities of Italy. On 1 August, the opening of the national parliament and the unity of Italy are celebrated. On 20 November, Cola defeats an uprising of the nobles led by the Orsini, Caetani, Frangipani and Colonna families. On 15 December, he abdicates and takes refuge among hermits in the Abruzzi region and later enjoins Charles IV, King of Bohemia, to become Rome's saviour and the new Holy Roman Emperor. His attempt fails, he is handed over to the Pope, declared guilty of heresy and imprisoned.
1348	Rome is struck by the Black Death and also by the worst earthquake in its history, which destroys or damages numerous monuments, ancient and modern. The façade of S. Giovanni in Laterano collapses.
1350	The Holy Year is celebrated, though Pope Clement VI remains in Avignon.
1352	Innocent VI, who succeeds Clement VI, is more favourable to Cola di Rienzo.
1354	Triumphal return of Cola di Rienzo to Rome with the title of Senator. His reinstatement proves brief as the arbitrariness of his rule leads to an outbreak of riots. Cola is seized by the mob and killed on October 8.
1367-1370	Brief return of the papacy from Avignon during Urban V's reign.
1377	Return of Pope Gregory XI to Rome, ending the so-called 'Avignon (or Babylonian) Captivity'.
1378	The Great Schism begins after the death of Gregory XI, with a Roman pope (Urban VI) and an Antipope (Clement XII) in Avignon.
1380	Death of St Catherine of Siena who, with St Bridget of Sweden, had been one of the strongest advocates of the papacy's return to Rome.
1383-1388	A further outbreak of the plague.

Chronology

1390	The third Jubilee is organized in a city devastated by the plague and internal strife. The interval between jubilees is changed from fifty to thirty-three years, the number of years of Jesus's life and also the average span of human life.
1400	Though not an official jubilee year, thousands of pilgrims visit Rome.
1409	The Council of Pisa deposes the two existing popes, Gregory XII and Benedict XIII, and elects another, Alexander V.
1420	*30 September.* Return to Rome of the Colonna Pope Martin V, elected at the Council of Constance (1414-1418).
1417-1431	Pontificate of Martin V Colonna, who attempts to restore the social, economic and cultural life of the city.
1423	Fifth Jubilee Year.
1447	With the accession of Nicholas V, 'the Christian Renaissance ascended the papal throne' (Gregorovius). He continues the programme of restoration initiated by Martin V. A great bibliophile, his library would become the foundation of the Vatican Library.
1450	Sixth Jubilee Year proclaimed by Pope Nicholas V. It is attended by vast crowds of pilgrims. Nearly 200 people are trampled to death on the Ponte S. Angelo.
1458-1464	Pope Pius II Piccolomini's attempts at a Crusade fail.
1471-1484	Pontificate of Sixtus IV Della Rovere. He is a munificent patron of letters and the arts, and a founder and restorer of numerous institutions; his town planning schemes transform Rome into a Renaissance city.
1475	Seventh Jubilee Year proclaimed by Pope Sixtus IV. With the exception of special Jubilees, the celebration would, henceforth, take place every twenty-five years.
1492-1503	Pontificate of Alexander VI Borgia, one of the great 'bad popes' whose worldliness, scandalous life, nepotism and neglect of things spiritual would lead to the development of the Protestant Reformation. He brings, however, the Romagna under papal control and is an enlightened patron of the arts.
1495	In January, the troops of Charles VIII of France occupy Rome.
1503-1513	Reign of Pope Julius II Della Rovere. One of the most powerful rulers of the Renaissance, this 'warrior pope' is also a patron of Michelangelo, Raphael and Bramante, and commissions some of the greatest artistic creations of the Renaissance.
1506	Foundation stone of the new basilica of St Peter's laid. Bramante created the new model which, in later years,

	would be elaborated by several other architects, including Michelangelo and Bernini. The reconstruction of the basilica would continue for more than a century.
1506	Discovery of the marble sculptural group of the Laocoon in a vineyard near S. Maria Maggiore. It is placed in the Cortile del Belvedere in the Vatican, where it would be joined by some of the most famous sculptures of antiquity, including the Apollo Belvedere.
1508-1512	Michelangelo's Sistine Chapel Ceiling.
1509-1517	Raphael's Vatican *Stanze*.
1510	Martin Luther visits Rome and is shocked by the worldliness of the clergy and the sale of indulgences.
1513-1521	Pontificate of Pope Leo X de' Medici. A great lover of literature, the arts and music and one of the most extravagant popes in history, he leaves the papal treasury depleted. Shortly before his death Leo excommunicates Martin Luther.
1523-1534	Pontificate of Pope Clement VII de' Medici. His vacillating policies and frequent shifts of support in the struggles between Francis I of France and Emperor Charles V for the domination of Italy has catastrophic results.
1527	Sack of Rome by the troops of Emperor Charles V. Much of the city is destroyed and a third of the population is slaughtered or dies of the plague. Clement VII is imprisoned in the Castel S. Angelo.
1534-1549	Pontificate of Paul III Farnese, the last of the great Renaissance popes and the first pope of the Counter-Reformation.
1536	*5 April*. Triumphal procession through Rome of Emperor Charles V. The event is the pretext for the creation of new thoroughfares. Pope Paul III authorizes the revival of the carnival.
1538	Transfer of the equestrian statue of *Marcus Aurelius* from the Lateran to the Piazza del Campidoglio.
1541	Completion of Michelangelo's *Last Judgement* on the altar wall of the Sistine Chapel.
1542	Formation of the Roman Inquisition (*Congregazione del Santo Ufficio*) to combat Protestantism and safeguard Catholic orthodoxy.
1545-1563	The Council of Trent in Northern Italy is convoked by Paul III to discuss theological, liturgical and ecclesiastical reform and clarify Catholic doctrines. It also discusses the status and role of the arts.

Chronology

1555	Establishment of the Roman Ghetto. The Jews are also compelled to wear a badge.
1564	Death of Michelangelo.
1585-1590	Pontificate of Sixtus V Peretti, the greatest of the 'Builder Popes'.
1592-1606	Caravaggio's years in Rome, where he produces his greatest masterpieces.
1597-1603	Annibale and Agostino Carracci decorate the main gallery of Palazzo Farnese.
1598	Birth of Gianlorenzo Bernini, the greatest artist of the Baroque era, whose genius would dominate artistic creation in Rome for almost half a century.
1600	*17 February.* Giordano Bruno is burned at the stake as a heretic in the Campo de' Fiori. Some 500,000 pilgrims visit Rome for the Jubilee celebrations.
1603	The Accademia dei Lincei is founded by Prince Federico Cesi. A forerunner of all scientific societies, its members would include Galileo Galilei, Francesco Barberini and Cassiano dal Pozzo.
1605-1623	Pontificate of Paul V Borghese.
1614	The Biblioteca Angelica, Rome's first public library, is founded.
1623-1644	Pontificate of Urban VIII Barberini.
1626	Consecration of the basilica of St Peter's.
1633	Galileo Galilei appears before the Inquisition and is sentenced to life imprisonment.
1650	Approximately 700,000 pilgrims visit Rome for the Jubilee.
1655	Queen Christina of Sweden, converted to Roman Catholicism in 1654, settles in Rome, where she would remain until her death in 1689 becoming one of the most important patrons of the arts.
1656-1667	Construction of St Peter's Square, Bernini's greatest architectural achievement.
1666	The French Academy (Accademia di Francia), the oldest foreign academy in Rome, is founded by Louis XIV. For three centuries it would be the home of painters, sculptors and (from 1720) architects, writers and composers, all winners of the *Prix de Rome* (the scholarships that allowed them a period of study in the Eternal City). Since 1803, the Academy has been housed in the Villa Medici. The *Prix de Rome* were abolished in 1968 and today the Academy's remit is the promotion of Franco-Italian cultural relations through exhibitions, concerts and conferences.

1726	Francesco de' Sanctis' Spanish Steps link the Piazza di Spagna to the church of the Trinità dei Monti and the Pincio.
1740	Piranesi moves to Rome where he would produce some of his greatest prints, notably the *Vedute di Roma* (Views of Rome) (*c.* 1746-1748) and *Le Antichità romane* (Roman antiquities) (1756).
1762	Inauguration of the Trevi Fountain.
1763	The German archaeologist Johann Joachim Winckelmann is named prefect of Roman antiquities.
1771	With the creation of Clement XIV's Museo Pio-Clementino, the transformation of the Vatican Palace into a museum complex begins.
1773	Pope Clement XIV orders the dissolution of the Jesuit Order. The Order would be reinstated in 1814.
1797	Pius VI signs the Treaty of Tolentino in which he renounces his rights over Bologna, Ferrara and Ravenna and is forced to give a large number of works of art to France. Most of these confiscated works (including *Laocoon* and *Apollo Belvedere*) would return to Italy in 1815.
1798	*February.* Anti-French riots in Trastevere. Execution in the Piazza del Popolo of twenty-two of the ring-leaders. Military occupation of Rome by the French under General Berthier following the murder of General Duphot. *November.* Troops of King Ferdinand of Naples march into Rome, outnumbering the French forces which withdraw to the north leaving a garrison at Castel S. Angelo. *December.* The French re-occupy Rome; Anton René Bertolio, the French civil commissioner, assumes the powers of a dictator. The Republic of Rome is declared; Pius VI is deposed and exiled to France, where he would die in 1799.
1799	*September.* The French garrison marches out of the city. Rome is re-occupied by Neapolitan troops.
1800	Pope Pius VII Chiaramonti enters Rome. The Jubilee is not celebrated.
1801	Concordat between the papacy and Napoleon.
1804	Pius VII presides over Napoleon's coronation in Notre-Dame in 1804.
1808	*February.* General Miollis is ordered to re-occupy Rome after Napoleon's decision to destroy the temporal power of the papacy.

Chronology

1809	A French administration is installed in Rome, which becomes the second capital of the French Empire and is ruled by the King of Rome, Napoleon's only son. Pius VII is exiled; he would return to Rome five years later, after Napoleon's abdication.
1814	The last French troops march out of Rome.
1815	Most of the works of art requisitioned by the French during Napoleonic rule are returned to Rome.
1821	*23 February.* Death of John Keats in the house near the Spanish Steps.
1847	*October.* Pius IX reorganizes the administration of the city, placing it in the hands of a council of 100 members. A Consultative Assembly, to assist in the work of the government, and the reorganization of the Council of Ministers follow.
1848	*March.* Pius IX grants a constitution – his Fundamental Statute for the Secular Government of the States of the Church – a compromise charter.
	29 April. Pius IX refuses to wage war on Austria and declares that his troops are only to defend the northern frontier of his states. Erosion of Papal popularity.
	15 November. Assassination of Pellegrino Rossi, the Pope's Head of Administration, and revolutionary upheaval in Rome. Pius IX flees to Gaeta, across the Neapolitan border, disguised as a simple priest.
1849	*9 February.* Proclamation of the Roman Republic. Elections take place and Mazzini's democrats win a majority. The elected assembly declares the Pope's sovereignty over the Papal States to have ended. The Republic is toppled later in the year by the intervention of the Catholic powers (France, Spain, Austria and Naples).
	30 April. Garibaldi's troops repulse the French forces under General Oudinot; Mazzini's rejection of Garibaldi's suggestion to pursue the French and attack again enables them to bring reinforcements.
	3 June. The French attack and capture Villa Pamphilj and Villa Corsini. Garibaldi's counter-attack leads to great losses and determined resistance and defence of the Republic.
	30 June. The French attack. Garibaldi favours a guerrilla campaign outside the City Walls. Mazzini resigns.
	3 July. French troops enter the city.
1850	*April.* Restoration and return of Pius IX to Rome. The Jubilee is not celebrated.

1856	Inauguration of the Rome-Frascati railway line.
1860	*17 March.* Victor Emmanuel II proclaimed King of Italy, having gained control of the entire peninsula with the exception of the Veneto and Rome.
1863	Death of Giuseppe Gioachino Belli, the greatest writer in Roman dialect.
1870	*20 September.* Italian artillery under General Raffaele Cadorna occupies the city.
1871	*1 February.* Rome is proclaimed capital of the Kingdom of Italy.
	2 May. The Italian Government passes the Law of the Guarantees to demonstrate that it does not wish to subjugate the papacy. The pope would retain the Vatican City and receive an annual allowance. Pius IX declares himself a prisoner and excommunicates the authors of the Act. His successors would adopt the same attitude.
1874	Inauguration of the new railway station in the Termini zone.
1875	The Jubilee is celebrated quietly without public ceremonies.
1876-1900	Construction of the Tiber Embankment in order to prevent the frequent flooding of the city.
1878	Deaths of Pius IX and Victor Emmanuel II.
1883	Opening of the Palazzo delle Esposizioni.
1885-1911	Construction of the Vittoriano, the huge monument in honour of Victor Emmanuel II.
1911	Rome hosts the International Exhibition, which celebrates the first fifty years of the Kingdom of Italy.
1922	The Fascists assume power after Mussolini's March on Rome.
1923	The assassination of Giacomo Matteotti, the Socialist leader, initially threatens to bring about the downfall of the Fascists.
1925	Establishment of the Governorship (*Governorato*) of Rome, making the administration of the city directly dependent on the Ministry of Interior.
1929	The Lateran Treaty (the *Conciliazione*) ends the strained relations between State and Church. It restricts the temporal sovereignty of the Pope to the Vatican City and some other extraterritorial possessions, but confirms Catholicism as the official religion of Italy.
1933	Opening of the Via dell'Impero (now called Via dei Fori Imperiali).
1937	Establishment of Cinecittà, the largest film studio complex in Europe.

Chronology

1938	*May.* Hitler's visit to Rome seals the Axis Alliance.
1939-1949	Excavations in St Peter's result in the discovery of the spot believed in the 2nd century to be the resting place of the saint.
1940	*10 June.* Mussolini declares war on England.
1943	*19 July.* Beginning of Allied air attacks on Rome.
	25 July. Mussolini is overthrown. Pietro Badoglio becomes Prime Minister.
	8 September. Armistice signed with the Allies.
	9 September. Victor Emmanuel III and Pietro Badoglio flee from Rome.
	10 September. German forces occupy Rome, which is declared an open city, i.e. a political neutral. This status is not recognized by the Allies.
	16 October. Over 1,000 Roman Jews are rounded up and deported to Auschwitz.
1944	*22 January.* The Allies land at Anzio, thirty-three miles south of Rome.
	23 March. Thirty-three Germans are killed in a partisan bomb attack on Via Rasella.
	24 March. 335 civilian hostages are shot in the Ardeatine Caves in retaliation.
	17 April. Deportation of 750 Romans.
	4 June. The Allies liberate Rome, ending the 268-day Nazi rule of the city.
1946	On 2 June, after a referendum, Italy is declared a republic. Rome becomes the capital of Italy and also the capital of Lazio (one of the twenty newly-created regions).
1950	Opening of the Via della Conciliazione.
1955	Inauguration of the first section of the Rome underground between Termini and EUR. The second section, between Ottaviano and Anagnina, would open in 1980 and the third, between Termini and Rebibbia, in 1990.
1960	The seventeenth Olympic Games are held in Rome. A new stadium, the Stadio Flaminio (designed by Pier Luigi and Antonio Nervi) is built in the area between Porta del Popolo and Ponte Milvio.
1975	*1 November.* Assassination of Pier Paolo Pasolini at Ostia.
1976	Election, for the first time, of a Communist administration.
1978	Abduction by the *Brigate Rosse* (Red Brigade) of Aldo Moro, the Christian Democrat prime minister. After being held captive for fifty-five days, during which a series of

	negotiations came to nothing, his body would be found in a car boot in the centre of Rome.
1978-	Pontificate of John Paul II, the first foreign pope in 455 years.
1980	Removal of the Via della Consolazione (created in the 19th century) that divided the Roman Forum in two.
1990	The football World Cup (Mondiale 1990) is held in Rome. The Stadio Olimpico is completely renovated.
	7 July. The Three Tenors' concert at the Baths of Caracalla is watched by 800 million people worldwide.
1991	The population of Rome is 2,777,888.
1993	Francesco Rutelli is elected Mayor of Rome. He would be re-elected in 1997.
2000	Jubilee Year. In preparation for the celebration of this Millennium Jubilee, an impressive programme of restorations of churches and monuments, and renovations of museums, is carried out.

THESES AND DISSERTATIONS ON ROME

Ancient Rome

Robert James Aitken. 'Piranesi-Vico: "il Campo Marzio" foundations and the Eternal City', MARCH thesis, McGill University, 1995.

Joseph Donella Alchermes. ' "Cura pro mortuis" and "cultus martyrum": commemoration in Rome from the Second through the Sixth century', PhD thesis, New York University, 1989.

Barbara Lee Ayanian. 'Foreign women in Livy's History of Rome: an analysis', MA dissertation, California State University, 1991.

Jean I. Bradford. 'Documentary evidence for libraries and book collectors in Ancient Rome and the Roman Empire', MA Dissertation, London University, 1974.

Nadine G. R. Brundrett. 'Thermae in Rome: a study of their development from the Republican period through to the first century A.D.', MA thesis, Queen's University at Kingston (Canada), 1993.

Christer Fredrik Magnus Bruun. 'The water supply in Ancient Rome: a study of Roman Imperial administration', FILTRI thesis, Helsingin Yliopisto, 1991.

Diane Atnally Conlin. 'The large processional friezes on the Ara Pacis Augustea: early Augustan sculptural styles and workshop traditions', PhD thesis, The University of Michigan, 1993.

J. R. Curran. 'Aspects of Rome as a pagan city and a Christian capital in the fourth century', DPhil thesis, University of Oxford, 1991.

Eve Dambra. '*Palladis artes*: the Frieze of the Forum Transitorium in Rome', PhD thesis, Yale University, 1987.

R. H. Darwall-Smith. 'Aspects of imperial building activity in Rome in 69-96', DPhil thesis, University of Oxford, 1990.

Penelope Jane Ellis Davies. 'Politics and design: the funerary monuments of the Roman Emperors from Augustus to Marcus Aurelius (28 BC-AD 193)', PhD thesis, Yale University, 1994.

Daniel Nathan Erickson. ' "Eutropius" *Compendium of Roman history*: introduction, translation, and notes', DA dissertation, Syracuse University, 1990.

Susan S. Fischler. 'The public position of the women of the Imperial household in the Julio-Claudian period', DPhil thesis, University of Oxford, 1989.

Charmaine Lynn Gorrie. 'The building programme of Septimius Severus in the city of Rome', PhD thesis, The University of British Columbia, 1997.

R. Haggo. 'The Good Shepherd: the character and origins of the pastoral theme in the Christian Catacombs at Rome', M.Litt, University of Edinburgh, 1976.

Linda Marie Hart. 'Decontextualizing the monuments of the Roman Forum: archaeological restoration drawings by the architecture students of the American Academy in Rome', PhD thesis, University of California, Los Angeles, 1997.

Samuel Alexander Hughes. 'Salamis on the Tiber: readings of the Mars Ultor temple's dedicatory games', PhD thesis, University of Pennsylvania, 1997.

Mary Katherine Jaeger. 'The poetics of place: the Augustan writers and the urban landscape of Rome', PhD thesis, University of California, Berkeley, 1990.

Ira Joseph Jolivet, Jr. 'The structure and argumentative strategy of Romans', PhD thesis, Baylor University, 1994.

Bernard Joseph Kavanagh. 'Gauls at the court of the Emperor: a prosopographical study of the service, promotion, and influence of Gauls in Rome and in the Imperial service, 31 BC-AD 54', PhD thesis, University of Alberta (Canada), 1993.

James Thomas Kearney, 'Ammianus Marcellinus and his Roman audience', PhD thesis, The University of Michigan, 1991.

Laurence Kern. 'La dynastie Julio-Claudienne: pathologies des Empereurs de César à Néron', Dr d'Etat, Université de Bourgogne, 1989.

Earl Dale Lavender. 'The development of Pelagius' thought within a late fourth-century ascetic movement in Rome', PhD thesis, Saint Louis University, 1991.

John Douglas Macisaac. 'The location of the Republican Mint of Rome and the topography of the Arx of the Capitoline', PhD thesis, The Johns Hopkins University, 1987.

Neville Daniel Gregory Morley. 'Metropolis and hinterland: the city of Rome and the Italian economy, 200 BC-AD 200', PhD dissertation, University of Cambridge, 1994.

Wendel William Meyer. 'The Church of the Catacombs: British responses to the evidence of the Catacombs, 1578-1900', PhD dissertation, University of Cambridge, 1985.

R. F. Newbold. 'Public disorders in Rome under the early principate', PhD thesis, University of Leeds, 1970-71.

Eric Michael Orlin. 'Deorum causa: the politics of Republican temple building', PhD thesis, University of California, Berkeley, 1994.

John Theodore Pena. 'Roman-period ceramic production in Etruria Tiberina: a geographical and compositional study', PhD thesis, The University of Michigan, 1987.

Leena Pietila-Castren. '*Magnificentia publica*: the victory monuments of the Roman generals in the era of the Punic Wars', PhD thesis, Helsingin Yliopisto, 1988.

Christine Renaud. 'Studies in the eighth book of the *Aeneid*: the importance of place', PhD thesis, The University of Texas at Austin, 1990.

David West Reynolds. 'Forma Urbis Romae: the Severan Marble Plan and the urban form of Ancient Rome', PhD thesis, The University of Michigan, 1996.

Connie Lynn Rodriguez. 'Poetry and power: studies in Augustan monuments and the poets of the Augustan age', PhD thesis, The Johns Hopkins University, 1990.

Leonard Victor Rutgers. 'The Jews in late Ancient Rome: an archaeological and historical study on the interaction of Jews and non-Jews in the Roman diaspora', PhD thesis, Duke University, 1993.

Francis Xavier Ryan. 'Precedence in the Republican Senate', PhD thesis, University of Pennsylvania, 1993.

P. W. H. Spring. 'The topographical and archaeological study of the antiquities of the city of Rome, 1420-1447', PhD thesis, University of Edinburgh, 1974-75.

Geoffrey Street Sumi. 'Public performances and political symbols: the rise of Octavianus in 44 B.C.', PhD thesis, The University of Michigan, 1993.

Rabun McDowell Taylor. 'Water distribution, the Tiber river, and the urban development of Ancient Rome', PhD thesis, University of Minnesota, 1997.

Mark A. Temelini. 'The function of Pompey's building complex in the Campus Martius', MA thesis, University of Ottawa, 1993.

Darryl William Turnbull. 'The living conditions and political role of the urban poor in late Republican Rome', MA thesis, Queen's University at Kingston (Canada), 1993.

James Christopher Walters. 'Ethnic issues in Paul's letter to the Romans: an analysis in light of the changing self-definition of early Christianity in Rome', PhD thesis, Boston University, 1991.

Architecture

Miroslava Marie Benes. 'Villa Pamphilj (1630-1670): family, gardens, and land in papal Rome', PhD thesis, Yale University, 1989.

Louise Smith Bross. 'The Church of Santo Spirito in Sassia: a study in the development of art, architecture and patronage in Counter-Reformation Rome', PhD thesis, The University of Chicago, 1994.

David Loran Butler. 'The Spada Chapel in Santa Maria in Vallicella, Rome: a study of late Baroque patronage, taste, and style', PhD thesis, Washington University, 1991.

Patrizia Cavazzini. 'Palazzo Lancellotti ai Coronari and its fresco decoration', PhD thesis, Columbia University, 1996.

Nicola Margot Courtrights. 'Gregory XIII's Tower of the Winds in the Vatican', PhD thesis, New York University, 1990.

Tracy Lee Ehrich. 'The Villa Mondragone and early seventeenth-century villeggiatura at Frascati', PhD thesis, Columbia University, 1995.

Terry Rossi Kirk. 'Church, state and architecture: the "Palazzo di Giustizia" of nineteenth-century Rome', PhD thesis, Columbia University, 1997.

Evonne Anita Levy. 'A canonical work of an uncanonical era: re-reading the Chapel of Saint Ignatius (1695-1699) in the Gesù of Rome', PhD thesis, Princeton University, 1993.

Andrea Laurel Mac Elwee. 'Allegory and the architecture of Francesco Borromini', MARCH thesis, McGill University, 1995.

Corinne L. Mandel. 'The Lateran Palace fresco cycle', PhD thesis, University of Toronto, 1991.

Robert Denton Meadows-Rogers. 'The Vatican Logge and their culminating decorations under Pius IV and Gregory XIII: decorative innovation and urban planning before Sixtus V', PhD thesis, The University of North Carolina at Chapel Hill, 1997.

Susan Scott Munshower. 'Filippo Juvarra's spatial concepts and Italian stage design: the consummation of a Renaissance discovery', PhD thesis, The Pennsylvania State University, 1995.

Debra Lyn Murphy-Livingston. 'The fresco decoration of the Pauline rooms in the Palazzo dei Conservatori', PhD thesis, Boston University, 1993.

Steven F. Ostrow. 'The Sistine Chapel at S. Maria Maggiore: Sixtus V and the art of the Counter-Reformation', PhD thesis, Princeton University, 1987.

Allison Lee Palmer. 'The Gesù e Maria on the Via del Corso: building in Rome after the Counter-Reformation', PhD thesis, Rutgers, the State University of New Jersey, 1994.

Carole Paul. 'The redecoration of Villa Borghese and the patronage of prince Marcantonio IV', PhD thesis, University of Pennsylvania, 1989.

Ann Edith Priester. 'The belltowers of Medieval Rome and the architecture of *renovatio*', PhD thesis, Princeton University, 1990.

Holly Marguerite Rarick. 'Pinturicchio's Saint Bernardino of Siena frescoes in the Bufalini Chapel, S. Maria in Aracoeli, Rome: an Observant Franciscan commentary of the late fifteenth century', PhD thesis, Case Western Reserve University, 1990.

Barbara J. Sabatine. 'The Church of Santa Caterina dei Funari and the Vergini Miserabili of Rome', PhD thesis, University of California, Los Angeles, 1992.

Robert Senecal. 'Chapel decorations in Rome from the reign of Pope Paul III until the year 1600', M.Phil thesis, University of Essex, 1990.

Gil R. Smith. 'Diplomacy by design: the aggregation and centenary competitions in architecture at the Accademia di San Luca in Rome and the Accademia's relations with the French Academy', PhD thesis, The Pennsylvania State University, 1987.

Leo Steinberg. 'San Carlo alle Quattro Fontane: a study in multiple form and architectural symbolism', PhD thesis, New York University, Institute of Fine Arts, 1960.

Manuel Vaquero Pineiro. 'An ecclesiastic heritage in Modern Rome: the church-hospital of San Giacomo degli Spagnoli (1450-1650)', HISTD thesis, Universidad de Cantabria, 1992.

Deborah Nelson Wilde. 'Housing and urban development in sixteenth-century Rome: the properties of the Arciconfraternità della Ss.ma Annunziata', PhD thesis, New York University, 1989.

Robin Brentwood Williams. 'Rome as state image: the architecture and urbanism of the Royal Italian Government, 1870-1900', PhD thesis, University of Pennsylvania, 1993.

History

Catherine A. Brown. 'The primacy of Rome: a study of its origin and development', PhD thesis, University of Manchester, 1987.

Margaret Angela Bruscia. 'Tiber Island in ancient and medieval Rome', PhD thesis, Fordham University, 1990.

Richard Joseph Ferraro. 'The nobility of Rome, 1560-1700: a study of its composition, wealth and investment', PhD thesis, The University of Wisconsin-Madison, 1994.

Thomas Charles Giangreco. 'Reform, renewal, and Renaissance: the thought of Cola di Rienzo in its historical context', PhD thesis, Fordham University, 1997.

Leopold George Glueckert. 'Between two amnesties: former political prisoners and exiles in the Roman Revolution of 1848', PhD thesis, Loyola University of Chicago, 1989.

Theses and Dissertations on Rome

Kenneth Veld Gouwens, 'Redefinition and reorientation: the curial humanist response to the 1527 Sack of Rome', PhD thesis, Stanford University, 1991.

Language and Literature

Jana Lyn De Benedetti. 'Dabbera in scionaccodesce (Speak giudaico-romanesco): keeping the Jewish-Roman dialect alive', DA thesis, State University of New York at Albany, 1997.

Betsy Kruizenga Emerick. 'Voices in the city: Joyce's Dublin and Pirandello's Rome', PhD thesis, University of California, Los Angeles, 1990.

Yongtae Kim. 'The Jacobean Roman tragedies of Shakespeare and Jonson in their political context', PhD thesis, The University of Nebraska-Lincoln, 1994.

Myrto Demeter Konstantarakos. 'Rome in the work of P. P. Pasolini: space and time in prose and films from 1950 to 1975', PhD thesis, The University of London, 1996.

Eric M. MacPhail. 'The voyage to Rome in French Renaissance literature', PhD thesis, Princeton University, 1989.

Henry Michael W. Russell. 'Community versus the Imperial mind: images of civil strife in Hawthorne's *The Marble Faun*', PhD thesis, The Louisiana State University and Agricultural and Mechanical College, 1992.

A. M. Scholar. 'Variety and variation in Du Bellay's Antiquitez de Rome', PhD thesis, University of Cambridge, 1976.

Alice Jewel Speh. 'The poet as traveller: Joseph Brodsky's Mexican and Roman poems', PhD thesis, Bryn Mawr College, 1992.

Bruce Carl Swaffield. 'Representations of Roman antiquities in Neoclassical literature', PhD thesis, University of Miami, 1988.

Laird D. Taylor. 'The ruins of Rome as literary topos', MA dissertation, University of Alberta, 1990.

George Hugo Tucker, 'A Frenchman's Rome, in Rome: a re-appraisal of Joachim Du Bellay's Antiquitez de Rome in the light of his poetic development and their relationship to Classical, Medieval Latin and Renaissance literature and scholarship', PhD dissertation, University of Cambridge, 1987.

Music

Kathleen Hickey Arecchi. 'Six political lament-cantatas by Luigi de' Rossi (*ca* 1597-1653)', MA Dissertation, University of Maryland College Park, 1993.

Richard Boursy. 'Historicism and composition: Giuseppe Baini, the Sistine Chapel Choir, and stile antico music in the first half of the 19th century', PhD thesis, Yale University, 1994.

Maureen Elizabeth Buja. 'Antonio Barre and music printing in mid-sixteenth-century Rome', PhD thesis, The University of North Carolina at Chapel Hill, 1996.

Jonathan Paul Couchman. 'Felice Anerio's music for the church and for the Altemps Cappella', PhD thesis, University of California, 1989.

Richard Eric Engelhart. 'Domenico Mazzocchi's *Dialoghi e sonetti* and *Magrigali a cinque voci* (1638): a modern edition with biographical commentary and new archival documents', PhD thesis, Kent State University, 1987.

Carolyn Jean Fraley. 'Selected masses of Angelo Berardi: an analytical study', PhD thesis, The Catholic University of America, 1989.

Robert Ray Holzer. 'Music and poetry in seventeenth-century Rome: settings of the canzonetta and cantata texts of Francesco Balducci, Domenico Benigni, Francesco Melosio, and Antonio Abati', PhD thesis, University of Pennsylvania, 1990.

Leslie Anne Korrick. ' "Ut Pictura Musica": observations on the reform of painting and music in post-Tridentine Rome', PhD thesis, University of Toronto, 1996.

Susan Gail Lewis. ' "Chi soffre speri" and the influence of the Commedia dell'arte on the development of Roman opera', MM dissertation, The University of Arizona, 1995.

Laura Williams Macy. 'The late madrigals of Luca Marenzio: studies in the interactions of music, literature, and patronage at the end of the sixteenth century', PhD thesis, The University of North Carolina at Chapel Hill, 1991.

Pamela F. Starr. 'Music and music patronage at the Papal Court, 1447-1464', PhD thesis, Yale University, 1987.

Douglas Edwin Weeks. 'Mario Marazzoli's music for Pope Alexander VII: an edition with commentary of Chigi Q VIII 178', PhD thesis, Washington University, 1996.

Painting and Sculpture

Laura Camille Agoston. 'Michelangelo's "Christ": the dialectics of sculpture', PhD thesis, Harvard University, 1993.

Lisa Passaglia Bauman. 'Power and image: Della Rovere patronage in late Quattrocento Rome', PhD thesis, Northwestern University, 1990.

Lars Bertil Berggren. 'Giordano Bruno on the Campo dei Fiori: a monument project in Rome, 1876-1889', FILDR thesis, Lunds Universitet, 1991.

Melissa Loring Bryan. 'Placido Costanzi and the art world of Settecento Rome', PhD thesis, University of Georgia, 1994.

Christine Jeannette Challingsworth. 'The 1708 and 1709 Concorsi Clementini at the Accademia di San Luca in Rome and the establishment of the Academy of Arts and Sciences as an autonomous building type', PhD thesis, The Pennsylvania State University, 1990.

Meredith Jane Gill. 'A French Maecenas in the Roman Quattrocento: the patronage of Cardinal Guillaume d'Estouteville (1439-1483)', PhD thesis, Princeton University, 1992.

D. M. Heath. 'The influences of Raphael on the Italian painters of the Cinquecento', M.Litt dissertation, University of Oxford, 1991.

Diana Norman. 'The patronage of Cardinal Oliviero Carafa, 1430-1511', PhD thesis, Open University, 1989.

Maria Antonietta Phillips. 'A reconstruction and contextual analysis of Ambrosiana Codex Sp 10/33: a Renaissance artist's sketchbook of the ruins of Rome', PhD thesis, University of California, Los Angeles, 1994.

Simon Jan Richter. 'Laocoon's body: pain and beauty in eighteenth-century German aesthetics', PhD thesis, 1990.

Carmen Roxanne Robbin. 'Ottavio Leoni and early Roman Baroque portraiture', PhD thesis, University of California, Santa Barbara, 1990.

Cynthia Jeanne Stollhans. 'Baldassare Peruzzi and his patrons: religious paintings in Rome, 1503-1527', PhD thesis, Northwestern University, 1988.

Cathy Ann Thomas. 'Domenico Cresti, "Il Passignano" (1559-1638), and the Roman "Rinascita": studies in his religious paintings for Rome between 1589 and 1616', PhD thesis, Case Western Reserve University, 1995.

Stefanie Walker. 'The sculptor Pietro Stefano Monnot in Rome, 1695-1713', PhD thesis, New York University, 1994.

Genevieve Ann Warwick. 'Padre Sebastiano Resta (1635-1714): collector, connoisseur, and critic of drawings', PhD thesis, The Johns Hopkins University, 1995.

K. Wells. 'The return of British painters to Rome after 1815', PhD thesis, University of Leicester, 1974.

Linda Jane Wolk. 'Studies in Perino del Vaga's early career', PhD thesis, The University of Michigan, 1987.

Carolyn Harwood Wood. 'The Indian summer of Bolognese painting: Gregory XV (1621-1623) and Ludovisi art patronage in Rome', PhD thesis, The University of North Carolina at Chapel Hill, 1988.

Shelley Elizabeth Zuraw. 'The sculpture of Mino da Fiesole: 1429-1484', PhD thesis, New York University, 1993.

Other

Susanna Kristina Akerman. 'Queen Christina of Sweden and her circle: a study in seventeenth-century political theology', PhD thesis, Washington University, 1988.

Caroline Frances Castiglione. 'Roman nobles and village communities: the Barberini family and the "stato" of Monte Libretti in Latium', PhD thesis, Harvard University, 1995.

Francesca Consagra. 'The De Rossi family print publishing shop: a study in the history of the print industry in seventeenth-century Rome', PhD thesis, The Johns Hopkins University, 1993.

Peta Dunstan. 'William Cornwallis Cartwright: a foreign correspondent in Rome in the 1860s', PhD dissertation, 1985.

Isabelle Jennifer Frank. 'Melozzo da Forlí and the Rome of Pope Sixtus IV (1471-1484)', PhD thesis, Harvard University, 1991.

Jack Freiberg. 'The Lateran and Clement VIII', PhD thesis, New York University, 1988.

Suzan Marie Germond. 'Florentine patronage in Rome in the church of San Giovanni dei Fiorentini (1583-1822)', PhD thesis, Stanford University, 1995.

Lesley Patricia Jessop. 'Pictorial cycles of non-biblical saints: the evidence of the 8th century mural cycles in Rome', PhD thesis, University of Victoria (Canada), 1993.

Maria Voutsinou Kiilia. 'Studies relating to the College of St Athanasios in Rome, together with a text and commentary on Ms Barb.Gr.138', PhD thesis, University of Southampton, 1987.

Melanie Fiona Knights. 'Migration in the new world order: the case of Bangladeshi migration to Rome', DPhil thesis, University of Sussex, 1996.

Gérard Labrot. 'Un instrument polémique, l'image de Rome au temps du schisme: 1534-1667', Thesis, Paris I, 1976.

Mary Alice Lee. ' "Hic Domus": the decorative programme of the Sala Barberina in Rome', PhD thesis, The Johns Hopkins University, 1993.

Michael William Maher. 'Reforming Rome: the Society of Jesus and its congregation at the church of the Gesù', PhD thesis, University of Minnesota, 1997.

H. J. Marchant. 'Papal inscriptions in Rome, 1417-1527', MPhil thesis, University of London, Warburg Institute, 1972-73.

Maria Louise Martin. 'Padre Sebastiano Resta: collector and connoisseur', MA thesis, Queen's University at Kingston, 1991.

John E. Moore. 'The Chinea, a festival in eighteenth-century Rome', PhD thesis, Harvard University, 1992.

Marjorie Ann Och. 'Vittoria Colonna: art patronage and religious reform in sixteenth-century Rome', PhD thesis, Bryn Mawr College, 1993.

Claudio Pellegrini. 'Comparative industrial relations at the local level in Rome and Chicago: the case of mass transit', PhD thesis, The University of Wisconsin, 1989.

Mark Robert Petersen. 'Pietro Torriti: critical study and catalogue raisonné', PhD thesis, University of Virginia, 1989.

Deborah King Robbins. 'A case study of medieval urban process: Rome's Trastevere (1250-1450)', PhD thesis, University of California, Berkeley, 1989.

D. T. Rotunda. 'The Rome embassy of Sir Eric Drummond, 16th Earl of Perth, 1933-1939', PhD thesis, University of London, London School of Economics, 1972.

Volker Schachenmayr. 'Points of connection among classical statuary, the Grand Tour, and stage performance in the age of Goethe', PhD thesis, Stanford University, 1997.

Amy Schwarz. 'Images and illusions of power in Trecento art: Cola di Rienzo and the Ancient Roman Republic', PhD thesis, University of New York at Binghamton, 1994.

Charles D. G. Spornick. ' The life and reign of Pope Eugene III (1145-1153), PhD thesis, University of Notre Dame, 1988.

Wesley Graves Rogers Tobey. 'Illusionistic ceiling painting: its fall from favor in sixteenth-century Rome', PhD thesis, The University of Texas at Austin, 1994.

Rome and Its People

General

1 Atti del Congresso nazionale di studi romani. (Proceedings of the National Congress of Roman Studies.)
Edited by C. Galassi Paluzzi. Rome: Istituto di studi romani, 1929-46.
The proceedings of five congresses organized by the then newly founded Istituto di studi romani in 1928, 1930, 1933, 1935 and 1938. Some 150 papers were delivered at each Congress on a wide variety of topics related to Rome. The sessions were divided into the following sections: antiquity, the Middle Ages, the Renaissance and modern period, the contemporary period, law disciplines, literature and philology, and science disciplines.

2 Panopticon romano. (Roman panopticon.)
Mario Praz. Milan, Italy: Ricciardi, 1967. 246p.
A collection of twenty-nine previously published essays and reviews by Mario Praz providing, as the title indicates, a panoramic view of Rome and its culture. In his preface, Praz laments Rome's transformation into a modern metropolis, and considers modern traffic, which has destroyed the city's former atmosphere of quietude and silence and is ruining its historic palaces and monuments, as the equivalent to the barbarian invasions or earthquakes of the past. The volume contains essays on artists and their relationship to Rome (Poussin, Richard Wilson, Piranesi), streets and quarters (the Corso, Via Veneto, the Macao quarter), squares (Piazza di Spagna, Piazza del Popolo, Piazza Navona, Piazza de' Ricci), aspects of the city (17th-century Rome, photographs of Rome, vanished Rome), the fountains of Rome, painted façades of palazzi, and a memoir on Eugénie Strong (Mrs Arthur Strong). A second volume by Praz and edited by Mariuma and Vittoria Gabrieli, *Panopticon romano secondo* (A second Roman panopticon) (Rome: Edizioni di storia e letteratura, 1977. 400p.) includes a bibliography of the writings of Praz from 1915 to 1977 (2,322 items), together with twenty-four essays on Roman palazzi (Palazzo Primoli, Palazzo Spada, Palazzo Braschi), G. G. Belli, the French in Rome, the Walls of Rome, the Tiber, Bernini, Piranesi, and Rome in the Renaissance.

3 **Roma: rivista di studi e di vita romana.** (Rome: a review of Roman life and studies.)
Rome: Istituto di studi romani (from 1926), 1923-44.

As well as articles on the city's history and antiquities, this monthly review on all aspects of Roman history and culture included features on its institutions and profiles of Roman artists, writers, composers and other personalities. It also had a listings supplement with information on museums and galleries, concerts, religious festivals and other events. It was the creation of Carlo Galassi Paluzzi, who also founded, in March 1925, the Istituto di studi romani, whose official organ this publication became from December 1926. After the war, the Istituto was restructured and in 1953 launched the publication *Studi romani*.

4 **Romans: their lives and times.**
Michael Sheridan. London: Orion, 1995. 258p.

This is a collection of ten essays presenting a personal vision of Rome and its inhabitants. Most focus upon a particular personality and read like a short story. The first essay is an account of the author's arrival in Rome by train, and a description of Stazione Termini and its surrounding area. There are essays on the Shelleys, Count Galeazzo Ciano (Mussolini's son-in-law), the papacy from Pius XII to John Paul II, Giulio Andreotti, as well as the kidnapping of Aldo Moro, the disappearance of Roberto Calvi, and other scandals.

5 **Rome: the sweet, tempestuous life.**
Paul Hofmann. London: Marvill Press, 1983. 245p.

In this book, thirty-three short pieces describe modern life in Rome, including New Year's Eve celebrations, flea markets, coffee and ice cream, the joys of the siesta, news stands and bureaucracy.

Books of photographs

6 **Album romano.** (Roman album.)
Silvio Negro. Rome: Gherardo Casini, 1956. 253p.

A collection of 265 photographs taken between 1840 and 1900. They include views of the city, ceremonies, buildings, interiors, works of art, genre scenes, views of ruins, and portraits (among others Cardinal Giacomo Antonelli, Francesco Saverio De Merode, Pope Pius IX, Ferdinand Gregorovius, Johann Friedrich Overbeck, and Mariano Fortuny). The introduction discusses the work of early photographers of Rome, such as Victor Prevost, Jacopo Caneva (who took the earliest dated photograph of Rome – a view of the temple of Vesta in 1847 – and also the only photograph of G. G. Belli), Antonio D'Alessandri (the principal photographer of the Rome of Pius IX), and Giuseppe and Luigi Primoli (great grandsons of Lucien Bonaparte and photographers of the Roman high society in the last decades of the 19th century). It also looks at the relationship between early photography and art and the influence of the new medium on painting and engraving. It evokes pre-1870 Rome, its picturesque appearance (some photographs show cattle grazing in the Forum), its society, and its superstitions (the scarcity, in the early years of photography, of photographic portraits of well-known people is here attributed to their fear of the *jettatura* [evil eye]). The radical changes in the appearance of the city after 1870 are also discussed, together with the survival of certain customs and traditions to the end of the century. The notes on the photographs are brief but informative. An edition published by Neri Pozzi in 1964 as *Nuovo album romano* (New Roman album) is essentially the same work with thirty-nine additional photographs. The quality of the reproductions is, however, preferable in the earlier edition, where they are in black and white, not in sepia.

7 **Roma fine secolo nelle fotografie di Ettore Roesler Franz.** (Turn-of-the-century Rome in the photographs of Ettore Roesler Franz.)
Bruno Brizzi. Rome: Edizioni Quasar, 1978. 247p.
In producing his water-colours recording picturesque views of Rome that were soon to disappear, Roesler Franz made use of photographs. A large cache of these photographs and also of quick sketches and colour notations taken on the spot was discovered in the 1970s and revealed Roesler Franz's talents as a photographer to equal his achievements as a water-colourist. A selection of these photographs and sketches forms the subject of this book. They were mostly taken in the 1880s and are a precious record of social conditions in the poorer quarters of Rome. The upper classes and political and celebratory events are totally absent from these photographs which concentrate, instead, on the life and occupations of the working classes. The excellent reproductions are accompanied by historical and topographical commentaries. The introductory essay describes the urban development of Rome in the 1880s, the creation of new quarters and the destruction of large segments of the city's historic centre and of the 'green belt' of patrician villas and parks. It also includes an interesting account of the construction fever and land speculation that gripped Rome in the early 1880s and the ensuing financial crisis.

8 **Roma ieri e oggi: immagini a confronto.** (Rome yesterday and today: comparative images.)
Armando Ravaglioli. Rome: Newton Compton, 1982. 342p. (Quest'Italia, 40.)
A photographic album comparing views of Rome in old and modern photographs, tracing the changes, over more than 100 years, in the city's appearance. There are chapters on the Walls and the Gates, the piazze, the streets, monuments and areas that have been destroyed (this section includes photographic sequences of the Villa Ludovisi and the Ghetto).

9 **Roma nelle fotografie della Raccolta Ceccarius presso la Biblioteca nazionale di Roma.** (Rome in the photographs of the Ceccarius Collection in the National Library of Rome.)
Edited by Piero Becchetti, Laura Biancini, Simonetta Buttò.
Rome: Colombo, 1991. 224p. maps.
The library and archive of the well-known romanist Ceccarius (Giuseppe Ceccarelli) was donated to the Biblioteca nazionale centrale di Roma in 1972. It includes books, prints and other material documenting all aspects of Rome, its history, urban development and folklore. Ceccarius's collection of photographs includes some 2,000 mostly rare and, in some cases, unique items dating from the mid-19th century to 1940. This edition brings together a cross-section of the collection. The first section includes examples of Rome's history and its artistic and cultural heritage and is introduced by an essay on Ceccarius, his contribution to Roman studies, and the formation of his collection. The second section concentrates on photographs commissioned by the Comune of Rome to record parts of the city that were soon to disappear as a result of the demolition campaigns between 1871 and

1931. An introductory essay describes these campaigns – the demolition of historic quarters and the 'green belt' of the city's villas and their gardens, the opening of major new arteries (Via Nazionale, Corso Vittorio Emanuele II), the creation of new quarters, and the demolition, in the 1920s and 1930s, of buildings in the historic centre to highlight individual ancient monuments and buildings – and divides them into three phases.

10   Roma primo Novecento nelle immagini di Alfredo de Giorgio. (Rome in the early 20th century in the photographs of Alfredo de Giorgio.) Texts and commentaries by Livio Jannattoni, technical and biographical notes by Piero Becchetti.   Rome: Editalia, 1988. 271p.

Like the Primoli brothers at the turn of the 19th century, Alfredo de Giorgio (1861-1926) was the chronicler of Roman life between 1908 and 1923. This is a selection of 200 photographs out of some 6,000 of his surviving 'stereoscopic' negatives. It is divided into the following sections with each group of photographs preceded by a short introduction: views and monuments, churches, museums, the city by night, Villa Borghese and the Pincio, the zoological gardens, the Vittoriano (views of its construction and its unveiling in 1911), the Campagna and Castelli romani, the Thermae of Fiuggi, theatres and concerts, portraits, popular feasts, cinema, the 1911 Exhibition, and the 'la Reginetta di Roma' (a contest in 1911 to elect a 'little queen' among 'princesses' representing each *rione*.)

11   Roma: i rioni storici nelle immagini di sette fotografi. (Rome: the historic *rioni* as seen by seven photographers.) Texts by Lucia Cavazzi (et al.).   Rome: Peliti Associati, 1990. 181p.

The catalogue of an exhibition held in Palazzo Braschi in 1990. It presents contemporary views of the fourteen historic *rioni* of Rome taken by seven professional photographers – Gabriele Basilico, Roberto Bossaglia, Giovanni Chiaramonte, Mario Cresci, Luigi Ghirri, Guido Guidi and Roberto Koch. Each section is preceded by a map of the *rione* and there is a mixture of colour and black-and-white photographs. There are biographical notes and pictures for each artist represented.

12   Rome from the air. Photographs by Guido Alberto Rossi, text by Franco Lefevre. London: Weidenfeld & Nicolson, 1989. 144p.

A collection of magnificent colour photographs of Rome, some showing abstract geometrical patterns (the pavements on the Campidoglio), others Piranesi-like accumulations of different types of structures (in one astonishing image the dome of the Pantheon is dwarfed by the gleaming white mass of the Vittoriano). There are impressive panoramic views showing the street network of whole areas of the city (the Tridente, the Campo Marzio), while others focus on single buildings (there are, predictably, several spectacular views of the Colosseum). The accompanying text is better avoided, the description of Stazione Termini as '…a strongbox of melancholy, an unfair salad of failed plans, education taken halfway and unresolved utopias' being typical.

13 Rome in early photographs: the age of Pius IX: photographs 1846-1878 from Roman and Danish collections.
Dyveke Helsted (et al.). Copenhagen: the Thorvaldsen Museum, 1977. 482p. bibliog. map.

This is the catalogue of an exhibition of 210 photographs shown in Copenhagen and Rome in 1977. Each photograph has a full-page reproduction with a detailed catalogue entry on the facing page. Introductory essays give an account of politics and social conditions in Rome during the reign of Pope Pius IX and describe, district by district, the changing townscape between 1846 and 1878. There is also a short history of early photography in Rome and biographies of all the photographers represented at the exhibition, with bibliographies where available.

14 I tetti di Roma: le terrazze, le altane, i belvedere. (The rooftops of Rome: the terraces, the loggias, the *belvedere.*)
Astra Zarina, Balthazar Korab, preface by Mario Praz. Rome: Carlo Bestetti, 1976. 79p. + *c.* 175p. of plates. bibliog.

A collection of black-and-white photographs of Roman 'roofscapes'. These include panoramic views of the city and views of individual buildings and architectural details, together with views of a wide variety of private and public terraces, pergolas and roof gardens. The volume includes a survey of views of Rome from above, with examples taken from ancient Roman frescoes and reliefs, plans of the city, topographical prints and drawings as well as aerial views. The preface by Mario Praz refers to a variety of panoramic descriptions of the city in art and literature.

Geography

General

15 Il Vaticano nell'antichità classica. (The Vatican in classical antiquity.)
Ferdinando Castagnoli.   Vatican City: Biblioteca apostolica vaticana,
1992. 278p. maps. bibliog. (Studi e Documenti per la Storia del
Palazzo Apostolico Vaticano pubblicati a cura della Biblioteca
Apostolica Vaticana, vol. 6.)
This is a study of the topography of the Vatican Hill (*Vaticanus ager* or *Vaticani montes*)
– the territory on the right bank of the Tiber below the juncture with the Cremera (a
tributary of the Tiber) – in antiquity. It examines references to the area in classical and
medieval texts, describing the origin of the name, the extent of the area, its special
geological features and its history. It also surveys medieval traditions (for example in the
Liber pontificalis) regarding its topography in antiquity. Separate chapters deal with
references to particular sites, buildings and monuments, including the Horti Agrippinae
and the Horti Domitiae, the Vatican obelisk, the Circus Gaii et Neronis, and burial
grounds. The study makes extensive use of excavations carried out in the area since the
1950s. An appendix provides a collection of inscriptions referred to in the text and
published here for the first time. There are 255 illustrations, including maps, plans, prints
and inscriptions).

Geology

16 La geologia del Monte Vaticano. (The geology of the Vatican Hill.)
Gioacchino De Angelis D'Ossat. Vatican City: Biblioteca apostolica
vaticana, 1953. 53p. + 9 leaves of plates. (Studi e Documenti per la
Storia del Palazzo Apostolico Vaticano pubblicati a cura della
Biblioteca Apostolica Vaticana, vol. 1, fasc. 1.)

Forming part of a series of studies on the history of the Palazzo apostolico vaticano, this
study of the geology of the Vatican Hill was facilitated by the excavations carried out in
the area during the 1930s, which brought to light new evidence regarding its rock
formation. It describes the morphology of the area from the Pliocene era to the present
and looks at the decisive phases of its development. It begins with a survey of earlier
publications on the geology of the city of Rome and its surrounding area. This is followed
by a systematic examination of the seven rock formations of the Vatican Hill, discussed
in chronological order beginning with the earliest, and a study of fossils (which are listed
and illustrated). The study also includes a geological plan of the Vatican City.

The River Tiber

17 Il Tevere e i suoi ponti. (The Tiber and its bridges.)
Giorgio Morelli, Associazione Amici del Tevere. Rome: Edizioni
Kappa, 1980. 262p. bibliog.

A photographic record of twenty-six bridges over the Tiber, from Ponte Tor di Quinto
(near Acqua Acetosa) in the north to Ponte della Magliana in the south. In each of the
twenty-six chapters, the photographs are preceded by information about the bridge
divided into four sections: name and reasons for its construction; date of construction and
later changes; technical data; and history and folklore of the area near the bridge. All the
photographs are in black and white.

18 The Tiber: the Roman river.
Nora Nowlan, map by Fred Kliem. London: Frederick Muller, 1970.
96p.

Nowlan follows the course of the Tiber from its source on the eastern side of Monte
Fumaiolo, through Umbria and Lazio, to Ostia and Fiumicino. The short text gives potted
histories and impressionistic descriptions of Perugia, Assisi, Todi, Orte, Bomarzo, Rome,
Ostia and Fiumicino, and is accompanied by a good selection of black-and-white
photographs.

Topography

General

19   Appunti di topografia romana nei codici Lanciani della Biblioteca apostolica vaticana. (Roman topographical comments in the Lanciani Codices in the Biblioteca apostolica vaticana.)
Edited by Marco Buonocore.   Rome: Edizioni Quasar, 1997- .

Rodolfo Lanciani (1846-1929), whose *Forma urbis*, a gigantic map of Ancient Rome (see entry no. 23), and *Storia degli scavi* (see entry no. 190) are fundamental texts on the topography of Ancient Rome and the history of the rediscovery of its antiquities, compiled a gigantic card index which contains, rigorously classified, the results of some fifty years of research (notes, inscriptions, drawings and photographs). This precious archive was donated by Lanciani to the Biblioteca apostolica vaticana in 1925. It was originally contained in forty-two files each containing information on one of Rome's fourteen *Regiones* and the city's surrounding area (*Suburbio*). These were later rearranged and bound in sixteen volumes (Vaticani latini 13031-13047). To these were added fourteen notebooks, also written by Lanciani (Vaticani latini 15216-15229). This edition gives a transcription of this important archive. The first two volumes (out of a projected five) have been published to date and these deal with the codices Vaticani latini 13031-13034 and 15216-15217 (Vol. 1) and Vaticani latini 13035-13038 and 15223 (Vol. 2).

20   Codice topografico della città di Roma. (Topographical codex of the city of Rome.)
Edited by Roberto Valentini, Giuseppe Zucchetti.   Rome: Tipografia del Senato, 1940-53. 4 vols. (389p., 405p., 510p., 638p.). maps. bibliog. (Fonti per la Storia d'Italia pubblicate dal R. Istituto Storico Italiano per il Medio Evo, 81, 88, 90, 91.)

A collection of texts on the topography of Rome dating from the beginning of the Empire to the end of the 15th century. Carl Ludwig von Urlichs' *Codex urbis Romae topographicus* (Topographical codex of the city of Rome), published in 1871, was a similar collection but the brevity of its commentaries and the discovery of new material on the topography of Rome in Antiquity and the Middle Ages made a new critical edition necessary. Each text is preceded by an introduction and copious notes.

21 Fontes ad topographiam veteris urbis Romae pertinentes.
(Sources related to the topography of Ancient Rome.)
Collected and edited by Giuseppe Lugli. Rome: Università di Roma, Istituto di topografia antica, 1952-69.

This compilation of literary sources to the topography of Ancient Rome was projected to be published in eight volumes but volumes five and seven were never published. It uses a wide variety of sources ranging from literary descriptions to coins and brick-stamps. The information is provided under convenient headings with numerous cross-references. Volume one contains general references to the city (its location and nature, its name, its origins, references ranging from the period of the early Kings to that of the Empire, explanations about the way the city was divided into *regiones*), descriptions and praise of the city, and sections on the Pomerium and the City Walls and Gates. Volume two contains sections on the Tiber, the Bridges, the Cloaca Maxima, the Insula Tiberina and the Aqueducts. The remaining volumes consist of a systematic survey of references to each of the fourteen *regiones* into which Augustus divided Rome when he reformed the municipal administration in 7 BC.

22 Forma Urbis Marmorea: aggiornamento generale 1980. (The Marble Plan of Ancient Rome: a general update 1980.)
Emilio Rodriguez Almeido. Rome: Quasar, 1981. 200p. + portfolio (51 folded plates).

Almeido presents the results of research carried out during the twenty years following the publication of the first edition of the Marble Plan of Ancient Rome. A number of other marble fragments have been placed in their positions since then, for example those related to the Southern Field of Mars (Campus Martius) or the large fragment with Vicus Patricius. The work is in two parts, the first addressing general questions about the plan and providing a chronology since its creation during the first decade of the third century AD, the second providing a commentary to the fifty-one plates which reintegrate the new discoveries into the plan.

23 Forma urbis Romae. (Plan of the city of Rome.)
Rodolfo Lanciani. Milan, Italy: E. Hoepli, [1893-1901]. 14p. + [47] leaves of plates (46 folded).

This magnificent plan of Rome, which ranks among Rodolfo Lanciani's greatest achievements, was issued in eight parts between 1893 and 1901. It is drawn at a scale 1:1000 and is in forty-six plates each measuring approximately 57 cm x 97 cm. It superimposes modern locations (delineated in red) on those of the ancient city (in black) and also contains indications of the date of excavation or restoration of ancient structures, written by their name. There are two indices, the first of buildings and monuments of Ancient Rome, the second (which is sub-divided into four headings) of the modern city.

24 La Galleria delle carte geografiche in Vaticano. (The Gallery of Maps in the Vatican.)
Edited by Lucio Gambi and Antonio Pinelli. Modena, Italy: Franco Cosimo Panini, 1994. 2 vols. (534p., 595p.), 1 portfolio (index of place names, 40 folded maps). (Mirabilia Italiæ, 1.)

The frescoes in the Gallery of Maps in the Vatican constitute the largest cycle of geographical images in Europe. The walls of the gallery are adorned with regional maps of Italy, which were drawn up between 1580 and 1581, at the wish of Pope Gregory XIII, and were the creation of the cosmographer Egnazio Danti, who was responsible for the overall design and was assisted by numerous painters and stucco-workers, notably the Flemish landscape painters Matthijs and Paul Brill, and also Gerolamo Muziano and Cesare Nebbia. In this sumptuous edition, the texts are in double columns with the Italian original on the left and the English translation in the right-hand column. The Atlas volume contains an introductory essay by Lucio Gambi and 790 mostly colour plates depicting the entire decoration of the Gallery: the maps on the walls and their inscriptions, the 'picture atlas of Christian history' and monochrome scenes on the ceiling, the 'grotesques', the amphoras and herms. The Texts volume contains seven essays discussing the historical background to the creation of the gallery, the circumstances of its construction and the contribution of Egnazio Danti, and its significance in the context of Counter-Reformation policies and Pope Gregory XIII's other commissions. They also examine the Gallery's elaborate iconography, its influence, and the history of its restorations and repaintings, which began as early as 1588. This volume also contains detailed notes on all the works, a full bibliography and an index of names and places. Finally, a separate portfolio contains forty folded maps and an index of all the place names found in the Gallery, with an abbreviation of the name of the map in which they feature. An English language edition by Lucio Gambi, *The Gallery of Maps in the Vatican* (New York: George Braziller, 1997. 208p.) contains Lucio Gambi's introductory text, 195 colour plates of the maps and a diagram of the Gallery.

25 Lexicon topographicum Urbis Romae. (A topographical dictionary of the City of Rome.)
Edited by Eva Margareta Steinby. Rome: Edizioni Quasar, 1993-99. 5 vols. bibliog.

This dictionary aims to replace Platner and Ashby's work, the *Topographical Dictionary of Ancient Rome*, published in 1929. It is substantially larger than its predecessor, both in the number of its entries and in its treatment of individual monuments. One notable feature is its inclusion of Christian antiquities (to the 7th century), whereas Platner/Ashby only treated classical antiquities (to 608 AD). Another difference is that the geographical area covered in the present work is that of Rome within the Aurelian Wall, omitting the Suburbio, as a separate volume is being planned for that. Each entry provides: the name(s) of the site, its definition (its region and its relationship with surrounding buildings), written sources, archaeological data, its changes of function, its restorations, and a bibliography. Illustrations include plans of the monuments, maps, depictions on coins, and other iconographical elements. The texts of the entries are in Italian, French, English, or German, the language in which contributions were originally submitted.

26 The Map of Rome, 1625 Paul Maupin: a companion to the facsimile reproduced from the original in the Pepys Library.

Sarah Tyacke. London: Nottingham Court Press; Cambridge, England: Magdalene College, 1982. 24p. maps.

Measuring over twelve feet in length and six in width, and printed on forty-eight sheets, this is the largest woodcut plan of the city. There are only two known copies, at the Bibliothèque nationale in Paris and the Pepys Library of Magdalene College, Cambridge, neither of which had been previously reproduced. This short text, which accompanies the facsimile of the Cambridge copy, provides a wealth of new information, especially about the respective roles of the cartographer and publisher. The map was drawn in the bird's-eye-view or plan-view style, showing the city as if viewed from above at an oblique angle from a high point to the west of the city. The buildings are drawn in elevation but do not obscure the ground plan of the city. It was published by Paul Maupin, a French stationer on the Ripetta, who largely used the unpublished plans of Giovanni Maggi, a talented draughtsman and cartographer who had died some seven years earlier, updating them to 1625. It seems that Maupin's contribution was mainly the dedication to Prince Wladislaw of Poland (1595-1648), who was then on a tour of Italy, and the explanatory text which describes the foundation and development of Rome, listing squares, churches and other notable buildings. Tyacke's introduction also compares the 1625 map to its better known 1774 reprint by Carlo Losi and gives an indication of the amount of information about the Rome of 1625 that was lost in the alterations made by Losi, which include a resetting in letterpress of the legends and place-names, a new title-cartouche and the removal of the dedication to Wladislaw and the explanatory text.

27 A new topographical dictionary of Ancient Rome.

L. Richardson Jr. Baltimore, Maryland; London: The Johns Hopkins University Press, 1992. 492p.

This dictionary is offered as a replacement for *A Topographical dictionary of Ancient Rome* by Samuel Ball Platner and Thomas Ashby (Oxford: Oxford University Press, 1929), until now the standard reference work on the subject. It takes into account the results of the excavations and research carried out since the publication of that work. Its geographical limits are those of the fourteen Augustan *regiones* and it includes all significant sites, monuments and buildings from the earliest occupation of Rome to the onset of the Middle Ages in the 6th century. Most Christian churches and tombs are excluded. Numerous entries include plans, and there is a glossary and a chronological list of dated monuments. The introduction provides a useful survey of topographical sources, from epigraphical material on surviving remains of ancient monuments, through medieval compilations such as the *Codex Einsiedelnsis*, the *Mirabilia urbis Romae*, and the works of Renaissance antiquarians, topographers and artists, to the archaeological writings of the 19th and 20th centuries. It points out the variety of material available to the topographer of Ancient Rome, which ranges from literary sources to the analysis of physical remains, and underlines the need for evaluating the reliability of the evidence they present. The work of the topographer is described as '...a path through a maze, beset with pitfalls and full of surprises, both pleasant and unpleasant'.

28 Nuova pianta di Roma, 1748. (A new map of Rome, 1748.)

Giovan Battista Nolli, edited by Stefano Borsi. Rome: Officina edizioni, 1994. [47p.].

A facsimile of the original 1748 edition of Giovanni Battista Nolli's 1748 ichnographic map. Nolli had worked as a surveyor in Lombardy and Piedmont before moving to Rome in 1736. His map, on which he worked for the next twelve years, assisted by, among others, Ferdinando Fuga and Michelangelo Specchi (who executed the plans of the churches), combines great accuracy and high artistic quality. It consists of twelve imperial format sheets, plus a table in which important monuments and buildings are individually numbered by *rione*, and an alphabetical index.

29 La pianta marmorea di Roma antica: Forma Urbis Romae. (The Marble plan of Ancient Rome: Forma Urbis Romae.)
Edited by Gianfilippo Carettoni (et al.). Rome: X Ripartizione del Comune di Roma, 1960. 265p. + 1 portfolio (6p., 64 plates). bibliog.

The Forma Urbis Romae is a plan representing the city at a scale of 1:240, incised on marble slabs during the reign of Septimius Severus. It was originally displayed on a wall in an annex of the Temple of Peace. Fragments of it were accidentally discovered in 1562 behind the church of SS Cosma e Damiano. Various other fragments were discovered in later centuries. The plan, on which the names of numerous buildings are also incised, sheds important light on Roman topography but, to date, only 160 of its 1,000 surviving fragments (10 per cent of the total) have been put in place. The plan has been the subject of intense interest, with drawings of some of its fragments first being made during the Renaissance. This magisterial edition incorporates new finds and research carried out since Heinrich Jordan's 1874 study and is in two parts. Part one traces the history of the discoveries of the plan's fragments and includes a catalogue containing 712 entries corresponding to 1089 items, i.e. 993 marble fragments and 96 drawings of lost parts. Part two includes a study on the hall and wall where the plan originally hanged, a technical analysis of the plan, a discussion of its date, purpose and precedents, and, finally, a reconstruction of it. The volume also contains topographical, epigraphic and name indices.

30 Le piante di Roma. (Maps of Rome.)
Amato Pietro Frutaz. Rome: Istituto di studi romani, 1962. 3 vols. (358p., 322 plates, 362 plates).

A catalogue of 245 maps dating from 203 AD to 1961. They are arranged as follows: Ancient Rome (1-60), 4th to 15th centuries (61-102), 16th century (103-142), 17th century (143-162), 18th century (163-177), 19th century (178-220) and 20th century (221-145). There are detailed analytical and chronological indexes.

31 Le piante di Roma dal Cinquecento all'Ottocento. (Maps of Rome from the sixteenth to the nineteenth century.)
Edited by Giovanna Aragozzini, Marco Nocca. Rome: Dino Audino, 1993. 157p.

A study of ten maps of Rome published between 1551 and 1829, all landmarks in the cartography of the city. Each has an introductory chapter in which the circumstances of its creation, artistic merits and special features are discussed. Since the maps are studied in chronological order, these chapters provide a continuous survey of urban developments from the 16th to the early 19th century, with references to the appropriate section in the plates that follow each chapter. It is a pity that the mediocre quality of the plates makes detailed consultation of the maps virtually impossible. The maps are by Leonardo Bufalini (1551), Ugo Pinard (1555), Etienne Dupérac (1574 and 1577), Antonio Tempesta (1593), Mattheus Greuter (1618), Giovanni Maggi (1625), Giovanni Battista Falda (1676), Giovan Battista Nolli (1748) and the Direzione generale del Censo (1829). In the introductory essay the editors describe the varied clientele of these maps – pilgrims, artists, and antiquaries. Depictions of modern Rome were favoured by popes for propaganda purposes as they showed (and often highlighted) the new urban and architectural wonders achieved during their pontificate. Humanist and antiquarian interests were reflected in plans of the ancient city – Dupérac's 1574 map is an example of this tendency. This is a generally admirable edition, though the editors seem to be unaware of the extant copies of the 1625 map by Giovanni Maggi (see entry no. 26), reproducing instead its 1774 reprint.

32 **Piante e vedute di Roma e del Lazio conservate nella raccolta delle stampe e dei disegni, Castello Sforzesco.** (Maps and views of Rome and Lazio in the prints and drawings collection of the Castello Sforzesco.)
Paolo Arrigoni, Achille Bertarelli. Milan, Italy: Edizioni d'arte Emilio Bestetti, 1939. 583p.
This catalogue lists 5,038 items. It includes a checklist of works cited, an index of locations (in two parts: Rome, and other locations in Lazio), an index of artists, and an index of authors of the works in which the engravings were published. The volume is enriched by numerous plates.

33 **Piante e vedute di Roma e del Vaticano dal 1300 al 1676.** (Maps and views of Rome and the Vatican from 1300 to 1676.)
F. Ehrle, H. Egger, illustrated by Amato Pietro Frutaz. Vatican City: Biblioteca apostolica vaticana, 1956. 25p. + 54 leaves of plates. maps. (Studi e Documenti per la Storia del Palazzo Apostolico Vaticano pubblicati a cura della Biblioteca Apostolica Vaticana. Tavole, vol. 1.)
This is a collection of fifty-four folio maps and views selected by Francis Cardinal Ehrle and Hermann Egger, the two eminent historians of the Vatican Palace and originators of this series of publications. The material is arranged in strict chronological order with a subject index (the two scholars originally planned a subject arrangement in several volumes but the project was left unfinished and finally published in this form some twenty years after their deaths). The views include both details from illuminated manuscripts and also independent works in a variety of media (paintings, frescoes, drawings and engravings). The earliest work dates from the 13th century and the latest, a detail from G. B. Falda's *Map of Rome*, from 1676. They include Pol de Limbourg's view of Rome (*c.* 1416), a panoramic view of Rome in the background of the Benozzo Gozzoli fresco in the church of S. Agostino at San Gimignano (1465), Marten van Heemskerck's drawn and painted depictions of S. Peter's and the Vatican (c. 1533-34), Pinard's map of Rome (1555), a panoramic view of Rome attributed to Joos Van Cleve (1560), frescoes by Cesare Nebbia and Giovanni Guerra (1588-90), and Antonio Tempesta's map of Rome (1664). The collection is a valuable record of the transformations of S. Peter's basilica and the Vatican over a period of four centuries.

34 **Pictorial dictionary of Ancient Rome.**
Ernest Nash. London: Thames & Hudson, 1968. rev. ed. 2 vols. (544p., 535p.)
The *Pictorial dictionary* presents the monuments of Ancient Rome in pictures and plans, with brief descriptions giving the main dates of their history and discovery. It follows, in the arrangement and denominations of its entries, the order established by Samuel B. Platner and Thomas Ashby in their *Topographical Dictionary of Ancient Rome* (1929), which adopted an

alphabetical rather than topographical arrangement, and includes numerous monuments and districts of Ancient Rome which came to light in the interval between the two works. The dictionary also includes monuments whose names cannot be ascertained, as they are not mentioned in literature or epigraphy, but which are important to the study of Roman topography. The photographs show the present state of the monuments, with an emphasis on the topographical aspect, though it also includes photographs showing inscriptions, architectural ornament and sculptured decoration. Old photographs, engravings and drawings are used to show changes in a monument's appearance or when a monument was destroyed or reburied. The bibliography complements the one in the *Topographical Dictionary*, while the introduction provides a survey of earlier depictions of the ruins of Ancient Rome, beginning with 16th-century collections of engravings.

35   Roma di Sisto V: la pianta di Antonio Tempesta, 1593. (The Rome of Sixtus V: the map of Antonio Tempesta, 1593.)
Stefano Borsi.   Rome: Officina edizioni, 1986. 170p. maps. (Fonti e immagini / architettura e città, 1.)

Tempesta's map is an important document on the topography of Rome at the end of the 16th century and a record of the urban changes carried out during the pontificate of Sixtus V. It consists of twelve sheets joined together, although in this edition each sheet is further subdivided into four sections. The introductory essay examines Tempesta's career in Rome and his output both as a painter and engraver. Having worked for Gregory XIII, he was out of official favour during the pontificate of Sixtus V and had to turn to engraving as a source of income, executing numerous battle and hunting scenes (Tempesta-engraved works number more than 1,500 prints). The production of this enormous map of Rome, which would show the extensive changes to the city's appearance brought about by Sixtus V (especially his creation of new arteries joining the major basilicas) is seen here as Tempesta's attempt to gain favour with the new pope. However, it took so long to complete that it was finally published after the death of Sixtus V, with a dedication to Clement VIII. Some of the unusual features of the map are pointed out, such as the inclusion of signs for inns and hostelries. Very few copies of the 1593 and 1606 editions have survived but there are revised editions by Mattheus Merian (1640) and Gian Giacomo de' Rossi (1648-60). The introduction is followed by a detailed, zone-by-zone, study of the map. The plates are of only average quality.

36   Roma di Urbano VIII: la pianta di Giovanni Maggi, 1625. (The Rome of Urban VIII: the map of Giovanni Maggi, 1625.)
Stefano Borsi.   Rome: Officina edizioni, 1990. 138p. (Fonti e Immagini. Architettura e Città, 2.)

This is the largest historical map of Rome, in forty-eight large sheets. This edition examines both its historical-documentary value and also its artistic qualities. The introductory chapter looks at the life and career of Giovanni Maggi (who, as well as an engraver, was also a landscape artist and theorist [he was the author of two unpublished architectural treatises]), his patrons and collectors. It is followed by a detailed, zone-by-zone, analysis of the map, outlining urban changes.

37   Rome 1748: the *Pianta grande di Roma* of Giambattista Nolli in facsimile.
Introduction by Allan Ceen.   Highmount, New York: J. H. Aronson, 1984. 8p. + 20 sheets. bibliog.

Ceen's introductory essay considers the position of Nolli's great plan (scale 1:2900) in the series of ichnographic images of the city, which began with the 3rd-century *Forma Urbis Marmorea* and ended with Rodolfo Lanciani's *Forma Urbis* (1893-1901). It also examines Nolli's debt to the *Forma Urbis Marmorea* (the fragments of which he arranged for display on the staircase of the Capitoline Museums in 1741) and also to Bufalini's 1551 woodcut, the first meticulously complete plan where every street and city block was clearly drawn. The differences between the original drawing, from which the plates of the plan were made, and the print are also discussed, as are the ruins and monuments that appear in the plan and the symbolism of the allegorical figures of ancient and contemporary Rome. It concludes by pointing out the excellent timing of the publication of the plan at the end of a period of urban vitality in the early 18th century, as opposed to the second half of the century, which was a period of comparative lethargy. The plan includes all projects completed or about to be completed at the time of its execution, such as the Trevi Fountain (completed 1762) and Palazzo Corsini (completed 1751). There is also a chronology of known events in the life of G. Nolli. See also *Gio. Battista Nolli, 1701-1756, e la sua gran 'pianta di Roma' del 1748* (Gio. Battista Nolli, 1701-1756, and his great 'plan of Rome' of 1748) (Clemente Faccioli. *Studi Romani*, vol. XI, no. 3 [July-September 1966], p. 415-42]. As well as discussing Nolli's map, this article also provides a biography of the cartographer and discusses his other work, such as his design for the church of S. Dorotea in Trastevere.

Modern maps

38   Artwise Rome: the art map.
Amagansett, New York: Streetwise maps, 1997. rev. ed.

This map is accompanied by brief entries for museums (the 'Rome art index'), churches and monuments, all of which are clearly indicated on the map by different colour codes.

39   Let's Go map guide Rome.
Edited by Emily M. Tucker.   New York: St Martin's Press, 1997. 27p. folded maps.

Provides maps of Greater Rome, the city centre, Vatican City, as well as the Rome underground. These are accompanied by a practical guide that gives general information for the casual visitor; it includes a complete street locator and city guide, essential phone numbers and addresses, restaurants and hotels, villas and parks, entertainment, sights and museums, and seasonal events.

40 Pianta monumentale a volo d'uccello del centro storico di Roma nell'anno del centenario, 1970. (Monumental bird's eye view map of the historic centre of Rome in the centenary year, 1970.) Edited by Armando Ravaglioli, drawn by Luigi Piffero. Rome: Linostampa Nomentana, 1972.

Seventy segments of this map were used in a later publication by Ravaglioli to form walks in the city. It includes two smaller maps, Rome in 1870 (taken from the map of Augusto Fornari, first printed in 1865 and corrected in 1868), and a map of the greater metropolitan area of Rome in 1970, showing the boundaries of the main map (enclosed by the Aurelian and Leonine Walls) and the wider area.

41 Roma: guidatlante. (Rome: a guide and atlas.) Milan, Italy: Touring Editore, 1997. 111p. maps.

This guide-atlas is divided into three sections. The first is a guide which, after a brief history of Rome and a note on food and drink, consists of thirteen itineraries. Each itinerary includes brief historical entries about the various sights while a map in the text indicates their exact location. The more important sights are also given map references, with the maps constituting the second section. There are seventy-five maps, their scale ranging from 1:1,000,000 (surroundings of Rome) to 1:6,000 (the city centre). The third section is an alphabetical index.

42 Roma: pianta e indice. (Rome: a plan and an index.) Milan, Italy: Michelin italiana, 1999. (Michelin Tourism, no. 38.)

This is an annually updated plan (scale 1:10,000) showing all major roads, one-way streets, main public buildings and car-parks. There is an alphabetical index and a useful information section.

43 Roma, Rome, Rom. Edited by Marco Ausenda. Milan, Italy: Touring Club Italiano, 1998.

The main plan is 1:12,500 in scale. There is also a plan of the historic centre (1:7,500) and a plan of the Greater Rome urban area (1:100,000). The three plans are accompanied by an index of street names, monuments and squares.

Guides and Companions

General

44 Baedeker Rome.
Madeleine Reincke, Heinz Joachim Fischer. New York: Macmillan;
Basingstoke, England: Automobile Association, 1995. 5th ed. 217p.
maps. (Baedeker's Travel Guides.)
The guide is divided into three parts. The first part has a history of Rome, a dictionary of
prominent figures in Roman history, facts and figures, a list of emperors and popes, and
quotations about Rome. The second, and most substantial, part describes the principal
sights of Rome in alphabetical order with practical information about times of opening
and how to get there, with the location shown in the margin. Each entry also gives the co-
ordinates of the square on the large folded map included where the particular feature can
be located. The third part contains practical information, also in alphabetical order, from
airlines and antiques to when to go and youth and student hostels. The guide is illustrated
in colour throughout and includes several plans and a large folded map.

45 Breviarium Urbis Romae antiquae. (Breviary of Ancient Rome.)
Compiled by Adrianus van Heck. Leiden, the Netherlands: E. J.
Brill; Rome: G. Bretschneider, 1977. 632p.
This guide is a collection of texts drawn from classical sources related to what was built in
Rome in the eleven centuries between when Romulus built his hut on Palatine Hill and the
completion of Constantine's Arch. Only a fraction of what was created remains and sometimes
there is an abundance of information about minor monuments and next to nothing about major
ones. The work does not include Greek sources and the texts are not accompanied by full
commentaries. They are arranged according to the division of Rome into fourteen regions, with
an introductory chapter of general texts on Rome and followed by an epilogue. At the head of
each chapter there is a catalogue, in Latin, of the monuments to be seen in the particular region.
Within each region, the monuments are presented in the order in which they would be
encountered on a walk from the centre of the city to the Aurelian Wall. The names of extant
monuments are given in capital letters. Where more than one text is cited, the first one provides

17

general information about the monument and is followed, in chronological order, by texts about the history of its exterior and then its interior, and finally texts about the events that took place in or around the monument. Each fragment includes the origin of the text (author and work) and, wherever useful, the precise date of each event. All fragments are numbered and additional numbers indicate where there are further references to the same monument. The publication also includes maps of the regions, with figures on maps referring to the text.

46   City secrets – Rome.
Series editor Robert Kahn.   New York: The Little Bookroom, 1999.
274p. bibliog.

An elegantly produced companion to general guidebooks on Rome, this volume consists of recommendations of a favourite work, building, shop, or stroll in the city by artists, archaeologists, classicists, historians and other scholars who have lived in Rome (many of them attached to the American Academy in Rome). The contributions are organized into ten city zones, each with an accompanying map on which the sites discussed are numbered. An eleventh chapter discusses the area outside Rome. The length of entries ranges from one sentence to several paragraphs. Many entries include recommended reading.

47   The companion guide to Rome.
Georgina Masson, revised by Jim Jepson.   London: Collins, 1998.
522p. + [28]p. of plates. maps.

This companion guide was originally published in 1965 and is now in its fifth revised edition. It begins by warning the reader that it does not pretend to cover all aspects of the city's 2,500 years of history, but aims instead to provide a starting point for the visitor's own personal discoveries. It more than fulfils this promise with its twenty-six itineraries designed to fill the two-week holiday of an extremely energetic visitor. Most days are divided into two walks, with the last afternoon of the visit left free for shopping! Each walk is accompanied by a useful map, and the author's enthusiasm and vast knowledge of her subject are evident in every page. The guide also includes a list of places of interest not mentioned in the text, general information, hotels, restaurants, and opening hours of museums, galleries, churches and monuments.

48   Essential Rome.
Jane Shaw.   Basingstoke, England: AA Publishing, 1998. 126p.
maps. (The Essential Series.)

This guide, for the visitor seeking 'essential' information about the city and its sights, is divided into five sections: an introduction to Rome, the author's choice of Top Ten places to visit (each with practical information), a 'what to see' guide (with an alphabetical listing and a brief description of the main attractions, suggested walks and tours, and practical information), a 'where to...' guide (listings of restaurants, hotels, shops, and events), and practical matters.

49   Fielding's Rome agenda.
Lynn V. Foster, Lawrence Foster.   Redondo Beach, California:
Fielding Worldwide, 1997. maps. 300p. (Fielding Travel Guides.)

This guide includes twelve walks ('the neighborhoods, the hills, and in-between'), suggestions for excursions outside Rome and for prioritizing time depending on the length of one's visit, a special section on 'the three great sights' (the Roman Forum and the Palatine, the Colosseum area, and Vatican City) as well as the three things to avoid (Via

Veneto – 'not "in" since the '50s', the beach at Ostia, and McDonald's). It also provides extensive sections on hotels, restaurants and practical advice. All sections have star and icon rating systems. There is one appendix on Rome's history and art and one on art in Italy.

50 Frommer's Rome.
Darwin Porter, Danforth Prince. Foster City, California: IDG Books Worldwide, 2000. 15th ed. 281p. folded map.

A popular guide, updated annually, with sections on planning a trip to Rome, practical information (which includes advice about what to do upon arrival, a description of the city's layout, and its transport system), accommodation, dining, shopping, strolling in Rome, the sights, Rome after dark, and 'side trips' from Rome. A new feature of the latest edition is the inclusion of an online directory (which includes information on travel-planning websites). The guide, which is aimed at the general visitor, is stronger on practical information and restaurants (with thirty-one pages of recommendations) than history and culture (an 'in-depth' history of Rome is given in an appendix).

51 Guida insolita ai misteri, ai segreti, alle leggende e alle curiosità di Roma. (An unusual guide to the mysteries, secrets, legends and curiosities of Rome.)
Claudio Rendina. Rome: Newton & Compton, 1998. 540p. (Guide Insolite, 1.)

The stated aim of this work, also reflected in its somewhat sensationalist title, is to provide an A to Z of the wonders of Rome making use of anecdotes, myths and legends illustrating the city's history and art. Though these elements feature in several of the entries (as, indeed, in any other guide to Rome!) this is a useful encyclopaedic manual to Ancient, Medieval, Renaissance, Baroque, Modern, and Contemporary Rome and its monuments, temples, churches, obelisks, walls, bridges, streets, libraries, cultural institutes, traditions, festivals and food. There are also numerous entries for Romans and other persons associated with Rome (for example Petrarch, Tasso, St Bridget of Sweden), the biographical information concentrating on their relationship to the city. Full lists of popes and emperors of Ancient Rome and of the Holy Roman Empire are also included.

52 Guide rionali di Roma. (Guides to Rome's *rioni*.)
Edited by the Assessorato alla Cultura, directed by Carlo Pietrangeli. Rome: Fratelli Palombi, 1967- . bibliog.

This is a series of detailed guides to Rome's 22 *rioni* (wards or quarters). The names of these quarters are as follows: *Rione* 1. Monti, 2. Trevi, 3. Colonna, 4. Campo Marzio, 5. Ponte, 6. Parione, 7. Regola, 8. Sant'Eustachio, 9. Pigna, 10. Campitelli, 11. Sant'Angelo, 12. Ripa, 13. Trastevere, 14. Borgo, 15. Esquilino, 16. Ludovisi, 17. Sallustiano, 18. Castro Pretorio, 19. Celio, 20. Testaccio, 21. San Saba, 22. Prati. The first fourteen are the historic *rioni*, the other eight were created in the 19th century to include the areas outside the historic centre of the city. Sixty-five parts have been published to date, as each historic *rione* is covered in several parts. Each part includes information about the population, extent and confines of the area, its coat of arms, and an itinerary with detailed descriptions of notable buildings, their history and works of art they house. There are numerous black-and-white illustrations, maps, name and place indexes, opening hours (to be used with caution), as well as a bibliography. There is also an accompanying volume, which is an index to streets, squares and monuments discussed in the guides.

53 Handbook for Rome and the Campagna.
Edited by Norwood Young. London: Edward Stanford, 1908. 17th ed. 582p.

This is the seventeenth edition of the popular *Murray's Handbook for Rome & the Campagna*. The first edition was published in 1858 and it quickly became an indispensable guidebook for English visitors in Rome. It is in three parts: Directory (which provides practical information), Introduction (a short history of Rome, articles on architecture, sculpture, painting, chronological tables, lists of emperors, famous men, popes, religious orders, artists, a glossary of technical terms, and coats of arms of famous popes and noble families), and Routes.

54 Holy Rome: a millennium guide to the Christian sights.
Edited by Luca Giannini. New York: Fodor's Travel Publications, 1999. 180p.

This well-presented guide includes sections on the saints and martyrs of Rome, a history of Rome's Jubilees, twelve thematic itineraries, information on the projects for the year 2000, a calendar of cultural events, and the official calendar of religious events. It also includes Jubilee itineraries, and an alphabetical listing of artists who worked in Rome with the locations in the city where their work can be seen. The guide is illustrated in colour throughout.

55 Lazio.
Milan, Italy: Touring Club Italiano, 1996. 4th ed. 830p. maps. bibliog. (Guida d'Italia del Touring Club Italiano.)

The first edition of this guide was published in 1924. This is the latest printing (1996) of the fourth edition, first published in 1981. Future editions will also incorporate the surroundings of Rome, which are no longer included in the Rome volume of this series. The introductory section of this guide includes chapters on: geography, including social and economic conditions (with sections on demography, administration, the relationship of the region to Rome); dialects; history; the Etruscans of southern Etruria (northern Lazio); and art. There is also a chapter providing useful information on thermal stations, excursions, antiquities, sanctuaries, abbeys, castles, museums, events and folklore, hotels and restaurants, camping, food and drink. There are twenty itineraries. Twenty-one maps, seventeen town plans and an exhaustive bibliography are included.

56 Living and working in Rome.
Frances Gendlin. London: Kuperard, 1997. 295p. (Cultureshock!)

Designed to offer advice and assistance on daily life in Rome for visitors planning a longer stay in the city, there are chapters on housing and settling in; formalities for staying; business and money matters; transport; food markets; shopping and services; and religion.

57 Michelin Green Guide to Rome.
Watford, England: Michelin Tyre, 1997. 315p. maps. (Michelin Tourist Guides.)

Contains thirty-two itineraries to the sights of Rome, classified according to the Michelin star-rating system. Excursions to the outskirts of Rome are also included (to Lago di Bracciano, Castelli Romani, Ostia antica, Palestrina and Tivoli). Three summary maps locate the principal sights, and there are over 100 colour illustrations, while the texts are complemented by 80 detailed local maps and floor plans. The introduction has essays on the history of the city from its legendary beginnings to the present, its visual arts, literature, music and cinema. The practical information section includes travel tips, a calendar of events and admission times and charges, information on hotels, public transport, food and drink, as well as a glossary of useful words.

58 Pilgrims in Rome.
Edited by Francesco Gioia. London: Chapman, 1999. 240p. maps.

This is the English translation of the official Vatican guide for the Jubilee Year 2000. It contains introductions to the spiritual and historical treasures of Rome – the basilicas, the historic churches, the martyrs' sanctuaries, the homes of the saints, the Vatican museums, the various national Catholic churches in Rome, and the places of worship of other churches and religious communities. Each section begins with a spiritual introduction and ends with a spiritual message, and each basilica is also preceded by a reflection on the saint it is dedicated to. The main part of each entry gives a brief account of the history, and a description of the art and architecture of each building. These are accompanied by colour maps, plans and other illustrations, and also include practical information.

59 I rioni di Roma. (The *rioni* of Rome.)
Luciano Zeppegno. Rome: Newton Compton, 1978. 1,098p. (Quest'Italia, 8.)

In this book, Zeppegno presents a series of walks through the fourteen traditional *rioni* and also the eight modern ones.

60 Roma. (Rome.)
Edited by Adriano Agnati. Milan, Italy: Touring Club Italiano, 1995. 8th ed. 939p. maps. bibliog. (Guida d'Italia del Touring Club Italiano.)

The first edition of this justly famous guide, *Roma e dintorni* (Rome and its environs), was published in 1925. This new and much enlarged edition is dedicated exclusively to Rome (i.e. the area under the jurisdiction of the Comune of Rome). The surroundings will henceforth be included in the volume on Lazio. The new edition provides more detailed coverage of the architecture of the 19th and 20th centuries, and also of industrial archaeology. The introductory section includes: a chronology, a list of popes and papal coat-of-arms, a detailed history of the city from its origins to the present, and a survey of art and culture from the Middle Ages to the present. There is also useful information about underground Rome, obelisks, columns, 'talking statues', and foreign culture in Rome (religious communities, academies and cultural institutes). The main part of the guide consists of thirty-eight itineraries contained in five chapters, each corresponding to a unified sector of the city – the *rioni* east of the Tiber; Vatican City and the *rioni* west of the Tiber; the Aurelian Wall; the Tiber from Ponte Milvio to Ponte Sublicio; and the city outside the Wall. Each chapter and itinerary is preceded by an introduction discussing the special features of the area. It also provides useful information, an extensive bibliography divided into subject subdivisions, author and place indices, thirty plans and a folded map (scale 1:12,500).

61 Roma nell'età di mezzo. (Rome in the Middle Ages.)
Pasquale Adinolfi. Rome: Fratelli Bocca, 1881-82; Florence, Italy: Le Lettere-Licosa, 1982- .

In 1847, Pasquale Adinolfi (1816-82) began his extensive archival research that was to culminate in a systematic, street-by-street, topographical description of Rome in the Middle Ages. His work was, however, left unfinished, with only two volumes (out of a projected eight) published shortly before his death in 1882. The first volume is divided into three books; the first of these gives a general view of the city, its walls, gates and bridges; the second looks at the various ecclesiastical and civic authorities and establishes the division of Rome into thirteen *rioni*; the third examines *rione* Monti. The second volume continues the study of *rione* Monti and also covers Lo Trejo (Trevi) (the second *rione*) and Colonna (the third *rione*). Adinolfi's work was taken up again a century later with a facsimile reprint of the sections on the first three *rioni* followed by four new volumes based on Adinolfi's papers in the Archivio Capitolino. The volumes published thus far are *Rione Trastevere* (edited by Emilia Carreras); *Rione Arenula* (edited by Emilia Carreras); *Rione Ponte* (edited by Clara Mungari and Emilia Carreras); *Rione Campo Marzo & Rione S. Eustachio* (edited by Clara Mungari).

62 Rome.
Ros Belford. London: Dorsley Kindersley, 1999. 432p. (Eyewitness Travel Guides.)

This popular guide is divided into four main sections. *Introducing Rome* gives an overview of the geography and history of Rome and its main sights – the chapter *Rome at a glance* shows 'Rome's best' museums and galleries, churches and temples, fountains and obelisks and where to find them in *Rome area by area*, the main sightseeing section. This describes the main sights with maps, photographs and a variety of other types of illustrative material. There are sixteen area chapters, another chapter ('for the more inquisitive visitor to Rome') on some of the more isolated churches (S. Paolo fuori le Mura, S. Agnese), tombs and catacombs, parks and gardens, as well as day trips around Rome (Tivoli and Ostia antica) and a chapter proposing six guided walks (by the Tiber, along Via Giulia, along Via Appia antica, a tour of Rome's Triumphal Arches, mosaics, and Bernini's Rome). The last two sections are *Travellers' needs* – hotels, restaurants and cafés, shops and markets, entertainment, and children's Rome – and *Survival guide* – practical information, getting to Rome, and getting around in Rome. There is a profusion of colour illustrations, indeed the user is bombarded with area and locator maps, photographs, colour-codings, 'star sights' boxes, cutaway plans, and a variety of other visual signs. The 'detailed information' on each sight is, however, rarely more than a single paragraph offering only general information for the casual visitor. For an in-depth account of Rome's buildings and monuments, the reader should look elsewhere.

63 Rome.
Dana Facaros, Michael Pauls. London: Cadogan Books, 1997. 3rd ed. 472p. maps. (Cadogan City Guides.)

The main part of this refreshingly irreverent and commonsensical guide is divided into fifteen walking tours, each falling into categories of interest (Ancient Rome, Medieval Rome, Renaissance and Baroque, Vatican City). Other chapters offer practical information, dealing with Roman topics ranging from cats, pasquinades and the Roman Carnival to 'seven preposterous buildings', the worst Pope, a day in Ancient Rome, history, art and architecture, food and drink, accommodation, shopping, and living and working in Rome. The illustrations and maps are only adequate.

64 Rome.
Edward Hutton. London: Hollis & Carter, 1950. 297p.

This companion to Rome was first published in 1911 at a time when, as the author says in his preface to this seventh edition, there was a King in Italy and the Pope was a prisoner in the Vatican. It was also before the dramatic transformations of Rome during the first half of the century, when whole quarters of the city were excavated and the solitude of the Campagna was invaded. Many more changes have also taken place since the publication of this revised and enlarged edition, but the work can still be read with profit. Of its thirty-seven chapters, eleven are devoted to ancient Roman sites, twenty-one to Christian antiquities and churches, and the remaining chapters are about the pontifical national colleges in Rome, the fountains, some palaces and villas, the galleries of sculpture (i.e. the Museo Capitolino, the Vatican Museums, the Museo nazionale etrusco di Villa Giulia, and the Museo nazionale romano), and the Campagna.

65 Rome.
Veit Mölter, Margit Bornmann.   Singapore: APA Publications, 1991.
133p. maps. (Insight Pocket Guides.)

Described as a 'perfect companion for travellers who want to make the most of a short stay', this guide suggests three one-day itineraries to the city as well as four day-trips (to the Etruscan cities of Cerveteri and Etruria, to Tivoli, to the Lago di Bracciano, and to Ostia antica). It also has information about hotels, restaurants, shopping and Rome's nightlife. The style of writing is chatty and jokey, though the information provided is generally sound. The same applies to the presentation – 'welcome refreshment' is the caption of a photograph of a fountain and 'the heir of Michelangelo' that of a pavement artist.

66 Rome.
Anthony Pereira, Nick Skidmore.   London: Mitchell Beazley International Ltd, 1992. 4th ed. 295p. maps. (The American Express Travel Guides.)

Though this guide proposes four itineraries in the historic centre, the main description of the sights has an A-Z arrangement. It also includes excursions both to the environs of Rome and further afield (as far as Pompeii, Herculaneum and Capri!). The larger part of the guide is, however, taken up by practical matters including basic information (useful addresses, getting around, emergency information), hotels, eating and drinking, nightlife and entertainment, sport, and words and phrases. The maps and plans are all in black and white, though reasonably clear.

67 Rome.
London: David Campbell Publishers, 1994. 555p. bibliog. maps.
(Everyman Guides.)

The main part of this guide consists of seventeen itineraries, each with maps showing the main sites of interest as well as mini-maps locating a particular itinerary within the wider area covered by the guide. There are also plans of the main museums and galleries, together with colour illustrations and cut-outs of their most famous works. Special symbols indicate sites of interest. In the margins of the main text are illustrations and comments providing additional information on historical figures, monuments and works of art. The itineraries are preceded by brief introductory sections on the fauna and flora of Rome, its history, architecture, arts and traditions and, finally, artists' and writers' impressions. The guide also includes some sixty pages of practical information as well as thirteen street maps of central Rome and an index of streets.

68 Rome and environs.
Alta Macadam.   London: A. & C. Black; New York: W. W. Norton, 1994. 5th ed. 512p. maps. (Blue Guide.)

This excellent guide is divided into three parts. The first part provides practical information, giving hotel and restaurant listings, and it has sections on transport; museums, collections and monuments; parks and gardens; churches and church ceremonies; plays, concerts and festivals; and on visiting Rome with children. The second part details twenty-seven walks in

23

different areas of the city with descriptions of monuments, churches and museums. The third part covers the environs of Rome, including Northern Lazio, with thirteen excursions. There is also a list of Roman Emperors and a chronological list of Popes, plus an introduction to Ancient Rome with suggestions for further reading. The text is accompanied by numerous maps and plans and there are fifteen maps at the end of the book.

69 Rome and the Vatican.
Texts by Gianni Eugenio Viola, Laura Giallombardo, Alessandra Andresen. Milan, Italy: Touring Club of Italy; Basingstoke, Hampshire: AA Publishing, 1999. 241p.

This is a welcome English translation of the Touring Club Italiano's shorter guide to Rome. It includes an introductory chapter on the history of Rome and a section – split into twelve areas, each with a description of the main general features of the area – giving information on hotels, restaurants, cafés and other places of interest. There are twenty-one itineraries. Three of these come under the general heading 'Entering Rome', ten cover the historical city (including the Vatican), one the Lungotevere and, finally, seven the city following the unification of Italy. The work is richly illustrated with drawings, colour photographs, floor plans of buildings and museums and an excellent thirty-five-page city atlas.

70 Rome: the comprehensive street-by-street guide with bird's eye-view mapping.
Peter Greene, Richard Dixon, maps by Langford Richards. London: Duncan, Petersen Publishing, 1994. 143p. maps. (3-D City Guides.)

A useful guide containing fifty isometric maps (running from North to South and from West to East) produced from aerial photographic surveys showing all buildings, whether near or distant, in similar detail, thus avoiding the diminishing effect of perspective. Numerals on each map cross refer to the text printed on the facing page. The texts aim to show the rich variety of Rome, providing information not only on historic buildings, museums and famous sights but also on shops, bars and restaurants. There are indexes of points of interest (listed under convenient headings such as shops, cafés, churches, etc.) and people described in the text, as well as an index of street names. The guide also includes, for the first-time visitor, 'Rome in a nutshell', a list of the city's unmissable attractions.

71 Rome for less: compact guide.
London: Metropolis publishing, 1999. 72p. maps.

A brief guide for the visitor in a hurry. Its special feature, which justifies its title, is the inclusion of discount coupons for some of the museums and other attractions described in the text. Another original feature is the presence of numerous postage stamp-size maps at the margin of each building's description showing its immediate vicinity. These are accompanied by practical information (opening hours, address, etc.). The text contains numerous misprints.

72 Rome in the nineteenth century.
Charlotte A. Eaton. London: Henry G. Bohn, 1852. 5th ed. 2 vols. (460p., 431p.) (Bohn's Illustrated Library.)

According to the author, this book 'contains a complete account of the ruins of the Ancient city, the remains of the Middle Ages, and the monuments of modern times with remarks on the fine arts, the museums of sculpture and painting, the manners, customs, and religious ceremonies, of the modern Romans'. There are ninety-seven chapters.

73 Time Out Rome guide.
Edited by Anne Hanley. London: Time Out Group Ltd, 1999. 4th ed. 298p. maps.

A guide that aims to give a complete picture of Rome, from architecture and major tourist sites to practical information about pubs and bars. Its focus is as much on the present as on the past. There are brief surveys of Rome's history and architecture. In the *Sightseeing* section, the city is divided into various areas in which sites of interest are listed under headings such as Ancient Rome, churches, museums & galleries, etc. There are separate articles on special features of the area or personalities associated with it. There is also a section on practical and consumer matters giving information on accommodation, restaurants, snack and wine bars, ice cream, shopping (antiques, bookshops, flea markets, etc.), and services. An additional section provides details on art and entertainment, with information on film, gay and lesbian Rome, music, nightlife, theatre and dance, sport, and media. The directory contains information on getting around, women's Rome, and living and working in Rome. Finally, this edition of the guide gives 'the low-down on how to enjoy – or avoid – Rome's festivities for the Jubilee Holy Year in 2000 and beyond'.

74 A traveller in Rome.
H. V. Morton. London: Methuen, 1984. 5th reprint. 432p.

This vivid account of Rome was first published in 1957. Each of its ten chapters describes a visit to a particular area of the city and combines historical and cultural information with anecdotes, conversations and the author's wry observations. The section on the Trevi Fountain in Chapter 1 is typical – with a few deft strokes, Morton provides the history of the fountain and of the Aqua Virgo, evokes the delighted reactions of visitors to its theatricality ('Why, it's a perfect little theatre...Come along, let's go and sit in the stalls'), refers to its appearances in literature and in films, and discusses the custom of tossing a coin in the fountain. The text is full of felicitous and amusing remarks such as the description of William Wetmore Story's set as ' ...a gentlemanly and predominantly Anglo-Saxon Montmartre; and everybody... sufficiently well-off to leave Rome in the summer and go into the hills' or the description of Lord Byron's attitudinizing and his encounter with Thorvaldsen who, portraying him as he saw him, failed to capture his 'unhappy' expression. The appendix provides a biographical account of Charles Andrew Mills (1760-1846), owner of the Villa Mills on the Palatine Hill. See also Elizabeth Bowen, *A time in Rome* (London: Penguin Books, 1989. 169p. [Penguin Travel Library]). First published in 1960, this is an account of the writer's three-month stay in Rome in which she describes the famous classical sites and evokes the city's moods, adding her own reflections on life, politics and religion.

75 Tutta Roma: sessanta passeggiate proposte per 'vedere e capire la città'. (Complete Rome: suggestions for sixty walks to 'see and understand the city'.)
Armando Ravaglioli, drawings by Sergio dei Tinger. Rome: Edizioni di "Roma centro storico", 1983. 288p.

These walks were originally published in weekly instalments in *Il Tempo*. They offer a methodical, zone-by-zone, exploration of the city, each centred around a well-known monument or landmark. Each chapter/walk includes a volumetric segment of the *Pianta monumentale di Roma* (Monumental plan of Rome) (which accompanies this book) with the area covered in the walk highlighted, and consists of a short history of the area followed by individual descriptions of its main sights.

76 Virago woman's guide to Rome.
Ros Belford. London: Virago Press, 1993. 355p. (The Virago Woman's Travel Guides.)

This guide offers women advice about their stay in Rome. It has a larger than usual chapter on practical information, with sections on police and crime, sexual harassment, dress, danger spots, health and sex, women and feminism in Rome, and addresses of women's organizations. It also includes recommendations of hotels, restaurants and bars where women can feel safe and welcome and there is a chapter on women with children and businesswomen. The historical sections of the guide emphasize women's contribution to the history, art and culture to be seen in Rome's museums, galleries and monuments. These are usually in the form of highlighted sections following the descriptions of individual monuments or areas and describing the contribution of a woman or providing information on a topic of interest to women. Women discussed range from St Catherine of Siena to Alessandra Mussolini, and topics from the cult of Isis to the women on the ceiling of the Sistine Chapel.

77 Visitiamo Roma mille anni fa: la città dei Mirabilia. (Let's visit Rome a thousand years ago: the city of the Mirabilia.)
Cesare D'Onofrio. Rome: Romana Società editrice, 1988. 215p. (Collana di Studi e Testi per la Storia della Città di Roma, 5.)

This work contains the texts of four medieval guidebooks to Rome: the 11th-century *Mirabilia Urbis Romae* (Marvels of Rome); a 13th-century vernacular translation called *Le miracole di Roma* (Wonders of Rome); the 12th-century *Graphia aureae urbis Romae* (Writings on the golden city of Rome); and the 15th-century *Anonimo Magliabecchiano* (or *Tractatus de rebus antiquis urbis et situ urbis Romae* [Treatise on matters relating to the ancient city of Rome and its site]). The text of the *Mirabilia*, which largely concentrates on Ancient rather than Christian antiquities, contains chapters discussing famous monuments and legends such as Octavian's vision at Aracoeli, the equestrian statue of Marcus Aurelius (then believed to be of Constantine), reasons for the construction of the Pantheon, the origin of S. Pietro in Vincoli, etc. The introductory essay discusses the *Mirabilia* and other, less famous, medieval guidebooks, such as the 8th-century *Itinerario di Einsiedeln* (which describes the city in eleven itineraries) and the 4th-century *Curiosum*. It discusses and rejects the attribution of the *Mirabilia* to Benedictus, Canon of S. Peter's, the compiler of *Liber politicus*, a collection of documents which includes an *Ordo Romanus*, a description of the itineraries to be followed during religious festivals. It also attempts to date the texts through an examination of the textual evidence.

78 Walks in Rome (including Tivoli, Frascati, and Albano.)
Augustus J. C. Hare, 22nd edition by St Clair Baddeley. London: Kegan Paul, Trench, Trubner, & Co., 1925. 719p. maps.

This guide first came out in 1871 and it soon established itself as an indispensable point of reference for the English tourist in Rome. It is generally considered to be one of the best guidebooks to the city that has ever been published in English. The material for the original edition was collected throughout the 1860s. Sixteen editions were published during the author's lifetime, and St Clair Baddeley continued to edit the text until this, its twenty-second and last edition. After the introduction and a chapter giving 'dull-useful' (i.e. practical) information, the guide provides twenty-two walks describing all the sights in minute detail and making excellent use of quotations from other writers. There are numerous maps and plans. Hare also wrote a companion volume on the Roman Campagna – see *Days near Rome* (Fourth edition by St Clair Baddeley. London: Kegan Paul, Trench, Trübner & Co., 1906. 310p.).

Children's guides

79   The Colosseum: how it was built and how it was used.
Peter Chrisp.   Hove, England: Wayland, 1997. 48p. (Great Buildings.)

After an introductory description of a gladiators' contest, the first chapter introduces Rome and the Roman Empire and the role of amphitheatres and amusements in the lives of the citizens. After two chapters on the plan for the Colosseum and its building, the remaining four chapters concentrate on the variety of entertainments provided (from mock sea battles to wild beast hunts), the composition of the audience, the gladiators, Christian martyrs and the fortunes of the building after the banning of gladiatorial games in 404. The volume is illustrated in colour throughout, with photographs of sculptures, mosaics and coins, as well as illustrations showing the various stages in the construction of the amphitheatre. A chronology ('timeline') from 73 BC to 1871 is included.

80   Living in Ancient Rome.
Written by Odile Bombarde and Claude Moatti, illustrated by François Place.   London: Moonlight Publishing, 1987. 35p. (Pocket Worlds; Human World.)

One of a series of books of discovery for six-year olds and upwards, describing Rome at the time of the emperors, the appearance of a Roman villa, Roman dress, food, games, and the Romans at war.

81   The Roman Colosseum.
Fiona Macdonald, Mark Bergin.   Hove, England: Macdonald Young Books, 1996. 48p. (Inside Story.)

Before concentrating on the Colosseum itself, this account includes chapters on the Roman world, the city and its people (with a plan of Ancient Rome showing some of its buildings and monuments with their function explained), Roman government, the structure of society and the respective roles of the ruling class and ordinary citizens, city life and the religious significance and civic importance of 'bread and circuses'. The Colosseum is then compared to other amphitheatres, its construction shown (the preparation of the site, layout and materials, decorations), and its seating arrangements explained. The following chapters concentrate on the performances and, finally, on the Colosseum in later centuries. The work is illustrated throughout with Mark Bergin's attractive colour reconstructions. A glossary and a Colosseum chronology are also provided.

82   The traveller's guide to Ancient Rome.
Written by John Malam, illustrated by Mike Foster.   London: Marshall Publishing, 1998. 46p.

This is a humorous and informative guide for children aged between ten and twelve. It offers a tour of Rome's sights and entertainments. It includes useful information about the Roman calendar, numerals, weights and measures, and coins.

Travellers' Accounts

83   American novelists in Italy: the Discoverers: Allston to James.
Nathalia Wright.   Philadelphia: University of Pennsylvania Press,
1965. 288p.

A study of the influence of their experiences of Italy on the first group of American writers
to be notably affected by their stay in the country. Thirteen novelists and one short-story
writer (among them Nathaniel Hawthorne and Henry James) who went to Italy before 1870
and wrote fiction inspired by the country are in this group. Each section includes an outline
of the novelist's Italian itinerary, a summary of his comments on his experiences in letters,
diaries and travel books, a survey of the use of Italian material in his published works and a
detailed analysis – but not evaluation of the literary worth – of the treatment of Italy in his
fiction. The introductory chapter discusses precedents set by American artists abroad and the
close relations between artists and writers in Italy. It also points out that though few American
poets visited or were influenced by Italy, more than twenty-five 19th and some fifty 20th-
century American novels have an Italian setting. The last chapter highlights the influence of
Nathaniel Hawthorne's *The Marble Faun* on later American writers and examines patterns in
the Italianate fiction of the writers covered.

84   America's Rome.
William L. Vance.   New Haven, Connecticut; London: Yale
University Press, 1989. 2 vols. bibliog.

A comprehensive survey of some two hundred years of American representations of Rome in
literature (including journals, letters, travel and autobiographical writing, aesthetic, political, and
religious commentary and polemics), paintings, and sculpture. The subject of Americans in Italy
is of secondary importance, the primary focus being the actual works that resulted out of their
creators' experience of Rome. The descriptions and analyses of the works are arranged around
Rome's most prominent sites while, at the same time, the author is careful to demonstrate the
multifaceted reality reflected by a wide variety of individuals with different reactions to matters
political, religious and aesthetic. Volume one examines the influence of classical Rome. It
includes chapters on the Forum, the Colosseum, the Campagna, the Pantheon, the Vatican and
Capitoline Museums. Volume two concentrates on Catholic Rome (medieval and Baroque) and
the city in which the artists and writers lived. It describes representations of the Santo Bambino,

the Mother of God, and the pope, contrasting the views of American Roman Catholics to those of anti-papal Protestants. It also looks at reactions to Roman Baroque sculpture and architecture and neo-classical sculpture, and to Italy's national unification with Rome as its capital.

85   A dictionary of British and Irish travellers in Italy, 1701-1800.
John Ingamells.   New Haven, Connecticut; London: Yale University Press, 1997. 1070p. bibliog.

This dictionary publishes the Brinsley Ford Archive, donated to the Paul Mellon Centre for Studies in British Art in 1988. It contains biographical data on more than 6,000 people who travelled or lived in Italy in the 18th century. The entries describe the travellers' experiences in Italy and the emphasis is on biography. Visitors include grand tourists and students of the fine arts, diplomats, merchants, Jacobite exiles, and British and Irish families living abroad. The main text of each entry is preceded by a chronology of the traveller's whereabouts and is followed by bibliographical references. The book also contains maps, a chronology of events affecting the movements of travellers, a table of the rulers of nine Italian states, chronological and alphabetical lists of all known British artists in Italy in this period and, finally, William Paton's 'Advice on travel in Italy' (1766).

86   Due passi a Roma con Goethe. (Strolling in Rome with Goethe.)
Introduced by Italo Alighiero Chiusano.   Milan, Italy: E.S.T.E., 1997. 123p. (Collana Viaggio in Italia.)

This bilingual edition has sections on Rome in Goethe's time, his friends and cultural circle (with portraits and brief biographical notes), his home at 17 Via del Corso (now housing the Goethe Foundation), and extracts from his diary. It also includes a detailed chronology of Goethe's travels.

87   En Italie avec André Gide. (In Italy with André Gide.)
François-Paul Alibert, edited by Daniel Moutote.   Lyons, France: Presses universitaires de Lyon, 1983. 112p.

André Gide's *Journal* is virtually silent about his journey to Italy in 1913 in the company of François-Paul Alibert, Henri Ghéon and Eugène Rouart. Alibert's lyrical diary, later used for his *Élégies romaines,* gives an account of the journey that the four friends made between 21 April and 5 May 1913 and his ecstatic discovery of the beauty of Italy and its artistic treasures. In Rome, Alibert was particularly impressed by the Forum, the Sistine Chapel, and Raphael's *Stanze*. See also Alibert's *Élégies romaines* (Roman elegies) (Paris: Éditions de la Nouvelle Revue Française, 1923. 81p.).

88   The English road to Rome.
Brian Barefoot.   Upton-upon-Severn, England: Images, 1993. 255p.

A survey of English travel to Rome from the 7th century to the entry of the Allied Forces into Rome on 4 June 1944. Faced with the decision of whom to leave out, the author decided to allot more space to travellers whose experience of Rome was important to their later development or subsequent career. There are five chapters dedicated to the Middle Ages (looking at pilgrims, mercenaries, diplomats and merchants visiting Rome, and the history of the English Hospice in Rome), the humanists and English Catholics of the 15th and 16th centuries, the Grand Tourists of the following two centuries, British and American artists, and writers in Rome from the end of the Napoleonic Wars to 1870.

89 The English Roman life.
Anthony Munday, edited by Philip J. Ayres.   Oxford: Clarendon
Press, 1980. 142p. (Studies in Tudor and Stuart Literature, 3.)

Anthony Munday (*c.* 1560-1633) was a prolific poet, dramatist and pamphleteer. *The English Romayne lyfe* (first published in 1582) is of value both as a historical document and as travel literature. Munday went to Rome in 1579 in the company of Thomas Nowell (who later became a spy against Catholics in England), and the pair stayed in the English College, newly established as a seminary. Munday remained in Rome for three months and his work provides a detailed record of daily life in the College and the rebellion of the English students against Maurice Clenocke, who was later removed from the rectorship. It also gives a first-hand account of Roman social history and contains descriptions of the Jewish Ghetto, the reception of the Jewish converts in S. Giovanni in Laterano on Holy Saturday, the Roman Carnival, the recently rediscovered Catacombs, and surveys of churches and their relics. Munday was to play an important part in the capture and imprisonment of Jesuit emissaries to England, beginning with the first mission in 1581 led by St Edmund Campion and Robert Persons.

90 Il fascino di Roma nel Medioevo: le "Meraviglie di Roma" di maestro Gregorio. (The charm of Rome in the Middle Ages: the "Marvels of Rome" of Master Gregorius.)
Cristina Nardella.   Rome: Viella, 1998. 208p. bibliog. (La Corte dei Papi, 1.)

The introductory essay traces the journey to Rome in Antiquity and the Middle Ages, and the development of the genre describing the city and its monuments, the *Mirabilia Urbis Romae.* It also examines Master Gregorius's background and personality and points out some of the special features of his text that distinguish it from other medieval descriptions of Rome – its freshness and spontaneity, the author's lack of interest in Christian antiquities and his enthusiasm for and aesthetic appreciation of classical antiquities, which make him a pre-humanist. Master Gregorius's sources are also indicated and there is a detailed examination of his descriptions of individual statues, monuments and buildings, some of which are also illustrated at the end of the volume. The Latin text is given with a parallel Italian translation.

91 Florence Nightingale in Rome: letters written by Florence Nightingale in Rome in the winter of 1847-1848.
Edited by Mary Keele.   Philadelphia: American Philosophical Society, 1981. 340p. (Memoirs of the American Philosophical Society, 143.)

Florence Nightingale was born in Italy in 1820 and named after the city of her birth. She grew up in Derbyshire and before her stay in Rome described in these letters, she had been with her family on a prolonged tour of the Continent between September 1837 and April 1839. During this time, she developed an intense interest in Italian unification. Though initially reluctant to spend a winter in Rome, she was later to remember her time in Rome as one of the happiest of her life. Her views on art are highly individual, often influenced by its 'moral' content. This edition includes sixty-three letters, mostly to her family. They are divided into four sections, the letters written in Rome forming the bulk of the collection and framed by those written *en route* to Italy and, on her way home, from Paris. The last section consists of letters to Henry Colyar, a friend who accompanied her on her sightseeing on a number of occasions.

92 The fortunate pilgrims: Americans in Italy, 1800-1860.
Paul R. Baker.   Cambridge, Massachusetts: Harvard University
Press, 1964. 274p. bibliog.

Baker analyses American responses to Italy during the early and middle years of the 19th
century, from the morally earnest 'explorers', who wanted to learn and take back to the United
States information about the country's social life and institutions, to the 'romanticizers' who had
lost the freshness of impressions and spontaneity of the earlier generation and whose reactions
were conditioned by their readings and preconceptions about Italy. It examines the variety of
visitors and the motives of their journey (study, religion, culture, health, fashion) and the
business of travel itself (preparations, timetables, guidebooks, travel arrangements and
itineraries). It traces their reactions to the Italian, and Roman, social scene, their sightseeing, and
looks at some American residents whose homes became nuclei of Rome's cosmopolitan social
life – the sculptor William Wetmore Story, the actress Charlotte Cushman, the painter William
Stanley Haseltine, and the essayist and literary critic Margaret Fuller. It also looks at social
contacts with Italian people and American estimates of the national character and responses to
the various classes of Italian society, social customs and institutions, religion, government,
economy, and art. The life and work of American artists working in Italy, their artistic tastes and
influence of Italian art (both ancient and modern) on their work is also surveyed.

93 Les Français à Rome. (The French in Rome.)
Maurice Andrieux.   Paris: Fayard, 1968. 498p. (Les Grandes Etudes
Historiques.)

A history of French visitors to Rome through the ages, from the invasion of the Gauls in 390
BC to the end of the 19th century. It includes sovereigns, writers, painters, composers, financiers,
and others. The selection was based on the importance of each visitor, the influence Rome
exercised on his work, or the interest of events related to his stay. It is an immensely readable
work, marred only by the lack of bibliography and notes, which is frustrating especially when
the title of a writer's work is not given (as, early on, in the section on Claudius Rutilius
Namatianus, whose name is, moreover, misspelled in two different ways!) and when it is not
clear whether a passage referred to comes from a writer's travel journals or a work of fiction (as
in the section on the Goncourt brothers). An appendix lists churches, palazzi, villas, streets and
squares with French connections, and notable French works in museums and galleries in Rome.

94 The French and Italian notebooks.
Nathaniel Hawthorne, edited by Thomas Woodson.   Columbus,
Ohio: Ohio State University Press, 1980. 1056p. (The Centenary
Edition of the Works of Nathaniel Hawthorne, vol. 14.)

Nathaniel Hawthorne had two lengthy stays in Rome with his family: from 20 January to May
1858 (pp. 46-230) and from October 1858 to June 1859 (pp. 480-524). His feelings about the
city were ambivalent. His first impressions were negative due to the adverse circumstances of
his journey and his uncomfortable first lodgings. In these notebooks, he describes Rome as a
dead and mostly decayed corpse. He dislikes the narrowness of its streets, the houses which,
though built with brick and stone from Ancient Rome, look like magnified hovels, and the beggars.
He admires, however, the Barberini, Borghese, and Doria Pamphilj palaces, and the churches
of S. Giovanni in Laterano, S. Maria Maggiore, and S. Peter's impress him with their richness,
magnificence, and splendour. He also likes the Corso, and the Pincio (his lodgings were at 37
Via di Porta Pinciana). He conceived the idea for *The Marble Faun* in April 1858, a few weeks
before the end of his first Roman sojourn. Many of the impressions described in the notebooks
find their way into *The Marble Faun*, such as his highly personal comments on works of art –

for example, Guido Reni's *Beatrice Cenci* in the Palazzo Barberini and *S. Michael overcoming Satan* in the Church of S. Maria della Concezione (the Cappuccini Church), which play such an important symbolic role in the novel, or the descriptions of the Carnival on the Corso.

95   Grand Tour: the lure of Italy in the eighteenth century.
Edited by Andrew Wilton, Ilaria Bignamini.   London: Tate Gallery Publishing, 1996. 328p. bibliog.

This is the catalogue of the exhibition shown in London and Rome in 1996-97 that celebrated the Grand Tour, the journey to Italy which, by the 18th century, had become an essential part of every European gentleman's education. As the vast majority of Grand Tourists were British, the exhibition highlighted their role as patrons and collectors. The catalogue begins with a sample of 17th- and early 18th-century views of Italy collected by earlier visitors which helped to establish the image of the country. This is followed by a series of portraits of travellers, ranging from royalty and the nobility to connoisseurs, writers (a separate section is devoted to Goethe's Italian journey) and artists. Subsequent sections look at the journey and the evolution of the guide book; the places visited; festivals and folklore; the lure of the antique; memories from Italy (in the form of paintings and water-colours, bronze statuettes, biscuit-ware, Roman micromosaics, and architectural *capricci* [i.e. depictions of real monuments in imaginary settings]). As Rome, in the words of one of the contributors to the catalogue, 'represented the sacred goal at the end of a long, arduous and often dangerous journey', a large number of the 265 works at the exhibition were related to city and its inhabitants. See also Christopher Hibbert's *The Grand Tour* (London: Thames Methuen, 1987. 256p.), a vivid and well-illustrated account that follows the tourists through Europe and uses the descriptions of their experiences and their impressions of the cities they visited.

96   Italian hours.
Henry James, edited with an introduction and notes by John Auchard. Harmondsworth, England: Penguin Books, 1992. 415p. bibliog.

Henry James' *Italian Hours* was first published in 1909, bringing together his essays on travels in Italy written between 1872 and 1909 and originally published in the *Atlantic Monthly* and elsewhere. It includes a number of essays on Rome: 'A Roman holiday', 'Roman rides', 'Roman neighbourhoods', 'The after-season in Rome' and 'From a Roman note-book' all date from 1873, while 'A few other Roman neighbourhoods' was first published in *Italian Hours*. John Auchard, in his excellent introduction, points out the social changes Italy has undergone since the publication of *Italian Hours* and also the enormous changes Rome was undergoing in the years after 1870 – the virtual captivity of the pope, the secularization of the city and the new spirit of commercialism which saw the sale and destruction of some of its most beautiful villas. This edition also provides, in an appendix, Henry James's reviews of Italian travel books or travel notebooks, including Hippolyte Taine's *Italy: Rome and Naples* (a translation of *Voyage en Italie*, published in New York in 1868), *Passages from the French and Italian Note-Books of Nathaniel Hawthorne* (published in Boston, 1872), and Augustus J. C. Hare's *Days near Rome* (published in Philadelphia, 1875).

97   Italian journey, 1786-1788.
J. W. Goethe, translated by W. H. Auden and Elizabeth Mayer. Harmondsworth, England: Penguin, 1970. 508p. (Penguin Classics.)

When Goethe arrived in Rome on 29 October 1786, he was thirty-six years old. Already famous as the author of *Werther*, he travelled incognito, though his anonymity did not remain a secret for long. He stayed in Rome until 21 February 1787 and, after a journey to Naples and Sicily, from June 1787 to April 1788. He shared lodgings on the Corso with Johann Heinrich Wilhelm Tischbein, the neo-classical artist whose monumental portrait of Goethe in the Campagna was to become the most familiar image of the poet. Through Tischbein, Goethe was introduced to the German artistic and literary colony in Rome and Naples, which included Angelica Kauffmann and Philipp Hackert (who gave him drawing lessons). Goethe's journey was one of self-discovery and he regarded the two years he spent in Italy as the happiest of his life. His impressions, which are based both on the letters he sent to his friends in Weimar and the journal he kept, were published some thirty years later and were very influential. They give a vivid account of the poet's discovery of the artistic treasures of Rome (both ancient and modern) and of his life in Rome. There are also notable descriptions of Roman ceremonies and festivals, for example the Roman Carnival and the race of the riderless (the *barberi*) horses on the Corso, and the illuminations and fireworks on the name day of St Peter and St Paul (the *Girandola*).

98 **Italies: anthologie des voyageurs français aux XVIIIe et XIXe siècles.** (Italies: an anthology of French travellers in the eighteenth and nineteenth centuries.)
Edited by Yves Hersant.   Paris: Robert Laffont, 1988. 1121p. maps. bibliog. (Bouquins.)

Includes extracts from the writings of seventy-five French or Swiss writers who visited Italy between 1700 and 1900. The work is divided into three broad sections. The first includes extensive segments from the work of seven of the most famous writer-visitors: Charles De Brosses, Charles Dupaty, François René de Chateaubriand, Stendhal, Théophile Gautier, Guy de Maupassant, and Maurice Barrès. The aim here is to include each writer's impressions from various parts of the Peninsula, for example the six letters by Charles De Brosses are from Genoa, Milan, Florence, and Rome. The second section includes extracts from the work of a much larger number of writers (including the seven in the first section) following a route from North to South. The third section adopts subject divisions, from 'Amour' to 'Zoologie'. Other subjects include: Beggars, Brigands, Brothels, *Castrati*, Death, Festivals, Gastronomy, Inns, Music, Popes, Religion, and Theatre. The work also includes biographical notices of the writers, and a chronology.

99 **Lettre à M. de Fontanes sur la campagne romaine.** (Letter to M. De Fontanes on the Roman Campagna.)
François-René (Vicomte de Chateaubriand), edited by J.-M. Gautier.
Geneva: Librairie Droz, 1951. 169p. (Textes Littéraires Français.)

This famous letter celebrating the beauty of Rome and the Roman Campagna was written at the end of Chateaubriand's first sojourn in Rome, from June 1803 to January 1804, as secretary of Cardinal Fesch, the French ambassador to the Holy See. The letter was written for publication, the only one out of the twenty letters Chateaubriand planned to write and publish in which he would describe Rome and the reflections it aroused in him. It appeared in *Mercure de France*, of which Fontanes was the publisher, on 3 March 1804. The long introduction to this critical edition of the text discusses the historical and biographical background, looking at the circumstances of Chateaubriand's appointment, his journey to Rome, his troubled relationship with Fesch, and the death of Madame de Beaumont. It also surveys the literary and artistic vogue for the description and depiction of ruins and compares Chateaubriand's work with other travellers' impressions of the Roman Campagna, assessing its literary influence. Finally, it looks at Chateaubriand's later reactions to Rome, especially during his second sojourn in the city, as French ambassador in 1828-29, and in his *Mémoires d'outre-tombe* (Memoirs from beyond the grave).

100   Lettres d'Italie du Président De Brosses. (The Letters from Italy
of Président De Brosses.)
Edited by Frédéric D'Agay.   Paris: Mercure de France, 1986.
2 vols. (519p., 585p.) (Le Temps Retrouvé, 46-47.)

Charles De Brosses (1709-77) spent a year in Italy, from May 1739 to April 1740, with a
group of other Burgundian men of letters and collectors. Only nine of his letters were actually
written in Italy and sent to friends in Dijon, the rest were written after his return and are based
on notes made while in Italy. They present a vivid picture of life in Italy during the first half
of the 18th century. In Rome, where he stayed for four months, De Brosses was received by
Pope Clement XII. A man of encyclopaedic interests, De Brosses visited methodically all
sites and monuments, libraries, collections of natural history, medals, and prints and
drawings. He also attended many musical and theatrical performances. A great admirer of
female beauty, he deplores the absence of women from the stage in Rome but his letters
include numerous descriptions of Roman theatrical and musical life and comparisons
between French and Italian music and musical practices. In art, he admires Raphael, Titian,
Veronese, Caravaggio, and the Bolognese classicists; he dislikes Gothic and 15th-century art.
The introduction to this well-annotated edition provides biographical information about De
Brosses and his travelling companions, describes his character and intellectual and artistic
interests, and oulines the historical and political situation in Italy at the time of his visit. It also
surveys 18th-century travel literature, and the complicated publishing history of these letters
(which first appeared in print in 1799), and critical reaction to them. It also includes an index
of painters, sculptors and architects mentioned in the text, and a general index.

**101   The lure of Italy: American artists and the Italian experience,
1760-1914.**
Theodore E. Stebbins Jr.   New York: Harry N. Abrams, 1992. 470p.

The catalogue of an exhibition held in Boston, Cleveland and Houston in 1992-93 which
surveyed the fascination Italy held for American artists, from Benjamin West to the eve of
the First World War. West was the first colonial artist to visit Italy and he admired its Roman
ruins and Renaissance works of art. Later American artists were fascinated by the landscape
of Italy and the tangible evidence of its past, which they interpreted in works produced
during their long sojourns in the country. After 1914, the journey to Italy ceased to be
considered an essential element in an artist's education. The catalogue includes 130
paintings and sculptures produced by 72 American artists during or after their Italian
sojourns. Those artists inspired by Rome include Thomas Cole, William Wetmore Story,
Sanford Robinson Gifford and Martin Johnson Heade. All the catalogue entries are
reproduced in colour and are accompanied by extensive commentaries, and there are
biographies of all the artists represented. The catalogue also includes a variety of other
material, which shows the context in which the works of art were made – photographs,
letters, guidebooks, maps, sketchbooks, travel journals, novels and souvenirs from Italy.

102   The marvels of Rome.
Master Gregorius, translated with an introduction and commentary
by John Osborne.   Toronto: Pontifical Institute of Mediaeval
Studies, 1987. 122p. bibliog. (Mediaeval Sources in Translation, 31.)

Magister Gregorius' *Narracio de Mirabilibus urbis Romae* (a Latin text of approximately 4,500
words known from a single manuscript copy now in the library of St Catherine's College,
Cambridge) is, like the popular *Mirabiliae urbis Romae,* an account of the marvels to be seen
in Rome, a genre popular in the late Middle Ages. The precise date of the document is uncertain

(though a date between 1226 and 1236 is proposed in the introduction of this edition), as is the identity of the author. What distinguishes Gregorius' text from other medieval accounts of Rome is the author's scant interest in the city's Christian past and his concentration on its ancient art and architecture, thus giving an idea of the vast number of classical structures which had survived until the demolitions of the 16th and 17th centuries. It is, consequently, of great importance to historians of the survival of the classical tradition. It is divided into thirty-three short chapters in which the author describes, among others, bronze statues (two chapters are taken by the equestrian statue of Marcus Aurelius – the only equestrian monument to have survived from Antiquity), marble statuary, buildings (the Pantheon, then called S. Maria Rotonda), triumphal arches and columns, pyramids and obelisks. The introduction considers the importance of the text and its special characteristics, while the detailed commentary contains a wealth of information about the works and places mentioned in the text.

103 Mémoires d'outre-tombe. (Memoirs.)
François-René (Vicomte de Chateaubriand), edited by Maurice Levaillant and Georges Moulinier. Paris: Éditions Gallimard, 1951 (latest edition 1991). 2 vols. (1274p.; 1496p.). (Bibliothèque de la Pléiade, 67, 71.)

Chateaubriand's *Mémoires d'outre-tombe* include two sections describing his two sojourns in Rome, in 1803-04 and in 1828-29. In 1803, Chateaubriand was appointed secretary of Cardinal Fesch, Bonaparte's uncle and ambassador to the Holy See. His description of his experiences in Rome, which include his uneasy relationship with Fesch, the death of his beloved Madame de Beaumont, and his discovery of the beauty of Rome, is contained in Books 14 and 15. Chateaubriand returned to Rome in 1828 as Ambassador and remained in the Eternal City for seven months (14 September 1828 to 16 May 1829). The description of this period is in Books 30 and 31. As Chateaubriand himself notes, the information they contain is of three types: his private life and feelings as revealed in his letters to Madame Récamier; his public life, contained in his dispatches; and, in the third category, a mixture of historical details about the popes, Roman society and the changes it has undergone over the centuries. They also include his reflections about Rome and his descriptions of the city and its countryside, the fruit of his walks. There are also descriptions of the funeral of Pope Leo XII in February 1829 and of the conclave that elected Pope. This edition includes a chronology and an analytical index of names and places mentioned in the text.

104 The memoirs of Hector Berlioz.
Translated and edited by David Cairns. London: Cardinal, 1990. 582p.

Berlioz was a Prix de Rome pensioner at the Villa Medici from January 1831 to May 1832, during the directorship of Horace Vernet, a kindly man who showed great patience with the young composer's impulsive decisions and sudden changes of mood. These memoirs include vivid descriptions of life at the Villa – escapades with other pensioners, the Thursday *soirées* at the director's quarters, Sunday excursions to the outskirts of Rome. Berlioz was bored in Rome – he went there half-heartedly during a period of great emotional turmoil, away from Paris – in his words 'the centre of civilisation' – to a city where he found himself cut off from music, the theatre (theatres in Rome were open only four months each year) and literature (most of the works he admired were on the Papal Index of books proscribed by the Roman Catholic Church). He disliked official functions, which he found insipid, but enjoyed his wanderings and adventures in the Roman Campagna and beyond. His accounts of musical practices and standards in Italy are scathing. He was fascinated, however, by the rustic music of the *pifferari* – the shawm and bagpipe players who came to Rome from the countryside during Advent and played traditional Christmas tunes in the streets of the city. The *Memoirs* contain an abundance of amusing episodes and situations, such as the author reading Lord Byron's *The Corsair* in a confessional in S. Peter's, sheltering from the summer heat. This translation is well annotated and has two useful appendices: Berlioz as seen by his contemporaries and a glossary.

105 Mes voyages, Lourdes, Rome: journaux inédits. (My travels, Lourdes, Rome: unpublished journals.)
Émile Zola, edited by René Ternois. Paris: Fasquelle, 1958. 302p.

Émile Zola's Roman journal covers the period between 31 October and 15 December 1894 (p. 121-292 of this edition). He was given a distinguished visitor's welcome in Rome, where he had come to research his next novel, entitled *Rome*. His requests for an audience with Pope Leo XIII were, however, rebuffed. He, nevertheless, managed to gather enough detailed information about the Pope and the Vatican Palace from friends. During his stay in Rome he visited ancient sites, churches and the Catacombs, and surveyed newly built neighbourhoods, always making notes of his impressions and trying to imagine what would be the impressions of Pierre Froment (the hero of his novel) in the various places he visited. The introduction to the text of the journal, which also explains the genesis of *Rome*, analyses Zola's stay in Rome, the development of his ideas and his reactions to the social and political conditions in the Eternal City that were to find their way into the novel.

106 Oeuvres intimes. (Private works.)
Stendhal, edited by V. Del Litto. Paris: Éditions Gallimard, 1981-82.
2 vols. (1676p., 1731p.) (Bibliothèque de la Pléiade, vols. 109, 304.)

This collection of Stendhal's autobiographical works contains two texts related to Rome: the *Journal,* and *Vie de Henry Brulard* (Life of Henry Brulard). The *Journal,* which Stendhal kept from 1801 to 1841, is of particular interest to the student of Rome for the entries written during the novelist's unhappy years as French Consul at Civitavecchia (1830-41), which contain numerous references to Rome. *Vie de Henry Brulard* begins with a famous description of Rome seen from S. Pietro in Montorio on the day of the author's fiftieth birthday, a view that triggers, like Proust's madeleine, the narration of his life. This edition is minutely annotated and contains excellent indices of persons, places and works of art.

107 Panopticon italiano: un diario di viaggio ritrovato, 1759-1761.
(Italian Panopticon: a newly discovered travel diary, 1759-1761.)
Jean-Claude-Richard de Saint-Non, edited by Pierre Rosenberg, with the collaboration of Barbara Bréjon De Lavergnée. Rome: Edizioni dell'Elefante, 1986. 447p. map.

This is the first publication of the Abbé de Saint-Non's diary of his journey to Italy. Until the reappearance at a sale in Paris of the copy of Saint-Non's text (on which this edition is based), the diary was thought to have been lost. The Abbé de Saint-Non (1727-91) is best known today as the patron of J.-H. Fragonard, Hubert Robert and other artists, and for the *Voyage pittoresque de Naples et de Sicile* (Picturesque journey from Naples and Sicily) (5 vols., 1781-86), one of the most beautiful illustrated books of the 18th century, which was published thanks to his efforts. On his journey to Italy, where he stayed for nearly two years (from 1 October 1759 to 26 September 1761), he was accompanied by the painter Hughes Taraval, and on his return journey to France, by Fragonard. The twenty-eight-year-old artist, who had previously gone with Saint-Non to Tivoli and Naples, had to study works of art and antiquities, and produce drawings of these and also of views of natural scenery. At the end of the journey these drawings remained with Saint-Non, who may have intended to engrave and publish some of them. Saint-Non's diary includes descriptions of all the important works of art, buildings and monuments of the places he visited, as well as observations on social life and anecdotes. There are few comments on contemporary events – for example the Seven Years War, or the election of a new pope (Clement XIII) – and few personal revelations, apart from a mention of a sentimental attachment in Rome which may account for the length of his stay in the city (from December 1759 to April 1760 and from June 1760 to April 1761). He shows interest in popular and religious festivals, music, architecture and town planning, but his main preoccupation is painting, especially Raphael, Michelangelo, Pietro da Cortona, and the Bolognese School. This bilingual edition (in French and Italian), includes a catalogue of 360 drawings Fragonard produced for Saint-Non, arranged by the location of the original works or the views Fragonard copied. Nos. 40-120 were done in Rome. The catalogue entries point out changes of attribution, and indicate the existence of engravings after Fragonard's drawings. All the drawings are reproduced, and some of the artist's remarkable red chalk drawings are also reproduced in colour in the text.

108 Pictures from Italy.

Charles Dickens, edited with an introduction and notes by Kate Flint. Harmondsworth, England: Penguin Books, 1998. 272p.

Dickens was in Italy for an extended stay during 1844 and 1845 and this account of his journey and impressions follows his route through France, Genoa, Central Italy, Rome and Naples. He arrived in Rome on 30 January 1845, during the Carnival season, but moved on to Naples on 6 February, returning to Rome for a more extended stay between 2 and 25 March. In the chapter on Rome (p. 116-161), he is an attentive but virulent observer of Catholic rituals, which he deflates mercilessly. He is equally sarcastic about most religious iconography, as in his trenchant description of the frescoes in the church of S. Stefano Rotondo showing scenes of martyrdom – 'Grey-bearded men being boiled, fried, grilled, crimped, singed, eaten by wild beasts, worried by dogs, buried alive, torn asunder by horses, chopped up small with hatchets... these are among the mildest subjects.' He enjoys the exuberance of the Roman carnival and the race of the riderless horses on the Corso. He is horrified by a public beheading he witnesses, condemning its cruelty and inhumanity but also showing a morbid interest in all its macabre details. He is fascinated above all by the grandeur and desolation of ruins, where 'the broken hour-glass of Time is but a heap of idle dust' and the fusion of the ancient and the modern, especially in the way pagan buildings and monuments have been assimilated into the fabric of the modern city and appropriated by Christianity, 'the false faith and the true are fused into a monstrous union', as in the various obelisks where statues of saints have replaced those of Roman Emperors.

109 Roba di Roma.

William W. Story. London: Chapman & Hall, 1863. 2 vols. (363p., 365p.).

William Wetmore Story settled in Rome with his wife in 1856. A man of independent means (he was the scion of a distinguished New England family) he lived in princely fashion in a large apartment in the Palazzo Barberini. This collection of essays on Roman society and mores, some of which originally appeared in the *Atlantic Monthly*, was published during his first years in Rome. The title of the work, he explains in the preface, would be intelligible to anyone who has been to Rome, 'roba' meaning everything 'from rubbish and riff-raff to the most exquisite product of art and nature'. It begins with his first impressions of Rome, and subsequent articles deal with a variety of subjects: street music and beggars in Rome (where he provides an astonishing portrait of Beppo, the 'king of the beggars'), cafés and theatres (including an account of theatrical and operatic censorship), Pasquino and pasquinades, the Colosseum, markets, the Ghetto, Roman games, field sports and races, fountains and aqueducts, saints and superstitions (including the evil eye), and births, baptisms, marriages and burials.

110 Rome au XIXe siècle, vue par les grands compositeurs pensionnaires à la Villa Médicis, et par leurs contemporains. (Rome in the 19th century, as seen by the great composer pensioners at the Villa Medici, and by their contemporaries.) Anne-Christine Faitrop-Porta. Moncalieri, Italy: Centre interuniversitaire de recherche sur le voyage en Italie, 1996. 308p. bibliog. (Bibliothèque du Voyage en Italie, 53.)

The Prix de Rome for music was established in 1803, enabling the winner to spend two years of study in Rome as a pensioner at the Villa Medici, the new home of the French Academy. As Rome was a musical backwater, the rewards of the prize were not obvious, unlike those of the prizes for painting, sculpture, engraving and architecture, which enabled young artists to profit from the Eternal City's immensely rich artistic heritage. It was accordingly accepted with bad grace by some of the winners, such as Berlioz, who only stayed for fourteen months (see also entry no. 104). Some of the greatest 19th-century French composers – Gounod, Bizet, Massenet, Debussy and Charpentier – were among the winners and their correspondence and memoirs provide a vivid picture of everyday life in Rome and the Villa Medici. This study also makes use of accounts about these composers provided by other contemporary visitors in Rome, often from different disciplines – writers such as George Sand talking about Bizet, Maupassant and Zola about Debussy and Charpentier, or the painter Regnault about Massenet.

111 Ye solace of pilgrimes: una guida di Roma per i pellegrini del Quattrocento. (Ye solace of pilgrimes: a guide to Rome for fifteenth-century pilgrims.) John Capgrave, edited and with an introduction and translation by Daniela Giosuè. Rome: Roma nel Rinascimento, 1995. 231p.

John Capgrave's description of Rome was written c. 1450 in the Norfolk dialect. The text was first published in 1911. Capgrave (1390-1464) was an Augustinian (Austin) friar and probably a prior at King's Lynn monastery. He visited Rome between 1449 and 1452 perhaps for official reasons (in 1449 the general chapter of the Augustinian order met in Rome). No record of his journey has survived. The editor considers this the best guide to Rome written in England before the modern era. It is in three parts: part 1 is an account of the origins of Rome, from Noah's visit to Italy to the founding of the city, with a description of its ancient monuments and the legends related to them, and a list of its rulers from Romulus to Frederick II. Capgrave's sources for this part are three texts: *Graphia aureae urbis, Mirabilia urbis Romae* and *Libellus de cerimonia aulae imperatoris*; part 2 is a tour of the Seven Churches and Stations of Lent; part 3 examines other famous churches. The text, which contains precise copies of inscriptions and lists of relics in the churches he visited, shows that the author was well-read and a careful observer. The text is translated from a 15th-century copy at the Bodleian Library and is incomplete. See also *Ye solace of pilgrimes: a description of Rome, circa AD 1450, by John Capgrave, an Austin friar of King's Lynn* (edited by C. A. Mills. London: Henry Frowde, 1911. 212p.).

112 Specchio di Roma barocca: una guida inedita del XVII secolo, insieme alle vedute romane di Lievin Cruyl. (A mirror of Baroque Rome: an unpublished 17th-century guide, together with the Roman views of Lievin Cruyl.)
Edited by Joseph Connors, Louise Rice. Rome: Edizioni dell'elefante, 1991 (2nd revised and enlarged ed.). 266p.

Reproduces (in the original French with an Italian translation) parts of the unpublished manuscript 'Description de Rome moderne' in the Avery Library, New York (Ms n. AA 1115.D456). The manuscript is anonymous and not dated, though internal evidence points to a date between 1677 and 1681. Though incomplete, it describes the most important monuments of Rome. The author was a traveller, well-introduced in Rome (he had an interview with Queen Christina of Sweden), well-read (there are various references to classical authors) and chauvinistically French (he has a low opinion of Italian gardens and Italian interior design). He lived in Piazza Navona and had an eye for street life and popular culture. As the editors point out in their excellent introduction, 'It is these descriptions of everyday life rather than the largely derivative attributions of works of art, that constitute the charm and merit of the *Description*...' The text is accompanied by prints and drawings of views of Rome by Lievin Cruyl, a Flemish artist active in Rome from 1664 to 1674. Cruyl also had a liking for the popular life of the streets and piazzas, which he recorded in his teeming views. In the drawings, which were intended for publication as prints, the view is reversed.

113 Stendhal's Rome: then and now.
Alba Amoia and Enrico Bruschini. Rome: Edizioni di storia e letteratura, 1997. 162p. bibliog. (Quaderni di Cultura Francese, 29.)

The authors of this work remark that the Rome of today is almost as remote from Stendhal's Rome as was the latter from the Rome of the Caesars. They point out the obliteration of the distinctive profile of the hills since Stendhal's time and the further acceleration in the levelling of hills and valleys, the disappearance of many of the characteristic sights, sounds and smells of the city (the smell of rotten cabbage and the sight of hanging rags seen through the windows of the buildings on the Corso that horrified Stendhal on his first visit to Rome, the sound of the bagpipes of the *pifferari* from the Abruzzi in the weeks before Christmas), and the loss of many of the artistic treasures that were in Rome in Stendhal's time. The study begins with a general consideration of Stendhal's writings on Rome, pointing out their unevenness and the alternation in them of brilliant perceptions or descriptions of contemporary Roman life and hackwork or enumerations of places of interest without comment. It surveys the wide range of Stendhal's sources, which include writers of memoirs and travel accounts (Cellini, de Brosses, Montaigne, Duclos), historians (Gibbon, Suetonius, Plutarch, Livy, Montesquieu), archaeologists (Antonio Nibby, Ennio Quirino Visconti). Subsequent chapters examine the writer's impressions of entering and leaving Rome; hotels, restaurants, and theatres; and Piazza Venezia and its surroundings. There is a discussion of the present status of the twelve palazzi Stendhal names in *Promenades dans Rome*, each with a splendid art gallery and open to visitors, and a similar discussion of the changes to the villas and gardens described by Stendhal, most of which have either been destroyed or now serve as embassies, cultural institutions, or Government buildings, and are closed to the public. Other chapters discuss the now destroyed Porto di Ripetta, the Tiber and its bridges; the Vatican; Basilicas and Baths; the Colosseum and its surrounding area; and the Capitoline and the Forum.

114 Travel journal.
Michel de Montaigne. In: *The complete works of Montaigne: essays, travel journal, letters*. Newly translated by Donald M. Frame. Stanford, California: Stanford University Press, 1957, p. 860-1039.

The text of Montaigne's *Journal de voyage* was discovered in 1770 and first published in 1774, nearly two centuries after the journey to Germany, Switzerland and Italy it describes, which lasted from 22 June 1580 to 30 November 1581. After five and a half months' sojourn in Rome, Montaigne went to the baths of La Villa (near Lucca), returning again to the Eternal City for a few days in October before his return home, where he was summoned to take up his duties as mayor of Bordeaux. Montaigne arrived in Rome on 30 November and lodged initially in the Albergo dell'Orso, enjoying a good view over the Castel S. Angelo and the Tiber, later moving to the Campo Marzio. Montaigne, who was steeped in classical literature, loved Rome. Its ruins moved him, however, less than they did Du Bellay, Montaigne finding instead greater interest in the contemporary life of the city, its streets, its inhabitants and their traditions. Insatiably curious about Roman society, manners and customs, he watches a circumcision at the Synagogue, and the public execution of a murderer who is hanged and quartered. He comments on Rome's renowned courtesans and on the city's religious life, and he visits churches which he finds less beautiful than those of France, but he is virtually indifferent about Rome' artistic treasures. The introductory note to this edition sketches the background to the writing of the *Journal*, lists and assesses previous editions (including translations into English) and studies and, in order to facilitate the reading of the text, provides an analytical table of the trip.

115 Travelling in Italy with Henry James.
Edited by Fred Kaplan. London: Hodder & Stoughton, 1994. 413p.

A collection of texts taken from James's essays on Italy and his letters. James visited Italy fourteen times over a period of forty years. He first visited Rome in 1869, in the last days of papal rule, and he remained for a long time hostile to changes wrought by the Risorgimento (the movement that led to the unification of Italy). The section on Rome contains a selection of letters and the following essays: 'A Roman holiday'; 'Roman rides'; 'Roman neighbourhoods'; 'The after-season in Rome'; 'From a Roman note-book'; 'A few other Roman neighbourhoods'; and 'The spirit of Rome'.

116 Travels through France and Italy.
Tobias Smollett, edited by Frank Felsenstein. Oxford: Oxford University Press, 1979. 588p.

Tobias Smollett (1721-71) published this work in 1766, the year after his journey to France and Italy, where he went with his wife for health reasons after the death of their only daughter. It is in the form of forty-one letters, eight of which are from Italy. Letters 29-33 describe his stay in Rome, where he arrived in late September 1764 and stayed for several weeks. He admires the great number of fountains in the city and praises the munificence of the popes who restored and repaired them, but regrets that this abundance of water has not induced the Romans to be clean and deplores the filth in the city and its palazzi and the smell of the putrefying bodies of hanged criminals. He visits the antiquities and admires the Colosseum more than the Pantheon (which he likens to 'a huge cockpit, open at the top'). His comments on works of art are equally idiosyncratic, Michelangelo's *Last Judgement* inducing '...the sort of confusion that perplexes my ears ...when a number of people are all talking at once'. He also dislikes paintings depicting scenes of martyrdom, such as St Lawrence, 'broiled like a barbecued pig', in that they encourage a spirit of religious fanaticism. He is scornful about Grand Tourists, their social rituals and pretensions and equally unflattering to Italians.

Laurence Sterne's *A sentimental journey through France and Italy* (London: T. Becket & P. A. De Hondt, 1768) satirizes Smollett's ill-temper and spleen. In this edition, the introduction discusses the 18th-century Grand Tour, the origin of the letters comprising the *Travels*, and the work's critical reputation. Smollett's major borrowings in his descriptions of Florence and Rome are collected in three appendices.

117 Two Englishwomen in Rome, 1871-1900.
Matilda Lucas. London: Methuen & Co., 1938. 292p.

Matilda Lucas and her sister Anne spent their winters in Rome every year from 1871 to 1900. This selection from the letters Matilda sent to relations in Hitchin was published when she was ninety and represents only one thirtieth of the whole output. The letters, which are full of anecdotes and amusing asides, are a marvellous evocation of Roman society and the Anglo-American community in the Eternal City. In her long introduction, the author reminisces about a world which had, by then, nearly passed away. This was still the Rome of Hawthorne, Hans Christian Andersen and William Wetmore Story, when the Tiber was still bordered by picturesque but unsanitary houses and there were frequent floods, and sheep passed through the city at night. She discusses archaeologists, the city, servants, pensions, food and restaurants, antiques shops, flowers of the Roman Campagna, royalty, art in Rome and introduces some artists they knew in Rome who feature in the letters – Giovanni Costa, Mario de Maria (a painter with a passion for scenes depicting cholera!), and Elihu Vedder.

118 'Very modern Rome' – an unpublished essay of Henry James.
Edited by Richard C. Harrier. *Harvard Literary Bulletin*, vol. 8 (1954), p. 125-140.

Written in 1877 after James's fourth visit to Rome, this essay was intended for the *Atlantic Monthly*. In it, the author further attempts to reconcile the charm and splendour of Rome with its squalor and modern vulgarity. Though it repeats a number of impressions that appeared in earlier sketches – of the Forum, the Colosseum, life on the Corso, a gallop over the flowered Campagna – it includes a number of new elements such as the interior of an artist's studio, and a sympathetic portrayal of Americans abroad. It describes his expectation to find Rome's charm and picturesqueness destroyed by the new administration at first confirmed by the new Via Nazionale ('a third rate imitation of the Boulevard Haussmann'), until he finds comfort in the Villa Medici, which has remained untouched by the reforming hand.

119 Viaggio in Italia, 1740. (Journey to Italy, 1740.)
Johann Caspar Goethe, edited by Arturo Farinelli. Rome: Reale Accademia d'Italia, 1932-33. 2 vols. (559p., 522p.)

Johann Caspar Goethe (1710-82) had studied law and was appointed Imperial Councillor though, a man of independent means, he devoted his later years to his family and to private scholarship. His account of his journey to Italy in 1740 was written in Italian and was based on notes he made in each of the many cities he visited. He had just completed the work when he was paralysed in 1768 and his manuscript remained unpublished, first in the collection of his son, the famous poet, and later in the Goethe-Nationalmuseum in Weimar, until the present edition. The journey is described in forty-two letters. His impressions of Rome and the Roman Campagna are contained in letters 29 to 33. In this edition, Goethe's text is in the first volume while the numerous inscriptions he copied are given in the second volume, which also includes detailed notes to the text, under the name of the city where they were copied (the ones from Rome are on p. 117-58).

120 **Vieille Rome: Stendhal, Goncourt, Taine, Zola et la Rome baroque.** (Old Rome: Stendhal, Goncourt, Taine, Zola and Baroque Rome.)
Jean-Pierre Guillerm. Villeneuve d'Ascq, France: Presses universitaires du Septentrion, 1998. 165p. (Peintures.)

A study of the mostly negative reactions to Baroque Rome – fascination mingled with malaise – of five prominent French 19th-century writers: Stendhal, in his *Promenades dans Rome*, the Goncourt brothers in their novel *Madame Gervaisais*, Hippolyte Taine in his *Voyage en Italie*, and Émile Zola in his novel *Rome*.

121 **A visit to Germany, Italy and Malta, 1840-1841. (A Poet's Bazaar I-II).**
Hans Christian Andersen, translated from the Danish with an introduction and notes by Grace Thornton. London: Peter Owen, 1985. 182p.

In 1840, Andersen, who had already been to Italy in 1833-34, took another long journey abroad, planning to visit Italy and then Greece and Turkey. This time his stay in Rome was not, however, a happy one. Plagued with a bad toothache, perhaps a result of his anxiety about the fate of his new play that was to be performed in Copenhagen, he spent a lonely Christmas in a bitterly cold Rome and his depression deepened when he was informed about the failure of his play. He stayed in Rome until the end of February 1841 and in early March a providential grant from King Christian VIII enabled him to continue his journey to Greece. In the chapters on Rome in *A Poet's Bazaar*, the record he kept of his journey, Andersen describes parts of the city which had featured so impressively in his novel *The Improvisatore* (published five years earlier) – the area around Piazza di Spagna and Piazza del Tritone and the Church of the Cappuccini with its macabre crypt. He also visits the Vatican and St Peter's (the riches of which he likens to those of palaces in Eastern fairy tales), the Tivoli waterfalls, and he describes Roman religious customs and festivals. His narrative includes numerous striking vignettes (as in the chapter 'Three Roman boys'), anecdotes (the discovery of a statue of Bacchus, the God of Pleasure, by two old men digging the grave of a young nun in the cloister garden of the church of the Trinità dei Monti), and one of the chapters ('My boots') is in the form of a short story.

122 **Voyage d'Italie.** (Journey to Italy.)
Pierre-Jacques-Onésyme Bergeret De Grancourt, introduction and notes by Jacques Wilhelm, drawings by J.-H. Fragonard. Paris: Éditions Michel de Romilly, 1948. 158p.

Bergeret de Grancourt, Trésorier-Général des Finances for Montauban and Comte de Négrepelisse in Languedoc, embarked on his journey to Italy and Northern Europe in 1773 and his retinue included Fragonard, whose duty was to provide a visual record of the journey. Bergeret himself kept a journal, of which this is an abridged version accompanied by some of the artist's works. Bergeret and Fragonard later quarrelled over the question of ownership of the artist's drawings. Bergeret's text is more interesting for the freshness of his observations about contemporary life in Rome than for his artistic judgements, often suggested by Fragonard and other artists he meets in Rome. He finds Italian cities provincial compared to Paris – Rome itself he describes as 'une vaste cité provinciale' (a vast provincial city). Highlights of the journal are the description of the Christmas Mass in the pope's chapel at the Quirinal Palace (which he calls 'jour de gala') and the chaos created by the arrival of cardinals each accompanied by at least three coaches, and also his trenchant comments about theatrical performances in Rome (he is bored by the inordinate length of the ballets and by the all-male casts).

123 Voyage de Gratz à la Haye. (Journey from Gratz to The Hague.) Montesquieu. In: *Oeuvres complètes* (vol. 1). Text presented and annotated by Roger Caillois. Paris: Gallimard, 1979, pp. 544-874.

Montesquieu's journey to Italy was part of a longer journey to various countries in Europe which he undertook in order to familiarize himself with their different political systems. He arrived in Rome on 19 January 1729 for a six-month sojourn which was to provide him with the background information for his *Considérations sur les causes de la grandeur et de la décadence des Romains* (Considerations of the causes of the greatness and the decadence of the Romans) (1734). The diary of his journey was discovered and first published in 1894. In this edition, the section on Rome is on pp. 661-717 and pp. 735-760. Montesquieu is an enthusiastic visitor to the city's antiquities, churches, libraries and art collections, to which he has easy access through his contacts with the French artistic community in Rome – Palazzo Farnese, Palazzo Strozzi, Villa Albani, Palazzo Borghese and the Farnesina are among the collections he visits. He also visits the Vatican and St Peter's, and is even taken to visit the workshop where the mosaics that were to replace the painted altarpieces at St Peter's were being made. He deplores the sale of Roman antiquities and works of art to foreign visitors and is critical of the church government, to which he attributes the poverty of the people, and of the administration of Pope Benedict XIII, whom he accuses of simony. His journal also includes descriptions of theatres in Rome, the Carnival and the race of the riderless horses on the Corso.

124 Voyage en Italie. (Journey to Italy.) François-René, vicomte de Chateaubriand. Lausanne, Switzerland: La bibliothèque des arts, 1995. 201p.

These texts were written during Chateaubriand's first sojourn in Rome in 1803 as a secretary of Cardinal Fesch, Napoleon's uncle and Ambassador of France to the Holy See. This appointment marked what was to prove a short-lived *rapprochement* with Napoleon, which ended after the assassination of the Duc d'Enghien in 1804. Chateaubriand was already famous as the author of *Génie du Christianisme* (Genius of Christianity), and his arrogance and lack of concern about official protocol quickly led to friction with the Cardinal, precipitating the writer's recall by Bonaparte seven months later, in January 1804. By then, Chateaubriand had already decided to leave Rome after the sad death, on her visit to Rome in November 1803, of Madame de Beaumont, his mistress, which affected him profoundly. The texts describe the author's arrival in Rome and his enthusiastic discovery of its beauty, his visits to the Colosseum, the Pantheon, the Column of Trajan, the Castel S. Angelo, the monastery of S. Onofrio (where Tasso died), St Peter's, and his audience with the pope (which was his first *faux pas* as he did not wait to be presented by his superiors). There are also descriptions of the Vatican, the Capitoline Museums, the Galleria Doria Pamphilj, a walk in Rome in the moonlight, and a visit to Tivoli. The second half of the work is taken with an account of Chateaubriand's journey to Naples before his departure from Italy. In this edition, the texts are accompanied by views of Rome from a sketchbook by Louis Gauffier, drawn during the artist's stay in Rome between 1784 and 1789.

125 Voyage en Italie. (Journey to Italy.) Hippolyte Taine. Paris: Julliard, 1965. 2 vols. (368p., 391p.) (Littérature, 26-27.)

Hippolyte Taine's journey to Italy was undertaken as a remedy to his state of intellectual and physical exhaustion induced by his work on *Histoire de la littérature anglaise* (History of

English Literature), which he completed in 1863 after seven years of intense study. He started his journey early in 1864 and stayed in Italy for three months. He disembarked at Civitavecchia and, after a few days in Rome, went to Naples, where he stayed for two weeks, returning to Rome on 6 March. He spent four weeks in the city, diligently visiting its museums, churches, villas and archaeological sites. His *Voyage en Italie* was first published in 1866 and takes the form of a diary addressed to a friend in Paris in which he describes his impressions. These are systematically set out in separate chapters – Antiquities, Paintings, Villas and Palaces, Churches, Society, and Holy Week. Taine's immediate reactions to the contemporary city were affected by the state of his health and the foul weather throughout his stay. He sees Rome as decadent, dirty and funereal, an untidy collection of bric-à-brac, and his reactions are constantly 'corrected' by his reading of its descriptions in literature and depictions in engravings. His account includes numerous penetrating descriptions and individual views such as his dislike for Canova and his less than exalted opinion about the Apollo Belvedere and Laocoon.

126 Voyages en Italie. (Journeys to Italy.)
Stendhal, edited by Vittorio del Litto. Paris: Gallimard, 1973.
1912p. (Bibliothèque de la Pléiade, 249.)

This is a remarkable edition of Stendhal's travel writings about Italy. It includes the four publications which embody most of his descriptions of Rome and his reactions to the city's artistic riches, ancient and modern. These are: *L'Italie en 1818*, the two editions of *Rome, Naples, Florence* (originally published in 1817, the text was substantially revised for the edition of 1826), and one of the author's greatest works, *Promenades dans Rome*. Stendhal visited Rome several times (1811, 1816-17, 1823, 1827 and he was later to spend long periods in the city during his years as French Consul at Civitavecchia, from 1831 to 1841) and, though his first impressions (described in the 1817 *Rome, Naples, Florence*) were mostly negative, he soon fell in love with the city, as his *Promenades dans Rome* testifies. Stendhal's travel writings are not mere guidebooks. As well as descriptions of ancient and modern Rome, its antiquities and works of art, they contain anecdotes and personal reminiscences, drafts for future novels, long digressions and borrowings from other writers and, notoriously, conversations with people he had never met, descriptions of lodgings he had never lived in and places he had never visited. The texts are extensively annotated and there are two indices, of people and fictional characters, and of places, works of art, literature and music.

127 William Wetmore Story and his friends: from letters, diaries, and recollections.
Henry James.   London: Thames & Hudson, [1957]. 2 vols. (371p., 345p.).

William Wetmore Story (1819-95), the American sculptor and writer, settled in Rome with his wife in 1856 (they had previously stayed there during the siege of Rome in 1849 and, again, in 1852). The Storys entertained lavishly in their luxurious forty-roomed apartment in the Palazzo Barberini and they cultivated an international circle of affluent friends who commissioned most of his sculptures. This biography was written by James at the request of Story's family and was originally published in 1903. This is a facsimile reprint of that edition. James makes extensive use of letters and other documentary material transcribed *in extenso*.

Archaeology and Antiquities

128   Ancient Rome in the light of recent discoveries.
Rodolfo Lanciani.   London: Benjamin Blom, 1967. 358p.

In his long preface, the author, secretary of the Comune of Rome Archaeological Commission, provides some staggering statistics concerning the works of art and antiquities brought up by the official excavations in the 1870s and 1880s. He also mentions the losses and sacrifices these discoveries have entailed but argues that the process of destruction and transformation is present throughout Rome's long history, which divides into four periods: from the fall of the Empire to the return of the papacy from Avignon (the least guilty of destruction), the Renaissance (which reused materials from ancient buildings), the 17th and 18th centuries (which destroyed much of the medieval remains of Rome, both by demolishing and by ruining, through restoration and embellishment, the original character of buildings), and the period from Napoleon's conquest to 1870. He laments the destruction of villas for the construction of new quarters, which he blames on the greed of the scions of the Roman nobility and speculators, but defends the work of archaeologists. The eleven essays, based on lectures delivered in England and the United States, cover a wide variety of topics. They include the renaissance of archaeological studies in the 14th century, the foundation and prehistoric life of Rome, sanitary conditions in Ancient Rome, the public libraries of ancient and medieval Rome, the House of the Vestal Virgins, the Palace of the Caesars, the Tiber and the Claudian Harbour, and the loss and discovery of works of art.

129   Antichità di Villa Doria-Pamphilj. (The collections of antiquities in the Villa Doria-Pamphilj.)
Edited by Raissa Calza.   Rome: De Luca, 1977. 648p. + 13 leaves of plates. bibliog.

The Villa Doria-Pamphilj is a magnificent example of a 17th-century villa, which originated in a vineyard purchased in 1630 by Pamphilo Pamphilj, the brother of the future Pope Innocent X and husband of the formidable Olimpia Maidalchini. In the 1640s, Camillo Pamphilj, his son, bought further land and the Casino del Belrespiro (now called Villa Doria-Pamphilj) was built as the family's villa for social and official entertaining and functions, in which the collections of antiquities and paintings were displayed. It was the work of Alessandro Algardi and Giovan Francesco Grimaldi. Successive generations continued to extend the property, which by the end of the 19th century covered an area of 210 hectares. The villa and its park (the largest in Rome)

Archaeology and Antiquities

were acquired by the Italian State and the Comune of Rome between 1965-1971. This catalogue contains entries for 467 works, all of which are reproduced in 264 plates. It includes not only the antiquities currently at the villa but also all those that once formed part of its collections or decoration but are now elsewhere (in the Palazzo Doria-Pamphilj, the Vatican museums, the Capitoline Museums, or in foreign collections). The arrangement is as follows: statues, reliefs, urns, altars, funerary steles, sarcophagi, portrait busts, trapezophores, decorative architectural elements, and modern sculptures inspired by the antique.

130 Antike Kunst und die Epoche der Aufklärung. (Ancient art and the era of the Enlightenment.) Edited by Herbert Beck and Peter C. Bol. Berlin: Mann, 1982. 577p. + 178 plates. (Forschungen zur Villa Albani, Frankfurter Forschungen zur Kunst, 10.)

Villa Albani (now Torlonia) on the Via Salaria was built by Carlo Marchionni between 1746 and 1762 to house and display the collections of ancient sculpture Cardinal Alessandro Albani amassed with the assistance of J. J. Winckelmann, who worked for him from 1758 to 1768. The Villa today houses part of the original Albani collection and also the collections of the Torlonia family, the owners of the Villa since 1866. The essays in this volume examine both the history of the villa, its architecture and collections and also the 18th-century intellectual and art historical background. Eva Maek-Gérard discusses the Antique in 18th-century artistic theory while Inga Gesche examines restoration practices of the period and Winckelmann's views. The most detailed essay (by Steffi Röttgen) discusses the Villa and its buildings and gives a detailed portrait of Cardinal Alessandro Albani. It also includes extracts from Winckelmann's letters, with observations on the building and on life at the Villa, other material from the Archivio di Stato di Roma, and a little-known description of the Villa by Giulio Cesare Cordara. Another essay (by Elisabeth Schröter) describes the programme of a decorative cycle by Antonio Bicchierari, which has been overshadowed by the fame of Anton Raphael Meng's *Parnassus*. The collections of antiquities in the Villa are studied in two essays: Agnes Allroggen-Bedel describes the collection at the time of Winckelmann while Carlo Gasparri examines its vicissitudes during the Napoleonic occupation of Rome, when part of the collection was taken to Paris, and the Restoration, when most of the confiscated works were sold to the King of Bavaria. Finally, Wolfgang Liebenwein discusses the history of the Villa and princely art collections from the Renaissance to Neo-classicism. The texts are accompanied by 178 plates, which contain 343 illustrations.

131 Die Antikensammlung des Kardinals Scipione Borghese. (The collection of ancient art of Cardinal Borghese.) Katrin Kalveram. Wormss am Rhein, Germany: Wernesche Verlagsgesellschaft, 1995. 294p. bibliog. (Römische Studien der Bibliotheca Hertziana, Band 11.)

No thorough or systematic groundwork on the Borghese collection exists. This study focuses on Cardinal Scipione Borghese's collection of ancient statues, with busts and reliefs only touched on where they highlight particular problems. It is largely based on primary sources, particularly accounts, order books and inventories of the Borghese family. It looks at the development of the collection, its display (which is compared to that of other similar contemporary collections), and the restoration of statues in the 17th century. The catalogue of the collection is based on descriptions of 1650 and 1700 and includes information related to provenance, restoration, etc.

132 The aqueducts of Ancient Rome.
Thomas Ashby, edited by I. A. Richmond. Oxford: Clarendon
Press, 1935. 356p.

The crowning achievement of Ashby's archaeological work, this classic work was the
fruit of many years of research and numerous expeditions in the Campagna. It was
published posthumously, five years after Ashby's untimely death. The work, which
includes an introductory survey of earlier topographical studies, is in two parts.
Part 1 describes the making and preservation of the aqueducts in Roman times; the
administration of the Imperial Water Board; the career of Sextus Iulius Frontinus, and his
treatise *De aquae ductui*; and the engineering of the aqueducts. Part 2, which forms the
longer part of the work, contains descriptions of the remains of eleven aqueducts: Aqua
Appia, Anio Vetus, Aqua Marcia, Aqua Tepula, Aqua Iulia, Aqua Virgo, Aqua Alsietina,
Aqua Claudia, Aqua Anio Novus, Aqua Traiana, and Aqua Alexandriana. The text is
accompanied by seven maps, twenty-four folded plans of the aqueducts, and twenty-four
plates.

133 The Ara Pacis Augustae.
Giuseppe Moretti, translated by Veronica Priestley. Congleton,
England: Old Vicarage Publications, 1989. 44p. map. (Itineraries of
the Museums, Galleries and Monuments in Italy, no. 67.)

This short study for the visitor to the site is divided into two sections. The first is a
historical note describing the discoveries of fragments from the altar in three different
locations from the 16th to the 19th century. The recognition of these fragments in 1879 by
Frederick von Duhn as part of the Ara Pacis Augustae, and the reconstruction by Eugene
Petersen in 1894, led to excavations in the area of the monument in 1903, which yielded
important results concerning the topography, architecture and decoration of the altar. Full
excavations had to wait, however, until 1937, which led to the further recuperation of
fragments and the recomposition of various panels of the walls of the precinct. The second
section is a description of the monument itself, the circumstances of its creation, its floral
decoration, the figured frieze and the altar. The text is accompanied by twenty-seven
plates which, as well as details of its decorations, also include a reconstruction of the
monument and photographs taken during the excavations.

**134 The Ara Pacis Augustae and the imagery of abundance in later
Greek and early Roman art.**
David Castriota. Princeton, New Jersey: Princeton University
Press, 1995. 271p.

A detailed study of the floral friezes of the altar. Vegetal attributes symbolize the support
of the gods to the stability of the Augustan regime. Precedents are to be found in
Pergamene relief sculpture and the Greek tradition of floral ornament, though no other
Greek work seems to have used so many plants and animals within one tendril
composition. The work considers the altar to be the culmination of artistic developments
that preceded it and emphasizes its Janus-like aspect and its blending of previous
traditions into something new and distinctive.

135 Archeologia di Roma nelle fotografie di Thomas Ashby, 1891-1930. (The archaeology of Rome in the photographs of Thomas Ashby, 1891-1930.) Thomas Ashby, texts by Peter Wiseman (et al.). Naples, Italy: Electa Napoli, 1989. 191p. bibliog. (British School at Rome Archive, 2.)

The biographical sketch of Thomas Ashby given in the preface of this catalogue explains both the subject of the photographs in this volume but also those of two companion volumes which were published later. Rodolfo Lanciani, who was in charge of the Forum excavations between 1882 and 1885, was a great formative influence on the young Ashby, who was then in Rome with his parents. When Ashby finished his studies at Oxford he returned to Rome becoming the first student to enrol at the British School at Rome but, as he was barred (as a foreigner) from conducting excavations in the archaeological centre of Rome, he aimed instead, through a series of books, articles and photographs, to establish the Roman Campagna as part of the great complex of ruins of the Roman Imperial age. The introductory essays in this volume describe Ashby's love of Rome and his work in documenting the far-reaching changes the city was undergoing at the time, the role of his photographs as working tools, and Ashby's relationship with Giacomo Boni, Lanciani's successor at the Forum excavations between 1898 and 1904. The catalogue is divided into sixty-three sections, each dealing with a particular zone or monument. The most extensive is the first section, showing the excavations of the Forum, both under Lanciani (the earliest photographs were taken when Ashby was only eighteen) and, later, under Boni. They provide a valuable record of the progress of the excavations, on which Ashby was also reporting in English reviews such as *The Builder*. The photographs in the catalogue are accompanied by extensive explanatory captions. The panoramic views of the Forum and of its individual monuments are followed by sections on other areas, including the Valley of the Colosseum, the Imperial Fora, the Palatine, the Pantheon, the Servian Wall, various aqueducts, and the Tiber. The volume also includes a bibliography of the writings of T. Ashby on Rome, and transcriptions from his notebooks.

136 The art of Rome c. 753 BC-337 AD: sources and documents. J. J. Pollitt. Englewood Cliffs, New Jersey: Prentice-Hall, 1966. 272p. (Sources and Documents in the History of Art Series.)

An anthology, in English translation, of the most important ancient literary testimonies, from the period of the kings to late antiquity, relating to Roman art. It is divided into three parts (the Roman Republic, the Roman Empire from 27 BC to 192 AD, and late antiquity), each subdivided into several sections, each introduced by extensive historical sketches of the period they cover. The introduction points out the commemorative nature of Roman art and its historical consciousness, both qualities reflected in the art criticism. Other aspects of Roman art criticism discussed are: the 'lament over decadence', i.e. the unfavourable comparison of the present to a distant, austere, and virtuous past, and aesthetic theories like the Vitruvian *ratio decoris* (the rational theory of appropriateness), considering the appropriateness of a building to its site and function, or that of a cult image to the temple in which it was placed. There is also a discussion of the literary sources of Roman art, indicating that in most cases authors do not deal directly and exclusively with art but in passing (exceptions to this are Vitruvius's treatise on architecture, descriptive poems and letters, and rhetorical display pieces describing paintings and statues), and the combination, in the work of authors from the time of the Empire and later, of first-hand observation of contemporary artistic developments with descriptions of events and monuments of earlier periods, for which they went back to the *annales,* the records of important civic, military, and religious events, and the work of earlier writers, such as Marcus Terentius Varro (116-27 BC).

137 The artists of the Ara Pacis: the process of hellenization in Roman relief sculpture.
Diane Atnally Conlin. Chapel Hill, Carolina; London: The University of North Carolina Press, 1997. 145p. bibliog. (Studies in the History of Greece and Rome.)

Scholarship on the Ara Pacis Augustae has tended to concentrate on the monument's iconography and the identity of the figures represented in its reliefs, rather than on the artistic identity of its sculptors. This study provides, instead, a stylistic and technical analysis of the carving techniques and tool marks used on the two large processional friezes of the exterior wall of the altar. This narrow focus is used as the starting point for a wider examination of the social, political and religious role of Augustan art. There is a survey of the historical background to the monument's creation and a lucid summary of the viewpoints and conclusions of earlier writers who considered the reliefs to be the work of a Greek master sculptor, partly as a reaction to Fascist and nationalist interpretations which saw them as the embodiment of *Romanità* (a term used to convey the spirit and ideals of Ancient Rome). The effects of earlier restorations that have altered the original appearance of the sculptures are also considered, especially Francesco Carradori's work in the late 18th century. The conclusions reached here are that the reliefs are the work of a Roman workshop, combining Attic and Asiatic figural and compositional styles and marble-carving techniques with indigenous Etrusco-Italic artistic traditions. There are 247 excellent black-and-white photographs of details of the reliefs and comparative illustrations.

138 Augustan culture: an interpretive introduction.
Karl Galinsky. Princeton, New Jersey: Princeton University Press, 1996. 485p. bibliog.

An overview of Augustan culture in its various manifestations, focusing on some of the major examples of literature (including sections on Virgil's *Aeneid*, Ovid's *Metamorphoses*, Horace, and Livy), art and architecture (including the Ara Pacis Augustea, the portraits of Augustus, and wall paintings), society (ideas, ideals, and values), politics and religion.

139 The Baths of Caracalla: a study in the design, construction, and economics of large-scale building projects in Imperial Rome.
Janet DeLaine. Portsmouth, Rhode Island: Journal of Roman Archaeology, 1997. 269p. folded plans. (Supplementary Series, no. 25.)

A detailed study of the Baths of Caracalla, this work was originally conceived as a study of large-scale construction in Imperial Rome and of the Roman building industry, but was eventually limited to the Baths because the building, though much cited, is little known. Implications to our understanding of Roman imperial architecture are threefold and demonstrate: the treatment of decoration as an integral part of the desired architectural effect; the importance of design and constructional 'blue-prints', which allowed variation on an established pattern even after a considerable lapse of time; and the continuing relevance of Vitruvius's precepts and their application in novel ways and on a large scale. The study looks at the history of the building, its design, decoration, the materials used in its construction, its cost, construction techniques and processes, and the building industry of Severan Rome.

140   Bullettino della Commissione archeologica municipale. (Bulletin of the Municipal Archaeological Commission.)
Rome, Italy: Commissione archeologica di Roma, 1872- .

The Commissione archeologica di Roma was established by the Comune of Rome in 1872, with responsibility for the monuments of the city and its territory. Its first secretary was Rodolfo Lanciani. The Commission's duties included the supervision of excavations, the execution of maps and ground-plans, the conservation of monuments, the transfer to the Capitoline Museums of newly discovered objects, the establishment of new collections of antiquities and, finally, the publication of a monthly bulletin that would give an account of its activities, especially the results of new excavations shedding new light on the history and topography of the city, and also publicize new acquisitions and donations. Between 1931 and 1943, the *Bulletin* was published in two parts, *Bullettino della Commissione archeologica comunale di Roma* (from 1939 as *Bullettino della Commissione Archeologica del Governorato di Roma*) and *Bullettino del Museo dell'Impero Romano*. The latter title ceased after the collapse of the Fascist regime and from 1947 the *Bulletin*'s title reverted to *Bullettino della Commissione archeologica comunale di Roma*.

141   Il Cardinale Albani e la sua villa: documenti. (Cardinal Albani and his villa: documents.)
Edited by Elisa Debenedetti.   Rome: Bulzoni, 1980. 404p.
(Quaderni sul Neoclassico, 5.)

A collection of documents related to Cardinal Alessandro Albani (1692-1779), one of the greatest collectors of antiquities in 18th-century Rome, other members of the Albani family and the villa in Via Salaria built to house and display his collections, both in its galleries and in its gardens. The documents presented are: the Cardinal's will; inventories of Albani households between 1790 and 1852 (these include a 1790 inventory of paintings and drawings in the Palazzo Albani alle Quattro Fontane, an 1817 inventory of the collection of paintings of Prince Carlo Albani in the Palazzo alle Quattro Fontane, the Villa Albani, and other properties of the family); documents related to the Villa and its land (1747-63); the fountains in its gardens; various guides, descriptions and inventories of the Villa compiled between *c.* 1785 and 1835; and documents related to the vicissitudes of the antiquities removed from the Villa by the French during the Roman Republic and their subsequent sale in 1815 to Ludwig I of Bavaria.

142   Il carteggio di Cassiano dal Pozzo: catalogo. (The correspondence of Cassiano dal Pozzo: a catalogue.)
Edited by Anna Nicolò.   Florence, Italy: Leo S. Olschki, 1991.
335p. (Quaderni di 'Rinascimento', 11.)

The bulk of Cassiano dal Pozzo's correspondence is in thirty-eight volumes now in the collection of the Accademia nazionale dei Lincei. Other holdings are in the École de Médecine at Montpellier and the Archivio segreto vaticano. This catalogue excludes material held in other collections. The introduction traces the history of the epistolary collection, which also includes autographs by famous contemporary and earlier authors, and stresses the importance of the collection for the identification of the sheets of Cassiano's Paper Museum and for the reconstruction of the guiding principles in his collecting policies and patronage. The catalogue is accompanied by a chronological index and an index of names of correspondents.

143 Cassiano Dal Pozzo's Paper Museum.
[Ivrea, Italy]: Olivetti, 1992. 2 vols. (168p., 179p.) (Quaderni Puteani, 2-3.)

Cassiano Dal Pozzo, one of the most important art patrons in 17th-century Italy, was famous in his lifetime for his knowledge of antiquities and natural history, and for his 'Paper Museum' (*Museo cartaceo*). This was a project to collect drawings and prints of all known remains of antiquity and also of geological, plant and animal specimens. Though accessible to artists and scholars, this 'Paper Museum' was never published. These two volumes contain the proceedings of a conference convened jointly by the British Museum and the Warburg Institute on 14 and 15 December 1989. The first volume covers the archaeological side of Cassiano's interests.

144 The Catacombs: rediscovered monuments of early Christianity.
J. Stevenson.   London: Thames & Hudson, 1978. 179p. bibliog. map. (Ancient Peoples and Places, 91.)

This volume provides an introduction to the history and art of the Catacombs, the underground burial complexes created principally around Rome from the 2nd to the 5th century AD. The term derives from the area near S. Sebastiano on the Via Appia Antica, called *ad Catacumbas* ('in the hollows') because of its topography, a centre of veneration for the Apostles Peter and Paul where, by the 4th century, there was an underground burial place. The first three chapters describe the making and development of the Catacombs, their rapid decline after the barbarian invasions which began in the 5th century, their transformation into places of pilgrimage in the Middle Ages, the archaeological interest which began in the 16th century – notably the work of Antonio Bosio (1576-1629), which led to their plundering in order to obtain relics, and the monumental discoveries of G. Marchi (1795-1860) and G. B. de Rossi (1822-94), which laid the foundations for subsequent investigators. The remaining chapters examine the decoration of the catacombs and the use of subjects from the Old and New Testament. A separate chapter looks at the burial places of heretics and schismatics and there is also a chapter on catacombs in Naples, Sicily, Malta, North Africa and Syria.

145 La collezione Boncompagni Ludovisi: Algardi, Bernini e la fortuna dell'antico. (The Collection Boncompagni Ludovisi: Algardi, Bernini and the critical reception of antiquities.)
Edited by Antonio Giuliano.   Venice, Italy: Marsilio, 1992. 256p. bibliog.

This is the catalogue of an exhibition held in Rome in 1992 marking the completion of the restoration of the Boncompagni Ludovisi collection before its installation in the Palazzo Altemps. One of the great collections of ancient sculptures in Baroque Rome, the Ludovisi collection had been drastically restored in the 17th century by, among others, Bernini and Algardi. The catalogue examines the critical reception of the works from the 16th to the 19th century. Its three introductory essays discuss the Villa Ludovisi (one of the most lamented casualties in the destruction of Rome's 'green belt' in the 19th century) and the formation of the collection, and the influence of the works on artists ranging from Poussin and Velázquez to Canova, Pompeo Batoni and John Singleton Copley. There are also essays on sculpture restoration practices in the 17th century, including extracts from Orfeo Boselli's 'Osservationi della scoltura antica' (Observations on Ancient sculpture), a contemporary treatise on the subject. The catalogue section provides detailed entries for twenty-five sculptures, each including information about previous restorations of the work and its present state of conservation, and discusses its history and iconography. Mimmo Jodice's black-and-white photographs of the sculptures are outstanding.

146   La Colonna Traiana. (The Column of Trajan.)
Edited by Salvatore Settis.   Turin, Italy: Giulio Einaudi, 1988.
616p. (Saggi, 716.)

The Column of Trajan is among the rare ancient monuments to have survived virtually intact, though, under Sixtus V, the Emperor's statue which crowned it was replaced by one of St Peter. Its shaft is about 130 feet tall and its low-relief frieze, which unfolds in a 656 feet long spiral, depicts Trajan's victories over the Dacians and has some 2,500 figures. The reliefs could originally be seen at eye level/close up from the surrounding buildings. This splendid volume is divided into four sections. Adriano La Regina examines Trajan's policies and their celebration in the buildings he commissioned in Trajan's Forum (of which the Column is the centrepiece), while Salvatore Settis provides a detailed study of the column itself. This is followed by 288 full-page colour plates of details of the Column's reliefs, specially photographed after its restoration, each with a caption explaining the action depicted. Finally, the influence of the Column from the Renaissance to the 20th century is studied by Giovanni Agosti and Vincenzo Farinella.

**147   La Colonna Traiana e gli artisti francesi da Luigi XIV a
Napoleone I.** (The Column of Trajan and French artists from
Louis XIV to Napoleon I.)
Edited by Philippe Morel.   Rome: Carte Segrete, 1988. 299p.

This is the catalogue of an exhibition held at the Villa Medici (the present seat of the French Academy in Rome) to celebrate, like entry no. 147 above, the recent restoration of the Column of Trajan. One of the first tasks of Charles Errard, the first Director of the Academy, was the execution of casts of the Column's reliefs, ordered by Louis XIV, a series of these casts remaining at the Academy. The exhibition examines the influence of these reliefs on French artists residing in Rome in the 17th, 18th and 19th century. Works inspired range from drawings and engravings copying specific figures, gestures or expressions from these reliefs (Jacques-Louis David spent six months studying them), to architectural projects using the Column as a model. Artists represented include Poussin, Boucher, Hubert Robert, Piranesi (who included the Column in several of his 'Views of Rome' and also executed a series of twenty-one etchings inspired by it), Étienne-Louis Boullée and Giuseppe Valadier.

148   The Colosseum.
Peter Quennell.   London: The Readers' Digest Association;
New York: Newsweek, 1971. 172p. (Wonders of Man.)

Built on the site of an ornamental lake of the Domus Aurea of Nero, the Colosseum (or Amphitheatrum Flavium) was dedicated by Vespasian before his death in 79 AD and completed by Domitian. This general history of the building looks at its architecture, the gladiatorial games and other blood sports it provided, the Christian martyrs who found their death in its arena, its fortunes after the fall of the Roman Empire and the inspiration it provided to countless painters, architects, poets and other visitors. It also includes a section on the Colosseum in literature, with extracts from Martial, Gibbon, Goethe, Lord Byron, Edgar Allan Poe, Charles Dickens, Nathaniel Hawthorne, Henry James, George Bernard Shaw and others. There are numerous well-captioned illustrations and, finally, a short guide to other Roman monuments and a chronology of Roman history.

149 **Da Pisanello alla nascita dei Musei Capitolini: l'antico a Roma alla vigilia del Rinascimento.** (From Pisanello to the birth of the Capitoline Museums: antiquities in Rome on the eve of the Renaissance.) Edited by Anna Cavallaro, Enrico Parlato. Milan, Italy: Mondadori; Rome: de Luca, 1988. 259p. map. bibliog.

This catalogue of an exhibition held in Rome in 1988 traces the development of the interest in the antique in 15th-century Rome after the return of the papal court from Avignon, the reversal of the policies of destruction of pagan antiquities initiated by Gregory I, and a programme of reconstruction of Rome. The period examined, from the beginning of the pontificate of Martin V Colonna in 1417 to that of Sixtus IV in 1472, saw the decline of the international late Gothic style and the birth of antiquarianism. The catalogue examines the work and influence of Ciriaco d'Ancona, Felice Feliciano, Giovanni Marcanova and Leon Battista Alberti, all of whom visited Rome during this period; and highlights the importance of the *Codex Marcanova* (Modena, Biblioteca estense), which contains numerous inscriptions related to the city of Rome as well as eighteen full-page drawings showing ancient Roman monuments and antiquities. The catalogue also discusses representations of Rome in illuminated codices of the early 15th century; these range from realistic to symbolic or fantastic depictions of the city; imperial iconographies in drawings and medals; the study of the antique in Pisanello's drawings and medals and his work at S. Giovanni in Laterano, where he completed Gentile da Fabriano's frescoes after the latter's death in 1427; Filarete's sculptures, including the bronze door of the main porch of the old St Peter's (1445), which combine classical and Christian elements, and his bronze statuettes after the antique, such as his copy of the equestrian statue of Marcus Aurelius; the works of Fra Angelico and Benozzo Gozzoli commissioned by Pope Nicholas V; and copies after ancient sarcophagi, the Arch of Constantine and the Column of Trajan and of the statues that came to symbolize Ancient Rome – the bronze she-wolf, the equestrian statue of Marcus Aurelius, and the Dioscuri or Horse-tamers of Monte Cavallo. There is also a note on the topography of Rome in the 15th century and a folded map reconstructing the appearance of the city in 1500 and indicating the most important ancient and Christian monuments.

150 **The Dal Pozzo-Albani drawings of classical antiquities in the British Museum.** Cornelius C. Vermeule III. Philadelphia: The American Philosophical Society, 1960. 78p. (Transactions of the American Philosophical Society: New Series, vol. 50, part 5.)

Dal Pozzo's Paper Museum (*Museum Cartaceum*) was the last major collection of drawings made before the statues and reliefs of Rome began to be dispersed, leaving Rome for France (with the Mazarin collection), Naples (with the Farnese collection) and England (with generations of visitors on the Grand Tour). This study includes a catalogue of the drawings now in the British Museum together with an index of subjects, index of locations (of the antiquities), and a concordance of the numbers of the drawings with the original numbering of Dal Pozzo's *Museum Cartaceum*.

151 The Dal Pozzo-Albani drawings of classical antiquities in the Royal Library at Windsor Castle.
Cornelius C. Vermeule III. Philadelphia: The American Philosophical Society, 1966. 170p. (Transactions of the American Philosophical Society: New Series, vol. 56, part 2.)

The Royal Library's collection of drawings from the Dal Pozzo collection is principally in ten volumes. This study includes a full catalogue of all the drawings in these volumes. It is accompanied by 270 plates and a concordance of the numbers of the drawings with the original numbering of Dal Pozzo's *Museum Cartaceum*, a subject index, and an index of present locations of the works depicted in the drawings.

152 The eagle and the spade: archaeology in Rome during the Napoleonic era.
Ronald T. Ridley. Cambridge, England: Cambridge University Press, 1992. 356p. bibliog.

The systematic excavation and restoration of all the classical monuments in Rome during the French occupation (1809-14) was the first large-scale archaeological programme in the city. This programme is set in context by an examination of the fate of the monuments since antiquity and the contemporary Napoleonic political and cultural history. The core of this study is a detailed account of the excavation and restoration work on the Forum Romanum, the Colosseum, and the Forum of Trajan. The work of leading administrators, archaeologists and architects is also assessed. A prologue surveys preceding literature and an introduction traces the background to the French occupation, the condition and history of the monuments from the end of antiquity to the arrival of the French, a history of the French antiquities and embellishments organizations, and includes a discussion of major monuments in turn in alphabetical order and an examination of the controversies which arose as a result of the archaeological work.

153 La fascination de l'antique, 1700-1770: Rome découverte, Rome inventée. (The fascination of the antique, 1700-1770: Rome discovered, Rome invented.)
Joselita Raspi Serra, François de Polignac. Paris: Somogy, Éditions d'art, 1998. 215p. bibliog.

This is the catalogue of an exhibition held in Lyons in 1998 demonstrating that the 18th-century revival of interest in excavations and the antique started at the beginning and not in the second half of the century. It looks at various aspects of antiquarian culture in Rome at the end of the 17th and the first half of the 18th century, the Museo Kircheriano and the establishment of the Capitoline Museums, and the discovery and diffusion of antique painting exemplified by the discovery in the Palazzo Rospigliosi in 1709 of the frescoes of a house dating from the 1st century AD. It also discusses the influence of antiquity on artists working in Rome, such as the sculptor Edme Bouchardon and the painter Pompeo Batoni, and the depiction of antiquities by Clérisseau, Hubert Robert, and other *pensionnaires* of the French Academy in Rome. Another section of the catalogue is dedicated to the influence of Winckelmann's ideas on the circle of Cardinal Alessandro Albani, and also looks at British collectors and antiquarians in Rome, and the activity of Piranesi and Cavaceppi as dealers of ancient marble sculptures. The last two sections move away from the Roman milieu and examine the influence of the antique on various aspects of French culture, from architecture to porcelain vases, and the fashion for classical subjects in the Paris Salon. There is a chronology listing, in three columns, political and culural events in Europe, excavations and antiquarian culture in Rome, and artists and connoisseurs in Rome. The volume is splendidly illustrated.

154 Fasti Anni Numani et Iuliani, accedunt ferialia, menologia rustica, parapegmata. (Calendars of the Numan and Julian periods to which are added festivals, monthly almanacs, and tables of astronomical calculations.)
Edited by Attilio Degrassi. Rome: Libreria dello Stato, 1963. 612p.

This is a magisterial edition of forty-four surviving *fasti* (the ancient Roman calendars which enumerate all the days of the year, with their festivals and events), coming from a variety of sites, mostly near Rome. They are all fragmentary and of various periods. The Fasti Antiates Maiores (the Major Calendar of Antium), for example, dates from 84-55 BC, while the Fasti Praenestini (the Calendar of Praenestum) is from AD 6-9. The edition contains numerous commentaries on, among others, the months, market days, tutelary deities, signs of the zodiac, and games. The *commentarii diurni* (daily commentaries) bring together the literary and epigraphical sources related to the religious observances for each day. There are eighty-nine plates showing various fragments of the calendars.

155 The Forum of Trajan in Rome: a study of the monuments.
James E. Packer, architectural reconstructions by Kevin Lee Sarring and James E. Packer. Berkeley, Los Angeles; Oxford: University of California Press, 1997. 2 vols. (528p., 114 plates + microfiches), 1 portfolio. (California Studies in the History of Art, 31, a Centennial Book.)

The Forum of Trajan and the Basilica Ulpia (its most famous building) are among the most important buildings of imperial Rome. The Forum, which is as large as all the other fora put together, was constructed to celebrate Trajan's victories in the Dacian campaigns of 101-102 and 105-106 AD. It was officially dedicated in 112 AD. This monumental study provides a general account of the architecture of the Forum as a whole. Part one reviews the history and destruction of the Forum, its later fortunes, and its excavations over the last two centuries, first by the French between 1811 and 1814 and by the Fascists in 1928, when demolitions started and the 'Markets of Trajan', the East Hemicycle and East Colonnade were cleared, and in the 1930s, during the opening of Mussolini's Fori Imperiali, when an enormous number of objects were unearthed and the West Colonnade and the Basilica Ulpia were cleared. It also focuses on the lesser monuments, some buried (the Equus Traiani, most of the West Colonnade and Hemicycle), some completely excavated (the East Colonnade and Hemicycle, the West Library). Part two assesses various previously published writings on the Basilica Ulpia and combines their findings with other evidence which jointly allows a more accurate reconstruction of the site. Part three discusses the techniques used to build the Forum, the special features of its architecture, and the significance of the complex as a whole. The accompanying catalogue arranges the surviving architectural remains according to type, while technical problems connected with the reconstruction of the excavated buildings are discussed in twelve appendices. Volume two contains 114 plates while the 11 accompanying microfiches contain 414 frames of supplementary views of the site, and photographs of architectural fragments. The portfolio contains 34 folios of technical versions of the reconstructions.

156 Frammenti di Roma antica nei disegni degli architetti vincitori del Prix de Rome, 1786-1924. (Fragments of Ancient Rome in the drawings of French architects winners of the Prix de Rome, 1786-1924.) Edited by Massimiliano David. Novara, Italy: Istituto geografico De Agostini, 1998. 223p. bibliog.

A selection of drawings made by winners of the Prix de Rome competition for architecture during their sojourn in the city as pensioners of the French Academy in Rome. The three introductory essays discuss: the Prix de Rome for architecture, a stepping stone to a brilliant career, which gave its recipients the privilege of studying the city's monuments; the use these students made of their sojourn; and their studies of the ancient monuments which now constitute the precious archive of architectural drawings of the École des beaux-arts, a treasure trove of faithful depictions and reconstructions of ancient buildings, works of art, and decorative details. The importance of these drawings is stressed in the last of the three essays, which discusses the urban development of Rome and the archaeological excavations carried out after 1870 that changed the face of the city and led to the sacrifice, in the name of progress, of entire historic quarters demolished to make way for new thoroughfares and also allow excavations. The catalogue section includes drawings after the Severan *Forma Urbis* (the Marble Plan of Rome), and views, plans and reconstructions of the buildings of the Capitol, the Roman Forum, the Imperial Fora, the Palatine, the Circus Maximus, the Colosseum, the Theatre of Marcellus and the Theatre of Pompey, the Temples, the Isola Tiberina, Campus Martius (including the Pantheon, and the portico of Octavia), the Baths (of Titus, Trajan, Caracalla, Diocletian), the Bridges, the Aqueducts, the Walls and Gates, Hadrian's Mausoleum, Via Appia, and the Villa of Maxentius. The large format of the publication allows for spectacularly detailed colour plates of the drawings (most of which are, themselves, of spectacular proportions), and also of photographs showing excavations in progress and plans of the city (which include fourteen plates from Rodolfo Lanciani's magnificent *Forma Urbis*). A French translation of this work was published in 1999 – *Fragments de la Rome antique dans les dessins des architectes français vainqueurs du Prix de Rome, 1786-1924* (Paris: Éditions Hazan, 1999. 222p.). See also *Roma antiqua: grandi edifici pubblici: 'envois' degli architetti francesi, 1786-1901* (*Roma antiqua*, great public buildings: 'envois' of French students of architecture, 1786-1901), edited by Paola Ciancio Rossetto et al. (Rome: Edizioni Carte Segrete, 1992. 320p.).

157 Hadrian's Villa and its legacy. William L. MacDonald and John A. Pinto. New Haven, Connecticut; London: Yale University Press, 1995. 392p. bibliog.

Situated near Tivoli, the villa constructed by the Emperor Hadrian between AD 118 and the 130s was one of the greatest architectural complexes of the ancient world. It covered 300 acres and encompassed scores of buildings: dwellings, temples, a library, underground passages, theatres (approximately 900 rooms are known) and was adorned with gardens, pools and fountains. Much of it still lies underground. This study is in two parts. The first part examines the architecture of the various buildings of the villa, its wide range of sculptural styles and subjects and decoration of mosaic and marblework (of which there is plentiful evidence), painting and stucco (of which the evidence is slight). It includes chapters on the setting of the villa, the personality of its creator, the function of its structures, both orthodox (i.e. common in pre-Hadrianic architecture) and unfamiliar ones (which have no counterpart in other surviving Roman buildings), and life at the villa. The second part examines the villa's survival and rediscovery, and its reception since the early Renaissance. It looks at the systematic survey of the antiquarian Pirro Ligorio, the architect of the Villa d'Este in Tivoli, at the influence of individual buildings on Italian Baroque architecture (notably on Francesco Borromini), the pastoral ideal and at the golden age of antiquarian and artistic study of the villa in the 18th century, when more systematic excavations were undertaken and the villa attracted the interest of numerous architects and *vedutisti* (painters or engravers of souvenir views). A separate chapter is dedicated to Piranesi's dramatic engravings showing its major buildings as well his enormous plan, which was published posthumously in 1781. Piranesi's commentary to the plan is given here in full. Only 25 statues of the 173 found on the site (and the additional 105 of more uncertain provenance) remain at the villa, the rest have been dispersed to collections all over the world. The final chapter, which includes Luigi Rossini's views and work by American and French Beaux-Arts students, looks at the villa from 1800 to the present.

158 Hadrian's Villa and Tivoli past and present and Villa d'Este: guide with reconstructions.
Catia Caprino, Luigi Salerno. Congleton, England: Old Vicarage Publications, 1993. 51p.

This short guide, originally published in Rome by Vision Editions in 1967, offers a coupling of the two villas at Tivoli, one dating from Imperial Rome, the other from the 16th century. Each has a short introduction and historical summary. The section on Hadrian's Villa includes illustrations of works of art originally housed there; it also offers a room-by-room description of the building with transparent colour restorations and outline drawings and photographs aimed at helping the visitor to visualize the original appearance of the villa and its grounds. There is also a short chapter on the Temples of Vesta and of the Sybil.

159 Hadrien: trésors d'une villa impériale. (Hadrian: treasures of an imperial villa.)
Edited by Jacques Charles-Gaffiot and Henri Lavagne. Milan, Italy: Electa, 1999. bibliog.

The catalogue of an exhibition shown in Paris in 1999, which included over 200 works from or about the villa. The twenty-five introductory essays include various contributions on Hadrian and the art of his time, the antiquities of the villa now in the Capitoline Museums, artists and other visitors to the villa in the 18th century, Marguerite Yourcenar, and a report on the restorations carried out over the last ten years and work in progress. The catalogue section begins with sculptures of Hadrian, depictions of him on coins and medals, and accounts of his life in Renaissance manuscripts. These are followed by a section on the architecture and decoration of the villa, which includes the model of the villa from the Museo della civiltà romana and Piranesi's enormous plan, as well as sculptures, vases and pavements from the villa. The main section of the catalogue is dedicated to Hadrian's collections and includes busts, statues of gods and heroes, sculpture showing Egyptian influences, garden sculpture, mosaics, gems and cameos, and the cult of Antinous. The following section examines the reception of the villa in the past 500 years and includes examples of the work of draughtsmen, engravers and sculptors, among them Charles-Louis Clérisseau, Robert Adam, Hubert Robert and Augustin Pajou. It also looks at the role played by antiquaries such as Piranesi, J. J. Winckelmann and Gavin Hamilton, at the influence of the mosaic of the doves now in the Capitoline Museums, at the iconography of Antinous, at 19th-century architectural drawings by students at the Villa Medici, at photographs by Pierre Gusman of architectural elements of the villa and at a sketchbook by Le Corbusier. Finally, there is a dossier on Marguerite Yourcenar's novel *Les mémoires d'Hadrien* (The memoirs of Hadrian).

160   Ianuculum – Gianicolo: storia, topografia, monumenti, leggende dall'antichità al rinascimento. (Ianiculum – Gianicolo: its history, topography, monuments, and legends from Antiquity to the Renaissance.) Edited by Eva Margareta Steinby. Rome: Institutum romanum Finlandiae, 1996. 274p. (Acta Instituti Romani Finlandiae, vol. 16.)

The proceedings of a seminar organized by the Istituto romano di Finlandia in 1994 to celebrate its fortieth anniversary. The seminar's theme was the history and topography of the Janiculum hill, the 'eighth' hill of Rome, from classical times to the end of the 16th century. The contributions examining the hill in antiquity are divided into two sections, the first looking at its topography and monuments, and the second at the cults, myths and legends associated with it (such as the cult of Syrian divinities, the Keraunian divinities, and the *Nymphae Furrinae*). The contributions dealing with the Renaissance examine various aspects of the decoration of the Villa Lante (Casino Turini, the present home of the Istituto romano di Finlandia). The villa was designed between 1518 and 1527 by Giulio Romano for Baldassare Turini (1485-1543). Giulio Romano's work is examined in two papers, and there is also a paper discussing Turini's career in the Roman Curia and his artistic patronage. Another paper looks at the paintings and stuccowork of the villa and their iconography of myths of the ancient Ianuculum. There is also a study of the frescoes by Polidoro da Caravaggio, now in the Palazzo Zuccari but originally part of Villa Lante's decorative scheme (they were removed – together with frescoes by Giulio Romano – in the 19th century, when the Istituto del Sacro Cuore was housed here and their mythological subject matter was considered unsuitable).

161   The influence of Rome's antique monumental sculptures on the great masters of the Renaissance. Edited by Pogány-Balás. Budapest: Akadémiai Kiadó, 1980. 115p.

An examination of the key role played by the monumental antique sculptures in Rome during the Renaissance. It begins with an introductory survey of sculptures known to Renaissance artists in the 15th century. These included statues that had never been buried and remained *in situ* for centuries, like the two horse tamers on the Quirinale. These were described in the various medieval guidebooks and in other descriptions of Rome in the 14th and 15th centuries by, among others, Petrarch, Flavio Biondo and Poggio Bracciolini. The study then looks at use of antiquity in Mantegna's engravings and their influence on other artists. It provides detailed analyses of the prototypes in Mantegna's engravings used by Leonardo and Michelangelo for the cartoons they designed for the great Council-Hall of the Palazzo Vecchio in Florence, which depicted, respectively, the Battle of Cascina and the Battle of Anghiari. There is also a discussion of Mantegna's fresco in Rome representing the Baptism of Christ (destroyed in the 18th century), which also exercised a strong influence on Michelangelo. The latter's *Battle of Cascina* cartoon is seen here as the inspirational source of the engraving *Massacre of the Innocents* by Raphael and Raimondi. Finally, there is a study of antique prototypes, again through Mantegna's mediation, in Dürer's engravings of Apollo and Adam. The text is accompanied by 265 illustrations.

162   Inscriptiones Christianae Urbis Romae septimo saeculo antiquiores. (Pre-seventh century Christian inscriptions of the city of Rome.) Giovanni Battista de Rossi. Rome: Ex Officina Libraria Pontificia, 1861- .

The first two volumes were published in 1861 and 1888, with a supplement edited by Giuseppe Gatti published in 1915. The new series began in 1872 and its tenth volume appeared in 1992.

163 Inscriptiones Graecae Urbis Romae. (Greek inscriptions of the
City of Rome.)
Luigi Moretti. Rome: Istituto italiano per la storia antica, 1968-90.
4 vols. (Studi Pubblicati dall'Istituto Italiano per la Storia Patria,
fasc. 17, 22, 28, 47.)

This is a catalogue of 1,705 Greek inscriptions found in Rome. It includes transcriptions
and detailed discussion of the texts. Numerous entries are accompanied by photographs
of the inscriptions.

164 Inscriptiones Urbis Romae Latinae. (Latin inscriptions of the city
of Rome.)
Edited by E. Bormann (et al.). Berlin: apud Georgium Reimerum,
1876-1996. (Corpus Inscriptionum Latinarum, vol. 6.)

This collection of Latin inscriptions found in the city of Rome includes sacred
inscriptions, inscriptions of emperors, magistrates and priests, inscriptions of soldiers,
minor officials and craftsmen, sepuchral inscriptions and false inscriptions. Indexes of
names and surnames are included in volume six, while volume seven contains word
indexes. The first six volumes were reprinted between 1959 and 1974.

165 Katalog der antiken Bildwerke. (Studies on Villa Albani: a
catalogue of the ancient sculptures.)
Edited by Peter C. Bol. Berlin: Mann, 1989-98. (Forschungen zur
Villa Albani: Schriften des Liebieghauses.)

Villa Albani (now Torlonia) on the Via Salaria was built by Carlo Marchionni between 1746
and 1767 as a private museum for the display of the magnificent collections of ancient sculpture
of Cardinal Alessandro Albani, the nephew of Pope Clement XI. Albani was advised on his
purchases by J. J. Winckelmann, his librarian and curator from 1758 to 1768. In 1817, the Villa
was bought by the Castelbarco family and in 1866 by Alesandro Torlonia. Today it houses both
the remaining Albani collection and the collection of the Torlonia family. The Villa consists of
a number of different buildings set in extensive formal gardens: the large two-storey Casino has,
on its ground floor, a sculpture loggia opening on to the garden, and, on the piano nobile, a suite
of magnificent rooms which includes the Salone with Anton Raphael Mengs' *Parnassus* fresco.
Other buildings include the Appartamento di Leda (Leda's Apartment), the Bigliardo (Billiard
Room), two Greek pavilions (*tempietti greci*), an artificial ruined temple composed of genuine
antique fragments and placed in a picturesque setting in the garden, and a *kaffeehaus* (Coffee
House) set in the exedra at the far end of the garden. The sculptures in the Villa have thematic
groupings: those of the emperors are in the Casino, the poets and philosophers in the wings, and
the gods in the exedra. These five volumes provide detailed catalogue entries for the massive
corpus of 1,112 sculptures in the Villa. All the works are reproduced in black and white.

166 Il Lazio di Thomas Ashby, 1891-1930. (The Lazio of Thomas
Ashby, 1891-1930.)
Edited by Emanuela Bianchi. Rome: Fratelli Palombi, 1994- .
(British School at Rome Archive, 4.)

Thomas Ashby (1874-1931), archaeologist, collector, and Director of the British School at
Rome from 1906 to 1925, was also an expert photographer, amassing an archive of over 9,000
photographs of the Roman Campagna which supplemented his archaeological researches. This

first volume of a projected catalogue of his photographs of Lazio is divided into sections, each of which covers a particular area: Etruria, Via Aurelia (including Cerveteri, Santa Marinella, Ponte del Diavolo, Tarquinia, and Vulci), Via Cassia, Via Clodia, Via Amerina (including Nepi, and Falerii Novi), Via Flaminia, Ostia, Southern Lazio (including Palestrina, Olevano, Anagni, Alatro, Terracina), and the Latin shore. There is a listing of some 300 photographs from the archive arranged by the name of the modern Comune in which the site is located and a listing of the plans Ashby used in his walks, now in the collection of the Unione accademica nazionale. In one of the introductory essays, the photographs and working methods of Ashby, an archaeologist using the camera as an aid to his researches, are contrasted to those of Giovanni Gargiolli, a professional photographer who, in 1892, also started to explore Rome and its countryside, his photographs later becoming the foundations of the Gabinetto fotografico nazionale. The volume also includes a bibliography of Ashby's writings on Lazio.

167 The legacy of Rome: a new appraisal.
Edited by Richard Jenkyns.   Oxford: Oxford University Press, 1992. 490p. bibliog.

A survey of ancient Roman influence on later centuries. In his introduction to the work, Jenkyns distinguishes between constitutive influence (where the source is the basis of what it influences, for example, classical models of Renaissance architecture), auxiliary influence (where the source provides support or coherence, for example, the shaping of social and political attitudes in 17th- and 18th-century England), and decorative influence (where the source provides elegance of surface, for example, classical quotations, subject-matter in art). Individual contributors look at the transmission of texts, the Middle Ages, the Renaissance, Virgil, the Pastoral, Horace, Ovid and other writers, Satire, Drama, Rhetoric, Art, Architecture, Language, Law, and the City of Rome. Each chapter includes a separate bibliography.

168 The marble wilderness: ruins and representation in Italian Romanticism, 1775-1850.
Carolyn Springer.   Cambridge, England: Cambridge University Press, 1987. 208p.

This study examines the revival of interest in ruins in the late 18th and early 19th centuries. It contrasts the elegiac mode of European Romanticism that reached its climax in the poetry of Lord Byron who, in *Chide Harold's pilgrimage* described Rome as a 'marble wilderness', with the prevailing mood of Italian literature from 1775 (the beginning of the papacy of Pius VI) to 1850 (the fall of the Roman Republic), which celebrated ruins and their restoration both as a symbol of the continuity between Pagan and Christian Rome and also of political rebirth. It looks at the literature of archaeological encomium, and gives a fascinating analysis of Vincenzo Monti's 'Prosopopea di Pericle' (1779), a poem celebrating the recovery of the bust of Pericles from the ruins of Tivoli and its inclusion in the Museo Pio-Clementino, the newly created museum of antiquities in the Vatican Palace created by Clement XIV and Pius VI as a demonstration of the papacy's renewed vigour and wealth. The iconographical programmes commissioned for the museum's galleries are also examined.

169 Marvels of Ancient Rome.
Margaret R. Scherer, edited and with a foreword by Charles Rufus
Morey. New York; London: Phaidon Press for the Metropolitan
Museum of Art, 1955. 439p.

Scherer compares the present aspect of Rome's ancient sites and monuments with their
appearance in earlier centuries before they were divested of their secular accretions (their
'accumulated past') by 20th-century archaeologists. An introductory chapter looks at Rome's
ancient ruins through the centuries and the way they were described by writers and depicted
on coins, reliefs, engravings, paintings and photographs. Subsequent chapters examine the
following: the Campidoglio, the Palatine, the Forum, surviving triumphal arches, the Basilica
of Constantine or Maxentius, the Colosseum, the Golden House of Nero, the Baths of
Caracalla, the Baths of Diocletian, the Forum of Nerva, the Forum and Column of Trajan,
ruins in the Colonna Gardens, the Theatre of Marcellus, unidentified temples by the Tiber, the
House of Crescentius, the Pantheon, the Pyramid of Cestius, Hadrian's Tomb, the Vatican
Obelisk, and, finally, statues that were never buried (among them Marcus Aurelius, the
colossal head and hand now in the Capitoline Museums, and the Horse Tamers of the
Quirinal). 223 plates show contemporary photographs of the monuments and sites discussed
alongside artistic representations of them. There is also a chronology.

170 Monumenti antichi di Roma nei disegni di Alberto Alberti.
(Ancient monuments of Rome in the drawings of Alberto Alberti.)
Giovanna Maria Forni. Rome: Accademia nazionale dei Lincei,
1991. 209p. + 1 portfolio (386 plates). (Atti della Accademia
Nazionale dei Lincei, anno 386 [1989]; (Memorie, Classe di Scienze
Morali, Storiche e Filologiche, series 8, vol. 23.)

A detailed study of four codices (nos. 2501-04) in the Gabinetto nazionale delle stampe
of the Uffizi, depicting ancient monuments in Rome. Though the importance of these
works was pointed out by Rodolfo Lanciani at a session of the Accademia nazionale dei
Lincei in 1882, they had remained unpublished until the present study. The catalogue
attempts to identify the subjects of the drawings, and compares them to the drawings of
other Renaissance artists. Moreover, the author establishes that the drawings are the work
of the sculptor and architect Alberto Alberti, and not of his sons Giovanni and Cherubino
Alberti, to whom they were previously attributed. They are dated between 1570 and 1598
and are accompanied by measurements and notes. They provide original evidence for
monuments which, in many cases, have since disappeared, such as the Septizonium, and
the Temple of Serapis on the Quirinal.

171 Notes from Rome.
Rodolfo Lanciani, edited by Anthony L. Cubberley. London:
British School at Rome, 1988. 478p.

The articles in this volume appeared in *The Athenaeum* between 1876 and 1913. They are a
series of eyewitness accounts and comments on archaeological activity in Rome and its
surroundings. In their apparent spontaneity and their author's ability to introduce anecdotes and
digressions while retaining his main theme they are not unlike Alistair Cooke's 'Letter from
America' broadcasts. Lanciani conducted excavations in Rome, Ostia and Tivoli and his
achievements include the identification of the Temple of Jupiter Capitolinus, the House of the
Vestal Virgins and most of Hadrian's Villa at Tivoli. From 1882, he held the Chair of Roman
Topography at the University of Rome. He was the author of numerous publications. The period

covered by these notes was one that saw massive destruction of the city's historical and artistic heritage but which also afforded great opportunities for archaeological discoveries. Lanciani's feelings are typically ambivalent when he laments, for example, in Note 45, the Government decision to construct the Vittoriano, which would necessitate the destruction of part of the Capitoline hill. His outrage is, however, tempered when he reflects that the excavations for the construction of the monument are bound to yield interesting archaeological discoveries.

172 The obelisks of Rome.
Erik Iversen. Copenhagen: G. E. C. Gad Publishers, 1968. 206p. map. bibliog. (Obelisks In Exile, 1.)

An introductory chapter outlines the role of obelisks as objects of cult, their mythical origins and historical development and also considers the various theories about their symbolism. Each of the thirteen surviving obelisks is accorded a chapter in which the monument's symbolism is discussed, its inscriptions transcribed, and its history traced. Ancient regional descriptions of Rome enumerate forty-eight obelisks, and the fate of most of the remaining thirty-five is obscure. Fragments of other obelisks still preserved attest, however, to the original existence of several other unrecorded monuments and some of these are discussed in the last chapter.

173 The Pantheon: design, meaning, and progeny.
William L. MacDonald. London: Allen Lane, 1976. 160p. bibliog. (The Architect and Society.)

The best preserved of all Roman monumental buildings, the Pantheon owes its survival to its consecration in 609 as a church (Sancta Maria ad Martyres, later becoming known as Santa Maria Rotonda). This excellent short study gives the history of the building and its vicissitudes (in 663 the Byzantine Emperor Constans II removed its gilded bronze tiles, while Urban VIII removed some 200 tons of ancient bronze from the support system of the porch roof using them chiefly to cast 80 cannons for the Castel S. Angelo and for Bernini's Baldacchino), describes its parts and structure, discusses the principles and historical background of its architectural design, and considers its various levels of meaning and symbolism. It also examines the far-reaching influence of the Pantheon upon subsequent architecture, beginning with the later Roman Empire, continuing with the Renaissance and the work of Bramante, Serlio, Michelangelo and Palladio, the 17th century and Bernini, the neo-classical movement, with examples of the building's influence on the work of Italian, English, French and American architects and, finally, more recent interpretations in churches, civic and academic buildings, libraries and capitols inspired directly or indirectly by it.

174 The Paper Museum of Cassiano Dal Pozzo.
Francis Haskell (et al.). [Ivrea, Italy]: Olivetti, 1993. 288p. bibliog. (Quaderni Puteani, 4.)

This is the catalogue of an exhibition held in the British Museum in 1993 showing 162 works originally in the collection of Cassiano Dal Pozzo. One of the greatest collectors and antiquarians in 17th-century Rome, Cassiano Dal Pozzo (1588-1657) aspired to have recorded for himself 'the collectable products of the natural world and of human creativity', employing draughtsmen to copy antiquities in the city. He also collected drawings and prints by earlier artists. His collection of drawings were bound in some twenty-three volumes, divided by subject matter, and constituted the so-called 'Paper Museum' (*Museo cartaceo*). The exhibition showed examples of all aspects of Cassiano's collections – archaeological, topographical and architectural drawings, natural history drawings, and prints. The introductory essay by Francis

Haskell in this volume outlines Cassiano's life and describes his various interests, while the later history of the Paper Museum is traced in the essay by Henrietta McBurney.

175 The Paper Museum of Cassiano Dal Pozzo: a catalogue raisonné: Series A, Antiquities and Architecture.
General editors: Francis Haskell, Jennifer Montagu, series editor: Amanda Claridge. London: Harvey Miller, 1996- .

The publication of the catalogue raisonné of drawings and prints originally in Cassiano Dal Pozzo's 'Paper Museum' and now in the Royal Library at Windsor Castle, the British Museum, the Institut de France and other collections is projected to be in eighteen volumes published in two series – Series A covering Antiquities and Architecture, and Series B Natural History. The first title published was volume 2, part 1 covering mosaics and wallpaintings in Roman churches. The catalogue proper is preceded by a general introduction to the Paper Museum of Cassiano Dal Pozzo, giving an account of the development of the collection and its subsequent changes of ownership and vicissitudes, and an essay on the Antiquities and Architecture series – which comprises some 4,200 drawings – explaining that its ten sections broadly reflect the subject-based groups in which the drawings are found today, though the order of the drawings in the catalogue is not necessarily that in which they are found in the various albums.

176 Piranesi e la cultura antiquaria: gli antecedenti e il contesto.
(Piranesi and antiquarian culture: its antecedents and their context.)
Edited by Anna Lo Bianco. Rome: Multigrafica, 1985. 439p.

This volume brings together papers presented at a conference held at the Palazzo dei Conservatori in 1979, the bicentenary of Piranesi's death. The conference aimed to demonstrate the relationship between Piranesi and the antiquarian tradition in Rome and the Veneto from the 15th to the 18th century. The twenty-four papers include discussions of the following: the Column of Trajan in 15th century antiquarian iconography (A. Cavallaro); 15th- and 16th-century drawings after ancient Roman architecture (S. Danesi Squarzina); Roman antiquarian culture in the second half of the 15th century and the typology of a cardinal's residence (M. G. Aurigemma); the relationship between Piranesi and Giovanni Gaetano Bottari, the librarian of Cardinal Neri Corsini (A. Monferini); Piranesi's role as archaeologist and his work in Hadrian's Villa (H. Lavagne); Piranesi's studies of the Walls and Gates of Rome (Luciana Cassanelli); Piranesi and the role of archaeological illustration (John Wilton-Ely); Piranesi and Egyptian taste (M. G. Messina); Piranesi's theoretical works and Etruscan antiquities (Mauro Cristofani); Piranesi and the Roman neo-classical milieu (S. Röttgen); Giuseppe Valadier's drawings and their relationship to Piranesi's techniques (E. Debenedetti); the role of the antique in P. L. Ghezzi's paintings (Anna Lo Bianco); the Roman works of Giovanni Volpato (E. Tittoni Monti); and Canova's *Perseus* (A. Pinelli). Most of the contributions are accompanied by numerous illustrations.

177 Pirro Ligorio, artist and antiquarian.
Edited by Robert W. Gaston. Florence, Italy: Silvana, 1988. 303p. bibliog. (Villa I Tatti, 10.)

Pirro Ligorio, architect, draughtsman, painter and antiquary, is best known as the architect of the Casino of Pius IV and of the gardens at the Villa d'Este at Tivoli, and also as the architect in charge at St Peter's after Michelangelo's death. Until recently his work was relatively little studied, a fact here attributed to the artist's difficult character and his engagement in polemics about antiquities and architecture. This collection of papers, presented (with one exception) at a seminar held at the Villa I Tatti in 1983 to commemorate the quatercentenary of Ligorio's death, assess his achievements as a serious and learned scholar of classical antiquity and archaeology, his iconographical interpretations of classical images, and his notebooks. They include a study on Ligorio's reconstruction of Ancient Rome in his *Anteiquae Urbis Imago* (The image of the ancient city) of 1561; on Ligorio and the temples of Rome on coins; his stucco decorations of the Casino of Pius IV; and on Ligorio's major change in Michelangelo's design of the elevation of St Peter's.

178 Pirro Ligorio's Roman antiquities: the drawings in Ms XIII B.7 in the National Library of Naples.

Edited by Erna Mandowsky and Charles Mitchell. London: The Warburg Institute, University of London, 1963. 160p. 76 plates. (Studies of the Warburg Institute, 28.)

Examines Pirro Ligorio's activity as painter, architect, decorator, topographer and antiquary. Ligorio was in charge of the excavations at Tivoli between 1549 and 1555, while in the service of Cardinal Ippolito II d'Este. In 1564, he succeeded Michelangelo as architect of St Peter's and in 1568 was appointed ducal antiquary in Ferrara. Like other artists and draughtsmen of his generation, he was equally at home in the painter's workshop, the court and the philologist's study. He was a lifelong investigator of antiquities on the site compiling, by 1553, some forty volumes of records of Roman antiquities. He restored defective monuments in the same way that contemporary classical scholars edited and emended defective texts. There are four main collections of Ligorio's drawings of Roman antiquities, representing only a fraction of his output (his other activities include printmaking and the publication of maps of Rome): these are in the Bibliothèque nationale, Paris (1 vol.), the Bodleian Library, Oxford (1 vol.), the Archivio di stato in Turin (27 vols.) and the Biblioteca nazionale in Naples (10 vols.). The catalogue, which contains 145 entries, deals exclusively with the drawings of figured monuments in this codex, most of which came from Rome or from the route between Rome and Naples. All the drawings are reproduced and Ligorio's often elaborate commentaries transcribed.

179 Pleasure of ruins.

Rose Macaulay. London: Thames & Hudson, 1966. 466p.

First published in 1953, this study explores attitudes towards ruins and the various kinds of impressions induced by their beauty, strangeness or picturesqueness. The section on Rome (pp. 165-204) looks at the dwindling of the city's external glory brought about by numerous sackings and the plundering and quarrying of its buildings. It is suggested that the Rome of Justinian was already taking the pattern it was to keep through the Middle Ages, of classical antiquity mouldering into picturesque decay, with grass and shrubs covering the ancient stones and new churches and monasteries growing out of 'ancient, spoiled magnificence'. It looks at the role of Cola di Rienzo, the first ruin enthusiast to make a close study of classical inscriptions, and Petrarch's reactions during his short visits to Rome, a mixture of admiration and rage about the wilful destruction of the ancient city. The poet was the most famous voice before Raphael against the wrecking of antique Rome. The reactions of Joachim du Bellay, and of numerous artists and writers of the 18th and 19th century, the great era of the appeal of ruins, are also surveyed.

180 Renaissance artists & antique sculpture: a handbook of sources.
Phyllis Pray Bober, Ruth Rubinstein, with contributions by Susan
Woodford. London: Harvey Miller; Oxford: Oxford University
Press, 1986. 522p. bibliog.

A reference guide to the ancient monuments used by Renaissance artists. It includes 203 statues
and reliefs and examines their history in the Renaissance: their discovery, display,
interpretations of their subject-matter, and the artists and antiquarians who recorded them or
profited from their presence. The guide can be used to identify a drawing after the antique; to
investigate whether a sculpture could have been known to a particular artist, either directly or
through another medium; to study the responses of different artists to the antique; and to survey
the iconographic contents of Renaissance collections. The guide, like the 'Census of antique
works of art known to Renaissance artists', an unpublished reference collection of
documentation and photographs at the Warburg Institute, from which it derives, concentrates on
antiquities known during the 15th century and up to the Sack of Rome in 1527. As well as
statues, it also includes relief sculptures but few small, portable antiquities, coins, gems, relief
ceramics, and bronzes. The arrangement is thematic and in two sections: Greek and Roman
gods and myths, and Roman history and life. Each entry includes a short explanation of the
theme in antiquity, and indications of literary sources and other antique representations of the
figure type elsewhere in the book or known in the Renaissance in other examples or media. The
volume also includes two useful appendices: an index of Renaissance artists and sketchbooks;
and a selective, annotated index of the major Renaissance collections mentioned in the book.

181 The Renaissance discovery of classical antiquity.
Roberto Weiss. Oxford: Basil Blackwell, 1988. 2nd ed. 245p. bibliog.

Originally published in 1969, this is a survey of the rise and early development of interest in the
tangible remains of classical antiquity and their study, which started in the late 13th century and
culminated in the work of Poggio Bracciolini and Flavio Biondo in the early 16th century. It
provides a study of archaeology in its early stages and an examination of the humanist study of
the statues, inscriptions, coins, and ruins of classical antiquity. An introductory chapter
demonstrates that interest in antiquity never waned altogether during the Middle Ages. The
following chapters look at the 14th-century and the interest of Petrarch in archaeology which,
though not as overwhelming as his interest in classical scholarship and bibliophily, nevertheless
manifested itself in various ways during his first visit to Rome in 1337 and his walks among its
ruins in the company of Francesco Colonna. The study of ancient inscriptions was a strong
interest of Cola di Rienzo and his short-lived rise to power in 1347 was coloured by his
antiquarianism. The contribution of humanist writers who, during the first half of the 15th
century, initiated a new approach to the study of ancient monuments, is examined next,
especially those of Poggio Bracciolini in his treatise *De varietate fortunae* (On the vicissitudes
of fortune) (1448), and Fabio Biondo, whose *Roma instaurata* (Rome restored) is a
comprehensive survey and reconstruction of Ancient Rome that combines the work of the
historian with that of the archaeologist. Other humanists who wrote on the topography of
Ancient Rome include the Florentine Bernardo Rucellai who in his treatise *de Urbe Roma* (On
the city of Rome) used a variety of sources, literary, historical, and epigraphic; Francesco
Albertini, whose popular *Opusculum novae et veteris Urbis Romae* (A short work about modern
and Ancient Rome) had five editions between 1510 and 1523; and Andrea Fulvio, whose
Antiquitates Urbis (The antiquities of the City of Rome) was published in 1527, shortly before
the Sack of Rome. During the second half of the 15th century, the Roman Academy of
Bartolomeo Platina and Pomponio Leto continued the antiquarian study of the city. The interest
in the topography of Ancient Rome is examined next and also the destruction of its ancient
remains which, ironically, was far greater during the Renaissance than in preceding centuries.

Archaeology and Antiquities

The discoveries and occasional restorations of masterpieces of ancient art are also considered, as are the rise of interest in classical epigraphy, the development of sylloges of inscriptions and their interpretation, and, finally, the collections of antiquities that began on a large scale during the 15th century. Notable collections in Rome included that of Pope Paul II (a large part of which was later acquired by Lorenzo de' Medici), the collection of bronze statues gathered in the Palazzo dei Conservatori (the seat of Rome's municipal government) and the collection of marble statues in the Vatican Belvedere.

182 Roma. (Rome.)
Filippo Coarelli. Milan, Italy: A. Mondadori, 1980 (latest reprint of the 3rd ed., 1999). 391p. maps. bibliog. (Guide Archeologiche Laterza, 6.)

This thorough, well-illustrated archaeological guide to Rome was first published in 1980. It is divided into: the great public works (the 'Servian' and Aurelian Wall, the aqueducts); the monumental centre (the Campidoglio, the Roman Forum, the Imperial Fora, the Palatine, the Valley of the Colosseum); the Augustan regions (the Caelian, Esquiline, the Quirinal and the Viminal, the Via Lata and the Pincian, Campus Martius, Foro Olitorio, Foro Boario, Circus Maximus, the Aventine, Isola Tiberina, Trastevere, Vatican); and the urban section of the Via Appia. An appendix describes building techniques and construction materials. Coarelli is the author of numerous other works on Roman archaeology and topography of Ancient Rome. See also *Il Foro romano* (The Roman Forum) (Rome: Edizioni Quasar, 1983-85. 2 vols. [320p., 364p.]) and *Il Foro Boario dalle origini alla fine della repubblica* (The Foro Boario, from its beginnings to the end of the Republic) (Rome: Edizioni Quasar, 1988. 503p.).

183 Roma e l'antico nell'arte e nella cultura del Cinquecento. (Rome and the antique in 16th-century art and culture.)
Edited by Marcello Fagiolo. Rome: Istituto della Enciclopedia italiana fondata da G. Treccani, 1985. 531p. (Biblioteca Internazionale di Cultura, 17.)

A collection of twenty-three studies originally presented at a series of seminars organized by the Accademia nazionale dei Lincei in October 1982. They are divided into four sections: i) *The idea of Rome in the fifteenth and sixteenth century* includes studies showing the influence of the classical tradition on Renaissance thought and culture, and on men of letters (Francesco Patrizi), historians (Francesco Baronio) and popes (Paul III); ii) *The rediscovery of the art of Ancient Rome* includes studies examining: the creation of the collection of antique sculptures in the Vatican and its importance; Bramante, Raphael and Peruzzi; the symbolism of 'grotesque' decorations and literature describing them in the second half of the century; the restoration of the Antonine Column; the frescoes of Tommaso Laureti, depicting scenes from the history of Ancient Rome, in the Sala dei Capitani of the Campidoglio; iii) *Architecture and the classical tradition* includes contributions on: the study of ancient Roman architecture during the 16th century; the influence on Renaissance architects of the Sanctuary of the Fortuna Medica at Palestrina and the complex of Ercole Vincitore at Tivoli; and demolitions and 'restorations' of antiquities in the sixteenth century; iv) *Rome beyond Rome* shows the influence of ancient Roman art on Venetian Renaissance art (for example, the paintings of Vittore Carpaccio); the zodiacal frescoes by the Veronese artist Giovanni Maria Falconetto in the Palazzo D'Arco in Mantua; and on Portuguese artists. The studies are accompanied by numerous illustrations in black and white and include bibliographies or bibliographical notes.

184   The Roman Forum.
Michael Grant, photographs by Werner Forman.   London; New
York: The Hamlyn Publishing Group, 1974. 240p.

The Forum was the heart of Ancient Rome, the nucleus of the business and commercial affairs of the city and Empire, the centre of its religious life, and the scene and route of the triumphal processions of generals. In imperial times it was called the Roman Forum (Forum Romanum) to distinguish it from the adjoining Imperial Fora built by Julius Caesar, Augustus, Vespasian, Nerva and Trajan. Its mass of ruins, enormous yet fragmentary, is one of the most imposing testimonies handed down by antiquity. This book attempts to explain their grandeur and significance from what is visible today. After offering a general survey of the development of the Forum it explains the role its various monuments had in the life of Rome and indicates events associated with them. The monuments are divided into shrines for the Gods, shrines for the Caesars, meeting-places of people and Senate, vaults and arcades, and the monumental arches. Lastly, it gives an account of the Forum's fate in later centuries. An appendix lists some of the most important monuments of the Forum which have either disappeared completely or have only survived in fragments or traces.

185   Roman Ostia.
Russell Meiggs.   Oxford: Clarendon Press, 1973 (2nd ed., 3rd
reprint 1985). 641p. + xl leaves of plates. map. bibliog.

Ostia, Rome's harbour town, was built on the mouth of the Tiber, fifteen miles from Rome. This study begins with a survey of the literary and material evidence (buildings, sculpture, inscriptions, the geographical setting) for the tracing of Ostia's history. It then traces its origin and early growth, its prosperity in the late Republic and early Empire, its development under Claudius and Nero and subsequent decline from the 3rd century onward, and finally its exploitation and excavation. The second, and larger, part of the work analyses the city and society, with chapters dedicated to its constitution and social structure, its houses, recreations (baths, theatres), cemeteries, and the arts (sculpture, painting and mosaics). There are eleven appendices which include information about Ostia officers taken from the *Fasti*, histories of families which played a leading role in Ostia's life, the Christian martyrs of Ostia and Portus, the population of Ostia, the dating of Ostian buildings and inscriptions, as well as a transcription of selected inscriptions. This edition also includes new evidence brought to light since the work's first edition in 1960. The forty plates at the end include descriptions of the views and monuments depicted and there is also a topographical index. See also *La civiltà dell'acqua in Ostia antica* (The water civilization in Ancient Ostia), by Maria Antonietta Ricciardi and Valnea Santa Maria Scrinari (Rome: Fratelli Palombi, 1997. 2 vols. [188p., 296p.]).

186   Rome.
Text by Filippo Coarelli.   London: The Reader's Digest
Association, 1979. 191p. maps. (Monuments of Civilization.)

This work, intended for the general reader, aims to evoke ancient Roman history, life and artistic achievements through a combination of text and images. The text is divided into four parts which examine: the origins of Rome; the formation of Roman culture during the Republican period (509-31 BC); the Imperial Age from Augustus to Marcus Aurelius (31 BC-193 AD); and the Imperial Age from the Severan dynasty to the era of Constantine (193-330 AD). The text is complemented by photographs (mostly in colour), captions, maps and plans, a chronological chart, and passages from ancient writers. A useful appendix looks at the transformation of Roman monuments through the ages, their integration into structures of different periods, their adaptation to different functions, their export and destruction in the late Middle Ages, and their use as quarries for building materials during the Renaissance. It is pointed out that the best-preserved monuments are those (like the Pantheon, which was transformed into a church in the 7th century) for which new uses were found during the city's long history. The changes in the ground level, a source of astonishment to visitors to Rome, are also explained.

187   Rome: an Oxford archaeological guide.

Amanda Claridge, with contributions by Judith Toms and Tony Cubberley.   Oxford; New York: Oxford University Press, 1998. 464p. bibliog. (Oxford Archaeological Guides.)

This is a guide to all the important archaeological sites of Rome from 800 BC to 600 AD. It is the only general account in English of recent scholarship and important finds such as the meridian line of the Augustan Sundial of 10 BC, discovered by German excavations in 1979-80 in Via di Campo Marzio. The sites are divided into nine main areas – the Roman Forum, the Upper Via Sacra, the Palatine, the Imperial Fora, the Field of Mars (*Campus Martius*), Capitoline Hill, Circus Flaminius to Circus Maximus, Colosseum Valley and Esquiline Hill, Caelian Hill and the Via Appia. A tenth section groups together sites in other areas, such as Monte Testaccio, the Lateran and the Viminal. The Catacombs and fifteen museums of antiquities are examined in the last two chapters. There is also a historical overview, a description of documentary sources (antiquarian and architectural drawings and maps, the Marble Plan, coins, reliefs, inscriptions, regionary catalogues, and classical texts from Plautus to Procopius), and a glossary of Rome's building materials, building techniques, architectural orders and dimensions, building-types, and major public works. It includes 200 useful black-and-white illustrations (site plans, maps, diagrams and photographs).

188   The Rotunda in Rome: a study of Hadrian's Pantheon.

Kjeld De Fine Licht.   Copenhagen: Gyldendal, 1968. bibliog. (Jutland Archaeological Society Publications, 8.)

A detailed survey of the building, aiming to clarify the circumstances of its erection and illustrate the problems and conditions of Roman architecture at the beginning of the 2nd century AD. It establishes that the examination of the Pantheon complex (the forecourt, pronaos, the intermediate block and its connection with the rotunda, the cupola) proves incontrovertibly that the whole was erected at the same time according to a master plan. The building south of the Pantheon, the walls and buildings around the rotunda are also examined, as are the relics of other buildings under the Pantheon. It offers a dating of the building considering both the written evidence from Antiquity and the Early Middle Ages and architectural and archaeological evidence. It also considers the Pantheon's place in the history of architecture – its construction and relation to contemporary architecture and to its immediate surroundings, its later history and the inspiration it gave to innumerable architects.

189   Sarcophagi from the Jewish catacombs of Ancient Rome: a catalogue raisonné.

Adia Konikoff.   Stuttgart, Germany: Franz Steiner Verlag, 1990. rev. ed. 58p. + 16p. of plates. bibliog. map.

This monograph attempts to catalogue all known sarcophagi used in the burial of Jews in the Roman catacombs. The sarcophagi, which are the largest group found anywhere in the Jewish Diaspora, indicate the departure of the Jews of Rome from their ancestral custom and their adoption of the practice of internment in coffins in the last century BC and the first century

AD. Though small in number, they range from those decorated solely with Jewish symbols to those with untraditional figurative designs. The catalogue contains twenty-two items: three recorded sarcophagi; sarcophagi found *in situ* (on Via Appia, in the Vicolo S. Sebastiano, on Via Portuense, and on Via Nomentana); sarcophagi found removed from their site; and, finally, a funerary couch from the Monteverde catacomb. Each entry contains a bibliography.

190 Storia degli scavi di Roma e notizie intorno le collezioni romane di antichità. (History of the excavations in Rome and notes concerning Roman collections of antiquities.)
Rodolfo Lanciani. Rome: Edizioni Quasar, 1989- .

This vast work was originally planned by Lanciani to be published in five volumes and give a detailed history of excavations in Rome from the year 1000 to 1870, together with an account of the formation and dispersal of collections of antiquities in Rome. Only the first four volumes were finally published, from 1902 to 1912, covering the period up to 1605. The arrangement of material in the first volume is in strictly chronological order; thereafter, Lanciani opted for a more narrative approach, grouping together all information about individual monuments. The completion of the work was prevented by Lanciani's other commitments and also by the cost of the publication, which was privately printed by the author. Unlike the original edition of the work, which was without illustrations, the text in the present edition is accompanied by some 1,000 illustrations (prints, drawings and maps). Six volumes of the present edition have been published so far. The first four reproduce the contents of Lanciani's published volumes – vol. 1, 1000-1530; vol. 2, the last years of Clement VII and the pontificate of Paul III (1531-49); vol. 3, from the election of Julius III to the death of Pius IV (1550-65); vol. 4, from the election of Pius V to the death of Clement VIII (1566-1605). The last two volumes are based on the drafts in Lanciani's archive, now in the Istituto di archeologia e storia dell'arte, together with his library and collection of prints and drawings. Vol. 5 covers the period from the election of Paul V to the death of Innocent XII (1605-1700); and vol. 6 covers the period from the beginning of the pontificate of Clement XI (1700) to the death of Pius IX (1878). Vol. 7 will include various analytical indices – of places (ancient and modern), archives and libraries, museums and collections, personal names, and also a general bibliography.

191 Subterranean Rome.
Ivana Della Portella, photography by Mark E. Smith. Cologne, Germany: Könemann, 2000. 278p.

A beautifully illustrated guide through the world of subterranean Rome – temples dedicated to the cult of the god Mithras, nymphea, columbaria, hypogea and underground passages under churches, palaces and ordinary buildings. It includes sacred places such as the Area sacra of Largo Argentina, the Syriac sanctuary on the Janiculum, S. Crisogono, S. Clemente and S. Cecilia in Trastevere and also secular buildings such as the Domus Aurea (the Golden House of Nero), the quarters of the Seventh Cohort of Guards, and the Stadium of Domitian. See also *Roma sotterranea* (Underground Rome), edited by Roberto Luciani (Rome: Fratelli Palombi, 1985. 298p. [Cataloghi.]).

192 Taste and the antique: the lure of classical sculpture, 1500-1900.
Francis Haskell, Nicholas Penny. New Haven, Connecticut; London: Yale University Press, 1982. 392p. bibliog.

An enthralling study of the antique sculptures that, between 1500 and 1900, were considered to have reached the summit of artistic achievement. Most of these were to be seen in Rome, and later also in Naples, Florence and Paris, and were copied or reproduced in various materials, and celebrated in literature from Du Bellay to Hawthorne. The work is in two sections. The first traces, in fifteen chapters, the rise and fall of the vogue for classical sculptures. It begins with 16th-century Rome and the development of the Belvedere Court in the Vatican Palace to house some of the most important statues, the discovery of important works – such as the statues (later moved to Naples) unearthed in 1545 on Farnese property in the Baths of Caracalla – and the development of other private collections of sculptures. The spread of the popularity of antique sculptures in the 17th century through plaster casts, prints and books is examined next and is followed by a chapter on their display in collections and museums in 18th-century Rome, such as the Villa Albani and the creation of the Museo Pio-Clementino in the Vatican, the greatest museum of antiquities in the world. The final chapters examine the proliferation of casts and copies in the 18th century, reinterpretations of antiquity by, among others, Johann Joachim Winckelmann, which led to a fall in the reputation of several previously admired works, and the fate of antiquities during the Napoleonic era. The catalogue section includes entries for ninety-five of the most famous sculptures, listed alphabetically under their most common name (most of them were known by a variety of names, which are also given). Each entry provides information about the statue's discovery, ownership and its movements, and discusses its rise and decline in popularity, its copies and interpretations. All the sculptures are excellently reproduced in black and white and the book also contains a profusion of comparative illustrations.

193 **Thomas Ashby: un archeologo fotografa la campagna romana tra '800 e '900.** (Thomas Ashby: an archaeologist photographs the Roman Campagna.)
Edited by Ferdinando Castagnoli.   Rome: De Luca, 1986. 257p. maps. (British School at Rome Archive, 1.)

This catalogue of Thomas Ashby's photographs of the Roman Campagna includes 203 entries. The photographs are arranged by area, and each area is described in an introductory note. They are as follows: Via Salaria, Via Nomentana, Via Tiburtina-Valeria, Via Collatina, Via Prenestina, Via Labicana, Via Latina, Via Appia, Via Ardeatina, Via Laurentina, Via Ostiense, Via Severiana, Via Aurelia, Via Clodia and Via Cassia, Via Flaminia and, finally, aqueducts. A biography of Ashby and a bibliography of his writings on the Roman Campagna are also included.

194 **The tombs of St Peter and St Paul.**
Engelbert Kirschbaum, translated from the German by John Murray.
London: Secker & Warburg, 1959. 247p.

This volume makes available the results of the excavation under the 'Confessio' at St Peter's, which was commissioned by Pope Pius XII and completed in 1951. Peter's tomb had previously been buried beneath the 'Confessio'. The excavation uncovered the ancient Roman road, the tombs lining it, and the spot where a monument was built to house the remains of the Saint. The study consists of a chronological and retrospective description of the excavation and an interpretative account of the results. As the question of actual relics of the apostle recurs in practically all debates about St Peter's grave, the study includes a chapter on the bones of St Peter and St Paul, prefaced with a note on St Paul's grave (which has not been excavated) on the Via Ostiense, suggesting parallels between the two.

195 Trajan's Column and the Dacian Wars.

Lino Rossi, English translation revised by J. M. C. Toynbee.
London: Thames & Hudson, 1971. 240p. bibliog. (Aspects of Greek
and Roman Life.)

This study gives a detailed description and interpretation of the Column of Trajan by means
of a series of 157 photographs of the frieze. The author argues that the frieze, a
commemoration of the Roman army's achievements in the two Dacian Wars (in AD 101-102
and AD 105-106) and 'a document in pictures', ought to be studied and understood as a
whole and not as a series of isolated scenes. He views the Column as a rich source of
information on military matters of the Middle Empire and, to assist its reading, he
provides an examination of the Roman army and navy, their composition, organization
and strength. The political and geographical background against which the wars were
fought is outlined and military standards, armour, arms and equipment are examined as is
the evidence on contemporary coins and inscriptions. The present author sees the reliefs
both as a narrative of the Dacian campaign but also as a series of symbolic scenes forming
a synthesis of the imperial virtues. See also *Trajan's army on Trajan's Column*, by Sir Ian
Richmond, with a preface and bibliography by Mark Hassall (London: The British School
at Rome, 1982. 65p.).

196 La Valle del Colosseo. (The Valley of the Colosseum.)

Text by Letizia Abbondanza, edited by Paola Urbani. Milan, Italy:
Electa, 1997. 53p. (Guide Electa per la Soprintendenza Archeologica
di Roma.)

A visitor's guide to the Colosseum and the Arch of Constantine, with briefer sections on
the Meta Sudans and the Temple of Venus and Rome. Each section is imaginatively
illustrated with diagrams, plans, paintings, and period and modern photographs.

History

General

197 The antiquarian and the myth of antiquity: the origins of Rome in Renaissance thought.
Philip Jacks. Cambridge, England: Cambridge University Press, 1993. 395p.

A study of the changing humanist perceptions, from the 13th to the 17th century, of the mythical and symbolic image of Rome and the evolution of the appreciation for the physical city when the new evidence offered by archaeology, inscriptions and attempts to measure and map the city was added to the literary. Its analysis of the changing archaeological, philological and historical methods used during this period demonstrates that the legendary and historical origins of Rome were constantly being re-interpreted. The work includes 103 plates of paintings, maps, architectural details and engravings.

198 Archivio della Società romana di storia patria. (The archive of the Society of the History of Rome.)
Rome: Società romana di storia patria, 1877- .

This is a six-monthly publication containing scholarly articles on the history of Rome and Lazio, reviews of books, announcements, obituaries and the minutes of the Society's meetings. During the journal's long history there have been slight variations in its title: *Archivio della R. Deputazione romana di storia patria*, *Archivio della R. Società romana di storia patria*. Numerous indices have been published, usually bound with an issue of the review or as separate volumes.

199 Castel S. Angelo e Borgo tra Roma e papato. (Castel S. Angelo
and the Borgo between Rome and the papacy.)
Cesare D'Onofrio. Rome: Romana società editrice, 1978. 350p.
(Studi e Testi per la Storia Della Città di Roma, 1.)
An examination of the role of the Castel S. Angelo and the Borgo in the history of Rome over
a period of nearly two thousand years. Both the monument and its surrounding area (the *Ager
vaticanus*, later becoming the Borgo) were of major strategic importance for the defence of the
city and, consequently, became the objects of ferocious fighting between the Romans, the
Empire and the papacy. The monument was at the centre of all historical events as its possessor
was *ipso facto* the possessor of Rome. The study begins with a description of Hadrian's
monument (the *Mausoleum Hadriani*) in antiquity, and the early history of the area. It follows
all the key events in the monument's history from the invasions of the barbarians, which began
with the Visigoths under Alaric in 410, through the Carolingian era and the later Middle Ages,
when it was the property of the Crescenzi family, to its becoming, in 1376, a private residence
of the popes. During the Sack of Rome in 1527, the fortress sheltered Pope Clement VII and
later in the 16th century, its defences were strengthened and its interiors splendidly decorated.
The work includes a chapter on the history of the statue of the archangel Michael that was
placed on top of the building (thus giving it its modern name) after the vision of Pope Gregory
the Great during the plague of 590. An appendix provides a list (with substantial quotations)
of documents that refer to the fortress, and numerous splendid illustrations.

**200 Chronicle of the popes: the reign-by-reign record of the papacy
from St Peter to the present.**
P. G. Maxwell-Stuart. London: Thames & Hudson, 1997. 240p. maps.
Brief accounts of all 366 popes are accompanied by 350 illustrations, documentary
gobbets, graphic chronologies and numerous 'sidebars'. The book provides information
on such topics as the Conversion of Constantine, the legendary Pope Joan, the Crusades
and the re-building of St Peter's, although there is inadequate coverage of the more recent
popes – for example, only 300 words on Pius IX. Unfortunately, it contains nothing
meaningful about the critical issues and choices facing the Church in the 20th century –
there is nothing, for instance, about the social question, the Roman question, Communism
and Fascism, the genocide, ecumenism, sex or morality.

**201 The history of the popes from the close of the Middle Ages:
drawn from the secret archives of the Vatican.**
Ludwig Pastor, edited by Frederick Ignatius Antrobus. Nedeln,
Liechtenstein: Kraus Reprint, 1968-69. 40 vols.
A facsimile reprint of the sixth English edition of Pastor's mammoth history of the papacy
from the middle of the 15th century to the end of the 18th, which was originally published
between 1885 and 1924. The work was greatly helped by Leo XIII's decision to open the
Secret Archives of the Vatican, which had formerly been inaccessible to scholars.

202 Lunario romano. (Roman almanac.)
Edited by the Gruppo dei cultori di Roma. Rome: F. Spinosi, 1971- .
This is a series of studies on the history and culture of Rome and Lazio. The original series
(nos. 1-20), which was published by Fratelli Palombi for the Gruppo dei cultori di Roma
(later renamed Gruppo culturale di Roma e del Lazio [Cultural Group of Rome and
Lazio]) was edited by Renato Lefevre and the new series, which is published by Newton

Compton, by Armando Ravaglioli. Topics covered have included Roman dwellings, Roman waterways, Roman vineyards, women, traditional festivals, farmhouses and castles, the Renaissance, villas and parks, music, art, architecture and trade.

203 Miscellanea della Società romana di storia patria. (Miscellaneous publications of the Society of the History of Rome.)
Rome: [the Society], 1882- .

An irregularly published series of monographs on the history of Rome. Subjects covered have included the Baroque period, the cardinals' conspiracy against Pope Leo X, the Vallicelliana library, the Schism of 1130, the Roman Senate during the early Middle Ages, and many others.

204 The origins of Rome in historiography from Petrarch to Perizonius.
Hendrik Johannes Erasmus. Assen, The Netherlands: Van Gorcum, 1962. 152p. bibliog. (Bibliotheca Classica Vangorcumiana, 11.)

This is an investigation of the origins of Rome and of early Roman history in the historiography of the period from the 14th to the 17th centuries. The author refutes the often repeated claim that humanist scholars regarded Greek and Latin writers as infallible authorities and argues that greater freedom from ancient writers developed during the 16th century (for example, Temporarius's rejection of the Romulus legend). Moreover, in the 17th century the sources available to early historians began to be discussed (Philip Cluverius).

205 The Oxford dictionary of popes.
J. N. D. Kelly. Oxford; New York: Oxford University Press, 1986. 347p.

In his preface, the compiler explains that this dictionary was written to fill a gap because, though there are numerous biographies of individual popes and massive surveys of the papacy, it is almost impossible to find a one-volume handbook in English containing summary biographies of all popes and antipopes. The arrangement is chronological, not alphabetical, enabling the reader to view each pope in his historical context. Where available, details are given of each pope's family background and pre-papal career. Each entry has a brief bibliography giving references to primary sources as well as to specialized and more general studies.

206 The Pope's Jews.
Sam Waagenaar. London: Alcove Press, 1974. 501p. bibliog.

The Jewish community in Rome is the oldest in the Western world. This study traces its history and social history, from the earliest Jewish immigrants from Judea who settled in Rome in the 2nd century BC to the aftermath of the Second World War and the conversion of Israele Zolli, the Chief Rabbi of Rome. It surveys all the major events involving Roman Jews and also their living conditions and the changes in their status, such as the pageant organized in 70 AD by the emperor Vespasian to celebrate his son Titus's destruction of Jerusalem, which included the spoils from the Temple of Solomon and hundreds of Jewish slaves (a scene commemorated on the Arch of Titus in the Forum), the creation of the ghetto in 1555 where Jews were confined until its walls were torn down in 1870, and their predicament in the 20th century during the Fascist era and the Nazi occupation of Rome. It also describes the role of Jews in Roman society, the forced sermons they had to attend during the Counter-Reformation, their compulsory participation in the Carnival races (bought off in 1667 for an annual tribute of 300 scudi paid to the Pope) and their tribute to each new pope.

207 Roman presences: receptions of Rome in European culture, 1789-1945.
Edited by Catharine Edwards. Cambridge, England: Cambridge University Press, 1999. 290p. bibliog.

A collection of interdisciplinary essays tracing Ancient Rome's presence in a number of different European cultural contexts from the late 18th century to the end of the Second World War. One of the aims of the collection is to re-evaluate the idea that in the early 19th century Greece displaced Rome from its position of dominant cultural authority and to demonstrate that Rome's impact was as strong during the last two centuries as in earlier periods. A number of essays examine Anglo-Saxon responses to Rome – in the work of Henry James and T. S. Eliot, in Macaulay's evocation of early Roman history in his once popular *Lays of Ancient Rome* (1842) and in depictions of Christians and pagans in Victorian novels. Other essays explore the presence of Ancient Rome in the visual arts of France, Britain and Italy (in the work of François-Marius Granet, Simeon Solomon, and the artists of the Fascist period). Other contributions look at the uses of Roman history and antiquity by Napoleon I, the display of the ancient Roman past in early Italian films, the Fascist cult of *Romanità*, and the Nazi concept of Rome.

208 Rome: the biography of a city.
Christopher Hibbert. Harmondsworth, England: Penguin Books, 1987. 396p. map.

This is a well-written survey of the history of Rome and the social history of its people from the city's legendary beginnings to Mussolini (with an epilogue giving an overview of post-Liberation developments). It is divided into two parts – from the city's mythical origins to the Sack of Rome and from its recovery in the mid-16th century to its Liberation in 1944 after another period of foreign invasion and captivity. A third part aims to act as a guide to the city by providing historical notes (but not practical information) about its buildings and treasures in the order they appear in the text. The author is particularly adept at evoking the life in the city at various historical periods and at enlivening his text with character sketches and anecdotes.

209 Saints and sinners: a history of the popes.
Eamon Duffy. New Haven, Connecticut; London: Yale University Press in association with S4C, 1997. 326p.

A history of the papacy from its beginnings to the reign of Pope John Paul II. It explores the origins and development of papal authority, the political and religious role of the papacy after the collapse of the Roman Empire, its launching of the Crusades in the Middle Ages and its espousal of spiritual reforms, the 'Babylonian captivity' in Avignon and the Schism in the 14th and early 15th century, the Renaissance popes whose artistic patronage turned Rome into the greatest city in the world but whose worldliness precipitated the Reformation, the Counter-Reformation and the great 'builder popes' of the 17th and 18th centuries whose policies radically changed the appearance of Rome, the challenges to the authority of the papacy since the French Revolution, and, finally, the role and influence of the papacy in the contemporary world. A recurring question throughout the work is whether spiritual authority can be reconciled with worldly power and, if not, whether it can manage without it without falling into a state of subservience to it. The work is abundantly illustrated and includes a chronological list of popes and antipopes, a glossary and a bibliographical essay.

210 **Storia di Roma.** (The history of Rome.)
Bologna, Italy: Cappelli; Rome: Istituto di studi romani, 1938-96.

This is a series of monographs on the history, art and topography of Rome, ancient and modern. Topics covered in the series include the Republic, Rome in the Punic Wars, military conquest, the age of Caesar and Augustus, the Severans, the fall of the Western Empire, Byzantium, the Medieval Empire, Rome in the Renaissance, Rome in the 16th, 17th, 18th and 19th centuries, literature, art, and Rome in the 20th century.

211 **Studi romani: rivista bimestrale dell'Istituto di studi romani.**
(Roman studies: bi-monthly review of the Istituto di studi romani.)
Rome: Istituto di studi romani, 1953- .

The object of the review as stated in its first issue was to study all aspects and all periods of the history and civilization of Rome. Each issue contains articles, reviews and items of current interest in the life and culture of the city.

Ancient Rome

212 **The Catacombs and the Colosseum: the Roman Empire as the setting of primitive Christianity.**
Stephen Benko, John J. Rourke. Valley Forge, Pennsylvania: Judson Press, 1971. 318p.

A collection of studies, most of which were originally presented at a seminar on the Imperial Roman background of primitive Christianity. They provide a comprehensive examination of Roman life in the first two centuries of the Christian era (from the Principate of Octavian Augustus to the death of Hadrian), analysing the social and historical background to the development of the Christian Church. Political and religious history, Roman society and social conflict, law, education, and the military system are all examined. There are contributions on: the sources of Roman history, 31 BC-138 AD; the history of the Early Roman Empire; religion and social class in the Early Roman Empire; social unrest and primitive Christianity; ancient education in the time of the early Roman Empire; Roman law and the early Church; religion and the early Roman Empire; persecution and toleration of Christianity until Hadrian; and Collegia, philosophical schools and theology. Each study includes an extensive bibliography.

213 **Daily life in Ancient Rome: the people and the city at the height of the Empire.**
Jérôme Carcopino, edited with bibliography and notes by Henry T. Rowell. Translated from the French by E. O. Lorimer.
Harmondsworth, Middlesex: Penguin Books, 1991. 364p. bibliog.

For his detailed portrait of life in Ancient Rome, the author selects a period when Roman power and prosperity were at their height, between the middle of the first century AD and the reign of Hadrian (117-138). This is a period rich in both material remains (among them the Forum of Trajan and the port of Ostia) and literary evidence (Petronius, Statius, Juvenal). Part one describes the physical and moral background of Roman life. There are chapters on the extent and population of the city, its houses and streets, its society and social classes and also on marriage, women and the family, education and religion. Part two follows the routine of a day in the life of an average Roman from dawn until night in the Rome of the first Antonine Emperors. It explains the days and hours of the Roman calendar, and looks at the morning toilet of the Roman dandy (at the barber's) and the Roman matron, the various occupations, the shows and spectacles (the races, the theatre, the amphitheatre) and, on days when no spectacles and shows were provided, strolling, gambling, or bathing at the *thermae*, and, finally, dinner.

214 A history of Rome.
Marcel Le Glay, Jean-Louis Voisin, Yann Le Bohec, translated by Antonia Nevill.   Oxford; Cambridge, Massachusetts: Blackwell Publishers, 1996. 631p. bibliog.

A survey spanning over 1,300 years, from the earliest recorded settlement in the 8th century BC, to the establishment of the Roman Republic, the transition to Empire, and the decline of Rome in the late 4th and 5th centuries AD. It provides both an historical overview and an analysis of social, economic, religious and cultural issues. The book also includes a glossary, and a chronological table charting (in separate columns) military, political and social, and cultural and religious events.

215 The history of Rome.
Theodor Mommsen, with a new introduction by Thomas Wiedemann.   London: Routledge/Thoemmes Press, 1996. 5 vols.

Theodor Mommsen was one of the most prolific historians of the 19th century. His areas of interest included Latin inscriptions (he was the editor of the *Corpus Inscriptionum Latinarum* [Corpus of Latin Inscriptions]), Roman coins, the Roman calendar and chronology and, above all, Roman law. His monumental *Römische Geschichte* (The history of Rome) was, with his *Römisches Staatsrecht* (Roman constitutional law), his most important work. It was published in three volumes between 1854 and 1856. Its English translation by William P. Dickson was first published between 1862 and 1875. This is a reprint of the 1894 edition. The work covers the early Republic and the conquests of the Imperial Republic. Volume 4 of the work, dealing with the political and military history of Rome under the Emperors, was left unfinished and was not published in Mommsen's lifetime, and volume 5, *The Provinces of the Roman Empire from Caesar to Diocletian*, was published in 1885.

216 History of Rome: a documented analysis.
R. T. Ridley.   Rome: 'L'erma' di Bretschneider, 1987. 696p. (Problemi e Ricerche di Storia Antica.)

An analytical history of Rome from its origins to Diocletian and Constantine, every statement of which is documented, an abbreviated reference referring to a source listed in chapter one. Sources include literary accounts, archaeological evidence, legal sources, and reference works, divided into fifteen headings such as: histories of Rome, bibliography, encyclopaedias, dictionaries, atlases, etc. The texts chosen are the fullest and more accessible accounts (i.e. works available in English translation), with emphasis on ancient evidence. Each chapter is prefaced by suggested reading. The work also has genealogical tables and fourteen appendices, which include a chronology and notes on Roman names, the Roman calendar, the Roman tribes, Roman colonies and roads in Italy.

217   **A history of Rome, down to the reign of Constantine.**
       M. Cary, H. H. Scullard.   London: Macmillan Press, 1975. 3rd ed.
       721p.

This is a comprehensive survey of Roman history to the end of the Empire of the West. It was first published in 1935 and was revised for this edition by H. H. Scullard, who expanded the earlier sections incorporating new archaeological evidence. The work is in forty-four chapters and begins, in fact, with pre-Roman Italy and a description of the geographical environment of Roman history. There are numerous illustrations and maps, a detailed chronological table, a list of the Roman Emperors from Augustus to Constantine, and a glossary.

218   **A history of Rome under the Emperors.**
       Theodor Mommsen, edited with the addition of a new chapter by
       Thomas Wiedemann.   London; New York: Routledge, 1996. 650p.

Mommsen never completed his monumental history of Ancient Rome as the manuscript of the fourth volume, the history of Rome under the emperors, was burnt in a fire in his house in 1880. It is also believed that the scholar's reluctance to complete it was due to his feeling that his account of a period that was uncongenial to him would lack the brilliance of his first three books on the history of Rome during the Republic. This is an edition of the recently discovered complete transcripts of the work by two of his students.

219   **The history of the decline and fall of the Roman Empire.**
       Edward Gibbon, edited by David Womerley.   Harmondsworth,
       England: Penguin Books, 1995. 3 vols. (1225p., 1014p., 1357p.).
       bibliog. (Penguin Classics.)

This monumental work was published in six volumes between 1776 and 1788. It covers thirteen centuries of Roman history, from the age of Trajan and the Antonines to the fall of Constantinople in 1453. The first three volumes cover about 300 years to the end of the Empire in the West *c*. 480. They consider the geographical extent and constitution of the empire under the Antonines, and follow events to the 5th century, describing the destruction of paganism; the barbarian invasions beginning with Alaric and the Goths in 408; the sack of Rome in 455 by Genseric, King of the Vandals; and the origins, progress, and effects of monastic life. The last three books compress 1,000 years of history. The conclusion gives an overview of the medieval papacy and a history of Rome up to the 17th century. This edition contains a long introduction with a biographical sketch of Gibbon, a discussion of the genesis of his work, and an analysis of its contents. There are also detailed tables of contents of all the books, a bibliographical index, and other ancillary documents. See also Gibbon's *The decline and fall of the Roman Empire: an abridged version*, edited and with an introduction by Dero A. Saunders (Harmondsworth, England: Penguin Books, 1985. 691p. [Penguin Classics.]). A compact version bringing Gibbon's work '...within the grasp of ordinary readers and busy students', it concentrates on the centuries from the age of the Antonines to the fall of the Empire in the West.

220   **Lives of the later Caesars.**
       Translated and introduced by Anthony Birley.   Harmondsworth,
       England: Penguin Books, 1978 (second printing). 336p. maps.

This edition comprises the first part of the *Augustan History*, a collection of biographies of Roman emperors possibly written towards the end of the 4th century, with newly compiled *Lives* of Nerva and Trajan. The addition of Nerva and Trajan restores the continuity between

Suetonius' *Lives of the twelve Caesars* and the *Augustan History*, covering the period between the accession of Nerva in 96 AD and the death of Heliogabalus in 222.

221   Makers of Rome: nine lives by Plutarch.
Plutarch, translated with an introduction by Ian Scott-Kilvert.
Harmondsworth, England: Penguin Books, 1975. 366p. maps.

A selection of nine Roman lives (their Greek pairings have been omitted) ranging from the earliest years of the Republic to the establishment of the Empire. They are: Coriolanus, Fabius Maximus, Marcellus, Cato the Elder, Tiberius Gracchus, Gaius Gracchus, Sertorius, Brutus, and Mark Antony. In his introductory note, the editor divides the Lives into four distinct groups: those undertaken at the request of Plutarch's friends (Gaius Gracchus, Marcellus), those composed for his own satisfaction and showing great men personifying a particular virtue (Fabius Maximus, Brutus), those of men whose careers may serve as a warning (Coriolanus, Mark Antony) and, finally, those of the semi-mythical founders of Greece and Rome. He points out Plutarch's attention to a wider range of actions and emotions than other historians and praises his sense of drama (likening him to a portrait painter who chooses a characteristic but somewhat dramatized pose for his subjects) and his capacity to show greatness manifest itself in small actions. The virtues he praises include courage, power of leadership, generosity and forbearance.

222   Remus: a Roman myth.
T. P. Wiseman.   Cambridge, England: Cambridge University Press, 1995. 258p. bibliog.

Examines the reasons behind the legend of Romulus's twin brother, often ignored as irrelevant by historians of Rome. All the ancient written and visual sources of the story, with their variants, contradictions and inconsistencies, are analysed, and a hypothetical reconstruction of the origin, development and exploitation of the legend is given. Important new insights are given, in the conclusion, into the history and ideology of pre-imperial Rome and into the methods and motives of myth-creation in a non-literate society.

223   The Roman Emperors: a biographical guide to the rulers of Imperial Rome, 31 BC-AD 476.
Michael Grant.   London: Phoenix, 1996. 380p. maps.

This work contains brief accounts of the lives and backgrounds of the Roman Emperors to AD 476, ninety-two names in all, in chronological order.

224   The Roman historians.
Ronald Mellor.   London; New York: Routledge, 1999. 222p.

A survey and critical analysis of historical writing in and about Ancient Rome. It examines various historical genres and places them within the context of Roman public life at the time of the late Roman Republic and the Roman Empire. It shows the influence of Greek antecedents (Herodotus, Thucidides) on the early Roman annalists and that of Polybius on later Roman historical writers. There are chapters on Sallust, Livy, Tacitus and Ammianus Marcellinus, which examine their life and career, output, historical method, rhetoric and literary style. There are also chapters on biography and autobiography – Suetonius' *Lives of the twelve Caesars* and Julius Caesar's *Commentaries on the Gallic War*. Censorship and the moralism of Roman historical writing are also examined.

225 The Twelve Caesars.
Michael Grant. London: Weidenfeld & Nicolson, 1996. 293p. maps.

This book provides brief biographies of the Twelve Caesars: Julius Caesar and the first eleven Roman emperors that followed him. It thus covers the same ground as Suetonius' *De Vita Caesarum* (Lives of the Caesars) but puts greater emphasis on background information about Roman institutions and history. In his introduction, the author asserts the importance in historiography of establishing what the leading personalities were like as opposed to attributing developments to general trends. He also points out certain permanent features influencing the behaviour of all Caesars, such as their dependence on the army, both an instrument of their power and a threat to their security, the senate and the populace.

226 The Victorians and Ancient Rome.
Norman Vance. Oxford; Cambridge, Massachusetts: Blackwell Publishers, 1997. 328p.

The author argues that Roman heritage in Victorian life and letters has remained largely unexplored as interest has tended to concentrate on the influence of Greece and the Middle Ages. He looks at Roman themes in painting, literature, religion, and public life, charting the change of emphasis during the century from Republican to Imperial Rome. A separate section examines the afterlife of some major Roman poets (Lucretius, Catullus, Ovid, Virgil and Horace) in the 19th century. British attitudes are not discussed in isolation but in the context of European culture and scholarship. Thus the section on Virgil covers not only Tennyson and Hardy but also Berlioz, Hugo and Huysmans' virulent condemnation of the poet in his novel *À rebours* (Against the grain).

227 The world of Rome: an introduction to Roman culture.
Edited by Peter Jones and Keith Sidwell. Cambridge, England: Cambridge University Press, 1997 (reprinted 1998). 416p. maps.

This introduction to the history and culture of Ancient Rome covers all aspects of the city, from its rise to power to its eventual decline. It is divided into three parts: ideology, history and administration; society and economy (including the economic and social life of the city, production and consumption, the family); and the Roman mind (ideology, literature, art and architecture). The epilogue discusses the continuing influence of Rome in a variety of cultural spheres. Every paragraph of the text is numbered and this allows extensive cross-referencing. The text also contains numerous quotations from ancient writers. An appendix provides an alphabetical list of Greek and Roman writers with brief biographical notes and lists of their works. There is also an index and a glossary of Latin terms.

300-1400

228 The English in Rome, 1362-1420: portrait of an expatriate community.
Margaret Harvey. Cambridge, England: Cambridge University Press, 1999. 288p. maps. bibliog. (Cambridge Studies in Medieval Life and Thought. Fourth Series, 47.)

A study based on the early archives of the Venerabile collegio inglese (the present English College) in Rome. It examines the social, political and commercial background in Rome, the beginnings of English institutions in the city and the role of the English community between 1362, the foundation date of the first English hospice for pilgrims and the poor, and 1420. It describes a group of forty English merchants and their wives, discovering important links between the laity in Rome and the city of London, including a failed attempt to advance English participation in commerce with Rome before 1420. It also looks at charitable activities of the English community, especially the establishment of the Hospice of St Thomas of Canterbury in 1362 and the hospice of S. Crisogono. The role of English members of the curia (papal administration departments) after the papacy's return in 1377 is also examined, with a separate chapter on one such curialist, John Fraunceys, and a detailed study of Cardinal Adam Easton, the opponent of John Wycliffe and the last English cardinal resident in the curia for over 100 years.

229 The Life of Cola di Rienzo.
Translated with an introduction by John Wright. Toronto, Canada: Pontifical Institute of Mediaeval Studies, 1975. 166p.

Cola di Rienzo (or Cola de Rienzi) was the revolutionary leader of medieval Rome. The most vivid and compelling portrait remains the contemporary biography known as *Vita di Cola di Rienzo, tribuno del popolo romano* (Life of Cola di Rienzo, Tribune of the Roman people), written in the Roman dialect *c.* 1358. It is an extract from an anonymous author's history of Rome from 1327 to 1355, published under the title *Historiæ Romanæ Fragmenta* (Fragments of Roman History). The introduction to this translation gives a brief examination of the historical background of 14th-century Rome, the personality of Cola and the nature of the revolution of 1347, and also looks at the literary qualities of the *Life* itself. Cola has variously been seen as a champion of the proletariat, a protofascist, a forerunner of Garibaldi, and as the founder of the entire Renaissance. The life of Cola di Rienzo inspired E. Bulwer Lytton's novel *Rienzi, the last of the Tribunes* (1835) and Richard Wagner's opera *Rienzi* (1842). See also *Tribune of Rome: a biography of Cola Di Rienzo*, by Iris Origo (London: The Hogarth Press, 1938. 265p.).

230 Medieval Rome: a portrait of the city and its life.
Paul Hetherington. London: The Rubicon Press, 1994. 127p.

This book is an excellent introduction to medieval Rome, its five chapters examining the history, topography, religious life, and arts of the city, and the institution of the papacy and the cardinalate. The first chapter is a survey of the history of Rome from the 4th century to the return of the papacy from Avignon in the 14th century. The second chapter looks at the form and appearance of medieval Rome. It also looks at some of the factors that governed the change in its shape and appearance – the location of some of the major Christian sites, the presence of gigantic survivals from the city's ancient past, their impact and their re-use in new functions. The third chapter discusses the development of the papacy and the ways it impinged on the life of the city. It refutes the notion that the papacy was working towards a plan of absolute power and universal authority. The fourth chapter examines the various forms of religious life in Rome – parochial, monastic, the pilgrimages, the papacy and the papal court, charitable institutions (hospitals providing shelter for the sick and for travellers), and the tradition of 'indulgences' that began in the late 11th century. The last chapter discusses the art and architecture of Rome, which is seen as a reflection of the aspirations and restrictions of their creators. It contrasts the succession of great basilicas built during the early Christian centuries to the mere refurbishing and rebuilding of earlier structures that was carried out in later centuries. As a result of this practice of renovation and renewal, and also because of various natural disasters, very few buildings in Rome have retained their medieval appearance – the original St Peter's and S. Paolo fuori le Mura being notable losses. There is also a survey of artistic production (mosaic and fresco painting, religious and secular sculpture, easel painting and manuscript illumination, and textiles and metalwork) and patronage.

231 The Papacy, 1073-1198: continuity and innovation.
I. S. Robinson. Cambridge, England: Cambridge University Press, 1990. 570p. (Cambridge Medieval Textbooks.)

A study of the papacy from the accession of Gregory VII to the death of Celestine III, a period that saw the transformation of the pope from a ruler of the diocese of Rome to a monarch of the universal Church. It begins with a discussion of the problems of governing the city of Rome and the lands of the church (the Patrimony of St Peter). The institutions of the papal government are discussed in the following chapters – the college of cardinals (the most powerful institution of the papal court, the cardinals being the pope's advisers, chief administrators, legates and electors); the curia; the papal council; the papal legation; the papal protection accorded to religious houses; and papal judicial and financial institutions. The second part of the study examines the papacy's involvement in the secular politics of western Christendom. It discusses political ideas, the papacy's role in the promotion of the crusades, and its relationship with the Empire and Norman principalities of Southern Italy. This was a period of important church reforms – such as the 'Gregorian reform' that aimed to eradicate simony by ending the secular control of ecclesiastical appointments and its subornation to the royal power. The three schisms that occurred during this period and their effects on the papacy – each of the antipopes involved was supported by a secular ruler powerful enough to drive the legitimate pope out of Rome and into exile – are also examined. Other problems faced by the papacy were the hostility of Roman noble families toward the pope, and, after 1143, the existence of a Roman commune that claimed jurisdiction over the city.

232 Rome and medieval culture: selections from *History of the City of Rome in the Middle Ages.*
Ferdinand Gregorovius, translated by Mrs Gustavus W. Hamilton. Edited and with an introduction by K. F. Morrison. Chicago; London: The University of Chicago Press, 1971. 493p. map.

The texts selected in this volume include the introduction to Gregorovius's *History of the City of Rome in the Middle Ages*, which provides an overview of the city of Rome in ancient times and in the Middle Ages, and sections from all eight books of the complete work. These include chapters on Byzantine Rome, Rome under Gregory I, the imperial coronation of Charlemagne in 800, the rise of papal supremacy in the 9th century, the coronation of Frederick Barbarossa, Cola di Rienzo, the pontificate of Urban VI (1378-89), the Borgias, Julius II, Leo X, the aftermath of the Sack of Rome in 1527, and the return of Clement VII to Rome. It also includes the conclusion of the work, in which Gregorovius recounts the circumstances that inspired its writing and his reasons for refusing to continue his account to the present. The texts are preceded by short introductions that set the scene. The introduction to this volume gives an outline of Gregorovius's life and politics and points out parallels between the events he describes in his history and contemporary ones, in the conflict, for example, between Pius IX and republicanism and the medieval controversies between the papacy and various experiments in republican government. It also points out errors of fact or emphasis in Gregorovius's text which, however, '...has held its own as the chief survey of civic and cultural life in medieval and Renaissance Rome, an enduring landmark in urban, as well as cultural, history'. The publication includes a map and a list of popes and western Emperors in the period treated by Gregorovius. The original eight-volume translation of the complete text from which this selection was made was published between 1894 and 1909.

233 Rome before Avignon: a social history of thirteenth-century Rome.
Robert Brentano.   London: British Museum Press, 1990. 340p. map.

A social history of Rome in the 13th century and an attempt to reconstruct the physical form of the city. It describes the structure of power, the intrigues of the great families (notably the Orsini and the Colonna), the nature of the family, and the importance of religion in society.

234 Rome in the Dark Ages.
Peter Llewellyn.   London: Faber & Faber, 1971. 324p.

This is a history of Rome from 500 AD, when it was under Ostrogoth rule, to the imperial coronation of Otto I in 962. The survival of Rome during these four and a half centuries was largely the work of the papacy and consequently the narrative revolves around the Roman Church, its relations with the Byzantine Empire, the Carolingian Empire and other powers in the West, and the spiritual, literary and administrative tradition upon which its power was built. It also looks at the various invasions of Rome, at the city of the pilgrims, and at the transformation of the monuments of the pagan world into those of Christianity.

235 Rome: profile of a city, 312-1308.
Richard Krautheimer.   New Jersey: Princeton University Press, 1980. 405p. bibliog.

Krautheimer presents a magisterial account of one thousand years of Roman history, from the time of Emperor Constantine to the removal of the papacy to Avignon, through the city's monuments. He shows the transformation of the pagan city first into the see of the papacy and then into the spiritual focus of the West, and demonstrates that the memory of Rome's ancient glory and its monuments were as important in shaping its dominant place in the medieval world as the growing power of the Church. The city's buildings and its art are studied in the context of political realities and the conflict between the papacy, foreign emperors and the Romans themselves.

1400-1600

236 **At the court of the Borgia, being an account of the reign of Pope Alexander VI written by his Master of Ceremonies Johann Burchard.**
Edited and translated by Geoffrey Parker. London: The Folio Society, 1996 (6th printing). 245p.

Johann Burchard was one of many contemporary commentators (others included Stefano Infessura, Paolo Giovio, Marino Sanuto, and Francesco Guicciardini) on the affairs of the papacy during the pontificate of Alexander VI, the Borgia pope. Burchard's secret diary is, however, the most extensive source of information for the Borgia period from an eye-witness of most of the events described. A native of Haslach, near Strasbourg, he was papal Master of Ceremonies from 1483 to his death in 1506. The diary, which covers the period from the closing days of Sixtus IV's pontificate to the first years of that of Julius II, was intended as a private record of official and public affairs and consequently reports facts and gives detailed descriptions of official ceremonies and ecclesiastical life at the Vatican. It is devoid of the rumours and scandals about the private lives of the Borgias and is silent about contemporary cultural and artistic events (there is no mention of Pinturicchio's decorations of the Borgia apartments). The introduction explains the reasons for the unpopularity of the Borgia family and its downfall on the death of Alexander VI – more due to their Spanish origins than to Alexander's nepotism and corruption, failings in which he was not markedly different to other popes. The present edition contains selections from Burchard's account of Alexander VI's reign (about a quarter of the original) leaving out repetitive details of ceremonies and lists of names. The historical background to the events described is given in introductory passages preceding each selection. There is also a biographical index. The definitive edition of the diary was published in two volumes edited by E. Celani, *Johanni Burchardi Liber Notarum ab anno 1483 usque ad annum 1506* (Johann Burchard's diary from 1483 to 1506) (Città di Castello, 1906).

237 **The Autobiography of Benvenuto Cellini.**
Translated and with an introduction by George Bull. Harmondsworth, England: Penguin Books, 1998. rev. ed. 492p.

The Florentine artist Benvenuto Cellini (1500-71) was a man of many talents. A goldsmith, sculptor and medallist, he was also an accomplished writer and his autobiography is one of the most important texts of the Renaissance. It was written between 1558 and 1562, and provides a vivid account of the artist's life and adventures in, among other places, the Rome of Clement VII and, in particular, of the Sack of Rome in 1527. Cellini, never the most modest of men, participated in the defence of the city and among other claims he makes about his achievements he says that it was he who shot dead Charles, Constable of Bourbon during the siege of the city and, a few days later, the Prince of Orange. During Clement's imprisonment in the Castel S. Angelo, Cellini also removed the papal jewels from their settings and melted down the gold. Cellini's descriptions of his life in pre-1527 Rome – his patrons, his friendships and relationships with other artists, his study of the city's antiquities – are also full of interest, especially since nothing of Cellini's output during this period seems to have survived. The work was first printed in Italy in 1728 and was translated into various languages during the Romantic era. Cellini's descriptions of his struggles against officialdom ensured him a place in the Romantic Pantheon and his autobiography inspired the opera by Hector Berlioz. This translation of the work includes an introduction, a chronology of Cellini, and notes to the text.

238 Beatrice Cenci.
Irene Musillo Mitchell.   New York: Peter Lang, 1991. 234p.
(American University Studies. Series IX – History, vol. 104.)

In 1598, Count Francesco Cenci was assassinated in the castle of Petrella in the Sabine mountains where he had fled with his daughter Beatrice and her stepmother Lucrezia. The two women were his virtual prisoners and he had almost certainly raped Beatrice, who organized the plot to kill him. Also involved were his son Giacomo and two servants, the castellan Olimpio Calvetti, who was Beatrice's lover, and Marzio Catalano. The murder was soon uncovered and Beatrice, Lucrezia and Giacomo were tried and executed in the Piazza del Ponte S. Angelo on 11 September 1599 – Calvetti and Catalano both died before the trial, the former assassinated and the latter perishing in jail. The trial took no account of Francesco's violent and debauched character, his continuous ill-treatment of his entire family and his rape of Beatrice. It was also widely believed that the confiscation of the family's property (the Cenci were one of the richest families in Rome) was one of the motives that decided the murderers' fate. The ferocity of the sentence – Beatrice and Lucrezia were decapitated and Giacomo quartered – together with Beatrice's great beauty helped to turn her into a martyr, and the legend of her life and death has inspired numerous accounts, historical and fictional. The present work is closely based on the monograph by Norberto Valentini and Milena Bacchiani, *Beatrice Cenci* (Milan, Italy: Rusconi, 1981. 275p.), large passages of which are translated and inserted into this narrative. In an introductory chapter, the author discusses the legend of Beatrice Cenci and the works it has inspired – literary, musical and pictorial – omitting, however, Berthold Goldschmidt's eponymous opera, now widely considered to be his masterpiece.

239 Beatrice Cenci.
Corrado Ricci, translated from the Italian by Morris Bishop and Henry Longan Stuart.   London: Peter Owen Limited, 1956. 331p.

This is the most detailed account of the Cenci family, the events leading up to the murder of Francesco Cenci in 1598, and the trial and execution of Beatrice. This translation is without the ample critical bibliography (dealing largely with the manuscript sources) of the original Italian edition of this work, first published in 1923.

240 The Borgias.
Marion Johnson.   London: Macdonald Futura Publishers, 1981. 232p. maps.

This account of the Borgias was the last book of Marion Johnson (who, as Georgina Masson, wrote numerous works on Rome) and was published posthumously. The opening chapter examines the Spanish origins of the family and the European and Italian 15th-century historical and political background. This is followed by a chapter on Pope Calixtus III, the founder of the Borgia fortunes. It gives an excellent description of Rome at the time of his arrival there in 1445 as a cardinal and of Roman politics and culture since the return of the papacy from Avignon, when the city was transformed into the intellectual and artistic capital of Italy. Unexpectedly elected pope in 1455 at the age of seventy-seven, Alonso Borgia's main ambition during his short reign (1455-58) was to unite Western rulers in a crusade against the Turks. The bulk of the book is devoted to an examination of the characters, actions and policies of Alexander VI, the second Borgia pope (1492-1503), and Cesare Borgia, his son and evil genius. Their various failings are weighed against their achievements, most notably their success in bringing, within a very short time span, the Romagna region under papal control. Alexander's patronage is also assessed, especially his numerous building works in Rome. The lives of the rest of the Borgia dynasty (Alexander fathered nine children) are also looked at, especially that of Lucrezia

Borgia. A pawn to her father's dynastic plans, her marriage to Alfonso d'Este was the last and most successful of her three politically expedient marriages. As Duchess of Ferrara from 1502 to her death in 1519, she was the patron of numerous men of letters and artists. This work, aimed at a popular market, is richly illustrated with contemporary views of Rome, maps, buildings associated with the Borgias, and portraits though, in several cases, the identity of the sitters is not securely established.

241 The Borgias: the rise and fall of a Renaissance dynasty.
Michael Mallett. London: The Bodley Head, 1969. 351p. bibliog.

An attempt to explain why the Borgias, a family that numbered two popes (Calixtus III and Alexander VI), eleven cardinals and numerous princes and dukes in Naples and central and northern Italy, were so hated, feared and maligned. It begins with an excellent overview of papal diplomacy after the return of Martin V to Rome in 1420 and a description of the papal states in the 15th century, explaining the workings of the vicariate system inherited by the Renaissance popes, their attempts to impose a centralized administration and the consequent transformation of Rome from an independent commune into the unified administrative capital of an extensive papal state. The examination of the various members of the Borgia family follows the same pattern as Marion Johnson's work (see entry no. 240). It also has numerous notes, a good bibliography, and genealogical tables not only of the various branches of the Borgia but also of the Colonna, Orsini, and Della Rovere families. In his assessment of the Borgia legacy, the author concludes that despite the apparent failure of Alexander VI's dynastic policies in the Romagna region he, and Cesare Borgia, were nevertheless successful in laying the foundations of papal authority over the Roman barons and the Romagna vicars that later popes, especially Julius II, Alexander's sworn enemy, would consolidate.

242 England, Rome and the papacy, 1417-1464: the study of a relationship.
Margaret Harvey. Manchester, England; New York: Manchester University Press, 1993. 303p. bibliog.

This is a study on Anglo-papal relations, both political and spiritual, before the tension of Henry VIII's divorce, beginning with the election of Pope Martin V that ended the schism which, since 1378, had divided western Christendom, and ending with the advent of Edward IV and the death of Pius II. It looks at English personnel in the curia (for example, royal representatives), identifying leading English *curiales,* sketching their careers and showing aspects of their life in Rome; it also looks at papal representatives in England – the papal collectors and subcollectors, for gathering payments, and their supporting networks. It examines the role of English hospices in Rome, their function and funding and their importance as centres for curial officials. It also traces Anglo-papal diplomacy and English involvement in the Council of Basel (1431) and the Council of Florence (1439).

243 The German community in Renaissance Rome, 1378-1523.
Clifford W. Maas, edited by Peter Herde. Rome; Freiburg, Germany: Herder, 1981. 224p. bibliog. (Römische Quartalschrift, 39. Supplementheft.)

A study of one of the most important foreign colonies in Renaissance Rome. The return of Martin V and the curia to the city in 1420 led to an influx of German artisans and craftsmen and the formation of various guilds. The author traces the development of the German community, making use of a variety of sources, such as membership rosters of brotherhoods and guilds. In particular, his use of the archives of S. Maria dell'Anima, the German national church in Rome, and of the Arciconfraternità di S. Maria in Camposanto Teutonico, enables him to trace the development of these two focal points of German life in the city. The 'Anima' was founded as a hospital for German pilgrims on the eve of the 1400 Jubilee, later becoming, through the generosity of Friedrich von Niem, a brotherhood, and the area around it (north of Piazza Navona) becoming the German quarter. The Brotherhood initially attracted membership from a wide social spectrum but by the second half of the 15th century had become dominated by the Church and the nobility. This led to the development of a second brotherhood, named after the Campo Santo area near St Peter's, in which members' contributions varied according to their income. German printers, goldsmiths and silversmiths were dominant in late 15th-century Rome and German clerics played an important role in the curia. The study also examines the lives of individual Germans in Rome, both laymen of various social backgrounds and members of the papal curia.

244 Historians and historiography in the Italian Renaissance.

Eric Cochrane. Chicago; London: The University of Chicago Press, 1981. 669p.

A comprehensive survey of Italian Renaissance historians. The section on Rome examines the group of humanists employed or associated with the Roman curia. It begins with a discussion of Fabio Biondo, the progenitor of curial historiography and founder of the scholarly investigation of Roman antiquities. His *Roma Instaurata* (Rome restored) (1443-46) and *Roma Triumphans* (Rome triumphant) (1452-59), which remained standard guides to the literature and monuments of Ancient Rome for over a century, are the results of his direct personal observations of the monuments of the ancient city, which he arranged by genre (gates, theatres, etc.) or place. Biondo's innovation formed the basis of the school of historiography at the Roman curia. The author points out the lack of a Roman chronicle tradition in the 14th century (only three texts) and discusses the development of the genre in the 15th century. He also looks at the development of humanism as a source of ideological support for the papacy during the reigns of Nicholas V and Pius II. The final section discusses biographical history (such as Platina's *The Lives of the Popes*), which became the most characteristic form of curial historiography and included both histories of the papacy and of individual pontificates.

245 The Jews in Rome.

Kenneth Stow. Leiden, The Netherlands; New York; Cologne, Germany: E. J. Brill, 1995-97. 2 vols. 951p. bibliog. (Studia Post-biblica, vol. 48. A Documentary History of the Jews in Italy, vol. 11-12.)

The history of the Jews in Rome is the longest continuous history of a Jewish community in Europe. These two volumes bring together the acts drawn up by Jewish notaries in Rome from 1536 to 1558. The 2,250 documents transcribed and presented here in calendar form are housed in the Archivio storico capitolino (Fondo Notai Ebrei); they were drawn up in Hebrew and subsequently in Italian. They deal mainly with the daily life of Jews in Rome during the crucial years shortly before and immediately following Pope Paul IV's bull *Cum nimis absurdum* and the establishment of the Roman ghetto in 1555. The acts permit a view of the Roman Jewish community and its activities; they deal with private life, apprenticeships, disputes, and communal and synagogal business. They are not, however, all encompassing, as some activities had to be registered before a Christian notary. In his introduction, the editor outlines the history of the Jews in Rome up to the middle of the 16th century and analyses some of the findings that emerge from the notarial acts.

246 Julius II: the Warrior Pope.
Christine Shaw. Oxford; Cambridge, Massachusetts: Blackwell, 1993. 360p. bibliog.

A biography of Julius II (1503-13), the epitome of the Renaissance pope. As the title suggests, the focus is on politics, diplomacy and warfare rather than spiritual matters or Julius's cultural and intellectual interests. As a cardinal, Giuliano della Rovere played an important role in Italian politics for some thirty years before his accession to the papal throne and this work examines in detail his career first as one of four papal nephews during the pontificate of Sixtus IV and his less than glorious early military undertakings and his mission as papal legate to France in 1476, and then his activities during the reigns of Innocent VIII (on whom he exerted considerable influence) and Alexander VI (when he was in exile from Rome instigating the French to invade Italy and depose the Borgia pope). As a pope, Julius conducted in person some of his military campaigns and one of his main preoccupations was to free Italy from foreign interference, though he was not averse to using the French or the Spanish to further his aims. The work, which is based on extensive research of archival sources, provides new information on the reigns of Julius's predecessors and its first chapter is an excellent introduction to the 15th-century political situation, the conciliar movement, the attempts of several popes to organize a crusade against the Turks and thus assert papal spiritual leadership, the uncertain control over much of the Papal States after the return of the papacy from Avignon (forming the background to Julius's policy to recover lost territories and acquire more), and, finally, nepotism (the greatest source of dissension between the Pope and the College of Cardinals). Julius's cultural interests and his patronage of Michelangelo and Raphael are dutifully examined, albeit somewhat summarily in a chapter which also dismisses the idea that Julius II saw himself as a second Julius Caesar. Curiously, the book finishes with Julius's death and there is no discussion of his immediate or long-term legacy.

247 Li nuptiali di Marco Antonio Altieri pubblicati da Enrico Narducci. (The Nuptiali of Marco Antonio Altieri published by Enrico Narducci.)
Introduction by Massimo Miglio, indices by Anna Modigliani. Rome: Roma nel Rinascimento, 1995. 131p., 244p. (RR inedita. Anastatica, 9.)

M. A. Altieri's (1450-1532) treatise on marriage is a celebration of family values and the role of the family in contemporary Roman society. Taking as its starting point and pretext the wedding of Giovangiorgio Cesarini and Marzia Sforza in 1504, and Gabriele Cesarini's asking a group of friends for advice on how to organize his son's wedding, it offers a panorama of contemporary Roman society and mores. This facsimile of Enrico Narducci's 1873 edition of the text is preceded by an introduction that elucidates the historical background to Altieri's text. Documentary material related to the Cesarini and Altieri families and, most importantly, an index of over 1,000 names mentioned in Altieri's text and Narducci's introduction, are also included.

248 Renaissance Rome, 1500-1559: a portrait of a society.
Peter Partner. Berkeley, California; Los Angeles; London: University of California Press, 1976. 241p. bibliog.

This study provides a portrait of Roman society during the first half of the 16th century. It attempts to explain the success of Renaissance Rome and examine how, at a time of apparent weakness, when the papacy was confronted with the Reformation, successive popes were able to plan and reorganize their environment on a grand scale. It also looks at the relationship of the papacy with humanism.

249 **Roma capitale, 1447-1527.** (Rome the capital, 1447-1527.)
Edited by Sergio Gensini. Pisa, Italy: Pacini, 1994. 640p. (Collana di Studi e Ricerche, 5.)

Twenty-three papers read at a conference held at San Miniato (Pisa) in 1992. They discuss various aspects of Renaissance Rome – the city as the seat of the papacy, as the capital of the papal states, as a centre of humanist, cultural and artistic activity, and as a commercial and financial centre. Various papers examine the foreign communities in the city during this period – the German, the Catalan-Aragonese and Castilian communities – as well as political exiles and communities from other parts of the peninsula, notably the Florentines, who enjoyed great influence during the reign of the two Medici popes. Finally, there are papers describing the political and economic ascent of the Roman nobility in the last years of the 15th century.

250 **Rome in the High Renaissance: the age of Leo X.**
Bonner Mitchell. Norman, Oklahoma: University of Oklahoma Press, 1973. 182p. bibliog. (The Centers of Civilization Series.)

An introduction to Rome from the beginning of the pontificate of Julius II in 1503 to the Sack of Rome in 1527, aiming to evoke the moral, material and intellectual atmosphere of the city during one of the most decisive periods in its history. It describes the characters and interests of the four popes who reigned during this period and Rome's unique government structure. It also outlines contemporary local and international politics and points out the failure of the papacy to promote peace in Europe, to protect Italy from foreign domination, or to preserve the unity of the Christian Church. There are chapters on social conditions in Rome, describing the cosmopolitan nature of the city and the various national and ethnic groups and their colonies, on public ceremonies and artistic manifestations, on literature, and on faith and morals.

251 **RR: Roma nel Rinascimento: bibliografia e note.** (RR: Rome in the Renaissance: bibliography and notes.)
Edited by Massimo Miglio. Rome: [Associazione Roma nel Rinascimento], 1984- . annual.

This annual publication was launched on the occasion of the conference *Un pontificato e una città: Sisto V, 1471-1484* (A pontificate and a city: Sixtus V, 1471-1484) (see entry no. 788). Its aim, as stated in its prospectus, is to record and review work published or in progress, and it includes monographs and articles, conference proceedings and exhibition catalogues. Items reviewed enter the collections of the Biblioteca dell'Istituto storico italiano per il Medio Evo. Each issue includes long articles analysing major contributions to Roman Renaissance studies published during the year, but its greater part is dedicated to reviews. These are arranged under author, irrespective of the type of publication. Two separate indices have been published to date for the years 1984-89 and 1990-94, providing full bibliographical references to works analysed, reviewed or cited, lists of contributors, personal names, and manuscript and archival sources mentioned in the reviews.

252 **Il Sacco di Roma: l'edizione Orano de *I ricordi* di Marcello Alberini.**
(The Sack of Rome: the Orano edition of Marcello Alberini's *Ricordi*.)
Marcello Alberini, introduced by Paola Farenga. Rome: Roma nel Rinascimento, 1997. 436p. (RR, Inedita. Anastatica, 12.)

This eyewitness account of the Sack of Rome was written by Marcello Alberini (1511-80) in 1547 and first published in 1558. It is both an historical reconstruction and an account of its effect on the author and his family. In an attempt to understand the reasons that brought this momentous event about, Alberini examines events leading up to it, using as his starting point the death of Pope Leo X in 1521, which unleashed the rivalry between Giulio de' Medici and Pompeo Colonna. His focus is more on internal conflicts between the papacy and baronial families and less on strategy and international politics. He attributes the weakening of Rome both to the authoritarianism of the ecclesiastical government and the squabbling and lack of municipal pride of the Roman nobility. Charles V and Francesco Maria della Rovere are also blamed, the first for his greed and the second for his strategic ineptitude, which prevented him, as Captain of the League, from taking advantage of the disarray of the foreign troops. He also describes the aftermath of the Sack and the exhilaration (soon giving way to disillusionment) that followed the election of Paul III (a Roman pope). The text finishes abruptly with the preparations for the entry of Charles V into Rome in 1536. The text is a facsimile reprint of Domenico Orano's edition published in 1901.

253   The Sack of Rome.
E. R. Chamberlin.   London: B. T. Batsford Ltd, 1979. 220p. bibliog.

A popular history of the Sack of Rome in three sections. The first section introduces the backgrounds, characters and politics of the three protagonists – Charles V, Francis I, and Pope Clement VII – and also provides portraits of other key players, such as Charles de Bourbon, who led the imperial troops to Rome and was killed during the assault on 6 May 1527, and Pompeo Colonna, the great rival of Clement VII. The second sets the stage with an account of events in the 1520s, with separate chapters on the battle of Pavia and the march on Rome. Finally, the third section describes the attack and sack of Rome and its aftermath up to the return of Clement VII to Rome on 6 October 1528.

254   The Sack of Rome.
Luigi Guicciardini, translated with an introduction and notes by James H. McGregor.   New York: Italica Press, 1993. 192p. maps. bibliog.

This contemporary account of the Sack of Rome is the work of Luigi Guicciardini (1478-1551), the elder brother of the better-known Francesco Guicciardini, historian and papal lieutenant. It begins with the formation of the alliance against Charles V, known as the Holy League, and the signing of the Treaty of Cognac on 22 May 1526, and ends in the summer of 1527. It is in two books, the first describing warfare in Northern Italy and the long march towards Rome of the imperial troops under Charles de Bourbon. The second book considers the attack, capture and sack of Rome. In the introduction to this first English translation of the work, McGregor describes Guicciardini's political career (at the time of the sack he was a *gonfaloniere* [magistrate] in Florence) and assesses his work as a historian. He also provides a conspectus of the events preceding the ones described by Guicciardini and, in an afterword, discusses aspects of Renaissance warfare. There is also a useful glossary.

255   The Sack of Rome, 1527.
André Chastel, translated from the French by Beth Archer.   Princeton, New Jersey: Princeton University Press, 1983. 339p. bibliog. (Bollingen Series, XXX, vol. 26.)

These six studies are the A. W. Mellon Lectures in the Fine Arts given at the National Gallery of Art in 1977. Their subject is the Sack of Rome and its implications in a wide variety of fields. The first lecture surveys the events of 1527, from the march on Rome of the Imperial troops led by Charles de Bourbon in the spring, to the siege of the city and its subsequent looting, and the political repercussions elsewhere on the Italian peninsula and in Europe. Subsequent chapters look at the cultural context both before and after 1527. There is a section on the propaganda war, in the years immediately preceding the Sack, waged through the use of artistic images – on the one hand, the monumental frescoes in the Sala di Costantino in the Vatican glorifying the papacy and, at the other extreme, German popular woodcuts (by Hans Holbein and Lucas Cranach among others) vilifying the pope as the Antichrist and Rome as the 'Whore of Babylon'. Popular predictions and anticipations of catastrophe and their iconography are also examined. The destruction of Rome's artistic and religious heritage is also surveyed. During the Sack, holy relics were stolen (among them the heads of St Peter and St Paul from S. Giovanni in Laterano and the Veronica), jewels removed from sacred vessels and artistic treasures pillaged, the removal of the tapestries of Raphael's cartoons from the Sistine Chapel being a notable example. The reactions of contemporaries are also examined – the despair of Francesco Guicciardini typifying the attitudes of humanists and men of letters. Interpretations of the Sack ranged from divine punishment for corruption or the pope's incompetence and lack of military power to Lutheran sacrilege. Chastel also examines the artistic scene in Rome after the death of Raphael in 1520 and he identifies a 'Clementine' style which was profoundly altered after the Sack and the consequent dispersal of Rome's artistic community. The sobriety of Michelangelo's later style (his *Last Judgement* and his frescoes for the Cappella Paolina) is seen as indicative of this change of mood. The text is extensively annotated and is enriched by 115 excellent illustrations and two maps.

256   The Sack of Rome, 1527.
Judith Hook.   London; Basingstoke, England: Macmillan, 1972. 343p. maps. bibliog.

Hook presents a thorough and engrossing account of the events leading up to the Sack of Rome, a description of the momentous event, and its aftermath, making use of contemporary writings (reports, histories, diplomatic material, eyewitness accounts and autobiographies). She begins with a description of Rome in 1523, Giulio de' Medici's election to the papal throne (as Clement VII) and the implications of his success against Pompeo Colonna. This is followed by an analysis of European power politics, the rivalry between Francis I and Charles V and their struggles for dominance in the Italian peninsula, and a sympathetic examination of the plight of Clement VII, whose difficult position was undermined by his lack of resources, which partly accounts for his shifting alliances with Emperor and King in his vain efforts to resist external domination of Italy. The strategic importance of the various independent states on the peninsula is also described, together with the varying outlooks of the members of the anti-Imperial League of Cognac (1526). The inexorable progress through Central Italy of the imperial troops under Charles de Bourbon (who was to be slain by an arquebus shot during the assault on Rome) is followed. The pillage and destruction of the city's churches and palaces, the huge loss of life (Rome's population was halved), and the Pope's incarceration in the Castel S. Angelo (where he remained for seven months) are graphically depicted, as is the aftermath of the sack – the desolate landscape of Rome and the suffering of its people, the occupying troops, the spread of plague, the repercussions of the sack in other parts of Italy, the reinstatement of the Colonna family, the exile of the Pope and his return to Rome in October 1528, and the final triumph of Charles V. It is a pity that a study of such excellence is marred by an abundance of misspelled names of persons, buildings and place names.

257 **Vie économique et sociale de Rome dans la seconde moitié du XVIe siècle.** (Economic and social life of Rome in the second half of the sixteenth century.)
Jean Delumeau. Paris: E. De Boccard, 1957. 1038p. bibliog.
(Bibliothèque des Écoles Françaises d'Athènes et de Rome, fasc. 184.)

A magisterial study of the economic and social history of Rome in the 16th century dealing with the relationship between the lay population and the ecclesiastical world (the papacy, the Roman curia and their various subordinate bodies).

258 **Words and deeds in Renaissance Rome: trials before the papal magistrates.**
Thomas V. Cohen and Elizabeth S. Cohen. Toronto, Canada: University of Toronto Press, 1993. 308p. map.

Translated and annotated records, followed by commentaries, of nine trials or preliminary investigations that took place in the tribunal of the Governor of Rome between 1542 and 1574. Seven of these are from the years 1558 and 1559, the last two years of the pontificate of Paul IV and the first months of that of Pius IV, his successor. All these cases have a rich cast of characters (among them an exorcist, assassins and courtesans) and include prosecutions for murder, adultery, prostitution and sorcery. The editors consider court records as the best introduction to vernacular culture '...like throwing back heavy shutters to open a window on the past'. In their introduction they explain the machinery of justice in Renaissance Rome including conventions regarding the transcriptions of the cases. They also point out distinguishing features of Roman society, its vertical alliances (for example, between master and servant, patron and client) and horizontal solidarities (guilds, learned societies, confraternities, the neighbourhood, home town), its institutions and its social values. The links between the texts of these trials and the literature and drama of the period are also examined.

1600-1800

259 **Christina, Queen of Sweden – a personality of European civilisation.**
Stockholm: Nationalmuseum, 1966. 592p. + 96p. of plates.
(Nationalmusei Utställningskatalog, 305.)

This is the catalogue of the eleventh exhibition of the Council of Europe. It examines all aspects of Christina's life from her childhood, through her years as Queen of Sweden to her abdication and move to Rome where, for three decades, she played an active part in the political, intellectual and artistic life of the city. A great lover of the fine arts and one of the most outstanding collectors of all time, Christina's interests included paintings and drawings, sculptures, numismatics, medals, jewellery, handicrafts, manuscripts and printed books. The catalogue, which includes some 1,500 items, is roughly divided into two parts: 'Christina's life' (in seventeen sections) and 'Christina's collections' (in ten sections), with a connecting *entr'acte* examining theatre (and opera) in Rome at the time of Christina's stay. Each section is prefaced by a general note and each item has a full catalogue entry adding up to a monumental work of scholarship providing a wealth of information on 17th century history, politics and culture. Introductory essays discuss Christina's life, her literary activities and relations with scholars and, finally, her interest in music and the theatre.

260 Daily life in Papal Rome in the eighteenth century.
Maurice Andrieux, translated by Mary Fitton. London: George Allen & Unwin, 1968. 223p. bibliog.

In his foreword, the author describes Rome in the 18th century as 'an old country past its prime, pleasant and peaceful, basking in a warm caressing glow… something of a beautiful autumn sunset'. His description of the city's society and social life in the hundred years before the radical changes brought by the French Revolution and its aftermath is divided into nine chapters that deal with a variety of subjects. It begins with a description of the appearance of the city, its government, the pope and the structure of society. There are chapters on economics (including sections on coinage and the cost of living, commerce, agriculture, the lottery and the Ghetto); crime and punishment; love and marriage; religion; sports and pastimes (including popular pleasures, the Carnival, the theatre); literature and literary academies; art; archaeology; music; and tourism.

261 Diario di Roma. (Roman diary.)
Giacinto Gigli, edited by Manlio Barberito. Rome: Colombo, 1994. 2 vols. 926p.

Giacinto Gigli (1594-1671) started to keep a diary at the age of fourteen and continued to do so until 1657. He was a careful observer of everyday events and his diary is an important record of life in 17th-century Rome. His role as *caporione* (i.e. head of one the fourteen *rioni* or quarters of Rome), an office he held several times between 1631 and 1644 and, on three occasions, as prior of the *caporioni*, meant that he was introduced to various important personages and was well-informed about contemporary events. He was an accurate chronicler of religious and civil ceremonies and major historical events are reported in passing, the emphasis being on the details of their reception in Rome (usually with a procession, a celebration, or a religious ceremony). There are two introductory essays, the first, by Giuseppe Ricciotti (originally published in his 1957 edition of the diary), looking at Gigli's life and writings and the manuscripts of his diary, the second, by Manlio Barberito, discussing Gigli's attitude to religion, science, superstition and contemporary events, and highlighting the special features of the diary. There is a chronological index, an index to personal and place names, and an index of notable subjects, as well as fifty-six plates reproducing views of Rome, portraits, proclamations, edicts, and other documents.

262 Diario romano. (Roman diary.)
Francesco Valesio. Edited by Gaetana Scano, assisted by Giuseppe Graglia. Milan, Italy: Longanesi & Co., 1977-79. 6 vols. bibliog. (I Cento Libri.)

Francesco Valesio (1670-1742) was a man of letters, a scholar of classical and Christian antiquities, and a censor of hagiographical literature. His house opposite S. Carlo al Corso was a meeting point for antiquaries and scholars. His main claim to fame, however, is his diary, which presents a vivid picture of the social, political, military, religious and artistic life of Rome in the first half of the 18th century. It covers the period from 9 August 1700 to March 1711 and, after a break of thirteen years, resumes on 24 December 1724 and continues uninterruptedly until 27 March 1742, two months before the death of Valesio. The first part of the diary is considerably more detailed than the second – it is suggested in the introduction that Valesio had less time to prepare more elaborate entries in later years as he was busy with other tasks. The manuscript of the diary, which is kept in the Archivio Capitolino, includes transcriptions of letters, papal speeches, reports and other material, all faithfully reproduced in this fine edition. Each of the three two-volume sets has its own detailed index and bibliography.

263 The popes and European Revolution.
Owen Chadwick. Oxford: Clarendon Press, 1981. 655p. bibliog. (The Oxford History of the Christian Church.)

Examines the effect of the European Revolution of 1789 on the papacy, and attempts to establish what were the differences and continuities after the momentous events of the period between 1789 and 1815. It begins with a survey of the church during the *ancien régime*, examining the superstitious religion of the common people, the privileges of the clergy, the declining institution of monasticism, and the papacy, providing sympathetic portraits of the popes from Clement XI to Leo XII but also denouncing their political ineptitude. The second half of the book is devoted to reform and revolution. It examines the fall of the Jesuits, the work of Catholic reformers such as Muratori and Pietro Tamburini, the French Revolution and its aftermath, and, finally, the decline of Catholic political power during the Restoration.

264 Queen Christina.
Georgina Masson. London: Secker & Warburg, 1968 (reissued 1974). 405p. bibliog.

The second half of this biography of Queen Christina deals with her life in Rome, where she arrived in December 1655, eighteen months after her abdication, and where, for the next thirty-four years, she was to become one of the most influential and munificent patrons of the arts. She lived first in the Palazzo Farnese and then, from 1659, in the Palazzo Riario (now Corsini), which housed her enormous collections of art, books and manuscripts and where she founded the Accademia dell'Arcadia for philosophy and literature. Her unconventional behaviour, particularly her lack of religious observances in public, scandalized and enthralled Rome. In 1657, she unsuccessfully attempted, with support from Cardinal Mazarin, to become Queen of Naples and, in 1667, Pope Alexander VII supported a likewise unsuccessful attempt to gain the crown of Poland. Through her relationship with Cardinal Decio Azzolino, Christina also became active in church politics and an ardent supporter of the Christian war against the Turks.

265 Roma giacobina: storia della Repubblica romana del 1798-99.
(Jacobin Rome: a history of the Roman Republic of 1798-99.)
Antonio Cretoni. Rome: Istituto di studi romani, 1971. 438p.

This study of the Roman Republic of 1797-98 begins with the accidental death of General Mathieu-Léonard Duphot near Palazzo Corsini (the residence of Joseph Bonaparte, the French Ambassador), where the papal troops were trying to contain a demonstration, an event that provided the excuse for the Directory to send in an army of occupation under General Berthier. It describes all the events that followed this incident: the French occupation of Rome, the exile and death of Pope Pius VI, the proclamation of the Republic, its organization and features of its administration, social life in Rome (the theatres and patriotic circles), the relations between the French and the clergy, the popular uprisings in the spring and summer of 1798, the invasion and short-lived occupation by the Neapolitan forces of King Ferdinand, and the return of the French.

266   Rome-Amsterdam: two growing cities in seventeenth-century Europe.
Edited by Peter Van Kessel, Elisja Schulte. Amsterdam: Amsterdam
University Press, 1997. 357p. maps.

The essays collected in this volume examine various aspects of the history and social
conditions of these two cities during a period of prosperity and growth. There are twelve
chapters, each divided into two essays presenting each city. Subjects covered include: the
image of the city, territory and development, population, family structures, the relationship of
the people to the authorities, the role of religion, welfare and poor relief, immigration and
acculturation (Netherlanders in early Baroque Rome, Italians in Amsterdam), food supply,
criminality and punishment.

**267   Rome in the age of Bernini. Vol. 1 From the election of Sixtus V to
the death of Urban VIII. Vol. 2 From the election of Innocent X to
the death of Innocent XI.**
Torgil Magnuson.   Stockholm: Almqvist & Wiksell International;
[Atlantic Highlands], New Jersey: Humanities Press, 1982-86. 397p.,
412p. (Kungl. Vitterhets Historie och Antikvitetes Akademiens.
Handlingar. Antikvariska Serien, 33, 34.)

A comprehensive study of 17th-century art and architecture in Rome and of the historical and
cultural background that conditioned their creation. It begins with the pontificate of Sixtus V
and ends with the death of Innocent XI in 1689, its six chapters more or less corresponding to
the reign of one or two popes. The first chapter typically covers a wide range of subjects: it
describes the personality of Sixtus V and the characteristics of the ecclesiastical administration
under his rule, urban development and building activities, palaces and churches, the death of
Sixtus V and his succession by Clement VIII, his foreign policy, the Aldobrandini family, the
trials of Beatrice Cenci and Giordano Bruno, the acquisition of Ferrara, the flooding of the Tiber
in 1598, painting during his pontificate, and the contrasting geniuses of Annibale Carracci and
Caravaggio. The epilogue mentions the economic decline in the Papal States during the last
thirty years of the 17th century and the consequent decline in artistic patronage. It also points
out the shift of interest towards science, literature and music and the greater prominence during
this period of other artistic centres. It concludes, though, on an upbeat note, with a mention of
the late flowering of Rome during the first half of the 18th century. The work is well illustrated
in black and white throughout.

**268   Rome in the age of Enlightenment: the post-Tridentine syndrome
and the ancien regime.**
Hanns Gross.   Cambridge, England; New York: Cambridge University
Press, 1990. 421p.

A comprehensive overview of the economic, political, artistic, and intellectual life of 18th-
century Rome (the *ancien régime* of the title is the period from the late 17th century to the
French revolution), attempting to show that this was a century of decline in the city's history –
'the post-Tridentine syndrome' being the decline and lethargy that followed the initial energy
and zeal issuing from the Council of Trent. The work is divided into two sections, the first
examining the material and institutional structures (with chapters on the state and city
government, population, the economy, public finance and currency, food supply, poor relief and
health, law enforcement and criminal justice, education, and the Agro Romano [Roman
Campagna]), the second part considering aspects of Rome's intellectual and cultural life,

including chapters on literature, antiquarianism and Neo-classicism, painting and sculpture, and Jansenism as a Roman phenomenon).

1800-71

269 Between two amnesties: former political prisoners and exiles in the Roman Revolution of 1848.
Leopold G. Glueckert. New York, London: Garland Publishing, 1991. 166p. maps. (Modern European History: Italy.)

The amnesty of 1846, the first political act of Pope Pius IX, was greeted as a 'liberal' beginning for the new Pope. The events of the Roman Revolution of 1848, whose leaders included people pardoned two years previously, changed, however, the Pope's attitude of enlightened political reform into religious conservatism and bitterness. This study examines the shift and also looks at archival sources providing information on the individuals who applied for amnesty in 1846, as well as those who were later indicted for violating its conditions, and establishes that the vast majority of the amnesty recipients did not support the 1848 Revolution, which resulted from new leadership and new issues.

270 Cardinal Giacomo Antonelli and Papal politics in European affairs.
Frank J. Coppa. Albany, New York: State University of New York Press, 1990. 307p. bibliog.

Cardinal Antonelli (1806-76), Papal Secretary of State under Pius IX, was one of the most powerful political figures in Rome from 1850 until its capture by the Italians in 1870. He has been the subject of accusations for his alleged ascendancy over Pius IX from both liberals (for steering his policy towards conservatism, after his initial liberal reformism before the revolutionary upheaval of 1848) and conservatives (for failing to prevent the loss of papal temporal power). This monograph attempts to establish whether the 'Red Pope' was a villain of the Risorgimento (because of his pro-Papal, anti-national stance) or a hero of the Counter-Risorgimento. It examines his role in the inspiration and execution of papal policies, and argues that Antonelli's actions mostly flowed from the Pope and that he served Pius and did not lead him. The contrasting characters of the two men are examined (Antonelli rational and pragmatic, Pius emotional and mystical), as is the heroic conduct of Antonelli and his unwavering support of the Pope in 1848, which earned him Pius' unshakeable trust in later years.

271 Garibaldi and his enemies.
Christopher Hibbert. Harmondsworth, Middlesex: Penguin Books, 1987. 439p. maps.

Garibaldi played a crucial role in the defence of the Roman Republic in 1849. The siege of Rome, the French attack, and the fall of Rome are described in chapters four to six of this monograph. In 1860, Garibaldi's military expedition with his Thousand (the name given to his troops) overthrew Bourbon control in Sicily and Naples, but when he decided to move against the papal government, Cavour, one of the leading figures of Italian unification, withdrew his support and Garibaldi's plans failed. Garibaldi tried again, unsuccessfully, to conquer Rome in 1862 and 1867.

272 Garibaldi's defence of the Roman Republic, 1848-1849.
George Macaulay Trevelyan.   London: Cassell, 1988. 313p. (Cassell History.)

Originally published in 1907, this is the first volume of the author's Garibaldi trilogy, giving an account of his early life in Italy and South America, his love affair with Anita Ribiero da Silva and, especially, his role in the establishment and defence of the Roman Republic in 1849. It ends with Garibaldi's embarkation for Elba on 2 September 1849, after the collapse of the Revolution.

273 A history of the Popes, 1830-1914.
Owen Chadwick.   Oxford: Clarendon Press, 1998. 624p. bibliog. (The Oxford History of the Christian Church.)

A volume about the four popes who reigned between 1830 and 1914 – Gregory XVI (1831-46), Pius IX (1846-78), Leo XIII (1878-1903) and Pius X (1903-14). It examines papal attitudes on politics and society. All four men were constrained by their obligation to preserve their temporal principality and by the bureaucracy of the curia. Other problems included modernism and liberal scholarship. The role of particular cardinals, such as Umberto Benigni and Raffaele Merry de Val, who controlled curial business, is examined in detail. The contents of major pronouncements, for example Leo XIII's *Rerum novarum*, which gave Social Catholicism its charter, are analysed and their circumstances explained.

274 Mazzini.
Denis Mack Smith.   New Haven, Connecticut; London: Yale University Press, 1994. 308p.

Mazzini was with other liberals in Rome in 1849 and was instrumental to the proclamation of the short-lived Roman Republic, which he headed with Carlo Armellini and Aurelio Saffi. He also inspired the Republican Constitution that attempted to change the relationship between church and state. He resigned on 5 July 1849. The section on the Roman Republic is on p. 64-76 of this biography of the statesman.

275 Mostra storica della Repubblica Romana del 1849. (The Roman Republic of 1849: a documentary exhibition.)
Istituto per la storia del Risorgimento italiano.   Rome: Fratelli Palombi, 1999. 118p.

The catalogue of an exhibition in Rome commemorating the short-lived Roman Republic of 1849. After an introductory section dedicated to the Roman Republic of 1798, a decisive turning-point in the history of papal temporal power, the exhibition concentrates on the three years between the election to the papal throne of Pius IX in June 1846 to the occupation of Rome by French troops on 4 July 1849. It follows the development of the popular image of Pius IX as a liberal pope after his granting, on 17 July 1846, amnesty to political prisoners and exiles and his initial support of Italian nationalism, the subsequent disillusionment when he upheld the temporal sovereignty of the Holy See and opposed the establishment of a constitutional state, his exile and the convocation of the Constituent Assembly, and the proclamation of a Roman Republic on 9 February 1849, the siege of Rome and its occupation by French troops on 4 July 1849. In parallel to this chronological survey, the catalogue also examines various aspects of the Republic – the production of banknotes and medals, the treatment of religious minorities, the municipal government of Rome and the popular clubs. 467 items are reproduced, including portraits of all the main protagonists, photographs of the siege of Rome, contemporary popular prints, paintings, newspapers, pamphlets, proclamations and other documents. There is also a chronology of the main events between 1846 and 1849.

276   The papacy in the age of Napoleon and the Restoration: Pius VII, 1800-1823.
Margaret M. O'Dwyer.   Lanham, Maryland: University Press of America, 1985. 295p. bibliog.

This book provides a balanced and generally positive assessment of Pope Pius VII Chiaramonti (1800-23), who had the task of steering the church through one of its most difficult periods and adapting it to the new political realities in the aftermath of the French Revolution. The first section looks at the early life of Gregorio Chiaramonti as a monk, bishop and, from 1785 to 1800, cardinal, and his election to the papal throne in 1800. This is followed by an examination of the beginnings of Pius's pontificate, his return to Rome and the restoration of the papal government, and the Concordat with Napoleon which restored Catholicism in France. Pius successfully resisted Napoleon's attempts at imperial domination of the Church. His relations with Napoleon take up the third section, which covers his journey to Paris in 1804 for the coronation of Napoleon, the deterioration in their relations which led to the Pope's imprisonment in Savona and France between 1809 and 1814, and his triumphant return to Rome in 1814. The final three sections examine papal policies during the restoration period, when Pius's programme of moderate reform was opposed by reactionary elements in the papal regime, and offer an overall assessment of Pius's pontificate.

277   Roma nel 1859. (Rome in 1859.)
Anna Maria Isastia.   Rome: Istituto per la storia del Risorgimento italiano, 1978. 325p. (Biblioteca Scientifica. Serie II, Memorie, vol. 332.)

Isastia examines political events in Rome in 1859 and the role of the Roman volunteers in the Franco-Piedmontese war against Austria. The failure of the Revolution of 1849, the paternalism of the papal regime, and the presence of the French troops are some of the reasons given for the general passivity of the Roman population on this particular occasion.

278   The Roman journals of Ferdinand Gregorovius, 1852-1874.
Edited by Friedrich Althaus.   London: G. Bell & Sons, 1911. 496p.

Gregorovius (1821-91), author of the monumental *History of the City of Rome in the Middle Ages*, was an eyewitness of the death-struggle of the temporal power of the papacy and the transformation of Rome into the capital of a united Italy, a process that also meant the gradual disappearance of the city he knew and loved and the ruthless destruction of its medieval monuments. His journals are particularly important in view of the fact that the scholar destroyed all his papers and correspondence. They begin with his departure from his native Köningsberg in 1852, describe his sudden (like Gibbon's) decision, while standing on the Ponte Fabricio in the autumn of 1854, to embark on his enormous undertaking, provide interesting comments on contemporary Roman society and politics, and end with his return to Germany after the completion of his life's work which, as he says in the touching last paragraphs of his text (where he also expresses his unwillingness to remain in Rome, where everything was becoming new and was being transformed), '...threw light on eleven dark centuries in the city, and gave the Romans the history of their Middle Ages'. The introduction includes an outline of Gregorovius's life and his work and the editor's reminiscences of his friendship with the historian.

279 The Roman question: extracts from the despatches of Odo Russell from Rome, 1858-1870.
Edited by Noel Blakiston. London: Chapman & Hall, 1962. 514p.

Odo Russell, the third of the three sons of Lord William Russell, was born in Florence in 1829. He followed his father into the diplomatic service and, after Paris, Constantinople and Washington, was posted to Rome from November 1858 to July 1870. His culture was cosmopolitan but with a German bias. He was an avid reader and his wide cultural interests are evident in his despatches. His musical and theatrical interests, his wit, charm, and geniality endeared him to a wide spectrum of Roman society, from cardinals to anti-clerical liberals. Russell's relations with the two English Consuls in Rome, Charles Newton, who left in 1860 to take up an appointment in the British Museum, and Joseph Severn (the friend and companion of Keats during the last months of his life in Rome), a good-natured but vain man and an inexperienced and inept diplomat, are recounted with great gusto in the excellent introduction. Though technically a mere spectator of the diplomatic scene as there was no officially accredited agent in Rome, Russell was effectively the English representative at the Vatican. His despatches were initially sent to the diplomatic mission in Florence, later to the one in Naples, and, from 1860, to the Foreign Office. Though his initial impressions of Rome were unfavourable, he soon fell in love with the city where he was to spend the happiest years of his life. Russell's despatches during his twelve years in Rome cover a crucial period that saw the creation of modern Italy and the collapse of the temporal power of the papacy. He was on good terms with Pope Pius IX and Giacomo Antonelli, the Cardinal Secretary of State. It was thanks to Russell's judiciousness and popularity that relations between England and Rome remained friendly during these difficult years. This edition contains about one quarter of Russell's despatches to the Foreign Office, the ones selected being those that shed light on Italian history.

1871 to the present

280 Benevolence and betrayal: five Italian families under Fascism.
Alexander Stille. London: Vintage, 1993. 365p.

One of the family histories included in this book, 'A family of the Ghetto: the Di Verolis of Rome', describes the lives of the four De Veroli brothers and their respective families, who lived and worked (the men were peddlers or shopkeepers and the women seamstresses) on or near Via del Portico di Ottavia in the Ghetto area. It gives a vivid picture of the Jewish community in Rome in the early years of the century, their experiences during the Fascist period and after the racial laws of 1938, the horrible uncertainty after the fall of Fascism in September 1943, and the events leading up to their roundup and deportation to Auschwitz. The work skilfully combines history with personal accounts (based on interviews with surviving members of the family). The text is accompanied by several photographs of the family.

281 Black Sabbath: a journey through a crime against humanity.
Robert Katz. London: Arthur Barker Ltd, 1969. 417p. bibliog.

An account of the fate of the Jews of Rome in the Second World War focusing on the events of September and October 1943 – the gold ransom collection on 27 September, the roundup in the Ghetto on 16 October, and deportation to Auschwitz and Birkenau. The author has made use of primary and unpublished sources (documents, trial records, private papers) and interviewed leaders and officials of the Jewish community in Rome, German officers and diplomats in Rome during the war, and eyewitnesses and survivors of the roundup and deportation. An appendix lists the names and ages of the 1,041 known passengers on the Rome-Auschwitz train who did not come back, and another appendix lists those who did return.

282 Il caso Kappler: dalle Ardeatine a Soltau. (The Kappler affair: from the Ardeatine Caves to Soltau.)
Guido Gerosa. Milan, Italy: Sonzogno, 1977. 206p. (Sonzogno Dossier.)

On 14 August 1977, Herbert Kappler, the dreaded head of the SS in Nazi-occupied Rome, who carried out the executions at the Ardeatine Caves in 1944 and who was subsequently sentenced to life imprisonment, was smuggled out of the Celio hospital in Rome, where he lay dying. This account examines the circumstances of this escape, which caused considerable embarrassment in Italy and elsewhere, together with Kappler's role in the massacre, and his trial. Kappler died a year later. The book includes an interview (originally printed in *L'Europeo* on 12 April 1964) of Carla Capponi and Rosario Bentivenga, the two partisans who planted the bomb in Via Rasella on 23 March 1944 that killed thirty-three soldiers, the incident which prompted the Nazi execution of 335 Italians in retaliation.

283 Death in Rome.
Robert Katz. London: Jonathan Cape, 1967. 351p. maps. bibliog.

On 23 March 1944 (the 25th anniversary of Fascism), a partisan bomb attack on a heavily armed column of SS police in Via Rasella killed thirty-three German soldiers. The next day, in retaliation, the Germans killed 335 Romans in the Ardeatine Caves, near the Appian Way. The victims were political prisoners and, to make up the required number, fifty-seven Jews awaiting deportation. Ten men were to be executed for each German killed – the five extra victims were the result of an administrative error. The enormity of the crime shocked Italy but failed to stop partisan actions against the Germans. The caves were not opened until after the liberation of Rome. This account provides a full, dramatic reconstruction of the events and is based on personal interviews, trial testimony and published and unpublished documents. There is also an account of the aftermath – the trials held in Italian and Allied courts throughout the 1940s and 1950s and the controversy about the Via Rasella attack (the partisans who carried it out were taken to court by relations of some of the Ardeatine Caves victims) that was to continue for two decades. In the epilogue, the author establishes that the massacre could have been prevented in the twenty-four hours after the Via Rasella attack and is particularly critical of Pope Pius XII who, he alleges, had known about the Nazis' planned retaliation but opted not to act. A list of men known to have died in the Ardeatine Caves is included.

284 Hitler's Pope: the secret history of Pius XII.
John Cornwell. London: Viking, 1999. 441p.

An account of the life and carer of Eugenio Pacelli (1876-1958), who became Pope Pius XII in 1939, on the eve of the Second World War, and an indictment of his silence about the massacre of European Jews and failure to publicly condemn Hitler's acts. Such a condemnation, the author argues, might have saved many millions of lives from death, including those of the Jews of Rome, whose fate is described in Chapter Seventeen, which follows events from the bombing of Rome by the Allies on 19 July 1943, through the gold ransom collection on 27 September, the roundup of the Jews in the Ghetto on 16 October, to the subsequent deportation of an estimated 1,060 people to Auschwitz and Birkenau, where only fifteen survived the war. It is argued that the price for the German occupiers' guarantee of the extraterritorial status of the

Vatican was compliance and 'non-interference', and therefore silence about Nazi atrocities. Pius XII's silence is also explained by his concern that any clash with the Nazis would benefit the Communists and his fear of the consequences of a Communist takeover in Rome. Pius XII's liturgical silence after the end of the war, and the lack of apology or act of reparation, are also condemned. The work also examines Pacelli's career from the beginning of the century, including his activities in the 1920s and 1930s in Germany, and finds evidence of his antipathy towards the Jews and his collusion with tyranny.

285   Inside Rome with the Germans.
Jane Scrivener.   New York: The Macmillan Company, 1945. 215p.

A diary recording day-to-day events in Rome in the nine months from the armistice signed on 8 September 1943 between Pietro Badoglio and the Allies, to the liberation of Rome on 4 June 1944, a period of great instability, suspense and increasing misery. The author, writing under the pseudonym of 'Jane Scrivener', was an American woman who had lived in Rome for many years where she was engaged in educational activities. During the war, she worked on prisoners' relief in the Vatican. Her diary conveys the horror of the air raids – see, for example, the description of the bombing of the Vatican on 6 November 1943 and of the Tiburtina, Prenestina, and S. Lorenzo stations (all clearance points for war material) on 14 March 1944, which also caused great damage to civilian dwellings and numerous deaths – and contains vivid, well-informed accounts of the rounding up of the Jews on 16 October 1943 and the Ardeatine Caves massacre on 23 March 1944 and, finally, a description of the celebrations after the liberation of Rome.

286   La legislazione speciale per la città di Roma, 1870-1944. (The special legislation for the city of Rome, 1870-1944.)
Claudio Schwarzenberg.   Naples, Italy: Morano, 1975. 175p.

A survey of special legislation about Rome, from the city's establishment as the capital of Italy in 1870 to the fall of Fascism in 1944. It begins with a description of Rome in the last years of papal rule, when it was a city of 170,000 inhabitants (of whom 20,000 survived on charity), with one of the highest levels of illiteracy in Italy (47.3 per cent), and no industry. It examines the 'Roman question' – the problems regarding the relations between church and state – both in the 1860s and later, the various town planning schemes and their effect on the expansion of the city (that of 1883, for example, made provisions for the creation of new quarters, like Prati di Castello, and for the sale and redevelopment of the villas surrounding Rome), the building fever in the early years of the new capital, and the financial crisis of the late 1880s. Various municipal laws adopted during the mayoralty of Ernesto Nathan (1909-13) which attempted to bring about greater efficiency and improvement of social services are also examined, as are the measures taken during the Governorato which replaced the Comune during the Fascist era. The second half of the publication provides the texts of the principal special legislation for the city of Rome, beginning with the law of 3 February 1871 which established Rome as the capital of the Kingdom of Italy. It also includes the texts of laws regarding construction works in the new capital, various measures intended to encourage the development of the city, the law of 28 October 1925 replacing the Comune of Rome with the Governorato, and the one abolishing the latter on 17 November 1944.

287   Mussolini.
Denis Mack Smith.   London: Paladin, 1983. 495p. bibliog.

A political biography of Mussolini which also shows all aspects of his complex personality, his ferociousness and incompetence. It includes a description of the march on Rome on October

27-29 1922, the political and military operation that led to his appointment as premier and a discussion of the Fascist rebuilding of Rome.

288 The race for Rome.
Dan Kurzman. Garden City, New York: Doubleday & Company, 1975. 526p. maps. bibliog.

An account of the events leading up to the Allied liberation of Nazi-occupied Rome on 4 June 1944, in particular the final battle for Rome, Operation DIADEM, which began on 11 May. The author describes this battle, which the United States entered reluctantly, as flawed in its conception though brilliantly conducted by the Allies. The work brings together unpublished or widely scattered material, which includes Nazi plots to kidnap the pope, burn down Rome, or set up a Nazi-sponsored Communist regime, the Pope's reaction to the rounding up of Rome's Jews, the Allied commanders' scramble to conquer Rome, and the threat of civil war between factions of the Roman Resistance. Though none of the material in this book is invented or fictionalized, the narrative includes much dialogue and descriptive detail. The volume also includes numerous contemporary photographs, a chronology from Mussolini's overthrow to the Allied liberation of Rome, and an extensive bibliography.

289 Roma, un'altra città. (Rome, a different city.)
Paolo Portoghesi. Rome: Newton & Compton, 1981. 296p. (Quest'Italia, 17.)

A collection of photographs taken between 1880 and 1940 showing parts of Rome that have since been indiscriminately demolished, victims first to the town-planning policies and building speculation of the Third Rome and, later, to the Mussolinian attempts to create a grandiose city of spectacular vistas focused on individual monuments isolated from all surrounding structures. In his excellent introductory essay, Portoghesi argues that these attempts to create an artificially centralized and closed plan layout destroyed the city's polycentricity and compromised its chances of an organic expansion. The illustrations are in six groups, showing: the green belt of patrician villas and their gardens that occupied the area between the Aurelian Wall and the built up area; the banks of the Tiber, later radically altered through the construction of the embankments; monuments later demolished – these include 16th century structures like the house of Giacomo Di Bartolomeo da Brescia (attributed to Raphael and Baldassarre Peruzzi), the tower of Paul III and the convent of Aracoeli, and Baroque churches (S. Adriano, SS Venazio e Ansuino, S. Lucia dei Ginnasi); monuments before they were isolated from the surrounding structures (S. Maria in Cosmedin and the temple of Vesta, the churches of the Cappuccini and SS Luca e Martina); areas seen before the great demolitions (opening of the Via del Tritone, Via Minghetti, Via Arenula, Via Zanardelli, demolitions of houses in the Ghetto, and the quarter of the Via dell'Oca, and in the Fascist era the areas around the Mausoleum of Augustus, the Campidoglio, the Colosseum, the opening of the Fori Imperiali, and the destruction of areas like the Piazza Montanara and the Foro Boario); and, finally, 19th-century buildings later demolished (the Hotel Bristol, the Teatro drammatico nazionale, and the old Stazione Termini).

290 Roma capitale, 1870-1911. (Rome the capital, 1870-1911.)
Venice, Italy: Marsilio, 1983-84.

The catalogues of a series of exhibitions organized in Rome between 1983 and 1984, which examined various aspects of the social and artistic life of Rome in the years following its creation as the new capital of Italy. Topics covered include fashion, archaeology, literature, photography, Rome Zoo, science, museums, architecture, and town planning, among others.

291   Rome '44: the battle for the Eternal City.
Raleigh Trevelyan.   Falmouth, England: Coronet Books, 1983. 400p. map. bibliog.

A narration of the Allied liberation of Nazi-occupied Rome by a participant in the events. It is arranged in four main chapters, each of the first three examining the events of a single month from January to March 1944 beginning with the landings at Anzio on 22 January, and the fourth those of April to June culminating in the entrance of the Allied forces into Rome on 5 June. It includes chronologies of the events of 1943 and January-July 1944, as well as a detailed listing of sources and notes, maps, and lists of the key players.

292   The Rome escape line.
Sam Derry.   London: George G. Harrap & Co., 1960. 239p.

The story of the British organization in Rome for assisting escaped prisoners of war in 1943 and 1944. Derry operated an underground aid service for escaped Allied war prisoners hiding in Rome.

293   The sixteenth of October, and other wartime essays.
Giacomo Debenedetti, translated and with an introduction by Judith Woolf and a preface by Alberto Moravia.   Leicester, England: University texts, 1996. 69p.

This book commemorates two of the worst atrocities in Nazi-occupied Rome: the rounding up of the Jews for deportation to Auschwitz and the Ardeatine Caves massacre. 'The sixteenth of October' was first published in 1944 and is a moving account of the plight of the Jews of Rome, beginning with the events leading up to the fateful date: the payment to the Nazis by the Jewish community of fifty kilograms of gold, and the confiscation of the Rabbinical College library. The essay highlights the lack of awareness among the Roman Jews about the imminent danger facing them and their sense of false security because of the status of Rome as an 'open city' and their belief in the protection of the Pope. The 'Eight Jews' of the second essay were the Jewish prisoners whose names were deleted (together with two other surplus ones) at the last moment from the list of prisoners that were to be shot in the Ardeatine Caves in reprisal for the Via Rasella bombing on 23 March 1944. Debenedetti makes the testimony of Raffaele Allianello at the trial of Pietro Caruso (the Rome chief of police and Allianello's superior) the starting point for a meditation on the likely status of Jews in post-war Europe. In his preface, Alberto Moravia gives an autobiographical account of the loss of identity and its replacement by terror that he suffered, as a Jew, during the German occupation of Rome.

294   A spy in Rome.
Peter Tompkins.   London: Panther, 1964. 317p. map.

The wartime memoirs (originally published in 1962) of Peter Tompkins, an O.S.S. (US Office of Strategic Services) agent who entered Nazi-occupied Rome disguised as a German policeman. It begins on the eve of the Allied landing at Anzio and ends with the liberation of Rome. In the preface, Tompkins is described as a mercurial literary and intellectual roughneck and is likened to Xenophon, Procopius, Marco Polo, Casanova, Cellini, Pepys, Gertrude Bell and T. E. Lawrence.

295 A Vatican lifeline: Allied fugitives, aided by the Italian resistance, foil the Gestapo in Nazi-occupied Rome, 1944.
William C. Simpson. London: Leo Cooper, 1995. 240p. maps.

An account of the author's experiences in the last stages of the Second World War, which include his escape in 1943 from Nazi-occupied Abruzzi, underground life in Nazi-controlled Rome, and his work for the Allied Screening Commission appointed after the war to recognize and reimburse those who had assisted Allied escapees in Italy. It pays tribute to the many Italians, especially Monsignor Hugh O'Flaherty and Prince Filippo Doria Pamphilj, who sheltered and gave underground help to Allied fugitives in Rome.

Population

296 **Caratteristiche demografiche e socio-economiche dell'area metropolitana di Roma.** (Demographic and socioecononic characteristics of the metropolitan area of Rome.) Enrico Del Colle. *Sociologia*, vol. 26, no. 1 (1992), p. 189-202.

Rome is one of the nine official metropolitan areas in Italy, designated by law 142/90 of the reform of local autonomy in an attempt to achieve better regional co-ordination of suburbs and city centres. This article analyses the official census data for Rome, which show that from 1971 to 1991 the suburbs increased in population by 4 per cent while urban Rome decreased by 0.32 per cent, and suggests that social planners should take into account the new forms of decentralized development in their consideration of spatial requirements.

297 **Problemi di una metropoli in trasformazione: il caso di Roma.** (Problems of a metropolis in transformation: the case of Rome.) Salvatore Di Riso. *Sociologia*, vol. 25, nos. 2-3 (1991), p. 223-236.

Di Riso looks at the various roles of Rome – as a political capital, as the spiritual centre of the Roman Catholic church, as a capital of the visual arts and cinema, and as a centre of tourism and other service industries. Over the past century, modernization brought about enormous transformations and an increase of its population from 200,000 to almost 3 million, half of it added since 1945. City planning remains crucial to the provision of an orderly growth environment. This article examines the problems of youth, the elderly and the homeless.

Language

298 Canti popolari di Roma e del Lazio. (Folk songs of Rome and Lazio.)
Giggi Zanazzo, edited by Giuseppe Vettori.   Rome: Newton Compton,
1977. 482p. bibliog. (I Sauri, 11.)

Giggi Zanazzo (1860-1911), the dialect poet and playwright, was a great admirer of G. G. Belli.
He had a lifelong interest in Roman folklore and popular traditions, publishing collections of
short stories, fables, legends, proverbs, and this collection of folk songs generally considered to
be among the best of its kind. It was first published in 1910 and contains 1,624 songs of Rome
and Lazio of various types – cradle and children's songs, prisoners' songs, religious, political,
patriotic and historic songs, love songs – and forms – tarantellas (bitingly satirical poems, hence
their name which refers to the bite of the tarantula), sonnets, and ritornelli. The collection is
divided into two parts, the first a collection of songs from Rome, the second from twenty-six
towns in Lazio and the province of Rome (this group is arranged by location, from Albano
Laziale to Zagarolo). This edition also includes an essay by Alessandro Parisotti on popular
Roman melodies, with music examples.

299 Dizionario romanesco. (Dictionary of the Roman dialect.)
Fernando Ravaro, introduction by Marcello Teodonio.   Rome: Newton
Compton, 1994. 684p. bibliog. (Quest'Italia, 212.)

Includes over 11,000 entries, ranging from archaic words to neologisms, with definitions of the
words accompanied by 18,000 citations, given in chronological order, from the work of Roman
dialect writers from the 14th century to the present, and some 7,000 sayings, adages, proverbs
and other popular expressions. The introduction surveys the development of the Roman dialect
and its use in various texts from the 13th century to the present (among them a comedy by
Gianlorenzo Bernini, *La Fontana di Trevi*). It also discusses the grammar, phonetics, spelling
and morphology of Romanesco, the Roman dialect.

300 Piccolo dizionario romanesco. (A short Roman dialect dictionary.)
Giuliano Malizia. Rome: Tascabili economici Newton, 1999. 120p.
(Roma Tascabile, 89.)

A dictionary of *c.* 1,000 words. Each entry has a short explanation of the meaning(s) of the word and several entries also include poetry lines (by G. G. Belli, M. Dell'Arco, and G. Malizia himself) featuring the word. In the short introduction, the compiler surveys other Romanesco dictionaries and pays tribute to Fernando Ravaro, whose dictionary was used as a model for the present work.

301 Proverbi e altre cose romanesche. (Proverbs and other Romanesco things.)
Nino Manfredi. Aosta, Italy: Musumeci, 1983.

This collection by the comedian Nino Manfredi concentrates on the satirical and humorous elements of Roman proverbs and other popular expressions. It is divided into proverbs, sayings, slang expressions, and poems by Belli, Trilussa and Pascarella. The texts are accompanied by a rich selection of paintings, popular prints and drawings depicting Roman life and traditions.

302 Proverbi romaneschi. (Roman dialect proverbs.)
Collected by Giggi Zanazzo. Bologna, Italy: Arnaldo Forni, 1990. 202p.

A facsimile reprint of the work originally published in Rome in 1886. In his introduction, the compiler, the well-known Roman dialect poet, remarks that though there have been collections of proverbs of other Italian regions, there has never been one of Roman proverbs. Roman proverbs have a varied provenance – Biblical, classical (reflecting the city's pagan and Christian past) but also foreign and from other parts of Italy. He also notes that, unlike pasquinades (lampoons or satires), Roman proverbs are not satirical of priests. The proverbs are grouped under thematic headings listed in alphabetical order, from *abitudini* (habits/customs) to *scherzi* (jokes).

303 Roma e il Lazio. (Rome and Lazio.)
Pietro Trifone. In: *L'Italiano nelle Regioni: lingua nazionale e identità regionali.* (Italian language in the regions: national language and regional identities.) Edited by Francesco Bruni. Turin, Italy: U.T.E.T., 1992, p. 540-93.

This is a study of the Roman dialect from its origins to the present. It examines the background to the texts and documents included in the following entry (no. 304). Subjects discussed include: the emergence of the vernacular from Latin; language and society at the time of the *Cronica* (*c.* 1357-60) and the tuscanization of the language in the 14th century after the return of the papacy to Rome in 1377; the cosmopolitanism of the curia and the language of the courtiers; the linguistic effects of the Sack of Rome in 1527, which greatly reduced the number of its inhabitants and was followed by a large influx of immigrants (both from other parts of Italy and other nations); 17th-century plays in Romanesco (the Roman dialect); Gioacchino Belli; non-literary texts; and the role of dialect in the 20th century.

304 Roma e il Lazio. (Rome and Lazio.)
Pietro Trifone. In: *L'Italiano nelle Regioni: testi e documenti.* (Italian in the Regions: texts and documents.) Edited by Francesco Bruni. Turin, Italy: U.T.E.T., 1994, p. 557-604. bibliog.

An anthology of texts in the Roman dialect from the 13th century to the present. The material is notable for the liveliness of its language and its variety (its authors represent all social classes – churchmen and noblemen, schoolmasters and merchants, notaries, and men of the people). The earliest texts are the 13th-century *Ritmo Cassinense* (Cassinese rhythm), a poem in praise of monastic life, and the *Storie de Troja e de Roma* (Histories of Troy and Rome), a vernacular version of *Multe ystorie* (Many histories), a popular 12th-century history of Rome. Other texts include: the anonymous *Cronica* (Chronicle), written *c.* 1357-60, a combination of autobiography and political history (which contains a famous description of the last hours of Cola Di Rienzo); religious literature of the late Middle Ages; letters and diaries of the 14th and 15th centuries; popular medicine texts; statutes and proclamations; the 'confession' of a witch (1527-28); 16th- and 17th-century literary texts – Cristoforo Castelletti's play *Stravaganze d'amore* (Love's whims) (1585) and Giovanni Camillo Peresio's *Il Maggio romanesco, overo il Palio conquistato* (The Roman May, or The conquered Palio) (1688); and various 19th- and 20th-century texts, by G. G. Belli, Trilussa, and others.

305 Roma e il Papa nei proverbi e nei modi di dire. (Rome and the Pope in proverbs and sayings.)
Marco Besso. Rome: Fondazione Marco Besso; Florence, Italy: Leo S. Olschki, 1971. 435p. (Collana della Fondazione Marco Besso, 4.)

This is the definitive edition of the work on which Marco Besso (1843-1920) had worked since he first went to Rome in 1863. An earlier version, *Roma nei proverbi e nei modi di dire*, was published in 1889 and later disowned by the author, who published an enlarged compilation in 1904. Besso carried on collecting further documentation, notably on the papacy and on individual popes, for the following fourteen years, intending this to be incorporated into his text posthumously. The preface of this edition provides a biographical sketch of Besso and evokes his love for Rome, the most tangible result of which is the Biblioteca della Fondazione Marco Besso. The work is an encyclopaedic compilation of proverbs and sayings about Rome, from all periods and in various languages, to which are added those about the papacy and individual popes. Besso points out in his introduction the relative scarcity of material from the Middle Ages and its abundance after the return of the papacy to Rome from Avignon in 1377, especially during the 16th century, which saw a flood of anti-papal propaganda from northern Europe. He also explains some of the characteristics and influence of the 'pasquinate', the Roman *vox populi*. The volume includes a chronology of popes and conclaves, and numerous illustrations.

306 Vocabolario romanesco. (A vocabulary of the Roman dialect.)
Filippo Chiappini, posthumous edition edited by Bruno Migliorini with additional contributions by Ulderico Rolandi. Rome: Leonardo Da Vinci, 1945. 2nd ed. 554p.

This was the first extensive vocabulary of the Roman dialect (Romanesco), published in 1933, twenty-eight years after the death of Filippo Chiappini (1836-1905), following a recommendation at the 1930 Congress of the Institute of Roman Studies. Some 5,200 index cards were used by Chiappini for the preparation of his vocabulary. In his preface, the editor points out the differences between the Roman vernacular of earlier centuries and the tuscanized Roman dialect used in Gioachino Belli's poems. Unlike earlier vocabularies of regional dialects, which concentrated on the dialect of the people excluding those of other social classes, the present work includes words of various provenance. The preface also includes a biographical sketch of Chiappini, a doctor by profession and also the author of works on popular culture and a collection of poetry in the Roman dialect.

Religion

307 The Chief Rabbi, the Pope, and the Holocaust: an era in Vatican-Jewish relations.
Robert G. Weisbord, Wallace P. Sillanpoa. New Brunswick, New Jersey; London: Transaction Publishers, 1992. 240p. bibliog.

In February 1945, Israele Zolli, since 1939 Chief Rabbi of Rome's Jewish community, converted to Catholicism undertaking to honour the Pope for his great humanitarianism to Jews during the Holocaust. This action shocked Jewish people throughout the world. Pius XII, on the other hand, was subsequently accused of not doing enough for Jewish people, as the head of an organized, supra-national power and for his inaction and complicity with the Nazi occupying forces. This book examines these two controversies. It looks at the background, motives and legacy of Zolli's conversion and the attitude of Pius XII toward the Holocaust. The epilogue looks at the uneasy Catholic-Jewish relationship since the Holocaust, notably Pope John Paul II's visit to the Rome Synagogue in 1986 which, however, was followed by the canonization of S. Giuseppe M. Tommasi, whose miracles included the conversion to Catholicism of Rabbi Mosé 'da Cave in 1698. This was seen as a violation of the nascent Christian-Jewish dialogue, which was also damaged by the state visit of Kurt Waldheim (the then President of Austria, who had been accused of war crimes in Yugoslavia in 1942) to the Vatican in June 1987. It suggests that the opening of the Secret Vatican Archives might provide more credible answers to questions of papal policy during the Second World War.

308 Das Collegium Germanicum in Rom und die Germaniker: zur Funktion eines römischen Ausländerseminars, 1552-1914. (The German College in Rome and its alumni: on the function of a foreign seminary in Rome.)
Peter Schmidt. Tübingen, Germany: Max Niemeyer Verlag, 1984. 379p. bibliog. (Bibliothek des Deutschen Historischen Instituts in Rom, Band 56.)

One of the oldest colleges in Rome, the German College was founded in 1552 thanks to the efforts of Cardinal Giovanni Morone and St Ignatius of Loyola. Though higher courses were given at the College itself right from the start, from 1553 students of the College were attending philosophy and theology at the Collegio Romano. After difficult beginnings, the fortunes of the College improved when, in 1573, Gregory XIII drew up a new set of regulations and endowed the College with the Abbey of S. Saba all'Aventino and all its possessions. In 1574, the College moved into the Palazzo di S. Apollinare and its adjoining church. The aim of this study is twofold: to give an account of the history of the College in the context of papal policy and to examine the background and careers of its graduates and the role they played in Church history. It includes an alphabetical list of students between 1552-1798 and 1818-1914, indicating their home town, their years of residence in the College and their matriculation number. It also includes numerous tables providing: the College's annual income, a list of rectors, numbers of students attending between 1552 and 1914, the bishoprics and regions its students came from, their social background, and their age and qualifications upon entering the College.

309 **To Hellēniko Kollegio tes Rōmēs kai hoi mathētes tou, 1576-1700: symvolē stē meletē tēs morphōtikēs politikēs tou Vatikanou.** (The Greek College in Rome and its alumni, 1576-1700: a study on the cultural policy of the Vatican.)
Zacharias N. Tsirpanlis. Salonika, Greece: Patriarchal Institute for Patristic Studies, 1980. 935p. bibliog. (Analecta Vlatadon, 32.)

This is a detailed study of the first 125 years of the Greek College in Rome. Founded, like several other foreign colleges in Rome, by Pope Gregory XIII, its purpose was to receive alumni from any nation in which the Greek rite was used who would later use their learning to contribute to the reunion of the schismatical churches. Its direction was entrusted to four Cardinal protectors, of whom the most active, Giulio Antonio Santoro, controlled the affairs of the College for the first twenty-five years of its life. The College has been administered by the Jesuits (1591-1604, 1622-1773, 1890-97), the Somaschians (1604-09), the Dominicans (1609-20), and the Benedictines (1897 to the present). At other times secular priests were in control, and the College was closed between 1802 and 1849. This work is in two parts. Part one surveys the history of the College, its formation, the nature and length of its courses, its teachers, its students and their obligations and subsequent careers. It also describes the various archival and published sources used in the biographical entries for 690 students contained in part two. These are arranged chronologically and each entry gives all known information about the student, with bibliographical references where appropriate. An appendix provides statistical information about the number of students in each year together with their nationality or place of origin (apart from Greece there were students from Cyprus, Malta, Albania, Dalmatia, Syria, Moldavia and elsewhere).

310 **The English Hospice in Rome.**
John Allen (et al.). Exeter, England: Catholic Record Press, 1962. 306p. (The Venerabile, Sexcentenary Issue, vol. 22, May 1962.)

The various essays in this commemorative volume provide valuable contributions to the history of relations between England and Rome. Apart from John Allen's introduction, which looks at the six-hundred-year history of the Hospice of St Thomas and the English College, its successor, all the essays deal with the years before the foundation of the College. They examine the Hospice's foundation (with the deeds transcribed in an appendix); its development (making use of the College archives and accounts of travellers and historians); the growth of the Hospice of St Edmund (originally St Chrysogonus) in Trastevere alongside St Thomas's; the growth of the Hospice in the 15th century and some of the students, humanists, churchmen and statesmen who were received into the confraternity; and the increasing royal interest in the Hospice, especially under Henry VII, who took it under his control. There are also essays on the fortunes of the

Hospice in the 16th century, when it suffered first during the Sack of Rome in 1527 and later from the repercussions of the Reformation. During the reign of Elizabeth I, it became a residence of English Catholic exiles. In 1579, Gregory XIII issued the Bull of the foundation of the College. Almost from the beginning, the new College was governed by the Jesuits and this was the cause of major disturbances during the first years of its life. The last essay examines the controversial figure of Owen Lewis and the role he played in effecting the transition from Hospice to College.

311 Peter in Rome: the literary, liturgical, and archaeological evidence.
Daniel William O'Connor. New York, London: Columbia University Press, 1969. 256p. bibliog.

An attempt to verify the tradition that St Peter resided in Rome, and that he was martyred and buried there. The last two would be superfluous if it were possible to prove that Peter had never been to Rome. The author points out that the almost complete silence of the New Testament (especially Paul's Epistle to the Romans, and the Book of Acts) cannot be taken as proof against the tradition and, in his investigation, he discounts later evidence unless directly dependent upon a primitive source. After a detailed examination of the literary, liturgical and archaeological evidence, the conclusions reached are that it is plausible that Peter did reside in Rome, probably near the end of his life, and was martyred there as a Christian, but that his body was never recovered and, in later centuries, the general area of his death was taken to indicate the precise location of his grave, marked by a simple monument. A chronological chart of sources from AD 90 to 405 is given in an appendix.

312 Pilgrimage to Rome in the Middle Ages: continuity and change.
Debra J. Birch. Woodbridge, England: The Boydell Press, 1998. 238p. bibliog.

Birch provides a study of pilgrimage to Rome from late Antiquity to the end of the 13th century, concentrating upon the period from Paschal II to Innocent III (1099-1216). The popularity of Rome as a pilgrimage centre grew with the development of the cult of saints in the 4th and 5th centuries and developed around the tombs of St Peter and St Paul. The examination of the journey to Rome analyses the motives of the pilgrims for visiting Rome, the itineraries to the various routes to Rome, practical matters related to the journey (time of the year, length, types of accommodation, cost), and the dangers involved. The range of privileges enjoyed by pilgrims (right to hospitality, safe passage, exemption from the payment of tolls) and their obligations (permission for their journey, letters of recommendation identifying them as genuine, their equipment – the scrip, staff and badge) are also examined. A separate chapter outlines the building campaigns carried out in Rome between the 7th and 10th centuries, which were designed to give access to the tombs and churches. Another chapter concentrates upon the 12th-century pilgrims and how they spent their time in Rome. Welfare provisions for pilgrims in Rome are also considered, including measures taken to protect dying pilgrims and their property and arrangements for their burial. The reasons for the decline in popularity of pilgrimage to Rome in the 12th century in the face of competition from other pilgrimage centres, and the subsequent 13th-century revival, are analysed in the last two chapters. As well as an extensive bibliography of manuscript and printed sources, the study provides an excellent survey of medieval sources, including narrative sources, a wide variety of documentary sources, archaeological and architectural evidence as well as the evidence left by the pilgrims themselves in the form of graffiti and badges (which they wore on their hat or collar). There are also three maps showing pilgrimage routes to northern Italy, Rome, and Roman churches listed in pilgrims' itineraries.

313 La Regola e la fama: San Filippo Neri e l'arte. (The Rule and fame: St Philip Neri and art.)
Milan, Italy: Electa, 1995. 629p. bibliog.

This is the catalogue of the exhibition held in Rome in 1995 to commemorate the quatercentenary of St Philip Neri's death. It examines the image of the Saint in art and also looks at works commissioned by the Oratorians. St Philip Neri, like other Counter-Reformation saints (e.g. St Charles Borromeo), has a vast iconography. All the important events in his life, his miracles, and the foundation of his Confraternity were popularized by prints and, after his death, he was depicted in numerous altarpieces. The organizers of the exhibition remark that most depictions of the Saint tend to underplay his jocundity. The catalogue has seventeen introductory essays and also examines: the role of Cesare Baronio, the historiographer of the Oratorians; commissions for works of art at the Chiesa nuova; St Philip Neri and Marian iconography; Rubens's paintings for the high altar of Chiesa nuova; Pietro da Cortona and the Oratorians; 18th-century patronage in the Oratorians, especially that of Pope Benedict XIII and Cardinal Pietro Ottoboni (Ottoboni wrote an oratorio which was set to music by Alessandro Scarlatti); and the artistic treasures in the Congregazione dell'Oratorio in Via delle Sette Chiese (Chiesa dei SS Isidoro ed Eurosia). The catalogue contains 141 fully catalogued works – coins and medals, paintings, prints, drawings, and sculptures – among them paintings by Caravaggio, Rubens, Lanfranco, and Maratti. There are also 327 illustrations accompanying the introductory texts.

314 Religious conflict in fourth-century Rome: a documentary study.
Brian Croke and Jill Harries. Sydney: Sydney University Press, 1982. 155p. (Sources in Ancient History.)

A collection of material (given in annotated translations) related to the conflict between paganism and Christianity in the city of Rome in the late 4th century. It includes laws, inscriptions, poems, letters, and public speeches and focuses on two key areas: the debate about the Altar of Victory – the removal of which from the Senate prompted a petition from Quintus Aurelius Symmachus, one of the most articulate defenders of paganism, and a sharp reply from Bishop Ambrose – and the public revival of pagan religious practices by Eugenius in 394, which was followed by anti-pagan reaction during the reign of Honorius (395-423). The collection also includes views of Rome – by the 4th century no longer the seat of government of the Roman Empire but still the seat of the Senate, a reservoir of administrative experience, and a stronghold of Christianity – held by both pagans and Christians, the texts of anti-pagan legislation and the edicts establishing Christianity as the state religion (the Edict of Milan of AD 313 which followed the Edict of Toleration of AD 311).

315 Roma cristiana. (Christian Rome.)
Edited by C. Galassi Paluzzi. Bologna, Italy: Cappelli, 1962-65. 18 vols.

A monographic series on the Christian heritage of Rome. It includes studies on church history, Christian antiquities, ceremonies, charitable institutions, saints' homes, churches and church architecture, and palaces.

316 *Roma sancta*, 1581.
Gregory Martin, edited by George Bruner Parks. Rome: Edizioni di storia e letteratura, 1969. 348p. map. bibliog.

This text, which gives a vivid description of the religious life of Counter-Reformation Rome and its organized charities, was written at Rheims in 1580 and 1581. It was the first English book on Rome. Its author, the Reverend Gregory Martin (1542?-82), was a friend of two other leaders of the English Catholic clergy, St Edmund Campion and William Allen, and the author of numerous books on religion and of an English translation of the Douai version of the Bible. He had lived in Rome from 1576 to 1578, where he assisted William Allen in the foundation of the English College and organized the course of studies at the new college. His removal from Rome when Allen recalled him to Rheims in 1578 caused him much disappointment and his great love for the city can be seen in this work. It is in two books, the first describing the city's churches and their holy relics, church and street preaching, and religious processions, and the second listing its new seminaries (especially of the Jesuits), the monasteries of the religious orders, the hospitals and hospices, and lay companies devoted to charity. The introduction describes the life and works of Gregory Martin and the vicissitudes of the manuscript of *Roma Sancta*, which is today in the National Library of Australia at Canberra (Ms. 1097/33). It also discusses other writers, such as Onofrio Panvinio, Marco Attilio Serrano and Pier Francesco Zino, upon whose work Martin may have drawn in the writing of his book. There is a detailed index and an index of authors and works cited by Martin.

317 The Roman Catacombs and their martyrs.

Ludwig Hertling and Engelbert Kirschbaum. London: Darton, Longman & Todd, 1960. rev. ed. 274p.

The Catacombs provide the most important material evidence about early Christianity because of the richness of their inscriptions and their direct relationship with persons and events. Estimates about the number of tombs in the Catacombs range from a conservative (as here) 500,000 to 2 million. The largest necropolis is that of Domitilla on the Via Ardeatina. This examination of the history of the Catacombs begins with an account of their exploration from the 16th century to the present, beginning with St Philip Neri and Cesare Baronio and the work of Onofrio Panvinio, who undertook a series of studies in Christian archaeology and Roman topography, and Antonio Bosio, who published his *Roma sotterranea* (Subterranean Rome) in 1629, through the work of Giuseppe Marchi and Giovanni Battista de Rossi, to more recent discoveries. The erroneous belief that all Catacombs date from the times of Christian persecution led to the assumption that all the liturgy of the community was carried on underground and that Christians lived there. The work shows the location of the Catacombs (in a wide circle around the city) and explains their construction. It also traces their history from the earliest Christian cemeteries, which had their origins before the middle of the 2nd century in the private sepulchres of wealthy Christian families, their transformation into places of pilgrimage in the 4th century, the development of the cult of martyrs and the erection of basilicas over the tombs of the Apostles Peter and Paul, and the removal, in later centuries, of the remains of martyrs from the Catacombs to save them from barbarian plundering. A separate chapter surveys the tombs of the popes who were buried in the Catacombs, from Zefirinus (AD 217) to Hilary (461-468). Other chapters discuss the persecution and martyrdom of Christians, and the evidence in the Catacombs that the Eucharist has been the focal point of the Church's liturgy and of personal piety. The final two chapters look at the art of the Catacombs, the main sources of early Christian art.

318 Rome, 1300: on the path of the pilgrim.

Herbert L. Kessler, Johanna Zacharias. New Haven, Connecticut; London: Yale University Press, 2000. 237p. bibliog.

During the first Holy Year of 1300, declared by Pope Boniface VIII, Rome was visited by 200,000 pilgrims who came to visit the sacred Christian sites. This book follows the route of a pilgrim of this first Jubilee through the medieval city and describes the churches and their holy relics, frescoes, icons and mosaics. It begins with the Lateran, the principal palace of the medieval papacy, and surveys the emblems of the papacy it housed. It then visits the Sancta Sanctorum, the private chapel of the popes. The core of the work is the description of the papal procession on 14 August, the eve of the Feast of the Assumption of the Virgin, from the Lateran to the basilica of S. Maria Maggiore (where the *Acheropita*, the Lateran icon of Christ, is joined with the icon of the Virgin) through the church of S. Clemente, the Roman Forum, and S. Prassede. The final chapter re-creates visits to the twin basilicas of S. Paolo fuori le Mura and St Peter's. There are 225 illustrations, several in colour.

319 Romei e Giubilei: il pellegrinaggio medievale a San Pietro, 350-1350.

(Pilgrims and Jubilees: the medieval pilgrimage to St Peter's, 350-1350.) Edited by Mario D'Onofrio. Milan, Italy: Electa, 1999. 473p. bibliog.

The catalogue of an exhibition held in Rome in 1999-2000 which aimed to reconstruct the historical background to one thousand years of pilgrimages through the use of a wide variety of documents and other material, such as pilgrims' phials, shells and badges. It includes thirty-two introductory studies on topics including: the significance of the Jubilee in the Biblical tradition; the importance of pilgrimages in the Middle Ages; the origins of the pilgrimage to the Tomb of St Peter and the cult of the Roman martyrs; Rome as the new Jerusalem; categories of pilgrims to Rome – Emperors, Byzantine monks, Saints (St Francis of Assisi, St Galgano, St William of Maleval), pilgrims from Northern countries; aspects of the journey: the itineraries, the earliest Roman guidebooks, the *Mirabilia Urbis Romae*, the hospitals for the accommodation and welfare of the pilgrims; artistic manifestations related to pilgrimages: the medieval iconography of St Peter, the art on the pilgrimage routes, reliquaries, the Veronica, maps of Rome, literature; and liturgical furnishings of St Peter's basilica during the Middle Ages. There are also studies on the first three Jubilees (1300, 1325 and 1350). The catalogue section has 271 entries for manuscripts, mosaics, sculptures, enamels, maps, coins and medals, and other artefacts. All the exhibits are reproduced, mostly in colour, and the catalogue is richly illustrated throughout.

320 St. Philip Neri and the Roman society of his times, 1515-1595.

Louis Ponnelle and Louis Bordet. London: Sheed & Ward, 1932. 633p.

This monumental study remains the best account of St Philip Neri's life, personality and times. A Florentine by birth, St Philip Neri (1515-95) came to Rome at the age of eighteen and, after a period of study of theology and philosophy at the Sapienza, he began seven years of solitary prayer and meditation in churches and catacombs (especially the Catacomb of S. Sebastian). In 1544, while praying, a globe of fire entered his mouth and passed into his heart, giving him a swelling without pain. Through his 'lay apostolate' he popularized the devotion of Forty Hours, in commemoration of the time Christ spent in the tomb, and the pilgrimage to the Seven Churches – St Peter, S. Paolo fuori le Mura, S. Sebastiano, S. Giovanni in Laterano, S. Croce, S. Lorenzo, and S. Maria Maggiore. In 1548, he founded the Confraternity of the Santissima Trinità (with S. Salvatore in Campo as its headquarters), whose members helped pilgrims visiting Rome and, after the 1550 Jubilee, the convalescents. In 1551, St Philip was ordained and shortly afterwards he founded the movement that became known as the Congregation of the Oratory, which started as a gathering of priests and scholars who organized religious services and informal meetings in which music was performed and poetry read, and eventually developed into the Oratorio. The work is particularly good in describing the changing fortunes of the Oratorians under variously disposed popes. In 1575, Pope Gregory XIII (a personal friend of St Philip) recognized the Congregation of the Oratory, and the church of S. Maria in Vallicella was given to it which, after its rebuilding and re-opening in 1577, became known as Chiesa Nuova. St Philip was its first Provost and he was succeeded by Cesare Baronio. The work also looks at the cult of St Philip in Rome (among the many miracles attributed to him was the raising from the dead of Fabrizio Massimi's son, Paolo, in 1583) and his legacy. See also *Filippo*

Neri: il santo dell'allegria (Philip Neri: the Saint of merriment) by Rita Delcroix (Rome: Newton Compton, 1989. 276p. [Quest'Italia, 140.]).

321 Saint, site, and sacred strategy: Ignatius, Rome and Jesuit urbanism.
Edited by Thomas M. Lucas. Vatican City: Biblioteca apostolica vaticana, 1990. 232p. bibliog.

The catalogue of an exhibition organized to mark the 500th anniversary of the birth of St Ignatius Loyola and the 450th anniversary of the papal approval of the Society of Jesus. It aims to show how the Society was a response to the changing relationship of the Church with the world and argues that its rapid growth was related to Ignatius' adaptablity and creativity. It also examines the reciprocal relationship between the Saint and the city and the Jesuit contribution to visual arts, theatrical representations (the *Opera pietatis*), and literature. The catalogue is in two parts, the 141 catalogue entries following the argument of the two introductory essays. The first essay examines both the life of St Ignatius Loyola (1491-1556) and the urban development of Rome in the 15th and 16th century and its transformation from a medieval into a Renaissance city. Ignatius settled in Rome in 1537, abandoning plans for a pilgrimage to Jerusalem, after a vision at La Storta on the Via Cassia of Jesus carrying the Cross and saying to him 'I will be propitious to you in Rome'. Ignatius had, by then, visited most of the major cities in Europe and spent seven years in Paris, where the first nucleus of the Society was formed. In 1541, Ignatius was elected the first Superior General of the Society. With the support of Pope Paul III, the Jesuits began a programme of preaching, teaching catechism and visiting the sick. By the time of his death in 1556, the Society had acquired a permanent church (S. Maria della Strada) on the site, in the heart of Rome, where the Gesù was built in the 1570s and the attached residence, the casa Professa, added in the 17th century. The strategies of the expanding Society for the purchase of property and the siting of urban works in desired locations are examined, the Society's diffusion in Rome being paradigmatic for other locations. By the mid-17th century, the Jesuits also owned large tracts of suburban land on the Coelian, Quirinal and Aventine hills, and Jesuit colleges and universities had been established in major cities throughout the world. The history of the much-delayed building of the church of Gesù, finally carried out through the efforts of Francesco Borgia and Cardinal Alessandro Farnese, is also examined. Other buildings discussed are the Collegio Romano-S. Ignazio complex, the church of S. Anastasia, and Bernini's S. Andrea al Quirinale (the church of the Jesuit noviciate). The second essay, and the last section of the catalogue, look at Jesuit church interiors in Rome between 1567 and 1700, examining both permanent and ephemeral decorations created for funerals and Forty Hours devotions, and investigating Jesuit attitudes regarding church decoration and the development of a visually and iconographically unified interior during the generalship of Gian Paolo Oliva (1664-81).

322 The Saxon pilgrims to Rome and the Schola Saxonum.
W. J. Moore. Fribourg, Switzerland: [Society of St Paul], 1937. 140p. bibliog.

An excellent account of the Anglo-Saxon pilgrimages to Rome in the 7th and 8th centuries and the origins and history of the Schola Saxonum. Contacts between Rome and Britain were established with St Augustine's landing in 597 but the first pilgrimage to Rome was undertaken fifty-seven years later by St Benedict Biscop and St Wilfrid. St Benedict made six pilgrimages between 654 and 685, during which he collected numerous relics, books and paintings with which he enriched the monasteries of Wearmouth and Jarrow; St Wilfrid also visited Rome in 654 and made a second journey there in 678 to appeal to the central authority of the Pope over his dispute with King Egfrid regarding his diocesan rights as Archbishop of York, and a third in 704 when he again sought Roman authority. Other early pilgrims included Cadwalla, King of Wessex, who began his pilgrimage in 688, two years after finally subduing the other claimants to the throne, was baptized in Rome in 689 but died soon afterwards and was buried in St Peter's. Religious pilgrimages increased during the pontificate of Sergius (687-701), which marked the beginning of the great missionary period of the Anglo-Saxon church and resulted in a widening of culture, a growing number of monastic foundations with important libraries, and an interest in Gregorian plainsong. By the mid-8th century, a considerable number of Anglo-Saxons lived in Rome. Notable pilgrims in the latter half of the century included Aelbert and Alcuin, the eminent scholars and theologians, who went in search of books for the York Library. The term *Schola Saxonum* (first mentioned in the *Liber pontificalis* in 799) indicates not only a pilgrim hospice but also a district, or quarter, of Saxon pilgrims which was situated alongside the Portico of St Peter's basilica and which suffered great damage in the great fires in the Borgo of 817 and 847. The Church of S. Maria in Saxia (now S. Spirito in Sassia) was built in this quarter after the second fire. It also refers to an organized, corporate body of Saxon pilgrims living in Rome. The Saxon militia fought the Saracens when the latter invaded Rome in 846. The probable beginnings of the *Schola Saxonum* are traced back to the period between 716 and 738, but the first description of it is in the Bull of Leo IX of 1053, a reissue (with additions) of the Bull of Leo IV, published in 854 after the completion of the Leonine City, the relevant section of which has not survived. During these centuries, the stream of pilgrims, lay and ecclesiastic, continued and the Schola Saxonum flourished. After the Norman Conquest in 1066, however, the number of visitors declined as a result of the changed social conditions in Europe, the conflict between the Empire and the Papacy, and the Crusades. The foundation of the Ospedale di S. Spirito in 1204 under the Confraternity established by Guy de Montpellier deprived the English of a national church or hospice until the foundation of the Hospice of St Thomas of Canterbury in 1360. The work includes a chronological list of pilgrims in the 7th and 8th centuries.

323 Storia degli Anni santi: da Bonifazio VIII ai giorni nostri. (History of the Holy Years: from Boniface VIII to the present.)
Paolo Brezzi.   Milan, Italy: Mursia, 1975. 222p. bibliog.

There have been twenty-five Holy, or Jubilee, Years, celebrated at irregular intervals. The first was instituted by Boniface VIII in 1300 with the Bull 'Antiquorum fida relatio', which granted remissions and indulgences for sins to those who went to Rome and during their stay fulfilled certain conditions, which included visits to St Peter's and S. Paolo fuori le Mura. Originally they were to occur every 100 years but Clement VI, perhaps influenced by, amongst others, Petrarch and St Bridget of Sweden, halved the interval and added S. Giovanni in Laterano to the other two churches. S. Maria Maggiore was added to the list in the next Jubilee, in 1390, when Urban VI also decreed that Jubilees should be celebrated every thirty-three years (the number of years Jesus lived). From 1475, Jubilees have been celebrated every twenty-five years, with the exception of 1800, 1850 and 1875 because of political disturbances. There have also been seventy-six extraordinary Jubilees, beginning in 1560, Urban VIII being the Pope with a record nine extra Jubilees celebrated during his reign. This volume begins with an introduction describing medieval pilgrimages and the pre-eminence of Rome, whose wealth of holy relics included the tombs of St Peter and St Paul. It then provides a chronological survey of all Jubilees up to 1975, pointing out the special character of each celebration or events that marked it, such as the death of some 200 pilgrims trampled to death on the Ponte S. Angelo in 1450, at the time the only route to St Peter's.

324 The Venerable English College, Rome: a history, 1579-1979.
Michael E. Williams. London: Associated Catholic Publications, 1979.
268p. bibliog.

A study published on the quatercentenary of the foundation of the English College (the Venerabile Collegio degli Inglesi). The College, the origins of which go back to the foundation of the Hospice of St Thomas of Canterbury in 1362 for the use of English pilgrims and other visitors to Rome, is the oldest existing British institution abroad. The study looks at the college's 14th-century beginnings, its development first into the spiritual centre of the English in Rome and, during the religious persecutions under Elizabeth I, into a home for exiles. Its transition from hospice to college is also examined, together with the College's early missionary ideals and also the internal dissension between the English and Welsh students and other disciplinary troubles. The Jesuits were responsible for the training of the students, the future missionaries to England, and relations between the Mission and the College were sometimes strained as, for example, during the rectorship of Thomas Fitzherbert (1618-40). The vicissitudes of the College after the suppression of the Society of Jesus in 1773, its own suppression during the Napoleonic occupation of Rome and re-opening in 1818, and the achievements and influence of rectors such as Robert Gradwell (1818-28), Nicholas Wiseman (1828-40) and Arthur Hinsley (1917-29), are also surveyed.

Society

325 Borgate di Roma. (Borgate of Rome.)
Giovanni Berlinguer, Piero Della Seta.   Rome: Editori riuniti, 1976. rev.
ed. 358p. (Ventesimo Secolo, 52.)

Originally published in 1960, this enlarged edition is an investigation of the new 'ghettos' of Rome created in the 1920s by the urban policy of the Fascist regime that brought about the 'gutting' of the populous and popular centre of Rome and the expulsion of its inhabitants to the periphery with few or no amenities. The Second World War and the subsequent internal migration from southern Italy swelled the population of these slum areas and led to the building of illegal dwellings.

326 Mercati, botteghe, e spazi di commercio a Roma tra medioevo ed età moderna. (Markets, shops, and commercial spaces in Rome from the Middle Ages to the Modern Era.)
Anna Modigliani.   Rome: Roma nel Rinascimento, 1998. 386p. bibliog. (Inedita, 16: Saggi.)

A study of the market areas and other commercial spaces in Rome, mostly situated in the zone between the Campidoglio and the Vatican, and their special features. The introduction describes their development during the Middle Ages and their use, by both civic and religious authorities to show their strength, for festivals, processions and executions. It also surveys their predominantly foreign clientele of pilgrims and other visitors to the city. Subsequent chapters concentrate on the major markets in the Campidoglio, the Campo de' Fiori and the Via Mercatoria, the area around St Peter's, and Piazza Navona. There is also a chapter on special markets, such as the Mercatello in the Jewish quarter, the fish and game markets at S. Angelo in Pescheria and elsewhere, the cattle market in the Campo Torrecchiano, the horse market (between the Campo de' Fiori and S. Lorenzo in Damaso), and a section on street pedlars such as water and oil sellers. 148 commercial establishments in the area around the Campo de' Fiori are listed in an appendix.

Local Government and Administration

327   European Municipal Directory.
London: Newmedia Publishing Ltd, 1992- .

This directory (latest edition 1997) is divided into two sections: the first contains information (on p. 299-300) about Communes (*Comuni*) in the Province of Rome (*Provincia di Roma*) with more than 5,000 inhabitants, giving the address, tel/fax number and name of the chief elected officer, usually the *sindaco* (mayor). The second section, which provides an in-depth analysis of the larger authorities with a population in excess of 100,000, has information (on p. 713-14) on the *Giunta regionale di Lazio* (Regional council of Lazio), with names of seventeen officials responsible for a range of specialized functions. These functions are defined in nine different languages.

Transport

328 Il filobus a Roma. (Trolleybuses in Rome.)
Vittorio Formigari. Cortona, Italy: Calosci, 1980. 165p. bibliog.

Trolleybuses were used for public transport in Rome for thirty-five years, between 8 January 1937 and 2 July 1972. The Roman trolleybus network was the biggest in continental Europe, in its heyday having 419 vehicles running over a length of 137 kilometres of rail tracks. This study describes the short life of this means of public transport and attempts to establish whether its demise was due to its own technical deficiencies or whether it fell victim to wider economic and political interests. It examines the history of the network and the expansion of its various lines between the 1930s and the 1950s, and looks at the various types of vehicle used, both single carriage models and articulated ones. It is suggested that the hybrid nature of the trolleybus – between a tram and a bus without the advantages of either and with the defects of both – ultimately accounted for its disappearance. There are numerous photographs showing the vehicles discussed.

329 La metropolitana a Roma. (The underground in Rome.)
Vittorio Formigari, Piero Muscolino. Cortona, Italy: Calosci, 1983. 297p.

The development of an underground network in Rome came late and has been delayed by a lack of funding and obstructed by the constant discovery of new archaeological finds. The first underground lines in Rome date from 1955, though they were preceded by a long series of abortive proposals and plans going back to 1881, when a circular line was proposed that would start from Trastevere and have stops at S. Giovanni, Termini, Piazza di Spagna, and Prati. Various other proposals are surveyed in this volume, up to the Regulatory Plan of 1974 which proposed 6 lines and 195 stations, only a fraction of which have been built to date. There are separate chapters on Line B (Termini-Laurentina) and on Line A (Ottaviano-Anagnina), both of which include a section describing the archaeological treasures discovered during excavations. There is also a chapter on the history of the Roma-Lido railway line, which corresponds to the proposed Line E of the Regulatory Plan, and a chapter on the metropolitan services of the Ferrovie dello stato (Italian State Railways). The volume is richly illustrated with period photographs of the trains, underground tunnels, timetables, and other material.

**330   La nuova Stazione di Roma Termini delle Ferrovie italiane dello
stato.** (The new Stazione di Roma Termini of the Italian State Railways.)
Texts by L. Iannattoni (et al.).   Rome: Collegio ingegneri ferroviari
italiani, 1951. 204p. maps.

This is a collection of articles originally published in the review *Ingegneria ferroviaria* during
the renovation works and the building of the new hall and reception area of the Stazione
Termini, inaugurated in 1950. It contains seven articles looking at the history of the original
station and its modernization. The belated creation of the station, some twenty-five years after
Cavour's prediction in 1846 that Rome would become the centre of a vast railway network, is
examined by I. Iannattoni in the first article. The station, which occupied part of the grounds of
Villa Peretti Montalto, was built on one of the highest levels in the city, its unsuitable position
dictated by reasons of financial speculation. The second article looks at some of the problems
created, on the one hand, by the rapid increase in the traffic of the station and, on the other, the
presence of historic structures in its vicinity which prevented its expansion. The 1931 town
planning scheme proposed the creation of two large termini in the north and south that would
cross the city underground, meeting at the point occupied by this station, which would be
transformed into a passing through station. Owing to technical difficulties and huge costs, this
proposal was not adopted and was replaced by a plan which led to the creation of several
auxiliary stations (the Ostiense, Tiburtina, Tuscolana, and Trastevere) and provided for the
rebuilding of Stazione Termini in a position further back from the one it originally occupied.
This plan was interrupted by the Second World War and after the war a public competition was
held among Italian architects for the construction of a new front building, which attracted forty
entries. The winning project is examined in detail in the remaining articles, which discuss
the aesthetic and functional character of the plan and describe the execution of the work, the
station's electrical and electromechanical plants, and the organization of its services. There are
numerous illustrations, folded maps and plans.

331   Storia delle ferrovie in Italia. (The history of Italian railways.)
Italo Briano.   Milan, Italy: Cavallotti, 1977. 3 vols.

In this general history of railways in Italy, the development of the service in Rome and Lazio is
discussed in the context of the overall development of the network throughout the Italian
Peninsula. A separate chapter discusses the initial resistance to the creation of railways in the
papal states, especially during the reign of Pope Gregory XVI, and the establishment (under
Pius IX) of the first lines, running between Rome and Civitavecchia and between Rome and
Ancona (the Pio Centrale line). The third volume, which includes descriptions of railway station
architecture, looks at Roma Termini at various periods of its existence, beginning with 1862-70
and ending with its renovation and restructuring, and the inauguration of the new station in
1951. There is also a section on the Roma Trastevere station (1907-10).

Labour

332 L'altra Roma: classe operaia e sviluppo industriale nella capitale.
(The other Rome: the working class and the industrial development of
the capital.)
Gaetano Congi.   Bari, Italy: De Donato, 1977. 256p. (Movimento
Operaio, 41.)

A study of labour movements in Rome from 1945 to the present. It examines the composition
of the labour force in the capital in the immediate post-war era and during the 1950s, the gradual
shift from skilled to unskilled labour in the 1960s and 1970s, and the new role assumed by the
state in the 1970s. It also analyses, through a survey of delegates to works councils in the Rome
region, the political, social and ideological composition of the labour force, its attitude toward
social protest, and the relationship between trade unions and political parties. The work also
surveys one hundred years of industrial development and legislation in Rome and traces the
history of two particular categories of workers – construction workers and printers – whose
contrasting fortunes were closely linked to the specific circumstances of Rome's development
in the years after 1870 – the first to the enormous expansion of the city within a short period of
time followed by periods of financial crises, and the second to the concentration of the
Government administration and bureaucracy in Rome.

Statistics

333 Descriptio Urbis: the Roman census of 1527.
Edited by Egmont Lee. Rome: Bulzoni, 1985. 394p. (Biblioteca del Cinquecento, 32.)

Compiled a few months before the Sack of Rome in 1527, this is the earliest surviving census of the city. It was first published in 1894 in the *Archivio della Società romana di storia patria* by Domenico Gnoli, who based his edition on two 19th-century manuscripts. The present edition is based on the most authoritative surviving version of the text, probably the original manuscript of the census, acquired by the British Museum Library in 1910 and now in the British Library (Add. Ms 38,025). The identity of its author is uncertain (Iacobo Hellin, a resident of the rione Parione, calls himself the author of the text but he may just be the writer of the present manuscript). In his introduction, Egmont Lee points out that several different persons may have been responsible for the collection of data, which may account for the fact that the final data (family names, patronymics, places of origins, etc.) in the document are not rigorously standardized. Though he underlines the importance of the work, he also warns against placing excessive faith in its comprehensiveness and accuracy, comparing it to other contemporary sources (for example lists of bakers, many of whom do not appear in the present text). The present edition is enriched by numerous indices: names of persons divided into their component parts – first names, surnames (family names and nicknames), patronymics and husband's names, origins, Jews, occupations, ecclesiastical officials and institutions, lay officials and institutions. There is also a concordance of first names, place names, and trades and occupations.

334 Le fonti della demografia storica in Italia. (Sources of historical demography in Italy.)
Rome: Comitato italiano per lo studio dei problemi della popolazione (CISP), [1974?]. 2 vols. 1177p. bibliog.

A collection of papers presented at six seminars during 1971-1972 discussing information sources on population from the 16th century to the unification of Italy. They cover a variety of documents both demographic (the 'stati delle anime' [registers of inhabitants]; parish baptismal, marriage and death registers; and censuses) and non-demographic (land registers and taxation rolls). The compilation of these records was regulated during the Counter-Reformation period though, in most cases, their collection had begun much earlier. The importance of the 'stati delle anime' – up to the 19th century the major source of information on population, often including details about the distribution of the sexes, age and civil status – is discussed by Athos Bellettini in the first chapter. They were originally collected by parish priests as a means of establishing the number of people requiring communion at Easter. There are four contributions specifically about Rome, which examine state registrations in Rome between 1550 and 1650, the registration of baptisms and marriages in Rome, the registration of deaths in Rome, and repositories of Roman parish records, 1531-1870.

335 Roma in cifre. (Rome in figures.)
Edited by Aldo Santori.   Rimini, Italy: Maggioli, 1996. 983p. (Materiali per Roma.)

This is the first commercial edition of this report prepared by the Ufficio Studi (Uspe) (Department of Studies) of the Comune of Rome, which previously had a more restricted circulation. It provides a global view of the activities of the municipal administration of Rome and a socio-economic analysis of the capital. One of the features of the report is the comparison it provides between the various territories under the control of the Comune, the metropolitan area and the outskirts. The report is divided into four parts: part one surveys the social, economic and environmental features of the area; part two examines the production resources of the Comune; part three surveys the principal public services; and part four analyses two recent surveys which examined the geography of social malaise and living standards in the areas ('*circoscrizioni*') administered by the Comune. Each section includes numerous charts and projections.

336 Gli 'stati delle anime' a Roma dalle origini al secolo XVII. (The 'stati delle anime' in Rome from their beginnings to the 17th century.)
Carla Sbrana, Rosa Traina, Eugenio Sonnino.   Rome: La Goliardica, 1977. 651p.

A study of 17th- and 18th-century demographic sources in Rome concentrating on the 'stati delle anime', the population records kept in the parish churches of Rome. It examines their origins and analyses their administrative and religious importance, their qualitative and quantitative evolution and their gradual development into an important tool for the study of Counter-Reformation Rome. The work includes a descriptive catalogue of the 'stati delle anime' up to 1650, listed in parish church order. Other types of parish documents, such as baptismal, marriage and death records, are also described in an appendix with their present locations and shelfmarks.

Environment and Urban Planning

General

337   Art and power: Europe under the dictators, 1930-1945.
Compiled and selected by Dawn Ades (et al.).   London: The South
Bank Centre, 1995. 360p.

The catalogue of an exhibition held in London, Berlin and Barcelona in 1995-1996 examining
the role of artists and architects under totalitarian rule between 1930 and 1945. It is structured
around the regimes of the four great dictators of the time and the four capital cities of Paris (with
an evocation of the Exposition Universelle of 1937 and, in particular, the Spanish Pavilion),
Rome, Moscow and Berlin. The section on Mussolini's Rome contains four essays discussing
architecture, painting and sculpture, cinema and culture. Tim Benton's 'Rome reclaims its
Empire' looks at post-Unification urban policies in Rome, noting that the key issues of urban
planning had been well established before the Fascist era. It analyses the Plan of 1931, which
dramatically reshaped the landscape of the city advocating, among other things, the demolition
of buildings in order to highlight individual antique structures such as the Mausoleum of
Augustus. Simonetta Fraquelli's 'All roads lead to Rome' looks at Fascist propaganda, the
concept of *romanità* (Roman character), and attitudes to culture – though artists were permitted
a degree of creative freedom, the gradual establishment of artists' federations ensured collusion
with the regime in order to be allowed to exhibit their work. Lutz Becker's 'Black shirts, white
telephones' discusses the Italian film industry in the 1930s and its use as an instrument of
propaganda and points out that Neorealism had its roots in films produced during this period.
Ester Coen's ' "Against dreary conformism": Giuseppe Bottai and culture during the Fascist
period' examines one of the most complex personalities of the Fascist period and his
complicated relationship with the regime. An enlightened and liberal man, Bottai became
increasingly disillusioned with the dictatorial and antidemocratic tendencies of Mussolini in the
late 1930s and he gradually distanced himself from Mussolini.

338   Cities and people.

Mark Girouard.   New Haven, Connecticut; London: Yale University Press, 1985. 404p.

This study of cities and their people through the centuries, focusing on individual cities at crucial periods in their history, includes a chapter about Renaissance Rome ('Rome resplendent'). It describes the transformation of the city after the return of the papacy from Avignon, the creation of splendid new buildings, the rise in its resident population, the traffic problems which were worsened by the huge influx of pilgrims during Jubilee Years, and the policies of improving existing roads and the creation of new arteries, which sought both to alleviate these problems and also provide spectacular effects exalting the name of the pope who built them. It also points out the contrast between the large areas of open land within the Aurelian Wall (including the areas around the Colosseum and the Forum) and the densely populated medieval city, an imbalance that led to the creation of the private villas and their gardens, that would be, until their destruction in the 19th century, one of the great features of Rome. Finally, the study looks at aspects of Roman society such as festivals and the importance of courtesans in Renaissance Rome.

339   La costruzione di una capitale. (The building of a capital.)

Mario Sanfilippo.   Milan, Italy: Amilcare Pizzi, 1992-94. 3 vols. (156p., 156p., 188p.) maps. bibliog.

These three volumes present a history of the urban development of Rome between its becoming the capital of Italy in 1870 and 1911 (the year of the International Exhibition in Rome celebrating the first fifty years of the Unification of Italy), 1911 and 1945, and 1945 to the present. The introductory chapter looks at Rome during the pontificate of Pius IX (1846-1878), a relatively small city still contained within a limited geographical area (out of the 1,470 hectares within the Aurelian Wall only 400 were built up, the rest being vineyards, villas and their gardens), its population of 130,000 during the Napoleonic occupation growing to 230,000 by 1870. The author refutes the view that pre-1870 Rome was a backward city, pointing out numerous developments such as the opening of the first railway stations and the creation of new quarters by Federico Francesco Saverio de Merode, a foretaste of the building boom after 1870. Subsequent chapters look at the development of a centralized administration housed in new, symbolically monumental buildings, the enormous influx of administrators and other workers and the consequent disorderly expansion of the city (with various town-planning schemes following rather than preceding the excesses of property speculation), the destruction of some of the most famous green areas of the city, the creation and political organization of new social classes, and the gradual expansion outside the Aurelian Wall. Each volume is in two parts, an historical overview of the period followed by thirty to forty chapters each focusing on a specific subject – an area significantly altered during the period discussed, or a particular urban development or event. The photographs accompanying the texts are exceptional visual documents but the maps are, unfortunately, too small and difficult to read.

340   Hadrian and the city of Rome.

Mary Taliaferro Boatwright.   Princeton, New Jersey: Princeton University Press, 1987. 332p. maps. bibliog.

A detailed topographical examination of Rome and the new physical constructions and changes in the city's life that occurred during the twenty-one years of Hadrian's reign. This is set against the more general history of Hadrian's principate and the politics, culture and religion of Rome in the first half of the second century AD. The focus is exclusively on the city of Rome, though Hadrian built extensively throughout the Roman world. Many of the best-known buildings of Ancient Rome – the Pantheon, Hadrian's Mausoleum (Castel S. Angelo), the temple of Venus and Roma, and Hadrian's Villa at Tivoli – date from this period. These and other edifices transformed the face and life of Rome, but Hadrian also transformed existing buildings and whole districts of the city and reorganized the building industry. The introduction provides a useful survey of recent studies in a variety of areas such as brick stamps, coins and medals, inscriptions, cartography, architectural history, artistic and antiquarian as well as scientific archaeology (i.e. the evidence provided by artists and antiquarians in the Renaissance and Baroque periods as opposed to the more professional excavators of the 19th and 20th centuries), and also of the literary evidence. The material is generally divided by location, each chapter focusing on one area of the city with the exception of the first chapter, which examines Hadrian's administrative and organizational changes in the city, and the seventh chapter, which discusses the missing and misidentified buildings and monuments attributed to the period of Hadrian's rule. The latter category includes the Anaglypha Traiani/Hadriani, and the Tondi Adrianei now on the Arch of Constantine. There are chapters on: the Campus Martius; the Imperial Fora; the Forum Romanum; Imperial residences; Hadrian's Mausoleum and the Pons Aelius. There is also an appendix on the Obeliscus Antinoi, which in the 16th century stood outside Porta Maggiore and is now in the gardens of the Pincio. At the end of the book there is a catalogue which provides a general chronology of Hadrian's public buildings and urban changes.

341 **In this most perfect paradise: Alberti, Nicholas V, and the invention of conscious urban planning in Rome, 1447-55.**
Carroll William Westfall. University Park, Pennsylvania; London: The Pennsylvania State University Press, 1974. 244p. bibliog.
This work examines the attempt of Nicholas V to give Rome a unified urban structure, joining the papal quarter to the city proper and transforming the city into a symbol of papal supremacy. The author argues that this master plan grew out of Nicholas's knowledge of, and admiration for, Alberti's work.

342 **Mussolini urbanista: lo sventramento di Roma negli anni del consenso.** (Mussolini's town planning: demolitions in Rome in the Fascist era.)
Antonio Cederna. Rome: Laterza, 1980. 289p. (Biblioteca di Cultura Moderna, 825.)
A study of Mussolini's town-planning policies, which radically changed the appearance of modern Rome. Included are eighty plates showing Rome before, during and after the demolitions as well as three plans of the demolitions carried out for the opening of the Via della Conciliazione, the Via dei Fori Imperiali, and the area west and south of the Capitoline Hill. Notable demolitions included the Baroque churches S. Adriano in the Curia del Senato and S. Rita. There are also biographies of the principal 'sventratori' (the men who planned these demolitions): Armando Brasini, Gustavo Giovannoni, Antonio Muñoz, Ugo Ojetti, Marcello Piacentini, Corrado Ricci and Virgilio Testa.

343 **Piazza Navona, centro di Roma.** (Piazza Navona, the centre of Rome.)
Armando Ravaglioli. Rome: Biblioteca romana, 1973. 199p.
The history of Piazza Navona spans some nineteen centuries. Originally Domitian's stadium, in the centre of Campo Marzio, a market place from the 15th century, it was turned, by Pope Innocent X Pamphilj, into one of the great stage-sets of the Baroque, thanks to its fountains and Borromini's architecture. In his short introductory note to this collection of views of the square, the author points out its different roles and functions – as open-air market, as a stage for theatrical

performances, religious and state occasions and festivals and, above all, as a meeting place for the people. He also compares it to other squares in Rome, and concludes that only Piazza Navona can lay claim to have been at the heart of Rome and Roman life throughout its history. The illustrations are divided into sections which include reconstructions of Domitian's stadium and photographs of its remains, views of the square in the Middle Ages and the Renaissance, the Baroque square, views of parts of the square, depictions of people and events in the square, the square in the last hundred years, popular life as seen in details from general views of the square, and the statue of Pasquino. The work includes a chronology from 86 AD, the date of the inauguration of Domitian's Stadium, to 1968, when the square was pedestrianized.

344 Piazze e nuovi luoghi di Roma: il progetto della conferma e della innovazione. (Squares and new spaces in Rome: the project of consolidation and innovation.)
Edited by Raffaele Panella. Rome: Fratelli Palombi, 1997. 231p. (Groma Volumi, 1.)

Post-war Rome has undergone many transformations. The centre of the city is now largely non-residential, while its sprawling suburbs offer housing without the necessary infrastructures. It has become a polycentric city, i.e. a metropolitan area containing numerous individual nuclei. 'Centopiazze per Roma' (One hundred squares for Rome) is a programme of the Comune of Rome promoting and co-ordinating various projects which attempt to transform these separate nuclei into a unified whole. Four projects are described: Porta San Paolo, Tuscolano Selinunte, Torre Angela, and the new 'Porta Trionfale'. The volume also contains essays examining similar projects elsewhere in Italy and in other European cities.

345 I ponti di Roma. (The bridges of Rome.)
Sergio Delli. Rome: Newton Compton, 1979. 2nd rev. ed. 282p. (Quest'Italia, 5.)

In his introduction, the author refers to the sacred nature of bridges in both Ancient and Christian Rome, pointing out the role of the *pontifex* as a bridge between the believer and God. The history of the bridges of Rome is related, with an abundance of anecdotes, in four chapters: from earliest times to the year 1000; 1000-1870; 1870-1940, and 1945 to the present. At the end of each chapter there is a list of the bridges constructed during the period examined and their present state (or, if no longer extant, their presumed location). A fifth chapter looks at bridges over the Aniene and other smaller rivers the history of which is related to Rome. There are two appendices: the first is an anthology of poems in Roman dialect having bridges as their subject matter, the second twenty-eight views of Roman bridges in old photographs.

346 I ponti di Roma: dalle collezioni del Gabinetto nazionale delle stampe. (The bridges of Rome: from the collections of the Gabinetto nazionale delle stampe.)
Edited by Maria Catelli Isola and Enrichetta Beltrame Quattrocchi. Rome: De Luca, 1975. 228p.

The catalogue of an exhibition held at the Villa Farnesina in 1975. It includes 226 prints and drawings from the 15th to the 19th century from the Gabinetto nazionale delle stampe at the Uffizi Gallery. These range from maps and bird's eye views of the city and its bridges to depictions of particular bridges or events (for example, the Ponte S. Angelo with the Girandola fireworks displays). Roman bridges also feature in historical, allegorical or religious subjects such as Marcantonio Raimondi's *Massacre of the Innocents*, in which Ponte Fabricio appears in the background. There are numerous indexes including subject and artist indexes.

347 The Protestant Cemetery in Rome, the 'Parte Antica'.
Edited by Antonio Menniti Ippolito, Paolo Vian. Rome: Unione internazionale degli istituti di archeologia, storia e storia dell'arte in Roma, 1989. 379p. bibliog.

The non-Catholic cemetery at Testaccio, known as the 'Protestant Cemetery', is in an exceptional location (near the pyramid of Caius Cestius) and the variety of its monuments and their inscriptions attest to the cosmopolitan nature of Rome. This publication is the result of a project carried out by the Unione internazionale degli istituti di archeologia, storia e storia dell'arte in Roma (International Union of the Institutes of Archaeology, History and History of Art in Rome) to record the monuments of the cemetery and preserve the evidence they offer. The core of the work is a section that provides an objective archaeological description of the monuments in the *Parte antica* (Old part) of the cemetery, recording their types and inscriptions and including indexes of places and words appearing in them. There are also essays on the cemetery's history, and biographies of English and Irish people buried there, among them Keats, and Joseph Severn, the poet's friend. Texts are mostly in English but with contributions also in Italian or German. See also *North American records in Italy: the Protestant cemetery in Rome*, by Revalee Stevens and Robert Kim Stevens (Baton Rouge, Louisiana: Oracle Press, 1981. 116p.).

348 The Rome of Alexander VII, 1655-1667.
Richard Krautheimer. Princeton, New Jersey: Princeton University Press, 1985. 213p.

Pope Alexander VII Chigi (1655-67) was one of the great builder popes who, more than any of his great predecessors from Julius II to Urban VII, changed the face and image of Rome. His remapping of Rome greatly contributed to ruining the finances of the 17th-century papacy. This study sets the scene with an examination of the concept of *teatro* (grand architectural design, 'showpiece') in Alexandrine Rome, and a biographical sketch and character portrait of Alexander VII pointing out his vanity, catastrophic financial short-sightedness, and artistic interests – he had little feeling for painting but a real passion for architecture and monumental sculpture. The following chapter looks at the urban substructure of Rome and the key elements in Alexander's policies – the creation of long, unencumbered streets providing far vistas, spacious squares dominated by monumental sculptures, and the realignment of buildings placed conspicuously within the fabric of the city. The work of Alexander's architects is examined next, and subsequent chapters examine not only the projects carried out during Alexander's reign but also those which – like the project for the Piazza Colonna – though well-documented, were never brought to fruition due to lack of time or funds but are nevertheless useful in outlining his vision. Among his successes are Saint Peter's Square, the Piazza del Popolo, the church of S. Maria della Pace and its square, S. Maria in Campitelli, and the Piazza del Pantheon. There are also chapters on the interweaving of city planning and stage design, especially in the case of the Piazza del Popolo, on Alexander's attitude toward the monuments of Ancient Rome, and on city planning and politics. The 111 accompanying illustrations (engravings, photographs, architectural drawings and maps) are magnificent and the work is further enhanced by the detailed notes, which include numerous references to archival and printed sources.

349 Stradario Romano: dizionario storico, etimologico-topografico. (A Roman itinerary: a historical, etymological and topographical dictionary.) Benedetto Blasi. Rome: A. F. Formíggini, 1933. 354p. maps.

The publisher's introductory note states that this is a revised, and much augmented edition of the work originally published in 1923 (as *Vie, piazze e ville di Roma nel loro valore storico e topografico* [Streets, squares and villas of Rome in their proper historical and topographical context]), incorporating the new streets and squares created in the intervening ten years thanks to the Fascist regime's town-planning policies. The entries provide useful information on the history and etymology of place names and indications about their notable features. The text is accompanied by 120 plates reproducing water-colours by Ettore Roesler-Franz and two maps.

350 Le strade di Roma. (The streets of Rome.) Sergio Delli. Rome: Newton & Compton, 1975. 895p. bibliog. (Italia Nostra, 1.)

A useful alphabetical guide to the streets of Rome, their history, folklore, notable buildings and works of art. The introduction surveys the development of the streets and their nomenclature from antiquity – when they were often named after a consul, a notable monument, the origins of their inhabitants, or their use as pasture ground – to the Middle Ages and the Renaissance – when they were often named after notable families whose palaces with their turrets were the dominant features. The 19th century saw the numbering of each individual house during the Napoleonic occupation of the city and, after 1870, the often unsuccessful attempts to tuscanize the names of certain streets. The main features of the two town-planning schemes (the 'piani regolatori') of 1873 and 1883 and the resulting demolitions that changed the appearance of the city are also analysed, as are later developments such as the creation of new residential areas. The text is accompanied by numerous illustrations (maps, plans, woodcuts and lithographs).

351 I suoli di Roma: uso e abuso del territorio nei cento anni della capitale. (The ground of Rome: land use and abuse during the first one hundred years of the capital.) Piero Della Seta, Roberto della Seta. Rome: Editori riuniti, 1988. 282p. (Biblioteca di Storia, 126.)

This is a chronological survey of town planning in Rome, beginning with the building fever and property speculation in the new capital in the 1870s and ending with the attempts at urban regeneration of the left-wing administration in the 1970s. It gives a vivid description of the main features of the so-called 'oil stain' expansion of the city. It discusses the sale, in 1873, of ecclesiastical property in Rome and the Roman Campagna; the destruction of the great aristocratic villas, the 'green belt' of the city; the property development policies of the progressive administration of Ernesto Nathan (1907-12); the town planning of the Fascist era and the creation of twelve borgate, the housing estates built to accommodate immigrants and the former inhabitants of the areas demolished in the centre of the city; and the policies of the post-war administrations. See also *Roma: la crescita metropolitana abusiva* (Rome: the abusive metropolitan growth) by Pietrenzo Piazzo (Rome: Officina edizioni, 1982. 257p.).

352 Three Christian capitals: topography and politics.
Richard Krautheimer. Berkeley, Los Angeles; London: University of California Press, 1983. 181p.

Four lectures demonstrating that the architectural monuments of Rome, Constantinople and Milan (the three Christian capitals of the 4th and 5th centuries) and their location reflect the political realities and ideologies of the time. The first and fourth lectures are on Constantinian and early papal Rome. The first examines the political motives behind Emperor Constantine's choice of site for the Cathedral of Rome, founded in 312 at the Lateran, far from the populous quarters and the monumental centre of the still predominantly pagan city. It points out the inherent contradiction between, on the one hand, the choice of sites for Christian churches on the outskirts of the city to avoid causing offence and, on the other, their enormous scale and conspicuousness. The fourth lecture looks at developments one century later. By then, Christianity had become the established religion of Rome and the Pope its de facto ruler. The remote location of the Cathedral was no longer politically expedient but inconvenient, as it isolated the Pope from the population. Attempting to remedy the situation and to bring the Pope closer to his flock, new sumptuous 'subsidiary cathedrals' were created around the Lateran (S. Maria Maggiore, S. Stefano Rotondo) and liturgical changes were introduced (baptism was no longer only performed in the Lateran basilica). This was, however, an abortive attempt and was counterbalanced by the growing importance of S. Peter's on the opposite edge of Rome, and the 15th century saw the final reversal of the map of Rome from S. Giovanni in Laterano in the south east to S. Peter's in the north east.

353 Urbanistica, edilizia, infrastrutture di Roma Capitale, 1870-1990: una cronologia. (Town planning, construction works, and infrastructures of Rome the Capital, 1870-1990: a chronology.)
Giuseppe Cuccia, edited by Vincenzo Calabrese, Sabrina Cantalini, Alessandra Criconia. Rome: Editori Laterza, 1991. 342p. bibliog.

A systematic chronological presentation of data related to the development of Rome from 1870 to the present. An introductory chapter gives an overview of Rome in 1870. This is followed by three chapters describing different phases of the city's development and comparing programmes and proposals with the actual results. The final chapter is a series of thoughts on the eve of the millennium. The descriptions in each of the three central chapters are followed by chronological tables with information about town planning, new buildings, and the evolution of infrastructures during the period, and also relevant information about politics, economics, and legislation. The three periods covered are 1870 to 1914, 1914 to 1944, and 1945 to 1990. The chronology is divided into six sections: politics and the economy; the expansion of the city and legislation; town planning; infrastructures, transport and services; public building works and monuments; and housing. The volume is richly illustrated with photographs, drawings, plans, and various tables. There is also a selection of documentary material (including texts of laws and decrees) and several indices.

Gardens

354 Gardens of Rome.
Gabriel Faure. London: Nicholas Kaye, 1960. 200p. map.

This work by the prolific travel writer and near-namesake of the famous composer was originally published in French as *Les jardins de Rome*. This English edition contains 168 splendid heliogravure illustrations which, however, do not always correspond to the garden described by the text. The author identifies three essential elements in the composition of Roman gardens: evergreen trees (ilexes, pines, cypresses and laurels), marble artefacts (vases, busts, statues, porticoes and balustrades arranged in carefully planned groups), and moving waters (fountains, waterfalls and basins). The gardens are examined in chronological order beginning with an evocation of the gardens of antiquity, followed by the gardens of the great Renaissance villas (Aldobrandini, Mattei, Medici, Madama, Farnesina, Colonna and Giulia), the 17th- and 18th-century gardens (Villa Doria-Pamphilj, Villa Albani-Torlonia, Villa Bonaparte and Priory of Malta), and the 19th-century parks and public promenades (Giardino Borghese, Pincio and Sciarra). The work also includes Rome's fountains and other green spaces and promenades, as well as the Protestant Cemetery and the Military Cemetery at Monte Mario. Finally, some of the famous gardens in the surroundings of Rome are also visited – the D'Este gardens at Tivoli and the gardens of Frascati, Albano, Ariccia, Genzano and Nemi.

355 Guida ai giardini perduti di Roma. (Vanished gardens of Rome: a guide book.)
Roberto Lucifero, edited by Luigi Berliocchi. Rome: Di Baio, 1995. 136p.

This book looks at the now lost landscape of vineyards, orchards, woods, villas and gardens that for centuries surrounded Rome. Some of these were destroyed in the post-1870 expansion of the city while others are now in a ruinous state. Seventeen of the most significant villas and their grounds are described in as many chapters. Each contains an historical outline describing the changing fortunes of the location and is accompanied by photographs showing its present state, an artist's impression attempting to 'reinvent' the original architecture and garden, drawings, engravings and period photographs. Villas discussed include Villa Mattei, the Orti Farnesiani, Villa Ludovisi, Villa Pamphilj, and Villa Corsini ai Quattro Venti. There is also a separate section with texts on the poetry of ruins, sculptures in villas and gardens, obelisks, labyrinths, the garden and Baroque theatre, and botanical collections. The text is in Italian with English translations.

Flora and fauna

356 Atlante degli uccelli nidificanti a Roma. (Atlas of breeding birds in Rome.)
Edited by Bruno Cignini and Marzio Zapparoli. Rome: Fratelli Palombi, 1996. 126p. maps. bibliog.

This work lists seventy-five species of birds.

357 Flora d'Italia. (Flora of Italy.)
Sandro Pignatti. Bologna, Italy: Edagricole, 1982. 3 vols. bibliog.
The flora of Italy is the richest in Europe. The introduction to this comprehensive guide to vascular plants in Italy gives a history of botanical studies in the peninsula from the 14th century to the present. It also describes earlier compilations of the flora of Italy edited by Antonio Bertoloni (1833-54), Filippo Parlatore (1848-96), G. Arcangeli (1882), V. Cesati, G. Passerini and G. Gibelli (1868-86), and Adriano Fiori (1923-29). The present work describes 5,599 plants. Each entry is accompanied by drawings (mostly original though some are taken from A. Fiori's work) and a map of the Italian peninsula indicating regional distribution. There is a vocabulary of technical terms, a list of protected plants, a list of the 168 families of plants described together with an analytical key, and an index of Italian and dialect names with cross references to their Latin names.

358 Guida alla natura del Lazio e Abruzzo. (A guide to the nature of Lazio and Abruzzo.)
Fulco Pratesi, Franco Tassi. Milan, Italy: Arnaldo Mondadori, 1977. 319p. maps. (Libri illustrati Mondadori.)
The first half of this guide is dedicated to the fauna and flora of Lazio. Twenty-three areas are examined, including Rome, the Roman Campagna, the Alban Hills, the Sabine mountains, and the Ciociara. At the end of the volume there is a section suggesting tourist itineraries which includes information on artistic and other notable features.

359 Gli insetti di Roma. (Insects of Rome.)
Edited by Marzio Zapparoli. Rome: Fratelli Palombi, 1997. 358p. maps. bibliog. (Quaderni dell'ambiente, 6.)
This work brings together the results of research carried out into the insect fauna of the urban and suburban area of Rome since the beginning of the 19th century. The area examined lies within the 'Grande Raccordo Anulare' – the 1950s ringroad surrounding the city – which has a surface of *c.* 360 square kilometres and includes urban, green and river areas. The species recorded are critically revised and listed. The main body of the publication is an annotated list of all the insect species in Rome, each entry illustrated and with its own bibliography. Entries are in Italian or English and there is also an English summary and numerous maps and plans showing the distribution of the various species.

360 The Paper Museum of Cassiano Dal Pozzo: a catalogue raisonné: Series B, Natural history.
Francis Haskell, Jennifer Montagu (general editors), David Freedberg (series editor). London: Harvey Miller, 1997- . bibliog.
The publication of the *catalogue raisonné* of drawings and prints originally in Cassiano dal Pozzo's 'Paper Museum' and now in the Royal Library at Windsor Castle, the British Museum, the Institut de France and other collections is projected to be in eighteen volumes published in two series – Series A covering antiquities and architecture, and Series B covering natural history. Series B will include eight volumes on: citrus fruit; fungi; geological collections; birds; animals, fish and other fauna; the 'Erbario miniato' and other flora; a 'Syntaxis Plantaria'; and the Mexican Herbal. The first volume of this series has been published to date. As in the companion series, the catalogue proper is preceded by a general introduction to the Paper Museum of Cassiano Dal Pozzo giving an account of the development of the collection and its subsequent changes of ownership and vicissitudes. This is followed by an essay on the Natural History

collections. These provide important visual documentation for some key developments in the study of mycology, botany, and zoology carried out by members of the Accademia dei Lincei; they are also one of the first attempts at a classification of the natural world through visual description. Some 3,000 natural history drawings survive from Cassiano's collection, only a portion of the material commissioned and collected. There is also an essay on the role of Cassiano's Paper Museum in citrus taxonomy. The catalogue has 118 items, all of which are reproduced in colour. As explained in another introductory essay, a large number of these are by Vincenzo Leonardi and were executed to illustrate Giovanni Battista Ferrari's *Hesperides* (1646), a sumptuous book on citrus fruit, an encyclopaedic combination of literature, mythology, botany, and etymology. It was produced in collaboration with Cassiano, who provided Ferrari with information he had gathered from various correspondents throughout Italy. All the plates in *Hesperides* are reproduced in the present catalogue, which also includes a glossary.

361 Where to watch birds in Italy.
Lega italiana protezione uccelli. London: Christopher Helm, A. & C. Black, 1994. 224p. maps. (Where to Watch Birds Series.)

This book includes a chapter on Lazio with sections on: Lago di Bracciano, Valle del Baccano and Lago di Martignano; Maccarese and environs; Lago Vico; Rome; Nazzano-Tevere-Farfa Regional Reserve; Valle Mignone and Tarquinia saltworks; Tolfa mountains; the area around Ladispoli; Circeo national park; and Monte Cairo and Fiume Melfa canyon. Each section includes itineraries, habitat, species to be seen at the site listed, timing (the best period to visit the site), access (the best routes to the site from the nearest large town), a calendar (species that may observed according to season), useful contacts, and a bibliography. Several itineraries include maps.

Monuments

362 Le fontane di Roma. (The fountains of Rome.)
Bruno Brizzi. Rome: Colombo, 1987. 335p.

In the preface, the author points out the state of dilapidation of the lesser-known fountains in Rome (for example, 'internal' fountains in convents, courtyards etc.) and indicates that this work is primarily a photographic record of monuments threatened with destruction. It is divided into two parts. The first part is a chronological survey and includes chapters on: fountains in Ancient Rome up to their demise in 537 AD, when Vitige destroyed the overground aqueducts; the renewed use in the 16th century of the Acqua Vergine (which served Campo Marzio), followed by the Acqua Felice (which served the higher areas); the 17th century; and, finally, the 19th and 20th centuries. The second part is a survey of fountains by *rione* or quarter. It includes 250 illustrations accompanied by informative captions.

363 Le fontane di Roma. (The fountains of Rome.)
Cesare D'Onofrio. Rome: Romana società editrice, 1986. 3rd rev. ed. 564p. (Collana di Studi e Testi per la Storia della Città di Roma.)

The first two parts of this enlarged edition cover the 16th century, the aqueduct and the fountains of the Acqua Vergine, and those of the Acqua Felice. Parts three and four examine the Aqueduct

Paolo and the 17th-century fountains, and the fountains of Pietro and Gianlorenzo Bernini. Part five considers the fountains of the following three centuries, and part six looks at fountains in villas, gardens and courtyards.

364   Le fontane di Roma. (The fountains of Rome.)
Willy Pocino, illustrated by Franco Zampetti.   Rome: Newton Compton, 1996. 511p. bibliog. (Quest'Italia, 229.)

This study of Rome's fountains is arranged alphabetically by location, with an analytical index by name of fountain.

365   Fountains of Rome.
Photographs by Francesco Venturi, text by Mario Sanfilippo.   New York: the Vendome Press, 1996. 191p. map.

This is described, in a note to the reader, as a photographic *volume d'auteur*, with an accompanying introduction and outlines providing a framework and commentary to Francesco Venturi's exceptionally beautiful colour photographs. The text is divided into two sections. The first examines the social uses of water in the three cities of Rome (Ancient, Christian/Papal, Capital of Italy), while the second examines different types of fountains. These include: major fountain groups in Rome's squares (Piazza del Popolo, Piazza Navona, Piazza S. Pietro and Piazza Farnese); the Villa fountains (Villa Madama, Villa Giulia, Quirinal Palace Gardens, Villa Medici, the Vatican, Villa Borghese and Villa Doria Pamphilj); 'ballerina' fountains – fountains that have been repeatedly relocated from one part of the city to another and have reused, either partially or entirely, material from antiquity (the fountains in Piazza Nicosia, Piazza San Simeone, at S. Andrea della Valle, at Ripetta, and the Fontana del Babuino); the 'neighbourhood' fountains (*fontanelle*) of Pietro Lombardi, which were constructed in the 1920s and 1930s celebrating the dominant craft of each neighbourhood; and, finally, various other fountains in roughly chronological order.

366   Papal epigraphy in Renaissance Rome.
Iiro Kajanto; the chapters on paleography by Ulla Nyberg.   Helsinki: Suomalainen Tiedeakademia, 1982. 143p. (Suomalaisen Tiedeakademian Toimituksia: Annales Academiæ Scientiarum Fennicæ, Ser. B, tom. 222.)

The epitaphs of the popes represent a long tradition, from classical antiquity to the present. Their length varies from the mere name of a pope to long, commemorative inscriptions. This study assesses the informative value of papal epitaphs from the period between Martin V (d. 1431) and Paul III (d. 1549) and examines the influence of classical antiquity and epigraphy on their form and content. It also discusses inscriptions other than epitaphs, such as literary funeral epigrams and inscriptions recording constructions and restorations ordered by a pope. The introduction includes a useful discussion of earlier collections of papal epigraphs of various periods, pointing out that, though meticulously edited, they nevertheless contain little analysis and interpretation.

367 **Roma delle delizie: i teatri dell'acqua, grotte, ninfei, fontane.** (The delights of Rome: theatres of water, grottoes, nymphaea, fountains.) Marcello Fagiolo, Maria Luisa Madonna, photographs by Araldo De Luca. Translated by Antony Shugaar. Milan, Italy: Franco Maria Ricci, 1990. 227p. (Quadreria.)

The publisher's note to the reader fancifully describes this book as an invitation to a theatre where water is the protagonist of the evening's entertainment. The text (in English and Italian) is, accordingly, in a prologue and five acts which describe: the history and archetypes of the Nymphaeum (the first 'theatre of water'); the idea of theatre in Roman villas and gardens of the 16th century; the Casino of Pius IV in the Vatican; the Villa d'Este at Tivoli; the 'theatres of water' in the villas of Frascati; and Baroque Rome as a stage setting for waters. The thirty-two colour photographs of gardens, grottoes, fountains and garden sculpture, and the numerous colour plates reproducing works of art, are magnificent. See also *Roma, la città dell'acqua* (Rome, the city of water), edited by Angela Adriana Cavarra (Rome: Edizioni De Luca, 1994. 471p.).

368 **Strada Giulia.** (Via Giulia.) Ceccarius. Rome: [s.n.], [1940]. 125p. + [61] leaves of plates.

Via Giulia was the first and longest (it is over one kilometre long) rectilinear street in Rome, constructed over the Via Magistralis by Bramante on the orders of Pope Julius II. The plan to extend it to the Vatican was never carried out and, at Bramante's death in 1511, his grandiose Palazzo dei Tribunali (the Law Court Palace) was also left unfinished. The street became an important thoroughfare in the 16th century, but later it declined because of the expansion of the city in other zones. Today, the street is characterized by a mixture of styles and the juxtaposition of patrician palaces and more humble buildings. This authoritative portrait of Via Giulia by the eminent historian of Rome gives an account of the street's prehistory and its development in the 16th century, evokes legends and traditions associated with it, and describes several of its palaces and their inhabitants, and its churches (including those now demolished). The text is accompanied by sixty-one plates of drawings by Lucilio Cartocci and also by numerous maps and sketches.

369 **The Trevi Fountain.** John A. Pinto. New Haven, Connecticut; London: Yale University Press, 1986. 338p. bibliog.

The Trevi Fountain is the best known and most spectacular monument of 18th-century Rome, its grandiose fusion of sculpture, architecture and water inspiring innumerable artists, from Piranesi to Fellini. This scholarly monograph is in two parts. The first part examines the early history of the fountain, setting forth the archaeological and literary evidence about the Acqua Vergine, the Roman aqueduct suppplying the Trevi (the name is thought to derive from *trivium*, three streets converging on the fountain). It also examines the changing relationship between the Trevi and the developing city between 1453, when a smaller fountain was inaugurated by Pope Nicholas V, and the competition to design the Trevi Fountain in 1730. Various unexecuted projects for the fountain (which included proposals by Carlo Fontana, Filippo Juvarra, Luigi Vanvitelli and Edme Bouchardon) are also considered. The second part looks at Nicola Salvi's executed design and its iconographical programme, the construction history of the fountain and its place in the history of art – its relationship to the art and architecture of preceding periods and to contemporary monuments in Northern Europe – and, finally, the subsequent critical responses to the fountain.

370 Urbs Roma: a source book of classical texts on the city and its monuments.

Donald R. Dudley. London: Phaidon Press, 1967. 339p. maps.

A selection of classical primary sources – texts, coins, inscriptions – for the city of Rome and its monuments. Its geographical and chronological limits are the Aurelian Wall and the death of Constantine in 337 AD. The texts are given in translation where the originals are readily available and are arranged in three sections. Section one is on the site of Rome and the growth of the city; section two (by far the most extensive of the three) is about buildings and monuments; and section three is an anthology of praises of Rome. Each group of texts within each section is followed by the compiler's comments. The 'notes to the text' at the end amplify certain points in the text, and suggest books and articles for further reading. There are 110 illustrations, mostly chosen as working documents, and some of them have extended captions. There are four indices – of ancient authors, inscriptions, names, and principal places.

371 Via del Corso.

Edited by the Cassa di Risparmio di Roma. Rome: Cassa di Risparmio di Roma, 1961. 353p. bibliog.

This is a monumental study of Via del Corso, or 'il Corso' as it is familiarly known, the long street (over a mile long) that runs from Piazza del Popolo to Piazza Venezia. It is one of the oldest streets in Rome, corresponding to the urban section of the ancient Via Flaminia and, its southern part, to Via Lata. The study is in three sections. The first is a history of the street in antiquity and a survey of the monuments in its vicinity, which include the Mausoleum of Augustus, the Ara Pacis Augustae, the Column of Marcus Aurelius. The second part examines the history of the street from the Middle Ages to the present and also surveys the palazzi and churches that line the street, considering their history, architecture and artistic treasures. Famous palazzi on the Corso include Palazzo Doria Pamphilj, Palazzo Ruspoli, Palazzo Rondinini, Palazzo Mancini (until 1803 the seat of the Accademia di Francia), Palazzo Sciarra and Palazzo Chigi. Among its churches are S. Maria di Montesanto and S. Maria dei Miracoli, SS Ambrogio e Carlo al Corso, S. Lorenzo in Lucina, and S. Marcello. The third part looks at the life of the street through the centuries, especially the carnival festivities and the race of the riderless horses (from Piazza del Popolo to Piazza Venezia) that, during the 18th and 19th centuries, made it one of the most animated streets in Rome. The text is accompanied by 360 black-and-white plates and 18 tipped-in colour plates of depictions of the street in paintings, prints, and early and contemporary photographs. The architecture and works of art of the churches and palazzi are also discussed.

372 Via del Corso: una strada lunga 2000 anni. (Via del Corso: a 2000 years-long street.)

Edited by Cesare D'Onofrio. Rome: Edizioni De Luca, 1999. 219p.

This exhibition catalogue (Rome, 1999) is an excellent complement to the study discussed in entry no. 371. After a survey of the street's long history, other essays focus on more specific topics: the history of Michelangelo's *Pietà Rondanini*, a sculpture, now in the Castello Sforzesco in Milan, which in the 19th century was in the Palazzo Rondinini (now the seat of the Banca nazionale di agricoltura); the Column of Marcus Aurelius before its restoration under Sixtus V and the removal of the relief sculpture from its pedestal and the installation of the statue of St Paul on its summit; the Augustan monuments in the northern Campo Marzio – the Ara Pacis and the Sundial (of which a section of its meridian line was rediscovered during excavations in 1979-80 in the cellar of a house in Via Campo Marzio); depictions of Via del Corso and its vicinity on coins and medals; the carnival, other festivals and daily life on the

Corso from the 17th to the late 19th century, including depictions of processions, the race of the riderless horses, the street as one of Rome's centres of fashionable life with is famous cafés (the Caffè nuovo at Palazzo Ruspoli, the Caffè Aragno) and theatres (Teatro Fiano and its marionettes); and the aqueduct of Agrippa and the fountains of Acqua Vergine. There is also a reprint of an article by Rodolfo Lanciani describing the Corso in 1538 after the works carried out under Pope Paul III.

373 Via Giulia: una utopia urbanistica del 500. (Via Giulia: a sixteenth-century urban utopia.)
Luigi Salerno, Luigi Spezzaferro, Manfredo Tafuri. Rome: A. Staderini, [1973]. 541p. bibliog.

This is a comprehensive study of one of Rome's most famous streets. It is divided in two parts, the first examining the creation and development of the street in the context of the urban evolution of Rome in the 15th and 16th centuries, and the second providing a systematic and detailed survey of the street's most important buildings. Part one consists of three essays. The first looks at the urban policies of the papacy from Nicholas V to Julius II, in particular those related to the Vatican area and the plans to connect it to the rest of Rome through the development of a 'trident' of rectilinear streets converging toward the Ponte S. Angelo, to which was added, under Julius II, Via Giulia. The second essay examines the history and changing fortunes of the street from the 16th to the 20th century, pointing out its variety. The third essay provides a survey of the artists and patrons associated with the street, from its heyday during the Mannerist and Baroque periods to the late 19th century. The second section is an exhaustive presentation of all the notable buildings and other structures of Via Giulia, from the church of S. Giovanni dei Fiorentini to Ponte Sisto. Each entry contains an account of the building's history, a description of its architecture and decoration, and a survey of the works of art it contains; it also provides a full bibliography of primary and secondary sources. The work contains a profusion of black-and-white illustrations, architectural drawings, maps, engravings, photographs and twenty-four garishly coloured plates.

374 Le Vittoriano: monumentalité publique et politique à Rome. (The Vittoriano: public monumentality and politics in Rome.)
Catherine Brice. Rome: École française de Rome, Palais Farnèse, 1998. 439p. bibliog. (Bibliothèque des Écoles Françaises d'Athènes et de Rome, fasc. 301.)

A study of the genesis, construction and role during the Fascist era of the Victor Emmanuel II monument, commonly known as the Vittoriano or Altare della Patria (the Altar of the Fatherland) and, pejoratively, as 'the Typewriter', or 'the Wedding Cake'. It examines the political and social context of post-1870 Rome, the choice of site and its symbolic significance, the hundreds of projects for the monument submitted to the two competitions in 1882 and 1883-84 (these ranged from single columns and triumphal arches to temples, pantheons and monumental squares), its construction and transformation from a monument to Victor Emmanuel II to Altar of the Fatherland and, in 1920, monument of the Unknown Soldier, and, finally, the monument during the Fascist period. Interpolated chapters look at Victor Emmanuel the man, and his monument. The author also offers various reasons for the monument's lack of popularity – its gigantic scale, the enormous cost of its construction (60 million lire instead of the original budget of 10 million), mismanagement and, most importantly, its association in the collective consciousness with fascist ceremonies. The work includes a list of the ceremonies (between 1913-35) involving the monument.

Education

375 I maestri della Sapienza di Roma dal 1514 al 1787: I rotuli e altre fonti. (The professors of the Sapienza University in Rome from 1514 to 1787: the rolls and other sources.) Edited by Emanuele Conte. Rome: Istituto storico italiano per il Medioevo, 1991. 2 vols. 1141p. (Fonti per la Storia d'Italia pubblicate dall'Istituto Storico Italiano per il Medioevo, 116.)

This edition of the lists of teachers at the University of Rome (the *Studium Urbis* or Sapienza), based on a variety of documents, is a major source of information about the history of the institution over a period of two-and-a-half centuries. The University was founded in 1303 by Pope Boniface VIII but the compilation of the official rolls began during the reign of Pius II. The first surviving text dates from 1514 and the first surviving original from 1539. The rolls are kept at the Archivio di Stato di Roma, which also holds the rest of the University's archives. They are on large vellum sheets, most of which are richly decorated, and for this reason in 1972 they were separated from the rest of the University archives. This security precaution failed, however, to prevent the subsequent theft of five sheets. Moreover, there are numerous gaps in the 16th-century holdings and during the 17th century, the annual compilation of the rolls stopped and the richly decorated ones were only executed in the year following the accession of a new pope and were signed by him during a ceremonial presentation. In order to fill the 16th-century gaps, the editor has also used information contained in payment orders, and reports sent between 1566 and 1580 by Alessio Lorenzani, the janitor (*bedello*) of the University, to the Commission of Cardinals overseeing the University. As well as the names of all professors, these reports contain other interesting information about academic activities, all of which is transcribed in this edition. Also used are printed calendars (*bandi a stampa*) published from 1615 giving information about hours and subjects of lectures, which gradually replaced the official rolls. There is an index of names, with subjects taught and the years of appearance in the documents, as well as an index of Chairs and other university posts. See also *La 'Sapienza' romana nel Settecento: organizzazione universitaria e insegnamento del diritto* (The Roman 'Sapienza' in the eighteenth century: university organization and the teaching of law), by Maria Rosa Di Simone (Rome: Edizioni dell'Ateneo, 1980. 304p. [Studi e Fonti per la Storia dell' Università di Roma, 1]).

376 **Roma e lo *Studium Urbis*: spazio urbano e cultura dal Quattro al Seicento.** (Rome and the *Studium Urbis*: urban space and culture from the fifteenth to the seventeenth century.)
Edited by Paolo Cherubini. Rome: Ministero per i beni culturali e ambientali, Ufficio centrale per i beni archivistici, 1992. 554p. (Pubblicazioni degli Archivi di Stato: Saggi, 22.)

The proceedings of a conference organized in Rome in 1989. The conference examined both the history of the University, its archives, and the architecture of the Palazzo della Sapienza, and also the wider social and cultural context – other centres of learning (libraries, colleges); life in the university, its students and teachers; the presence of foreigners; the growth of activities related to the University (book printing and book selling); and the establishment of the first academies at the beginning of the 17th century. The papers amount to a reconstruction of the cultural environment of the *rione* S. Eustachio, between the Pantheon and Piazza Navona, and its various cultural institutions, its printers, booksellers and other artisans operating in the vicinity of the University. There are three indices: of names, places and manuscript locations.

377 **University of the Nations: the story of the Gregorian University of Rome from 1551 to Vatican II.**
Philip Caraman. New York; Ramsey, New Jersey: Paulist Press, 1981. 157p.

The Gregorian University was founded by St Ignatius of Loyola in 1551 as the Collegium Romanum (with the Germanicum – a hall of residence for students from Germany attending classes at the Collegium – opening eighteen months later). Its aims were both pastoral and missionary. Both its professors and students come from all over the world and its graduates have included several great figures of the Catholic Church, among them nineteen canonized saints and sixteen popes. This history of the university examines the development of the institution against the background of the social and political events which affected the Society of Jesus. The University, originally located in Via Capitolina, in 1557 moved to Palazzo Salviati, on the corner of the Via Lata and Via della Strada. In 1582, a new building was erected between the church of S. Maria sopra Minerva and the Corso, thanks to the munificence of Pope Gregory XIII, who had already assured a firm financial basis for the College through the endowment of an annual income from the papal treasury. The study also looks at the personalities and influence of the various teachers that made the College famous throughout the world. The Roman College became renowned as a clearing house of scientific information as Jesuits from all corners of the globe sent reports of their theoretical and practical discoveries. The work also describes student life in the various Jesuit colleges, the role of the *repetitore* and the spiritual director and also the Jesuit involvement in various theological controversies. The University's sister institutions, the Pontificio Istituto Biblico (established in 1909) and the Pontificio Istituto Orientale (established in 1917), are also discussed. An appendix lists alumni of the University, which include numerous saints and popes.

Science and Philosophy

378 Galileo Galilei and the Roman Curia.
Karl von Gebler. London: C. Kegan Paul & Co., 1879. 356p.

This account remains the most detailed examination of Galileo's relations with the Roman Curia and his trial and condemnation. It makes ample use of original documents, which include Galileo's correspondence, the acts of the trial, and the reports of Francesco Niccolini (the Tuscan ambassador to Rome) during and after the trial. It also gives a broad outline of Galileo's aims and achievements as a whole. It is in three parts, the first describing Galileo's early years, his discoveries, and his first conflict with the Roman Curia in 1616, and Cardinal Bellarmine's admonition, and assumed order, to abandon the Copernican system. It also describes the character of Pope Urban VIII (Maffeo Barberini), a friend of Galileo, who refused his suggestion to rescind the edict of 1616 banning the work of Copernicus but who also, unaware that Galileo had been ordered never to teach Copernicanism again, gave him permission to write a book comparing the old and new astronomies. Part two discusses the publication of the *Dialogues concerning the two principal systems of the world* (1632), the discovery of the assumed prohibition of 1616, Galileo's summons to Rome, his trial before the Inquisition, his sentence to life imprisonment (later commuted to house arrest), and his recantation. Part three looks at Galileo's last years at Siena and Acetri. See also Giorgio de Santillana's *The crime of Galileo* (London: Heinemann, 1958. 354p.).

379 Il processo di Giordano Bruno. (The trial of Giordano Bruno.)
Luigi Firpo, edited by Diego Quaglioni. Rome: Salerno, 1993. 404p. (Profili, 15.)

This is a collection of seventy-six documents related to the trial of Giordano Bruno, accompanied by a reprint (with corrections) of Luigi Firpo's essay on the trial originally published in 1948-49 in the *Rivista storica italiana*. The introduction surveys Firpo's numerous works on the philosopher and pays tribute to his forty years of research on the documentary evidence of the trial, which involved the collection and transcription of the documents, the establishment of a critical apparatus, and a new chronology for the trial (which lasted over eight years, from Bruno's arrest in May 1592 to his execution at the stake on 17 February 1600). The introductory essay by Firpo describes the various stages of the trial and its conclusion, examines and summarizes the three explanations offered by various scholars about the trial's outcome – Bruno's absolute conviction about his philosophical credo; his total failure to accept any compromise and religious reform; and a psychological fault in Bruno's character made up of a mixture of contempt about his judges, despair, pride, and madness.

Literature

General

380   Gabriele D'Annunzio: defiant archangel.
John Woodhouse.   Oxford, England: Clarendon Press, 1998. 417p.

This biography of Gabriele D'Annunzio (1863-1938) gives a lively account of his formative years in Rome, his journalistic activities, numerous liaisons, his marriage in 1883 to Maria Hardouin Gallese (the daughter of the then owner of Palazzo Altemps), and his first literary works. The poet arrived in Rome in 1881 and soon became a regular contributor to Eduardo Scarfoglio's weekly *Il Capitan Fracassa*. He also wrote for a number of other newspapers – *Domenica del Fracassa*, *Il Fanfulla*, *Il Fanfulla della Domenica*, and Angelo Sommaruga's *Cronaca bizantina*. In 1884, he became the editor of Prince Maffeo Sciarra Colonna's *Tribuna*, to which he contributed, over the following four years, some 260 articles on a bewildering variety of subjects, in different styles, and under different sobriquets. In 1885, he also directed Sciarra's short-lived *Cronaca bizantina*, which appeared after the cessation of Sommaruga's publication. *Il Piacere*, D'Annunzio's first novel, set in the fashionable quarters of Rome, was published in 1889 to wide acclaim. Rome also features prominently in other works by D'Annunzio, both in prose and poetry. In his prose works, the evocation of the Villa Ludovisi (destroyed during the urban expansion of Rome in the 1870s) in *Le Vergini delle Rocce* is justly famous. His collection *Elegie romane* (Roman elegies), written between 1887 and 1891 and first published in 1892, also evoke the city, as does the much later *Notturno* (1921).

381   Rerum familiarium libri I-VIII. (Letters on familiar matters. Books I-VIII.)
Francesco Petrarca, translated by Aldo S. Bernardo.   Albany, New York: State University of New York Press, 1975. 471p.

The *Letters on familiar matters*, which Petrarch addressed to a circle of intimate friends, were written between 1325 and 1366 and collected by the poet himself into twenty-four books, in non-chronological groupings. The first eight books cover the period up to 1350 and include several letters addressed to the Colonna family, charting the preparations for his first visit to Rome (II, 9), his arrival in 1337 and first impressions of the city (II, 14), and his coronation as Poet Laureate on the Campidoglio in 1341 (IV, 3-8). The poet was undecided as to whether to choose Paris, where he had been invited by his friend Roberto de' Bardi, the Chancellor of the University of Paris, or Rome, where he had been invited by the Senate. Rome, his spiritual home, finally won. The letters also show the poet's initial enthusiasm for Cola di Rienzo (VII 5, 7).

382 Rome: a literary companion.
John Varriano. London, England: John Murray, 1991. 286p. maps.

This guide is arranged as a series of ten walks through the city. These are preceded by an introductory chapter which describes the lure of Rome through the ages, the practicalities of the journey and accommodation, the travellers' guides and cultural baggage, and a miscellany of Roman impressions, from Petrarch to Virginia Woolf. In each chapter the author provides both his own description of the sights of Rome and also evokes the impressions and reactions of past visitors to the Eternal City. These include artists, writers (including other travel writers), historians and poets. Descriptions by writers (like Edgar Allan Poe) who never visited Rome are also included. The juxtaposition of opinions from different periods occasionally highlights the changing reputations of particular artists and styles and it is ironic that in describing the changing fortunes of the portrait of Beatrice Cenci, in the 19th century attributed to Guido Reni and one of the most famous works in Rome, and the artist's later eclipse, Varriano, whose dislike of 17th century art is also expressed elsewhere in the book, seems to be unaware that a major reassessment of the art of the Baroque era, which in the nine years since the publication of this book has brought artists like Reni, Guercino and Carracci back into favour, was already gathering impetus. Occasional inaccuracies – Baudelaire, who never visited Italy, is included among the illustrious patrons of the Caffè Greco – and omissions (François-Marius Granet) do not spoil the pleasure of reading the text. The bibliography is divided into primary and secondary sources.

383 Stendhal, Roma, Italia. (Stendhal, Rome, Italy.)
Edited by Massimo Colesanti (et al.). Rome: Edizioni di storia e letteratura, 1985. 607p. (Quaderni di Cultura Francese, 23.)

The proceedings of an international conference held in Rome in 1983, the bicentenary of the birth of Stendhal. Several of the 32 papers are specifically about Rome in Stendhal's travel writings or fiction. They include an overview of 'the Rome of Stendhal' by Massimo Colesanti, and papers on the writer's responses to Roman classicism, Neo-classicism, Roman theatre, puppet theatre, and Italian opera, as well as studies of his *Chroniques italiennes* (Italian chronicles). An appendix provides a useful chronological table of theatrical and operatic performances in Rome during Stendhal's sojourns.

384 Torquato Tasso a Roma: ricerche storiche. (Torquato Tasso in Rome: historical researches.)
Virginio Prinzivalli. Rome: Libreria Desclée Lefebvre, 1895. 195p.

Astonishingly, this study, published on the occasion of the tercentenary of the death of the poet, still remains the only monograph to have been written about Tasso in Rome. It examines in turn each of the nine sojourns of Tasso in the city, from the first one in 1554 at the age of seven to his last in 1594-95, which ended with his death on the eve of his coronation on the Capitol. The study also describes all the locations and people in Rome associated with the poet. It also lists works of art in public collections inspired by Tasso's work, and enumerates and discusses manuscripts and rare editions of his work in Roman libraries or books annotated by him.

385 Writing Rome: textual approaches to the city.
Catharine Edwards.   Cambridge, England: Cambridge University Press, 1996. 158p. (Roman Literature and Its Contexts.)

An examination of the relationship between ancient Roman literature and the city of Rome, both as a place and an idea, as a symbol of eternity and also of the fragility of all human achievement, of the triumph of Christianity and the lasting authority of the pagan literature. Its focus is literature written about the city in antiquity, interpreting the city in a multiplicity of ways – stories of its foundation, praise of its buildings, and the laments of those obliged to leave it. The study explores the relationship between written and material Romes, bringing together different disciplines – history, archaeology and literary criticism. It discusses: Rome as a repository of personal or communal memories (for example, places associated with Romulus, Rome's founder); the city's religious identity, and its relationship with its mythical predecessor Troy; the changing symbolism of the Capitoline Hill; associations of Rome's great public buildings; and perspectives of Romans in exile compared to perspectives of visitors to Rome in later centuries. It also discusses the disappearance of some of the most famous buildings of antiquity (for example the Temple of Jupiter Capitolinus) and of some of the treatises on the antiquities of Rome, notably Marcus Terentius Varro's *Antiquitates rerum humanarum* (On human antiquities) (twenty-five books) and *Antiquitates rerum divinarum* (On divine antiquities) (sixteen books), which were sources for many ancient writers on the city of Rome (for example St Augustine in his *De Civitate Dei* [The City of God]), although only fragments have survived to the present. It also considers descriptions of the city in writers from Livy and Horace to Petrarch, Gibbon and Byron.

Fiction

386 The agony and the ecstasy.
Irving Stone.   New York: New American Library, 1996. 776p.

Irving Stone (1903-89) called his novels studying the life and work of a historical character, based on exhaustive research on his subject's period and background, 'bio-histories'. *The Agony and the Ecstasy* is, with *The Lust for Life* (on Van Gogh), his most popular work. It is an account of Michelangelo's genius and of the political, social and spiritual issues that influenced his art. The artist's years in Rome begin with chapter five. This edition includes a bibliography, a glossary and a list of the artist's works and their present locations. The 1965 film based on the novel and focusing on the creation of the Sistine Chapel ceiling and Michelangelo's often stormy relationship with Pope Julius II was directed by Carol Reed, with Charlton Heston (Michelangelo) and Rex Harrison (Julius II).

387 Alì dagli occhi azzurri. (Blue-eyed Alì.)
Pier Paolo Pasolini.   Milan, Italy: Garzanti, 1996. 515p. (Gli Elefanti.)

A collection of short stories and other works set in Rome written between 1950 and 1965. They include stories Pasolini later turned into the screenplays of his films *Accattone* (1960), *Mamma Roma* (1961), and *La ricotta* (the episode directed by Pasolini in the film *RoGoPaG* in 1962 – a portmanteau film whose acronymic title is made up of the names of the four contributing directors: Rossellini, Godard, Pasolini and Gregoretti). Another short story in this collection, *La notte brava* (1957), became the screenplay of the film directed by Mauro Bolognini.

388 Bicycle thieves.
Luigi Bartolini. London: White Lion Publishers, 1972. 127p.

The fame of the Vittorio de Sica film, one of the great neorealist masterpieces, has obscured that of the novel on which it was based, published two years earlier, in 1946. Luigi Bartolini (1892-1963) is now better known as an engraver rather than as a novelist and a poet. *Bicycle thieves* is partly an autobiographical work. It is the simple story of a search for a stolen bicycle, set against a background of the streets and slums of Rome.

389 Catch 22.
Joseph Heller, with an introduction by Malcolm Bradbury. London: Everyman's Library, 1995. 608p.

Joseph Heller's absurdist novel (first published in 1961) is a satire of military madness and stupidity inspired by the author's experiences in Italy as a bombardier during the last phases of the Italian campaign. It is set in a bomber base on a fictional Italian island in 1944, when Italy was being liberated by the Allied forces and the German occupying troops were fleeing. Part of the novel takes place in Rome, the Eternal City becoming the surreal setting of the soldiers' escapades and where Yossarian, the hero of the novel, spends the night when he finally refuses to fly more combat missions and where he is met with a succession of appalling scenes. This edition provides a chronology from 1923 to 1994 (with columns showing the author's life, the literary context and historical events). Malcolm Bradbury's introductory essay provides an analysis of the novel and discusses the novel in the context of the 20th-century war novel. For a less anarchic view of Americans in wartime Rome see Alfred Hayes' *The girl on the Via Flaminia* (Bath, England: Lythway Press, 1949. 152p.).

390 Chroniques italiennes. (Italian chronicles.)
Stendhal, texts arranged, annotated and with a preface by Victor Del Litto. Geneva, Switzerland: Édition Édito-Service, 1968. 2 vols. (590p., 297p.) (Stendhal *Œuvres Complètes.*)

During his years as French Consul at Civitavecchia, Stendhal copied some Italian manuscripts he discovered in the house of a friend and used the plots of the real life tragic tales of love and death they related for six short stories. Four of these – *Vittoria Accoramboni, Les Cenci, La Duchesse de Palliano* and *L'Abbesse de Castro* – were published in *La Revue des Deux Mondes* between 1836 and 1839, while two others – *Trop de faveur tue* and *Suora Scolastica* – were left unfinished on his death. Fourteen folio volumes of Italian manuscripts, which include the 'chronicles' that inspired these stories, were later bought by the Bibliothèque nationale. The title was given to the collection by their first editor – Stendhal thought of calling them *Pièces tragiques* or *Historiettes romaines*. The stories have a Roman setting, except *Suora Scolastica*, which is set in 18th-century Naples. This edition includes the text of the original Italian manuscripts in an appendix, thus enabling the reader to appreciate the extent of Stendhal's liberties with his original sources. The tragic story of Vittoria Accoramboni also inspired Webster's *The White Devil*, while the story of the Cenci was used by numerous other writers, painters and composers.

391   Corinne, or Italy.
Madame de Staël (Anne-Louise-Germaine), translated by Sylvia
Raphael; introduction by John Isbell.   Oxford; New York: Oxford
University Press, 1998. [500p.] (Oxford World's Classics.)

Corinne, ou l'Italie (1807) was Madame de Staël's most popular novel and one of the most
important works of early French Romanticism. It is the tragic story of the love between the
beautiful and talented Italian poetess of the title and Oswald, Lord Nelvil, a Scottish lord who
ultimately decides to obey his dead father's wishes and marry Lucile, an English woman (and
also Corinne's half-sister), a decision that destroys the heroine and leaves a disconsolate
Oswald to revisit alone the sites of their past happiness. The novel was inspired by the
author's journey to Italy in 1804-05 and it shaped the romantic myth about Italy, the country,
as the title indicates, personified by the heroine. The novel contains numerous descriptions of
Italian customs and character, literature, art and architecture and parts of it read like a
travelogue. Much of it is set in Rome where Oswald first sees Corinne when, like Petrarch,
she is crowned on the Campidoglio. A mutual affection blossoms and Corinne becomes
Oswald's guide in Rome. There are interesting descriptions of the Pantheon, St Peter's, the
Capitoline Hill, the Forum, the Colosseum, and other landmarks of ancient history.
Subsequent chapters describe tombs, palaces and churches in Rome and their statues and
paintings. As the action of the novel takes place between 1794 and 1803, Mme de Staël had
to operate a kind of cultural restitution by relocating many works of art – which had, in the
meantime, been removed to Paris by Napoleon – to their original homes, an implied criticism
of the Emperor, like the idea of Italian nationality expounded in the novel. In this English
edition of the novel, the short introduction discusses its originality and its place in Mme De
Staël's work. There is also a chronology of the author, a select bibliography and numerous
explanatory notes to the text, in addition to Mme De Staël's own notes.

392   Daisy Miller.
Henry James, edited with an introduction by Geoffrey Moore and notes
by Patricia Crick.   Harmondsworth, Middlesex: Penguin Books, 1986.
126p. (Penguin Classics.)

First published in 1878, this novella is one of James's most popular works and the one that
established him as the master of the 'international situation', the confrontation between old
Europe and new America. Daisy is an innocent abroad, misunderstanding European
conventions and refusing to change her behaviour in order to conform. Rome is the setting of
the second half of the story and there are important scenes in S. Peter's, the Pincio, the Palace
of the Caesars and the Colosseum, her heedless nocturnal visit to the last one proving fatal.

393   Death in Rome.
Wolfgang Koeppen.   Harmondsworth, England: Penguin Books, 1994.
214p. (Penguin Twentieth-Century Classics.)

First published in 1957, this is a powerful dissection of German post-war malaise. The plot is a
chance reunion of a German family in Rome with tragic results. They are: Siegfried Pfaffrath,
a young composer of serial music whose new symphonic work is to be premiered in Rome, his
cousin Adolf Judejahn, who is to become a Catholic priest and, of the older generation,
Friedrich Wilhelm, Siegfried's father, a burgomaster who would rather bury his Nazi past
which, however, has resurfaced in the person of his brother-in-law Gottlied, an unrepentant
former SS high-ranking officer. Rome has different associations for each of these characters,
who symbolize four different areas of the German psyche – music, religion, bureaucracy, and

force. Their wanderings and encounters in the Eternal City have been described as 'a macabre ballet of outrageous contrivance'.

394 The fall of the axe.
Philip Lindsay. London: Hutchinson Library Services, 1974. 423p.

A novel on the Cenci family, originally published in 1940. In his dedication, the author acknowledges his debt to Corrado Ricci's biography of Beatrice Cenci. He also alludes 'to certain acts of old Francesco's which no novelist would dare write, at least in English', a fact which he regrets, as he feels that the full extent of his villainy should be shown if sympathy is to be won for the other characters. He concedes that only Zola could have done justice to old Cenci.

395 The heart of Rome: a tale of the 'Lost Water'.
Francis Marion Crawford, illustrated by Mary Tyler. Sevenoaks, England: Fisher Press, 1992. 290p.

Francis Marion Crawford (1854-1909) was one of the most popular novelists of the 1890s and the Edwardian era. A friend of Henry James, Nathaniel Hawthorne and other writers and artists from the United States and the Continent, he had an unrivalled knowledge of Italian society as he lived in Italy for most of his life. He was a prolific writer and of his forty-five novels, one third have a Roman setting (these include *The Saracinesca* trilogy, *A Lady of Rome* and *A Roman singer*). *The heart of Rome*, first published in 1903, is set in Rome in the 1880s and its plot is about the collapse of the property market and its effect on the aristocratic Conti family.

396 History: a novel.
Elsa Morante, translated from the Italian by William Weaver.
Harmondsworth, Middlesex: Penguin Books, 1980. 729p.

La Storia, Elsa Morante's epic novel set in Rome between 1941 and 1947, was first published in 1974. It quickly became a bestseller and also the object of ferocious criticism. The story unfolds in the poor quarters of Rome – S. Lorenzo, Testaccio, Porta Portese, the Ghetto and Pietralata. It relates the story of Ida Ramundo, a timid, half-Jewish elementary school teacher, and her two sons: Nino, who first joins the Blackshirts, then the Partisans and after the war becomes a black marketeer; and Useppe, born of her rape by a German soldier. Ida's struggles for survival form the core of the work, which has a large cast of unforgettable characters and numerous digressions. The novel contains several memorable descriptions of wartime Rome – the Ghetto before and after the deportation of the Jews, the Stazione Tiburtina platform with the sounds of weeping and moaning coming out of the sealed freight carriages packed with Jews about to be sent to the concentration camps, and the return to Rome of the few survivors. Each chapter covers a year and is introduced by an enumeration of contemporary historical events demonstrating man's inhumanity to man. The novel was filmed by Luigi Comencini in 1985 with Claudia Cardinale.

397 I, Claudius; and Claudius the God.
Robert Graves. Harmondsworth, England: Penguin Books, 1986. 839p.

First published in 1934, this vast reconstruction of Rome during the reign of four Emperors (Augustus, Tiberius, Caligula and Claudius) has been called the most successful historical novel of the 20th century. Claudius has been a puzzle to his contemporaries and to historians. An Emperor with republican views, a learned writer and historian, he escaped assassination at the hands of claimants to the succession through his physical infirmities, and cultivated weak-mindedness. Forcibly acclaimed Caesar in AD 41 after the assassination of Caligula, he accepted the role at the insistence of the soldiers hoping one day to restore the Republic. The novel, based on Suetonius and Tacitus, is a successful evocation of Rome in Claudius's time: its sociology, politics, geography, military practices and brutal history. In a gallery of thousands of memorable portraits, those of Livia, Caligula, Messalina and Claudius himself are outstanding. The novels were made into a popular television series in the 1970s.

398 The Improvisatore.
Hans Christian Andersen, translated from the Danish by Mary Howitt. Boston, Massachusetts: Houghton, Mifflin & Co., [1890]. 348p. (Andersen's Works.)

This was Andersen's first novel, published in 1835, the year after his return from Italy where he had spent fifteen months between 1833 and 1834 during his first long journey away from Denmark, when he visited Germany, Switzerland, France and Italy. He was full of enthusiasm about the works of art he saw and his discovery of the warm South. The novel, which is partly autobiographical, is set in Rome, the Campagna, Naples and Capri and includes numerous memorable sequences in the area around Piazza Barberini, the Crypt of the Church of the Cappuccini and its macabre décor, the Catacombs, the Spanish Steps – where the narrator's uncle, a legless beggar based on a famous real-life figure (Beppo, 'the king of the beggars') who appears in numerous journals and travel accounts of the time, has his post, the Roman Carnival, and the flower festival at Genzano. The work was a great success in Denmark and was quickly translated into several other languages. It is hardly read today, as the lack of a more recent English edition shows. There is, however, a recent French edition of the novel accompanied by a long introduction, which describes the genesis of the work and its importance in the author's output. See L'Improvisateur (In: Oeuvres, vol. 2. Hans Christian Andersen, edited by Régis Boyer. Paris: Éditions Gallimard, 1995. p. [133]-445. [Bibliothèque de la Pléiade, 414]).

399 Madame Gervaisais.
Edmond de Goncourt, Jules de Goncourt, edited by Marc Fumaroli. Paris: Gallimard, 1982. 344p. (Collection Folio.)

Madame Gervaisais was the last novel written by the Goncourt brothers. It was published in 1869 only a few months before the tragically early death of Jules and was based on the life of Nephtalie de Courmont, the authors' aunt, who in 1844 died of consumption in Rome, where she had settled two years earlier and where, like the heroine of the novel, she was converted to Catholicism. The work is virurently anti-Catholic, the heroine's conversion being accompanied by her moral and physical decline. It is the only work by the Goncourts which does not have a Parisian setting, the action taking place in Rome throughout, beginning with Mme Gervaisais' arrival and ending with her dramatic death at the feet of the Pope. Its unique focus is Mme Gervaisais and her spiritual awakening triggered by her experiences in the Eternal City. The city is, in fact, the only other protagonist of the work and a geographical metaphor of the heroine's condition and state of mind. A wealthy Parisian, she takes lodgings in a fashionable area of Rome, near Piazza di Spagna, frequents high society, visits the 'smiling' attractions of Rome – Via Condotti, Villa Borghese and Villa Pamphilj – and admires Rome's innumerable works of art, ancient and modern. Her conversion is carefully prepared and is accomplished during a performance of Allegri's Miserere in the Sistine Chapel while she is looking at Michelangelo's Last Judgement. After this 'entrapment', the image of Rome becomes increasingly sombre and sinister as the heroine's life follows a downward spiral that takes her from Piazza di Spagna to Trastevere where, under the direction of her terrifying trinitarian confessor, she abandons all social intercourse, and renounces all human feelings. The splendour of the Gesù is replaced by the gloom of S. Crisogono and S. Maria in Trastevere and the contemplation of death in the Catacombs and cemetery of the Cappuccini. The present edition is outstanding and proves that this unjustly neglected work (it has never been translated into English) is one of the authors' greatest achievements. Its preface is a masterly analysis of the novel's background, structure and of the philosophical, religious and literary sources used by the authors. There are also extracts from the preparatory notebook and comments on the work by the Goncourts' contemporaries – Sainte-Beuve, Zola, Serret, Barbey d'Aurevilly, Asselineau and Léon Daudet.

400 The Marble Faun: or, the romance of Monte Beni.
Nathaniel Hawthorne, edted with an introduction by Richard H. Brodhead. Harmondsworth, England: Penguin Books, 1990. 517p. (Penguin Classics.)

The story of four young people, two American artists – Hilda and Kenyon – and their European friends Miriam and Donatello, and their transformation from innocence to experience. The plot unfolds in Rome, with an Umbrian interlude sandwiched between the first twenty-three chapters that set the scene and lead to a tragic climax and the last fourteen, which provide the denouement. Rome is not just a setting for the story; its history and culture illuminate and set off the characters of the protagonists. There are numerous memorable descriptions of Roman locations: the Capitoline Museums; the Catacombs of St Calixtus; the Borghese Gardens; a walk on the Pincio; a moonlight walk in the Colosseum, the Forum and the Capitoline Hill which leads to the central episode in the novel, the murder of Miriam's 'spectre'; and St Peter's (where the conflict between Puritanism and Catholicism in Hilda's mind reaches its climax and leads to her spiritual transformation). The novel also contains descriptions of numerous works of art in Rome; these play a crucial role in describing character: the resemblance between Donatello and the Faun in the Capitoline Museums gives the novel its title, while Guido Reni's portrait of Beatrice Cenci – at the time one of the most famous works of art in Rome but now only ascribed to Reni and its subject questioned – is associated with Hilda, the innocent victim and witness of a crime.

401 Open city: seven writers in postwar Rome.
Edited by William Weaver and Kristina Olson. South Royalton, Vermont: Steerforth Press, 1999. 450p.

This is an anthology of prose works by seven writers who were working in Rome during the 1940s and 1950s – Ignazio Silone, Giorgio Bassani, Alberto Moravia, Elsa Morante, Natalia Ginzburg, Carlo Levi and Carlo Emilio Gadda. Three of the works are complete (Moravia's novella 'Agostino', Elsa Morante's 'The Nameless One', and Natalia Ginzburg's 'Valentino'), the rest are excerpts from novels. They do not necessarily have a Roman setting (Bassani' s *The Garden of the Finzi-Continis*, for example, is set in Ferrara) but they are all the products of the same intellectual milieu, the one described by William Weaver in his long introductory memoir. Weaver, one of the foremost translators of Italian literature, served as an ambulance driver for the British Army in Southern Italy during the Second World War but returned to the United States just before the Liberation of Rome. He returned to Italy in 1947 and settled in Rome, where he stayed until he moved to Tuscany in the mid-1960s. In Rome he joined the circle of Princess Marguerite Caetani, publisher of the international literary review *Botteghe oscure*, becoming acquainted with all the writers anthologized here whose personalities he vividly, and often amusingly, evokes. Weaver also evokes Roman life and contemporary politics (notably the elections of 1948, a landslide for the Christian Democrats), Italian cinema and its shift from neorealism to *neorealismo rosa* (same settings and characters but seen through rose-tinted lenses). He also describes his relations with American writers who began to visit Rome in the late 1940s and, in the final, melancholy paragraphs evokes a Rome that has long since disappeared. The volume also includes biographical notes (by Kristina Olson) about the seven writers.

402 Il Piacere. (Pleasure.)
Gabriele D'Annunzio. Milan, Italy: Arnoldo Mondadori, 1998. 359p.
(Oscar Classici Moderni.)

D'Annunzio's first novel, published in 1889, is a portrait of Rome's high society in the 1880s, and its idle pleasures. The hero of the novel is Count Andrea Sperelli, a poet, etcher and aesthete, and his relationship with the beautiful and voluptuous Elena Muti and, after she abandons him, with the pure Maria Ferres, whose resemblance to Elena arouses his passion. The work's geographical setting lies between the Trinità dei Monti and Palazzo Farnese, the Corso and the newly constructed Via Nazionale, and its protagonists inhabit famous Roman buildings like the Palazzo Zuccari and the Palazzo Barberini. The novel contains several magnificent evocations of Rome and is much influenced by Huysmans's *À rebours* in its detailed descriptions of interiors and its depiction of a self-absorbed, hermetically sealed world in which the rare intrusions of contemporary political and social reality are all the more resonant. The only English translation of the novel should be avoided. It is a bowdlerized version by Georgina Harding first published in 1898 as *The Child of Pleasure*, which also omits much of the aesthetic reflections that play such an important role in the original. This was reissued in 1991 by Dedalus (in a series called 'Decadence from Dedalus') without any indication of the translation's original date of publication and omissions.

403 Pictures of Fidelman: an exhibition.
Bernard Malamud. London: Chatto & Windus, 1983. 208p. (The Collected Works of Bernard Malamud.)

Bernard Malamud's novel (1959-68) is a variant of the 'innocent abroad' myth. Fidelman is a failed painter from the Bronx who has come to Italy to study Giotto. His initial reaction to Rome is one of awe and exaltation when, on emerging from Stazione Termini and discovering that across the crowded piazza are the Baths of Diocletian, which Michelangelo helped to convert into a church and a convent which is now a museum, he exclaims 'Imagine all that history.' His exaltation soon evaporates and ends in alienation when he meets his nemesis, a 'Jewish refugee from Israel' who shadows him, and when he discovers the elusive nature of the reality of Rome.

404 The Pope's rhinoceros.
Lawrence Norfolk. London: Minerva, 1997. 753p.

The complex plot, which interweaves the stories of the Baltic pagan Niklot/Salvestro, the German monks of Usedom, and an African princess, Usse, and leads to the search for a near legendary beast, is centred on a vivid evocation of Rome in the early 16th century, which forms the core of the book. Graphic descriptions of a city in turmoil and its multifarious life, from the rats gnawing at its foundations up to the gilded squalour of the papal court, culminate in a naumachia (mock sea battle) staged for Leo X in the Vatican, at which the rhinoceros is destined to make its climactic appearance. Other historical novels set in Rome include Hella S. Haasse's *The scarlet city: a novel of 16th-century Italy* (London: Allison & Busby, 1997. 367p.) and *Threshold of Fire: a novel of 5th-century Rome* (London: Allison & Busby, 1997. 255p.).

405 Portrait of Lozana, the lusty Andalusian woman.
Francisco Delicado, translation with introduction and notes by Bruno M. Damiani. Potomac, Maryland: Scripta Humanistica, 1987. 308p. (Scripta Humanistica, 34.)

First published in Venice in 1528, where the author moved after the Sack of Rome in 1527 (he had settled in Rome after the Edict of Expulsion of Jews from Spain in 1492), Delicado's *Loçana andaluza* is a novel in dialogue form and a valuable historical and sociological document of Renaissance Rome. It relates the picaresque adventures of Lozana, an Andalucian courtesan active in early 16th-century Rome, and includes vivid descriptions of the city (Piazza Navona, Campo de' Fiori, Piazza Giudea, Ponte Sisto) and its corrupt inhabitants (street vendors, thieves, go-betweens, etc.). It also contains numerous references to contemporary historical events. The structure of the work is episodic (it is divided into sixty-six 'sketches' or books) and the heroine takes on a variety of professions in a short span of time, ending her days on the island of Lipari in pious solitude. The epilogue evokes the destruction of Rome in 1527 and the pestilence that followed it and considers it as God's punishment for this modern Babylon. The introduction to the present translation points out the relationship of this work to Fernando de Rojas' *La Celestina* and suggests that it was known to Pietro Aretino and Cervantes and that it may have influenced later novels of roguery like *Lazarillo de Tormes* and Daniel Defoe's *Moll Flanders*.

406   Quo Vadis?
Henryk Sienkiewicz.   Gloucester, England: Alan Sutton, 1989; New York: Hippocrene Books, 1993. 455p.

First published in 1896, this huge historical fresco by the Polish novelist and patriot Henryk Sienkiewicz (1846-1916) won its author the Nobel Prize in 1905. It is a vivid portrayal of the luxury, power and corruption of Imperial Rome under Nero and the clash between Paganism and Christianity. It is also typical of the enormously popular genre of the early Christian epic novel, better known today through its popular Hollywood and Cinecittà film adaptations. Other novels in this category include *Ben-Hur: a tale of the Christ* (1880) by General Lew Wallace (latest edition published by Wordsworth Books, 1996), *The Robe* (1942) by Lloyd C. Douglas (latest edition: Corgi, 1976), *The Fall of the Roman Empire* (1964) by Harry Whittington, and *The Blood of the martyrs* (1939) by Naomi Mitchison (latest edition, Edinburgh: Canongate Classics, 1988). *Spartacus* (1951) by Howard Fast (latest edition: G. K. Hall, 1984) may also be included here though, in this case, the conflict is between rebel slaves and Romans.

407   Racconti romani. (Roman tales.)
Alberto Moravia, introduction and bibliography by Piero Cudini.   Milan, Italy: Bompiani, 1998. 433p. (I Grandi Tascabili: Romanzi e Racconti.)

First published in 1954, this is a collection of sixty-one short stories originally published in *Corriere della sera*. A later collection, *Nuovi racconti romani* (More Roman tales), followed in 1959 (also available in this series) bringing the total number to 150. They all have simple and concise plots, usually highlighting a foible or idiosyncrasy of the narrator (the tales are all related in the first person by people of the Roman working class or lower-middle class, including taxi drivers, swindlers, barmen, shop keepers, clerks and mechanics). Moravia said that the inspiration for these tales was G. G. Belli's poetry. Twenty-seven of these short stories have been translated into English by Angus Davidson as *Roman tales* (Oxford: Oxford University Press, 1988. [Oxford paperbacks]), and a selection and translation, also by Angus Davidson, from *Nuovi racconti romani*, was published by Secker & Warburg in 1963.

408   The ragazzi.
Pier Paolo Pasolini, translated from the Italian by Emile Capouya. Manchester, England: Carcanet, 1986. 256p.

Pasolini began to write *I ragazzi di vita*, about slum life in the suburbs (the *borgate*) of Rome, soon after his move to Rome in 1950, following his expulsion from the Communist Party and removal from his teaching post in his native Friuli when he was charged with obscene behaviour. The novel was published in 1955 and caused a scandal. Its various episodes, held together by the character of Ricetto, describe the futile lives of the sub-proletarian youths in the shanty towns and tenements on the edge of the city, their petty crimes and tragic deaths. The *borgata* is the unifying element in these episodes, a bleak landscape of rubbish tips, building works and ruins, populated by vagabonds, beggars, prostitutes and criminals.

409 Roderick Hudson.

Henry James, with an introduction by Tony Tanner. Oxford: Oxford University Press, 1999. 442p. (The World's Classics.)

Roderick Hudson was Henry James's first major novel. He began writing it in Florence in 1874 and it was serialized in the *Atlantic Monthly* throughout 1875. The novel is permeated with the atmosphere of Rome and, like the novelist's later fiction, the theme of the work is that of Americans in Europe and their different responses and fates. Roderick Hudson is a young American sculptor, gifted but unstable, who is brought to Rome by his friend and patron Rowland Mallet, a wealthy young man who believes that Roderick's genius will be nourished through contact with the Eternal City's rich sculptural heritage. Rowland's experiment will have fatal results – after an initial burst of creativity and momentary fame Roderick's output becomes fitful and his romantic attachments unhappy. He is eventually reduced to creative paralysis which leads to his suicide. The novel is a rich evocation of Rome, the society of which is contrasted to that of puritan New England. The descriptions of the Roman artistic milieu were based on James's own encounters in Rome. A number of other artists appear in the novel with different aspirations and methods of working – Sam Singleton (the landscape painter), Augusta Blanchard (the flower painter) and Gloriani (the academic artist).

410 Roman blood: a mystery of Ancient Rome.

Steven Saylor. London: Robinson, 1997. 370p. map.

First published in 1991, this was one of the author's most successful murder mysteries set in Ancient Rome. Other novels in the series so far include *Catilina's riddle* (London: Robinson, 1998. 466p.), *The Venus throw* (London: Robinson, 1995. 368p.), *The House of the Vestals* (London: Robinson, 1999. 275p.) and *Rubicon* (London: Robinson, 1999).

411 Roman nights and other stories.

Pier Paolo Pasolini, with an introduction by Jonathan Keates. Translated from the Italian by John Shepley. London: Quartet Books, 1994. 134p. (Quartet Encounters.)

Five short stories taken from Pasolini's *Alì dagli occhi azzurri* (Blue-eyed Ali – see entry no. 387), a collection of miscellaneous writings. They span the period between 1950, when Pasolini left Friuli and settled in Rome, and 1965. They are 'Roman nights' (1950), 'A night on the tram' (1951), 'Studies on the life of Testaccio' (1951), 'A rustic story' (1956-65), and 'Rital and Raton' (1965). The introduction discusses Pasolini's ability to provoke people of all political persuasions, his complex response to his homosexuality, and his ability to transmute urban squalor and suburban poverty, notable in his lyrical and unconventional evocations of Rome in these stories.

412 The Roman spring of Mrs Stone.

Tennessee Williams. London: Vintage, 1999. 116p.

This novella was first published in 1950, growing out of the author's trip to Italy in 1948; it was made into a successful film, in 1961, starring Vivien Leigh, Warren Beatty and Lotte Lenya. It traces the decline and fall of a wealthy American actress whose career and beauty are on the wane, alone in Rome after her husband's death, haunted by the onset of middle age and drifting into the world of high-class prostitution. Her affair with a young gigolo ends disastrously when he abandons her for a young starlet and she surrenders herself, in a kind of death pact, to a young, ragged man who has been following her ominously throughout the work. The title of the work is ironic, contrasting the heroine's cold and sterile life and her gradual decadence with the warmth and rejuvenating power of the Roman spring. There are also contrasts between age and youth, and the Eternal City and the transitory nature of human youth and beauty. The characters move in the same Via Veneto milieu that was to be made famous a few years later by Fellini's *La dolce vita.*

413 Romanzi e racconti. Vol. 1 1946-1961. (Novels and short stories. Vol. 1 1946-1961.)
Pier Paolo Pasolini, edited by Walter Siti and Silvia de Laude, with a chronology by Nico Naldini. Milan, Italy: Arnoldo Mondadori, 1998. 1959p. (I Meridiani. Pier Paolo Pasolini *Tutte Le Opere.*)

This is the first in a projected eleven-volume edition of Pasolini's complete works in this prestigious series. In a career that spanned over thirty years, from his first collection of poetry in the Friulian dialect in 1942 to his controversial film *Salò* shortly before his violent death in 1975, Pasolini worked incessantly in a variety of forms and media. This volume focuses on his prose narrative written between 1946 and 1961. The texts are presented in chronological order of composition. They include the posthumously rediscovered and published autobiographical fragments of the novels *Amado mio* and *Atti impuri* (Impure acts), material published here for the first time – *Il disprezzo della provincia* (The contempt for the provinces) (1952-1953), the two Roman novels *Ragazzi di vita* (The Ragazzi) (1955) and *Una vita violenta* (A violent life) (1959) that established Pasolini's reputation, and finally, short stories, sketches, and autobiographical notes which originally appeared in newspapers and reviews and were never published in volume form. The works are extensively annotated and the volume also includes a detailed, sixty-five-page-long, chronology of Pasolini's life and works.

414 Rome.
Émile Zola, edited by Henri Mitterand. Paris: Éditions Stock, 1998. 565p.

Rome, first published in 1896, is the second part of Zola's trilogy *Les trois villes* that started with *Lourdes* in 1894 and would be completed with *Paris* in 1898. The three novels follow Pierre Froment, a priest, in a journey of disillusionment across Catholic Europe. Pierre, who has come to Rome to seek an audience with Pope Leo XIII to prevent his book from being put on the Index (of proscribed books), discovers the coexistence of three different cities – Ancient Rome, Christian Rome and the modern metropolis – which unfold before his eyes. Zola added a number of secondary plots to the main story – a tragic love affair among the aristocracy, financial scandals, intrigues among cardinals – and included numerous long descriptions of Rome. Though these interrupt the flow of the work they provide a vast panorama of Rome and its social and intellectual life in the last years of the 19th century. Perhaps because of its hybrid nature, the novel is not one of Zola's popular works and until the appearance of this edition it was unavailable even in France. The excellent introduction describes the genesis of the work, its place in the overall body of Zola's writing, and its place in the contemporary debate about faith versus science. There are numerous notes elucidating the topographical, artistic and literary references contained in the novel. The only English translation of the work is the recently re-issued original translation by Alfred Vizetelly, first published in 1896 (Stroud, England; Dover, New Hampshire: Alan Sutton, 1993. 600p. [Pocket Classics]).

415 A street in Rome.

Ugo Moretti, translated from the Italian by William Weaver. London: The New English Library Limited, 1962. 160p. (Ace Books.)

A series of vignettes set in and around Via del Babuino, traditionally the artists' quarter in Rome, in the immediate post-war years. In both subject matter and style the work resembles Henry Murger's *Scènes de la vie de bohème* (Scenes of Bohemian life). In his preface, Moretti points out the autobiographical nature of the work and indicates that a number of contemporary artists and writers (such as Ugo Turcato, Renato Guttuso, Ennio Flaiano and Emilio Villa) appear as characters in it, some of them with their real names.

416 That Awful Mess on Via Merulana.

Carlo Emilio Gadda, translated from the Italian by William Weaver and with an introduction by Italo Calvino. London, Melbourne, New York: Quartet Books, 1985. 409p. (Encounter.)

On the surface a murder novel, Gadda's *Quer pasticciaccio brutto de Via Merulana*, the writer's only work with a Roman setting, is also an exercise in style. Gadda's language combines folk expressions, learned speech, various dialects (especially the Roman dialect), and literary quotations. The work was written in 1946 and was inspired by a crime recently committed in Rome (though the action of the novel takes place in 1927). In a large apartment block on Via Merulana, two crimes (a robbery and a murder) are committed within three days of each other. The murder remains unresolved as Gadda is more interested in the multiplicity of (often interconnected) causes behind each effect. As Italo Calvino points out in his introduction, the Eternal City – with its social classes and its various dialects, and its blend of the present with the mythical past – is the true protagonist of the work. Calvino also stresses the cultural, historical and mythical dimension the city assumes in the novel, noting Gadda's numerous references to Roman Renaissance and Baroque art. William Weaver, in his translator's foreword, provides a portrait of Gadda and his many contradictions, discusses the novel which, he says, occupies in contemporary Italian literature the same position that the masterworks of Proust, Joyce and Musil enjoy in their respective countries, and explains his decision to translate the work into straightforward spoken English rather than attempt a dialect rendition. The novel was filmed by Pietro Germi in 1959, without Gadda's collaboration.

417 A violent life.

Pier Paolo Pasolini, translated from the Italian by William Weaver. Manchester, England: Carcanet, 1985. 320p. (Carcanet Collection Series.)

Pasolini's second Roman novel was first published in 1959, four years after *Ragazzi di vita* (The Ragazzi). Like the earlier work, it describes life in the Roman *borgate*, the tenement areas on the outskirts of the city. The protagonist is Tommaso Puzzilli and the novel charts his progress from petty thieving, thuggery and a spell in prison to new-found respectability when he and his family are housed in a municipal apartment; his attempt to join the Christian Democrat establishment is abandoned after he witnesses an example of violent police repression after a labour dispute, and he joins the Communist Party. Already suffering from tuberculosis, he dies after saving a prostitute in a flood.

Poetry

418 The Aeneid.
Virgil, translated into English prose with an introduction by W. F. Jackson
Knight. Harmondsworth, England: Penguin Books, 1970. 361p.
(Penguin Classics.)

Virgil's Aeneid, the great Roman epic poem of the Augustan era, is an account of the flight of
Aeneas from Troy and his struggles to found a new home in Italy, the origin of Rome. Though
the whole work is permeated with the glory of Rome, its future power is prefigured in two
places: in Book 6, which describes Aeneas' visit to the Underworld, where he is offered a vision
of the future of Rome and most of its great future heroes; and Book 8, in which, advised by the
god of the river Tiber, Aeneas visits the Arcadian king Evander, who lives on the future site of
Rome, and receives a gift of armour from Venus, his mother, which includes a shield that depicts
future events in the history of Rome. See also *The Aeneid*, a new prose translation by David
West (Harmondsworth, England: Penguin Books, 1990. 353p. [Penguin Classics]).

419 Amours de voyage.
Arthur Hugh Clough, edited by Patrick Scott. St Lucia, Australia:
University of Queensland Press, 1974. 82p. (Victorian texts, 1.)

Arthur Hugh Clough visited Rome in April 1849 in order to see the Roman Republic which had
been proclaimed two months earlier. At the time of his arrival other visitors, expecting the
imminent collapse of the Republic, were leaving Rome. Clough remained throughout the
French siege of the city, during which he befriended the few remaining English speakers, the
Americans William Wetmore Story and Margaret Fuller, and wrote a report on the French
bombardment (included here in an appendix). He also wrote *Amours de voyage*, a poem in five
cantos and in epistolary form, which describes the feelings of Claude, a liberal intellectual
caught up in a real revolution, and his reflections on art, ancient and modern Rome, politics, and
love. The present edition also includes selected journal entries from April to July 1849 from
Clough's Roman notebook.

420 Childe Harold's Pilgrimage.
Lord Byron. Oxford: Clarendon Press, 1980. 341p. (The Complete
Poetical Works, Vol. 2.)

Lord Byron's *Childe Harold's Pilgrimage* (1818) was one of his most popular works and would
condition the reactions of generations of visitors to Italy. In Canto IV, the poet wanders among
the principal sites and antiquities of the peninsula reflecting on the decay of Italian civilization
and the irreversible erosion of the classical past. The famous section of the canto devoted to
Rome (stanzas 78-163, lines 694-1467) is an elegiac representation of Roman ruins. Byron
explores the remains of the ancient city and comments in turn upon each of its monuments. He
compares Rome to the statue of Niobe (in the Uffizi) lamenting the death of her children. For
the poet, ruins are a metaphor for the human condition and resist historical explanation or human
reconstruction. Any archaeological elucidation might impede the poetic imagination. The six
stanzas devoted to Cecilia Metella and her tomb (stanzas 99-105, lines 883-954) are a series of
conjectures about the identity of the woman buried there, her looks and her age when she died.
The poem contains the most famous description of the Colosseum by moonlight, which
includes the often-quoted lines (sometimes attributed to the Venerable Bede) 'While stands the
Coliseum, Rome shall stand; When falls the Coliseum, Rome shall fall; And when Rome falls
– the World'.

421 Epigrams.
Martial, edited and translated by D. R. Shackleton Bailey. Cambridge,
Massachusetts; London: Harvard University Press, 1993. 3 vols. (The
Loeb Classical Library, 94, 95, 480.)

Martial was born in Bilbilis in north-eastern Spain *c.* 40 AD and moved to Rome in 64, where
he remained until 100 when the assassination of Domitian, his chief patron, made his position
increasingly uncomfortable. His epigrams, the only literary form he practised, may have started
as a means of finding patrons. Their publication began in 86 AD and the twelfth and final book
came out after the poet's death. They contain around 1,175 poems which present a vast fresco
of contemporary Roman society. This edition also includes the *Liber de Spectaculis* (Book on
shows) on the games presented by Emperor Titus in the recently inaugurated Colosseum in 80
AD – only an incomplete selection of thirty-seven poems from the original work has survived.

422 Goethe's Roman elegies.
Translated with an introduction and notes by David Luke. London:
Chatto & Windus, 1977. 101p.

This edition has parallel German and English text, with an English introduction and notes.
The introduction sketches the background to Goethe's journey to Italy, his life in Rome in the
colony of German painters and his new appreciation of the ancient classics, especially the
Latin erotic poets, which inspired this cycle of poems, written between 1788 and 1790,
originally called 'Erotica Romana', and finally published in 1795 and considered scandalous
by his contemporaries. The rejuvenating contact of the poet with the Mediterranean world
and the monuments of both its ancient civilization and later centuries is pointed out, as is his
sexual emancipation in Rome. It is also suggested that the 'Faustina', the beloved in the
Elegies, whose identity remains a mystery, is not an Italian woman with whom Goethe had
an affair during his sojourn in Rome but Christiane Vulpius, the 23-year old woman whom
Goethe met in July 1788 shortly after his return from Italy, even though in the poems she is
a widow and has a small boy by her deceased husband. The poet's relationship with
Christiane, who was of a lower intellect and social extraction, scandalized the small-town
sensibilities of Weimar society. The influence of the Latin poets, especially Propertius,
Catullus and Ovid, is also brought out, together with the recurring themes – Rome and its
splendours, the contrast between the North and Italy, the happy liaison with a loving woman,
the conflict between art and life, the intellect and the senses – and the fusion of three different
worlds: that of Ancient Rome, the Rome of the 18th century, and Weimar. It is also explained
that the term 'elegy' refers to the metrical metre and not to the content of the poems, which
is happy love. The notes are, like the introduction, excellent, elucidating the mythological and
historical allusions in the poems. The collection has also been translated by Michael
Hamburger as *Roman elegies and other poems* (London: Anvil Press Poetry, 1996. 117p.).

423 Keats, Shelley & Rome: an illustrated miscellany.
Compiled by Neville Rogers. London: Johnson, 1970 (4th
impression). 76p.

This miscellany was originally published in 1949 to contribute to the effort of preserving the
Keats-Shelley Memorial House and some of the contributions are marked by the post-Liberation
mood, like the brief and moving testimony of A. C. Sedgwick, *New York Times* correspondent
attached to the American Fifth Army, describing a visit to the Keats-Shelley Memorial Museum
on the day the Allied Forces entered Rome and his relief at discovering that the house – a haven
of tranquillity – and its contents had miraculously survived the war. The house's popularity in
the first year of it re-opening (when it attracted 15,000 visitors, compared to the pre-war average

of 800) and its identification as 'some corner of a foreign field that is forever England' is mentioned elsewhere in the volume, while another contribution gives an account of the work of the exiled anti-Fascist poet Lauro de Bosis who, in a gesture interpreted here as a reflection of the Shelleyan ideals of justice and liberty, on 3rd October 1931 flew a private aeroplane over Rome and dropped 400,000 pamphlets addressed to the King and people of Italy before his plane was pursued and shot down. The book also includes essays on the posthumous fame of Keats and Shelley, an extract from Gabriele D'Annunzio's novel *Il Piacere* (Pleasure) describing the Protestant Cemetery and the graves of Joseph Severn, Keats and Shelley, a translation of Rainer Maria Rilke's poem on Severn's drawing depicting Keats on his deathbed, a note on the death-mask of Keats, and a history of the Memorial from its inception in 1903 to 1946.

424 The Lays of Ancient Rome.
Lord Macaulay. In: *The works of Lord Macaulay*. With an introduction by Donald Hawes. London: Wordsworth Poetry Library, 1995, p. 1-70.

First published in 1842, Lord Macaulay's once popular *Lays of Ancient Rome* are an evocation of heroic early Roman history. Macaulay believed that the tales about the early history of Rome in the first books of Livy were based on lost ballads. Accordingly, in each of the four lays the story is narrated by a popular bard. 'Horatius' and 'The Battle of the Lake Regillus' relate Tarquin's attempts to recover the throne of Rome, 'Virginia' the killing of a young woman by her father to save her from dishonour, and 'The Prophecy of Capys', like the prophecy of Anchises in Book 6 of Virgil's *Aeneid*, foretells Rome's future glories.

425 Leopardi a Roma. (Leopardi in Rome.)
Edited by Novella Bellucci and Luigi Trenti. Milan, Italy: Electa, 1998. 422p.

This remarkable publication is the catalogue of an exhibition held in Rome in 1998, the bicentenary of Giacomo Leopardi's birth. It provides a detailed examination of the poet's three sojourns in Rome (in 1822-23, in 1831-32, and in 1833) and a panoramic view of the social and intellectual milieu of Rome during the early years of the 19th century, which included salient figures like B. G. Niebuhr, Stendhal, Angelo Mai and Guiseppe Gioachino Belli. It is divided into three sections, each corresponding to a sojourn. The first two sections are subdivided into 72 and 44 chapters respectively, and each chapter is introduced by a few lines by Leopardi (mostly extracts from his letters) describing his experiences in Rome – things he has seen, people he has met, books he has read, etc. – which form the subject of the chapter. Thus there are chapters on Leopardi's contemporaries – Ennio Quirino Visconti, Antonio Nibby, Giuseppe Tamboni, among others, opera, Roman literature, Roman palazzi, churches, monuments, and works of art. Each chapter includes one or more illustrations – portraits, views of the city, books and manuscripts. There are also essays on Leopardi and the Bonaparte family, especially Charlotte Bonaparte; Leopardi, Canova and Neo-classicism; Leopardi and Stendhal; and Leopardi's letters in the Vatican Library. See also *Leopardi e Roma* (Leopardi and Rome), edited by Luigi Trenti and Fernanda Roscetti (Rome: Carlo Colombo, 1991. 449p.), which consists of seventeen papers read at a conference organized in Rome in 1988 to commemorate the 150th anniversary of Leopardi's death. Among the topics discussed are: Leopardi's image of Rome before his first journey; his letters from Rome; Leopardi and the 1822-23 theatre season in Rome; Leopardi's readings in Rome; and Perticari and Leopardi.

426 **Lettere, giornali, zibaldone.** (Letters, journals, notebook.)
Giuseppe Gioachino Belli, edited by Giovanni Orioli, introduction by
Giovanni Muscetta. Turin, Italy: Giulio Einaudi, 1962. 668p. bibliog.
(Saggi, 300.)

This collection brings together a miscellany of Belli's writings. The selection of letters includes
two long, autobiographical letters addressed to Filippo Ricci and Gaetano Bernetti, and his
correspondence with the actress Amalia Bettini, whom Belli first saw when she performed in
Rome in 1835 and who became a close friend and inspired several of his poems. The travel
journal covers the years 1827-29. The *Zibaldone* (in the Biblioteca nazionale Centrale di Roma)
consists of 4,525 numbered and several unnumbered entries in eleven volumes. It covers the
period between 1824 and 1840 and includes a wide variety of material ranging from
transcriptions of newspaper articles or extracts from books, to quotations, anecdotes and
detailed descriptions of new scientific discoveries. In the selections included in this volume the
emphasis has been on items that reflect the literary interests of the poet. There are also reviews
of theatrical performances and comments on plays he wrote in 1852-53 for the censorship
authorities. See also *Giuseppe Gioachino Belli nel bicentenario della nascita, 1791-1991*
(Giuseppe Gioachino Belli in the bicentenary of his birth, 1791-1991), edited by Muzio
Mazzocchi Alemanni (Rome: Istituto poligrafico e zecca dello stato, 1991. 165p.).

427 **The people of Rome in 100 sonnets by Giuseppe Gioachino Belli.**
Giuseppe Gioachino Belli, presented by Fabrizio Di Giacomo, translated
into English by Allen Andrews, with drawings by Ron Sandford.
Rome: Bardi, 1984. [400p.]

In his preface, Fabrizio Di Giacomo praises Belli's satire as 'wounding yet caressing, rocking
with scornful laughter and shaken with sobs' and describes the poet's taste for the risqué quip,
ranging from the vulgar to the obscene and spoken for the pleasure of saying it, as characteristic
of the Roman people. The poems are preceded by lines from Belli in which he describes his
purpose to set down the verbal idiom of the Roman people without ornament or alteration, and
without corrections to its syntax or its licence. The poems are given in the original Roman
dialect and in English and there are several explanatory notes. Ron Sandford's drawings, which
face the poems, stylistically lie somewhere between those of Picasso for 'The Vollard Suite' and
Hockney for 'A Rake's Progress'.

428 **Les regrets,** *précédé de* **Les antiquités de Rome.** (The Regrets,
preceded by The Antiquities of Rome.)
Joachim Du Bellay, edited by S. de Sacy. Paris: Éditions Gallimard,
1975. 318p. (Poésie, 109.)

Joachim Du Bellay was in Rome for four years between 1553 and 1557 as the private secretary
of Cardinal Jean Du Bellay, his uncle, on a diplomatic mission to the papal court. Though
initially enthusiastic about Rome and its antiquities he soon grew dissatisfied with the menial
duties he had to perform and grew nostalgic of France. These two collections of poems, both
published in 1558, show this shift of mood. *Les antiquités de Rome* is a grave meditation on
Rome's ancient glory seen in its ruins, whereas *Les regrets* express his boredom and are
caustically satirical. The present edition includes a biographical outline of Du Bellay, a
vocabulary, notes, and an index of the recipients of *Les regrets*. For a detailed reading of *Les
antiquités de Rome* and a study of texts, ancient and modern, that were probably known to Du
Bellay, see George Hugo Tucker's *The poet's odyssey: Joachim du Bellay and the Antiquitez de
Rome* (Oxford: Clarendon Press, 1990. 318p. bibliog.).

429 The ring and the book.
Robert Browning, edited by Richard D. Altick.   London: Penguin
Books, 1990. 707p. (Penguin Classics.)

Robert Browning's long narrative poem in twelve books is based on a collection of pamphlets and hand-written documents collected by Francesco Cencini, a Florentine lawyer, on the trial of Count Guido Franceschini for the murder of his wife (whom he accused of adultery), discovered by Browning in a second-hand market in Florence in 1860. Though Browning soon decided to base a long poem on the case, the work was not completed until 1868, when it was published in four volumes between November 1868 and February 1869. The narrative offers versions of the events given from various viewpoints. This extensively annotated edition opts for the text of the first edition of the work rather than the revised edition of 1872.

430 Roma del Belli: la città, i luoghi e i monumenti nei *Sonetti romaneschi* e nelle illustrazioni del tempo. (The Rome of Belli: the city, the places and the monuments in the *Sonetti romaneschi* and in contemporary illustrations.)
Roberto Vighi.   Rome: Fratelli Palombi, 1963. 407p. maps.

This is an anthology of poems by Guiseppe Gioachino Belli which refer to the topography of Rome. The introductory essays describe the city at the time of Belli and record some of the drastic changes in the character and appearance of each of its fourteen *rioni*, the result of Rome's development after 1870. The sonnets are presented in nine sections, each covering one aspect of the city: general references to the city's topography; squares; streets; antiquities; churches and oratories; hospitals and hospices; theatres and spectacles; museums and works of art; and beyond the city gates. The poems are well-annotated and the work is handsomely illustrated with contemporary topographical and popular prints (including the work of Pinelli) and maps. The illustrations, however, are not as comprehensive as one would have hoped as most of the buildings and monuments described in the poems are not shown.

431 Roman poems.
Pier Paolo Pasolini, translated by Lawrence Ferlinghetti and Francesca Valente, with a preface by Alberto Moravia.   San Francisco, California: City Lights Books, 1986. 145p. (Pocket Poets Series, no. 41.)

A selection of poems, originally published between 1957 and 1975, ranging from the poet's early impoverished days on the outskirts of Rome, where he fled after his expulsion from the Italian Communist Party in 1949, to his death in 1975. They are both deeply personal and politically engaged. The texts are in the original with parallel English translations. In his preface, Alberto Moravia identifies nostalgia for rural civilization, destroyed by mass emigration to the big cities, as one of the main themes of Pasolini's poetry.

432 Roman satirical poems and their translation.
Trilussa, edited by Grant Showerman.   New York: S. F. Vanni, 1945. 185p.

Forty-nine poems by Trilussa (pen-name of Carlo Alberto Salustri) with their English translations on facing pages. The poems are preceded by an introduction on the Romanesco dialect, the Roman dialect periodical *Rugantino*, and the work of Giuseppe Gioachino Belli, Cesare Pascarella, and Trilussa himself.

433 I sonetti, Storia nostra, Le prose. (The sonnets, Our history, The prose works.)
Cesare Pascarella, edited by the Accademia nazionale dei Lincei, with a preface by Emilio Cecchi.   Verona, Italy: Arnoldo Mondadori, 1955.
823p. (I Classici Contemporanei Italiani: Opere di Cesare Pascarella.)

This is a collection of the published works by Cesare Pascarella (1858-1940), with Belli and Trilussa the most important Roman dialect poet. His most famous, and ambitious, work is *Storia nostra*, a poem relating, in 267 sonnets, the history of Rome from its foundation to the unification of Italy. Its composition began in 1895 and the work acquired legendary status as Pascarella used to recite finished sections of it to friends. It remained, however, unfinished and was published posthumously in 1941. Other collections include *Er morto de campagna* (The dead man in the countryside) (1881), *La serenata* (The serenade) (1882), *Villa Gloria* (1886), and *La scoperta dell'America* (The discovery of America) (1894). The prose works were written between 1880 and 1890 and belong to the tradition of journalistic descriptions of literary and artistic bohemian life in Rome (there are articles on the Caffè Greco and on artists' models), travels (*In Ciociaria*), descriptions of nature and popular customs. Pascarella was also an accomplished artist – he was a member of the group of landscape artists *XXV della Campagna romana* – and this edition is embellished with sixteen of his drawings.

434 Sonnets of Giuseppe Belli.
Translated, with an introduction, by Milner Williams.   Baton Rouge, Louisiana; London: Louisiana State University Press, 1981.

Giuseppe Gioachino Belli (1791-1863) wrote some 2,250 sonnets in Romanesco, the language of the Roman common people, between 1820 and 1849, with the ambition of leaving a lasting monument to Rome. In her introduction, the translator describes Belli as 'the only writer of genius that Rome ever gave birth and education to' and likens the sensuality and lustiness of his vocabulary and imagery to those of Rabelais, Boccaccio, Chaucer and Molière. He also mentions the admiration writers like D. H. Lawrence, Gogol, Sainte-Beuve and James Joyce had for the poet. This is a bilingual edition of seventy-five poems with the translations given on facing pages. The poems are not rendered into dialect and the arrangement is not chronological but according to subject.

435 Studi belliani. (Belli studies.)
Edited by Ercole Marazza (et al.).   Rome: Colombo, 1965. 1050p. + 84p. of plates.

This volume contains the proceedings of a conference on Belli organized by the Istituto di studi romani on the anniversary of his death, together with other studies on the poet. The contributions are divided into three sections: the life and times of Belli (which includes studies on Rome during the reign of Gregory XVI, Belli's genealogy, houses he inhabited in Rome, and Belli and politics); Belli's work (romanticism and realism, originality, structure, language, and attitude to religion); Belli and contemporary culture (Belli and Porta, Manzoni, Thorvaldsen, and Baudelaire) and the poet's influence. There is also a chronological register of all the poems of Belli (both in Romanesco and in Italian), and detailed comments to the thirty-six plates in the text and the eighty-four plates at the end of the volume showing manuscripts, portraits and other material related to the poet.

436 Tutti i sonetti romaneschi. (The complete sonnets in Romanesco.)
Giuseppe Gioachino Belli, edited by Bruno Cagli. Rome: Newton
Compton, 1975. 2nd ed. 5 vols. bibliog. (Paperbacks Poeti, 36-40.)
This edition, originally published in 1964-65, includes 2,250 sonnets and a supplement of 50
poems either left unfinished or rejected by Belli. The long introductory essay outlines Belli's
life and career and analyses his poetry. The poems are accompanied by Belli's original notes
and supplementary ones by Bruno Cagli.

Drama

437 Beatrice Cenci.
Alberto Moravia, translated by Angus Davidson. London: Secker &
Warburg, 1965.
Moravia's version of the Cenci story was first staged in 1955. The play takes place entirely at
La Petrella castle and it ends with the arrest of Beatrice, Lucrezia and Marzio. Moravia leaves
out their trial and execution. See also *The Cenci* by Antonin Artaud, translated from the French
by Simon Watson-Taylor (London: Calder and Boyars, 1969. 60p. [Playscipt, 12]).

438 The Cenci.
Percy Bysshe Shelley. In: *Shelley: poetical works.* Edited by Thomas
Hutchinson, corrected by G. M. Matthews. Oxford; New York: Oxford
University Press, 1970, p. 274-337.
Shelley's single stage play was inspired by Guido Reni's 'Portrait of Beatrice Cenci', in the 19th
century one of the most popular paintings in Rome. Both attribution and identification have
since been rejected (the work, which now hangs in the Galleria nazionale d'arte antica at the
Palazzo Barberini, is now ascribed to a pupil of Reni and the figure is thought to depict a Sibyl).
In the play, which was written in two months in the spring and summer of 1819, Shelley adapts
the original characters and invents new ones – Beatrice becomes a symbol of ruined innocence
and a victim of paternal oppression.

439 The representative: a Christian tragedy.
Rolf Hochhuth, translated with a preface by Robert David MacDonald.
London: Oberon Books, 1998. (Modern Playwrights.)
Der stellvertreter, produced at the time of the Second Vatican Council (1962-65), strongly
censures Pope Pius XII, partly attributing a pro-Nazi bias to him, not due to anti-semitism or to
any pecuniary consideration of the Vatican but to character flaws and his preoccupation with the
afterlife and his corresponding devaluation of the importance of earthly suffering. An appendix
provides some of the playwright's sources for the creation of his characters and some of the
controversial happenings and statements in his play.

440   Shakespeare's Rome.
Robert S. Miola.   Cambridge, England: Cambridge University Press, 1983. 244p.

A study of all Shakespeare's plays which have a Roman setting or were inspired by Roman history – *Titus Andronicus, Julius Caesar, Antony and Cleopatra, Coriolanus* and *Cymbeline*, and also the narrative poem *The rape of Lucrece*. Each work has a chapter dedicated to it. An introductory chapter looks at the sources of information about Ancient Rome available during the Elizabethan era. The author points out that the chronological examination of the Roman canon shows that Ancient Rome occupies a special position in Shakespeare's art and that his vision of the city and its people, though it evolved dynamically throughout his career as he reworked dramatic situations and scenes, retains an overall coherence.

441   *La Tosca*: the drama behind the opera.
Victorien Sardou, edited and translated by W. Laird Kleine-Ahlbrandt. Lewinston, New York: The Edwin Mellen Press, 1990. 143p. (Studies in the History and Interpretation of Music, vol. 19.)

Victorien Sardou's once popular drama, written for Sara Bernhardt, is now chiefly remembered as the source of Puccini's opera. As this well-annotated edition shows, the play contains a wealth of historical references and anecdotes about the Napoleonic period (in the words of the editor 'it abounds with references to *philosophes,* to opera houses, rulers, generals, composers, cutthroats, battles, wines, arcane customs, card games, hair and clothing styles') which were removed from the opera. It is also fascinating to note some other alterations made by Puccini and his librettists, such as the astute change of the Act 1 setting from S. Andrea al Quirinale to S. Andrea della Valle. The introduction includes a discussion of Sardou as a playwright and a detailed survey of the historical background to the plot of the play. It also includes a biographical index of all the historical characters mentioned in the play, divided into: kings, queens, emperors and popes; army commanders, statesmen and politicians; philosophers and writers; and artists and musicians.

Visual Arts

General

442 Art and architecture in Italy, 1600-1750.
Rudolf Wittkower. Fourth edition revised by Jennifer Montagu and
Joseph Connors, with John Pinto.   Yale, New Jersey; London: Yale
University Press, 1999. 3 vols.

This classic survey of Italian Baroque art and architecture was first published in 1958. In this
edition, the work has been divided into three volumes dealing with early, high and late Baroque.
The text is accompanied by a critical introduction, a substantial new bibliography, and, for the
first time, numerous colour illustrations. In each volume, painting, sculpture and architecture are
examined in separate sections each beginning with chapters looking at artistic developments in
Rome, the centre of Baroque art, and followed by chapters on other parts of Italy. In their
introductory note and appreciation of Rudolf Wittkower (1901-71), the editors remark that
when this book was first published the Baroque was largely unfamiliar to the general public and
that this work was crucial to its revival and present popularity. They also point out the
alternation in the text between chapters which deal with dozens of artists and ones which focus
on individual geniuses, such as Caravaggio, Bernini and Borromini.

443 Art in Rome in the eighteenth century.
Edited by Edgar Peters Bowron, Joseph Rishel.   London: Merrell, 2000.
628p. bibliog.

This is the sumptuous and erudite catalogue of the exhibition 'The splendor of eighteenth-
century Rome' held in Philadelphia and Houston in 2000. It is the culmination of the process of
re-evaluation of the art of 18th-century Rome that has reassessed the view that Rome declined
as an artistic centre in the late 17th and the 18th century. The catalogue provides a panoramic
view of the cultural life of the city. Subjects discussed include: student competitions in the
Accademia di S. Luca, church restoration, urban planning, festivals and ephemeral architecture,
archaeology, Roman libraries and museums, collecting and patronage, and the aristocracy and
clerical elite. There are biographical entries for some 150 key figures in 18th-century Rome and
a chronology. The catalogue section, which includes the work of Italian artists like Maratti,

Pannini, Piranesi, Canova and Batoni, and foreigners like Fragonard, Subleyras, J.-L. David, Kauffmann, Flaxman and Fuseli, contains 444 entries divided into: architecture, decorative arts, sculpture, paintings, drawings, and prints. There are biographies of all the artists represented, and each entry is accompanied by a bibliography and lists provenance and exhibition history.

444 Artisti e artigiani in Roma al tempo di Martino V e di Eugenio IV.
(Artists and artisans in Rome at the time of Martin V and Eugenius IV.)
Anna Maria Corbo. Rome: De Luca, 1969. 257p. (Raccolta di Fonti per la Storia dell'Arte diretta da Mario Salmi: Seconda Serie, 1.)

This study was originally planned as an update of Eugène Muntz's *Les arts à la cour des Papes* (The arts at the papal court), a compilation of archival information on artists, mostly foreigners, employed by the papal court in the period between the return of the papacy from Avignon and the beginning of the 16th century. It was subsequently decided to limit it chronologically to the pontificates of Martin V (1417-31) and Eugenius IV (1431-47) and to include artists and artisans whose work was commissioned by the nobility and the middle classes. Both local artists and also large numbers of immigrants (from central and southern Italy) are included in this category. Archival sources used include documents related to the construction of new buildings and those related to the restoration of houses, churches, towers, etc. As these documents indicate the *rione* of residence of the persons mentioned, they give a picture of the geographical distribution of artists in the city and the concentration of nationalities in particular areas. The work includes chapters on individual groups of artists and artisans such as painters, stone cutters, carpenters, goldsmiths and armourers.

445 Baroque art: the Jesuit contribution.
Edited by Rudolf Wittkower and Irma B. Jaffe. New York: Fordham University Press, 1972. 155p.

This volume comprises papers originally presented at a symposium organized at Fordham University in 1969 and revised in the light of new information that emerged during the symposium. They explore various aspects of Jesuit involvement in art, architecture, theatre and music. This involvement, as Rudolf Wittkower points out in his overview, was already strong during the last decades of the 16th century, which explains why a number of the following papers deal with the 16th rather than the 17th century. In answer to the often asked question as to the existence of a Jesuit style and a specific artistic strategy, Wittkower suggests that there was a Jesuit strategy in artistic matters, especially in the architecture of the early period, through the control of a *consiliarius aedificiorum*, an officer responsible for all building matters and ensuring a degree of stylistic conformity. However, in matters of style, it was the artists that influenced the Jesuits during the course of the 17th century, as the latter abandoned their earlier spirit of austerity and militancy and also principles of artistic simplicity and decorative bareness. Other topics considered are the work of non-Jesuit artists who collaborated with the Order (such as Rubens, Cortona, Borromini and Bernini), the Gesù (one of the most imposing Baroque churches and a symbol of the Jesuit Order's emergence after its early struggle for survival), the role of Jesuit art patronage, the careers of various architects (such as Giuseppe Valeriani) who worked for the Order, Jesuit theatre as a vehicle of instruction and indoctrination, and the importance of the German College in Rome as a centre for Baroque music.

446   Il Cardinale Francesco Maria Del Monte, 1549-1626. (Cardinal
      Francesco Maria Del Monte, 1549-1626.)
      Zygmunt Wazbinski.   Florence, Italy: Leo S. Olschki, 1994. 2 vols.
      (697p. + 59p. of plates). bibliog. (Studi, Accademia Toscana di Scienze e
      Lettere "La Colombaria", 136.)
Cardinal Del Monte is chiefly known as one of Caravaggio's most important patrons in Rome.
This study examines the wide-ranging artistic, cultural and political activities of this complex
and attractive personality. It looks at his formative years in Venice, Urbino and Padua, his
experiences in numerous courts (among them Mantua, Ferrara, Modena and Naples), his
contacts with foreign statesmen, his friendship with Ferdinando de' Medici and his role as his
artistic adviser when Ferdinando became Grand Duke of Tuscany enabling him to reside at
Palazzo Madama, his role as protector of the Accademia di S. Luca, and his participation in
various congregations and conclaves. His advice was sought during the restoration of churches
in Rome for the Jubilee of 1600, and he was instrumental in securing Caravaggio the decoration
of the Contarelli Chapel in S. Luigi dei Francesi, the Cerasi Chapel in S. Maria del Popolo, and
the Cherubini Chapel in S. Maria della Scala. Del Monte was an avid collector of paintings,
sculptures, prints and drawings, glass, textiles, musical instruments, and books. One feature of
his collection was its large number of portraits. Other interests included medicine, botany, and
precious stones. This study is divided into two parts: a biographical study and a *corpus* of
documents. These are complemented by a rich iconography of works of art in the Cardinal's
collection and of portraits of Del Monte and his circle.

447   High Renaissance art in St. Peter's and the Vatican: an
      interpretative guide.
      George L. Hersey.   Chicago; London: The University of Chicago Press,
      1993. 318p.
This study aims to be '...something more readable and enlightening than an ordinary guidebook
and more accessible than the professional scholarship'. It concentrates on four Renaissance
popes – Julius II, Leo X, Clement VII and Paul III, and the work of Bramante, Raphael and
Michelangelo. It begins with an introduction on the Renaissance papacy which provides a brief
outline of European power politics and biographies of the four popes. This is followed by
chapters on the visual personality each of these popes created for himself, the new St Peter's,
the Cortile del Belvedere, Raphael's *Stanze*, Michelangelo's Sistine Ceiling and *Last
Judgement*, Raphael's *Logge*, and Michelangelo's planned tomb for Julius II. As the book is
intended for the visitor to the Vatican, areas not currently accessible, such as the Cappella
Paolina with Michelangelo's two late frescoes, the Sala Regia, and the loggia and stufetta of
Cardinal Bibbiena, are not discussed.

448   L'Idea del Bello: viaggio per Roma nel Seicento con Giovan Pietro
      Bellori. (The Idea of Beauty: a journey through seventeenth-century
      Rome with Giovan Pietro Bellori.)
      Edited by Evelina Borea and Carlo Gasparri.   Rome: Edizioni De Luca,
      2000. 2 vols. 763p. bibliog.
Giovan Pietro Bellori (1613-96) was the subject of a massive exhibition held in Rome in 2000
which examined all aspects of his output and interests. Over 700 items were shown and they
included ancient sculpture, paintings and other artefacts, as well as 17th-century paintings,
sculptures, prints, drawings, and plans. These two volumes, which include contributions by
some forty scholars, are the permanent record of the exhibition. Volume one is a collection of

seventeen essays which discuss Rome in Bellori's time, the study of the antique in the 17th century, Bellori's aesthetic theories, his views on contemporary sculpture, his use and collection of drawings, and his *Vite de' pittori, scultori, e architetti moderni* (Lives of the modern painters, sculptors, and architects) (1672). Volume two consists of twenty-eight sections reflecting the arrangement of the exhibition. The first fifteen are dedicated to the artists discussed in the *Vite*, each of whom is given a separate section with a representative selection of his work. The remaining sections deal with other aspects of Bellori – his relationship to the Accademia di S. Luca, his collections of drawings and antiquities, his library, his publications on the *Forma Urbis Marmorea* and on the Column of Trajan. There is also a section on the rediscovery of ancient painting in the 17th century. All exhibited works are reproduced and discussed in individual entries. There is also a detailed chronology from 1630 to 1696 listing, in separate columns, political events; science, literature and music; visual arts in Italy; visual arts in Europe; and art literature. See also *L'Idea del Bello: viaggio per Roma nel Seicento con Giovan Pietro Bellori: cinque itinerari nella città seicentesca* (The Idea of Beauty: a journey through seventeenth-century Rome with Giovan Pietro Bellori: five itineraries), edited by Angela Negro (Rome: Edizioni De Luca, 2000. 54p.). This is a useful, and well-illustrated, supplement to the catalogue. It contains five walks to archaeological sites and churches in Rome related to Bellori's work.

449 **"Il se rendit en Italie": Études offertes à André Chastel.** ("He went to Italy": a Festschrift for André Chastel.)
Edited by Giuliano Briganti (et al.). Rome: Edizioni dell'elefante; Paris: Flammarion, 1987. 698p.

This collection of forty-five essays presented to the famous scholar of Renaissance art and Franco-Italian artistic relations includes a number of contributions on Rome, one of Chastel's many research interests.

450 **Die Kunsttätigkeit unter Urban VIII.** (Art activity during the pontificate of Urban VIII.)
Oskar Pollak, edited by Dagobert Frey and Franz Juraschek. Vienna: Dr Benno Filser Verlag, 1928-31. 2 vols. (503p., 664p.) (Quellenschriften zur Geschichte der Barockkunst in Rom.)

This collection of archival sources from the pontificate of Urban VIII is based on the papers of Oskar Pollak who, prior to his tragic death in the First World War, had been collecting material for a series of major works on Baroque art in Rome. The entries are arranged thematically, as follows: Vol. 1. Excavations, bridges, fountains, churches, monasteries, colleges, oratories, palaces, squares, hospitals, streets (1,862 entries); Vol. 2. St Peter's (2,474 entries). Each entry includes a brief indication of the location of the document and there is a full listing of repositories and shelfmarks of the documents at the end of each volume.

451 **Lectures.**
F. Saxl. London: the Warburg Institute, University of London, 1957. 2 vols. (390p; 26p. + 243 plates). bibliog.

This collection of twenty-six lectures, most of which were written between 1933 and 1948, when Fritz Saxl (1890-1948) taught at the Warburg Institute, includes three masterly lectures related to Rome. 'The Appartamento Borgia' (1945) examines the decorations executed for Pope Alexander VI Borgia (1492-1503) by Pinturicchio and his assistants in the six rooms in the 'Torre Borgia', in the Vatican Palace. 'The Villa Farnesina' (1935) examines the complex iconography of the frescoes by Sodoma, Raphael and Baldassare Peruzzi in Agostino Chigi's 'villa suburbana' and explains the astrological meaning of the mythological scenes depicted. 'The Capitol during the Renaissance – a symbol of the Imperial idea' (1938) maps out the history of the Campidoglio as a religious and political symbol of ancient Roman greatness.

452   Un mecenate in Roma barocca: il Cardinale Benedetto Pamphilj, 1653-1730. (A patron of the arts in Baroque Rome: Cardinal Benedetto Pamphilj, 1653-1730.)
   Lina Montalto.   Florence, Italy: Sansoni, 1955. 592p. (Critica e Storia.)

Cardinal Benedetto Pamphilj (1653-1730), the younger son of Don Camillo Pamphilj and Olimpia Aldobrandini, Princess of Rossano, was a man of wide-ranging interests. A bibliophile and a discriminating art collector, he was also a distinguished man of letters – a member of the Arcadian academy (writing under the pseudonym 'Fenicio Larisseo') and a writer of numerous oratorio librettos and cantatas set to music by Alessandro Scarlatti, Bernardo Pasquini, Handel and other composers who worked in his household. This work, based on both published sources and also on Pamphilj's account books which cover a period of over sixty years, is both a biography and a study of his munificent patronage. The study is divided into four sections looking at Benedetto's role as prince, man of letters and poet (with a complete list of all his works and a selection of his poetry in an appendix), patron of the arts, and cardinal.

453   Patronage in Renaissance Italy: from 1400 to the early sixteenth century.
   Mary Hollingsworth.   London: John Murray, 1994. 372p. bibliog.

The premise of this work, and its companion volume, is that in the Renaissance it was the patron who was the real initiator of works of art, his role being crucial in determining both their form and content. Art played a central role in the construction of images for powerful and ambitious patrons and this survey shows the diversity of patronage in different regions of Italy. It is in four parts, the first three discussing Florence, Venice, and the Italian Courts and the last one Rome. After a brief outline of the historical and cultural situation in the 14th century, it examines papal patronage from the final return of the papacy to Rome in 1420, with short sections on each pope's contribution, from Martin V (1417-31) to Alexander VI (1492-1503). These are followed by a chapter discussing the papal court and the role played by cardinals (especially cardinal nephews). Often criticized for their extravagance and their unclerical lifestyle, they commissioned palaces, altarpieces and frescoes, portraits and sculptures. The last chapter is dedicated to Julius II (1503-1513), the patron of Bramante, Raphael and Michelangelo. His pontificate was a Golden Age in the cultural history of Rome and his programme of urban renewal was the culmination of his predecessors' attempts to turn Rome into a city that would demonstrate the renewed power and prestige of the church. Julius's decision to demolish and rebuild on a massive scale St Peter's, one of Christianity's most venerable buildings, shows the extent of his overarching ambition. See also the same author's survey of papal court patronage in 16th-century Rome in *Patronage in sixteenth-century Italy* (London: John Murray, 1996. 462p.).

454 Pawnshop and palaces: the fall and rise of the Campana art museum.
Helen Borowitz, Albert Borowitz. Washington, DC; London: Smithsonian Institution Press, 1991. 288p. bibliog.

Giovanni Pietro Campana (1808-80) was the director of the Roman Monte di Pietà, the deposit bank established by the Church to help the poor, from which he borrowed large sums of money for the purchase of classical vases, sculpture and Italian 14th- and 15th-century paintings. His collection was one of the largest amassed in 19th-century Europe and was much visited by artists and connoisseurs in Rome. Campana was, however, arrested, tried and imprisoned in 1857 for misappropriation of funds and his collection was confiscated and sold to museum collections in France, England and Russia. The Louvre, the Victoria & Albert Museum, and the Hermitage now have important holdings from the Campana collection and in the 1950s some 300 Italian paintings previously allocated to various museum collections in France were brought together and are now displayed in the Musée du Petit Palais in Avignon. This study examines all aspects of the Campana affair and its aftermath. It includes an account of the development of the Monte di Pietà, an examination of Campana as a financial genius and compulsive collector, and considers the wider implications of the affair. Its sixty-four illustrations include portraits, views of the Campana museum, and several works from the collection.

455 Pietro da Cortona, 1597-1669.
Edited by Anna Lo Bianco. Milan, Italy: Electa, 1997. 511p. bibliog.

This is the catalogue of an exhibition held in Rome in 1997-98 to celebrate the quatercentenary of the birth of Pietro da Cortona, one of the greatest artists of the Roman Baroque. Cortona came to Rome in 1623, and his studies of the Antique were encouraged by Cassiano dal Pozzo, who commissioned drawings for his 'paper museum'. Cortona was soon established as one of the most talented artists working in Rome and he had many illustrious patrons. In this volume, the fourteen introductory essays dedicated to Cortona include a survey of his career, the influence of early Baroque art on his work, his relation with the Sacchetti, Barberini and Pamphilj families, his workshop, his output as an architect, and his influence. A further fourteen essays examine the work of some of his most prominent followers (Giovanni Francesco Romanelli, Giacinto Gimignani, Ciro Ferri, and others). The catalogue includes 125 works: 54 paintings by Cortona, paintings and sculptures by artists who were active in Rome when he arrived there (Guercino, Lanfranco, Vouet) and by his numerous pupils, and also 20 architectural drawings by Cortona. Pietro da Cortona's work as a draughtsman is examined in the catalogue of a complementary exhibition, also held in Rome, which includes sections on his studies after the Antique, and preparatory drawings for the vault of the Gran Salone of Palazzo Barberini. See *Pietro da Cortona e il disegno* (Pietro da Cortona and drawing) (Milan, Italy: Electa, 1997. 279p.).

456 Queen Christina of Sweden: documents and studies.
Edited by Magnus von Platen. Stockholm: Kungl. Boktryckeriet P. A. Norstedt & Söner, 1966. 389p. bibliog. (Analecta Reginensia, 1; Nationalmusei Skriftserie, no. 12.)

A collection of twenty-six essays published in connection with the eleventh exhibition of the Council of Europe, held in Sweden in 1966, examining various aspects of Queen Christina's life and times. Several contributions concentrate on her activities in Rome, where she lived for nearly thirty years after her conversion to Roman Catholicism and subsequent abdication. The main emphasis is on individual areas of her various collections and spheres of patronage. Her book and manuscript collections (now in the Vatican Library) are discussed by Christian Callmer in 'Queen Christina's Library of printed books in Rome', by Sten Lindberg in 'Queen Christina bindings' and by Jeanne Bignami Odier in 'Les manuscrits de la Reine Christine au Vatican' (The manuscripts of Queen Christina at the Vatican). Her painting collections are discussed by Ellis Waterhouse in 'Queen Christina's Italian pictures in England' and Frans Baudouin in 'Deux tableaux de Rubens de la collection de la Reine Christine: "Hercule et Omphale" et "La mort d'Adonis" ' (Two Ruben's paintings from the collection of Queen Christina: "Hercules and Omphale" and "The death of Adonis"). Other contributions examine her collection of tapestries and armoury while Ruth Stephan, in 'A note on Christina and her Academies' discusses Christina's reputation as the 'Minerva of the North', her relationship with scholars and scientists and her role as a founder of various academies, which included the *Accademia Reale* in Rome, later renamed the *Accademia degli Arcadi*.

457   The Renaissance in Rome, 1400-1600.
Loren Partridge.   London: Weidenfeld & Nicolson, 1996. 184p. bibliog.
This is a study of the urban development of Rome in the 15th and 16th centuries and its transformation, thanks to the patronage of a succession of 'builder-popes', from its state of neglect during the Middle Ages into a city of magnificent palaces, churches and piazzas. It also surveys painting and sculpture and the work of artists ranging from Fra Angelico and Masolino to Botticelli and Pinturicchio, and culminating in the great decorative cycles of Michelangelo and Raphael. The book's six chapters examine: urbanism, churches, palaces, chapel decoration, and halls of state. There is a chronology in four columns: politics and culture, religion, urbanism and architecture, and painting and sculpture.The American edition of this work is called *The art of Renaissance Rome, 1400-1600* (New York: Harry N. Abrams, 1996).

458   Roma 1300-1875: l'arte degli anni santi. (Rome 1300-1875: the art of the Holy Years.)
Edited by Marcello Fagiolo, Maria Luisa Madonna.   Milan, Italy: Arnoldo Mondadori, 1984. 494p. bibliog.
The catalogue of an exhibition held in Rome in 1984-85 which included a huge number of works produced during the Holy Years from 1300 to the end of the pontificate of Pius IX. They are presented in eleven sections. The first six sections examine various themes or types of artefact. They include: signs and symbols of the pilgrimage (with chapters on the symbolism of the pilgrimage, the costume and items worn by pilgrims, the Veronica, and the Holy Gate); liturgical treasures from the great basilicas; coins and medals; and printed material related to pilgrimage, from the *Mirabilia Urbis Romae* to engravings. Sections seven to eleven are a chronological presentation of works from the 14th to the 19th century. The catalogue includes hundreds of illustrations.

459   Roma, 1918-1943. (Rome, 1918-1943.)
Edited by Fabio Benzi, Gianni Mercurio, Luigi Prisco.   Rome: Viviani, 1998. 365p. (Viviani Arte.)
This is the catalogue of an exhibition held in Rome in 1998, examining artistic production in Rome during the inter-war years. During this period, Rome was one of the most important centres of the 'return to order' tendencies, advocated by the review *Valori plastici*, which followed the avant-garde movements of the pre-war years. The city also played a major role in the development of Futurism, Metaphysical painting and, in the 1930s, saw the development of two local schools, the 'Scuola di Via Cavour' (the School of Via Cavour) and the 'Scuola romana' (Roman school). The fifteen introductory essays examine numerous aspects of artistic

and cultural activity in Rome during this vital period. They include an overview of artistic developments, and discussions of individual subjects: architecture, music, dance, cinema, literature and the role of literary reviews, Roman galleries, Roman cafés, the relationship between art and power between 1930 and 1943, the Fori imperiali, and the EUR (Universal Exhibition of Rome). The catalogue includes over 200 works (all reproduced in colour) by fifty different artists. There are bio-bibliographical entries for all the artists represented and the volume also contains an abundance of comparative illustrations, portraits and contemporary photographs of the city. See also *École romaine, 1925-1945* (The Roman School, 1925-1945) (Paris: Paris Musées, 1997. 159p.) and *Scuola romana: artisti tra le due guerre* (Scuola romana: artists during the inter-war years), coordinated by Domenico Pertocoli (Milan, Italy: Mazzotta, 1988. 315p.). Both of these volumes also show examples of the work of several of the artists represented in the volume above and include useful chronologies.

460 Roma di Sisto V: le arti e la cultura. (The Rome of Sixtus V: arts and culture.)
Edited by Maria Luisa Madonna. Rome: Edizioni De Luca, 1993. 602p. bibliog.

This massive publication, part of the celebrations for the quatercentenary of the pontificate of Pope Sixtus V (1585-90), is a *catalogue raisonné* of all the works produced during the reign of this pope, who transformed Rome more drastically than any other pope in history. It is divided into six sections dedicated to: painting, drawing, sculpture, coins and medals, the Biblioteca vaticana, and publishing and culture (the last section with chapters on book production, theological controversy, the wars of religion in France, the Oratory of St Philip Neri, musical life, and heraldry). The section on painting is the most extensive, containing chapters on iconology, painters' workshops, patronage, and the fresco cycles in the Biblioteca vaticana. These are followed by detailed descriptions of all the paintings produced during this period: papal commissions for painted cycles in churches and other religious buildings, altarpieces, municipal commissions, and painted cycles in secular buildings. The two appendices provide biographies of all the artists (painters, engravers, sculptors, stucco workers, medallists, and goldsmiths) whose work is discussed in the text. See also *Roma di Sisto V: arte, architettura e città fra Rinascimento e Barocco* (The Rome of Sixtus V: art, architecture and the city from the Renaissance to the Baroque), edited by Maria Luisa Madonna (Rome: Edizioni De Luca, 1993. 63p.). This is the catalogue of an exhibition held in Rome celebrating the same anniversary.

461 Rome 1630: l'horizon du premier baroque. (Rome 1630: the horizon of early Baroque.)
Yves Bonnefoy. Paris: Flammarion, 1994. bibliog.

A revised and updated edition of Bonnefoy's classic essay first published in 1970, this focuses on artistic activity in Rome around 1630, the years that saw the first flowering of Baroque art. It provides a kaleidoscopic view of all the artistic trends prevalent in the city at the time and their exponents – artists from different parts of Italy (none of the great 'Roman' artists of the 17th century was Roman by birth) and of different nationalities (Flemish, Dutch, French), and their patrons, who ranged from the Pope, religious orders like the Jesuits, the Theatines and the Oratorians, wealthy noblemen and cardinals and also antiquarians (such as Cassiano dal Pozzo) and ordinary people. It looks at the contrasting art and personalities of Annibale Carracci and Caravaggio, the dominant figures of the first thirty years of the century, the work of Bernini (in particular the creation of the Baldacchino), Pietro da Cortona and his great decorative schemes for the Barberini family, Domenichino, Poussin, Claude Lorrain, and the Bamboccianti. This edition also includes another text by Bonnefoy on

Baroque art – 'Un des siècles du culte de l'image' – which was originally published in 1989 in the catalogue of the exhibition *Seicento, le siècle de Caravage dans les collections françaises* (The seventeenth century, the age of Caravaggio in French collections). See also *Roma 1630: il trionfo del pennello* (Rome 1630: the triumph of the brush), edited by Olivier Bonfait (Milan, Italy: Electa, 1994. 259p. bibliog.).

462 Römisches Jahrbuch für Kunstgeschichte. (Rome yearbook for the history of art.)
Leipzig, Germany, 1937- .

This prestigious publication of the Bibliotheca Hertziana started life in 1937 as *Kunstgeschichtliches Jahbuch der Bibliotheca Hertziana* (The art history yearbook of the Bibliotheca Hertziana), but its title changed to the present one two years later when its publication moved to Vienna. It is currently published in Tübingen. Thirty-one volumes of the yearbook have been published to date, making a significant contribution to the study of Roman art and architecture (the coverage of the yearbook is predominantly, but not exclusively, Roman). The articles are written in English, French, German or Italian.

463 Studies in the Italian Baroque.
Rudolf Wittkower. London: Thames & Hudson, 1975. 304p.

A collection of fifteen papers and articles (all but two previously published) on Roman and Piedmontese sculpture and architecture, by one of the greatest writers on Baroque art. It includes four essays relating to Bernini as both architect and sculptor, and three essays on Piranesi.

464 Tomb of Julius II and other works in Rome.
Edited by William E. Wallace. New York, London: Garland Publishing, 1995. 480p. (Michelangelo: Selected Scholarship in English, 4.)

This is a collection of reprints from various sources focusing on Michelangelo's work in Rome between 1534 and his death in 1564. During these years, Michelangelo reached maturity as an architect and, consequently, a number of articles here deal with his architecture – there are studies on his projects for the Capitoline Hill, the Porta Pia and the new St Peter's. The volume also includes essays on the completion of the tomb of Julius II, the fresco of the 'Last Judgement', the Pauline Chapel, and several sculptures, including the two late *Pietàs*.

465 The Vatican and Christian Rome.
Vatican City: Libreria editrice vaticana, 1975. 537p. bibliog.

Published on the occasion of the Holy Year in 1975 and written by a team of internationally renowned experts, this is a lavishly produced guide to the collections of the Vatican and to churches and other Christian sites in Rome. The section on the Vatican contains chapters on the Pope and the history and structure of the Roman Curia; St Peter's; the Tomb of Peter; the remains of the Apostle's body; the new St Peter's; the Apostolic Palace; the Vatican City State; the Teutonic College in Campo Santo and the Ethiopian College; the Vatican Monuments and Museums; the Biblioteca apostolica vaticana; the Papal Choirs; and the Vatican's means of social communication – the newspaper *L'Osservatore romano*, Vatican Radio, and the Vatican Press Office. The section on Christian Rome has chapters on S. Giovanni in Laterano and the Administrative and Pastoral Centre of the Diocese of Rome; S. Maria Maggiore; S. Paolo fuori le Mura; a chapter containing shorter descriptions of thirty other churches; the Catacombs; Pontifical institutes of higher education; and Pontifical academies. The volume is abundantly illustrated in colour throughout and most of the illustrations still look impressive (especially those of sculptures), with the exception of those showing paintings and frescoes, for which the reader should look elsewhere. There are also fold-out plans of the Necropolis and the Constantinian basilica and a map of the Catacombs. See also *Art treasures of the Vatican: architecture, painting, sculpture*, edited by D. Redig De Campos (New York: Park Lane, 1974. 398p.).

466 Villa Medici: il sogno di un cardinale: collezioni e artisti di Ferdinando de' Medici. (Villa Medici: a cardinal's dream: the collections and artists of Ferdinando de' Medici.)
Edited by Michel Hochmann.   Rome: Edizioni De Luca, 1999. 323p. bibliog.

The catalogue of the exhibition held at the Villa Medici in 1999-2000 exploring the personality, patronage and collections of Cardinal Ferdinando de' Medici before his departure from Rome in 1587 when he succeeded Francesco de' Medici, his brother, as Grand Duke of Tuscany. Eleven introductory essays discuss the collections of antiquities and paintings, the architecture and gardens of Villa Medici and the recent restoration of its façades. Three essays look at Jacopo Zucchi, who executed numerous decorative schemes for the Cardinal, and other Florentine artists working in Rome at the time. The catalogue section has ninety works all reproduced in colour – paintings, drawings, marble and bronze sculptures, *pietre dure* (hardstones), and architectural drawings for the decoration of Villa Medici.

467 Le vite de' pittori, scultori e architetti moderni. (The lives of modern painters, sculptors and architects.)
Giovan Pietro Bellori, edited by Evelina Borea, with an introduction by Giovanni Previtali.   Turin, Italy: Giovanni Einaudi, 1976. 867p. 33 plates. bibliog. (I Millenni.)

Giovan Pietro Bellori (1613-96) has been called 'the greatest art scholar and archaeologist of his time'. His main claim to fame is this collection of lives of artists, first published in 1672, one of the great sources for the study of 17th-century Roman art. The fifteen biographies are as follows: Annibale Carracci (with a detailed commentary on the frescoes of the Farnese Gallery), Agostino Carracci, Domenico Fontana, Federico Barocci, Caravaggio, Rubens, Van Dyck, François Duquesnoy, Domenichino, Giovanni Lanfranco, Alessandro Algardi, Nicolas Poussin, and the posthumously published biographies of Guido Reni, Andrea Sacchi, and Carlo Maratti. The three notable omissions in Bellori's text are those of Bernini, Pietro da Cortona, and Borromini, an indication of his lack of interest in Baroque theatricality and exuberance. The long introduction provides a biography of Bellori and traces the development of his aesthetic theories, which determined his choice of artists. It also analyses the contents and structure of his work and his critical method. This edition reproduces the etchings used for the first edition. There is also a detailed chronology of Bellori's life and works, as well as name and place indices (the latter indicating, if known, the present whereabouts of the works).

Paintings, prints and drawings

468 Adam Elsheimer: paintings, drawings, prints.
Keith Andrews. Oxford: Phaidon, 1977. 178p.

An excellent study and *catalogue raisonné* of the work of Adam Elsheimer, a German artist who lived in Rome from 1600 until his early death in 1610. Elsheimer specialized in small, highly-wrought cabinet pictures painted on copper. In Rome, he moved in the circle of Johannes Faber, the herbalist of the Pope, and Kaspar Schoppe, whose humanist interests may have contributed to his adoption of unusual classical themes. He was influenced by Annibale Carracci's use of landscape and by Caravaggio's chiaroscuro effects (though Andrews points out that some of these effects were already used by Elsheimer before going to Rome). There is no record of Elsheimer's patrons or commissions in Rome, where he died in abject poverty. His fame was posthumous, partly through a series of prints Hendrick Goudt executed after his paintings and partly through younger Netherlandish artists in Rome, such as Pieter Lastman (Rembrandt's teacher) and Cornelis van Poelenburch. The catalogue lists fifty-nine known works, nearly half of which date from the artist's time in Rome.

469 After Raphael: painting in central Italy in the sixteenth century.
Marcia B. Hall. Cambridge, England: Cambridge University Press, 1999. 365p. bibliog.

This is an overview of Mannerism (the style developed from the late work of Raphael in Rome and influenced by antique Roman relief sculpture) in Rome, Florence and other artistic centres in central Italy. The opening chapter sets the scene by discussing developments during the first two decades of the 16th century, concentrating on works (the frescoes in the Sala di Costantino in the Vatican) or tendencies (Pinturicchio's taste for antiquarian profuseness) that were to influence the next generation of painters. Subsequent chapters examine the years between the death of Raphael in 1520 and the Sack of Rome in 1527, the diaspora of the Roman style brought about by the move of artists to other cities, the revival of artistic activity in Rome later in the century (in Michelangelo's *Last Judgement* and the frescoes in the Cappella Paolina, the work of Perino del Vaga [a pupil of Raphael who returned to Rome in 1537], Salviati and Vasari), the effects of the Counter-Reformation on painting and the development of a new style and decorum in sacred painting, and, finally, the end of the century in Rome, the influence of Sixtus V and the new religious orders and the first works by Caravaggio and the Carracci. Though the work is profusely illustrated (there are 32 colour plates and 188 black-and-white illustrations) the quality of the reproductions is only average.

470 The Age of Caravaggio.
New York: The Metropolitan Museum of Art; Milan, Italy: Electa International, 1985. 367p. bibliog.

The catalogue of an exhibition held in New York and Naples in 1985, this volume includes 100 paintings by Caravaggio and his contemporaries in Lombardy, Rome and Naples. The exhibition focused on the relationship of Caravaggio with his precursors and his contemporaries, and this study examines the work of Counter-Reformation artists who constituted the artistic establishment when Caravaggio arrived in Rome from Lombardy in 1592. The work of Annibale and Agostino Carracci, who arrived in Rome shortly before Caravaggio and whose reform of painting predates his own revolutionary naturalism, is singled out, and there is also a representative selection of paintings by other young artists active in Rome during Caravaggio's lifetime – Rubens, Reni, Elsheimer, Domenichino, Gentileschi, and Saraceni. The work of these diverse artists provides the background to the work of Caravaggio, represented here by forty canvases. Work by the artist's followers was excluded. The three introductory essays look at the critical reception of Caravaggio, recent scholarship on the artist, and his Roman patrons and admirers. Each catalogue entry is a short essay and most of the works are reproduced in colour.

471 Angelika Kauffmann e Roma. (Angelika Kauffmann and Rome.)
Edited by Oscar Sandner. Rome: Edizioni De Luca, 1998. 230p. bibliog.

This is the catalogue of an exhibition held in 1998 at the Accademia nazionale di S. Luca, an institution of which Kauffmann was one of the few women members. Born in Switzerland in 1741, Kauffmann spent most of her life in Italy and England. She first went to Rome in 1763 and over the next two years she painted numerous portraits and also her first subject pictures. After a fifteen-year stay in London (from 1766 to 1781), she returned to Italy with her second husband, the painter Antonio Zucchi, and quickly became an important figure of Roman society and, after the death of Pompeo Batoni in 1787, the most successful portrait painter in Rome. A long introductory essay surveys Kauffmann's life and work, focusing on her Roman years, the intellectual and artistic circles in which she moved, and her relations with Goethe. Another essay discusses her relations with English artists and visitors in Rome. The catalogue contains sixty-three paintings by Kauffmann, which include portraits and also subject paintings, and thirty-two drawings. There are also 105 works by her contemporaries in Rome, including works by Batoni, Canova, David, Goethe, Mengs, Piranesi, Thorvaldsen, and others. Finally, there are thirty-two engravings after Kauffmann's work.

472 Artemisia Gentileschi: the image of the female hero in Italian Baroque art.
Mary D. Garrard. Princeton, New Jersey: Princeton University Press, 1989. 632p.

Artemisia Gentileschi (1593-1652/3) was the only woman follower of Caravaggio, whose naturalist style of painting and often violent subject-matter she adopted. She was taught by Orazio Gentileschi, her father, and Agostino Tassi, one of his assistants, who, in 1611, seduced and raped her. A public trial ensued which lasted for seven months and became a public scandal. Tassi was imprisoned for eight months, while Artemisia was soon married to a Florentine and moved to Florence. She later worked in Genoa, England and Naples. Artemisia's work has often been read in psychoanalytical terms, the suffering or vengeful heroines (for example Susanna or Judith) that dominate her work seen as reflections of, or revenge for, her own humiliation. The first part of this monograph examines the artist's early years in Rome, the artistic milieu in which she grew up, dominated by the revolutionary art and personality of Caravaggio, especially his paintings in S. Luigi dei Francesi and S. Maria del Popolo. The circumstances of the rape and its aftermath are also examined. This volume also includes an English translation of the testimony of the rape trial of 1612 that resulted from the suit brought by Orazio Gentileschi against Tassi, an important document of social history. The painter's life has been the subject of a novel by Anna Banti, first published in 1953 (English translation published in 1988 by Nebraska University Press).

473   Artists working in Rome, c. 1550 to c. 1640.
J. A. Gere and Philip Pouncey, with the assistance of Rosalind Wood.
London: British Museum Publications, 1983. 2 vols. (255p.; xv, 370
plates). bibliog. (Italian Drawings in the Department of Prints and
Drawings in the British Museum.)

This is a sequel to the catalogue of drawings by Raphael and his immediate Roman circle
published in 1962, dealing with the mannerist era. The Roman High Renaissance came to an
abrupt end in 1527, seven years after Raphael's death, with the Sack of Rome, which drove
artists to other parts of Italy. Some of them, like Perino Del Vaga, later returned and pursued
successful careers, influencing a new generation of Roman artists. In their preface, the authors
of this catalogue point out that very few of the artists working in Rome during this period were
Roman by birth and that the rapid succession of popes and their tendency to employ artists from
their own native cities made for discontinuity of patronage and inhibited the development of a
local school of painting. The main criterion for inclusion of non-Roman artists was whether the
examples of their works in the Museum's collections were from their Roman years. The
biographical prefaces to each artist's works provide a wealth of information about artistic
activity in Rome as they concentrate on the part of the artists' careers spent in the city, omitting,
however, works no longer extant. The catalogue contains 398 drawings by 47 artists (including
Barocci, Pirro Ligorio, Cesare Nebbia, Pellegrino Tibaldi, and Federico and Taddeo Zuccaro).
There is an appendix of works by the artists included in the earlier volume that have been
recently acquired by the Museum or newly attributed to them, and indexes to related works,
references to drawings in other collections, and subjects.

**474   The Bambuoccianti: the painters of everyday life in seventeenth-
century Rome.**
Giuliano Briganti, Ludovica Trezzani, Laura Laureati.   Rome: Ugo
Bozzi, [1983]. 414p. bibliog. (The Collectors' Series.)

The Bambuoccianti is the name given to a group of Northern artists who worked in Rome in the
17th century and specialized in small paintings showing low-life scenes from everyday life. This
monograph examines the work of fifteen artists – among them Jan Both, Karel Dujardin,
Sébastien Bourdon, Johannes Lingelbach, Michelangelo Cerquozzi (the only Italian artist in the
group) and Pieter van Laer, called il Bamboccio (after whom the group was named). Each artist
is given a chapter and the text is accompanied by numerous examples of his work. An
introductory chapter examines the subject matter of the artists' paintings, the nature of their
realism and their underlying ideology of a 'contented poverty', and their patrons (paradoxically
the Roman aristocracy and bourgeoisie). Their work is also compared to the output of other 17th-
century artists who depicted the poor – Georges de La Tour, the Le Nain brothers, and Callot.

475   Baroque painting in Rome.
Hermann Voss, revised and translated by Thomas Pelzel.   San
Francisco, California: Alan Wofsy Fine Arts, 1997. 2 vols. (198p., 216p.)

This is a translation of *Die Malerei des Barock in Rom*, originally published in one volume in
1925. This pioneering study examined a period of Italian art that was at the time rather
unfashionable but has since returned to favour. The first volume looks at the period between
1585 and 1640 and the work of Caravaggio, the Carracci, Domenichino, and their followers,
while the second volume covers a much longer date-span (1620-1790), from High Baroque to
Rococo and early Neo-classicism. Each section consists of a general survey followed by entries
on individual artists with accounts of their life and work, followed by selected and updated

bibliographies (which, however, should be used with caution as they omit key works), comments on the works illustrated (there are 357 full-page plates and the illustrations, of only average quality, are indexed by artist and location) and lists of works not illustrated (arranged by present location).

476 British artists in Italy, 1920-1980.
Penelope Curtis, Alan Powers, Roger Mills.   Canterbury, England: Kent County Council, 1985. 55p.

The catalogue of a travelling exhibition organized by the Canterbury College of Art in 1985, this volume examines the influence of Italy on the work of British artists that received the Prix de Rome scholarship, which allowed them to reside in Rome for three years and also travel to other artistic centres in Italy. It includes introductory studies on: modernist sculptors such as John Skeaping, Barbara Hepworth (who both went to Rome in 1924), and Henry Moore; the Rome scholarship in decorative (i.e mural) painting from 1912 to 1939 (recipients include Winifred Knights, Thomas Monnington, Edward Halliday and Colin Gill, who all later provided mural decorations for public buildings in England, such as the Palace of Westminster, the Bank of England and Canterbury Cathedral); and Rome scholarships after the Second World War at a time when, from the avant-garde point of view, studying in Italy seemed almost an anachronism (artists in this group, painting from the motif and usually producing a variety of drawings, include Euan Uglow, Patrick Proctor and Michael Andrews). There are short biographical notes, lists of exhibitions and examples of the work of each of the twenty-three artists represented in the exhibition.

477 Caravaggio.
Howard Hibbard.   London: Thames & Hudson, 1983. 416p. bibliog.

Caravaggio (1571-1610) worked in Rome from *c.* 1592 to 1606, when he had to flee the city after killing a man in a brawl. This study concentrates on paintings known to be by Caravaggio himself, with some of the more important attributions discussed in an appendix. There are short sections on his early works, both secular and religious. These include several easel paintings, allegorical scenes depicting sensuous, half-length youths, commissioned by Cardinal Del Monte. These are followed by chapters on the first religious works and the major public commissions – the Contarelli Chapel in S. Luigi dei Francesi (*The calling of St Matthew* and *Martyrdom of St Matthew*) and the Cerasi chapel in S. Maria del Popolo (*Crucifixion of St Peter* and *Conversion of St Paul*), which established Caravaggio as one of the most exciting and innovative artists working in Rome during the reign of Pope Clement VIII – and on the later Roman paintings, which include altarpieces like *The Entombment of Christ* (painted for S. Maria in Vallicella, now in the Pinacoteca vaticana), *The Madonna di Loreto* (S. Agostino), and *The death of the Virgin* (painted for S. Maria della Scala, now in the Louvre). There is also a chapter discussing Caravaggio's borrowings from Michelangelo (especially in *St John the Baptist* and in *Amor vincit omnia*), which are seen as reflections of Caravaggio's ambivalent reaction to artistic tradition. A number of early texts on Caravaggio are given, in the original and in translation, in an appendix.

478 Caravaggio and his Italian followers: from the collections of the Galleria nazionale d'arte antica di Roma.
Catalogue by Claudio Strinati and Rossella Vodret.   Rome: Marsilio, 1998. 141p. bibliog.

This is the catalogue of an exhibition held at the Wadsworth Atheneum, Hartford in 1998 of the rich holding of works by Caravaggio and his followers in the Galleria nazionale d'arte antica at the Palazzo Barberini. The gallery, as well as two paintings by Caravaggio – *Judith beheading Holophernes* and *Narcissus*, has over seventy paintings by his followers which show the development of naturalistic painting in Rome and Naples during the first three decades of the 17th century. In their introductory essay, the two editors indicate the provenance of the works from the Torlonia collection that was presented to the Galleria nazionale in 1892, the collection of the Monte di Pietà, and through deeds of trust made by various Roman aristocratic families like the Barberini and the Mattei. The catalogue includes twenty-nine paintings, all of which are reproduced in colour. Among the artists represented are: Giovanni Baglione, Orazio and Artemisia Gentileschi, Carlo Saraceni, Orazio Borgianni, Simon Vouet, Lionello Spada, Luca Giordano, and Jusepe Ribera. The catalogue also includes a number of paintings from American collections, one of which, Jacopo Zucchi's *The bath of Bathsheba*, once belonged to the Galleria nazionale and was returned to it on the occasion of this exhibition. The story of its loss and recovery is related in an introductory article.

479 **Caravaggio and his two cardinals.**
Creighton E. Gilbert. University Park, Pennsylvania: The Pennsylvania State University Press, 1995. 335p. bibliog.

The two cardinals of the title are Cardinal Del Monte and Cardinal Girolamo Mattei, two of Caravaggio's major patrons in Rome. Del Monte was the first to discover the artist's talent and among those who acquired the largest number of his paintings, all of them before 1600. Caravaggio lived in Del Monte's household from 1595 to 1601, when he moved to the house Cardinal Mattei shared with his brother Ciriaco, where he was to remain for the following two years. The Mattei owned three paintings by him, the *Supper at Emmaus* (National Gallery), the *Taking of Christ* (National Gallery of Ireland) and *St John the Baptist* (Pinacoteca Capitolina). This last painting is the subject of a long examination occupying the first seven chapters of this book, which argue that its present title is erroneous and that the painting depicts, uniquely in Caravaggio's work, a classical subject, namely Paris of Troy as a shepherd, painted for the Marchese Ciriaco Mattei, an avid collector of classical antiquities. The work also looks at other patrons of the artist: Vincenzo Giustiniani, owner of some fifteen canvases; the Genoese Ottavio Costa; and Scipione Borghese (whose works by the artist were, however, acquired second hand).

480 **Caravaggio e la collezione Mattei.** (Caravaggio and the Mattei collection.)
Edited by Rossella Vodret. Milan, Italy: Electa, 1995. 183p.

The catalogue of an exhibition held at the Palazzo Barberini in 1995 examining the relationship of Caravaggio with the Mattei family, who were, with Cardinal Del Monte and Vincenzo Giustiniani, his most important patrons in Rome. The exhibition brought together three paintings Caravaggio executed for Ciriaco Mattei and his brother, Cardinal Girolamo Mattei – the recently rediscovered *Taking of Christ* (on loan to the National Gallery of Ireland), *St John the Baptist* (Pinacoteca Capitolina), and *The Supper at Emmaus* (The National Gallery). It also included other works in the picture gallery of a third Mattei brother, Asdrubale, whose patronage in the 1620s also had a strong naturalist and Caravaggesque element. These include paintings by Paul Brill, Bartolomeo Passarotti, Gaspare Celio, Giovanni Serodine, Valentin de Boulogne, and Pietro da Cortona. Introductory essays examine Caravaggio's relationship with the Mattei brothers and, through them, the Oratorians, to whose influence the spirituality of the artist's later works is attributed, and Scipione Borghese; the paintings collection of Ciriaco Mattei; and the gallery of Palazzo Mattei and its decoration by Pietro Da Cortona.

481   Caravaggio: a life.
Helen Langdon.   London: Chatto & Windus, 1998. 448p.

An account of the artist's life and times in which the author makes use of the three early biographies of Caravaggio, as well as information taken from a wide range of sources – archives, *avvisi* (proclamations), criminal records, transcripts of trial proceedings and police investigations. Caravaggio (1571-1610) was born in Lombardy and spent his formative years in Milan, moving to Rome in 1596. After a brief period of penury he was taken up by Cardinal Francesco Maria Del Monte and moved into his household in the Palazzo Madama. Caravaggio painted a series of sensuous allegorical scenes depicting semi-naked youths for Cardinal Del Monte, who was the first of a series of patrons that included some of the wealthiest and most powerful men in Rome (others included Vincenzo Giustiniani, Ciriaco Mattei, and Scipione Borghese). It was the loyalty and influence of these men that helped Caravaggio time and again in his brushes with the authorities until he was finally forced to flee Rome in 1606 after killing Ranuccio Tommasoni in a street brawl. The last four (and most adventurous) years of his life were spent in Naples, Malta and Sicily, and he died in mysterious circumstances on his way back to Rome, where he was hoping to receive a pardon. Langdon's work is particularly strong in its descriptions of Caravaggio's paintings, their subject matter and their revolutionary naturalism. Langdon also succeeds in establishing the artistic, social, political and religious context of the Rome of Clement VIII and the contrast between the different spheres in which Caravaggio moved – the sophisticated cultural circles of his aristocratic patrons, and the poverty and violent life of the streets and the city's underworld. Unlike other writers on the artist, she tends to underplay the erotic charge of several of Caravaggio's works and is circumspect about the artist's sexual orientation. There are forty-two excellent colour plates (though two of the paintings are reversed) and black-and-white illustrations.

482   Caravaggio studies.
Walter Friedlaender.   Princeton, New Jersey: Princeton University Press, 1974.

Originally published in 1955, in the wake of the 1951 Caravaggio exhibition in Milan that brought together nearly all known canvases by the artist and was both the culmination of intense scholarly activity since the beginning of the century and the starting point for the modern popularity of the artist, this is one of the landmarks in Caravaggio scholarship. As well as a *catalogue raisonné* of the artist's work, it brings together a wealth of documentary material both in the original and in translation – the texts of five early biographies of the artist (by Giovanni Baglione, Pietro Bellori, Giulio Mancini, Karel van Mander and Joachim von Sandrart) and also miscellaneous documents on his life and work. It includes studies on Caravaggio and the artistic milieu of Rome, some special problems concerning his earlier Roman works, the Contarelli Chapel in S. Luigi dei Francesi, and the Cerasi Chapel in S. Maria del Popolo. All the essays examine Caravaggio's sources and are accompanied by a large number of comparative illustrations (unfortunately of mediocre quality).

483   Claude Lorrain.
Helen Langdon.   Oxford: Phaidon, 1989. 159p.

The landscapes of Claude Lorrain (1600-81) celebrate the beauty of Rome and its surrounding countryside and evoke the city's glorious mythical and historical past. Like Poussin, Claude spent most of his long working life in Rome and this study of his life and work begins with an examination of his work in the 1620s, when he settled in Rome. He lived in the lively artistic colony around Piazza di Spagna and Via Margutta, and there he befriended Flemish and Dutch artists (the so-called *Bamboccianti*), whose influence can be seen in his early works; he initially worked in the studio of Agostino Tassi, and executed works in fresco until his establishment as an independent painter of cabinet pictures in the early 1630s. Each subsequent chapter examines one decade of the artist's life: the ambitious landscapes of the 1630s; the more classical landscapes of the 1640s; his move from the pastoral into a more heroic vein in the 1650s; the elegiac beauty of the mythological scenes inspired by Virgil, Apuleius and Ovid in the 1660s; and the final flourishing of his art, in the 1670s, in the series of episodes from the life of Aeneas. Claude was impervious to the reversals of fortune suffered by most other artists after the death of a pope, his fame always guaranteeing new patrons. These included popes (especially Urban VIII Barberini and Clement IX Rospigliosi), emperors (Philip IV commissioned eight pictures for the Buen Retiro palace), French ambassadors and diplomats, and Roman nobles. The description of their personalities and their relationship to the artist is one of the strengths of this fine monograph. Most of the works discussed are reproduced, though the quality of the colour plates is uneven.

484 Le collezioni private romane attraverso i tempi. (Roman private
collections through the ages.)
Carlo Pietrangeli. Rome: Fratelli Palombi, 1985. 27p. bibliog.
(Quaderni del Circolo della Caccia, 2.)

Between the 16th and the 19th century, Rome had the world's richest private collections of ancient and modern art, formed by cardinals, noblemen, bankers and antiquaries. A catalogue published anonymously by Giovan Pietro Bellori in 1664 lists about 150 such collections. These were later divided through succession, sold to foreign collectors or bought by the Italian State. Only a few still survive (for example, the Doria Pamphilj collection), though numerous famous works, now the pride of foreign museums, are still familiarly known by their provenance as, for example, the Borghese Gladiator (in the Louvre) or Raphael's Colonna altarpiece (in the Metropolitan Museum). This study traces the development of Roman private collections and examines the character and fate of twenty-one of the most famous collections, ranging from the Giustiniani collection, formed by the marchese Vincenzo Giustiniani (1564-1637), which rivalled the Vatican and Capitoline collections, to the collection of Giovanni Campana, a collector of ancient sculptures, vases and Renaissance art, whose unbridled passion for collecting led to his ruin and the sale of his various collections in 1859.

485 La Collection Lemme: tableaux romains des XVIIe et XVIIIe siècles.
(The Lemme Collection: Roman paintings of the 17th and 18th century.)
Edited by Stéphane Loire. Paris: Réunion des musées nationaux, 1998.
335p. bibliog.

A catalogue of an exhibition held in the Louvre in 1998 on the occasion of the donation to the museum of twenty Roman Baroque paintings from the collection of Fabrizio and Fiammetta Lemme. The collection, which includes religious and mythological subjects as well as portraiture, had been assembled over the previous thirty years and consists of works painted in Rome from the middle years of the 17th century to the advent of Neo-classicism, a still relatively unexplored period. 130 works were shown at the exhibition and the catalogue also reproduces the remaining 135 paintings of the collection. Introductory essays include a description of the creation and development of the collection, the donation to the Louvre, a survey of artistic developments in Rome in the 17th and 18th centuries, and an examination of the cycle of paintings executed in the early years of the 18th century in the church of S. Clemente, which owe their existence to the patronage of Pope Clement XI. A number of preparatory paintings for this cycle feature in the collection. Each catalogue entry includes a detailed discussion of the painting together with a note on provenance and a bibliography. There are also biographies of all the artists represented.

486 Corot in Italy: open-air painting and the classical landscape tradition.
Peter Galassi. New Haven, Connecticut; London: Yale University Press, 1991. 266p. bibliog.

Jean-Baptiste-Camille Corot (1796-1875) spent three years in Rome at the outset of his career, between 1825 and 1828, painting and drawing the city and its surrounding landscape. This richly illustrated monograph (it has 294 illustrations, many of them in colour) examines both the work Corot produced during this period (more than 200 drawings and 150 landscape paintings) and also the work of other young landscape artists from the North working in Rome at the time. The author considers Corot's art as the synthesis of two different types of painting – neo-classical landscape painting and open-air painting. The latter emerged as an autonomous practice in the 1780s in the work of Pierre-Henri de Valenciennes and Thomas Jones and by the time of Corot's arrival, Rome was the centre of an international school of outdoor painting. This artistic milieu is wonderfully evoked here – the gatherings in the Caffè Greco, the painting excursions in the Campagna during the summer months, with the winter months spent in Rome. The work of Corot is examined in detail and its originality and freshness is made all the more evident when compared to the more finished compositions prepared for the Salon. Corot's single-mindedness and total concentration on landscape painting can be seen in the fact that during his three years in Rome, he does not seem to have visited the Sistine Chapel.

487 David e Roma. (David and Rome.)
Arranged by Jean Leymarie (et al.). Rome: De Luca, 1981. 252p. bibliog.

This catalogue of the exhibition held at the Villa Medici in 1981-82 examines David's two stays in Rome, both crucial to the development of his art. He first went to Rome in 1775 having won, in 1774, after a number of unsuccessful attempts, the much coveted Prix de Rome, which entitled him to a five-year stay in Rome as a pensioner at the French Academy (then housed in the Palazzo Mancini, on the Corso). During his years in Rome, the young artist drew from the antique and studied the art of the great 17th-century masters (Poussin, Caravaggio, the Carraccis and Reni). Both of these influences led to the gradual evolution of his work from rococo animation and clutter to neo-classical grandeur, clarity and simplicity. He also drew street scenes, landscapes and cityscapes, filling twelve sketchbooks from which he reused drawings as motifs in future compositions. Four of these sketchbooks survive intact while the rest have been dismembered or lost. David returned to Rome in 1784 to execute the *Oath of the Horatii*, which established him as the leader of the neo-classical school in France. The catalogue includes some fifty paintings and drawings by David showing the development of his style from his earliest works to the great pre-Revolutionary canvases. It also looks at the work of two contemporaries of David at the French Academy in Rome – Jean-François-Pierre Peyron and Jean-Germain Drouais. There is a detailed chronology of the artist's years in Rome.

488 **Les dessins italiens de la reine Christine de Suède.** (The Italian drawings in the collection of Queen Christina of Sweden.)
J. Q. Regteren Altena. Stockholm: A. B. Egnellska Boktryckeriet, 1996. 135p.

After her conversion to Roman Catholicism and subsequent abdication, Queen Christina of Sweden (1626-89) moved to Rome, eventually settling in the Palazzo Riario (the present Palazzo Corsini) where she was to live for nearly thirty years, becoming a munificent patron of artists, musicians, writers and scholars and assembling one of the greatest art collections of all time. Drawings formed an important part of her collections and Italian drawings held pride of place. Though her collecting began before moving to Rome, her collection was augmented in Rome through the acquisition of contemporary artists' works – Bernini, Pietro da Cortona, Salvator Rosa and Guercino were all among her friends. After her death, her collection was left to Cardinal Decio Azzolino, her friend and adviser, and after an unsuccessful attempt to sell it to Louis XIV, it was purchased by Livio Odescalchi (1653-1713), whose remarkable collection was bought in 1790 by the Teyler Foundation in Haarlem. As there is no complete inventory of Queen Christina's collection it is not always certain which works in the Odescalchi collection were originally part of it. This richly illustrated work, published in conjunction with the Council of Europe exhibition in 1966, attempts to provide a chronological survey of the Italian drawings from the 15th to the 17th century in the Teyler Foundation that may have been in Christina's collection.

489 **Domenichino, 1581-1641.**
Richard E. Spear (et al.). Milan, Italy: Electa, 1996. 592p. bibliog.

Domenichino was born in Bologna, but he went to Rome in 1602 to work with Annibale Carracci in the decoration of Palazzo Farnese. He remained in Rome for the next thirty years, becoming renowed as one of the major representatives of early Baroque classicism. He produced numerous fresco cycles in the city and the great merit of this publication is that, as well as being the catalogue of a major exhibition of the artist's paintings and drawings, held in Rome in 1996-97, it also marks the completion of an extensive programme of restoration of the artist's major frescoes in Rome, Naples and Bologna. It includes separate, splendidly illustrated articles discussing his frescoes in the following locations in Rome: Palazzo Farnese, S. Onofrio, S. Luigi dei Francesi, S. Maria in Trastevere, S. Andrea della Valle, S. Maria della Vittoria, S. Silvestro al Quirinale, Palazzo Giustiniani-Odescalchi (at Bassano di Sustri Romano), and the Abbazia di Grottaferrata. There are also numerous scholarly contributions on every aspect of the artist's work and the catalogue section includes ninety-two works by Domenichino and some additional paintings by his contemporaries (among them Giovanni Lanfranco – the artist's great rival in the decoration of S. Andrea della Valle, Agostino and Annibale Carracci, Giovanni Battista Viola and Guido Reni).

490 **I Farnese: arte e collezionismo.** (The Farnese: art and collecting.)
Edited by Lucia Fornari Schianchi, Nicola Spinosa. Milan, Italy: Electa, 1995. 533p. bibliog.

The Farnese collections, which by the early 18th century were divided between Rome and Parma, began to be transferred to Naples in 1735, after the accession to the throne of Naples of Charles III, the son of Philip V of Spain and Elizabeth Farnese, who had previously inherited from his uncle the Duchy of Parma and Piacenza. The removal of the Roman collections began in 1787 after Ferdinand IV was granted permission by the Pope. The loss of the collections, which included some of the most renowned antique sculptures in Rome (the Farnese Bull and the Farnese Hercules), was much lamented at the time. Today the collections are divided between the Museo di Capodimonte and the Archaeological Museum in Naples. This massive catalogue accompanied an exhibition shown in Parma, Munich and finally Naples, celebrating the renovation of the galleries displaying the Farnese collections in the Museo di Capodimonte. Its twelve introductory essays look at the history of the Farnese family, their role as patrons of the arts, and their collections of paintings, drawings, antique sculptures, coins and medals, and armour. There is a separate chapter on the Roman collections. The catalogue includes entries on 292 works, all illustrated. It is particularly rich on Farnese portraiture, which includes the famous portraits of Pope Paul III by Titian.

491   Fiamminghi a Roma, 1508-1608: artisti dei Paesi bassi e del Principato di Liegi a Roma durante il Rinascimento. (The Flemish in Rome: artists from the Netherlands and the Principality of Liège in Rome during the Renaissance.)
Nicole Dacos (et al.).   Milan, Italy: Skira, 1995. 367p. bibliog.

A catalogue of an exhibition held in Brussels and Rome in 1995 examining the work of the artistic colony of Flemish artists in Rome from the reign of Pope Julius II to the works executed by Rubens during his sojourn in the city. It includes three introductory essays, one of which discusses Flemish and Dutch institutions in Rome during the Renaissance. The catalogue contains entries for 253 works (paintings, sculptures, drawings, prints and tapestries) and includes works by artists from other countries of Northern Europe also active in Rome.

492   Giovan Battista Gaulli, il Baciccio, 1639-1709.
Edited by Maurizio Fagiolo dell'Arco, Dieter Graf, Francesco Petrucci.
Milan, Italy: Skira, 1999. 368p. bibliog.

Gaulli was one of the most graceful artists working in Rome in the second half of the 17th century and one of the greatest colourists of the High Baroque. This magnificent catalogue of the exhibition held in Ariccia in 1999-2000 is a worthy complement to Richard Enggass' *catalogue raisonné* of the artist's paintings published in 1964 (see no. 507). Not only does it include a number of discoveries made in the intervening thirty-five years but it also examines Gaulli's output as a draughtsman and his graphic work. The sixty-one paintings in the exhibition represent all aspects of Gaulli's activity – portraiture, the great decorative cycles, altarpieces, and works for private collectors. The selection of his graphic work includes book illustrations (portraits, allegorical illustrations for theses, and frontispieces for opera libretti), etchings, and devotional images, while some thirty drawings include preparatory sketches, figure studies, and caricatures. There is also a detailed chronology, an index of Gaulli's paintings, and essays examining aspects of his art (notably his frescoes in the Gesù), his influence on 18th-century painting, and a survey of literature on the artist.

493   Giulio Romano.
Essays by Erst H. Gombrich (et al.).   Milan, Italy: Electa, 1989. 597p. bibliog.

Giulio Romano was the most brilliant of Raphael's pupils and the range of his activities nearly matches that of Gianlorenzo Bernini. This massive and sumptuously illustrated catalogue of the exhibition held in Mantua in 1989 examines all aspects of his work – as painter, architect, stage designer, and draughtsman – first in Rome and, from 1523, in Mantua. Giulio was born in Rome and received his artistic formation in Raphael's studio, collaborating on decorative cycles commissioned from Raphael, among others the Vatican *Stanze* and *Logge* and the Farnesina frescoes. The section examining the works of the artist's Roman period looks at his drawings and paintings. These include his contributions to the Sala di Costantino, the decoration of which was left unfinished on Raphael's death, as well as a number of paintings of difficult attribution, some formerly attributed to Raphael. Also included are *I modi* (The positions), a series of erotic drawings for woodcut illustrations to Pietro Aretino's *Sonetti lussuriosi* (Lascivious sonnets). Giulio's work as an architect is also examined in detail. In this field too, Giulio contributed to Raphael commissions such as Palazzo Branconio, Palazzo Alberini, and Villa Madama. After Raphael's death, he designed a number of residential buildings in Rome – Villa Lante, Palazzo Stati Maccarani, Palazzo Adimari Salviati, and Giulio's House at Macel de' Corvi (near the Column of Trajan). The sections of the catalogue dealing with Giulio's activities as an architect have been published in English as: *Giulio Romano* (Cambridge, England: Cambridge University Press, 1998. 338p.). See also Frederick Hartt's *Giulio Romano* (New Haven, Connecticut: Yale University Press, 1958. 2 vols. bibliog.).

494 'Il Gran Cardinale': Alessandro Farnese, patron of the arts.
Clare Robertson. New Haven, Connecticut; London: Yale University Press, 1992. 256p. bibliog.

Alessandro Farnese (1520-89), the grandson of Pope Paul III, was the most important individual patron of the visual arts in 16th-century Rome. One of the wealthiest men in the city, he commissioned works of art and buildings for over fifty years (he was made a cardinal at the age of fourteen). This study concentrates on his development and influence as a patron and establishes that, in his early years, he was more interested in costly works of decorative art – medals, engraved gems, *maiolica* (tin-glazed earthenware) and metalwork – than painting and sculpture. The masterpieces he commissioned during these years were the Farnese Hours (now in the Pierpont Morgan Library, New York) by Giulio Clovio, an artist who worked for Alessandro for some forty years, and the Farnese Casket (now in the Museo di Capodimonte, Naples). These were followed by secular commissions, culminating with his sumptuously decorated villa at Caprarola. It was relatively late in life that he began to commission religious works, in response to Counter-Reformation pressures, building a number of new churches, among them the Gesù.

495 Hubert Robert.
Jean de Cayeux, assisted by Catherine Boulot. Paris: Fayard, [1989]. 433p. bibliog.

A biography of the landscape artist and draughtsman. The first part covers the eleven years the artist spent in Rome (1754-65) under the protection of the Comte de Stainville (the future Duc de Choiseul), the French ambassador to the city. It gives a vivid portrait of artistic life in mid-18th-century Rome, its cosmopolitanism, the Académie de France (then housed in the Palazzo Mancini on the Corso) and its pensioners, and the various influences on the young artist, notably that of Giovanni Paolo Pannini and Giovanni Battista Piranesi. Robert, an exceptionally prolific artist, was to reuse in later works motifs he accumulated during his Roman sojourn and he later became known as 'Robert des ruines'.

496 Imagining Rome: British artists and Rome in the nineteenth century.
Edited by Michael Liversidge, Catharine Edwards. London: Merrell Holberton, 1996. 172p.

This catalogue of an exhibition held in Bristol in 1996 examines how British artists from Turner to Alma-Tadema viewed Roman antiquity in works ranging from picturesque representations of the city and its remains to imaginary, anecdotal reconstructions of Roman life and history. The catalogue entries are preceded by four essays examining: the complexity of British attitudes to

Ancient Rome, both in its Republican virtue and Imperial decadence; the city as a symbol of the transience of human endeavour; the triumph of Christianity; and changes of artistic and intellectual responses and social attitudes to Rome during the 19th century. All sixty-three works at the exhibition have full entries and are reproduced, mostly in colour. Artists represented include J. M. W. Turner, Samuel Prout, John Martin, Charles Eastlake, David Roberts, J. F. Lewis, Samuel Palmer, Edward John Poynter, Frederick Leighton and Lawrence Alma-Tadema.

497 Ingres in Italia, 1806-1824, 1835-1841. (Ingres in Italy, 1806-1824, 1835-1841.)
Michel Laclotte (et al.). Rome: De Luca, 1968. 218p. bibliog.

Ingres first arrived in Rome in 1806 as a winner of the Prix de Rome competition, which entitled him to a four-year stay as a pensioner at the Académie de France à Rome, at the Villa Medici. He remained in Rome for fifteen years (the last three years of his first Italian stay were spent in Florence). He returned to the Villa Medici in 1835, this time as its director. This exhibition of 130 paintings, water-colours and drawings executed during his two Italian sojourns, was held at the Villa Medici in 1968 to commemorate the centenary of the artist's death in 1867. It included painted and drawn views of Rome and the Roman Campagna and some of the numerous portraits of visitors to Rome which Ingres executed when the Grand Tour resumed after the Napoleonic Wars. These were rapidly drawn in pencil and their spontaneity and freshness of observation makes them among the artist's most appealing works. Works inspired by Italian culture, both classical and modern, were also shown (for example *Paolo and Francesca, The Sistine Chapel in 1820*).

498 J. H. Fragonard e H. Robert a Roma. (J. H. Fragonard and H. Robert in Rome.)
Edited by Jean-Pierre Cuzin, Pierre Rosenberg, Catherine Boulot.
Rome: Fratelli Palombi, 1990. 311p. bibliog.

The catalogue of an exhibition held at the Villa Medici in 1990-91 comparing the work executed in Rome by two of the most spirited artists of the 18th century – Jean-Honoré Fragonard and Hubert Robert. Robert was in Rome from 1754 to 1765 under the protection of the Comte de Stainville, the new French ambassador, who obtained for his unqualified protégé an exceptional residence at the Académie de France, where he met Fragonard who, having won the Prix de Rome in 1753, was a resident there between 1756 and 1761. Rome made an overwhelming impression on the two young artists and was a decisive influence on the development of their art. They drew and painted the city and its surroundings, its ruins, its Renaissance villas, its people and their festivals. Their work has often been confused in the past (to the extent that one of Fragonard's most enchanting paintings, *The Waterfall at Tivoli*, was, until 1933, attributed to Robert), and one of the aims of this catalogue is to attempt to establish more secure attributions. The catalogue includes 191 works all reproduced (42 in colour) and accompanied by numerous comparative illustrations. They include: paintings and drawings (both artists are renowned for their magnificent red chalk drawings) from the period 1756-61, when they were both together in Rome; Robert's works after Fragonard's departure (1761-65); works both artists produced after their departure from Italy but re-using Italian motifs; Fragonard's works from his second journey to Italy, in 1773-74, when he accompanied the wealthy financier Bergeret de Grancourt to Italy, acting as his guide and recording the various stages of their journey; and, finally, works by other artists influenced by Fragonard and Robert.

499   I luoghi di Raffaello a Roma. (Places associated with Raphael in Rome.)
Edited by Luciana Cassanelli, Sergio Rossi.   Rome: Multigrafica, 1983.
196p. bibliog.

This catalogue was part of the 1983 quincentenary celebrations of Raphael's birth, which was
marked by five documentary exhibitions in Rome built around works by the artist. The aim of
the exhibitions, which were held at the Villa Farnesina, S. Eligio degli Orefici, S. Maria del
Popolo, S. Maria della Pace, and S. Agostino, was to provide in-depth analysis of the works,
their iconography, historical and cultural background, and their relationship to works by other
artists on the same sites. Thus the examination of Raphael's work in the Chigi Chapel in S.
Maria del Popolo includes a discussion of the works of other contemporary or later artists – such
as Sebastiano del Piombo and Gianlorenzo Bernini, who contributed to the decoration of the
chapel. The catalogue also includes studies on five major paintings by Raphael in museums in
Rome (in the Galleria Borghese, the Galleria Doria-Pamphilj, and the Accademia di S. Luca).

500   Melozzo da Forlì: *pictor papalis.*
Nicholas Clark.   London: Sotheby's Publications, 1990. 167p.

The fame of Melozzo da Forlì (1438-77), papal painter under Sixtus IV (1471-84), has been
somewhat eclipsed by his great successors in 16th-century Rome, the depletion of his works,
and the misattribution of those surviving to other artists. This monograph traces his career from
his early years in Urbino, where he was influenced by Piero della Francesca, to his work in the
Vatican Library between 1476 and 1477 alongside Domenico and Davide Ghirlandaio, where
he executed his most famous work, the fresco (later transferred to canvas and moved to the
Pinacoteca Vaticana) depicting Sixtus IV founding the Vatican Library surrounded by four
nephews and Bartolomeo Sacchi da Piadena, called Platina, his librarian. The detailed analysis
of this work contains much useful information about the building of the Vatican Library and the
role of Platina. The only other work executed by Melozzo in Rome, here considered to be the
summit of the artist's achievement, is also given a detailed analysis. This is the fresco of the
Ascension for the apse of SS Apostoli, commissioned by Cardinal Giuliano della Rovere, the
future Julius II and one of the nephews depicted in Melozzo's fresco. Only fragments of this
work, which include the musical angels (now in the Pinacoteca Vaticana), survive. All the
surviving works by Melozzo are illustrated in colour and there are many comparative plates of
the work of Melozzo's contemporaries, including Mantegna, Piero della Francesca, and Justus
of Ghent and Pedro Berruguete, the two artists whose decoration of Federico da Montefeltro's
studiolo (a private domestic room) was once attributed to Melozzo.

501   The mosaics of Rome from the third to the fourteenth centuries.
Walter Oakeshott.   London: Thames & Hudson, 1967. 388p. bibliog.

A survey of the style and technique of Roman mosaics from the classical period to the early
Renaissance. The problem of authenticity (as later restorations have considerably altered the
appearance of the original works) is discussed in the introductory chapter, which also examines
the materials (stone and glass) and colours used, as well as techniques of setting the *tesserae* (the
small stones used in mosaics). The various methods of repair, restoration and replacement of
mosaics used in later centuries and various mosaic decorations destroyed (among them famous
works like Giotto's *Navicella* in St Peter's) are also surveyed. Thereafter the examination is
chronological, beginning with a chapter on the great decorations from the 4th to the 6th centuries.
These are characterized by ornaments showing the survival of classical style (for example, figure
elements like river gods and *amoretti* (cupids), acanthus scrolls, festoons and other motifs)
incorporated in the medieval Roman tradition. The 4th century is represented by decorations in
S. Costanza, S. Pudenziana, S. Giovanni in Laterano and S. Paolo fuori le Mura, the 5th century

by decorations in S. Maria Maggiore, and the 6th century by decorations in SS Cosma e Damiano. The impact of Byzantine iconographic features in Roman art of the 6th to the 8th centuries is also examined. A more linear technique was adopted during the Paschalian period (the late 8th and early 9th centuries), when Rome was at the crossroads between the iconoclastic controversy of the East and the artistic ideas of the Carolingian court – as shown in S. Prassede, SS Nereo ed Achilleo, S. Maria Domnica, S. Cecilia in Trastevere and S. Marco. After a gap of three centuries from which no major work in mosaic has survived, the next great period of artistic creation began in the 12th century (with examples in S. Clemente and S. Maria in Trastevere) and the 13th century (in S. Paolo fuori le Mura, the Cappella Sancta Sanctorum, S. Tommaso in Formis, and S. Maria in Aracoeli). The last chapter looks at the use of mosaics during the Renaissance period with examples, among others, in S. Sabina, S. Maria sopra Minerva, and S. Giovanni in Laterano. There are 33 excellent colour and 244 monochrome plates.

502   The Nazarenes: a brotherhood of German painters in Rome.
Keith Andrews.   Oxford: Clarendon Press, 1964. 165p.

This is an excellent monograph on the artistic brotherhood of the Nazarenes, a group of German artists reacting against academic teaching routines and united by their admiration for Raphael and 15th-century German and Italian art. In 1809 they formed the Brotherhood of St Luke and the following year they moved to Rome and settled in the deconsecrated monastery of S. Isidoro on the Pincio, where they lived in monastic isolation and were known as the Fratelli di S. Isidoro. The leading artists of the group were Friedrich Overbeck and Franz Pforr and, after the latter's early death in 1812, Peter Cornelius. Other notable artists who later joined the group were Carl Philipp Fohr, who executed a series of portrait drawings of the artists that gathered in the Caffè Greco shortly before his tragic death from drowning, and Julius Schnorr von Carolsfeld. The group revived the practice of fresco painting, first in the Palazzo Zuccari decorations commissioned in 1815 by Barthold Georg Niebuhr, the German ambassador in Rome, and then in 1817, following the success of the Palazzo Zuccari decorations, in the garden house of the marchese Carlo Massimo, which they decorated with scenes from Dante, Ariosto and Tasso. The Casino Massimo frescoes were the climax of the Nazarenes' activities in Rome and, unlike those of the Palazzo Zuccari, which were removed in 1887 to the National Gallery at Berlin, they are still *in situ*. After the completion of the decoration (which took twelve years) the group broke up and, with the exception of Overbeck, its various members pursued their careers away from Rome. The final section of the work examines the influence of the Nazarenes on European art (for example, on the Pre-Raphaelite Brotherhood).

503   I Nazareni a Roma. (The Nazarenes in Rome.)
Edited by Gianna Piantoni, Stefano Susinno.   Rome: de Luca, 1981. 476p. bibliog.

The catalogue of an exhibition held in 1981 at the Galleria nazionale d'arte moderna in Rome. The catalogue section provides biographies of all the artists represented in the exhibition together with detailed entries for the 148 paintings and drawings exhibited, all of which are illustrated. Eight introductory essays examine various aspects of the group's art: they range from the birth of the Brotherhood of S. Luke in Vienna and the artistic theories of its members to their impressions of Italy and Rome, the fresco cycles they executed in Rome and the elements of Italian popular culture in their works. There are also ten essays on the Casino Massimo frescoes, their iconography and restoration, and the critical reception of Dante, Ariosto and Tasso (the three poets whose work is the subject of the frescoes) in Germany in the 17th and 18th centuries. Finally, there is a detailed chronology of historical, cultural and artistic events from 1794 to 1830.

504 Nicolas Poussin, 1594-1665.
Edited by Pierre Rosenberg and Louis-Antoine Prat.   Paris: Réunion des
musées nationaux, 1994. 558p. bibliog.

This magnificent volume, a milestone in Poussin scholarship, is the catalogue of the exhibition organized in Paris in 1994 to celebrate the quatercentenary of Poussin's birth. Poussin moved to Rome, perhaps at the suggestion of the poet Giambattista Marino, in 1624 and remained there to the end of his life, except for the years 1640-42 when he was summoned back to France by Louis XIII. The catalogue includes 245 paintings and drawings, among them some of the artist's most famous works (notably the *Martyrdom of St Erasmus*, the altarpiece he executed for St Peter's – now in the Pinacoteca Vaticana – and the two series of the *Seven Sacraments*, the first of which was commissioned by Cassiano dal Pozzo). The catalogue entries contain a wealth of information about Poussin's Roman patrons. There are also fifteen introductory essays examining various aspects of the artist's life, work and influence. A different catalogue edited by Richard Verdi was published in English when a reduced version of the exhibition (with eighty-eight paintings) was shown at the Royal Academy in London in 1995. Also see *Nicolas Poussin, 1594-1665*, edited by Alain Mérot (Paris: La documentation française, 1996. 2 vols. 965p.). These two volumes contain over thirty papers read at a colloquium held in the Louvre on the occasion of the exhibition, which examine various aspects of the artist's life and work. A section is dedicated to the Roman artistic milieu and Poussin's Roman patrons.

505 Nicolas Poussin: i primi anni romani. (Nicolas Poussin: his first years
in Rome.)
Sir Denis Mahon (et al.).   Milan, Italy: Electa, 1998. 157p. bibliog.

The catalogue of an exhibition held in Rome in 1998 which concentrated on the artist's first years in Rome, highlighting his recently rediscovered *The sack and destruction of the Temple at Jerusalem by Titus*, an important early work which secured the artist Roman and French patronage of the highest level (bought by Cardinal Francesco Barberini, it later entered the collection of Cardinal Richelieu). The exhibition's aim was to demonstrate the artist's early development, a subject of some controversy, and his rapid progress during the second half of the 1620s. The introductory essay by Sir Denis Mahon gives an account of Poussin's work from his arrival in Rome in March 1624 to 1628-29, and the patronage of Marcello Sacchetti, Cassiano and Carlo Antonio dal Pozzo, Francesco Barberini, and Giovanni Stefano Roccatagliata. It suggests numerous new datings, in some cases changing the author's own earlier conclusions, based on new documentary evidence. An English version of this catalogue was subsequently published by Quadri e sculture and the Israel Art Museum in 1999; it has the same catalogue entries and Sir Denis Mahon's introductory essay but more colour illustrations (mostly of details of the paintings); it omits, however, two additional essays on Poussin and his patrons as well as a listing of references in 17th- and 18th-century Roman archives to Poussin and his works.

506 Painting in Italy, 1500-1600.
S. J. Freedberg.   New Haven, Connecticut; London: Yale University
Press, 1993. 3rd ed. 761p. bibliog. (Yale University Press/Pelican
History of Art.)

This is a comprehensive study of painting in Italy from Michelangelo and Raphael to Caravaggio. There are five sections dealing with Rome. The first examines the period of the High Renaissance up to the death of Raphael in 1520, a period that saw the creation of Michelangelo's Sistine Chapel ceiling and Raphael's *Stanze*. The work of Sebastiano del Piombo and Baldassare Peruzzi is also examined here. The second section looks at the school of Raphael after the master's death and the third the dissemination of Roman Mannerism after the Sack of Rome in 1527 and the departure of most of the artists who worked there (Giulio Romano moved to Mantua, Perino del Vaga to Genoa, Parmigianino to Bologna and then Parma). The fourth covers the period between 1535 and 1575, which saw the return of many artists to Rome and the development of a more sober style in accordance with Counter-Reformation dictates. The later work of Michelangelo (the *Last Judgement* in the Sistine Chapel and the frescoes in the Cappella Paolina), and the Roman output of Salviati, the Zuccari, and Muziano are the major works here. The final section looks at the period 1570-1600 and the move toward the classical style of the Carracci. The work was first published in 1971 and this edition includes minor textual revisions taking into account the results of recent research – the dating of some pictures has been changed, the bibliography updated and a number of colour illustrations introduced.

507 The painting of Baciccio: Giovanni Battista Gaulli, 1639-1709.
Robert Enggass. University Park, Pennsylvania: The Pennsylvania State University Press, 1964. 219p. bibliog.

This study and *catalogue raisonné* is an attempt to establish the corpus of paintings of the finest colourist of the Roman High Baroque and trace the lines of his stylistic development. Born in Genoa, Gaulli went to Rome in the late 1650s. His rise to fame was rapid – he was elected to the Accademia di S. Luca in 1662 and by 1667 he was working for the Chigi family, the family of the reigning pope. He painted numerous altarpieces for churches in Rome (S. Andrea al Quirinale, S. Maria in Campitelli, SS Apostoli) but his chief claims to fame are the radiant frescoes he executed for the church of the Gesù and a chapter is devoted to the commission in 1672 which Gaulli won in competition and with the support of Bernini. The work, which consists of nine large frescoes in the dome, pendentives, nave and transept vaults of the church, was executed between 1672 and 1683. In his lifetime, Gaulli was also famous as a portraitist and a chapter is devoted to his output in this field. The catalogue is in two sections: Gaulli's paintings (listed alphabetically by location), and erroneous attributions. There is also a section on lost works and a listing of documents related to the artist, which are either wholly or partially transcribed.

508 Patrons and painters: a study in the relations between Italian art and society in the age of the Baroque.
Francis Haskell. New Haven, Connecticut; London: Yale University Press, 1982. rev. ed. 492p.

First published in 1963, this hugely influential study of art patronage in Italy during the Baroque era concentrates on two cities: Rome during the 17th century and Venice during the 18th century. The first section of the book deals exclusively with Rome, in the early 17th century the artistic capital of Italy through the generous patronage of the popes and their families, first Paul V Borghese, followed by Urban VIII Barberini. The patronage of Urban VIII is one of the most important chapters in the book. The examination of patronage by the religious orders (the Jesuits, the Oratorians and the Theatines) reveals how little the Jesuits influenced the development of Baroque painting and the important role individual cardinals (in the case of the Gesù, Cardinal Alessandro Farnese) played in the decoration of their churches, their wishes often conflicting with those of the order. The work also investigates the role of private patrons – Vincenzo Giustiniani, Camillo Massimi, Cassiano dal Pozzo and his influence on Baroque classicism, and Lorenzo Onofrio Colonna and his interest in landscape painting. It also looks at the vogue in the mid-17th century for the *Bamboccianti*, the Northern painters of popular scenes, and the role of the wider public. In this revised and enlarged edition of the work, the author explains that the decline in the finances of the Vatican in the latter half of the 17th century and the consequent decline of artistic patronage were his reasons for leaving out 18th-century Rome from his examination, a decision criticized in some quarters.

509   The Picture Gallery of Vincenzo Giustiniani.
Luigi Salerno.   *The Burlington Magazine*, vol. 102, nos. 682, 684, 685 (Jan., March, April 1960), pp. 21-27, 93-104, 135-48.

These articles contain a transcription of an inventory of the collection of paintings and sculptures of marchese Vincenzo Giustiniani (1564-1637), drawn up on 9th February 1638 shortly after his death, which, unlike other inventories of his collection, gives the names of the artists and hence provides a more trustworthy source than later literature for the attribution of the various works in the collection. Vincenzo Giustiniani was one of the most important, erudite and richest art patrons of the 17th century. As well as collecting, he also wrote on a variety of subjects ranging from painting, sculpture, architecture and music to etiquette and hunting. Giustiniani was a connoisseur who also had the capacity to discover young artists and he exerted a strong influence on the artists who worked for him. He was a patron of Caravaggio and Carracci and, in the 1630s, the group of French painters in Rome who shared his interest in archaeology – Poussin, Claude Lorrain, Jean Lemaire and François Perrier. A catalogue of his collection, *Galleria Giustiniana*, was published in 1631 with engravings by Italian, Flemish and French artists. The collection was later dispersed and a large number of paintings were bought *en bloc* by the King of Prussia in Paris in 1812. The inventory contains nearly 600 items and this exemplary edition gives the subsequent history and attributions of the works with bibliographical references and line engravings (from the Paris sale catalogue) of paintings that have since disappeared. There is also an index of artists.

510   Pier Leone Ghezzi: Settecento alla moda. (Pier Leone Ghezzi: fashionable eighteenth century.)
Anna Lo Bianco.   Venice, Italy: Marsilio, 1999. 207p. bibliog.

The exhibitions *I Ghezzi dalle Marche all'Europa* (The Ghezzi family from the Marches to Europe), organized in Comunanza and Ascoli Piceno in 1999, celebrated the achievements of three generations of the Ghezzi family. Pier Leone Ghezzi (1674-1755) was, like his father Giuseppe, a man of many talents. A painter, draughtsman, antiquarian, and musician, he is best known for his innumerable caricatures. His patrons included Pope Clement XI (a fellow Marchigiano), churchmen, the Roman nobility and French and English Grand Tourists. This catalogue includes sixty-five works representing most aspects of Ghezzi's artistic output – religious and history paintings, portraits, genre scenes, drawings and caricatures. It also includes examples of the work of some of Ghezzi's contemporaries in Rome – Carlo Maratti, Marco Benefial, Pierre Subleyras, Benedetto Luti, and his father Giuseppe Ghezzi. The five introductory essays include an overview of Ghezzi's life and times, as well as studies focusing on the subject matter of his paintings and his work as a draughtsman.

511   Pietro Cavallini: a study in the art of late medieval Rome.
Paul Hetherington.   London: The Sagittarius Press, 1979. 203p. bibliog.

Pietro Cavallini (*c*. 1240-*c*. 1330) was active in Rome at a time when the Papacy was trying to re-establish its presence in the city through large-scale decorative projects. He is best known for his mosaic cycle in S. Maria in Trastevere and his *Last Judgement* fresco in S. Cecilia in Trastevere (the rest of his work in this church was destroyed in the 18th century). Though his fame was subsequently eclipsed by that of Giotto, it is now established that Cavallini was actually active in Rome before Giotto and that he probably influenced his work. This monograph examines Cavallini's life and posthumous reputation, his works, both extant and destroyed (for example, the paintings in S. Paolo fuori le Mura, almost totally destroyed by fire in 1823 but known through water-colour and engraved copies) and the relation of his art to the work of his contemporaries and its influence on his successors. It also reproduces up to 1,550 documents and texts relating to the artist and includes, in an appendix, a list of rejected attributions. There is a full bibliography and 165 plates, some of which provide reconstructions of destroyed decorative schemes.

512   La pittura del '700 a Roma. (Eighteenth-century painting in Rome.) Edited by Stella Rudolph.   Milan, Italy: Longanesi & Co., 1983. 815p. bibliog. (Repertori Fotografici Longanesi & Co.)

This catalogue contains black-and-white illustrations of 732 works by 272 artists born or working in Rome in the 18th century. There are biographical and bibliographical notices for all the artists represented, making this a useful bibliographical as well as iconographical tool. With its coverage of all genres of painting and the predominance of religious subjects it complements the work by G. Sestieri (see no. 520) in which religious art, landscapes and *vedute* (topographical views) are represented in fewer numbers.

513   Pompeo Batoni: a complete catalogue of his works, with an introductory text.
Anthony M. Clark, edited and prepared for publication by Edgar Peters Bowron.   Oxford: Phaidon, 1985. 416p. bibliog.

Pompeo Batoni (Lucca 1708-Rome 1787) moved to Rome in 1728 where he studied under Sebastiano Conca, Agostino Masucci and Francesco Imperiali. He drew from the antique and copied Raphael and Annibale Carracci. By 1740 he was at the forefront of Roman painters and was patronized by the great figures of the period. Though his output includes religious and historical paintings and decorative schemes, notably in the Villa Borghese, Palazzo Colonna, and the Casino of Benedict XIV on the Quirinal, Batoni is best known today for his portraits, especially of noble Englishmen on their Grand Tour, often posed in front of a Roman setting or with emblematic examples of Roman antiquities attesting their presence in the Eternal City. The introductory study gives an excellent biographical sketch of the artist and his life in Rome and also outlines Batoni's career and artistic development, dividing his activity in Rome into five distinct periods. His drawings and studio practices are also examined, as are his British portraits and the Grand Tour. By the middle of the 18th century, Rome had become the main centre of the European Grand Tour and for many British visitors having their portrait painted by Batoni was a major feature of their travels. There is also a discussion of Batoni's uses of the antique, his collaboration with contemporary Roman landscapists, his miniatures, and his copies of other artists' works. The reasons for the rapid decline in Batoni's reputation in Britain after his death are also explained. The catalogue contains 464 autograph paintings, around 160 untraced paintings for which documentation exists in the form of drawings, engravings or copies, over 80 doubtful, wrongly attributed or unverified paintings, and 324 drawings. There are two indices of works by subject and by location, and an index of persons and places.

514   Poussin: the early years in Rome: the origins of French classicism.
Konrad Oberhuber.   Oxford, England: Phaidon-Christie's, 1988. 367p. bibliog.

Nicolas Poussin (1594-1665) arrived in Rome in 1624, at the instigation of the poet Giambattista Marino, and, apart from a brief sojourn in France between December 1640 and November 1642, spent the rest of his life in the Eternal City. This study assesses his work during his first ten years in Rome, examining his development, sources and influences, and working methods. It also looks at his relationship with his patrons in Rome, especially Cassiano Dal Pozzo, the archaeologist-scholar to whose Paper Museum he contributed, and Francesco Barberini, who commissioned the St Erasmus altarpiece for St Peter's. Poussin's work during this period includes a wide variety of subject matter – mythological, biblical and historical scenes as well as landscapes, pastoral scenes and copies of architecture and sculpture. The catalogue section reproduces 277 paintings and drawings, the total of Poussin's known output during this period.

515 **Poussin et Rome: actes du colloque de l'Académie de France à Rome, 16-18 novembre 1994.** (Poussin and Rome: proceedings of the conference at the Académie de France à Rome, 16-18 November 1994.) Edited by Olivier Bonfait, Christoph Luitpold Frommel, Michel Hochmann, Sebastian Schütze. Paris: Réunion des musées nationaux, 1996. 414p.

A collection of papers read at the colloquium organized by the Académie de France à Rome and the Bibliotheca Hertziana examining the Roman artistic and intellectual milieu in Poussin's time. The twenty-two papers it contains are divided into three sections. The first section looks at Poussin's models (especially Raphael) and the influence of the Roman scene (for example, Roman architecture or the Farnese collection of antique sculptures) on his art. The second section examines the work of Charles Mellin and Simon Vouet (Poussin's French contemporaries in Rome), Poussin's role in Cassiano dal Pozzo's 'Paper Museum', the art market in Rome *c.* 1630 and the collections of Lelio Guidiccioni and Francesco Angeloni. The third section looks at contemporary art theory and criticism (Giovanni Battista Agucchi and his circle, Giovan Pietro Bellori's treatment of Poussin in his *Vite dei pittori, scultori e architetti moderni* [Lives of modern painters, sculptors, and architects]) and Poussin's interpretations of Tasso.

516 **Raffaello e la Roma dei papi.** (Raphael and the Rome of the popes.) Edited by Giovanni Morello. Rome: Fratelli Palombi, 1986. 221p. bibliog.

The catalogue of an exhibition organized by the Biblioteca apostolica vaticana in the wake of the major exhibition *Raffaello in Vaticano* (Raphael in the Vatican – see entry no. 517), drawn from the Library's own collections of manuscripts, books and coins.

517 **Raffaello in Vaticano.** (Raphael in the Vatican.) Fabrizio Mancinelli (et al.). Milan, Italy: Electa, 1984. 400p. bibliog.

This major catalogue of the exhibition held at the Vatican in 1984-85 which celebrated the five hundredth anniversary of Raphael's birth includes all aspects of the artist's intense activity in the Vatican during the last twelve years of his life. It is divided into four sections, three of which are subdivided into more specific areas, each preceded by a short introductory essay. The first section examines works by the master in the Vatican collections but executed before his arrival in Rome in 1508. The second examines the Roman cultural scene during the pontificates of Julius II and Leo X and includes sections on papal medals and ceremonies, the courtiers who shaped contemporary Vatican culture (among them Pietro Bembo, Pietro Aretino and Baldassar Castiglione), and contemporary interest in science, music and the antique. The third, and most extensive, section looks at various aspects of Raphael's work in the Vatican Palace – as architect, painter and sculptor – with separate sections on the *Stanze*, the *Logge* and the Stufetta del

Visual Arts. Paintings, prints and drawings

Cardinal Bibbiena (a private room with frescoes formerly attributed to Raphael, much engraved because of the erotic subject matter of the mythological scenes depicted). The fourth section surveys Raphael's activity in Rome, the output of his workshop, prints and maiolica after his works, and his posthumous fame and idealized image of the artist in the 19th century.

518 Raphael.
Roger Jones, Nicholas Penny.   New Haven, Connecticut; London: Yale University Press, 1983. 256p.

A comprehensive and authoritative study examining all aspects of the work of Raphael, one of the greatest artists of the Italian Renaissance. The study is chronological and after a discussion, in the first two chapters, of the artist's early years in Umbria and Florence it concentrates on his activities in Rome, where he arrived sometime in early 1509 and where, until his untimely death in 1520, he was to execute a staggering body of work. His first commission, which established him as one of the leading artists in Rome, was the decoration of the private library of Julius II (now known as the Stanza della Segnatura) in the Vatican, for which he created three of his most famous works – *the Parnassus, the School of Athens*, and the *Disputa*. Raphael's output during his early years included: commissions by Agostino Chigi, one of the richest men in Rome, for the decoration of his luxurious villa outside the city walls, now called la Farnesina, for which he painted the fresco depicting the Triumph of Galatea (and, in 1517-19, a loggia with scenes depicting the fable of Cupid and Psyche); and chapel decorations in S. Maria della Pace and S. Maria del Popolo. Raphael's fame was further spread through the execution of engravings after his work by, among others, Marcantonio Raimondi. Other major commissions included a series of ten cartoons for tapestries to cover the lower walls of the Sistine Chapel, the decorations of two more papal apartments in the Vatican, the Stanza d'Eliodoro (1512-14) and the Stanza dell'Incendio (1514-17), the loggia of Cardinal Bibbiena, and the private loggia of Leo X. Raphael's oil paintings (which, as well as numerous religious paintings, include several famous portraits) and his achievements as an architect (which included work for S. Peter's) and archaeologist are also examined. The volume is lavishly illustrated with 271 illustrations, many of them in colour and generally of high quality.

519 Raphael and his circle.
Philip Pouncey and J. A. Gere.   London: The Trustees of the British Museum, 1962. 2 vols. (215p., xviiip. + 278 plates). (Italian Drawings in the Department of Prints and Drawings in the British Museum.)

The British Museum's holding of thirty-nine Raphael drawings is only exceeded by the collections of the Ashmolean Museum, Oxford and the Musée des beaux-arts, Lille. This catalogue includes 293 drawings by the master and his circle in Rome. The compilers refute the tendency to overemphasize the studio share in the design of important late commisssions such as the Logge and the Stanza dell'Incendio. The latter include not only his immediate followers but also Baldassare Peruzzi, his close associate, and Timoteo Viti, his older contemporary and fellow countryman. Sixty additional drawings of little interest (copies, etc.) are summarily listed in an appendix. There are also indexes of related works, subjects, former owners, and related prints.

520   Repertorio della pittura romana della fine del Seicento e del Settecento. (Index of Roman paintings of the end of the seventeenth and of the eighteenth centuries.)
Giancarlo Sestieri.   Turin, Italy: Umberto Allemandi & Co., 1994. 3 vols. bibliog. (Archivi di Arte Antica.)

A catalogue of 1,166 works painted in Rome between 1680 and 1800, from the end of the Baroque era to the advent of Neo-classicism. It includes works by 126 artists, listed in alphabetical order. Each entry has a short introductory note, a chronology, a bibliography and a list of works arranged by location. The catalogue does not aim to be comprehensive, concentrating instead on figure paintings, especially mythological and historical subjects, as landscapes and *vedute* (topographical views) have been studied in other recent publications. The work of foreign artists working in Rome during this period is also included, while less space has been given to artists (such as Pompeo Batoni) whose work has been the subject of monographic studies or exhibitions. 1,166 paintings are reproduced in volumes two and three.

521   Roma e lo stile classico di Raffaello, 1515-1527. (Rome and Raphael's classical style.)
Edited by Konrad Oberhuber, catalogue by Achim Gnann.   Milan, Italy: Electa, 1999. 425p. bibliog.

This is the catalogue of an exhibition in Mantua and Vienna examining the development of Raphael's classical style during his years in Rome and its influence on artists working in Rome in the seven years between his sudden death, at the age of thirty-seven, in 1520 and the Sack of Rome in 1527. It includes 310 items, mostly prints and drawings, by the master himself and by twenty-one of his followers including Baldassare Peruzzi, Giulio Romano, Polidoro da Caravaggio and Parmigianino. It demonstrates, in particular, the importance of Rome as a printmaking centre in the early years of the 16th century, which is shown through the work of engravers such as Marcantonio Raimondi, Agostino Veneziano (Agostino dei Musi) and Marco Dente (Marco Da Ravenna).

522   Roman Baroque drawings, c. 1620 to c. 1700.
Nicholas Turner, with the assistance of Rhoda Eitel-Porter.   London: British Museum Press, 1999. 2 vols. (294p., 428p.). bibliog. (Italian Drawings in the Department of Prints and Drawings in the British Museum.)

The British Museum's collection of Roman drawings from one of the most brilliant periods in the history of Italian art covers all the major as well as many lesser-known artists working in Rome in the 17th century. It is particularly strong in finished compositional drawings and has a great variety of material including print, tapestry and medal designs, portraits, landscapes, caricatures and drawings of catafalques, designs for altarpieces, preparatory studies for paintings and decorations. The preface points out the competing trends of the 'Classical' and the 'Baroque' throughout this period, first in the work of Domenichino and Lanfranco, the technical flair of Bernini and the more restrained style of Algardi, and later in the exuberance of Pietro da Cortona and the composure of Sacchi and, finally, in the work of G. B. Gaulli and Carlo Maratti. It also gives a short history of the British Museum's collection of Roman drawings. All the artists mentioned above are well represented in the collection, which also has important holdings of the work of Pietro Testa, Pier Francesco Mola and Giovanni Francesco Grimaldi. The catalogue has 511 entries and there are 370 black-and-white plates. The great Bolognese artists (Annibale Carracci, Guido Reni and Guercino) who worked in Rome at the time and also

Poussin and Claude are not included in this catalogue. There are numerous appendices, indices (subjects, drawings in other collections, former owners), and a concordance.

523 Roman Baroque painting: a list of the principal painters and their works in and around Rome, with an introductory essay.
Ellis Waterhouse.   Oxford: Phaidon Press, 1976. 163p. bibliog.

A revised edition of a study originally published in 1937, one of the pioneering works in the re-evaluation of Baroque art. The list of artists and their paintings is preceded by a study of painting in Rome from the later 16th century to 1700, which includes illuminating sections on Annibale Carracci, Caravaggio, the development of the Baroque style and the Jesuit aesthetic. The list includes sixty-nine artists and works whose attribution is either documented or attested by early evidence. Only those painters who worked after the accession of Urban VIII in 1623, were born before 1660 and executed commissions of some importance for the decoration of churches and palaces are included (thus Claude Lorrain, whose work was of a more domestic nature, is omitted). Each entry contains a short biographical notice, a bibliography, and a list of works and their locations. There is also a topographical index and eighty-one plates.

524 Rubens and Italy.
Michael Jaffé.   Oxford: Phaidon, 1977. 128p. + [192]p. of plates.

Rubens was in Italy between 1600 and 1603 in the service of Vincenzo I Gonzaga, Duke of Mantua. He was free, however, to travel and accept commissions from other patrons, often spending extended periods in other cities. He first visited Rome in 1602, studying and copying the antique and also the work of the great 16th-century masters, especially Michelangelo and Raphael. He also executed three works for S. Croce in Gerusalemme. He was in Rome again between 1606 and 1608 when he obtained, through the influence of Cardinals Jacopo Serra and Scipione Borghese, a commission to paint an altarpiece for the high altar of Chiesa Nuova, the recently built church of the Oratorians. This was to prove a problematic but ultimately successful undertaking and its completion was followed by the artist's departure from Italy. His complex dealings with the Oratorians in drawing up the terms of his contract and during the execution of the work (which he had to replace with a new version of the same subject as the original painting proved unsatisfactory) are described in great detail, using original documents.

525 Le sculture del Seicento a Roma. (Seventeenth-century sculptures in Rome.)
Oreste Ferrari, Serenita Papaldo.   Rome: Ugo Bozzi, 1999. 722p. bibliog.

During the 17th century, Rome was enriched by an enormous number of sculptures that embellished the spectacular architectures created by Bernini, Borromini, Pietro da Cortona, and others. They include portrait busts of patrons and saints, sculptured altarpieces (in lieu of painted ones), stuccowork, and reliefs. This volume examines the whole range of sculptures produced during the Baroque era. It begins with those in churches and other places of worship, arranged alphabetically, then those in palaces, villas, and urban sites. These are followed by a listing of sculptures in museums and galleries, in private collections, and, finally, in the Vatican. There are two indices, of names and places. The work of some 170 sculptors is analysed, with information about patronage, changes in critical fortunes, and attribution. There are some 1,750 black-and-white illustrations as well as forty-seven colour plates.

526 Sebastiano e Giuseppe Ghezzi, protagonisti del Barocco. (Sebastiano and Giuseppe Ghezzi, protagonists of the Baroque.)
Edited by Giulia de Marchi.   Venice, Italy: Marsilio, 1999. 124p.

The exhibitions *I Ghezzi dalle Marche all'Europa* (The Ghezzi family from the Marches to Europe), organized in Comunanza and Ascoli Piceno in 1999, celebrated the achievements of three generations of the Ghezzi family. The archival researches undertaken on the occasion of the exhibitions brought to light new facts related to the biography of these artists. This catalogue looks at the life and work of Sebastiano Ghezzi (158?-1647), a little-known local artist who worked mostly in the Marches but also in Portugal, but its greater part is devoted to Giuseppe Ghezzi (1634-1721), his son, who moved to Rome in 1651 (not in the late 1660s as was previously believed) where he played a key role in the artistic life of the city during his long and distinguished career as a painter, illustrator and administrator. As well as pursuing an artistic career, he also trained as a lawyer, soon becoming a notary in the Reverenda Camera Apostolica (a department of the Holy Roman Church), a role that increased his social standing and influence. The catalogue examines his relations with important figures in the Roman scene like Cardinal Decio Azzolino (and through him Queen Christina of Sweden), Carlo Fontana, Carlo Maratti, Cardinal Ottoboni, Sebastiano Resta, and Cardinal Giovanni Francesco Albani (later Pope Clement XI). It also examines his work as a draughtsman and the role he played at the Accademia di San Luca (where he held the post of Permanent Secretary from 1678 to 1719), the Compagnia dei Virtuosi del Pantheon and the Accademia degli Arcadi. The last chapter looks at Ghezzi's collection of drawings.

527 Studies in Roman eighteenth-century painting.
Anthony Morris Clark, selected and edited by Edgar Peters Bowron. Washington, DC: Decatur House Press, 1981. 203p. (Art History Series, 4.)

A. M. Clark was a key figure in the re-evaluation of 18th-century Roman art and of the city's continuing importance as the major artistic centre in Italy (thus refuting the prevailing critical orthodoxy upholding the pre-eminence of Venice). As explained in the introduction of this volume, Clark's untimely death in 1976 at the age of fifty-three left a large corpus of work in progress, notably a biography of Pompeo Batoni and a history of 18th-century painting, the completion of which will be undertaken at a later stage. The present volume is a collection of fourteen papers originally published in books and journals. In some cases the editor has altered texts, basing his amendments on the author's manuscript drafts and notes. They include studies of little-known artists such as Nicola Pio, Placido Costanzi, Pietro Bianchi and Agostino Masucci, and also of better-known ones such as Marco Benefial, Cristoforo Unterberger, Francesco Imperiali and Pompeo Batoni. There are 205 illustrations and the volume also includes a bibliography of A. M. Clark's writings.

528 Turner in the South: Rome, Naples, Florence.
Cecilia Powell.   New Haven, Connecticut; London: Yale University Press, 1987. 215p. bibliog.

J. M. W. Turner visited Rome twice, in 1819 and 1828. Though he had been prevented from visiting Italy earlier in his career by the Napoleonic Wars, the painter had nevertheless been much influenced by Claude Lorrain and his depictions of Rome and the Campagna, and also by 18th-century English artists, notably Richard Wilson. The work looks at the influences that determined Turner's first journey in 1819, which included the patronage of Sir Richard Colt Hoare, and the publication in 1818 of Lord Byron's Book

IV of *Childe Harold in Italy*. The details of the journey and the sketches he executed on the way are described in a separate chapter, which also examines the practicalities of travel to Italy in the early years of the 19th century and explains the painter's method of executing from the carriage quick pencil sketches in pocket-sized sketchbooks and larger water-colour sketches in places were he was staying for some time. In Rome, Turner used eight sketchbooks which, as he kept no journal during his visit, constitute a valuable record of things seen during his stay in the city. He sketched, in a variety of techniques, all the major antiquities but also less famous or less central sites too (the Pyramid of Cestius, the walls and city gates). In addition, he sketched Renaissance and Baroque buildings and sites (St Peter's, the Trevi Fountain, the Piazza del Popolo), and panoramic views of Rome from the Aventine, the Pincio, Monte Mario, and the Janiculum. He also copied antique sculpture (both reliefs and free-standing sculptures), with an eye to using them in future paintings. His reactions to paintings he saw in Rome (where he was elected a member of the Accademia di S. Luca) are also surveyed, as are his explorations of the landscape of Tivoli and the Alban Hills. A separate chapter examines the oil paintings and water-colours of Italy Turner produced in the 1820s, in particular *Rome from the Vatican* and *Forum Romanum* (both now in the Tate Gallery). During his second journey to Rome in 1828-29, Turner sketched less (he filled only ten sketchbooks as opposed to the twenty-three of 1819) and painted more pictures, including three large canvases exhibited in Rome in 1828 – *Vision of Medea*, *Regulus*, and *View of Orvieto* (all in the Tate Gallery) – which are discussed in detail. Though Turner did not visit Rome and the South again, between 1829 and 1840 he produced several paintings of central and southern Italy which are examined in the last chapter. The epilogue summarizes the artist's intellectual reaction to Italy and assesses the wealth of works it inspired, comparing Turner's love for Italy to the stages of a love affair: anticipation, realization, and recollection. There are 180 black-and-white and 40 colour plates, the latter of uneven quality.

Sculpture

529   Alessandro Algardi.
Jennifer Montagu.   New Haven, Connecticut; London: Yale University Press, in association with the J. Paul Getty Trust, 1985. 2 vols. 511p. bibliog.

An investigation of the nature of Algardi's work and its position in the art of his time. The author suggests in the preface that, thanks to Bellori, Algardi has been wrongly pigeon-holed as a classical artist (as a kind of sculptural counterpart to the classicism of Annibale Carracci) and that there is a dichotomy between his large marble sculptures and his bronzes and drawings. The first volume of this work provides a detailed study of Algardi's life and work in roughly chronological order, but with chapters dedicated to Innocent X and Camillo Pamphilj's patronage of the artist, the reliefs, and the portraits. Volume two is a *catalogue raisonné* arranged by subject, rather than by date, as very few works are securely dated. The arrangement is as follows: religious subjects (under various sub-divisions), restorations, mythology, allegorical personifications, catafalques, history, portraits and tombs, decorative schemes, decorative objects, miscellanea, and medal reverses. There are 219 works accepted as by Algardi (with various gradations of status), and 59 rejected works. A checklist of 97 drawings (and 9 rejected ones) is also given. The work is richly illustrated – volume one contains 268 comparative illustrations and 8 colour plates and volume two contains 225 plates of Algardi's sculptures.

530 Algardi: l'altra faccia del barocco. (Algardi: the other face of the Baroque.)
Edited by Jennifer Montagu.   Rome: Edizioni De Luca, 1999. 326p. bibliog.

This is the catalogue of an exhibition of over 100 works by one of the great sculptors of the Roman Baroque. Alessandro Algardi (1598-1654) was born in Bologna but moved to Rome in 1625 and stayed there for the rest of his life. Less extrovert but more poetic than Bernini, his main rival, his work has often been seen as the sculptural equivalent of the paintings of the Bolognese artists (Agostino and Annibale Carracci, Domenichino and Guido Reni), who were also active in Rome during the first half of the 17th century. As well as a selection of smaller sculptures – magnificent busts like the portrait of Innocent X, and terracotta or bronze models of some of the artist's famous marble sculptures (for example, the *Encounter of St Leo the Great and Attila* at St Peter's) – it also includes a selection of his drawings, some of them designs for decorative art. The introductory essays examine Algardi's life, the contemporary artistic scene in Bologna and Rome, the artistic patronage of the Pamphilj family during the pontificate of Innocent X, Algardi's work at the Villa Pamphilj and, finally, his busts, bronzes, and drawings.

531 Bernini.
Howard Hibbard.   Harmondsworth, England: Penguin Books, 1976 (latest reprint). 255p. (Pelican Books.)

Originally published in 1965, this monograph attempts to give an idea of the growth and development of Bernini's artistic genius through an examination of his work as a sculptor. The sculptures are introduced in chronological order omitting doubtful, minor, or secondary works. Bernini's architecture is dealt with only in connection with his sculpture, and his other activities are mentioned only in passing.

532 Bernini: genius of the Baroque.
Charles Avery, special photography by David Finn.   London: Thames & Hudson, 1997. 287p. bibliog.

A study of the many-sided genius of Bernini. It covers all aspects of the artist's enormous body of work and looks at the various areas of his diverse activities. These included sculpture, architecture, urban planning, fountain displays, interior decoration, theatrical design and festival decorations, painting, and medal design. He was also a good draughtsman and one of the first caricaturists. The artist's work is treated more or less chronologically in twelve chapters. They discuss the early works which he executed in partnership with his father Pietro Bernini; the first portrait busts; the great mythological groups which he executed for Cardinal Scipione Borghese; the patronage of Pope Urban VIII Barberini and the mature portrait busts of popes and prelates; the architectural commissions for the basilica of St Peter, which include the Baldacchino, the Cathedra Petri and the papal tombs; the later religious sculptures which include works that combine architecture with sculpture and painting to form a 'beautiful whole'; the Roman fountains; the architectural and urban planning work, which include St Peter's Square and S. Andrea al Quirinale; and, finally, the work commissioned by Charles I and Louis IV. There is also a chapter examining Bernini's working methods in various disciplines – his modelling in clay and terracotta, his technique of carving in stone, his designs for the theatre, for coins and medals and for presentation drawings. The final chapter provides a portrait of the artist and discusses his posthumous reputation. The work is lavishly produced, with 400 illustrations (80 in colour), many of them specially commissioned photographs by David Finn showing spectacular views of the works and their locations, and also details which are scarcely visible *in situ* (see, for example, the section on the Cathedra Petri).

533 Bernini: the sculptor of the Roman Baroque.
Rudolf Wittkower. London: Phaidon, 1999. 4th ed. 320p.

This classic work, first published in 1955, was a ground-breaking re-evaluation of the greatest genius of the Baroque era. It focuses on Bernini's sculpture, leaving out his architecture and various other activities. The artist's achievements are outlined in the introduction while the critical material is supplied in a *catalogue raisonné* of his work. In the introduction there is a systematic arrangement of Bernini's output: early works and the sculpture groups executed for the Borghese family; religious imagery; portrait busts; work in St Peter's and the Vatican; the Cornaro Chapel; other chapels, churches and the Baroque stage; fountains and monuments; and, finally, a chapter on Bernini and his period, the organization of his studio, and his theory and practice. The catalogue has eighty-two detailed entries, some of them grouping together similar types of works (for example, sculptures for fountains) or summary listings of lost, destroyed and occasional works. Attributions made to Bernini after the appearance of the first edition of this work and not acceptable to the author are also included. The addenda to the third and fourth editions are given at the end of the entries. This edition also contains numerous new illustrations, including thirty colour plates.

534 Bernini scultore: la nascita del barocco in Casa Borghese. (Bernini as a sculptor: the birth of the Baroque in the Borghese House.)
Edited by Anna Coliva, Sebastian Schütze. Rome: De Luca, 1998. 473p. bibliog.

The catalogue of an exhibition celebrating the quatercentenary of Bernini's birth, this volume focuses on the works commissioned by Cardinal Scipione Borghese for the Villa Borghese. These include some of the sculptor's most famous works, such as *Apollo and Daphne, David, Eneas and Anchises* and *The Rape of Proserpina*. Each of the nineteen sculptures included in the exhibition is discussed in great detail, reproduced in a number of splendid colour plates and accompanied by a wealth of comparative material. The role of Cardinal Scipione Borghese as a patron of the arts is also discussed and an inventory of his collection of paintings is copied in an appendix, while all the documents related to the Bernini commissions are copied in another appendix. The catalogue also examines the work of Giovanni Lanfranco, who painted the ceiling fresco in the Galleria Borghese.

535 Canova in Rome.
Andrea Zanella. Rome: Fratelli Palombi, 1993. 77p. map. (Art and Culture Programme – Places.)

Two introductory chapters look at the political upheavals and changes in taste between 1779 and 1822, and at Canova's work during the forty years he lived in Rome. A chronology of the artist is also given but the core of the book is the catalogue of the sculptor's works in thirteen churches and public collections in Rome. This is divided into two groupings – places associated with Canova's activity, and public collections housing his works but not connected with the artist's activity. The first group includes: the Vatican museums, especially the Museo Pio-Clementino which, as well as housing one of the artist's masterpieces (*Perseo trionfante*), owes to Canova the recovery of its masterpieces, in 1815, from the French; St Peter's basilica; and the Chiesa di SS Apostoli, for which Canova executed the work that consecrated his name, the funerary monument to Clement XIV. The second group includes the Galleria Borghese, home of one of Canova's masterpieces – *Paolina Borghese come Venere Vincitrice*. All the works are illustrated.

536 Early eighteenth-century sculpture in Rome: an illustrated catalogue raisonné.
Robert Enggass. University Park, Pennsylvania; London: The Pennsylvania State University Press, 1976. 2 vols.

This work covers the period between 1695 and 1750, which saw the emergence of a new style in sculpture, free from the influence of Bernini. It examines the work of twenty-one sculptors, each treated in a separate section consisting of a life of the artist, a catalogue of his works in Rome and a bibliography. Illustrations of the works discussed appear in the volume of plates.

537 Effigies & ecstasies: Roman Baroque sculpture and design in the age of Bernini.
Edited by Aidan Weston-Lewis. Edinburgh: National Gallery of Scotland, 1998. 215p. bibliog.

The catalogue of an exhibition held in Edinburgh in 1998 to mark the quatercentenary of Bernini's birth. It examines the nature of artistic creation in 17th-century Rome, focusing on Bernini, but also looking at the work of Alessandro Algardi, his great rival, and other contemporary artists. Inevitably, as most of Bernini's sculptures are site-specific, his major works are represented here by preparatory drawings, models, or bronze replicas. There are sections on: portraits of Bernini, portrait drawings and caricatures; portrait busts; paintings; small bronze reliefs and reductions; projects for St Peter's and its Piazza; architectural and decorative designs and architectural medals; designs for fountains and outdoor monuments; designs for tombs and church monuments; designs for ephemera (festival decorations, catafalques); designs for applied art objects and engravings; medals and designs. The four introductory essays discuss Bernini's life; the social, economic, political and religious background in Rome; decorative arts in the age of Bernini; and Bernini and Britain.

538 Gian Lorenzo Bernini: regista del Barocco. (Gian Lorenzo Bernini: stage director of the Baroque.)
Edited by Maria Grazia Bernardini, Maurizio Fagiolo Dell'Arco.
Milan, Italy: Skira, 1999. 496p. bibliog.

This is the catalogue of an exhibition organized in Rome in 1999 as part of the celebrations of the quatercentenary of Bernini's birth in 1598. Bernini, more than any other artist, was the creator of Baroque Rome, the 'stage' of his prodigious creations. It includes over 200 works demonstrating his versatility and achievements as a sculptor, architect, painter, draughtsman, and town planner. It also aims to show his influence on the work of his contemporaries. The catalogue is divided into eight sections each introduced by one or more essays. They are as follows: a biographical section with numerous self-portraits and portraits of the artist; the works Gianlorenzo executed in the workshop of Pietro Bernini, his father, and his first independent works; a series of portrait busts of popes, cardinals, aristocrats, and sovereigns; architecture, fountains, and 'il bel composto' ('the beautiful whole', i.e. works combining sculpture, architecture, and painting); Bernini and Baroque decoration; the artist as propagandist – books, prints, and festival decorations; Bernini's paintings and works by his pupils; and his last years. It also includes a useful dictionary providing biographical information on popes, cardinals and artists associated with Bernini.

539 Gold, silver & bronze: metal sculpture of the Roman Baroque.
Jennifer Montagu. New Haven, Connecticut; London: Yale University
Press, 1996. 279p. bibliog.

This study is derived from the Andrew Mellon lectures, delivered at the National Gallery of Art
in Washington in 1991. They concentrate on a relatively neglected type of artefact: small-scale
gold, silver and bronze sculptures from the 17th and early 18th centuries. It examines all aspects
of their production and the relationship between, on the one hand, the designer and the sculptor
(who provided the drawings or models) and the bronze-founder and chiseller (who produced
the finished sculptures) on the other. It also looks at the relationship between the sculptor and
his patrons. There are studies on: the tabernacles of S. Maria Maggiore, S. Maria in Vallicella,
and St Peter's; medals and their designs (which, unlike those of the other types of sculptures
examined here, were mostly provided by the executants); and the work of Giardini and
Giardone, the leading founders and silversmiths of the early 18th century. The work is richly
illustrated with 267 black-and-white figures and 12 colour plates.

540 Roman Baroque sculpture: the industry of art.
Jennifer Montagu. New Haven, Connecticut; London: Yale University
Press, 1992. 255p.

This book is based on the author's Slade Lectures in the History of Art, delivered in
Cambridge in 1980. It examines various aspects of the sculptor's profession and sculptural
practice in 17th-century Rome. These include: the training of the sculptor and practical
matters related to the creation of a sculpture; the relationship between bronze-founders and
sculptors; the sculptor as executant of the work of other artists (painters or architects) and the
types of designs from which he was expected to work; the relationship between the master
and his assistant and the ways sculptors collaborated in the creation of major projects; the
restoration of antique sculptures in the 17th century (practised by some of the greatest
sculptors of the period, such as Bernini and Algardi); and the sculptors' contribution to
Baroque festival decorations. The work contains 278 black-and-white illustrations.

541 Roman sculpture.
Diana E. E. Kleiner. New Haven, Connecticut; London: Yale
University Press, 1992. 489p. bibliog.

A study of Roman sculpture and its cultural, political, and social contexts, this work discusses
all the major public and private monuments as well as many lesser-known ones. Its emphasis is
on sculpture in the city of Rome but it also examines significant monuments erected in the
provinces. The long, thematic introduction looks at the patrons, the artists and the materials they
used, the architectural context of the sculptures, the typology of the monuments, Roman
eclecticism (due to the wide variety of patrons and the differing regional tastes), the
historiography of Roman art, types of sculptures (major monuments and state relief sculpture,
imperial and private portraiture, funerary art and the art of freemen), Roman copies of Greek
originals, and the identity of Roman artists. The remaining chapters provide a chronological
examination from the foundation of Rome in 753 BC to the transfer of the capital to
Constantinople in 330 AD. Each chapter begins with a survey of the historical and political
background followed by a study of the monuments, which are divided by type (portraiture, state
relief sculpture, and provincial art). A bibliography of the period and the individual items
discussed is also included in each chapter. The texts are accompanied by 421 excellent black-
and-white illustrations and there is also a glossary of Latin and Greek terms.

542 Thorvaldsen: l'ambiente, l'influsso, il mito. (Thorvaldsen: his times, influence and myth.)
Edited by Patrick Kragelund and Mogens Nykjær. Rome: L' 'Erma' di Bretschneider, 1991. 236p. (Analecta Romana Instituti Danici, Supplementum 18.)

The Danish sculptor Bertel Thorvaldsen was the foremost neo-classical artist in Rome after the death of Canova in 1822. He arrived in Rome in 1797 with a scholarship from the Copenhagen Academy and, like many other artists, remained there after completing his studies, eventually establishing an international clientele and playing a key role in the artistic life of the city until 1838, when he returned to Denmark. This collection of sixteen essays in Italian, English or German, originally read at an international conference organized on the occasion of an exhibition of the artist's works held in Rome in 1989-90, covers a wide range of subjects. These include individual works such as his enormous stucco relief frieze of *Alexander the Great's entry into Babylon* in the Palazzo del Quirinale; his relationship with other artists, such as Canova, Abildgaard and the Russian artistic colony in Rome; his role as a teacher and officer of art institutions in Rome (one of the posts he held was that of the president of the Accademia di San Luca, ususally held by Roman artists); his views on the contemporary debate regarding the restoration of antique sculpture; his relations with Roman patrons like the Torlonia family (including an essay on why the sculptor's work does not feature in the Torlonia Chapel in San Giovanni in Laterano); and his influence in Denmark and in America. Curiously, there is nothing on his private art collection, one of the finest collections of contemporary art in Rome at the time (also including ancient sculpture, Renaissance and later paintings and drawings), now in the Thorvaldsens Museum in Copenhagen.

543 The tomb and the tiara: curial tomb sculpture in Rome and Avignon in the later Middle Ages.
Julian Gardner. Oxford: Clarendon Press, 1992. 207p. bibliog.

Gardner explores the authorship and stylistic evolution of the monuments and also the historical and legal context. He also looks at their relocation, dispersal (as, for example, the monuments in St Peter's, which were dispersed in the 16th century during the rebuilding of the basilica), and wholesale destruction by revolutionary fervour.

Decorative arts

544 The Cosmati: the Roman marble workers of the XIIth and XIIIth centuries.
Edward Hutton. London: Routledge & Kegan Paul Ltd, 1950. 74p. + 64p. of plates.

Arte Cosmatesca (Cosmati work) is the name given to Roman art of the 12th and 13th centuries, characterized by order, balance, beauty of design and colour. It is the product of a well-defined school of master decorators who handed down the traditions of their craft from father to son. Their centre of activity was Rome, where they found their most precious materials (porphyry, verde antico) among the ruins of the ancient city and where they studied forms and objects (sculptured capitals, architraves, lions and sphinxes). This monograph examines the diversity of Cosmati work in Rome: campanili (S. Maria in Cosmedin), cloisters (S. Giovanni in Laterano and S. Paolo fuori le Mura), porches and porticoes (S. Lorenzo fuori le Mura and San Giorgio in Velabro), ciboria (notable examples at S. Giorgio in Velabro and at San Lorenzo fuori le Mura), altar screens, episcopal thrones, ambones (S. Maria in Cosmedin, S. Clemente, S. Lorenzo fuori le Mura), paschal candelabra, and tombs (S. Maria in Aracoeli, S. Maria sopra Minerva). Perhaps the greatest achievements of Cosmati art are the polychrome pavements. These have a framework, generally of white marble, filled with great rounds of discs of coloured marble, generally porphyry, set with mosaics of coloured marble *tesserae*, fitted together in geometrical patterns. There are examples in many churches in Rome, notably S. Clemente, S. Maria in Cosmedin, S. Maria in Trastevere, S. Maria Maggiore, and S. Lorenzo fuori le Mura. Production of the pavements did not, like the rest of the Cosmati work, come to a halt when the school came to an end following the departure of the papacy to Avignon (Renaissance examples can be seen in the Sistine Chapel). The work includes a list of signed inscriptions under artists' names, and an index of places in Rome and outside Rome.

545 La découverte de la Domus Aurea et la formation des grotesques à la Renaissance. (The discovery of the Domus Aurea and the formation of the grotesques during the Renaissance.)
Nicole Dacos.   London: The Warburg Institute, University of London; Leiden, the Netherlands: E. J. Brill, 1969. 223p. + 116 plates. bibliog. (Studies of the Warburg Institute, vol. 31.)

The rediscovery, in the late 15th century, of rooms from one wing of the Domus Aurea, the huge (it was twenty-five times the area of the Colosseum) palace Nero built after the fire of Rome in 64 AD, and their wall paintings, exercised a strong influence on Renaissance artists. These paintings (which were in underground chambers, or grottoes (Nero's palace was buried beneath the ruins of the Baths of Trajan), led to the development of a type of decoration called 'grotesque' with decorative forms, half-animal and half-vegetal (griffons, sphinxes, centaurs, tritons). Landscapes and still-lifes were also copied and were later developed into separate genres. This scholarly study examines in detail the decorations of the Domus Aurea and their influence on the work of painters such as Pinturicchio, Perugino, Signorelli, Raphael (in his *Logge*) and his followers (especially Giovanni da Udine). It also looks at their influence on engravings, marquetry and ceramics. An appendix lists the graffiti in the Domus Aurea.

546 The house of life.
Mario Praz, translated by Angus Davidson.   London: Methuen & Co., 1964. 360p.

Mario Praz (1896-1982) lived in the Palazzo Ricci-Sacchetti in Via Giulia between 1934, the year of his appointment as Professor of English Literature at the University of Rome, and 1969, when he moved to a flat in the Palazzo Primoli (which now houses the Museo Praz and also the Museo napoleonico). Each piece of furniture, porcelain or painting sparks off an anecdote, a reminiscence, or philosophical speculation. Hugh Honour called this work the fullest and most penetrating account any collector has given of his ruling passion.

547 Inside Rome: discovering Rome's classic interiors.
Joe Friedman and Marella Caracciolo, with photographs by Francesco
Venturi. London: Phaidon Press, 1993. 128p.
This is not a comprehensive survey but an attempt to evoke the wealth and diversity of historic
interiors, which are a vital part of Rome's architectural heritage. It focuses on privately owned
buildings that are closed to the public and never or rarely published. Some of the *palazzi* of the
old Roman nobility are still occupied by the families who built them, though more often they
passed into other hands and uses. The book also includes examples of 18th- to 20th-century
interiors, often neglected in general surveys. These include: the art nouveau Palazzo dell'
Agricoltura, an example from the Quartiere Coppedè – the luxury apartments and villas built in
1919-23; and examples of interiors from the 1920s and 1930s, such as the Palazzo
dell'Aeronautica, Palazzo dell'Industria, the Casa Madre dei Mutilati (Headquarters of the War
Invalids Association), and the Foro italico. The work is illustrated in colour throughout, with
one or more colour illustrations for each building and a brief note about its special features. A
gazetteer provides brief information about the original construction of each building and the
creation of interiors specifically mentioned in the text, and also contains addresses and details
of whether the building is open or closed to the public.

548 Life and the arts in the Baroque palaces of Rome: *ambiente barocco*.
Edited by Stefanie Walker, Frederick Hammond. New Haven,
Connecticut; London: Yale University Press, 1999. 300p. bibliog.
The catalogue of an exhibition held in New York and Kansas City in 1999 examining the
decorative arts and domestic life of the palaces of 17th-century Rome, which were major centres
of artistic and social activity in the city during the Baroque era. The exhibition included various
types of decorative arts, such as furniture, silver and textiles, and attempted to reconstruct the
environment of artistic production during the period (the *ambiente barocco* of the title) and also
to explain the context and function of these works through the evocation of aspects of social and
cultural life, such as festivals, musical events, and the reception and entertainment of guests.
There are seven introductory essays examining: the artistic sources and development of Roman
Baroque decorative arts; the palace, its furnishings (wall hangings, furniture, plates) and the way
they were moved, exchanged, and rearranged; the interior and exterior of the palace as a stage
for the power struggles that dominated the city; the Barberini celebrations for Christina of
Sweden; Roman still-life painting of the 17th century; arms and armour; and Cardinal Pietro
Ottoboni (1667-1740) in the Palazzo della Cancelleria. The catalogue includes ninety-seven
magnificent objects and is arranged in the following thematic sections: approach to the palace
and introduction to its residents; the display of princely magnificence in the Audience Hall and
State rooms; musical entertainment in the palace; banqueting and secular silver; and private
devotion. The publication is richly illustrated throughout.

549 Studies in Cosmatesque pavements.
Dorothy F. Glass. Oxford: B.A.R., 1980. 163p. + 80p. of plates.
bibliog. (International Series, 82.)
This first detailed study of one particular aspect of Cosmati art looks at the distinctive features
in the design of Cosmatesque pavements, the materials used in their composition (porphyry,
serpentine, *giallo antico*, and white marble). It attempts to provide a secure chronology for
Cosmatesque pavements through a systematic analysis of signed pavements, establishing at
least three families of 12th and 13th-century Roman marbleworkers who for generations were
active in pavement design. It also investigates the stylistic sources of the pavements, rejecting
the assumption that they were influenced by Eastern models through Byzantine marbleworkers

who imparted their skills to Italian workers. Instead, it suggests a combination of ancient Roman, Late Antique and early Christian North Italian influences. It also explains the iconology of the pavements, and concludes with a *catalogue raisonné* of all Cosmatesque pavements in Italy. There are eighty black-and-white plates, numerous illustrations of geometric patterns, and plans.

Frescoes

550 Annibale Carracci, the Farnese Gallery, Rome.
Charles Dempsey. New York: George Braziller, 1995. 103p. (The Great Fresco Cycles of the Renaissance.)

Annibale Carracci's frescoes in the main gallery at the Palazzo Farnese were executed between 1597 and 1603. They were seen by contemporaries as the beginning of a new era in Roman painting after the period of decline following the death of Raphael. This excellent short study describes the architecture of the gallery and Annibale's exuberant ceiling decoration with its ingenious illusionist devices that weave together nature and artifice, and examines the precedents of its sculptural, architectural and painted elements in earlier Renaissance and Mannerist decorative schemes by Pellegrino Tibaldi, Michelangelo, and Raphael, as well as in ancient Roman art. It also elucidates the narrative scenes and demonstrates the unity of their subject matter – the power of love, exemplified by the loves of the gods. Love is also the subject of the two paintings on the lower end walls, executed after the ceiling and the stucco decorations of the rest of the gallery, while the long walls' decorations (painted with studio assistance) illustrate the devices of the Farnese family. All the main elements of the frescoes are illustrated in colour and a magnificent frontispiece gives a spectacular view of the ceiling, enabling the reader to see all its components at a glance.

551 Art and politics in Renaissance Italy: British Academy lectures.
Selected and introduced by George Holmes. Oxford: Oxford University Press, 1993. 327p.

A collection of eleven essays on the Italian Renaissance originally presented as lectures at the British Academy and later published, in an expanded form, in the *Proceedings of the British Academy* and, in some cases, elsewhere. Florence and Rome are the dominant subjects; the essays on Rome include Denys Hay, 'Flavio Biondo and the Middle Ages', a study of the life and work of one of Rome's most important Renaissance historiographers focusing on the *Decades*, his monumental history of Rome from 410 to 1441. There are also three major studies of High Renaissance art in Rome: John Shearman, 'The Vatican Stanze: functions and decoration', considers the relationship in the three *Stanze* painted by Raphael between the design and subject matter of their decoration and their functions; Johannes Wilde, 'The decoration of the Sistine Chapel', considers all three fresco cycles, executed in three distinct periods, in their relation to each other and to the overall decoration of the chapel; and Edgar Wind, 'Michelangelo's Prophets and Sibyls', discusses the iconography of Michelangelo's seven Prophets and five Sibyls which occupy the zone between the ceiling (which depicts the Creation of the World) and the walls depicting the Genealogy of Christ and their significance as connecting elements, through the theme of their prophesies, of the two cycles.

552 The Cinquecento chapel decorations in S. Maria in Aracoeli in Rome.
J. E. L. Heideman. Amsterdam: Academische Pers B. V., 1982. 159p.

In this book, the author revises the dating, attribution, iconography, style and patronage of the extant decorations of several chapels in the church of S. Maria in Aracoeli and provides new information about the use to which the chapels were put. The book also includes a chapter on the history of the church, whose origins as a Christian monastery go back to the 8th century. The chapels examined were created during the outburst of building activity in the second half of the 16th century and the artists involved included Girolamo Muziano, Taddeo Zuccaro, Pier Francesco Mola, and Cristofano Roncalli. There are separate chapters on the following chapels: the Cappella dell'Immacolata Concezione (of the Serlupi family), the Cappella di S. Matteo (of the Mattei family), the Cappella della Pietà, and the Cappella di S. Paolo (of the Della Valle family). Four other chapels whose original 16th-century decoration is much mutilated are examined in the last chapter. There are eighty-four black-and-white plates.

553 The Farnese Gallery.
John Rupert Martin. Princeton, New Jersey: Princeton University Press, 1965. 307p.

A comprehensive study of this masterpiece of early Roman Baroque decoration. It is in three parts, the first giving a brief account of the Farnese dynasty and the construction of their Roman palace and the artists they employed for the decoration of its main gallery, Annibale and Agostino Carracci. It also discusses the Camerino Farnese, also decorated by Annibale immediately before the commission for the decoration of the main gallery. The second part is entirely devoted to the decoration of the gallery; it examines the chronology of the execution of the works and the role of Annibale's assistants, and analyses the style of the decorative scheme, its iconography and literary and artistic sources. It also looks at the influence of the frescoes on other 17th-century artists. Finally, the third part is devoted to the preparatory drawings for both the Camerino and Gallery cycles and includes a catalogue of 151 works, all of which are reproduced together with numerous other plates of the finished frescoes and comparative illustrations.

554 Filippino Lippi's Carafa Chapel: Renaissance art in Rome.
Gail L. Geiger. Kirksville, Missouri: Sixteenth Century Journal Publishers, 1986. 208p. bibliog. (Sixteenth-Century Essays & Studies, 5.)

The Carafa Chapel in the church of Santa Maria sopra Minerva was the only commission Filippino Lippi carried out in Rome between 1488 and 1493 and his first personal large-scale work in fresco. It was commissioned in 1488 by Cardinal Oliviero Carafa, the wealthy and politically influential cardinal of Naples who had a deep interest in letters, as his own burial place and as a site for the Dominicans and the College of Cardinals to honour St Thomas, the Order's primary theologian. This study examines the importance of the chapel as a manifestation of the resurgence of the importance of Thomism and the Dominicans during the second half of the 15th century. It analyses the iconography of Lippi's work, pointing out his translation of subjects based on 13th-century theology and hagiography into imagery of contemporary relevance (for example, his depiction of the *Assumption of the Virgin* in the spirit of contemporary festival decorations) and his adaptation of ancient Roman art to the visualization of theological ideas. Lippi's monumental figures and Sibyls and his application of antique ornament to painted friezes and pilasters are seen as the precursors of Michelangelo and Raphael. The study also gives a portrait of Oliviero Carafa as a humanist and art patron.

555 Francesco Salviati: affreschi romani. (Francesco Salviati: Roman frescoes.)
Edited by Anna Coliva. Milan, Italy: Electa, 1998. 117p. bibliog.

Published as a supplement to the catalogue of a major exhibition of Salviati's work held in Rome and Paris in 1998, this work looks at the frescoes the artist executed in Rome between 1531 and 1563. An introductory essay discusses artistic trends in Rome after the Sack of 1527 and the influence on Salviati of the art of Michelangelo, Raphael and their followers, notably Perino del Vaga and Parmigianino. The following nine chapters examine the subject matter, style and iconography of Salviati's extant work in nine different locations in Rome, with colour illustrations of details of the works together with plans showing their position within each decorative scheme. These include the frescoes at: the Oratory of S. Giovanni Decollato (the chapel of a Florentine confraternity in Rome, executed in 1538), the Cappella dei Margravi in S. Maria dell'Anima (the church of the German community, executed between 1541 and 1548), two important commissions from Cardinal Alessandro Farnese – the Cappella del Pallio in the Palazzo della Cancelleria (1548), and the Sala dei fasti farnesiani in the Palazzo Farnese (1549-56), the Sala delle Udienze in the Palazzo Ricci-Sacchetti in Via Giulia (1553, one of the artist's masterpieces), the Palazzo dei Penitenzieri (now Hotel Columbus, 1552), the refectory of the convent of S. Salvatore in Lauro (1552-53), the Chigi Chapel in Santa Maria del Popolo (*c*. 1548), and the Griffoni Chapel in S. Marcello al Corso (*c*. 1554).

556 Images of nepotism: the painted ceilings of Palazzo Barberini.
John Beldon Scott. Princeton, New Jersey: Princeton University Press, 1991. 256p. bibliog.

The focus of this study is the fresco cycles in the Palazzo Barberini, commissioned during the apogee of the papacy of Urban VIII (Maffeo Barberini) and Barberini family fortunes in the 1620s and 1630s. They constitute the most extensive series of ceiling frescoes in Rome outside the Vatican. The most famous fresco in the palace is that painted by Pietro da Cortona in the Gran Salone depicting *Divine Providence*, a masterpiece of optical illusionism and the largest ceiling painting in Rome since Michelangelo's Sistine ceiling. The other two major piano nobile frescoes were Andrea Sacchi's *Divine Wisdom* and Andrea Camassei's *Creation of the Angels*. After an introductory chapter describing the conventions of Italian Baroque ceiling painting, the author examines the chronology of the execution of the frescoes, explains their thematic unity (all three assert the divine election of the Barberini family to rule the Church) and analyses the form and content of their imagery, demonstrating how the scenes depicted functioned as social and political propaganda for the Barberini. The text is accompanied by 174 illustrations and 4 colour plates.

557 Michelangelo, la Cappella Sistina: documentazione e interpretazioni.
(Michelangelo, the Sistine Chapel: documentation and interpretations.)
Carlo Pietrangeli, Fabrizio Mancinelli, Kathleen Weil-Garris Brandt.
Novara, Italy: Istituto geografico de Agostini, 1994. 3 vols. ([387]p., 424p., 435p.). bibliog.

These volumes are the fullest account of the controversial restoration of Michelangelo's ceiling of the Sistine Chapel, which was carried out between 1980 and 1989. Volume one consists of colour plates showing the restored frescoes and a bibliography of works about the restoration of the ceiling and lunettes published between 1980 and 1993. Volume two contains a scientific report on the restoration; it also includes a fully illustrated report on the condition of the frescoes before restoration, making for an interesting comparison with the plates showing the restored works, a technical report on how the restoration was carried out and information about Michelangelo's technique and working methods revealed during restoration. Volume three contains forty-eight papers read at the conference organized in 1990. It includes 100 pages of comparative illustrations, mostly in colour.

558 Michelangelo, the Last Judgment: a glorious restoration.
Texts by Loren Partridge, Fabrizio Mancinelli, Gianluigi Colacucci.
New York: Harry N. Abrams, 1997. 207p.
Michelangelo's *Last Judgement* fresco in the Sistine Chapel was unveiled in 1541, twenty-nine years after the completion of the chapel's ceiling decoration, and divided critics who either saw it as the artist's greatest achievement as a painter or condemned it for the immorality of some of its images. Following the dictates of the Council of Trent concerning religious images, the passages deemed to be offensive to public decency were covered after Michelangelo's death. The restoration, which began in 1990 and was completed in March 1994 removed, where possible, the post 16th-century additions. This lavishly illustrated publication contains an essay by Fabrizio Mancinelli, the director of the restoration, on the development of Michelangelo's composition, his fresco painting technique and problems encountered during its restoration, while Luigi Colacucci reflects on his ten years of involvement in the restoration of Michelangelo's frescoes in the Sistine Chapel. The longest essay is by Loren Partridge, who examines the work's history and controversial theology and analyses its iconography in nine chapters each dealing with a section of the fresco and containing numerous colour illustrations of individual figures or groupings.

559 Raphael's cartoons in the collection of Her Majesty the Queen and the tapestries for the Sistine Chapel.
John Shearman.   London: Phaidon Press, 1972. 266p. (The Pictures in the Collection of Her Majesty the Queen.)
Raphael's cartoons (now at the Victoria & Albert Museum, on loan from the Royal Collection) were commissioned by Pope Leo X in 1515 and were designed for tapestries to hang on the lower walls of the Sistine Chapel below the frescoes executed under Pope Sixtus IV by Botticelli, Ghirlandaio and other painters. The tapestries were made in the workshop of Pieter van Aelst in Brussels. Eight of the ten executed cartoons survive (it is thought that sixteen were originally intended but it is not known why the commission was never completed). The subject of the cartoons and tapestries are the acts of Peter and Paul. This scholarly study examines the patron and the commission, attempts a reconstruction of the position of the works in the Sistine Chapel, and discusses their subject matter and design and subsequent history. There are three colour plates, forty-six black-and-white plates of the cartoons, and also ninety comparative illustrations. See also Sharon Fermor's *The Raphael tapestry cartoons* (London: Scala Books in association with the V. & A. Museum, 1996. 96p.). This is a shorter study published after the completion of a research programme and examination of the cartoons.

560 Raphael, the Stanza della Segnatura.
James Beck.   New York: George Braziller, 1993. 95p. (The Great Fresco Cycles of the Renaissance.)
The Stanza della Segnatura contains Raphael's most famous frescoes – the *School of Athens, Parnassus,* and the *Disputa* – executed during his first years in Rome between 1509 and 1511, while Michelangelo was working less than fifty yards away on the ceiling of the Sistine Chapel. The rivalry between the two painters and their very different characters and artistic geniuses are described in the introductory essay, which also outlines Raphael's life and work before his Roman years and gives a brief character study of Pope Julius II, the artist's patron.

The unity of the complex iconographic programme of the room – the private library of Julius II – is explained both in the essay and also in the commentaries accompanying the thirty-three colour plates (photographed before the recent cleaning of the frescoes) of overall views and also details of each work.

561   Raphael's School of Athens.
Edited by Marcia Hall.   Cambridge, England: Cambridge University Press, 1997. 194p. (Masterpieces of Western Painting.)

This examination of one of the greatest paintings of the Italian High Renaissance, Raphael's *School of Athens* in the Stanza della Segnatura, includes both early criticism of the work (by Giovan Pietro Bellori and Heinrich Wölfflin) and new interpretations written for this volume. In her introductory essay, Marcia Hall surveys the history of the commission and the iconography of the scheme of the Stanza, early interpretations of the work, Raphael's later critical fortune as the embodiment of the academic tradition in art, and recent scholarship. Other articles in the book examine the religious and intellectual background, the role of the architecture in the work (variously interpreted as the reflection of Bramante's new St Peter's, the evocation of the architecture of the ancient world, a stage set, or the ideal city), as well as Raphael's use of colour and chiaroscuro.

562   The Sistine Chapel before Michelangelo: religious imagery and papal primacy.
L. D. Ettlinger.   Oxford: Clarendon Press, 1965. 141p. + 44p. of plates. (Oxford-Warburg Series.)

A study of the frescoes on the side and entrance walls of the Sistine Chapel, executed in 1481 and 1482 by some of the best painters of the day – Botticelli, Perugino, Rosselli, Ghirlandaio, Pinturicchio, and Signorelli – summoned to Rome by Pope Sixtus IV. The frescoes by Perugino on the altar-wall were destroyed in the 16th-century and replaced by Michelangelo's *Last Judgement*. The frescoes occupy the middle zone of the walls and depict scenes illustrating the life of Moses and Christ (on the south and north wall respectively). Each fresco contains within one frame a number of separate scenes (between two and seven). This study examines the order of execution of the paintings and suggests that the unity and homogeneity of the paintings show that there was an artistic masterplan and strict supervision of its execution. It also includes an iconological study both of the individual scenes and of their arrangement in cycles, drawing on comparative pictorial material, current Bible commentaries, theological writings of the period (including works by Sixtus himself) and on other examples of typological decorations (i.e. ones showing the prefiguration of events in the New Testament through those of the Old). The frescoes' role as political and historical manifesto is also examined, demonstrating that all scenes show Moses and Christ in their triple role as leader, lawgiver and priest. This is seen in the context of the 15th-century revival of the doctrine of papal supremacy, argued in contemporary treatises which sought to extend the claim to absolute power to secular matters at a time when the papacy was trying to re-establish its full power after a period of decline in the 13th century.

563   The Sistine Chapel: a glorious restoration.
English language edition edited by Diana Murphy.   New York: Harry N. Abrams, 1994. 271p.

The nine-year restoration (1984-93) of Michelangelo's frescoes on the ceiling of the Sistine Chapel revealed the artist's original vivid colours. This splendidly illustrated publication celebrates the completion of the task with nine essays on various aspects of Michelangelo's work. These include an account of the restoration by Carlo Pietrangeli, an essay by John Shearman on Michelangelo's use of colour, and a chapter on the construction of the Chapel and the restoration, then under way, of Michelangelo's *Last Judgement*.

564 La volta affrescata della Loggia Mattei. (The frescoed vault of Loggia Mattei.)
Simonetta Baroni. Milan, Italy: Electa, 1997. 79p. bibliog.

Villa Mattei (or Villa Spada) was situated on the Palatine Hill in the ruins of Domitian's Palace (the site of Augustus' House, the *Domus Augustana*). Built in the 14th century for Cristoforo Stati, it subsequently became the property of the Mattei family (16th century), the Spada family (17th century), and, in the 19th century, was acquired by Charles Andrew Mills and William Gell, who gave it a Neo-Gothic exterior (it was known, at the time, as Villa Mills). In 1856, it became a Convent of the Order of the Visitation and the frescoes depicting mythological scenes were sold and replaced by new decorations. Between 1926 and 1936, the villa, with the exception of the former convent (now the Antiquarium) and the richly decorated loggia, was demolished to enable archaeological excavations. The loggia was built in 1519-20 and its vault (*volta lunettata*) was decorated with grotesque ornament. The decoration, which was influenced by that of the Domus Aurea, has been variously attributed to Raphael, Giulio Romano, or (as here) Baldassare Peruzzi and his assistant Pietro d'Andrea. The loggia was restored in 1989 and the twenty-two panels depicting mythological scenes, which had been sold between 1846 and 1860 and subsequently purchased by the Metropolitan Museum in New York, were returned on long-term loan. This study examines the history of the villa, the iconography and the technique of the decoration of the vault and the lunettes of the loggia. It contains seventy-four illustrations, mostly in colour.

Views of Rome / Artists in Rome

565 Abraham-Louis-Rodolphe Ducros: un peintre suisse en Italie.
(Abraham-Louis-Rodolphe Ducros: a Swiss painter in Italy.)
Jörg Zutter. Milan, Italy: Skira; Lausanne, Switzerland: Musée cantonal des beaux-arts, 1998. 131p.

The Swiss artist Abraham-Louis-Rodolphe Ducros first visited Rome in 1776 and settled there in 1779. After producing, in collaboration with the engraver Giovanni Volpato, a series of hand-painted etchings of views of Rome for the tourist market and genre scenes in acquatint with Jacques Sablet, he opened in 1783 a print shop in Strada della Croce (near Piazza di Spagna), which acquired an international clientele. His water-colours were particularly popular with English connoisseurs such as Sir Richard Colt Hoare. After the outbreak of the French Revolution and the consequent cessation of the Grand Tour, Ducros lost most of his clients and, finally, like other Francophone artists living in Rome at the time, he fled from Rome after the events of 1793. After a stay in the Abruzzi, he settled in Naples and between 1801 and 1806 divided his time between Naples and Rome, returning to Switzerland in 1807. His work influenced the younger generation of English water-colour artists, in particular J. M. W. Turner, who knew Colt-Hoare's collection of water-colours. This catalogue of the exhibition held at Lausanne and Quebec in 1998 follows the artist on an imaginary journey from Rome to Naples,

Sicily and Malta. All the works are from the collection of the Musée cantonal des Beaux-Arts in Lausanne. Of the sixty-four works in the exhibition (all magnificently reproduced), thirty-six are views of Rome and the Campagna, the rest of the Abruzzi, Sicily and Malta. There is a detailed chronology of the artist's life and travels.

566   Bartolomeo Pinelli, 1781-1835, e il suo tempo. (Bartolomeo Pinelli, 1781-1835, and his times.)
Maurizio Fagiolo, Maurizio Marini.   Rome: Centro iniziative culturali Pantheon, Rondanini galleria d'arte contemporanea, 1983. 346p. bibliog.

Bartolomeo Pinelli adapted the language of Neo-classicism to the depiction of the people and landscape of contemporary Rome. All aspects of the work of this prolific draughtsman, engraver, illustrator and sculptor are represented in this sumptuous catalogue. It includes entries for 145 drawings and water-colours, 14 terracotta figurines, and reproductions of all the plates in the collection *L'Istoria romana* (1816).

567   Exploring Rome: Piranesi and his contemporaries.
Catalogue by Cara D. Denison, Myra Nan Rosenfeld, and Stephanie Wiles.   New York: The Pierpont Morgan Library; Montreal, Canada: Centre Canadien d'Architecture, 1993. 285p. bibliog.

The catalogue of the exhibition held in Montreal in 1993-94 which explored the work of artists, architects, antiquarians, and collectors active in 18th-century Rome on the eve of the establishment of Neo-classicism. It focuses on the work of Piranesi and on his relationship with English, French, and Italian artists, architects and patrons. The introductory essays discuss Roman architecture at the time of Piranesi (1740-76), the evocation of ancient and modern Rome in the work of artists and architects who had studied at the French Academy in Rome, and the influence of Piranesi's work. The 128 works in the catalogue include panoramic and other views of Rome, architectural and theatrical designs, *capricci* (i.e. depictions of real monuments in imaginary settings), and furniture designs. Artists represented include: Giovanni Paolo Pannini, Giuseppe Vasi, Giovanni Battista Nolli, Richard Wilson, and Charles-Louis Clérisseau.

568   Gaspar van Wittel.
Giuliano Briganti, edited by Laura Laureati and Ludovica Trezzani.   Milan, Italy: Electa, 1996. 463p. bibliog.

A revised edition of the *catalogue raisonné* (originally published in 1966) of the work of this Dutch artist (1652/53-1736) who spent most of his working life in Rome, where he was one of the most prominent painters of topographical views ('*vedute*'). It includes 465 paintings and 491 drawings, all of which are illustrated, several in colour. 268 of the paintings are views of Rome and the Roman Campagna, the remainder views of other Italian cities (Florence, Venice, Naples, Urbino, Verona, Bologna, Messina) or imaginary views ('*vedute ideate*'). The drawings, which are listed under their present location, are divided into three categories: preparatory studies, sketches and notations from life, and imaginary views. In his magisterial, and richly illustrated, introductory essay, Briganti surveys the work of a host of Northern artists (painters and engravers) working in Rome in the 16th and 17th centuries, and the evolution of the views of ruins set in generic italianate landscapes into the 18th-century topographical view documenting the most up-to-date aspects of the modern city. There is a discussion of the major influences on van Wittel's work, notably that of Viviano Codazzi, and an examination of his life and work and its relation to the art of Venetian artists such as Canaletto and Carlevarijs. In another introductory essay, Laura Laureati discusses some notable collectors of van Wittel's work. There is a chronology of the artist, a full bibliography and a name index but, unfortunately, no subject index.

569   Géricault in Italy.
Wheelock Whitney.   New Haven, Connecticut; London: Yale University Press, [1997]. 256p. bibliog.

In 1816, Théodore Géricault (1791-1824) failed to win the Prix de Rome competition which would have allowed him a three-year stay at the Villa Medici. He nevertheless left for Italy in October 1816 and, after a short stay in Florence, arrived in Rome the following month, remaining there until 1817 when he suddenly departed a year earlier than originally planned. In Italy, Géricault produced a series of works in a variety of media and with subjects ranging from copies after the antique and earlier masters to contemporary Italian genre subjects based on scenes directly observed in the streets of Rome and elsewhere. This detailed study of Géricault's Italian journey examines the artistic milieu in Rome at the time and the influence of other artists, both earlier masters (especially Michelangelo, whose work in Rome had an overwhelming effect on the young artist) and contemporaries (such as Antoine Jean-Baptiste Thomas and Bartolomeo Pinelli), on his work. Géricault's most important Italian project was a large canvas showing the annual race of riderless horses down the Corso, the highlight of the Roman Carnival. Various preparatory studies have survived showing the development of his ideas from a contemporary crowd scene with figures in picturesque modern dress to a more classically balanced, frieze-like composition. The final work was never completed, as Géricault suddenly left Rome a year earlier than originally planned.

570   Giovanni Battista Piranesi: the complete etchings.
John Wilton-Ely.   San Francisco, California: Alan Wofsy Fine Arts, 1994. 2 vols. 1264p. bibliog.

This is the only catalogue of Piranesi's complete etchings, containing a staggering total of 1,008 plates. The arrangement is by series and type, each series introduced by a brief summary of its history. The works are divided into seven groups as follows: the etched catalogue of works; early architectural and decorative fantasies; views of Rome and its environs; archaeological works; theoretical and polemical works; works for decorative design and antique dealing; and miscellaneous works. There are indices of titles and captions, places, subjects, names and collections, a concordance between the numbers of etchings in the Focillon catalogue and the present edition, as well as various appendices which include: a list of Piranesi's published works by Arthur M. Hind, Andrew Robison's dating of combination volumes, watermarks, and a list of Piranesi's copperplates in the Calcografia nazionale in Rome.

571   Giuseppe Vasi, 1710-1782.
Luisa Scalabroni.   Rome: Multigrafica, 1981. 133p. bibliog.

Giuseppe Vasi, Piranesi's teacher in Rome, was one of the most prolific etchers of the 18th century. Born in 1710 at Corleone in Sicily, he moved to Rome in 1736. His work consists almost exclusively of topographical views of Rome, the most famous of which are the *Magnificenze di Roma*, published in ten books between 1747 and 1761. After the completion of this collection, Vasi published, in 1763, a guide to Ancient and Modern Rome divided into eight parts, richly illustrated with small etchings. The work soon became extremely popular and various subsequent editions of it were published. In 1765, Vasi published an enormous (265 x 100 cm) panoramic map of Rome seen from the Janiculum, upon which notable sites bore numbers referring to their depiction in the *Magnificenze di Roma*. Although Vasi's work lacks the visionary qualities of his famous pupil, it nevertheless has the merit of presenting a more

213

accurate and objective view of Rome. This is a catalogue of 427 etchings, all of which are reproduced. The introduction surveys the artist's life and works, and discusses problems of dating and attribution and Vasi's relationship to Piranesi.

572 Goethe a Roma: disegni e acquerelli da Weimar. (Goethe in Rome: drawings and water-colours from Weimar.)
Edited by Paolo Chiarini. Rome: Artemide edizioni, 1988. 207p.

The catalogue of an exhibition at the Museo napoleonico in Rome commemorating the bicentenary of Goethe's journey to Italy, one of the happiest periods in the writer's life. It includes forty-eight drawings and water-colours of Rome and the Roman Campagna by Goethe himself, together with fourteen by J. H. W. Tischbein, J. P. Hackert, C. P. Kniep, and A. C. Dies, his friends in Rome. The accompanying essays include an appreciation of the great archaeologist and antiquarian Ludwig Pollak (1868-1943) and his admiration for Goethe, and also a note about his collection of Goethe manuscripts, now in the Museo Barracco in Rome, together with a list of the collection. There is also a chronology of Goethe's Roman sojourn. See also the exhibition catalogue *Goethe in Italia* (Goethe in Italy), edited by Jörn Göres (Milan, Italy: Electa, 1988. 115p.), which includes 298 items related to the poet's Italian journey.

573 Granet: peintre de Rome. (Granet: painter of Rome.)
Isabelle Neto Daguerre, Denis Coutagne. Aix-en-Provence, France: Association des amis du Musée Granet, 1992. 300p.

A catalogue reproducing over 260 paintings, water-colour sketches and drawings mostly from the collections of the Musée Granet at Aix-en-Provence, the artist's birthplace. Granet (1775-1849) produced these during his stay in Rome from 1802 to 1819 and they include views of the city and the Roman Campagna, and depictions of cloister and church interiors for which the artist became renowned. The text examines Granet's early output in the studio of David and discusses the artistic circles he frequented in Rome, his patrons and his work in the context of French landscape art.

574 Images of the Grand Tour: Louis Ducros, 1748-1810.
Luc Boissonas (et al.). Geneva, Switzerland: Editions du Tricorne, 1985. 111p. bibliog.

The catalogue of this travelling exhibition (it was shown in London, Manchester and Lausanne) assesses Ducros's position among foreign artists working in Italy in the late 18th century. Introductory essays examine the Swiss artists' colony in Rome between 1775 and 1793, the fourteen large views of the Museo Pio-Clementino in Rome published by Ducros and Giovanni Volpato between 1787 and 1792, and English patrons of Ducros (notably Sir Richard Colt Hoare). There is also a detailed chronology and historical and biographical notes.

575 In the light of Italy: Corot and early open-air painting.
Philip Conisbee, Sarah Faunce, Jeremy Strick. Washington, DC: National Gallery of Art; Yale, New Haven, Connecticut: Yale University Press, 1996. 288p. bibliog.

The catalogue of a travelling exhibition in the United States in 1996-97 on the work of the first school of open-air landscape painting, which originated in Rome and southern Italy at the end of the 18th century in the works of Pierre-Henri de Valenciences and Thomas Jones and culminated in the Italian landscapes painted by Corot (represented here by twenty items) in the

1820s. It includes 131 works by forty-eight French, British, German, Belgian, and Danish artists, most of them painted in and around Rome. One of the introductory essays discusses the early history of open-air painting, which can be traced back to the work of Northern artists working in Rome in the 17th century and, in the 18th century, to the work of artists such as Claude-Joseph Vernet and Richard Wilson. Another essay considers descriptions of Rome and its environs by travellers of the Romantic era and traces the increase in the number of landscape painters in the early years of the 19th century, becoming, by the 1820s, part of the Roman scene. It also discusses some of these artists and surveys the sites they chose to paint, both in Rome and in the surrounding Campagna. The catalogue includes biographical notes for all the artists represented in the exhibition. All the paintings are reproduced in colour and there are numerous additional illustrations accompanying the introductory essays.

576 **Incisioni romane dal 500 all'800 nella collezione Muñoz: il catalogo informatizzato della Raccolta grafica comunale.** (Roman engravings from the sixteenth to the nineteenth century in the Muñoz collection: the computerized catalogue of the print collection of the Rome Comune.) Edited by Massimo Riposati. Rome: Edizioni Carte Segrete, 1993. 145p.

A catalogue of 121 prints of views of Rome ranging from Nicolas Béatrizet's 1550 engraving of the statue of Pasquino to Eugène Ciceri's 1870 lithograph depicting the Basilica of Maxentius. Other artists represented include: Étienne Duperac, Giovanni Battista Falda, Matteo Gregorio De Rossi, Alessandro Specchi, G. B. Piranesi, Giuseppe Vasi, Luigi Rossini, and Bartolomeo Pinelli. The introductory essays present the new computerized catalogue of the Raccolta grafica comunale, and discuss the art collection of Antonio Muñoz (1884-1960).

577 **Ingres in Rome.** Introduction and catalogue by Hans Naef. Meriden, Connecticut: printed for the International Exhibitions Foundation by the Meriden Gravure Co., 1971. 152p.

This is the catalogue of an exhibition of 140 landscape drawings from the Musée Ingres at Montauban and from American collections, shown in the National Gallery of Art and other American museums. These magnificent landscape drawings had been overlooked in earlier inventories, exhibitions and studies on the artist. Ingres himself attached little importance to them. They date from his first sojourn in Rome, first as a *pensionnaire* (pensioner) at the Villa Medici from 1806 to 1810, and then trying to earn his living by executing portraits of visitors to the city. In the Villa Medici he occupied the Pavillon S. Gaetano in the north-west corner of the villa, enjoying a sweeping view of Rome. A group of drawings were executed as gifts for his then fiancée Julie Forestier and her family, and sent to them in Paris. Others act as a kind of guide to the villa and depict all its important landmarks. There are also panoramic views of Rome that Ingres executed after his departure from Villa Medici, and pencil portraits with views of Rome in the background. The exhibition also included the only landscape paintings Ingres ever painted. The three small panels depict the Casina del Raffaello (on the grounds of the Villa Borghese, destroyed during the siege of 1849), the Casino dell'Aurora of the Villa Ludovisi, and the Orangerie of the Villa Borghese.

578   Italy in the age of Turner: 'The Garden of the World'.
Cecilia Powell.   London: Merrell Holberton, 1998. 120p.

The catalogue of an exhibition held in London in 1998 examining the work of British artists in Italy in the five decades following the end of the Napoleonic Wars, which had put a temporary end to the Grand Tour. It looks at various aspects of Italy which influenced their work – its ancient ruins and their appeal to the Romantic generation; its picturesque scenes of modern life and customs; the idyllic landscape of the Roman Campagna and the enduring influence of Claude on generations of artists, including Turner; and the vision of the Warm South and Italy as 'the Garden of the World'. There is also a survey of lithographs, engravings and illustrations in guidebooks and literary works, showing Italian life and landscapes. There are biographical entries for the twenty-eight artists represented at the exhibition – who included J. W. M. Turner, Edward Lear, Richard Parkes Bonington, William Etty, John Martin, Samuel Palmer, Samuel Prout, and John Ruskin – highlighting their journey to Italy and the works it inspired.

579   Luigi Rossini incisore: vedute di Roma, 1817-1850. (Luigi Rossini engraver: views of Rome, 1817-1850.)
Edited by Paola Hoffmann, Lucia Cavazzi, Maria Elisa Tittoni.   Rome: Multigrafica, 1982. 199p.

This is the catalogue of an exhibition held at Palazzo Braschi in 1982 of Luigi Rossini's views of ancient and modern Rome and Lazio. Rossini (1790-1857) was born in Ravenna, spent his formative years in Bologna and, after winning a prize for architecture, settled in Rome in 1817 with a three-year pension, residing at Palazzo Venezia. In 1817, he published his first collection of etchings of views of Roman antiquities. He was to produce ten more, the last one begun in 1850 but left unfinished as a result of the tragic death of Rossini's son in a coach accident and the subsequent decline of the artist's health. Rossini's style is less visionary and more factual than that of Piranesi. An edition of Rossini's complete etchings was published in ten volumes in 1856 containing a total of 613 plates. The present publication includes a selection of 167 works from all eleven collections, each of which is preceded by an introductory note. The three introductory essays examine Rossini's life and work in Rome, archaeological excavations, and the print market in Rome during the first half of the century. There is also an index of places depicted in Rossini's etchings.

580   Maarten Van Heemskerck *Inventio Urbis*.
Edited by Elena Filippi.   Milan, Italy: Berenice, 1990. 121p. (Le Grandi Raccolte dei Disegni di Architettura.)

Maarten van Heemskerck visited Rome in 1532, where he stayed for the next five years. He was much influenced by the work of other artists he met there and also by the antiquities of the city, which he recorded in numerous studies that he later used as background material for his paintings and prints. This album contains a selection of sixty-three drawings, reproduced in their original dimensions, from a sketchbook which was later dismembered. Its leaves are now in two albums in the collection of the Berlin Kupferstichkabinett known as *Römische Skizzenbücher* (Roman sketchbooks). They show classical antiquities, views of the city and architectural fragments.

581 Le magnificenze di Roma nelle incisioni di Giuseppe Vasi. (Rome's
magnificence in the engravings of Giuseppe Vasi.)
Paolo Coen. Rome: Newton & Compton, 1996. 311p. bibliog.
(Quest'Italia, 235.)

This is an edition of Giuseppe Vasi's most famous collection of etchings, the *Magnificenze di
Roma*, published in ten books between 1747 and 1761. All 200 etchings have full-page
reproductions with explanatory texts on the facing page. The ten books are as follows: Book 1,
The Walls and the Capitoline Gates (1747); Book 2, The main squares of Rome (1752); Book
3, The basilicas and ancient churches of Rome (1753); Book 4, The most famous palaces and
streets (1754); Book 5, Bridges and buildings on the Tiber (1754); Book 6, Parochial churches
on the Capitol (1756); Book 7, Convents and houses of Clerks Regular; Book 8, Monasteries
and convents (1758); Book 9, Religious colleges, hospitals, and charitable institutions (1759);
and Book 10, The most remarkable villas and gardens (1761).

582 The mind and art of Giovanni Battista Piranesi.
John Wilton-Ely. London: Thames & Hudson, 1988. 304p.

The author suggests that recent studies on Piranesi have tended to emphasize his Romanticism
and overshadow his roots in the stylistic language of the Baroque and Mannerism – he compares
Piranesi to Borromini and Pirro Ligorio and their equally inventive use of antique forms – and
Neo-classicism. This study examines all aspects of Piranesi's varied output, underlining his
practical activities as a pioneer of Roman archaeology, universally acknowledged in his time
and recognized by his election to the Society of Antiquaries in London in 1757. He was the
creator of a range of technical illustrations of far-reaching importance in the history of
antiquarian publications. His output as an architect is also examined through the complete
building accounts of his reconstruction of S. Maria del Priorato and the recently discovered
presentation drawings for the projected tribune of S. Giovanni Laterano. The influence of his
designs for furniture and his decorative schemes is also demonstrated. The work is sumptuously
illustrated with examples from all published collections of engravings, preparatory drawings,
and photographs of Piranesi's architecture. It includes full-page plates of the complete sets of
Vedute di Roma (137 plates) and the second states of the *Carceri* (16 plates).

583 Ottocento romano. (Nineteenth-century Rome.)
Renato Mammucari. Rome: Newton & Compton, 1997. 2nd ed. 525p.
bibliog. (Quest'Italia, 247.)

This richly illustrated monograph examines all types of artistic activity in Rome from the late
18th century to the end of the 19th century. There are chapters on the Grand Tour, Neo-
classicism and the Accademia di S. Luca, the Romantic movement (including the work of the
Nazarenes), foreign academies in Rome, *plein air* painting, Risorgimento art, Roman water-
colourists, Nino Costa and Roman pre-Raphaelism, D'Annunzio and art, the painters of the
Roman Campagna, and Divisionism. The second half of the work is a biographical dictionary
of artists who worked in Rome in the 19th century.

584 Paesaggi perduti: Granet a Roma, 1802-1824. (Lost landscapes:
Granet in Rome, 1802-1824.)
Edited by Maureen B. Fant, Sarah Hartman. Milan, Italy: Electa, 1996.
158p.

The catalogue of an exhibition of Granet's views of Rome held at the American Academy in
Rome in 1996. It includes eighty-six small oil sketches from the Musée Granet at Aix-en-

Provence of views of the city with its buildings and abstract geometry and its surrounding landscape of vineyards, fields and gardens dotted with ancient monuments. The latter landscape largely disappeared during the transformation of Rome in the second half of the 19th century and the surviving monuments now appear in different urban settings. There are six essays in English, Italian or French.

585   Pannini.

Michael Kiene.   Paris: Réunion des musées nationaux, 1992. 183p. bibliog. (Les Dossiers du Musée du Louvre, 41.)

Giovanni Paolo Pannini (1691-1765) was one of the great 18th-century *vedutisti* (painters of topographical views) and the creator of the genre of paintings commemorating a particular event. He was born in Piacenza but moved to Rome in 1711. There, he established close links with French artists and patrons, eventually becoming the official painter of the French ambassadors in Rome. This is a catalogue of an exhibition of works mostly from the Louvre (which has the world's largest collection of the artist's works); it includes all aspects of Pannini's output, mainly his depictions of Roman festivities and ceremonies, in particular three famous paintings commissioned by Cardinal Polignac, French ambassador to the Holy See – *Preparations in Piazza Navona to celebrate the birth of the Dauphin of France* (1729), *Cardinal Melchior de Polignac visiting St Peter's* (1730) and *Musical and theatrical performance in the Teatro Argentina, on 15 July 1747, on the occasion of the second marriage of the Dauphin*. The detailed discussion of these works provides a wealth of information about contemporary society and customs. The catalogue also includes examples of Pannini's views of the monuments of ancient and contemporary Rome, interiors of buildings (*Interior of St Peter's*), *capricci* (i.e. depictions of real monuments in imaginary settings), and 'gallery' paintings (i.e. paintings of interiors stacked with famous views of Rome) – all the painted views and antique sculptures included in *Interior of an imaginary picture gallery with views of Ancient Rome* and *Interior of an imaginary picture gallery with views of Modern Rome* (65 and 56 respectively) are identified. Works by Pannini's pupils are also included.

586   Piranèse et les français. (Piranesi and the French.)

Edited by Georges Brunel.   Rome: Edizioni dell'elefante, 1978. 611p. (Collection Académie de France à Rome, 2.)

A collection of twenty-eight papers originally read at a colloquium organized on the occasion of an exhibition shown in Rome (and later in Dijon and Paris) in 1976-77. The papers, which have been substantially supplemented with archival material, deal with various aspects regarding the diverse activities of Piranesi and his relationship with French artists and collectors also working in Rome. The subjects covered include: Piranesi as archaeologist and French architecture in the late eighteenth century; Charles Percier and the Egyptian Room at the Villa Borghese; the early years of Piranesi in Rome – the brothers Pagliarini and Nicola Giobbe; the architecture of Claude-Nicholas Ledoux and its relation to Piranesi; Nicolas-Henri Jardin's stay in Rome; the Villa Albani as seen by an artist of the 18th century; Piransesi and Clérisseau's vision of classical antiquity; the group of French 'Piranesians' (1740-50); and Piranesi's 'fantasia' and the Graeco-Roman controversy.

587   Piranesi.

Jonathan Scott.   London: Academy Editions; New York: St Martin's Press, 1975. 336p.

A full account of Piranesi's life and work. Each chapter follows the artist's development in roughly chronological order and also focuses on one aspect of his output, with the tenth and final chapter giving an appreciation of his achievement. The work includes a great deal of background information on 18th-century Rome, Piranesi's involvement in contemporary artistic debates (for example, the Graeco-Roman controversy) and his relationship with patrons and collaborators – there is, for instance, a detailed examination of the intrigues involved in the failed patronage of Lord Charlemont, the original dedicatee of the *Antichità romane*, and his more successful relationship with the Adam brothers. There are 353 plates, several of them full page. Some of the plates are located in the text but each chapter is followed by several pages of plates from the collection discussed – forty-one pages of plates follow chapter three, showing a selection of engravings from the *Prima parte di Architetture e Prospettive* (First part of Architectures and Perspectives), *Opere varie* (Various works), *Grotteschi* (Grotesques), and, on facing pages, the two states of the *Carceri* (Prisons).

588 **Piranesi and the grandeur of Ancient Rome.**
Peter Murray. London: Thames & Hudson, 1971. 72p. (Walter Neurath Memorial Lecture 1971.)

This is an excellent, lucid introduction to the work of Piranesi, one of the greatest and most prolific engravers of all time (he executed over 1,000 etchings). It focuses on the series of views of Rome he produced between 1745, when he settled in Rome, to the end of his life. It begins, however, with an examination of his formative years and a survey of early influences on his art. These include the work of Venetian *vedutisti* (topographical landscape painters) such as Gaspar van Wittel, Luca Carlevarijs and Canaletto, the Roman views of Pannini, which ranged from strictly accurate delineations of buildings to *capricci* (depictions of buildings in unusual settings), and the tradition of stage-set etchings of Antonio Juvarra and Ferdinando Bibiena (Piranesi made great use of the latter's major theatrical innovation, the *scena per angolo* [a scene set at an angle so that the perspectives run off diagonally at either side]). Piranesi began etching views of Rome on single sheets for the tourist market in 1745. These were published as *Varie vedute di Roma antica e moderna* (Various views of ancient and modern Rome), a volume consisting of ninety plates, fifty of which are by Piranesi (other artists represented are Paolo Anesi and French pensioners at the French Academy in Rome). In 1748, he started producing his *Vedute di Roma* (Topographical views of Rome), a series of etchings planned to provide large, beautiful and cheap souvenirs of the main sights of Rome; these included both modern and popular subjects and subjects from Ancient Rome. At the same time, he began work on his *Antichità romane de' tempi della Repubblica e de' primi Imperatori* (Roman antiquities from the times of the Republic and the first Emperors), which are among the largest plates ever etched. Another set, called *Antichità romane*, was published in four volumes in 1756. Piranesi's shift, in the mid-1750s, from simple *vedute* to the investigation of the problems of construction and aesthetics of ancient buildings is also examined, as well as the tension in his work between antiquarianism and full-blooded Romanticism, more concerned with effect than with truth and accuracy.

589 **Piranesi nei luoghi di Piranesi.** (Piranesi in the locations of Piranesi.)
Rome: Multigrafica; Fratelli Palombi, 1979. [598]p.

This volume contains the five catalogues for each of the five sections of a Piranesi exhibition, held at Castel S. Angelo, the Calcografia Nazionale, the Istituto di studi romani (in the complex of S. Maria del Priorato), the Orti Farnesiani, and the Palazzetto Luciano in Cori. The exhibitions aimed to demonstrate the relationship between Piranesi's work and the locations in Rome that inspired it, and provide a comparison between his etchings and the architecture or monuments that inspired them. The exhibitions also attempted to show his work in archaeological locations. All five sections are richly illustrated and include essays on various aspects of Piranesi's work.

590   La Roma di Bartolomeo Pinelli. (The Rome of Bartolomeo Pinelli.)
Bartolomeo Rossetti. Rome: Newton Compton, 1981. 205p. bibliog.
(Quest'Italia, 20.)

A study of Bartolomeo Pinelli (1781-1835), 'the painter of Trastevere', who was, like Gioachino
Belli, a prolific chronicler of early 19th-century Rome and its people. The introductory chapter
provides an outline of Pinelli's life and work, looking at his enormous output as a book illustrator,
especially his illustrations for Giuseppe Berneri's poem in Roman dialect *Meo Patacca* (1822)
and Giovanni Camillo Peresio's *Maggio romanesco* (1835), which epitomize his characterization
of the 'bullo romano', the fiery, proud and tough Roman. It also describes Pinelli's larger-than-
life personality, making ample use of anecdotes about the artist, and looks at his affinities to Belli.
The following seven chapters provide a selection of Pinelli's prints. Each print is given a full-
page reproduction that is accompanied by a description of the scene or character depicted. The
chapters are as follows: Roman people; occupations (barbers, butchers, harvesters, carters,
scriveners, etc.), street vendors and street-cries (such as the *acquavitaro* (spirit-vendor), the
scoparo (broom vendor), and the *cocomeraro* (watermelon seller); festivals and popular games;
festivals and religious traditions; inns and tavern games; Pinelli's contribution to Luigi Rossini's
1827 collection *I sette colli di Roma e vedute di Roma* (Rome and its seven hills and views of
Rome), for which he provided staffage; and spectacles of the piazza.

**591   Roma romantica: vedute di Roma e dei suoi dintorni di A.L.R.
Ducros, 1748-1810.** (Romantic Rome: views of Rome and its
surroundings by A.L.R. Ducros, 1748-1810.)
Edited by Pierre Chessex, with an introduction by Francis Haskell.
Milan, Italy: Franco Maria Ricci, 1985. 136p. (Quadreria.)

This sumptuous volume includes thirty-four hand-tipped colour plates of water-colours by
Ducros and twenty-three coloured etchings of views of Rome and its surroundings that he
produced in collaboration with the printer Giovanni Volpato between 1779 and 1784.
Each plate is accompanied, on the facing page, by an explanation of the landscape
depicted and by comments of contemporary travellers.

592   Roma sparita e dintorni negli acquerelli di Ettore Roesler Franz.
(Vanished Rome and its surroundings in the water-colours of Ettore
Roesler Franz.)
Pier Andrea De Rosa, Paolo Emilio Trastulli. Rome: Newton &
Compton, 1994. 261p. (Quest'Italia, 211.)

Ettore Roesler Franz (1845-1907) was born in Rome into a family of Swiss hoteliers and
bankers established in Rome at the end of the 18th century. This study offers a revaluation of
his prolific output, concluding that his best water-colours were the landscapes he executed in
the countryside around Rome, especially his views of the olive groves at Tivoli. There is also a
long essay surveying, year by year, Roesler Franz's life and works, and his role in the artistic
life of Rome in the last decades of the 19th century. It also points out the artist's numerous links
with England, his friendship with Joseph Severn, Keat's close friend who, after years of
absence, returned to Rome in 1861 as English Vice Consul, his filiation to the English water-
colour tradition, and his participation in numerous exhibitions in London. Ninety-six water-
colours are reproduced in colour and the accompanying commentaries discuss both the works
themselves and the sites depicted. As the three series of '*Roma sparita*' ('Vanished Rome') were
reproduced in an earlier volume in this series (see no. 593), the emphasis here is on views of
Tivoli and the Roman Campagna.

593 Roma sparita negli acquerelli di Ettore Roesler Franz. (Vanished Rome in the water-colours of Ettore Roesler Franz.) Livio Jannattoni. Rome: Newton & Compton, 1983. 295p. (Quest'Italia, 24.)

This publication reproduces the artist's most famous works, the 120 water-colours included in the three series of 'Roma sparita'. They record picturesque views of Rome that were to disappear or be transformed in the post-1870 demolitions and urban development of the city. Roesler Franz started painting these views in 1881, initially calling them 'Roma pittoresca' ('Picturesque Rome'), producing, over the following fifteen years, 120 views in three series. All three were purchased by the Comune of Rome, the first after their exhibition in 1883 and the other two posthumously after years of prolonged negotiations. Twenty-seven of them are now in the Museo del Folklore and the remainder (with the exception of one water-colour that was stolen in 1966) are in the Museo di Roma. The water-colours, all of which are reproduced in colour, are here divided into ten sections by subject depicted. They include views of the banks of the Tiber before the construction of the barriers (the 'muraglioni'), the Tiber bridges and the Isola Tiberina, the Ghetto, Prati di Castello, and Testaccio. The accompanying captions discuss the locations depicted, their history and their subsequent fate. There is a useful index of streets, houses, monuments, etc. demolished or 'vanished', and an introductory essay on the artist and his work.

594 Vedute di Roma dai dipinti della Biblioteca apostolica vaticana. (Views of Rome from the paintings of the Biblioteca apostolica vaticana.) Giovanni Morello, Pierluigi Silvan. Milan, Italy: Electa, 1997. 171p. bibliog.

The two introductory essays in this volume survey the painted areas in the Biblioteca apostolica vaticana – among them the library of Sixtus IV, the Salone Sistino, the Sale Sistine, the Sale Paoline, and the Gallery of Urban VIII – and their decorative cycles. These include depictions of Church Councils, allegories, and important events of the pontificate of Sixtus V and, in the Sale Paoline, of Paul V. The views of Rome examined in the second part include piazzas, basilicas, obelisks, and fountains. The work is lavishly illustrated in colour throughout.

595 Vedute di Roma dal medioevo all'Ottocento: atlante iconografico, topografico, architettonico. (Views of Rome from the Middle Ages to the nineteenth century: an iconographical, topographical and architectural atlas.) Jörg Garms. Naples, Italy: Electa Napoli, 1985. 2 vols. (223p., 557p.)

This massive corpus of views of Rome ranges chronologically from Cimabue's view of Rome in the Basilica of S. Francesco at Assisi to views produced in the 18th century, the apogee of the Grand Tour which had Rome as its epicentre. It includes a wide range of painted and printed material – panoramic views, maps, capricci (i.e. depictions of real monuments in imaginary settings), church facades and interiors, monuments, palaces, ephemeral festival decorations (from a variety of sources), sketchbooks, architectural treatises, and the great print cycles of Piranesi, Falda and Vasi. The first volume contains an introduction and 113 colour plates in chronological, thematic order, followed by their catalogue entries which include bibliographical references. The second volume contains a further 992 black-and-white plates and their captions, again including bibliographical information. There are sections on panoramic views, the Tiber, Castel S. Angelo, St Peter's and the Vatican, Campidoglio, Aracoeli, the Roman Forum, the Palatine, the Colosseum, the first fourteen rioni, the Walls, the Gates, and places outside the Walls.

596 Viaggio a Roma e nella sua Campagna. (Journey to Rome and its Campagna.)
Renato Mammucari. Rome: Newton & Compton, 1997. 526p. bibliog. (Quest'Italia, 254.)

Mammucari describes the fascination Rome exerted on artists and writers from the late 18th to the beginning of the 20th century. The work is divided into three sections. The first section describes the fascination with the antiquities of Rome and the landscape of the Roman Campagna of generations of visitors. Various categories of visitors and their reasons for coming to the city are examined – Grand tourists, the international artistic community living in the orbit of the foreign academies or independently, and Italian artists catering for the tourist market. The second section is a dictionary of some 1,000 artists working in Rome during this period, each entry concentrating on information about the artist's activities in Rome. The third section contains extracts from the writings on Rome of 171 writers, from Edmond About to Émile Zola, each extract preceded by biographical information about the author. Rather annoyingly, however, there are no indications about the exact provenance of the cited extracts. The work is richly illustrated throughout with paintings, engravings, portraits and photographs of the artists and writers.

597 Views of Rome from the Thomas Ashby collection in the Vatican Library.
Raymond Keaveney. London: Scala Books, 1988. 304p.

Thomas Ashby (1874-1931), Director of the British School at Rome, was the author of numerous works on the archaeology and topography of Rome. He was also an expert photographer, amassing an archive of over 9,000 photographs of the Roman Campagna, which supplemented his research. His collection of *c.* 6,000 prints and 1,000 drawings, mostly about the Roman countryside, was acquired by the Vatican Library in 1933. This is the catalogue of a travelling exhibition in the United States of a selection of eighty-one drawings and water-colours from the collection. The works are representative of many different national schools and range from the Renaissance to the early 19th century. All are reproduced in colour and there are numerous comparative illustrations. The accompanying commentaries by Raymond Keaveney are supplemented with extracts from earlier writers' work describing the monument or view depicted. Biographies of the artists are also included. The three introductory essays describe the circumstances of the purchase of the collection, discuss the dual role of the drawings as works of art and as sources for the study of radically altered or vanished archaeological sites and landscapes, and consider the theme of renewal and continuity in the Eternal City.

598 Views of Rome then and now: 41 etchings by Giovanni Battista Piranesi.
Herschel Levit (corresponding photographs and text). New York: Dover Publications, 1976. 109p. bibliog.

An interesting juxtaposition, on facing pages, of Piranesi's etchings with corresponding photographs by the author – taken, as far as possible, from the viewpoint of the etchings. The photographs not only show the changes effected over the intervening two hundred years but also reveal the devices Piranesi used to create the grandiose effects that characterize his work, for example the enhancing of the scale of the architecture by diminishing the size of the figures populating the etchings. There are notes to the plates which compare each etching with its accompanying photograph.

Museums and Galleries

599 **L'Angelo e la città: la città nel Settecento.** (The Angel and the city: the city in the eighteenth century.)
Edited by Giovanna Curcio. Rome: Fratelli Palombi, 1988. 2 vols. (293p., 320p.). bibliog.

A two-volume catalogue of an exhibition held in Rome in 1987 to celebrate the restoration of one of the landmarks of Rome – the bronze statue of the Archangel Michael that crowns the Castel S. Angelo. The first volume looks at the history of the statue (unveiled in 1752, the statue replaced the statue by Raffaello da Montelupo which had, itself, replaced an earlier statue that disappeared during the Sack of Rome in 1527), the work of its creators (the Flemish sculptor Peter Anton von Verschaffelt [1710-1793] and Francesco Giardoni [1692-1757], who cast it in bronze), and gives a technical examination of its restoration. It also studies the iconography of the Archangel in the pose of sheathing his sword, traditionally thought to symbolize his victory over the plague of 590, and analyses its cultural, historical and religious significance. Other works carried out during the pontificate of Benedict XIV – in S. Maria Maggiore, the Palazzo del Quirinale, S. Giovanni in Laterano, and S. Apollinare – are also examined. The second volume provides a major survey of 18th-century Roman dwellings; it focuses on the parish of S. Lorenzo in Lucina in the *rione* Campo Marzio (between the Porto di Ripetta and the Trinità dei Monti) and provides a detailed analysis of the houses of 52 *isole* ('islands' of buildings). The critical edition of the various editions of Filippo Titi's guide to works of art in Roman churches (see entry no. 702) was published in conjunction with these catalogues.

600 **Catalogo sommario della Galleria Colonna in Roma: dipinti.**
(Summary catalogue of the Galleria Colonna in Rome: paintings.)
Edited by Eduard A. Safarik, with the assistance of Gabriello Milantoni.
Busto Arsizio, Italy: Bramante, 1981. 157p.

The Galleria Colonna houses one of the most important collections of paintings collected by the Roman nobility. Most of its rich holdings of 16th- and 17th-century works were acquired by Lorenzo Onofrio Colonna (1637-1689) and largely reflect the tastes of the painter Carlo Maratti, his adviser. In the 18th century the collection was further enriched, through marriage, with numerous paintings from the Salviati collection. This catalogue contains 210 paintings, all of which are reproduced. Each entry contains technical data, provenance, references in earlier catalogues and inventories, and a full bibliography. There is also a room-by-room listing of the works with number references to the main part of the catalogue, and a list of inventories and catalogues of the Colonna collection. An introductory essay by Fabrizio Lemme examines and elucidates the *fedecommesso* (entail) and its application to the collections of art of the Roman nobility. In Roman law, the *fedecommesso* was a recommendation or request by the maker of a will to his heirs to preserve and transmit intact to a succeeding generation specified goods. This later become a binding condition and from the 17th century onward it was adopted by the Roman nobility as a means of preventing the dispersal of their art collections. Abolished during the Napoleonic occupation, the law was reinstated by Pope Pius VII in 1816. This article usefully lists the present legal status of the art collections of the great Roman families.

601   Catalogo sommario della Galleria Colonna in Roma: sculture.
(Summary catalogue of the Galleria Colonna in Rome: sculptures.)
Edited by Filippo Carinci (et al.).   Busto Arsizio, Italy: Bramante,
1990. 316p.

A catalogue of 151 ancient sculptures and eighteen 16th-century bronzes in the Galleria Colonna. The catalogue entries and their numbering follow the location of the works in the various rooms of the gallery, making the work a useful companion on a visit to the collection. Each entry includes a detailed discussion of the work as well as technical information (type of material, measurements, state of conservation, restorations), provenance, and full bibliographical and archival references. All the works are reproduced. The introductory essays, written by a team of scholars, provide a detailed history of the development of the Colonna collections from the 15th century to the present, making ample use of archival evidence. In the 15th and 16th centuries, a number of sculptures were discovered in lands owned by the Colonna family on the slopes of the Quirinal. However, with the exception of Cardinal Prospero Colonna, the Colonnas did not attempt to form a collection of antiquities to rival those of other patrician families. They tended, instead, to give away important works for political reasons – to establish new political alliances or as gifts to important personages. This tendency continued as late as the 18th century, with the gift to Pope Pius VI Braschi of four important sculptures which were removed from the Galleria Colonna. The bulk of the collection was formed during the 17th century and was magnificently displayed, together with the collection of paintings, in the sumptuous gallery which was completed in 1703, where they can still be admired today.

602   '- finalmente in questa capitale del mondo': Goethe a Roma. ('- at
last in this capital of the world': Goethe in Rome.)
Edited by Konrad Scheurmann and Ursula Bongaerts-Schomer.   Rome:
Artemide edizioni, [1997]. 2 vols. (232p., 230p.).

This is a catalogue published on the inauguration of the Casa di Goethe in Rome in the building (on Via del Corso, 18) where the poet lived during his sojourn in Rome between October 1786 and April 1788. The first volume contains eighteen essays on various aspects of Goethe's life in Weimar, the reasons for his sudden departure, the Italian journey and its importance to the poet's subsequent development. Goethe's experiences in Rome are compared to those of Winckelmann and Humboldt. Other essays examine Rome in Goethe's time – there is a study of the *rione* Campo Marzio at the end of the 18th century, and another on the history of the Casa di Goethe and its restoration. The second volume is the catalogue of the exhibition and is divided into eight sections/rooms, beginning with a biographical section including numerous portraits of Goethe, together with manuscripts and other documents related to the social and intellectual life in Weimar and Goethe's activities as a civil servant and statesman. This is followed by a room dedicated to Goethe's journey from Karlsbad – from where he departed secretly on 3 September 1786 – to Italy; it includes drawings by the poet, accompanied by extracts from his diary and views of Italy and Rome by Jakob Philipp Hackert, Johann Heinrich Wilhelm Tischbein and others. The third room concentrates on the *rione* Campo Marzio, Piazza del Popolo and Via del Corso, the quarter where Goethe, Tischbein and other German artists lived. The fourth room is taken by the journey to Naples and Sicily in the spring of 1787 and Goethe's studies from nature and of natural specimens, as well as those of Tischbein and Christoph Heinrich Kniep, his travel companions. The fifth room documents Goethe's theory of colour, first elaborated during his Italian sojourn. The sixth room examines his attitude to antiquity while the seventh looks at the lively circle of Goethe's artist and writer friends in Rome. The final room surveys the poetical and literary results of the poet's Italian journey. The catalogue also includes a short biography of Goethe and an extensive bibliography.

603   Galleria Borghese.
Edited by Anna Coliva.   Rome: Progetti museali, 1994. 399p. bibliog.
(Luce per Arte.)

The Galleria Borghese houses one of the richest collections of fine and decorative art in Rome. The core of the collection was formed by Camillo Borghese (Pope Paul V) and his nephew Scipione Borghese, who expanded the family's original 'Vigna vecchia' on the Pincio into a park (designed by Flaminio Ponzio) and built the *palazzina*, which they started filling with works of art, ancient and modern. The collection's rich holdings of 16th-century mannerist art and the works by Caravaggio and Bernini's famous early sculpture groups (*Apollo and Daphne*, *Aeneas, Anchises and Ascanius*, *Pluto and Proserpina*) were acquired during this period. Later in the 17th century, the collection was further enriched by the Salviati and the d'Este collections, inherited by the Aldobrandini branch of the family. Little was acquired in the 18th century which, moreover, saw the sale of several works during the Revolutionary period to English dealers. Even more disastrous was Prince Camillo Borghese's sale of the most important antique sculptures to Napoleon (his brother-in-law). During this period, the Gallery was redecorated in the rich neo-classical style, giving it the sumptuous interiors that can still be admired today. In 1902, the Villa and the collection became State property, while the park was ceded to the Comune of Rome. This lavishly produced and profusely illustrated publication is a celebration of the collections of the Gallery. There are chapters on the history of the collection and its transformation from princely collection to state museum, Scipione Borghese as a collector, and the Gallery's famous collection of works by Raphael, Caravaggio and, above all, Bernini.

604   Galleria Borghese: i dipinti. (Galleria Borghese: the paintings.)
Paola Della Pergola.   Rome: Istituto poligrafico dello Stato, Libreria dello Stato, 1955. 2 vols. bibliog. (Cataloghi dei Musei e Gallerie d'Italia.)

A catalogue of 557 paintings in the collection of the Borghese Gallery. The first volume covers the Emilian, Genoese, Lombard, Neapolitan, Umbrian and Veneto schools, as well as anonymous paintings, while the second covers the Tuscan, Roman and Foreign Schools. Each entry gives information about the work's state of conservation, a detailed discussion of its provenance (the provenance of Raphael's *Deposition* is notorious – the work, which was wanted by Cardinal Scipione Borghese for his collection, was smuggled out of the Baglioni Chapel in the church of S. Francesco in Perugia for which it was painted), and a full bibliography. Each volume also includes a bibliography divided into three sections: documents (many of which are transcribed), inventories and books. There are indexes of artists, subjects, persons portrayed, and places. All the paintings are reproduced in black and white. The preface traces the formation and later fortunes of the collection.

605   La Galleria Corsini a cento anni dalla sua acquisizione allo Stato.
(The Galleria Corsini on the hundredth anniversary of its acquisition by the State.)
Edited by Dante Bernini, Sivigliano Alloisi.   Rome: Multigrafica, 1984. 96p.

In 1883, Palazzo Corsini alla Lungara was sold to the Italian State by Prince Tommaso Corsini on condition that the building would house the Accademia dei Lincei. The family's library and art collection were donated. This catalogue of the centenary exhibition held in Rome contains six essays on the history of the Corsini family and their collections. The first essay looks at the history of the building, which as Palazzo Riario had counted among its illustrious occupants Queen Christina of Sweden. It was bought by Cardinal Neri and Bartolomeo Corsini after the election of Lorenzo Corsini as Pope Clement XII (1730-40) and was one of a number of building projects undertaken by the family (others included the façade of S. Giovanni in Laterano and the 'manica lunga' of the Palazzo del Quirinale). The Palazzo is remarkable for its imposing size, location, and vast gardens. The role of Neri Corsini as a patron of the arts is examined next, both as a private collector (he had a special interest in Flemish and French art), and his crucial role in preventing the dispersal of important collections – hence the creation of the Museo Capitolino (which saved the collection of antiquities of Cardinal Alessandro Albani) and the Calcografia apostolica (through the acquisition of the copperplates of the De' Rossi family). Another essay examines the role of Giovanni Gaetano Bottari, the erudite librarian and Neri's artistic adviser. The library, which opened to the public in 1754, saw its second period of development in the 19th century thanks to the munificence of Prince Tommaso Corsini and the erudition of Luigi Maria Rezzi, his librarian, who acquired some of the collection's greatest treasures in manuscripts, incunables, rare books and prints. The print collection was later detached from the library and, as the Gabinetto nazionale delle stampe, is now housed in the Villa Farnesina, opposite Palazzo Corsini. The transformation of the Galleria Corsini into the Galleria nazionale d'arte antica (1895), which also incorporated the Torlonia collection and that of the Monte di Pietà, is examined in another essay. The Galleria is now shared between Palazzo Barberini and Palazzo Corsini.

606   Guida alla Galleria Spada. (A guide to the Galleria Spada.)
Edited by Maria Lucrezia Vicini.   Rome: Gebart, 1998. 92p.

The Galleria Spada is housed in the 16th-century Palazzo Capodiferro, which was bought in 1632 by Cardinal Bernardino Spada and extensively rebuilt, two of the additions being a gallery to house the Cardinal's art collections, and Borromini's famous *trompe l'œil* colonnade in the garden. The Palazzo was bought by the Italian Government in 1926 and today is the seat of the Consiglio di Stato (Council of State). The Gallery was first opened to the public in 1927 and, after a period of closure during the 1940s, it reopened in 1951. The collections are presented in their original setting in four rooms, all of which have retained their contemporary décor and furnishings. They include paintings from the 15th to the late 17th century, among them masterpieces by Andrea del Sarto, Guido Reni, Guercino, G. B. Gaulli, Orazio Gentileschi, and Simon Vouet. This useful publication provides a brief history of the place and the collection, and a room-by-room guide, with some 100, mostly excellent, colour illustrations.

607   Guide to the Borghese Gallery.
Kristina Hermann Fiore.   Rome: Gebart, 1998. 127p.

A room-by-room guide published on the occasion of the gallery's reopening after a fourteen-year total or partial closure necessitated by structural problems.

608   The Keats-Shelley Memorial House guide book.
Bathsheba Abse.   Rome: The Keats-Shelley Memorial House, [1998].
12p.

This is a brief guide to the Keats-Shelley Memorial House, with a general introduction and sections on Keats, Shelley and Byron.

609   Musei capitolini. (The Capitoline Museums.)
Texts by Margherita Albertoni (et al).   Milan, Italy: Electa, 2000.
207p.

This guide to the Capitoline Museums was published on the occasion of their re-opening in April 2000 after a period of closure during which the buildings were refurbished and the display of the collections vastly improved. It outlines the history of the Capitoline hill, describes the architecture of the buildings on the Campidoglio, and discusses the development of the municipal collections (the oldest public collections in the world), which started in 1471 with the symbolic donation by Sixtus IV of four famous bronze statues (the She-wolf, the Spinario (the Thorn-picker), Camillus, and the monumental head of Constantine). There is a room-by-room visit to the Palazzo Nuovo (which houses most of the sculptures), the Palazzo dei Conservatori and the Pinacoteca Capitolina, and also the Tabularium (Ancient Rome's Record Office). There is also a section on the Centrale Montemartini, a former power station on the Via Ostiense in which sculptures from the Capitoline collections are displayed alongside industrial archaeology.

610   Il Museo di Roma: documenti e iconografia. (The Museum of Rome: documents and iconography.)
Carlo Pietrangeli.   Bologna, Italy: Cappelli, 1971. 322p. bibliog. (Roma Cristiana, 15.)

A guide to the Museum of Rome and its varied collections, which range from topographical prints and drawings to carriages and the train of Pius IX. An introductory chapter outlines the history of the museum and the formation and growth of its collections. The museum was founded at a relatively late date, in 1929, thanks to the efforts of the Istituto di studi romani, though the need for a collection that would preserve the appearance of parts of the city that were rapidly disappearing had been felt much earlier. The museum opened in 1930 and its original collections included *Roma sparita* (Vanished Rome), a series of 120 water-colours by Ettore Roesler Franz, an important collection of Roman prints, and a collection of contemporary views of the city before the demolitions of the 1920s. Major acquisitions during the following years included an important collection of drawings by Bartolomeo Pinelli, and a series of works from the Rospigliosi collection showing scenes of everyday life in 18th-century Rome and the Campagna. After the War, the museum moved into a more spacious home, Palazzo Braschi, and during the 1950s it acquired several important collections, such as the Antonio Muñoz collection of some 5,000 prints, drawings, and manuscripts. The guide to the collections is preceded by a listing of its various constituent collections, which include: prints and drawings, ceramics, coins and medals, sculptures, costumes, coaches, plaster casts, and the studio of the poet Trilussa. The guide is divided into three parts: from the Middle Ages to the 16th century, the 17th and 18th centuries, and the 19th century. Each of these is subdivided into several sections showing various aspects of the city, its society, its artistic and cultural life, and its religious and secular festivals. There are 221 illustrations and 8 colour plates.

611   Il Museo nazionale etrusco di Villa Giulia. (The National Etruscan
Museum of Villa Giulia.)
Edited by Giuseppe Proietti.   Rome: Edizioni Quasar, 1980. 360p. map.
bibliog.

Villa Giulia was designed by Giacomo Barozzi da Vignola for Pope Julius III Del Monte
(1550-55). It originally extended from Porta del Popolo to Ponte Milvio and from Parioli to the
Tiber. The Casino and the Nymphaeum are the only surviving buildings today and only parts of
the original stuccos and painted decorations remain. The Museo nazionale di Villa Giulia was
founded, together with the Museo nazionale romano, in 1889. It is one of the most important
collections of Etrusco-Italic antiquities in the world. Excavations in southern Etruria (northern
Lazio) undertaken during the first half of the 20th century have yielded important finds which are
displayed in topographical sections in the museum. The present displays date from the 1950s and
1960s, when there was a thorough reorganization of the collections. Their presentation in this
catalogue is by area of excavation, with the exception of three special collections, which are
introduced separately – the Castellani collection of ceramics, the Pesciotti collection of ceramics
and bronzes, and the Castellani collection of jewellery – and the Antiquarium, which contains
items of various provenance. The geographical areas covered are Vulci, Bisenzio, Veio, Caere,
Pyrgi, Capena and Agro Falisco, Latium, Praeneste, and Todi. Each is introduced by a description
of the location and its antiquities. There are 537 illustrations, several in colour. The publication
also includes a brief description of the architecture of Villa Giulia and an essay on the Etruscans.

612   Museo nazionale romano. (The National Roman Museum.)
Rome: De Luca, 1979- .

A catalogue of the collections of the museum. There are fifteen volumes, eleven covering
sculptures and four dealing with paintings.

613   Il Museo Praz. (The Praz Museum.)
Patrizia Rosazza Ferraris.   Rome: Edizioni S.A.C.S., 1996. 45p. (Le
guide dei Musei S.A.C.S., 1.)

The Museo Praz in the Palazzo Primoli opened to the public in 1995, thirteen years after
the death of the great scholar, connoisseur, and collector. Mario Praz (1896-1982) lived in the
apartment which is now his museum for the last thirteen years of his life. His collection of over
1,200 items of Neo-classical, Empire and Restoration art, which can now be admired in this
display, is described in his *La casa della vita* (The house of life), which is both his
autobiography, the history of his collection and the history of the apartment in Palazzo Ricci-
Sacchetti in Via Giulia where Praz lived from 1934 to 1969. This is a guide to the eight rooms
of the museum, which recreate the collector's original arrangement and include furniture,
paintings, sculptures, porcelain, fans, engravings, water-colours, prints, miniatures, books, and
gems, reflecting some sixty years of collecting focused on the period and styles Praz also
championed in numerous publications. The library of Mario Praz (15,000 volumes) was
bequeathed to the Biblioteca della Fondazione Primoli, which is also housed in the Palazzo
Primoli together with the Museo Napoleonico. For a representative selection of works from
the Praz collection see *Le stanze della memoria* (The rooms of memory), edited by Stefano
Susinno and Elena Di Majo (Milan, Italy: A. Mondadori, 1987). This is the catalogue of an
exhibition shown at the Galleria nazionale d'arte moderna in Rome to mark the acquisition of
the collection in 1986 by the Italian State. The catalogue also includes a biographical profile
of Praz, an essay about his role as a collector and an anthology from his writings.

614 The National Gallery of Modern Art (Rome, Valle Giulia).
Palma Bucarelli. Rome: Istituto poligrafico e zecca dello stato, 1976.
276p. (Itineraries for Italian Museums, Galleries and Monuments, 13.)
This is a useful guide to the Galleria dell'arte moderna of Rome and its collections of 19th- and 20th-century art. It includes a historical survey describing the foundation of the Gallery after the success of the national exhibition of 19th-century art held in Rome in 1883, which led to a state grant for the purchase of works by contemporary artists, later supplemented by grants to cover the whole of the 19th century. The survey gives a succinct account of the successive enrichment and expansion of the collection, through purchase or donation, during the 20th century. Though the description of the Gallery's seventy-four rooms is, to a certain extent, outdated because of the recent refurbishments and rearrangement of the displays, it nevertheless remains the only detailed account of the collection currently available. The guide also includes a list of artists and their works and 197 black-and-white illustrations.

615 Paintings in the Vatican.
Carlo Pietrangeli, essays by Guido Cornini, Anna Maria De Strobel, Maria Serlupi Crescenzi. Boston, Massachusetts; London: Little, Brown and Co., 1996. 605p.
This volume provides an overall survey of paintings in the Vatican including, in addition to the works in the Pinacoteca vaticana (the Vatican Picture Gallery), the paintings in the Pontifical Apartments and the cycles of frescoes of the Apostolic Palace. An introductory chapter by Carlo Pietrangeli gives the history of the collections, describing the evolution of the private collection of paintings in the Palazzo del Quirinale (which in the early 17th century became the papal residence) and the opening of a public collection on the Campidoglio (now the Capitoline Picture Gallery). Over the next three centuries, parts of the collections were moved several times between four different locations: the Palazzo del Quirinale, the Vatican Palace, the Capitoline Museums and the Palazzo Lateranense. In 1797, 506 paintings were confiscated by the French and taken to Paris, where they were displayed as war booty. The most important of these were recovered in 1815 but 248 remained in France and 9 were declared lost. The present Pinacoteca vaticana was inaugurated in 1932. The catalogue of the paintings is arranged by century, with separate chapters for paintings and frescoes. Each chapter consists of a short introduction to the works and the circumstances of their commission and execution followed by mostly excellent colour illustrations and, for the paintings, technical information and provenance. There are 539 illustrations, ranging chronologically from the 11th to the 19th century. The frescoes include some of the greatest masterpieces of world art: Fra Angelico's Chapel of Nicholas V (the Cappella Niccolina); Michelangelo's ceiling and *Last Judgement* in the Sistine Chapel (which also includes frescoes by Botticelli, Perugino, Pinturicchio, Ghirlandaio, and Piero di Cosimo); Pinturicchio's frescoes in the Borgia apartments; Raphael's *Stanze* and *Logge*; the Gallery of the Maps (Galleria delle carte geografiche). Works destroyed over the centuries evoked in the text include fresco cycles by Fra Angelico, Mantegna, and Lorenzo Lotto. There are biographical entries of the artists with particular emphasis on their works in the Vatican collections.

616 Palazzo Altemps: Museo nazionale romano.
Francesco Scoppola and Stella Diana Vordemann. Milan, Italy: Electa, 1997. 67p. (Guide Electa per la Soprintendenza Archeologica di Roma.)
Since 1997, the newly restored Palazzo Altemps (named after Cardinal Marco Sittico Altemps, who owned it in the 16th century) has displayed part of the collections of the Museo nazionale romano – the collection of Egyptian antiquities, the Mattei collection, the remaining sixteen sculptures from the Altemps collection, and, above all, the famous Boncompagni Ludovisi

collection of ancient sculptures (which may include some of the sculptures formerly in the Altemps collection, later dispersed). This guide provides a brief history of the palazzo and a room-by-room description of the collections accompanied by fifty-eight colour illustrations. See also, in the same series, guides to the following sites: *La Valle del Colosseo, Il Palatino, Il Foro Romano, Carcer Tullianum, Terme di Caracalla, Terme di Diocleziano, Fidene: una casa dell' età di Ferro,* and *Palazzo Massimo alle Terme.*

617 Palazzo Barberini: capolavori della Galleria nazionale d'arte antica. (Palazzo Barberini: masterpieces of the National Gallery of Old Master Paintings.)
Lorenza Mochi Onori, Rossella Vodret.   [Rome]: Edizioni De Luca, 1998. 152p. bibliog.

This guide includes an introduction outlining the history of the building and that of the collections it now houses. The building was bought from Paolo Sforza in 1625 and it served both as a suburban villa and as prestige town residence of the Barberini, the family of Pope Urban VIII (Maffeo Barberini). Four architects were involved in its enlargement: Carlo Maderno, Gianlorenzo Bernini, Francesco Borromini, and Pietro de Cortona (who also painted his masterpiece, *The Triumph of Divine Providence,* for its main salon). The building's heyday was during the reign of Urban VIII (1623-44), when lavish entertainments were held there. It later lost some of its prominence as a result of changes to its surrounding area, especially the opening of the Via del Tritone in the 19th century. The Galleria Nazionale d'Arte Antica was founded in 1895 after a number of important collections were acquired by the state, notably those of the Corsini, Torlonia and Odescalchi families and that of the Monte di Pietà. However, a suitable gallery to house these collections was needed, and this need was eventually fulfilled by the Palazzo Barberini, which was bought in 1949 and finally opened to the public in 1952. In 1984, the Corsini collection was transferred to the Palazzo Corsini, in Via della Lungara. The present collection housed in the Palazzo Barberini has 1,445 paintings, though relatively few of these come from the Barberini collections, as the family was allowed to sell one third of them in the 1930s. It includes works from the 12th to the 19th century, but its main strengths are 16th and 17th century paintings with, among others, masterpieces by Raphael, Titian, Lotto, Caravaggio, Guercino, and Guido Reni. 107 works are examined in this guide, each reproduced in colour. The accompanying text includes medium, provenance and changes in attribution.

618 Il Palazzo Doria Pamphilj al Corso e le sue collezioni. (The Palazzo Doria Pamphilj on the Corso and its collections.)
Edited by Andrea G. De Marchi.   Florence, Italy: Centro Di, 1999. 262p.

The Doria Pamphilj is, with the Colonna collection, the most important private collection of old master paintings in Rome. Its treasures include masterpieces of 16th- and 17th-century painting by Raphael, Titian, Lotto, Caravaggio, Guercino, Claude Lorrain and Velázquez, as well as antique sculptures and two busts of Pope Innocent X by Bernini and Algardi. This volume examines the history of the Palazzo, which for three centuries was constantly being enlarged through the acquisition of adjacent properties, its decoration and its works of art. The first building was constructed in 1505 by Fabio Santoro who, in 1507, was forced by Julius II to hand it to Francesco Maria della Rovere, his nephew. It remained a della Rovere property until 1601, when it was bought by Cardinal Pietro Aldobrandini. In 1647, Camillo Pamphilj's marriage to Olimpia Aldobrandini brought him the palazzo, and also Cardinal Pietro Aldobrandini's splendid collection of 16th-century paintings. To the inherited works were soon added his own purchases of 17th-century masterpieces. The collection was further enriched later in the century through the acquisitions of Prince Giovanni Battista and Cardinal Benedetto Pamphilj. The

1725 inventory of the collections of Cardinal Benedetto Pamphilj (since 1709 the owner of all the family collections) in the various Pamphilj properties is published here for the first time. The work also examines specific, and less well-known, areas of the collection: the still-life paintings collected by Cardinal Benedetto, the portraits, and the landscape paintings of Giovan Battista Giovannini (an artist who worked exclusively for the family). See also Francesca Cappelletti, *Nuova guida alla Galleria Doria Pamphilj* (A new guide to the Galleria Doria Pamphilj) (Rome: Àrgos, 1996. 134p.).

619 **Palazzo Massimo alle Terme: Museo nazionale romano.** (Palazzo
     Massimo alle Terme: the National Museum of Roman Art.)
     Edited by Adriano La Regina.   Milan, Italy: Electa, 1998. 291p. bibliog.

In the 1990s, the collections of the Museo nazionale romano were extensively restored and divided between four different locations: Palazzo Altemps, the Baths of Diocletian (Terme di Diocleziano), Crypta Balbi, and Palazzo Massimo alle Terme. Further locations may be used in future for the display of other parts of the collections. Palazzo Massimo takes its name from the Massimo family, who, in 1789, bought the famous Villa Peretti Montalto, the private villa of Cardinal Felice Peretti (later Sixtus V) adjoining the Baths of Diocletian. The villa was destroyed in the 19th century to make way for the new railway station and most of its grounds are now occupied by the Stazione Termini. Palazzo Massimo was built in the 1880s on the area that remained in the possession of the family. Until 1960, the imposing, six-storey building housed the Istituto Massimiliano Massimo, a Jesuit college. In 1981, it was bought by the Italian State to house part of the collections of the Museo nazionale romano, which was in urgent need of new spaces for the display of its collections, which had been constantly growing since its foundation in 1889. After a thorough renovation, one floor of Palazzo Massimo opened in 1995 and the entire new museum, on four floors, opened in 1998. The museum displays antiquities from the Republican period to the fourth century AD. The ground floor and first floor house mainly sculptures, including numerous portrait busts, groups of sculptures from the Horti sallustiani, and antique Greek statues found in Rome. They also include the Fasti Antiates, fragments of an ancient calendar, discovered at Anzio in 1915, recording events during 84-55 BC, and the Fasti Praenestini, found in Palestrina in 1907. The second floor is dedicated to the display of paintings and mosaics, which include famous examples of domestic decoration, such as the paintings from the Villa of Livia at Prima Porta and the paintings and stuccoes from the 1st-century-BC villa discovered in 1879, during the construction of the Tiber Embankment, on the grounds of the Villa Farnesina. The basement is occupied by a display of jewellery, coins and medals. This splendidly illustrated volume contains descriptions of the various displays in the museum and entries for individual works which, as well as a description, include information about the exact place of discovery and a bibliography. See also *Palazzo Massimo alle Terme: Museo nazionale romano* (Palazzo Massimo alle Terme: the National Museum of Roman Art) by Marina Sapelli (Milan, Italy: Electa, 1998. 75p. [Guide Electa per la Soprintendenza Archeologica di Roma]).

620 **A room in Rome.**
     Vera Cacciatore.   New York: Keats-Shelley Association of America,
     [1970]. 56p.

The room in question is the one where John Keats lived during the last months of his life, from November 1820 to February 1821, now part of the Keats-Shelley House in Piazza di Spagna in Rome. This work evokes the poet's stay in Rome through the use of his letters and Joseph Severn's writings, and surveys impressions of later visitors to the house, such as E. Sinclair Lewis, who confessed that the only time he cried was when he visited Keat's house in Rome. It also traces the history of the house (which was purchased by the Keats-Shelley Memorial

Association and officially inaugurated by Vittorio Emanuele III in 1909), its survival during the Second World War and the German occupation of Rome (when the author was the curator of the house), the first Allied visitors on 5 June 1944, and the reinstatement on the wall of the building of the plaque which had been removed during the war years. It quotes extracts from the diaries of the poet's contemporaries who also stayed in the house, which evoke early 19th-century Rome – Robert Gray, Lady Morgan, and Robert Finch. An Italian edition of this work was published in Rome in 1987, entitled *C'è una stanza a Roma* (There is a room in Rome).

621 Il Seicento a Roma: Caravaggio a Salvator Rosa. (Seventeenth-century [painting] in Rome: from Caravaggio to Salvator Rosa.)
Edited by Sergio Guarino. Milan, Italy: Electa, 1999. 93p. bibliog.

The Pinacoteca Capitolina is one of the oldest museums in the world. It was founded in 1749 by Pope Benedict XIV after the acquisition by Cardinal Silvio Valenti Gonzaga of the collections of Giberto Pio di Savoia and the Sacchetti family. All but one of the twenty-three works included in this catalogue of an exhibition of 17th-century paintings shown at the Pinacoteca di Brera in 1999 come from these two collections. They include some of the Gallery's most treasured possessions, such as Caravaggio's *Fortune teller*, Pietro da Cortona's *Triumph of Bacchus*, Van Dyck's *Portrait of Pieter de Jode the Elder and Younger* (the one exception, acquired in the 19th century), Guercino's *Persian Sibyl*, as well as works by Guido Reni, Salvator Rosa, and Gaspar van Wittel. The three introductory essays give a history of the collection and its changes of fortune.

622 The Vatican collections: the papacy and art.
Carlo Pietrangeli (et al.). New York: The Metropolitan Museum of Art, 1982. 255p.

The catalogue of an exhibition shown at three venues in the United States in 1983-84. It contains 237 works of art (catalogued as 168 entries) from the entire range of the artistic holdings of the Vatican, including some of the most famous works in its collections, such as the Apollo Belvedere, the Belvedere Torso, and Caravaggio's *Deposition*. The scholarly entries (which all have their own bibliographies) are arranged in fourteen sections, each with an introduction providing the history of the relevant Vatican museum or monument represented by the exhibits. See also Allen Duston and Arnold Nesselrath, *Angels from the Vatican: the invisible made visible* (New York: Harry N. Abrams, 1998. 320p.). This is a sumptuously produced and scholarly catalogue of a touring exhibition in the United States, with ninety-eight works from the Vatican collections on the depiction of angels in art. An introductory essay discusses papal patronage and collecting through the ages.

623 Velázquez, el Papa Inocencio X de la Galeria Doria Pamphilj, Roma.
(Velázquez's *Pope Innocent X* of the Galleria Doria-Pamphilj in Rome.)
Edited by Isabel Morán Suárez. Madrid: Museo del Prado, 1996. 123p.

Velázquez's portrait of Pope Innocent X Pamphilj is one of the most penetrating portraits ever painted – the sitter, when confronted by the severity of his features, is reputed to have said that it was 'troppo vero' (too true). It is the most important work in the Galleria Doria-Pamphilj and, as such, is never allowed to travel. Exceptionally, during the gallery's four-month closure for renovations in 1996, it was lent to the National Gallery in London, where it was shown with other works from the collection, and to the Prado Museum in Madrid, where it joined the museum's rich collection of this artist's works. This is the catalogue of the latter exhibition. It includes essays on the history of the Doria-Pamphilj collection, Velázquez in Italy (the artist visited Italy on two occasions, in 1629-30 and 1649-51, when his status as painter to the King of Spain gained him access to the Vatican, where he painted Innocent X, a self-proclaimed Hispanophile), and art in Rome at the time of Innocent X (taken from Torgil Magnusson's monograph).

624   Via Tasso: carcere nazista. (Via Tasso: the Nazi prison.) Arrigo Paladini.   Rome: Istituto poligrafico e zecca dello stato, 1986. 123p.

A guide to the former Nazi prison in Rome, now housing the Museo storico della liberazione di Roma (Historical Museum of the Liberation of Rome). It includes a chronology of the main events in Rome from 8 September 1943 to 4 June 1944, and various documents related to the Ardeatine Caves massacre, including a list of the victims, and partisan warfare between 1943 and 1945. There are also sixty-five illustrations showing some of the cells of the prison, now rooms of the museum, and their graffiti, official documents, and musical scores composed by prisoners.

Architecture

General

625   An architect in Italy.
Caroline Mauduit, with a foreword by Sir Hugh Casson.   London:
Bloomsbury, 1988. 112p.

The author, a recipient of a scholarship in architecture at the British School at Rome in 1983, calls this book a working record of her time in Rome, a visual diary and an attempt to understand the architecture of Renaissance Italy. In her introduction she describes life at the School, where she stayed for the first nine months of her visit, and her wanderings in Rome – 'this extraordinary *millefeuilles* of a city' – with her sketchbook, water-colour box, bottle of water and measuring tape. The drawings are divided into four groups – Ancient Rome, Renaissance Rome, a journey from Lazio to the river Po, and, finally, the Veneto – each preceded by a short commentary.

626   The architecture of Michelangelo.
James S. Ackerman.   Harmondsworth, England: Penguin Books, 1970
(2nd rev. ed., 1995). 373p. (Pelican Books.)

A survey of Michelangelo's architectural output, which includes his Roman works – the Capitoline hill complex, the Farnese Palace, St Peter's, San Giovanni de' Fiorentini and the Sforza Chapel in S. Maria Maggiore, the Porta Pia, and S. Maria degli Angeli. A catalogue of Michelangelo's works, compiled by J. S. Ackerman and John Newman, is included.

627   Architettura del Settecento a Roma nei disegni della Raccolta grafica comunale. (Eighteenth-century Roman architectural drawings of the Collection of Graphic Art of the Comune of Rome.)
Edited by Elisabeth Kieven.   Rome: Edizioni Carte segrete, 1991. 185p.
bibliog.

The Gabinetto comunale delle stampe of the Museo di Roma (Palazzo Braschi) has a resource of some 30,000 items on the iconography of Rome from the 16th to the 20th century. This exhibition catalogue concentrates on its holdings of 18th-century architectural drawings and includes 112 works aiming to show the diversity of the material, which encompasses both monumental and smaller-scale projects. There are works by well-known artists such as Filippo Juvarra (views of the Campidoglio), Nicola Salvi (proposals for the Trevi Fountain), Luigi Vanvitelli (proposals for the facade of San Giovanni in Laterano), and Luigi Valadier (a group of proposals for the redevelopment of the Piazza del Popolo), as well as fascinating groups of drawings by the obscure Lorenzo Possenti and Francesco Ferruzzi. All the works discussed are reproduced, sixteen of them in full colour. An introductory essay gives an overview of the changes to the architectural landscape of Rome in the 18th century.

628   Art in Rome from Borromini to Canova.
Mario Rivosecchi. Rome: Editalia, 1978. 245p.

This volume examines the work of architects who succeeded in giving a new appearance to Rome, interpreting the wishes of their patrons according to their own respective temperament. It includes chapters on Borromini 'the supreme artificer of Catholic Rome', Bernini's public sculptures and architecture, Carlo Fontana, Pietro da Cortona, Alessandro Specchi, Nicola Salvi, Luigi Vanvitelli and the monuments of Canova. It also looks at building in Rome in the 17th and 18th centuries and at town planning solutions such as S. Maria del Popolo, Porto di Ripetta (now destroyed), and the Spanish Steps. See also two works edited by Franco Borsi, *Arte a Roma dal neoclassico al romanticismo* (Art in Rome from Neo-classicism to Romanticism) (Rome: Editalia, 1979. 244p.) and *Arte a Roma dalla capitale all'età umbertina* (Art in Rome from 1870 to the Umbertine age) (Rome: Editalia, 1980. 244p. bibliog.).

629   Baldassare Peruzzi: pittura, scena e architettura nel Cinquecento.
(Baldassare Peruzzi: painting, stage design and architecture in the sixteenth century.)
Edited by Marcello Fagiolo and Maria Luisa Madonna.   Rome: Istituto della Enciclopedia italiana fondata da G. Treccani, 1987. 773p.
(Biblioteca Internazionale di Cultura, 20.)

The Sienese artist Baldassare Peruzzi (1481-1536) was, with Bramante and Raphael, the greatest architect working in Rome in the early 16th century. He was also a painter and a prolific draughtsman and was strongly interested in classical antiquities. This volume brings together thirty-two papers, originally read at a conference on Peruzzi held in Rome in 1981, which explore all aspects of his multifaceted genius. They are divided into three sections: drawing and architecture; painting, perspective and stage design; and Peruzzi's influence on 16th- and 17th-century art and architecture. All three sections include contributions dealing specifically with Peruzzi's work in Rome. In the first section, three essays examine Peruzzi's work in the Villa Mills (also known as Villa Mattei), the Palazzo Massimo alle Colonne, and three unexecuted projects for churches in Rome. In the second section, there is an examination of Peruzzi's and Raphael's study of antiquities, as well as two essays on the work of Peruzzi and his workshop on the decorations executed for Villa Farnesina and Palazzo della Cancelleria, and the Sala delle Prospettive. Finally, the third section includes studies on Peruzzi's influence on the early architectural work of Giulio Romano, Polidoro da Caravaggio's painted building façades, and the problems of conservation and restoration of Peruzzi's painted façades of Villa Farnesina and Palazzo Massimo alle Colonne. The volume contains numerous black-and-white illustrations.

630 Bernini: flights of love, the art of devotion.

Giovanni Careri.   Chicago; London: The University of Chicago Press, 1995. 127p.

A study of Bernini's use of architecture with sculpture and painting in such a way that together they form a beautiful whole (a *bel composto*). This is exemplified in three ensembles the artist created in Rome between 1658 and 1675: the Fonseca Chapel in S. Lorenzo in Lucina (1664-75), the Albertoni Chapel in S. Francesco a Ripa (1665-75), and the high altar in the church of S. Andrea al Quirinale (1658-70). The author explores Bernini's integration of different forms into a coherent space for devotion and the ways the spectator-worshipper reassembles these disparate elements.

631 Borromini.

Anthony Blunt.   London: Allen Lane, 1979. 240p. bibliog.
(The Architect and Society.)

This is a lucid study of the life and work of Francesco Borromini (1599-1667), one of the great architects of the Roman Baroque. It discusses his early life and initial training as a stone-carver and architectural draughtsman, Borromini's relationship with Bernini (his hated rival), and the extent of his contribution to the Baldacchino in S. Peter's and the construction of Palazzo Barberini. His sources (particularly the influence of Michelangelo and ancient Roman architecture) are explained in a separate chapter. Borromini's major works are examined in order of commission, beginning with the cloister and church of S. Carlo alle Quattro Fontane (San Carlino), his first work, in 1634, as an independent architect, and where he first displayed his skill in making good use of the limited potential of small and irregular sites. Other buildings examined are the Oratory of S. Filippo Neri, S. Ivo della Sapienza, S. Giovanni in Laterano, S. Agnese in Agone, Palazzo Spada, Collegio di Propaganda Fide, and S. Andrea delle Fratte. The last chapter examines Borromini's influence and reputation.

632 Borromini.

Paolo Portoghesi.   London: Thames & Hudson, 1967. 459p. bibliog.

This is a detailed and sumptuously illustrated (with 400 monochrome plates, 147 drawings and 158 illustrations in the text) examination of Borromini's output. His buildings are studied in three sections – the early works, the works of maturity, and the late works. In each, the text is followed by a full complement of photographs and architectural drawings of the buildings discussed. An introductory chapter looks at influences on Borromini, which range from classical antiquity to Mannerism; the final chapter discusses his architectural language and its blend of reason and feeling, calculation and emotion. This work is a translation of *Borromini, architettura come linguaggio* (Borromini, architecture as language), originally published in 1967.

633 Borromini and the Roman Oratory: style and society.

Joseph Connors.   New York; Cambridge, Massachusetts; London: The Architectural History Foundation, 1980. 389p. bibliog.

The Church of S. Maria in Vallicella and the adjacent Casa dei Filippini are among the buildings of the new religious groups that sprang up in the wake of the Counter-Reformation in which the austere ideals of their founders sometimes clashed with the demands of their princely patrons or, as in this case, with the exuberant ideas of their architect. This monograph, though its main focus is Francesco Borromini's contribution and his often turbulent relationship with the Oratorians, is a detailed study of the development of this important architectural complex. It examines the impact of St Filippo Neri on the society of late Renaissance Rome, the early history of S. Maria in Vallicella (built between 1594 and 1606) and early projects for the Casa dei Filippini by Marco Arconio (1621-23) and Paolo Maruscelli (1624-36). Borromini obtained the commission for the Oratory in 1637 after Maruscelli's resignation, the circumstances of which are explained here. This was the commission that launched Borromini's career and it occupied him for some thirteen years. In it, he used for the first time some of what would become his future trademarks although, as in some later commissions, he was constrained by a pre-existing plan (in this case Paolo Maruscelli's) to which he had to adhere. Borromini's work at the Casa dei Filippini is compared to a later institutional design, for the building of the Propaganda Fide, in which he reused and refined motifs from the Casa and where he similarly revised and enriched his original thoughts over a number of years. The work includes a catalogue of 115 architectural drawings of the Oratory by Paolo Maruscelli, Carlo Rainaldi, Borromini, G. B. Falda, Giuseppe Vasi, and others. There is also an appendix describing Paolo Maruscelli's works in other buildings in Rome, and transcriptions of numerous documents from the archives of the Congregazione dell'Oratorio di Roma.

634 Borromini e l'universo barocco. (Borromini and the Baroque universe.) Edited by Richard Bösel and Christoph L. Frommel. Milan, Italy: Electa, 1999-2000. 2 vols. (236p., 415p.). bibliog. (Documenti di Architettura, 127.)

The catalogue of an exhibition, held in Rome and Vienna, celebrating the quatercentenary of the birth of the architect Borromini. Volume one contains eleven introductory essays that examine various aspects of Borromini's life and work, and the historical, social and political background. They include studies on: his life; his relations with other contemporary artists, especially Bernini; the influence of antiquarian culture and tradition; his drawings; his use of hieroglyphics and heraldic emblems; his influence on late Baroque and modern architecture; and interpretations of his work during the last 350 years. Volume two contains the catalogue entries for over 600 items included in the exhibition. They are divided into twenty-four sections, each looking at a particular period of the architect's life or an individual building designed by him.

635 Bramante. Arnaldo Bruschi, foreword by Peter Murray. London: Thames & Hudson, 1977. 208p. bibliog.

This is a shorter version for an English-speaking public of the author's monumental *Bramante architetto*, originally published in 1969. It covers all periods of the architect's activity, beginning with his apprenticeship at Urbino and his works in Lombardy. The greater part of the book deals with Bramante's work in Rome, where he moved, according to Vasari, just before 1500 and spent the last fourteen years of his life, becoming the official papal architect. His first work in Rome that has survived is the cloister of S. Maria della Pace commissioned by Oliviero Carafa, Cardinal of Naples. Other works examined here include the Tempietto of S. Pietro in Montorio (marking the supposed site of St Peter's crucifixion), the Cortile del Belvedere in the Vatican (linking the palace of Nicholas V to the Belvedere of Innocent VIII and the spiral stairway ramp near the sculpture court), and his project for S. Peter's, only a part of which was executed, though Bramante's designs formed the basis for other architects' work. The study also includes a chapter on Bramante's personality and influence and there is a chronological list of his works which includes both documented projects and urban schemes for Rome (Via Giulia, Via della Lungara, Via dei Banchi) and works attributed to him without definite evidence.

636 Carlo Maderno and Roman architecture, 1580-1630.
Howard Hibbard. London: A. Zwemmer, 1971. 404p. bibliog.

A nephew of Domenico Fontana, the favourite architect of Pope Sixtus V, Carlo Maderno (1555/6-1629) was involved in many of his projects, including the completion of the Palazzo del Quirinale and the re-erection of the Vatican obelisk. His independent commissions after Fontana's departure for Naples in 1594 included the renovation of S. Susanna (1597-1603), S. Andrea della Valle (1608-12), and the completion of St Peter's. Equally important were his numerous designs for secular buildings: the Palazzo Mattei di Giove (1598-1617), the Palazzo Borghese (1611-14), the Palazzo Ludovisi (now Chigi-Odescalchi), and the Palazzo Barberini (begun in 1628). This study begins with a history of Roman architecture and papal patronage during the second half of the 16th century and then moves onto a discussion of Maderno's career, with separate chapters devoted to his contribution to the construction of the new St Peter's and to the commissions he received from the Borghese, Ludovisi and Barberini families. The core of the work is the catalogue, which contains over sixty items. It discusses all the works of architecture with which Maderno was actively concerned as a designer, the length of each section roughly reflecting the importance of the building (the section on St Peter's is naturally the longest and it also includes documentary sources for the planning and construction of the basilica). Many of the buildings catalogued are only partially by Maderno. There are 104 plates (photographs of the buildings, architectural drawings, and engravings). There is also a list of works erroneously attributed to Maderno and a chronological overview of his career.

637 The City Wall of Imperial Rome: an account of its architectural development from Aurelian to Narses.
Ian A. Richmond. Oxford: Clarendon Press, 1930. 291p.

This detailed study of the great defensive wall which Emperor Aurelian began to built around Rome in 271 collects ancient, medieval and Renaissance literary traditions about the structure, examines its architectural evolution, and attempts, by bringing the two sets of data together, to establish the architectural history of the Wall, its gates and its posterns from 271 until the arrival of Narses in 552, which brought Rome under Byzantine rule.

638 The Cortile del Belvedere.
James S. Ackerman. Vatican City: Biblioteca apostolica vaticana, 1954. 269p. (Studi e Documenti per la Storia del Palazzo Apostolico Vaticano pubblicati a cura della Biblioteca Apostolica Vaticana, vol. 3.)

This work describes the expansion of the Vatican palace during the reigns of Pope Nicholas III and Nicholas V, the building of the Villa Belvedere by Pope Innocent VIII, and the piecemeal building of the palace and its fortifications under their successors, until the grandiose reorganization of St Peter's basilica, the palace and the gardens under Julius II, which determined the course of developments for the next eighty years. Julius II's masterplan, with Bramante as sole director of the building project, involved a greatly expanded basilica and the creation of the Belvedere Court, a garden-theatre between the palace and the villa of Innocent VIII. The concept and design of the Court (which reached its maturity in 1580-85, when it was enclosed on all sides) were destroyed by later developments – under Sixtus V it was bisected by the building of the Library and today exists only in name, hence the necessity to reconstruct the Cortile from surviving clues, both as it was planned and as it was executed. The first chapter, therefore, attempts to reconstruct Bramante's plan, whereas each subsequent chapter examines the development of the project under a different pope and is followed by a summary chronology of the construction. The style and sources of the Cortile are discussed in the final chapter. The work is completed by three appendices giving written descriptions of the Vatican palace, listing

226 sources referring to its construction during the period 1503-85, and cataloguing sixty-one views of it.

639 Ferdinando Fuga e l'architettura romana del Settecento. (Ferdinando Fuga and eighteenth-century Roman architecture.) Edited by Elisabeth Kieven. Rome: Multigrafica, 1988. 309p. bibliog.

Ferdinando Fuga was one of the most successful architects of the 18th century. This exhibition catalogue examines his Roman work between 1730, when he was appointed architect to the papal palaces, and his departure from Rome in 1748, when he was summoned to Naples by Charles III. Projects examined here include the extension of the Palazzo del Quirinale (the *manica lunga* executed in 1731), the Palazzo della Consulta (1732), S. Maria dell'Orazione e Morte (1733-37), Palazzo Corsini (1736-58), the portico of S. Maria Maggiore (1735), and the Coffee House in the garden of the Palazzo del Quirinale (1741-43). Also included are designs for unexecuted projects (the facade of S. Giovanni in Laterano, the Trevi Fountain). In addition, the catalogue contains drawings by Fuga's contemporaries, including Nicola Salvi (the architect of the Trevi Fountain), Luigi Vanvitelli and Giuseppe Valadier. There are 206 entries, all reproduced by one or more plates. The introductory essay discusses Fuga's early years, his activity in Rome and the evolution of his style.

640 Il giovane Borromini: dagli esordi a San Carlo alle Quattro Fontane. (Young Borromini: from his beginnings to San Carlo alle Quattro Fontane.) Edited by Manuela Kahn-Rossi, Marco Franciolli. Milan, Italy: Skira, 1999. 528p. bibliog.

This monumental catalogue of the early work of Francesco Borromini was published to accompany an exhibition of his work in the Ticino, his birthplace, organized as part of the celebrations of the quatercentenary of the architect's birth. It provides an indispensable tool for the study of his early life, formative influences, and first years in Rome up to the construction of his first commission as an independent architect, the church of S. Carlo alle Quattro Fontane. The catalogue also examines the work of the network of families of trained building workers (which included masons, stuccoworkers, and architects) from Ticino that dominated building sites in Rome in the 17th century. Domenico Fontana and Carlo Maderno were among this group and Borromini, upon his arrival in Rome, was enabled to work on the façade and nave of St Peter's as an assistant to Maderno, to whom he was related, and who was then in charge of the operations. Initially, Borromini worked as a craftsman, but he soon became an architectural draughtsman, and in 1624 he worked alongside Bernini on the Baldacchino in S. Peter's and, from 1627, on the Palazzo Barberini. Borromini's relationship with Bernini, and the extent of his contribution to the Baldacchino are examined. There is also a section on Carlo Maderno and his work at S. Andrea della Valle, and chapters looking at the work of other Ticinese architects in Rome – Giovanni Battista Mola, Martino and Onorio Longhi, and Flaminio Ponzio. There are 289 illustrations and 68 colour plates.

641 Guida di Roma moderna: architettura dal 1870 a oggi. (A guide to modern Rome: architecture from 1870 to the present.) Irene de Guttry. Rome: De Luca, 1978. 132p. map.

This photographic guide to modern architecture in Rome shows buildings erected since 1870, during a century that saw Rome's population grow from 200,000 to over 3 million and when more buildings were built than in all previous centuries put together. It is divided into four sections, showing developments between: 1870 and 1900, 1900 and 1922, 1922 and 1942, and 1945 to the present. Each section has a succinct introduction that lucidly describes the history of urban planning in Rome, from the building boom of the 1870s which brought with it the destruction of Rome's 'green belt' of villas and their gardens, through the continuous outward expansion of the city and the creation of new quarters to house both the middle classes and those who lost their homes when whole areas in the historic centre of the city were demolished to make way for new thoroughfares and for the grandiose urban schemes and excavations of the Fascist era, to the creation of EUR suburb and the post-Second World War *borgate*, the notorious popular quarters in the extreme periphery of Rome. The texts are accompanied by well-chosen, telling descriptions in literature of some of the types of housing surveyed here. All the photographs are accompanied by explanatory captions that include the date of the building, and the publication also includes itinerary suggestions and an index of architects, listing their major buildings.

642 Guide to Baroque Rome.

Anthony Blunt. London; Toronto; Sydney; New York: Granada, 1982. 335p. bibliog.

This extremely useful guide deals mainly with the churches of Rome, the greatest achievements of the Roman Baroque, though it also includes chapters on the palaces, villas, fountains, the Vatican, the Alban Hills and, finally, miscellaneous other buildings. Each chapter has individual entries that include information about the buildings and their contents and the sources from which the information is derived, for example the monographic series *Le chiese di Roma illustrate* (The churches of Rome illustrated). It wisely avoids giving practical (and usually quickly outdated) information about the buildings. It also includes 119 plates of engraved views or plans of the buildings discussed. The period covered is that between the election of Gregory XV as pope in 1621 and the beginning of the neo-classical movement in the middle of the 18th century. The emphasis is on architecture and, to a certain extent, the work is complemented by Ellis Waterhouse's *Roman Baroque painting* (see entry no. 523).

643 Michelangelo architect.

Giulio Carlo Argan, Bruno Contardi. London: Thames & Hudson, 1993. 388p.

A translation of *Michelangelo architetto*, originally published in 1990. This sumptuously produced publication examines the entire architectural output of Michelangelo. It includes the various designs and sculptures made for the Tomb of Julius II, which were begun in 1505-06 and continued throughout Michelangelo's life; the painted architectural divisions of the ceiling of the Sistine Chapel, 1508-12; and the aedicula for the Chapel of Saints Cosmas and Damian in the Castel S. Angelo, *c*. 1514. The second half of the volume is dedicated to Michelangelo's work in Rome from 1534 to the end of his life. It includes: the renovation of the Capitoline complex, 1538-64; the Palazzo Farnese, 1546-49; St Peter's, 1545-64; designs for the Vatican fortifications, 1546-48; model for the church of Il Gesù, 1558; design for the renovation of the area around the Column of Trajan, 1558; designs and model for S. Giovanni dei Fiorentini, 1559-60; design for the Sforza Chapel, in S. Maria Maggiore, *c*. 1560; Porta Pia, 1561-64; and S. Maria degli Angeli, 1561-64. The volume contains 522 excellent illustrations, mostly in black and white.

644 Il Palazzo delle finanze di Roma capitale. (The Palazzo delle finanze of Rome, capital of Italy.)

Edited by G. Tartarini. Rome: Libreria dello stato, 1979. 123p.

The Palazzo del Ministero delle Finanze was built by Raffaele Canevari (1828-1900) between 1872 and 1879 and formed part of the new administrative centre created along Via XX

Settembre. It occupies an area 300 x 118 metres along Via XX Settembre (its main longitudinal façade) and Via della Cernaia (its rear façade) and houses a number of different departments, libraries, archives, meeting rooms, and areas for ceremonial purposes. Its architecture consists of a series of joined pavilions with a central courtyard. This monograph, marking the first one hundred years of the building's life, looks at the transfer of the Government administration to the new capital and the development of Via XX Settembre, the influence of Quintino Sella (the Minister of Finance) and his choice of architect, Canevari's plans and their modifications, an appreciation of the architecture and decoration of the building, and its critical reception. The volume has numerous illustrations and architectural plans in the text and also contains eighty colour plates showing exterior and interior views of the building, architectural and decorative details (including six views of Cesare Mariani's painted ceiling in the Sala della Maggioranza), works of art, and some spectacular views of the surrounding area and the Roman skyline seen from the top of the building. There are also lists of Finance and Treasury ministers from the 1860s to the 1970s.

645 **Pictures of Montecitorio, the Chamber of Deputies.**
Edited by Franco Borsi. Rome: Palazzo Montecitorio, 1971. 152p.

The Ludovisi Palace was built before Pope Alexander VII decided to make Piazza Colonna the centre of the city. The building of a grandiose Bernini structure began in 1650 but because of the slow pace of the operation, the Ludovisis acquired a nearby palace in S. Lorenzo in Lucina. The deaths of Pope Urban VIII (1655) and Niccolò Ludovisi (1664) brought the construction to a halt. In 1694, Carlo Fontana proposed the centralization of the law courts into a single curia, claiming that during the Roman Empire the Montecitorio had the same function. The piazza was completed in 1695 and in 1789 the obelisk was raised in its centre. After 1870, the law courts were expelled from the palace and, after the construction of the Assembly Hall, the building became the Chamber of Deputies. There are fifty-six black-and-white and twelve colour plates of views of Piazza Colonna and the Palazzo del Montecitorio, dating from the 16th to the 19th century. Artists include Dupérac, Fontana, Piranesi, Pannini, Rossini, and Thomas.

646 **Piranesi architetto.** (Piranesi, the architect.)
John Wilton-Ely, Joseph Connors. Rome: Edizioni dell'Elefante, 1992. 115p. bibliog.

The catalogue of the exhibition held at the American Academy in Rome in 1992 which included the Piranesi drawings in the Avery Architectural Library of Columbia University, which were discovered and presented to the library in 1972. The subjects of the thirty-five drawings exhibited are the two substantial commissions for architecture Piranesi received from Pope Clement XIII and his nephew Cardinal Giambattista Rezzonico, for a projected tribune to the west of the transept at S. Giovanni in Laterano and for the remodelling of S. Maria del Priorato. In his introductory essay, John Wilton-Ely gives an overview of Piranesi's career, pointing out that his training and concerns as an architect are fundamental in understanding his multi-faceted genius. He examines in detail the two commissions, comparing Piranesi's proposals for S. Giovanni in Laterano to Borromini's scheme, carried out between 1646 and 1649, which was a source of inspiration to him. (Borromini's work in S. Giovanni in Laterano is also examined in the essay by Joseph Connors.) The abandonment of this commission in 1767 was a major source of disappointment for Piranesi, but the commission in 1764 to renovate and enhance S. Maria del Priorato, the priory church of the Knights of the Grand Order of Malta, was a brilliant achievement. There are full-page colour plates of all twenty-three exceptionally beautiful presentation drawings in the Avery Architectural Library related to the S. Giovanni in Laterano commission. The catalogue entries and essays are in English, while the latter are also translated into Italian.

647 Piranesi as architect and designer.

John Wilton-Ely. New York: The Pierpont Morgan Library; New Haven, Connecticut; London: Yale University Press, 1993. 186p. bibliog. (Franklin Jasper Walls Lectures.)

This volume sets out to examine Piranesi's achievements as an architect and versatile decorative designer, which have been somewhat overshadowed by his fame as a topographical engraver and graphic fantasist. Piranesi was an important architectural theorist, whose published writings span some twenty-five years and who played a key role in the development of international Neo-classicism. His influence can be seen in the work of other architects and designers such as the Adams brothers Sir John Soane, Boullée, Ledoux, and Schinkel. His originality in the applied and decorative arts can also be seen in the surviving works based on his original designs. The five lectures examine Piranesi's architectural fantasies, his polemical works, the projected tribune for S. Giovanni in Laterano, the remodelling of S. Maria del Priorato, and his work as a decorative designer. The text is accompanied by 160 black-and-white and 7 colour plates of outstanding quality.

648 Piranesi e l'Aventino. (Piranesi and the Aventine.)

Edited by Barbara Jatta. Milan, Italy: Electa, 1998. 235p. bibliog.

An exhibition catalogue examining Piranesi's only architectural creation, the church and headquarters of the Knights of Malta on the Aventine, which he renovated during 1764 and 1766, completely transforming the original façade and interior of S. Maria del Priorato and creating a new ceremonial piazza. The work was commissioned by the Grand Prior of the Knights of Malta, Cardinal Giovanni Battista Rezzonico (1740-83). Piranesi also received a number of other commissions from the Rezzonico family (the family of Pope Clement XIII) in the 1760s, such as the project for the tribune of S. Giovanni in Laterano, and for furniture and decorative schemes, and these are examined in two introductory essays. Other essays look at the history and topography of the Priory and the Aventine. There is also a catalogue of the Piranesi holdings of the Biblioteca apostolica vaticana. The catalogue section is divided into four parts: the priory before Piranesi's work (which includes paintings and engravings showing the Aventine and S. Maria del Priorato); Piranesi and the patronage of the Rezzonico family (engravings of decorative work [such as clocks and candelabra] that Piranesi executed for the Rezzonicos, as well as portraits by other artists of members of the family); Piranesi's work at the Priorato (which includes numerous preparatory drawings for the decoration of the church); and other works Piranesi executed in the 1760s, and portraits and busts of the artist. There is also a section on coins and medals produced during the reign of Clement XIII (1758-69), and photographs of the Priorato, the interior of the church, and Piranesi's emblematic monuments in the Piazza dei Cavalieri di Malta.

649 Raffaello architetto. (Raphael, the architect.)

C. L. Frommel, S. Ray, M. Tafuri. Milan, Italy: Electa, 1984. 475p. bibliog.

This remarkable catalogue of an exhibition held in Rome on the occasion of the quincentenary of the artist's birth examines every aspect of Raphael's activity as an architect, often considered marginal compared to his work as a painter. It is largely confined to the last six years of his life, after Leo X appointed him architect of St Peter's following Bramante's death in 1514. The catalogue also examines Raphael's response to the antique, which is of major relevance not only to his architectural output but also to his overall work. This was the first attempt to present in an exhibition all the original material available and investigate the methods of work of Raphael and his assistants, the complex elaboration of the design of St Peter's and Villa Madama, and also establish the extent of Raphael's responsibility for the design of the church of S. Giovanni dei Fiorentini, and assess his involvement in the design of Palazzo Alberini. The volume also looks at the depiction of architecture in his paintings and the relation of his architectural projects to the urban planning policies of Leo X. The catalogue contains a total of thirty-one essays, which range from overall appreciations to studies of individual works.

650 **Ragguagli borrominiani.** (New documents about Borromini.)
Edited by Marcello Del Piazzo. Rome: Archivio di Stato di Roma, 1968. 377p. bibliog. (Pubblicazioni degli Archivi di Stato, 61.)

The catalogue of an exhibition of documents on Francesco Borromini organized by the Archivio di Stato di Roma in 1968 (the tercentenary of his death) and held at the Biblioteca Alessandrina (which still retains the bookstacks designed by the architect). The exhibition included material from the archives of families, religious orders, the University of Rome, and the Camera Apostolica, as well as notarial acts containing first-hand accounts of the execution of Borromini's works or information about his artistic milieu. The catalogue is in two parts. The first part provides descriptions of 257 documents and is divided into four sections: biographical information about Borromini and his family; his early years in Rome, his work as a sculptor and his relationship to Carlo Maderno and the Ticinese community of stonemasons with whom he collaborated; the architecture of Borromini's artistic maturity, from S. Maria di Loreto (1634) to S. Giovanni in Oleo (1660-68); and his work at the Sapienza (this section makes ample use of the diaries of Carlo Cantari, which shed light not only on Borromini's work but also on the Studium Urbis). The second part of the catalogue provides full transcriptions of sixty-two documents. The catalogue includes thirty-two plates of 17th-century prints showing Borromini's architecture and forty-eight plates of documents. There are also chronological and location indices of documents exhibited or cited and a genealogical table of the Borromini family.

651 **The Renaissance from Brunelleschi to Michelangelo: the representation of architecture.**
Edited by Henry A. Millon and Vittorio Magnago Lampugnani.
London: Thames & Hudson, 1994. 731p. bibliog.

There is one article specifically about Rome ('St Peter's: the early history' by Christoph Luitpold Frommel) but Roman architecture is also discussed in most of the other twelve introductory articles of this volume. The catalogue has 421 entries (architectural drawings, paintings depicting architecture, and models). Roman buildings and artists discussed include: Bramante; the Belvedere Court and the Tempietto; Michelangelo and the Porta Pia; urban planning in Rome under the Medici popes; St Giovanni dei Fiorentini; the Villa Madama; and the various projects related to the large-scale renovation of St Peter's and the contribution of Bramante, Raphael, Michelangelo and Antonio da Sangallo the Younger. An abridged version of this work, omitting the entries for the exhibited works, was published in 1996.

652 **Roma: palazzi, palazzetti, case, 1200-1870: progetto per un inventario.** (Rome: palaces, small palaces, and houses, 1200-1870: a project for an inventory.)
Ferruccio Lombardi. Rome: Edilstampa, 1992 (2nd rev. ed.). 557p.

An inventory of 900 buildings built between 1200 and 1870 in the fourteen historic *rioni* of Rome. The entries are in fourteen sections, one for each *rione*. Each section includes: a short introduction outlining the history of the *rione*, a numerical and a chronological index to the buildings, the *rione* as it appears in Nolli's 1748 plan and as it is today, and finally the entries for the buildings. Each entry consists of a colour photograph of the building, an outline of its history and a description of its principal architectural features. There are three indexes: an alphabetical index of all the buildings, a chronological index (by century), and an index of popes. A selection of buildings between 1870 and 1950 is also given in an appendix, and there is a plan showing the major demolitions carried out between 1870 and 1950 and two plans showing the fourteen ancient Roman *regiones* and the twenty-two post-1870 *rioni*. See also *Roma: le chiese scomparse* (Rome: the churches that have vanished) by Ferruccio Lombardi (Rome: Fratelli Palombi, 1996. 492p. bibliog.).

653 Roma, 1300-1875: l'arte degli anni santi: atlante. (Rome 1300-1875: the city of the Holy Years: an atlas.)
Edited by Marcello Fagiolo, Maria Luisa Madonna.   Milan, Italy: Arnoldo Mondadori, 1985. 399p. bibliog.

This is the catalogue of an exhibition held in Rome in 1985. It was preceded by *Roma 1300-1975: l'arte degli anni santi*, a massive display of the art of the Holy Years (see entry no. 458). It provides a systematic survey charting (in twenty chapters) all the artistic and architectural works executed in Roman churches on the occasion of each Jubilee year. It also includes all town planning schemes carried out during these years, shown on a series of maps. A separate sequence of maps shows the architectural development of the 'Via Mercatoria', the important commercial and administrative area lying between the Ponte S. Angelo and the Ponte Quattro Capi, with information about all the notable buildings. The volume is profusely illustrated.

654 Roma barocca. (Baroque Rome.)
Paolo Portoghesi.   Rome: Laterza, 1998. 568p. bibliog. (Grandi Opere.)

This survey of one of the most glorious periods of architecture in Rome, from the early years of the 17th century to the mid-18th century, was first published in 1966. It is in two parts. Part one examines the birth of the new architectural language and some of its features (for example, optical illusionism) against the background of Roman culture and the urban development policies of the papacy. It also looks at the work of the three geniuses of the first generation of architects – Gianlorenzo Bernini, Borromini, and Pietro Da Cortona. Part two investigates the development of the Baroque style during the latter half of the 17th century in the work of a number of other architects, such as: Carlo Rainaldi (S. Maria in Campitelli, S. Andrea della Valle, and the two churches in Piazza del Popolo – S. Maria dei Miracoli and S. Maria di Montesanto); Carlo Fontana (S. Marcello al Corso); Alessandro Specchi; Francesco De Sanctis (the Spanish Steps); and Gabriele Valvassori (Palazzo Doria-Pamphilj on the Corso). The final section looks at early 18th-century architects, including: Giuseppe Sardi; Filippo Raguzzini; Carlo De Dominicis; the pupils of Carlo Fontana (including F. Juvarra); Domenico Gregorini and Pietro Passalacqua (S. Croce in Gerusalemme); Nicola Michetti; Gaetano Chiaveri; Ferdinando Fuga (S. Maria dell'Orazione e Morte, the facades of Palazzo della Consulta and S. Maria Maggiore); Nicola Salvi (the Trevi Fountain); Alessandro Galilei; and Luigi Vanvitelli. There is also a chapter on the restorations of the early Christian basilicas carried out during this period, and one on later influences of the Baroque style. An index of architects and a chronological listing of their works is also included.

655 Rome: the biography of its architecture from Bernini to Thorvaldsen.
Christian Elling.   Copenhagen: Gyldendal, 1975. 586p. maps. bibliog.

Originally published in Danish in 1950, this is a personal reaction to Rome and its buildings from the end of the High Baroque period to the beginning of the Empire style. It includes 212 full-page photographs.

656 Rome of the Renaissance.
Paolo Portoghesi. London: Phaidon, 1972. 450p. bibliog.

This study of Roman architecture in the first half of the 16th century (1503-63) was originally published in 1970 as *Architettura di Roma nel rinascimento*. It is divided into the following periods: the reign of Julius II and the Roman activity of Bramante, the ideal interpreter of Julius's '*renovatio urbis*', symbolizing the restoration of the papacy's political prestige; the reigns of Leo X, Hadrian VI and the first years of Clement VII, the summit of the period of Roman classicism; from the Sack of Rome in 1527 to the 1540s, when Antonio da Sangallo reigned supreme; and the triumph of classical conservatism in the 1550s. Architects whose work is discussed include: Raphael, Baldassare Peruzzi, Antonio da Sangallo, Pirro Ligorio, Andrea and Jacopo Sansovino, and Bartolomeo Ammannati. There are 446 black-and-white plates, 57 architectural drawings, and numerous illustrations in the text.

657 Studi sul Borromini. (Studies on Borromini.)
Rome: De Luca, 1967. 2 vols. (544p., 299p.).

The proceedings of a conference organized by the Accademia nazionale di S. Luca in 1967, together with a series of exhibitions and other events, to commemorate the tercentenary of Borromini's death. It includes a lecture by R. Wittkower on the character of Borromini in which his personality and temperament are contrasted with those of Bernini, his greatest rival and the last in the tradition of universal geniuses as opposed to Borromini's single focus on architecture.

658 Studi sul Settecento romano. (Studies on Rome in the eighteenth century.)
Rome: Multigrafica, 1985- .

A series of volumes covering various topics concerned with Roman architecture of the 18th century. Subjects covered include: the commissions of the Albani family; stage illusion and archaeological myths in villas and palazzi; the work of Carlo Marchionni; architecture from Clement XI to Benedict XIV; decorative themes; patrons, artists and theorists from Classicism to Neo-classicism; Bourgeois Rome: houses and palazzetti for renting; paintings, drawings, sculptures and correspondence in the Rome of the Curia; and 18th-century draughtsmanship.

659 Tutto Borromini a Roma. (The complete works of Borromini in Rome.)
Rome: Rotundo, 1988. 175p. maps. (A Roma.)

This is a useful general guide to twenty-four Borromini buildings in Rome. Each entry is accompanied by a map, a drawing and a photograph of the building, its address and information on how to get there, and a note about Borromini's contribution. A chronology of Borromini's work and a biographical note are included. The text is in Italian and English.

660 Valadier: segno e architettura. (Valadier: drawing and architecture.)
Edited by Elisa Debenedetti. Rome: Multigrafica, 1985. 444p.

A catalogue of an exhibition held in Rome in 1985-86. It brings together Giuseppe Valadier's architectural drawings executed between 1773 and 1838, which are now held in public collections in Rome. It also reproduces three recently discovered sketchbooks of the architect held in the Biblioteca nazionale centrale di Roma, which date from 1775, 1799-1806, and 1832. Valadier was one of the most important exponents of Neo-classicism in Italy. His work in Rome includes the Villa Poniatowski on the Via Flaminia, and the restoration of Ponte Milvio and of various churches (for example, S. Pantaleo). The French occupation of Rome gave Valadier great opportunities as an architect and restorer. His greatest achievements, however, were the redevelopment of Piazza del Popolo (which unified its diverse components, including the 15th-century church of S. Maria del Popolo and the Baroque churches of S. Maria dei Miracoli and S. Maria di Montesanto, built in the 1670s) and the formal garden and coffee house (the Casina Valadier) on the Pincio, completed in 1824. The 596 drawings exhibited are all illustrated here and are listed chronologically. The catalogue also includes short biographies of three other artists of the Valadier dynasty: Luigi Valadier (1726-85), Luigi Maria Valadier (born 1791), and Andrea Valadier (born 1815).

661 The Walls of Rome.
Malcolm Todd. London: Paul Elek, 1978. 91p. bibliog.
This short and well-illustrated monograph examines the city walls of Rome from the earliest defences of the city in the mid-5th century BC – a rampart with a broad ditch outside it that surrounded part of the city – to the construction of the Aurelian Wall. It is now established that the 'Servian Wall', believed to have been constructed during the reign of Servius Tullius (578-535 BC), was built c. 386 BC, shortly after the Gaulish attack on the city. Work on the Aurelian Wall began in 271 AD; it measured some 18 kilometres in length and had 18 gates and 381 towers. During the reign of Maxentius (306-312) its height was raised through the addition of a galleried structure. The development of, and alterations to, the towers and gates, as well as later restorations of the Wall (up to the 6th century) are outlined and the influence of the Aurelian Wall on later fortifications in other parts of the Roman Empire is examined in the final chapter. The study does not examine the Leonine Wall (enclosing the *civitas Leonina*), constructed by Pope Leo IV in 852, which enclosed the Vatican into the circuit of the Aurelian Wall.

Palazzi and villas

662 L'architettura di Villa Borghese: dal giardino privato al parco pubblico. (The architecture of Villa Borghese: from private garden to public park.)
Beata Di Gaddo. Rome: Università degli studi di Roma "La Sapienza", Dipartimento di architettura e analisi della città, 1997. 218p. maps. bibliog. (Groma Quaderni, 5.)
A revised edition of *Villa Borghese, il giardino e le architetture*, originally published in 1984. The villa was built in the outskirts of Rome on grounds ('vecchie vigne') purchased by the Borghese family between 1574 and 1606. It was a princely residence and home to the art collections of Pope Paul V and Scipione Borghese, his nephew. The villa is now the Borghese Gallery, recently restored and still housing the Borghese collections, while the gardens, which were originally enclosed by a wall and where the ancient sculptures were displayed, were turned into a public park at the beginning of this century. This work traces the evolution and transformations of the villa and its grounds from the beginning of the 17th century to the present century. It includes numerous detailed plans and maps showing the development of the grounds. The various buildings on the grounds are described.

663 **Bernini's *Scala regia* at the Vatican Palace: architecture, sculpture, and ritual.**

T. A. Marder. London: Cambridge University Press, 1997. 336p. bibliog.

This is a detailed study of the Scala Regia, the ceremonial staircase leading to the Vatican palace and the principal link between the palace and St Peter's. It examines its structure, function, and symbolism. It sets Bernini's achievement within the context of the earlier history of the palace, and recreates the development of its design and its construction through the use of documentary and literary evidence. It also interprets the creation of the staircase as a development of Bernini's schemes for St Peter's Square. A separate chapter discusses the design and execution of the statue of Constantine. The work includes 78 full-page plates and also 212 illustrations in the text.

664 **The Casino of Pius IV.**

Graham Smith. Princeton, New Jersey: Princeton University Press, 1977. 141p. + [51]p. of plates. bibliog.

The Casino of Pius (today the seat of the Pontificia Accademia delle Scienze) is set in the Vatican gardens to the west of the Belvedere Court. It consists of a richly decorated pavilion and a loggia linked by an oval courtyard. It was built by Pirro Ligorio for Paul IV but completed under Pius IV and named after him. Its decoration was entrusted to a great number of painters, mosaicists, stone masons, and stucco decorators. Its two decorative programmes combine antiquity (the stucco decoration) and Catholicism (the fresco decoration). Ligorio, the antiquarian and archaeologist, was in charge of the external stucco decorations and the fresco decorations were entrusted to Marcantonio Da Mula, the Venetian ambassador and later Vatican librarian. This study looks at the history of the building and its architectural sources, the iconography of the stucco decorations, and the interior decoration, its iconography and its meaning. It rejects the suggestion that the casino was a miniature reconstruction of an antique *naumachia* (the setting of a mock sea battle) and compares its architecture to other 16th-century buildings: Baldassare Peruzzi's Palazzo Massimo alle Colonne and Palazzo Lancellotti, and to another *villa suburbana*, the Villa Giulia. It establishes that though the exterior and interior decoration programmes have a certain autonomy they are not independent from each other, as they both contain complimentary allusions to Pius and themes of the exterior decoration (for example, baptism) are carried into the interior. The special character of Federico Barocci's, Federico Zuccaro's and Gerolamo Genga's decoration in the Casino is brought out through their comparison to other painting cycles commissioned by Pius IV.

665 **The Falconieri Palace in Rome: the role of Borromini in its reconstruction, 1646-1649.**

Elizabeth G. Howard. New York; London: Garland Publishing, 1981. 360p. bibliog. (Outstanding Dissertations in the Fine Arts.)

The 16th-century Falconieri palace is situated in Via Giulia, to the north-west of the garden of Palazzo Farnese. It originally belonged to the Odescalchi and then the Farnese family who, in 1638, sold it to Orazio Falconieri, who entrusted its enlargement and remodelling to Borromini. The building later housed the celebrated art collection of Cardinal Fesch. Today it houses the Hungarian Academy in Rome. This study investigates, in the light of new documentary evidence, the nature and extent of Borromini's role in the reconstruction, enlargement and decoration of the palace. It is in four sections comprising: a history of the Falconieri family and the palace before Borromini's work, an analysis of the building programme of 1646-49, an examination of Borromini's decoration seen in the context of contemporary palace decoration and, finally, the symbolism of Borromini's decorative programme. As in other commissions,

Borromini was hampered by the need to incorporate a pre-existing structure to his plans and he was also unable to complete the interior decorations. He nevertheless managed to transform the relatively modest building into an imposing Baroque structure in which he combined features of the formal Roman city palace and the suburban Renaissance villa. In the last years of his life, Borromini worked again for the Falconieri, on their chapel of the high altar of the church of S. Giovanni dei Fiorentini and also on the restoration of their villa at Frascati.

666   Introduction au Palais Farnèse. (Introduction to the Palazzo Farnese.)
Anne Puaux.   Rome: École française de Rome, 1983. 274p.

This volume is a useful alternative to the first three volumes of the massive work on the Palazzo Farnese also published, between 1980 and 1994, by the École française de Rome (which is housed, together with the French Embassy, in the palazzo). Though it covers the same ground as the other work, it adopts a more narrative approach. The history of the palazzo is told in five sections, beginning with a study of the site and its surrounding area in antiquity and ending with the restorations carried out in the 1970s. The various phases of the palazzo's construction and decoration are analysed and there are interesting character portraits of its various inhabitants. The work is well-illustrated and has four useful appendices giving descriptions of the fresco cycles in the Galleria and the Camerino, genealogies of the Farnese, a list of the French ambassadors who resided in the palazzo and directors of the École française de Rome since 1875, and ground plans of the building.

667   Palaces of Rome.
Fabio Benzi, Caroline Vincenti Montanaro, photography by Roberto Schezen.   London: Thames & Hudson, 1997. 323p.

A sumptuously illustrated survey of Roman palaces and villas from the Renaissance to the end of the 18th century. The vital role played by Rome in the evolution of the palaces and the villas as concepts and architectural realities is discussed in the introduction, which also points out the architectural and functional differences between the two types of structure. There is a chronological survey of their development, beginning with the return of the papacy from Avignon at the end of the 14th century and the creation, in the 15th century, of urban gardens (*vigne*) and pavilions in the open spaces within the walls and beyond, eventually becoming part of the fabric of the city and being transformed into palaces (for example, the Palazzo del Quirinale, and Palazzo Barberini). It looks at the antiquarian origins of Renaissance villas (the design of their gardens being inspired from ancient sources and embellished with statues and inscriptions which themselves became objects of humanistic meditation), and the contribution of architects of the stature of Donato Bramante and Antonio da Sangallo the Younger to the development of the princely home, which evolved into the grandiose structures of the Baroque era created by Carlo Maderno, Gianlorenzo Bernini, Francesco Borromini and Pietro da Cortona. The survey ends with Villa Albani and Piranesi's villa of the Knights of Malta on the Aventine. There are individual sections on twenty-five palaces and villas, giving a brief outline of each building's history and special features and accompanied by colour photographs showing details of its architecture and decoration. Though the selection is not exhaustive and does not include all the major examples, a number of lesser-known buildings are included (for example, the Palazzo Pecci Blunt – a 16th-century palace standing opposite Michelangelo's Campidoglio stairs, or the neo-classical Palazzo Rondinini on the Corso) in order to convey the idea of the enormous wealth and variety of buildings still preserved.

668   Le Palais Farnèse – École française de Rome. (Palazzo Farnese –
French School in Rome.)
Rome: École française de Rome, 1980-94. 3 vols. in 6.

This massive and exhaustive study of one of the greatest buildings in Rome is arranged in three
volumes and six parts. Volume one is in two parts: the first examines the history of the site and
the evolution and transformations of the Arenula quarter in Campo Marzio (the quarter
dominated by the palazzo) during antiquity and the Middle Ages. It then focuses on the palazzo
itself, its construction (which took nearly as long as that of St Peter's) and the contribution of
various architects: Giuliano Da Sangallo and Michelangelo (1513-50); and Vignola and Giacomo
della Porta (1550-89). This is followed by a survey of its decorations, by Daniele Da Volterra,
Francesco Salviati and Federico and Taddeo Zuccaro in the 16th century and by the Carraccis in
the early 17th century. The second part looks at the Farnese collections – antiquities, inscriptions,
coins, paintings, modern sculpture, furniture and *objets d'art*, printed books (with the inventory
of 1653 in an appendix), and Greek manuscripts. It also includes the history of the palazzo in the
17th and 18th centuries. Volume two contains over 1,000 photographs (out of a corpus of 5,000
taken by the École française de Rome) depicting the palazzo and its collections. It also moves
from the surrounding area to the palazzo, first its exterior and then its interior (from the cellar to
the loft), and includes reproductions of works of art that were once housed in the palazzo. Volume
three is divided into three parts. The first part is a study of financial documents (1535-1612)
related to the palazzo. The second part is a history of the Farnese library and a detailed study of
its Latin and Italian manuscripts, based on the surviving inventories. Each entry includes a
description of the manuscript, its provenance and a bibliography. The third part is an edition of
the 1644 inventory of the palazzo and other Farnese properties in Rome. This is the earliest
surviving inventory, and was rediscovered in 1953. It lists 7,320 items, including furniture,
paintings, statues, etc. There is a concordance (from present location and catalogue/inventory
number to the Farnese inventory number) and numerous indexes.

669   I Palazzi di Roma. (The palazzi of Rome.)
Giorgo Carpaneto.   Rome: Newton Compton, 1993. 574p. bibliog.
(Quest'Italia, 175.)

A dictionary of notable, and still standing, buildings from the 15th to the 19th century, with
information about their architecture, their various inhabitants and anecdotes. In a brief
introduction, the author gives a general account of the development of the Roman palazzo from
the classical equilibrium of the early Renaissance to the eclecticism of the 19th century.

670   Palazzi of Rome.
Text by Carlo Cresti and Claudio Rendina, photography by Massimo
Listri.   Cologne, Germany: Könemann, 1998. 398p.

This beautifully illustrated volume (originally published in Italian as: *Ville e palazzi di Roma*)
introduces thirty Roman villas and palazzi. Each chapter introduces a particular building, giving
an account of its construction, architecture, decoration, and changing fortunes and functions.
The text is accompanied by several stunning colour photographs showing views of each
building and its grounds, and details of its decoration or works of art created for or housed in it.
These are unerringly well chosen to highlight particular distinctive features of the building and
to indicate the variety of artistic treasures or the beauty of its natural setting. There are six
introductory essays examining the architecture of the Roman palazzo from Nero's *Domus
Aurea* to the palazzi of the Third Rome, their sumptuous interiors with their decorations,
furnishings and picture galleries, and their courtyards and gardens, and also on descriptions of
Roman palazzi by landscape painters and travel writers.

671 **Il Palazzo apostolico lateranense.** (The Lateran Apostolic Palace.)
Edited by Carlo Pietrangeli. Florence, Italy: Nardini, 1991. 338p.
bibliog. (Chiese Monumentali d'Italia e Palazzi Apostolici.)

The introduction to this volume discusses the Basilica del Salvatore (later renamed S. Giovanni) in Laterano, the Cathedral of Rome, and its relationship to St Peter's in the Vatican. Satellite cities developed around both churches – the 'Città leonina' (the Borgo), protected by the Castel S. Angelo and surrounded by the Leonine Wall (built after the sacking of St Peter's by the Saracens in 846) and, in the Lateran, around the Patriarcate (*Patriarchio*), the residence of the Bishop of Rome (the Pope), with its assembly rooms, triclinia, archives, etc. The publication has chapters on the history, topography, and architecture of the old Patriarcate which, under Sixtus V, was demolished and replaced by a new building designed by Domenico Fontana. There is a detailed examination of the architecture of the new palace and the painting cycles executed in 1588-89, which cover a surface of over 10,000 square metres, and also the tapestries collection in the palace. The Scala Santa – traditionally believed to be the staircase of the house of Pontius Pilate – and its sanctuary (the Sancta Sanctorum), which were moved to a nearby site when the new palace was built, are also discussed. The Scala Santa is richly decorated in the mannerist style by, among others, Giovanni Baglione, Cesare Nebbia, Andrea Lilio, Paul Brill, Ventura Salimbeni, and Antonio Viviani. The Sancta Sanctorum is also rich in mosaics and frescoes and its treasure includes the Acheropita (*Acheropoieton*), the miraculous icon of Christ the Saviour shown only on special occasions. There is also a chapter discussing monuments of the Classical era in the Patriarchio – a number of bronzes were transferred from the Lateran to the Campidoglio in 1471, among them the bronze she-wolf *Mater Romanorum* and the Spinario, followed in 1538 by the equestrian statue of Marcus Aurelius (in the Middle Ages believed to be of Constantine). Finally, there is a chapter on the three sections of the Museo storico vaticano (inaugurated in 1973), which are housed in the Lateran. All the chapters are splendidly illustrated.

672 **Palazzo Braschi.**
Carlo Pietrangeli. Rome: Istituto di studi romani, 1958. 75p. + 44p. of
plates. (Quaderni di Storia dell'arte, 8.)

A study of the history and architecture of Palazzo Braschi, the last Roman palazzo to be built for the family of a pope. It also relates the history of the Palazzo Orsini-Santobono, which was purchased by Pope Pius VI in 1790 and demolished, together with adjacent houses, to make way for the present palazzo. Situated on the Via Papalis, Palazzo Orsini was the first great example of 15th-century civil architecture in Rome. It was built in 1432 by Francesco Orsini, the Prefect of Rome, and remained Orsini property until the 18th century, though it had a number of other distinguished occupiers. In the early 1500s it was given to Cardinal Oliviero Carafa (the patron of Bramante in S. Maria della Pace and Filippino Lippi in S. Maria sopra Minerva) who installed the Pasquino statue in Via di S. Pantaleo. Due to the close links of the Orsinis with France, the Palazzo was periodically used as the residence of French ambassadors in Rome. Its most splendid period was in the 17th century under Don Flavio Orsini, Duke of Bracciano, when the Salon of Anna de la Trémoille, his second wife, became the centre of Roman artistic, literary and political life. The building of the Palazzo Braschi was interrupted by the French occupation of Rome in 1798, the deposition and exile of Pius VI and the arrest of don Luigi Braschi. It was finally completed after don Luigi's return to Rome in 1800. It was the work of Cosimo Morelli, who was replaced in the later stages by Luigi Valadier. It was richly decorated in the neo-classical style with scenes from Greco-Roman mythology and Etruscan and Roman history. The Braschi art collections were later dispersed (they are given here in an appendix) and the Palazzo's subsequent history and fortunes have been varied: since becoming a state property in 1871 it has housed, among others, the Ministry of Interior (1871-1922), the

Federazione fascista (1927-44) and, since 1952, the Museum of the History of Rome (Museo di Roma) and the Comune's collection of Italian art from 1800 to the present.

673   Il Palazzo del Quirinale. (The Quirinal Palace.)
Texts by Franco Borsi (et al.), introduction by Giovanni Spadolini.
Rome: Editalia, 1974. 286p. bibliog.

The Quirinal Palace has always been used as an official residence. Between 1592 and 1870 it was the principal summer residence of the pope, then it became the residence of the king of Italy and, since 1947, it has been the official residence of the president of the Italian Republic. Accordingly, this volume begins with a look at the role of the palace in the history and public life of Italy. This is followed by an examination of its history and architecture – its construction and expansion were the work of various architects including Ottaviano Mascherino (who designed the first papal residence in the grounds of Cardinal Ippolito d'Este's original villa), Giovanni and Domenico Fontana, Carlo Maderno, Gianlorenzo Bernini and Ferdinando Fuga (who lengthened the *manica lunga* [the long wing]). The palace's decoration, to which some of the greatest artists of the 17th and 18th centuries contributed, contains a great variety of materials and styles ranging from ancient Roman mosaics to Rococo interiors and chinoiseries. There are also chapters on the art treasures housed in the palace, its gardens and, finally, a list of documents, from 1533 to 1871, related to the palace and its grounds. The volume is lavishly illustrated.

674   Il Palazzo Doria Pamphilj. (The Palazzo Doria Pamphilj.)
Giovanni Carandente.   Milan, Italy: Electa, 1975. 359p. maps. bibliog.

Built over four centuries, the Palazzo Doria-Pamphilj occupies a huge block extending between Via del Corso, Piazza del Collegio Romano, Via del Plebiscito, Via della Gatta and Via Lata. In 1505, Fabio Santoro built his residence on land he bought from the chapter of S. Maria in Via Lata but he was soon forced by Pope Julius II to give it to Francesco Maria della Rovere, his nephew. The palazzo was enlarged, later in the century, through the acquisition of other adjacent properties, and in 1601 it was bought by Cardinal Pietro Aldobrandini. In 1647, it passed to the Pamphilj family when Camillo Pamphilj, nephew of Pope Innocent X, married Olimpia Aldobrandini. The palazzo was further extended with the building of two new façades on the Piazza del Collegio romano and Via della Gatta, and the decoration of the interior rooms continued under Prince Giovanni Battista and Cardinal Benedetto Pamphilj, a great patron of the arts, especially music. The façade on the Via del Corso was constructed between 1731 and 1734 by Gabriele Valvassori. Giovanni Doria Pamphilj IV (1747-1820) (the son of Cardinal Benedetto's sister) moved to Rome in 1760 after the Pamphilj family was threatened with extinction. During the Napoleonic occupation of Rome, the palazzo became the residence of General Miollis, who hosted many lavish receptions. The last remodelling was carried out under Prince Alfonso Doria-Pamphilj (1851-1914). This lavishly illustrated volume follows the evolution of the building and examines the work of various architects, which include Antonio del Grande (1610?-71?), Gabriele Valvassori (1683-1761), and Andrea Busiri Vici (1818-1902). Its 263 illustrations show interior and exterior views of the building, architectural details, furniture, works of art, topographical prints and architectural plans.

675   Roman mornings.
James Lees-Milne.   London: Collins, 1988. 167p.

Eight essays, originally published in 1956, dealing with buildings representative of six phases of the architectural history of Rome – Ancient Roman, Early Christian, Romanesque, Renaissance, Baroque, and Rococo. The buildings are: the Pantheon, S. Costanza, S. Maria in

Cosmedin, il Tempietto, Palazzo Massimo alle Colonne, S. Andrea al Quirinale, S. Carlo alle Quattro Fontane, and the Trevi fountain.

676 Rome palaces and gardens.
Texts by Sophie Bajard, photographs by Raffaello Bencini. Paris: Editions Terrail, 1997. 207p. map.

An introduction to eighteen villas and palaces in and around Rome built from the early 16th century to the 19th century. It looks at the origins of the villa in the summer retreats for church dignitaries and the *vigne*, country retreats within or without the Aurelian Wall consisting of a small *casino*, a garden and a few vines. The Roman nobility's passion for hunting during the Renaissance led to the creation of game reserves (*barchi*), and the building of villas on their sites or in their vicinity – the Villa Lante at Bagnaia, Villa d'Este at Tivoli and Villa Farnese at Caprarola. The buildings are examined in chronological order, beginning with the Villa Farnesina and ending with the Villa Bonaparte. Though villas and their gardens, or just gardens (the Sacro Bosco at Bomarzo, and the Orti farnesiani on the Palatine) form the main subject of the book, there are also chapters on the Palazzo Farnese, Palazzo Madama and Palazzo del Quirinale. The numerous colour illustrations are good, except those of works of art.

677 Rome's first national state architecture: the *Palazzo delle finanze*.
Eberhard Schroeter. In: *Art and architecture in the service of politics.* Cambridge, Massachusetts; London: The MIT Press, 1978, p. 128-49.

This article provides a study of the Ministry of Finance building, including an analysis of the historical factors that determined its construction, an examination of the architecture of the building, and a discussion of its political meaning. It considers the historical and ideological situation around 1870, and the role Quintino Sella, the Minister of Finance, played in its construction. Sella, a follower of Auguste Comte, saw Rome as an unindustrialized capital without a proletariat and run by an intelligentsia who would make decisions and balance the different interest groups of the country. Sella was instrumental in the development of the administrative centre of Rome along the axis of Via XX Settembre and its choice as the site of the Ministry of Finance building; he also chose its architect (Raffaele Canevari). The article examines in detail the construction of the building (1872-79) and the modifications imposed by the administration to Canevari's original plan, which drastically altered its entire structure. It is argued that the need to reduce costs influenced the artistic quality of the building. It also discusses the eclectic architectural character of the building and suggests that its adaptation of the Roman Baroque, a style associated with papal Rome, indicates 'a continuity with papal Roman social and power structures'.

678 Der Römische Palastbau der Hochrenaissance. (The building of Roman palaces of the High Renaissance.)
Christoph Luitpold Frommel. Tübingen, Germany: Verlag Ernst Wasmuth, 1973. 3 vols. map. bibliog. (Veröffentlichung der Bibliotheca Hertziana [Max-Planck-Institut in Rom].)

This work aims to provide an overview of the building of Renaissance palaces as a phenomenon. Few other writers have attempted this task, though numerous works exist on individual palaces. The period covered is that from Bramante's first Roman palace to the death of Pope Paul III; the geographical scope is restricted to Rome, with a few exceptions of buildings by Roman masters outside the city itself. Because of the impossibility of covering the whole range of Roman palaces from the chosen period, an attempt has been made to include all buildings of the most important architects (for example, Bramante and G. da Sangallo) and only the most important and characteristic ones of lesser artists. The work is divided into two parts. The first is a general introduction discussing style, function and typology, the façades, and twenty-six palaces. The second volume contains detailed studies of the thirty-six most important palaces, including a chronological list of written references to them, a list of the most important pictorial references, details of architects and owners, the history of each building, and a reconstruction of its original plan. The plates are arranged alphabetically by name of palace.

679 Seventeenth-Century Roman palaces and the art of the plan.
Patricia Waddy.   New York: The Architectural History Foundation,
1990. 469p. bibliog.

The first part of this work attempts to reconstruct, by making extensive use of contemporary handbooks on etiquette and household management, the general programme of activities of any large 17th-century palace. The second examines in detail five palaces: Palazzo Borghese, Palazzo Chigi in Piazza SS Apostoli, and three houses of the Barberini family ('a virtual paradigm of the well-managed Roman family') – Palazzo Barberini, the Casa Grande at Giubonnari and the Palazzo Colonna-Barberini at Palestrina.

680 Villa Aldobrandini a Roma. (The Villa Aldobrandini in Rome.)
Carla Benocci.   Rome: Àrgos, 1992. 254p.

This volume examines the history of the Villa Aldobrandini and its various changes of fortune since the 16th century. Built on the slopes of the Quirinal hill by Carlo Lombardi for the Vitelli family, the villa in 1601 became the property of Cardinal Pietro Aldobrandini, the nephew of Pope Clement VIII, and housed his rich collections of paintings and antiquities (later dispersed). These included the *Nozze Aldobrandini* (The Aldobrandini Wedding – now in the Vatican Museums), one of the most famous examples of ancient Roman painting and discovered in the vicinity; Titian's *Bacchus and Ariadne* (now in the National Gallery, London); and Giovanni Bellini's *The Feast of the Gods* (now in the National Galley of Art, Washington DC). During the Napoleonic period, the villa was the residence of General François Alexandre Sextius Miollis, Lieutenant-Governor of the Roman States, who had it decorated in the neo-classical style. With the opening of Via Nazionale (1875-76) the villa lost part of its splendid gardens and since 1926 it has been the property of the Comune of Rome. The work concludes with a list of the art collections housed in the villa from the 17th to the 19th century (based on a number of different inventories of the Vitelli, Aldobrandini, Pamphilj, Borghese and Miollis collections), comprising 787 paintings and 716 sculptures.

681 The Villa d'Este at Tivoli.
David R. Coffin.   Princeton, New Jersey: Princeton University Press,
1960. 202p. (Princeton Monographs in Art and Archaeology, 34.)

The Villa d'Este at Tivoli and its lavish gardens with their famous fountains and waterworks is the one surviving example of the patronage of one of the greatest 16th-century private art patrons, Ippolito II d'Este, Cardinal of Ferrara (1509-72). He was appointed Governor of Tivoli in 1550 and he immediately decided to rebuild the run-down governor's residence and transform it into a luxurious country villa, a worthy setting for his collections of antiquities and his splendid court. This study begins with a chapter on the early history of the villa and the tensions created by the cardinal's numerous purchases of additional land for the new gardens and the efforts to provide a sufficient water supply for the fountains, and describes the architecture of the villa. The following chapter looks at the gardens and fountains and the use

Architecture. Palazzi and villas

of ancient and contemporary sculpture to create an iconographical programme, devised by Pirro Ligorio, celebrating the Cardinal and the Este family. Though the architecture of the villa is of minor interest, its sumptuous interior fresco decoration – painted by the workshops of Girolamo Muziano, Federico Zuccaro, Cesare Nebbia and Livio Agresti – is a good example of mannerist art and its programme, which is related to the symbolism of the exterior decoration formed by the gardens and fountains, is examined in a separate chapter. Pirro Ligorio's sixteen tapestry designs illustrating the life of the Greek hero Hippolytus, accompanied by commentaries (which are transcribed in an appendix) are also studied, as is the villa's overall symbolic meaning. The work concludes with a study of the later history and influence of the villa and its gardens. There are 137 black-and-white illustrations at the end and also four appendices which include a list of the personifications of the Virtues, with their attendant symbols, in the Cardinal's apartment, and transcriptions of several unpublished manuscripts.

682 **Villa Farnesina alla Lungara, Rome.**
Elsa Gerlini.   Rome: Istituto poligrafico e zecca dello stato, Libreria dello stato, 1990. 85p. bibliog. (Guides to Italian Museums, Galleries and Monuments. New Series, no. 2.)

The villa, built for the Sienese banker and humanist Agostino Chigi in 1510 by Baldassare Peruzzi, takes its name after the Farnese family who bought it in 1577, planning to annex it to Palazzo Farnese through a bridge over the Tiber. Since 1944, the villa has formed part of the Accademia dei Lincei. This is an exemplary study/guide of the villa and its history, its architecture and its decoration (by Raphael, Peruzzi, Sebastiano Del Piombo, and Sodoma), as well as its subsequent restorations and their impact. The complex astrological and astronomical symbolism of the mythological scenes depicted in Peruzzi's frescoes in the vault of the Galatea Room is elucidated and the problems regarding the attribution and chronology of other works in the villa are explained. The accompanying illustrations are excellent.

683 **Villa Madama.**
R. Lefèvre.   Rome: Editalia, 1973. 302p. bibliog.

Villa Madama, on the slopes of Monte Mario, was one of the major architectural undertakings of the early 16th century. It was commissioned by Cardinal Giulio de' Medici (the future Pope Clement VII) and was meant to provide a Medici residence at the outskirts of Rome to welcome important visitors to the city. Raphael and, after his death, Giulio Romano and Giuliano da Sangallo, worked on it. The villa's name comes from the title of Margaret of Austria, natural daughter of Charles V and wife of Alessandro de' Medici, Duke of Florence and later of Ottavio Farnese, Duke of Parma and Piacenza. Since 1940, it has been used by the Ministry of Foreign Affairs for state receptions and high-level meetings. This study traces the history of the villa and attempts to establish the extent of Raphael's role in its construction, which began in 1517 and continued during the pontificate of Clement VII. Owners of the villa also included the Bourbons of Naples, and Maurice Bergès, a French engineer, who acquired the by-then dilapidated villa in 1913 from the heirs of the Bourbons and began its restoration. His work was completed by Carlo Dentice Di Frasso, who bought the property in 1925, and Dorothy Caldwell Taylor, his American wife.

684 **Villa Madama: a memoir relating to Raphael's project.**
Guy Dewez.   London: Lund Humphries Publishers, 1993. 184p.

Raphael was commissioned to build Villa Madama in 1518 but at his death in 1520 he had only completed one half of the project and left no definite plans in respect of the other half, though a number of pointers exist as to his intentions. On the occasion of the exhibition *Raffaello architetto*, held in Rome in 1984, a model was built attempting to show how Raphael might have brought his plan to completion. This publication is divided into two main parts: a memoir and a series of illustrations with accompanying commentaries. The illustrations are divided into 19th-century plans, elevations and early photographs, and views of the villa as it stands today. A series of architectural plans tentatively brings the project to completion. It also contains the text of a letter by Raphael describing his project, together with a translation and commentary.

685 Villa Medici: Académie de France à Rome. (Villa Medici: the French Academy in Rome.)
Text by Philippe Morel, photographs by Araldo de Luca, co-ordinated by Michel Hochmann.   Milan, Italy: Franco Maria Ricci, 1998. 105p. bibliog. (Grand Tour, 12.)

This richly illustrated work gives a short history of the villa and an itinerary to its nine levels, followed by some fifty full-page plates. These include views of the garden façade and its antique reliefs and excellent details of the most famous decorations in the villa, such as those of the 'Camera turca' and the frescoes by Jacopo Zucchi in the 'Stanza delle Muse' and the 'Stanza degli Elementi'.

686 The Villa Medici in Rome.
Glenn M. Andres.   New York; London: Garland publishing, 1976.
2 vols. bibliog. (Outstanding Dissertations in the Fine Arts.)

The Villa Medici is a major monument on the Roman scene and in the development of the Italian villa, described by the author of this thesis as 'the accreted and metamorphosed product of pre-existent conditions, politics, personalities, and changing tastes and function'. Its history is followed from antiquity to the end of the 18th century when, having been virtually abandoned for a number of years, it was used to quarter Napoleonic troops who plundered and ruined much of what had remained. In 1803, a new chapter in the history of the Villa was to begin, when it was bought by the French and became the new seat of the Académie de France, previously housed in the Palazzo Nevers, which had been sacked and burned down during the French Revolution.

687 La Villa Médicis. (The Villa Medici.)
Directed by André Chastel, co-ordinated by Philippe Morel.   Rome: Académie de France de Rome, 1989- .

The first three volumes (out of the five projected) of this monumental work have been published to date. Volume one, *Documentation et description* (Documentation and description), by Bernard Toulier, provides an exhaustive pictorial documentation (through some 1,200 paintings, prints and drawings and 250 plans showing the Villa, its gardens and collections of antiquities) and a methodical description of the building and its grounds. Volume two, *Études* (Studies), by Glenn M. Andres and others, looks at the history of the Villa and its transformation from an ancient villa into a Renaissance suburban villa first of Marcello Crescenzi (1543), then of Cardinal Giovanni Ricci de Montepulciano (1564), a great collector of antiquities, and finally of Cardinal Ferdinand de' Medici, when it became a museum of antiquities second only to the Vatican. There are studies on the architects Nanni di Baccio Bigio and Ammannati, the gardens of the Villa, its decoration, and the art collections of its various owners. These were dispersed in the 17th and 18th centuries. Volume three, *Le parnasse astrologique: les décors peints pour le cardinal Ferdinand de Médicis. Étude iconologique* (Astrological Parnassus: painted interiors for Cardinal Ferdinand de' Medici. Iconological study), by Philippe Morel, examines the principal painted decor of the

Villa by Jacopo Zucchi and his assistants in the bedroom of Ferdinard de' Medici, and the recently discovered and restored *Stanza degli uccelli*, elucidating Zucchi's astrological and politico-mythological imagery. Volume four is planned to provide a catalogue of the collections of antiquities and paintings and, finally, volume five will consist of a catalogue of written sources.

688   Le ville di Roma. (The villas of Rome.)
Carlo Zaccagnini.   Rome: Newton Compton, 1984. 346p.
(Quest'Italia, 3.)

A chronological survey of Roman villas and their gardens from their origins in Ancient Rome to the end of the 19th century. They are examined in three sections: the villas and gardens of Ancient Rome; the Middle Ages and the Renaissance; and from the 17th century to the end of the 19th century. The three main sections both examine the historical development of the villa and also have separate sections on the most important villas of the period under review – there are, for example, nineteen descriptions of 17th-century villas and gardens, and seventeen of the 18th century. The work also gives, in an appendix, brief descriptions of fifty-six lesser-known villas and gardens, and there are other useful appendices listing: destroyed private villas and gardens; extant private villas and gardens, their location and present condition or ownership; and parks and public gardens.

Churches

689   The altars and altarpieces of new St. Peter's: outfitting the Basilica, 1621-1666.
Louise Rice.   Cambridge, England: Cambridge University Press, in association with the American Academy in Rome, 1997. 494p. bibliog.

This is a detailed study of the monumental altarpieces commissioned during the first half of the 17th century, mostly during the reign of Urban VIII, to decorate the altars of the new St Peter's. Some of the most famous artists working in Rome at the time – including Domenichino, Guercino, Reni, Pietro da Cortona, Lanfranco, Poussin, Valentin and Vouet – were invited to submit proposals. The works were later removed and replaced by mosaic copies or works by different artists, or destroyed to make way for papal tombs. The study is in three parts followed by a catalogue. Part one traces the early history of the altars in St Peter's and the work of the Congregazione della reverenda fabbrica di San Pietro – a committee whose work was to supervise the construction, outfitting, and maintenance of the new basilica – and of the Chapter of St Peter's, the clerics in charge of the liturgical and ceremonial life of the basilica. It also looks at the altars in old St Peter's and the commission by Gregory XV of Guercino's St Petronilla altarpiece in 1621. Part two examines the fifteen altarpieces commissioned during Urban VIII's pontificate, and part three provides a detailed discussion of Barberini patronage and describes the creative process and initial public reaction. The catalogue is a series of detailed essays on the history and iconography of each of the nineteen commissions, and is followed by a documentary appendix. There are 186 illustrations at the end of the volume; however, the total absence of colour plates from a publication of this importance is deplorable.

690 **Le chiese di Roma dalle loro origini sino al secolo XVI.** (The churches
of Rome from their origins to the sixteenth century.)
Mariano Armellini. Rome: Tipografia editrice romana, 1887. 808p.

In his preface to this monumental catalogue, Armellini, lamenting the loss of a large part of
Rome's Christian heritage, states that in the 13th century Rome numbered more than 1,000
churches. The present volume contains a total of 918 churches (800 within the walls), more than
half of which had been destroyed in the intervening centuries. It is in two parts, the first of which
gives a historical survey of the churches and discusses catalogues published between the 12th
and the 16th century. Part two is an alphabetical listing of the churches, each entry providing
information about the history and topography of the church. There are two indices – the first
listing the churches by *rione*, the second in alphabetical order.

691 **Le chiese di Roma illustrate.** (The churches of Rome illustrated.)
Rome: Casa editrice 'Roma', [1923?]- .

A series of monographs on the churches of Rome. Each volume is dedicated to one church
and gives an outline of its history and a detailed description of the building, its architecture
and works of art. The text is accompanied by numerous black-and-white illustrations and
plans together with a full bibliography. The original series was founded and edited by Carlo
Galassi Paluzzi (1893-1972), who was succeeded by Carlo Pietrangeli when the series was
taken over (from volume 126) by the Istituto di studi romani and published by Fratelli
Palombi. The first series comprised 135 volumes; some 30 volumes have so far appeared in
the new series, although some of its earlier volumes, which bear a double numeration, were
reprints of titles from the original series.

692 **Le chiese di Roma nel Medio Evo: cataloghi e appunti.** (The churches
of Rome in the Middle Ages: catalogues and notes.)
Christian Huelsen. Florence, Italy: Leo S. Olschki, 1927. 755p. maps.
(Associazione Artistica fra i Cultori di Architettura in Roma.)

This massive volume is a study and transcription of early catalogues of the churches of Rome. It
is in two parts, preceded by a long introduction in five chapters which describe the catalogues,
discuss the work of authors of works on Roman churches written from the 16th to the 20th
century, establish a chronology of the churches, and discuss their names. Part one is a
transcription of the lists of churches in fourteen catalogues dating from the 7th to the 16th century.
Part two is a study of the topography, nomenclature, and history of the medieval churches of
Rome. The churches are listed in alphabetical order and each entry cites references to the church
in the earlier catalogues. There are two folded maps and two indices, the first a topographical
index of the churches in the urban *regiones* (*rioni*), the second a general alphabetical index.

693 **Le chiese sconosciute di Roma.** (Unknown churches of Rome.)
Mario Escobar. Rome: Newton Compton, 1988. 319p. bibliog.
(Quest'Italia, 125.)

A guide to fifty lesser-known churches in Rome which, though not included in the usual tourist
itineraries, nevertheless have interesting histories and contain important works of art. Each
church has a chapter to itself.

694 The churches of Rome.
Roloff Beny, Peter Gunn. London: Weidenfeld & Nicolson, 1981.
288p. map.

In an introductory chapter, the author discusses some of the characteristics of churches in Rome – the predominance of Baroque architecture and the reasons behind the comparative scarcity of Romanesque and Renaissance churches, and the palimpsest-like quality of several churches (successive places of worship having been built one on top of the other). Subsequent chapters examine the churches in Rome chronologically, from the Early Christian Churches to the late 18th century. The volume is richly illustrated though the plates rarely correspond to the text. There is a useful gazetteer of the principal churches in Rome and a map showing their location, a glossary and a list of popes since 1417.

695 Corpus basilicarum christianarum Romae. (The Early Christian basilicas of Rome.)
Richard Krautheimer. Vatican City: Pontificio istituto di archeologia cristiana, 1937-77. 5 vols. (Monumenti di Antichità Cristiana, ser. 2, vol. 2.)

In his preface, Krautheimer points out the existence of systematic classifications for Early Christian churches in provinces of the Roman Empire and attributes the lack of a corpus for Rome to the plethora of material in different fields of Christian archaeology which, since the 17th century, developed independently, with the result that the history of the monuments from the architectural point of view was neglected. This Corpus aims to provide an analysis of the structure of the buildings and an examination of the architectural history of the monuments deriving from this analysis. It seeks to establish the original aspect of each monument, to analyse the transformations that have taken place and separate the different superimposed layers of the construction. Other fields of research connected with the churches, such as topography, epigraphy and the history of mosaics, are referred to only if important to the clarification of the architectural history of the monuments. The analysis is accompanied by specially commissioned ground plans of sections of the churches. Chronologically, the collection deals with the churches from the beginning of a Christian architecture in Rome until the middle of the 9th century (i.e. to the end of the last flourishing period of early Christian architecture). The churches are grouped in alphabetical order under their Italian names. Geographically, the churches included are those situated in Rome and in the *suburbium* (suburbs) to the fourth milestone.

696 Il Gesù di Roma. (The church of Gesù in Rome.)
Pio Pecchiai, preface by Pietro Tacchi Venturi. Rome: Società grafica romana, 1952.

This detailed study of one of Rome's most important churches is divided into two sections, one historical and the other descriptive. The first examines the history of the church: it was built on the site of an earlier and smaller church, S. Maria della Strada. Work on the first two plans, by Nanni di Baccio Bigio (1550) and Michelangelo (1554), was quickly suspended and work resumed in 1568 thanks to the patronage of Alessandro Farnese, who was instrumental in acquiring the adjacent properties of the Astalli and Muti families, which had earlier prevented the expansion of the church. The architects of the third and definitive plan of the church were Jacopo Vignola, Giacomo della Porta, and Giovanni Tristano. The church opened during the Holy Year of 1575 and was consecrated in 1584. Between 1672 and 1685 it was radically renovated with Gaulli's spectacularly illusionistic frescoes. Other artists who worked there include Pietro da Cortona, Giacomo Cortese (il Borgognone) – the original choice for the decoration of the tribune, and Andrea Pozzo. Pozzo executed the frescoes in the corridor of the rooms of St Ignatius in the Casa professa (1681-86) and the altar for the tomb of St Ignatius. The fortunes of the church declined during the 18th century with the dissolution of the Society in 1776 and the Napoleonic looting, but revived during the 19th century when Alessandro Torlonia funded the renovation of the decorations of the great nave. The second section is a description of the Church and its Casa professa – it examines their importance in the history of religious art and considers their art treasures, which include works by notable exponents of Roman Mannnerism such as Federico Zuccaro, Niccolò Pomarancio and Girolamo Muziano, as well as by the artists mentioned above. Various documents related to the history of the church are included in an appendix together with an inventory of the furnishings of the church.

697   **The Lateran in 1600: Christian Concord in Counter-Reformation Rome.**
Jack Freiberg.   Cambridge, England: Cambridge University Press, 1995. 333p. bibliog.

The subject of this study is the revival of the Lateran in the second half of the 16th century and the architectural and decorative projects carried out during the reign of Pope Clement VIII (1592-1605). Initially an ambitious renovation of the entire Lateran complex was envisaged but finally only the transept of the Basilica of San Giovanni in Laterano (the *Nave Clementina*) was decorated and it forms one of the most representative projects of the Counter-Reformation period. This study includes a detailed examination of the iconography of the decoration, which was conceived in response to three concepts: the Lateran's venerable history as the spiritual centre of the Christian world until the 15th century, the function of the transept to honour the Eucharist, and the celebrations of the Holy Year in 1600.

698   **Roma: chiese, conventi, chiostri: progetto per un inventario, 313-1925.** (Rome: churches, convents, cloisters: a proposal for an inventory, 313-1925.)
Ferruccio Lombardi.   Rome: Edilstampa, 1993. 492p. maps. bibliog.

This work includes entries for 416 buildings, 314 of which are in the twenty-one *rioni* within the walls. They are divided into twenty-two sections by *rione* (the *rione* Prati is outside the walls), the Vatican, and the outskirts. The entry for each building includes historical and artistic data. The volume also contains an index by *rione*, a general index by type of building, as well as G. B. Nolli's 1748 map of Rome and maps of the *rioni* after 1870. There are over 800 colour photographs, plans of the buildings and hundreds of prints by Piranesi, Rossini and others.

699   **Roma sacra: guida alle chiese della Città Eterna.** (Sacred Rome: a guide to the churches of the Eternal City.)
Edited by Antonio Federico Caiola, Oreste Ferrari, Sergio Guarino. Rome: Elio De Rosa, 1995- .

This work is projected to be in fifty parts, each published as a separate fascicle covering the churches of a particular area of the city. Each part contains articles on ten to fifteen churches and each entry includes the history of the building and a description of its architecture and the works of art it houses. The text is accompanied by excellent photographs (several of them in colour) of works of art which are often little known and rarely reproduced. There is also a bibliography, adding to the usefulness of the publication.

700 Rome's historic churches.

Lilian Gunton. London: George Allen & Unwin, 1969. 220p. bibliog.

A guide to the stational churches of Rome, i.e. the churches included in the practice of inter-parochial visitations that started in the 6th century, in which members of different parishes met in a pre-named church (the *collecta*) and walked in a procession led by the Pope to a further church, where they attended a communal service. The order of the churches in which the 'station' was to be held at Lent was fixed by Pope Gregory the Great (590-604). The forty-five short chapters (one for each church) follow the order of the liturgical sequence in which the churches were visited, from S. Sabina on Ash Wednesday to S. Maria Maggiore on Easter Sunday. Some churches became Lenten stations much later, replacing other churches as, for example, S. Agostino after the destruction in the 15th century of the church of S. Trypho. Each chapter includes information on the name of the church, architectural features, decoration, works of art, restorations, and other points of interest. Most chapters also include a plan of the church. This is a well-planned and useful work which, unfortunately, contains errors that should have been spotted at the editing stage (for example, *theokotos* instead of *theotokos*; a view of S. Paolo fuori le Mura after the fire of 1823 is described as an engraving by Paranesi [*sic*]) and, worse, factual errors (S. Giovanni in Laterano is described as taking its name after St John the Baptist rather than after both St John the Baptist and the Evangelist; in the same chapter there is some confusion between Alessandro Galilei, the architect of the 18th-century façade of the church and Galileo Galilei).

701 San Giovanni in Laterano.

Edited by Carlo Pietrangeli. Florence, Italy: Nardini, 1990. 336p. bibliog. (Chiese Monumentali d'Italia.)

This volume examines the basilica of S. Giovanni in Laterano, the Cathedral of Rome, and the monuments closely related to it – the Baptistery and its chapels, the Cloisters by the Vassalletto family, the obelisk and its fountain. Originally dedicated to Christ the Saviour, the dedication to St John the Baptist and the Evangelist dates from the time of Pope Gregory I (590-604). The introduction gives a brief history and examines the changing fortunes of the basilica from the 4th century to the present. It is followed by an examination of the prehistory of the site, which makes use of archaeological evidence about the surrounding area, its buildings and monuments – the houses of the Laterani (*Aedes Laterani*), the *Horti* of Domitia Lucilla (the mother of Marcus Aurelius), the *Domus* of Fausta and the *Castra nova equitum singularium*, the barracks that occupied part of the site on which the basilica was later built. The following chapters examine the architecture of the basilica and works of art it housed at different periods of its long history, beginning with the 4th-century Constantinian basilica and its development over the next five centuries, and continuing with its rebuilding after the earthquake of 896 which destroyed its entire central nave, the painted decoration of the 13th and 14th centuries (which includes a fragment of a fresco by Giotto, as well as the great mosaic cycle in the apse), the medieval sculptures (popes were buried here until the 14th century and there are notable sepulchral monuments including works by Arnolfo di Cambio), the Renaissance (the frescoes by Gentile da Fabriano and Pisanello, destroyed by Borromini in the 17th century, have been among the greatest losses in the basilica's history), and from the 16th century to the present (including Borromini's radical renovations in the 17th century and Alessandro Galilei's Corsini Chapel in 1734 and the new façade in 1735). A separate chapter looks at Roman monuments re-used in the Basilica (among them the statue of Constantine – transferred here from the Capitoline Hill, the sarcophagus of St Helena, and the bronze doors from the Curia in the Forum). The final chapters examine the Treasure (in the Museo di S. Giovanni), the Organ and the Obelisk (the oldest and most imposing in Rome). The work is lavishly illustrated and the colour plates are outstanding.

702 **Studio di pittura, scoltura, et architettura, nelle chiese di Roma, 1674-1763.** (A study of the paintings, sculptures, and architecture in Roman churches, 1674-1763.)
Filippo Titi, edited by Bruno Contardi and Serena Romano. Florence, Italy: Centro Di, [1987]. 2 vols. (331p., 421p.).

The Abbate Filippo Titi (1639-1702) was a noted cartographer but his main claim to fame is this work, the first great guide to the art treasures in Roman churches. It combines new information about the works described with knowledge of earlier guides to Rome and Giovanni Baglione's *Le vite de' pittori, scultori e architetti moderni* (1642). It was first published in 1674 and updated editions (which included references to recently executed works of art) came out in 1675, 1686 and, after Titi's death, in 1708, 1721, and 1763. Giovanni Bottari was mainly responsible for the updating of the sixth and final (and much augmented) edition of the work, which included numerous corrections and descriptions of the contents of palaces and villas. The sixth edition also reflects Bottari's admiration of earlier Italian art and his interest in contemporary classicism. The present work is a critical edition of the six editions of Titi's guide. The second volume provides 1,630 illustrations of works mentioned in the text and an introductory essay examines Titi's life and work.

703 **Umanesimo e primo Rinascimento in S. Maria del Popolo.**
(Humanism and early Renaissance in S. Maria del Popolo.)
Edited by Roberto Cannatà (et al.). Rome: De Luca, 1981. 112p.
bibliog. (Il Quattrocento a Roma e nel Lazio.)

This is the catalogue of one of the twelve exhibitions held under the general title *Il Quattrocento a Roma e nel Lazio*. It does not include separate entries for individual items in the exhibition. It is, instead, divided into chapters, written by different scholars, each describing a different area of artistic activity – the architecture of the church, its sculptures, paintings (including wall paintings), and a reconstruction of Andrea Bregno's high altarpiece. There are also separate sections on the major 15th-century chapels in the church – the Della Rovere, Cybo, Costa, and Mellini chapels, as well as Pinturicchio's decorations.

704 **Der Vaticanische Palast in seiner Entwicklung bis zur mitte des XV. Jahrhunderts.** (The Vatican Palace and its development to the middle of the fifteenth century.)
Franz Ehrle, Hermann Egger. Vatican City: Biblioteca apostolica vaticana, 1935. 147p. (Studi e Documenti per la Storia del Palazzo Apostolico Vaticano, vol. 2.)

A history of the architecture of the Vatican Palace to the death of Nicholas V in 1455. The palace is an enormous, sprawling complex of buildings. The first buildings date back to the 5th century but the extension of the complex to the north of St Peter's began when, after the Saracen invasion of 846, Pope Leo IV built a wall enclosing the whole hill as protection against future invasions. Nicholas III Orsini (1277-80) was the first pope to make the palace his residence, enlarging and remodelling the existing buildings and linking the palace through a passageway to the Castel S. Angelo. The second part of the volume is a detailed examination of the Chapel of St Nicholas (Cappella Niccolina), decorated by Fra Angelico during the reign of Nicholas V.

Money, Coins and Medals

705 Annali della Zecca di Roma. (Annals of the Mint of Rome.)
Edoardo Martinori. Rome: Istituto italiano di numismatica, 1917-22.
24 fascicles. bibliog.

The series of papal coins issued by the Mint of Rome began with the return of the papacy from Avignon in 1377 and continued until 1870, the end of the temporal power of the Pope. Until 1439, coins were also issued by the Roman Senate and the papal coins themselves usually contained some reference to the Senate and the people. With the monetary reform of Pope Eugenius IV in 1439, all mention of the latter disappeared. This work consists of separate chapters for each pope, each introduced by a summary of the main events of his reign (many of which had a bearing on coinage) followed by a section on the Mint, its organization, its officials and engravers, and an examination, in chronological order, of all the known coins from the period with reproductions of their obverse and reverse sides.

706 La medaglia annuale dei romani pontefici, da Paolo V a Paolo VI, 1605-1967. (The annual medal of the Roman popes, from Paul V to Paul VI, 1605-1967.)
Franco Bartolotti. Rimini, Italy: Cosmi, 1967. 500p.

The *annuale* was a medal issued on 29 June, the Feast of S. Peter and S. Paul. It had a portrait of the pope on the obverse while the reverse depicted the single, most important event of the year. This is a catalogue of all the medals issued between 1605 and 1967. Each entry includes a reproduction of both sides, a transcription of the motto, information about the engraver and an explanation of the allegory or event depicted.

707 La moneta dei papi e degli Stati pontifici. (The coins of the popes and of the Papal States.)
Francesco Muntoni. Rome: Urania, 1996. 2nd ed. 4 vols. bibliog.

This detailed catalogue aims to provide a comprehensive and up-to-date survey of papal coinage, and improve on previous catalogues which contained various inaccuracies and lacunae. Its preparation entailed extensive research in private and public collections. The introduction describes the various monetary systems adopted over twelve centuries (from

262

Hadrian I) and the monetary reforms carried out by individual popes. The descriptions are divided into five sections: coins issued by popes, coins issued by antipopes, coins issued anonymously, coins issued by the Roman Senate, and coins issued during occupations and revolts. 240 types of previously unrecorded coins are published here for the first time, as well as numerous variants of known types. The locations of coins of extreme rarity are indicated in the catalogue. In each section, coins are listed under the issuing mint, beginning with coins issued in Rome and followed by those of the provinces, listed in alphabetical order. Within each area, the arrangement is by type of metal and in decreasing value and, within each type, by legend. The catalogue includes a glossary, a bibliography, a general index and several other indexes (saints, legends, coiners, etc.).

708 *Roma resurgens*: **papal medals from the age of the Baroque.**
Nathan T. Whitman, in collaboration with John L. Varriano. Ann Arbor, Michigan: University of Michigan Museum of Art, 1983. 188p. bibliog.

This exhibition catalogue examines the historical and artistic importance of the series of commemorative medals issued by the Vatican from the 1540s – when medals for the first time were used as instruments of state propaganda, celebrating victories, proclaiming doctrines, and celebrating urban renewal – to the middle of the 18th century. Papal medals are unique in that they were issued uninterruptedly for several centuries and are distinguished by their high artistic quality. Their interest is both historical and art historical (as miniature relief sculptures issued in small editions of gold, silver or bronze). Various types of medals are examined: the *annuali*, issued on 29 June, the feast day of Saint Peter and Saint Paul and commemorating, on the reverse, the single most important event of the year; medals celebrating a *possessio* (the Pope taking possession of the cathedral of the Lateran as bishop of Rome); those celebrating Holy Years or Jubilees; and those commemorating special events. The catalogue also examines the problem of reissues (the dies or *coni* were not subject to the rigid controls applied to coinage and remained in the possession of the medalist or his successors without any restrictions as to their use; a series of high quality reissues were, moreover, produced by the papal mint [the *zecca*] in the 19th century) and of *mules* (the arbitrary obverse/reverse combinations in reissues, the results of substitutions for badly worn sides). 172 medals are catalogued, each entry reproducing both obverse and reverse sides, and including a description of their iconography and a transcription of their inscriptions, a note on strike and style, a explanation of the historical event depicted and, finally, bibliographical references. There is also a biographical list of medalists.

Music

709 Alessandro Scarlatti: an introduction to his operas.
Donald Jay Grout. Berkeley, Los Angeles; London: University of
California Press, 1979. 161p.

Alessandro Scarlatti's works were produced between 1679 and 1725. A prolific composer in all
musical forms, he is best known today for his vocal works, especially his cantatas and operas, of
which he composed some 700 and 114 respectively. Half of his operas have entirely disappeared
and the author of this study, who is also the editor of the collected edition of Scarlatti's operas
which is in progress, estimates that between thirty and thirty-five of them are salvageable. He
presents here a general survey of the composer's operatic output, beginning with an examination
of the *dramma per musica* (early opera) in Scarlatti's time, its form and content, the relationship
between composer, librettist, and singers, and performance practices of 18th-century Italian
opera. This is followed by an account of Scarlatti's early years in Rome, where he was sent from
his native Palermo in 1672 at the age of twelve, the social milieu in which he moved, his patrons
(including Cardinals Benedetto Pamphilj and Pietro Ottoboni, and Queen Christina of Sweden),
and theatrical life in the city. Musical influences on the young composer are also examined,
together with the operas produced in Rome to great acclaim between 1679 and 1684, the date of
his move to Naples where he remained until 1702 when he returned to Rome and the renewed
patronage of Cardinal Ottoboni. Scarlatti continued to produce operas both for Naples and Rome
to the end of his life and though he is sometimes thought of as the father of Neapolitan opera, he
is here considered a Roman composer too, as he began and ended his professional life in Rome
and spent some of his more active and productive years there.

710 Alessandro Stradella, 1639-1682: his life and music.
Carolyn Gianturco. Oxford: Clarendon Press, 1994. 347p. bibliog.

An account of the sensational life of Alessandro Stradella (1639-82) and his original and varied
output. Stradella became famous in Rome during the pontificate of Pope Clement IX as a
composer of *concerti grossi*, oratorios, cantatas, and operas for the Tordinona theatre. Stradella
had to flee from Rome in 1677 after a scandal concerning his involvement as a go-between in
an arranged marriage. Over the following five years he lived in Venice, from where he fled with
the mistress of a Venetian nobleman, Turin and, finally, Genoa, where he was assassinated by
hired *bravi* (thugs), perhaps the victim of a vendetta (there had been a similar attempt on his life

in Turin). Stradella was a prolific composer. The second part of this study is an examination of his work, with separate chapters on his cantatas, theatre music, oratorios, arias, duets, madrigals, sacred vocal music, instrumental music, and a pedagogical piece. An appendix provides a list of the works (including lost works) and a second appendix presents Stradella's extant writings (letters, opera dedications, motet texts) in the original and in English translation.

711 Berlioz Benvenuto Cellini.
Léon de Wailly, Auguste Barbier, literary and musical commentary by Hugh MacDonald. Paris: L'avant-scène, 1991. 121p. bibliog. (Opéra, 142.)

Berlioz, who was later to write his own *Mémoires* (1848), was profoundly impressed by Benvenuto Cellini's *Autobiography*, which inspired his first opera – first performed in 1838. The work is in two acts and four tableaux and is set in Rome during the carnival of 1532. Its plot includes a love story between Cellini and Teresa (an invented character), the daughter of Giacomo Balducci, the papal treasurer, and the sculptor's struggles against officialdom and professional rivalry with Fieramosca (another invented character). The second scene of the opera is a magnificent evocation of the Roman Carnival. It takes place in Piazza Colonna on the Corso on Shrove Tuesday and includes crowds of carnival revellers, a pantomime performance, a goldsmiths' chorus and the famous Roman Carnival (better known as an independent orchestral overture). It ends with the cannon shot at Castel S. Angelo at midnight signalling the end of carnival, the ensuing blowing out of the *moccoli* (candles) and darkness proving providential to our hero. The climax of the work is Cellini's triumphant casting of the bronze statue of Perseus, which is transposed from the Florence of Cosimo I de' Medici to the Rome of Clement VII, in a foundry set up in the Colosseum, with the operation watched by the Pope himself. This edition includes the libretto by Léon de Wailly and Auguste Barbier with a detailed literary and musical commentary, as well as introductory essays discussing the genesis of the work and its libretto, its depiction of the artist as hero, and its initial failure but also its influence on Wagner's *The Mastersingers of Nurenberg*. There is also a discussion of recordings and a performance history with full casts.

712 Berlioz. (Vol. 1. The making of an artist, 1803-1832. Vol. 2. Servitude and greatness, 1832-1869.)
David Cairns. Harmondsworth, England: Allen Lane, the Penguin Press, 1999. 2 vols. (586p., 906p.).

Having won the Prix de Rome in 1830, Berlioz was required to spend two years as a pensioner at the Villa Medici, since 1803 the home of the French Academy in Rome. Though he was unhappy to leave Paris for a musical backwater such as Rome, his stay in Rome was to have a profound effect on his art. The relative freedom he enjoyed at the Villa (his only official obligation was to submit a composition every year) enabled him to explore the city and its surrounding countryside, and the impressions from his walks and rides in the Campagna were to reappear in a number of later works, especially *Les Troyens* (The Trojans) and *Harold en Italie* (Harold in Italy), while *Benvenuto Cellini* was inspired by the adventures of the Florentine sculptor in Rome. This excellent account of the composer's early years ends with his return to France after his fourteen-month stay in the Eternal City and forms an essential companion to the composer's memoirs.

713   'Cantate spirituali e morali', with a description of the papal sacred
       cantata tradition for Christmas 1676-1740.
       Carolyn Gianturco.   In: *Music & letters*, vol. lxxiii (1992), pp. 1-31.

This piece examines the tradition of the papal Christmas Eve cantata performed at the Palazzo
Apostolico on Christmas Eve between the First Vespers of Christmas and Matins. The
performance was attended by the Pope, cardinals, members of the papal court and the Roman
aristocracy, and any foreign rulers or diplomats visiting Rome at the time. A strict protocol was
attached to the preparations for this event. The choice of poet, composer and performers,
together with the arrangements for the printing of the libretto, which was distributed to the
audience, were the responsibility of the Reverenda Camera Apostolica, as were the costs of the
lavish banquet and accommodation for visiting cardinals. This tradition lasted for sixty-five
years until Pope Benedict XIV abandoned it in 1740. As well as discussing the social
background to this important social, and uniquely Roman, function, this article also provides
full documentation for almost all the years it took place, listing all works performed and, in a
separate appendix, passages from contemporary accounts of the event. Though the librettists are
relatively unknown, the composers include Alessandro Scarlatti (who set the cantatas for 1695,
1705-1707), Domenico Scarlatti (1714 and 1717), and Antonio Caldara (1713). It also discusses
other types of non-secular cantatas performed elsewhere in Rome.

714   The composer Michelangelo Rossi: a 'diligent fantasy maker' in
       seventeenth-century Rome.
       Catherine Moore.   New York; London: Garland Publishing, 1993. 201p.
       (Outstanding Dissertations in Music from British Universities.)

Michelangelo Rossi (1601-56) was one of the leading composers of keyboard music in 17th-
century Italy. A pupil of Frescobaldi, he was equally renowned during his lifetime as a violinist
(he was nicknamed the 'Michelangelo del violino') and as a composer. His compositions
include works in three genres then at different stages of their development: opera, in its infancy;
keyboard toccata, at its height; and madrigal, in its decline. Though this study is predominantly
a musicological study of Rossi's work, it also examines the composer's life in Rome and his
relationship with the Barberini family in the 1630s – *Erminia sul Giordano* (Erminia by the
banks of the river Jordan), his one extant opera, was spectacularly staged at the Barberini Palace
in 1633 with sets designed by Gianlorenzo Bernini and with Rossi himself cast as a violin-
playing Apollo – and the Pamphilj family in the 1640s and 1650s.

715   Corelli: his life, his work.
       Marc Pincherle, translated from the French by Hubert E. M. Russell.
       New York: W. W. Norton and Company, 1956.

Arcangelo Corelli (1653-1713) acquired great fame during his lifetime, both as composer and
violinist and also as teacher and director of instrumental ensembles. He also exercised a great
deal of influence in matters of musical form, style and technique. Though born at Fusignano, he
spent most of his mature years in Rome where his presence is attested from 1675 and where his
patrons included Cardinal Benedetto Pamphilj, Queen Christina of Sweden and Cardinal Pietro
Ottoboni. This study, originally published in 1933 and revised and expanded in 1954, is
astonishingly (both in view of the composer's fame and the popularity of Baroque music in
recent years) the most recent monograph on the artist. As well as a detailed study of Corelli's
works (which consists of only six collections of instrumental music and a few other authentic
works) it includes an account of the composer's life and the various anecdotes about it (for
example, his supposed stay in France, where he aroused Lully's jealousy).

716 Giacomo Puccini *Tosca*.

Mosco Carner.   Cambridge, England: Cambridge University Press, 1985. 165p. (Cambridge Opera Handbooks.)

Puccini's work is a story of love, lust and politics. Its action takes place in Rome in June 1800 shortly after the collapse of the Roman Republic. Its main characters are Tosca, an opera singer, Cavaradossi, her lover, a painter with liberal sympathies, and Scarpia, the sadistic chief of police who finally tricks Tosca. Each of the opera's three acts takes place in a well-known Roman location – act 1 in the church of S. Andrea della Valle, act 2 in the Palazzo Farnese, and act 3 in the Castel S. Angelo. Appropriately, the work was first performed at the Teatro Costanzi (now Teatro dell'Opera) on 14 January 1900 and has become one of the most popular works in the operatic repertoire. This volume includes articles on Sardou's original play and a comparison between the play and the opera, the genesis of the opera, a discussion of its first production and critical history (it has been famously described as 'a shabby little shocker'), a detailed synopsis, and an analysis of the work's style and technique and its musical and dramatic structure.

717   The history of a Baroque opera: Alessandro Scarlatti's *Gli equivoci nel sembiante*.

Frank A. D'Accone.   New York: Pendragon Press, 1985. 197p. (Monographs in Musicology, 3.)

Gli equivoci nel sembiante (Mistaken appearances) was the first of Alessandro Scarlatti's 114 operas. It was premiered in Rome during the carnival season of 1679 and its great success launched the career of the eighteen-year-old composer. This detailed study of the work makes use of contemporary sources (for example, the *Avvisi di Roma*, broadsheets providing news and gossip) and recently discovered documents which make possible the reconstruction of its early and subsequent performance. The author gives a lively account of the circumstances in which it was first performed, during the reign of Pope Innocent XI Odescalchi, who was ferociously opposed to all forms of staged entertainment, prohibiting all performances before a paying public. Scarlatti's work was given as a 'private' theatrical entertainment in the house of the architect Giambattista Contini (perhaps a relation of the librettist of the work, Domenico Filippo Contini), with designs by Pietro Filippo and Domenico Bernini, two of Gianlorenzo's sons. Later performances given during Lent, violating the solemnity of the penitential season, caused a great scandal. Scarlatti counted among his supporters Queen Christina, whose household he was soon to join as *maestro di cappella* (director of music). The work was revived several times over the next twenty years, both in Rome (at the Palazzo Farnese) and other cities and with different librettos (listed in an appendix).

718   A history of the oratorio.

Howard E. Smither.   Chapel Hill, North Carolina: the University of North Carolina Press, 1987. 3 vols.

The first and third volumes of this magisterial study deal with the Italian oratorio, a musical genre that evolved in Counter-Reformation Rome, taking its name from St Philip Neri's Congregazione dell'Oratorio (Congregation of the Oratory), its history and social context. Volume one looks at the Baroque era and investigates antecedents and origins of the oratorio in staged and unstaged dramatic genres. It gives a detailed account of St Philip Neri (1515-95) and the Congregation of the Oratory, which he founded and which was officially recognized as a religious order in 1575. The informal meetings, or sacred exercises, included music (intended to attract people and also to provide edifying entertainment), eventually using narrative and dramatic texts. The development of the genre in Italy between *c.* 1640-1720 is also examined, as are the differences between Latin and Italian oratorio and their respective audiences (the former has a more exclusive, aristocratic audience). There is a survey of a number of oratories (such as S. Girolamo della Carità and the Oratorio del SS. Crocifisso) and their special features, as well as separate chapters discussing the work of notable composers active in Rome, such as Domenico Mazzocchi, Marco Marazzoli, Luigi Rossi and, especially, Giacomo Carissimi. Volume two examines oratorio in England and Northern Europe and though Rome features in the examination of Italian oratorio during the classical era, in volume three, the city had by then ceased to be the epicentre of this particular genre.

719 Jesuits and music: a study of the musicians connected with the German College in Rome during the 17th century and of their activities in Northern Europe.
Thomas D. Culley. Rome: Jesuit Historical Institute; St Louis, Missouri: St Louis University, 1970. 401p. bibliog. (Sources and Studies for the History of the Jesuits, vol. 2.)

A study about the students and singers at the German College in Rome between 1630 and 1674 and their later activities in other European countries. The period covered is that of Giacomo Carissimi's tenure of the post of *maestro di cappella*, the apogee of the college's fame and influence as a musical centre. The work is divided into three sections. The first describes the development of a programme of liturgical music in the period between 1573 and 1600 and the activities of the musicians who directed (the *maestri di cappella*) and performed it (the singers and organists), their musical training and performance practice, and the reputation and influence of the college. The following two sections examine the development of this tradition in the years between 1600 and 1630, and 1630 and 1674.

720 The motets of Carissimi.
Andrew V. Jones. Ann Arbor, Michigan: UMI Research Press, 1982. 2 vols. (371p., 523p.). (British Studies in Musicology, 5.)

Giacomo Carissimi is better known today as a composer of oratorios and cantatas, whereas his motets have remained in relative obscurity. Moreover, the lack of autograph manuscripts (which were largely destroyed when the Jesuit order was dissolved in 1773) has created various problems of authenticity, to which are added problems of definition, as there is disagreement among scholars as to which sacred works by the composer are 'oratorios' and which are 'motets'. This monograph, based on the author's doctoral thesis, attempts to distinguish between the two genres and establish their different functions and characteristic musical features. It suggests an approximate chronology for seventy-two motets and offers a transcription of thirty-three motets believed to be authentic. It also includes a biography of the composer, explaining his duties as teacher, composer and choir trainer at the Collegio germanico in Rome, where he was *maestro di cappella* (director of music) for forty-five years (1629-74), an analysis of his style and technique, and appendices of the printed and manuscript sources. See also Graham Dixon's *Carissimi* (Oxford; New York: Oxford University Press, 1986. 84p. [Oxford Studies of Composers, 20]).

721 Le muse galanti: la musica a Roma nel Settecento. (The gallant muses: music in Rome in the eighteenth century.)
Edited by Bruno Cagli. Rome: Istituto della Enciclopedia italiana, 1985. 187p.

A collection of revised and expanded versions of papers originally read at a conference on the theatre in 18th-century Rome. They cover a wide range of subjects related to musical theatrical life in Rome. They include: Nino Pirotta on stagings of Metastasio's works in Rome; Lowell Lindgren on operas and oratorios by Alessandro Scarlatti and other composers performed in Rome between 1660 and 1725 (with a detailed appendix listing performances of Scarlatti's works); Ellen T. Harris on Handel's Roman cantatas; Rodolfo Celletti on some famous singers in Rome and the works in which they performed; Letizia Norci Cagiano de Azevedo on French travellers (De Brosses); Pierluigi Petrobelli on the caricatures of musicians by Pier Leone Ghezzi; Bruno Cagli on the relationship between music production and the papal government; and Giancarlo Rostirolla on music publishing, an important contribution which includes an index with biographical entries for music printers, booksellers, engravers and composers-publishers active in Rome during this period, each entry accompanied by bibliographical references.

722 Music and spectacle in Baroque Rome: Barberini patronage under Urban VIII.

Frederick Hammond.   New Haven, Connecticut; London: Yale University Press, 1994. 393p. bibliog.

A wide-ranging examination of the Barberini family's patronage of music and spectacles involving music during the reign of Urban VIII (1623-44). It is divided into three parts. The first part (*Mirabili Congiuntura*: the Barberini and their program) provides an overview of Roman patronage during the first half of the 17th century, and includes a wealth of information about the social, financial and religious background that governed the commissioning of works of art. It also introduces the personalities of the *dramatis personae* – Maffeo Barberini (Urban VIII) and his nephews – and their artistic interests. It finally looks at works commissioned by the family – the Barberini Palace and its frescoes celebrating the virtues of the Pope and his family, the completion of St Peter's and the Tomb of Urban VIII, the Barberini Tapestries – and considers the place of music in Barberini patronage. The second part examines the musical establishments of the Barberini, their collections of musical instruments, the musicians they employed and the events they performed for and, finally, the academies and their repertory. The third part is a detailed account of the musical events sponsored by the papal nephews. These included the *feste* (sacred, secular and popular festivals and celebrations, including the Roman Carnival), the musical patronage of churches, and the Cappella Pontificia. The last two chapters concentrate on Baroque opera, its origins and development, its political, social and artistic context, and the mechanics of its performance. The circumstances of the production, the symbolic nature and the music of the various operas sponsored by the Barberini between 1628 and 1644 are examined in great detail. An appendix provides a year-by-year conspectus of the most important musico-festal events of the reign of Urban VIII.

723 The New Grove Italian Baroque masters: Monteverdi, Frescobaldi, Cavalli, Corelli, A. Scarlatti, Vivaldi, D. Scarlatti.

Denis Arnold (et al.).   London: Macmillan, 1984. 376p. (The New Grove Composer Biography Series.)

This volume includes the entries from the *New Grove Dictionary of Music* on the following composers who dominated the musical scene of 17th and 18th-century Rome: Girolamo Frescobaldi (by Anthony Newcomb); Arcangelo Corelli (by Michael Talbot); and Alessandro Scarlatti (by Donald J. Grout). Though Claudio Monteverdi never worked in Rome he, nevertheless, composed one of the great operas with a Roman subject – *L'incoronazione di Poppea* (The coronation of Poppea). Each entry examines the composer's life, personality and reputation, and works, and each also contains a list of works and a bibliography.

724   **Papal music and musicians in late medieval and Renaissance Rome.**
Edited by Richard Sherr.   Oxford, England: Clarendon Press;
Washington, DC: Library of Congress, 1998. 367p.

The conference at which most of the twelve contributions included in this volume were presented was held in the Library of Congress in 1993 in conjunction with the exhibition *Rome Reborn*. They cover the period from the re-establishment of the papacy in the city in the late 14th century to the end of the 16th century and they are divided into three sections: music for the Pope and his chapel, the papal choir as institution, and studies of individual composers and singers who were members of the papal choir, including its most famous member, Pier Luigi da Palestrina. Contributions include: Margaret Bent, 'Early papal motets', a survey of 14th and 15th-century motets written specifically for popes, in which she analyses texts and extant music and suggests possible reasons for their composition; Giuliano Di Bacco and John Nádas, 'The papal chapels and Italian sources of polyphony during the Great Schism', in which the authors identify a number of previously unknown singers and provide new information on two important composers who worked in Rome at the time, Johannes Ciconia and Antonio Zacara da Teramo; and Jeffrey Dean and Mitchell Brauner, who survey the repertory of the papal singers in the late 15th century and the 16th century, a period that witnessed an interest in contemporary large-scale settings of masses and motets and a number of important composers (Josquin, Morales, Arcadelt, etc.) as members of the papal choir.

725   **Papal patronage and the music of St. Peter's, 1380-1513.**
Christopher A. Reynolds.   Berkeley, California: University of California Press, 1995. 456p. bibliog.

This monograph gives a detailed account of the music associated with St Peter's from the final return of the papacy from Avignon in 1420 to the death of Julius II in 1513. It traces the policies of various popes – notably those of Nicholas V (1447-55), Sixtus IV (1471-84) and Julius II (1503-13) – to make the Vatican Palace the principal papal residence and St Peter's the principal basilica in Rome. These included the establishment of the Sistine Chapel in around 1475, the private chapel of Sixtus IV, and the founding by Julius II of the Cappella Giulia at St Peter's and his grandiose plans to demolish the old basilica and replace it with an imposing new structure symbolizing the splendour of the Roman church. The work is divided into three parts. Part one looks at the singers and organists who served at St Peter's during this period and includes a description of a manuscript choirbook (San Pietro B 80), dating from around 1475, which shows the musical repertoire performed in the basilica. It contains masses, motets and hymns, mostly by Northern composers such as Dufay, Binchois, Dunstable, and Josquin. Part two is a detailed examination of the contents of this choirbook, and it provides attributions to anonymous works. Part three considers the importance of Northern singers in St Peter's and their influence on Italian secular and religious music and also looks at the gradual shift from Northern to Italian patronage in the 16th century. There are five appendices with information, taken from the Vatican Archives, about music and musicians.

726   **Prince of music: Palestrina and his world.**
R. J. Stove.   Sydney: Quakers Hill Press, 1990. 120p.

A short biography of Pierluigi da Palestrina (1525/6-1594), one of the great figures of the Counter-Reformation, and a study of his music. Palestrina's numerous papal appointments included that of *maestro di cappella* at St Peter's *Cappella Giulia* (1551-55), a post from which he was dismissed when a decree passed during Pope Paul IV's reign forbade the employment of married men in the papal chapel, and at S. Giovanni in Laterano (1555-60). In 1561 he took up a more congenial appointment at S. Maria Maggiore where he remained until 1567 when he entered the private service of Ippolito II d'Este at Tivoli. He remained there until his return to the Cappella Giulia in 1571. Palestrina's output was enormous – it includes 104 securely attributed masses, 375 motets, and 140 madrigals. A selective discography is included. See also Henry Coates, *Palestrina* (London: J. M. Dent, 1938. 252p. [The Master Musicians]). Palestrina's life and work inspired Hans Pfitzner's opera – see *Pfitzner's Palestrina: the 'musical legend' and its background* by Owen Toller, with a preface by Dietrich Fischer-Dieskau (London: Toccata Press, 1997. 310p. [Other operas, 1]).

727 Rome: the power of patronage.

Malcolm Boyd. In: *Music and society: the late Baroque era, from the 1680s to 1740*. Edited by George J. Buelow. Englewood Cliffs, New Jersey: Prentice Hall, 1993, p. 39-65.

This overview gives a clear account of the various forms of music patronage in 17th- and 18th-century Rome. As in the previous volume in this series, the tensions between sacred and secular music are underlined, manifesting themselves, for example, in the papal interference in secular music-making, especially opera, with periods of opposition alternating with periods of encouragement depending on the personality and interests of the reigning pope. The section on church music looks at the Cappella Sistina, the upholder of tradition and Tridentine tenets, and the Congregazione (later Accademia) di S. Cecilia, which supervised musical standards in the city's churches and controlled the activities of musicians. The patronage of ecclesiastical and lay aristocracy is surveyed, looking at: the contribution of three cardinals – Carlo Colonna (1665-1754), Benedetto Pamphilj (1653-1730), and Pietro Ottoboni (1667-1740) – who sponsored numerous operas, cantatas and oratorios, often from composers who were *maestri di cappella* in their households; exiled monarchs, such as Queen Christina of Sweden and Queen Maria Casimira of Poland; and noblemen, such as Prince Francesco Maria Ruspoli. The work of the academies and their role in the development of various musical forms such as the sonata, the concerto and the cantata is also examined, as is the development during this period of the oratorio, the *serenata* (a secular composition, performed in the open, usually with spectacular forces and effects), opera and, finally, the opening of the first public theatres in Rome (the Tordinona, Alibert, Valle, and Argentina), their vicissitudes, special features and repertoire.

728 Rome: sacred and secular.

Silke Leopold. In: *Music and society: the early Baroque era, from the late 16th century to the 1660s*. Edited by Curtis Price. Englewood Cliffs, New Jersey: Prentice Hall, 1993, p. 49-74.

In this article, Leopold provides a good overview of music patronage in Rome from the years after the Council of Trent to the death of Queen Christina in 1689 and the tension between spiritual and temporal influences in music, which was far greater in Rome than in any other European city. It explains the importance of church music in the post-Tridentine attempt to renew the Catholic Church – hence the excellence of the choirs of the Cappella Sistina, Cappella Giulia (at St Peter's), the Cappella Pia (S. Maria Maggiore) and the Cappella Liberiana (S. Giovanni in Laterano) – and how innovations in sacred music were introduced by the Jesuits, who recognized the importance of didactic drama as useful propaganda, and the Oratorians, who made music a basic component of their meetings. The musical patronage of the Barberini family between 1623 and 1644 forms the core of the discussion. Urban VIII Barberini was a lover of music and his poetry was set to music by composers such as Johann Hieronymus Kapsberger and Domenico Mazzocchi who worked in his entourage. During his long reign (1623-44), the Barberini Palace became the musical centre of Rome. Lavish spectacles were staged in its theatre (the first in Rome), which was inaugurated in 1632 with Stefano Landi's *San Alessio*, the libretto of which was written by Giulio Rospigliosi, the future Pope Clement IX. In the years that followed the death of Urban VIII, secular music was on the wane whereas a new sacred style was developed using a *cappella* polyphony with multiple choirs. The arrival in Rome of Queen Christina of Sweden in 1656 led to a revival of secular music, her household becoming the centre of Rome's artistic and intellectual life for more than thirty years. Among the composers who worked for her were Giacomo Carissimi, Alessandro Stradella, Alessandro Scarlatti and Arcangelo Corelli. It was also thanks to her efforts that the Teatro Tordinona became the first public opera house in Rome. After her death, musical patronage continued through cardinals Benedetto Pamphilj and Pietro Ottoboni, who dominated Roman musical life in the last years of the 17th century.

729 Rossini a Roma – Rossini e Roma. (Rossini in Rome – Rossini and Rome.)
Edited by Francesco Paolo Russo. Rome: Fondazione Marco Besso, 1992. 251p. (Collana della Fondazione Marco Besso, 11.)

Papers presented at a conference organized by the Fondazione Marco Besso in 1992, the bicentenary of Gioacchino Rossini's birth, on the composer's Roman sojourns between 1816 and 1822 and his relationship with Rome. It includes studies on the following: the works Rossini wrote for Rome (*Torvaldo e Dorliska*, *The Barber of Seville*, *La Cenerentola*, *Adelaide di Borgogna*, *Matilde di Shabran*) and the stagings he supervised of other works; the opera *Demetrio e Polibio*, first performed at the Teatro Valle on 18 May 1812, the composition of which may date back to 1808, and the role played by the tenor-impresario Domenico Mombelli in its success; an unpublished cantata Rossini composed in honour of Pope Pius IX in 1846 after the latter's edict granting amnesty to all political prisoners, for which he reused pieces from four earlier operas composed between 1817 and 1826 and which had long disappeared from the operatic repertory, adapting them to their new context; the relationship of Rossini with the three musical academies active in Rome between 1822 and 1842 (Congregazione e Accademia di S. Cecilia, Accademia Filarmonica, and Accademia 'Antifilarmonica') and the key role these academies played in the performance of his works in Rome, especially in cases where censorship had prevented their performance in Roman theatres (*William Tell*); reviews of first nights of Rossini operas in contemporary Roman newspapers (1812-21); Rossini and G. G. Belli – the poet, Rossini's contemporary, was a keen opera- and theatre-goer and though Rossini does not figure in his sonnets in dialect, he is often mentioned in the rest of his output – in the travel writings, the *zibaldone* (notebook) and other prose works, the correspondence, and also in his work as censor between 1852 and 1853 (this contribution includes, in an appendix, the chronology of all performances of Rossini's works at the Valle, Argentina, and Apollo theatres between 1823 and 1840); and Rossini manuscripts and printed editions in the Biblioteca musicale 'S. Cecilia'. The publication also includes the catalogue of an exhibition of Rossiniana held at the Fondazione Marco Besso.

730 The Ruspoli documents on Handel.
Ursula Kirkendale. *Journal of the American Musicological Society*, vol. xx, no. 2 (Summer 1967), pp. 222-73.

During his extended sojourn in Italy between 1707 and 1711, Handel spent the longest time in Rome where he stayed for approximately a year, between May 1707 and the end of April 1708, and where he returned in July 1708 after a brief stay in Naples. During this period he composed his first masterpieces, which included the oratorio *Il trionfo del tempo e del disinganno* (The triumph of time and truth), on a libretto by Cardinal Benedetto Pamphilj. Other patrons of the young composer included the Cardinals Carlo Colonna and Pietro Ottoboni, and, above all others, the Marchese Francesco Maria Ruspoli, for whom he composed the motet *Dixit Dominus*, several secular cantatas, and *La Resurrezione* (The Resurrection), his second oratorio.

There are numerous unresolved problems about Handel's precise activities in Italy – it is not known, for example, whether he served an apprenticeship with an established Italian composer, whether he had regular employment, whether his 'Italian' works were all produced in Italy and whether they represent the total output of his Italian years. The present study attempts to shed light on some of these problems, making use of documents from the Fondo Ruspoli in the Archivio Segreto Vaticano, which contain a wealth of information about the composer's whereabouts during most of 1707-08, his agreement with the Marchese Ruspoli, the works he wrote for this important patron, and relative dates for some fifty undated compositions. The documents between May 1707 and October 1711 contain thirty-eight entries related to Handel. These are transcribed here in chronological order and are preceded by a detailed analysis of their contents, a discussion of the time limits, the amount, and the character of Handel's work for Ruspoli, and the latter's role as patron of the arts. The material falls into four distinct chronological groups recording: various activities for Ruspoli between May and October 1707 (nos. 1-6); a continuous period of work at the Ruspoli household from February to April 1708 (nos. 7-20); another period of work for Ruspoli in the second half of 1708 (nos. 21-33); and isolated entries from February 1709 (when the employment had ceased) to 1711 (nos. 34-38).

731 Tosca.

Giacomo Puccini.   London: John Calder; New York: Riverrun Press, 1982. 80p. (Opera Guides, 16.)

This is the libretto of the opera, by Puccini's regular collaborators Giuseppe Giacosa and Luigi Illica, with parallel English translation, introductory essays on the significance of the historical themes and on the quality of Puccini's music, a thematic guide, musical examples and numerous illustrations from productions of the work.

732 Tosca's Rome: the play and the opera in historical perspective.

Susan Vandiver Nicassio.   Chicago: University of Chcago Press, 1999. 344p.

An examination of Puccini's opera, premiered in Rome in 1900, Victorien Sardou's 1887 play on which it was based, and the historical background and politics in the Rome of 1800 and the locations which inspired both the opera and the play. The author attempts to identify historical figures who might have provided Sardou and Puccini's librettists with the models for their characters. She also describes, in separate chapters, Rome as each of the protagonists would have seen it – a painter (Cavaradossi), an opera singer (Tosca), and a chief of police (Scarpia) – and lists operas performed in Rome in 1800 which Tosca could have sung in. An appendix provides parallel summaries of the play and the opera.

Dance

733 The arrival of the great wonder of ballet.
Claudia Celi.   In: *Rethinking the Sylph: new perspectives on Romantic ballet.*   Edited by Lynn Garafola.   Hanover, New England; London: Wesleyan University Press, 1997, p. 165-181.

An article examining ballet in Rome between 1845 and 1855, a period during which the most celebrated ballet dancers appeared on the stages of Rome. These included Fanny Elssler, Fanny Cerrito, Lucile Grahn, Marie Taglioni and Carlotta Grisi, Arthur Saint-Léon, Francesco Penco, Domenico Ronzani. The author outlines the social and political background to the performances – this was the period that saw liberal aspirations crushed by the failure of the Roman Republic – and the theatrical life of the capital. She describes the influence of the Torlonia family who controlled Rome's theatres, the role of impresarios such as Antonio Lanari and Vincenzo Jacovacci (who combined the role of agent, producer, and artistic director) and the problems of censorship, greater in Rome than elsewhere in Italy. She also looks at the work of some of the period's most famous choreographers, such as Giovanni Galzerani, Francesco Ramazzini, and Antonio Coppini.

Theatre

734 Cinquant'anni del Teatro dell'Opera, Roma 1928-1978. (Fifty years of the Teatro dell'Opera, Rome 1928-1978.)
Edited by Jole Tognelli.   Rome: Bestetti, 1979. 293p.

This volume was published to celebrate the fiftieth anniversary of the Teatro dell'Opera but also, judging from the somewhat defensive tone of the preface, the achievements of the management appointed during the reorganization of the theatre after the crisis of the early 1970s. An essay by Marcello Fagiolo looks at the history of the construction of the theatre, which formed part of the 'Third Rome' campaign, and the arguments in the 1870s for building an opera house that would cater for the interests of a cultural élite or a popular theatre (a *politeama*) that would stage a variety of shows, from circus performances to opera. The latter option was finally dropped following the tireless campaign of Domenico Costanzi, the entrepreneur after whom the theatre was named when it opened in 1880 (it was renamed Teatro Reale dell'Opera after its enlargement and restoration by Marcello Piacentini in 1928). There are numerous short chapters on the orchestra, opera, ballet, the Terme di Caracalla summer seasons, stage design, and great singers who appeared at the theatre. These are followed by a rich selection of photographs accompanying each section, illustrating key moments in the theatre's history. Among the artists, composers and performers in these are Beniamino Gigli, Maria Callas, Luchino Visconti, Giorgio De Chirico, Darius Milhaud and Eduardo De Filippo. There is also a chronology with detailed programmes of each season as well as indexes of composers and works performed, conductors, directors, choreographers and singers. Operas first performed in this theatre include *Tosca* and *Cavalleria rusticana*.

735 Corpus delle feste a Roma. Vol. 1. La festa barocca. Vol. 2. Il Settecento e l'Ottocento. (Corpus of Roman festivals. Vol. 1. Baroque festivals. Vol. 2. The eighteenth and nineteenth centuries.)
Edited by Maurizio Fagiolo dell'Arco (vol. 1) and Marcello Fagiolo (vol. 2).   Rome: Edizioni De Luca, 1997. 607p., 500p.

An account of festivals and ceremonies organized in Rome from 1585 to the end of papal temporal power on 20 September 1870. It charts the evolution of taste from the Baroque to Neo-classicism and Eclecticism (including, among others, revivals of Egyptian, Chinese, and Gothic styles). The festivals (religious, civic or popular celebrations) are presented in chronological order, each entry with a description of the event and information about its patrons, together with references to descriptions and depictions of the ephemeral architectures and decorations created for the celebration. The publication also has entries for artists and artisans employed by the architects and the *festaroli* (masters of revels), each giving a short biography, bibliography and a list of the artist's contributions. It includes a survey of contemporary accounts of the celebrations and a full bibliography. The first volume is an expanded and revised version of the two-volume *L'effimero barocco: struttura della festa nella Roma del '600* (The ephemeral Baroque: the structure of festivals in seventeenth-century Rome), edited by Maurizio Fagiolo dell'Arco and Silvia Carandini (Rome: Bulzoni, 1977).

736 **Due secoli di musica al Teatro Argentina.** (Two centuries of music at the Teatro Argentina.)
Mario Rinaldi.   Florence, Italy: Leo S. Olschki, 1978. 3 vols. 1664p. bibliog. (Storia dei Teatri Italiani, 1.)

This is a detailed history of Teatro Argentina, one of the oldest theatres in Rome, inaugurated on 13 January 1732. It was built in the gardens of Duke Sforza Cesarini and its name, like that of the surrounding area, derives from a tower built on the grounds by Johann Burchard (Giovanni Bucardo) (died 1506), master of papal ceremonies, which had the word *Argentina* (the Latin name of his native Strasbourg) inscribed on it. Shaped like a horseshoe, and smaller and more compact than the auditorium of the Alibert theatre, Argentina in the 18th century housed prose theatre, opera and ballet productions. One of the most glittering occasions in the theatre's history was the spectacular celebration organized on 12 July 1747 by Cardinal De La Rochefoucauld in honour of the marriage of Louis, the Dauphin of France to Maria Josepha, Princess of Saxony. The works of Alessandro Scarlatti, Cimarosa, Gluck, and Paisiello were first performed here and Rossini's *Il Barbiere di Siviglia* (The Barber of Seville) had a disastrous premiere in 1816, conducted by the composer. After a period of decline in the 1830s, the theatre was acquired by Alessandro Torlonia who restored the building to its former glory. Verdi wrote *I due Foscari* (The two Foscari) (1844) and *La Battaglia di Legnano* (The battle of Legnano) (1849) especially for Argentina. In 1869, the theatre was sold to the Comune and, after the closure in 1888 of Teatro Apollo, its main rival, the newly restored Argentina briefly became Rome's premier music theatre where Puccini's *La Bohème*, Giordano's *Andrea Chénier* and Wagner's *Die Walküre* (The Valkyrie) and *Götterdämmerung* (The Twilight of the Gods) had their first Roman performances. Competition from the Teatro Costanzi, which later became Rome's opera house, meant that Argentina had to concentrate on prose theatre becoming, from 1905, the home of the Compagnia Stabile di Roma company. The theatre is associated with the first performances of works by D'Annunzio, Pirandello, Marinetti and actors such as Emma Gramatica, Vittorio De Sica, Eduardo and Peppino De Filippo, and Ruggero Ruggeri. There is a detailed chronology of performances from 1732 to 1978, with information about composers, librettists, choreographers, theatre directors and soloists. The numerous indices include indices of works, composers, conductors, stage-managers, stage designers, choreographers, singers, ballet dancers, impresarios, and instrumental soloists.

737 **Feast and theatre in Queen Christina's Rome.**
Per Bjurström.   Stockholm: Nationalmuseum, 1966. 154p. (Analecta Reginensia III, Nationalmusei Skriftserie, 14.)

After her abdication in 1654, Queen Christina eventually settled in Rome where she arrived in September 1655. Being fascinated by theatrical and ecclesiastical events she appears in numerous contemporary illustrations of Roman spectacles. This volume aims to provide a picture of Queen Christina's Rome and makes use of drawings collected by the Swedish architect Nicodemus Tessin the Younger (Christina's protégé). There are chapters on Christina's entry into Rome in December 1655, where she was received in splendour by Pope Alexander VII, the celebrations during the carnival of 1656, her attendance at canonization ceremonies, banquets arranged for her and other dignitaries, and her role as a patron of theatrical representations and, in the epilogue, her funeral procession and ceremony. There are numerous contemporary illustrations of stage sets, processions and banquets.

738 La festa a Roma: dal Rinascimento al 1870. (Roman festivals: from the Renaissance to 1870.)
Edited by Marcello Fagiolo.   Turin, Italy: Umberto Allemandi, 1997.
2 vols. (284p. + 103p. of plates, 277p. + 15p. of plates). bibliog.

The catalogue of an exhibition held in Rome in 1997. Volume one contains nineteen essays which examine the festivals in chronological order and also the locations (for example, St Peter's and other basilicas, squares, streets) where they occurred, a catalogue of the works exhibited, and a bibliography. Among other issues discussed, the essays point out the political and diplomatic importance of the festivals, their mixture of the sacred and profane, the involvement of a wide variety of artists in their organization, and the reuse in more permanent works of innovative artistic ideas first expressed in the festivals. Volume two is a collection of essays examining the nature of Roman festivals, such as canonizations, the *Chinea* (the tribute of a white hackney paid to the Pope by the Kingdom of Naples), and the Pope's possession of the Lateran (the *Possesso*). It also provides a thematic presentation of elements derived from prints and drawings.

739 Orfeo in Arcadia: studi sul teatro a Roma nel Settecento. (Orpheus in Arcadia: studies on the theatre in Rome in the 18th century.)
Edited by Giorgio Petrocchi.   Rome: Istituto della Enciclopedia italiana fondata da G. Treccani, 1984. 305p. (Biblioteca Internazionale di Cultura, 14.)

This collection of papers read at the conference 'Roma e il teatro nel Settecento' includes essays on both general aspects of 18th-century theatrical culture in Rome and on individual playwrights and plays performed in Rome. The latter include Metastasio's *Ezio* (the last play he wrote before his departure for Vienna), Alfieri's *Antigone*, Goldoni's stay in Rome in 1758-59, and the use of dialect in the plays of Gherardo de Rossi. There are also three essays on foreign visitors (the French, the English and Goethe). Finally there is a useful list of theatrical spaces in 18th-century Rome, arranged under the city's fourteen *rioni*, with brief indications of the type of plays performed there and notable performances.

740 I teatri di Roma. (The theatres of Rome.)
Stefania Severi.   Rome: Newton Compton, 1989. 271p. bibliog.
(Quest'Italia, 144.)

A survey of Roman theatres from the 2nd century AD to the present. An introductory chapter discusses theatrical and musical life and representations, establishing 1513 as the year in which modern theatre was born in Rome, with the construction by Baldassare Peruzzi of a theatre on the Campidoglio for the celebrations in honour of Giuliano de' Medici. The variety of theatrical performances – private or public, high or low – is demonstrated and special features peculiar to Rome are highlighted, for example the banning of women from the stage between 1558 and 1798, the shortness of theatre seasons (limited to the months between Christmas and Lent), the closure of theatres during Jubilee years, the fate of theatres depending on the attitude of the reigning pope (Pope Clement IX, a writer of opera libretti, was a notable supporter whereas Innocent XII, who hated theatrical entertainments, ordered the demolition of the Tordinona theatre). Thereafter the various theatres are examined in chronological order, with the exception of the five great theatres of Rome – the Alibert, Argentina, Capranica, Tordinona (later Apollo), Valle, and the Opera (formerly Costanzi) theatres – which are discussed in a separate section. The survey begins with the theatres of Ancient Rome (the Theatre of Marcellus, the theatre at Ostia antica, and other theatres that have disappeared) and these are followed by a century-by-century arrangement, beginning with the 16th century.

741   Il teatro a Roma nel Settecento. (Theatre in Rome in the eighteenth century.)
Edited by Luciana Buccellato and Fiorella Trapani.   Rome: Istituto della Enciclopedia italiana fondata da G. Treccani, 1989. 2 vols. (814p. + index). (Biblioteca Internazionale di Cultura, 21.)

These volumes contain revised versions of papers originally read at the international conference on *Roma e il teatro nel Settecento* (Rome and the theatre in the eighteenth century) held in Rome in 1982. They are divided into three sections: theatre and the visual arts; festivals and popular spectacles; and sources. The first section includes papers on the evolution of Baroque theatre, the relationship between real architecture and stage design, architectural ruins in 18th-century stage sets, the theatricality of garden design in the Bosco Parrasio on the Janiculum, Villa Albani and the neo-classical concept of the garden, and Carlo Fontana and the Teatro Tordinona. The second section includes papers on Goethe and Goldoni's *La Locandiera*, the carnival and French festivals, theatrical relations between Spain and Rome, popular theatre in Rome, and the protagonists of Roman theatrical life in the eighteenth century – the theatres, performers, companies, financial backers, and the public. The third section includes papers on the theatre collections of the Biblioteca Casanatense and the Archivio di Stato di Roma, theatrical performances in Roman palaces, the theatre of Cardinal Ottoboni in the Palazzo della Cancelleria, the Colonna family's theatre patronage, comments on theatrical life in Roman periodicals, and President De Brosses' comments on the theatrical season of 1739-40.

742   Il Teatro Alibert o delle Dame, 1717-1863. (The Teatro Alibert *later called* Teatro delle Dame, 1717-1863.)
Alberto de Angelis.   Tivoli, Italy: Arti grafiche A. Chicca, 1951. 320p.

During the one and a half centuries of its life (it burned down on 15 February 1863), the Teatro Alibert was, with the Tordinona, Argentina, Valle and Capranica, one of the most important theatres in Rome. Artists whose work was performed there included the librettists and playwrights Pietro Metastasio, Apostolo Zeno and Vittorio Alfieri, the singers Carlo Broschi ('Farinelli') and the tenor David, and the ballerinas Fanny Elssler and Fanny Cerrito. In the 18th century, the theatre was associated with composers of the Neapolitan school – works by Francesco Gasparini, Nicolò Porpora, Leonardo Vinci, Jommelli, Galuppi, Paisiello, and Piccinni were first performed here. Some of the most famous stage designers, architects and painters also worked here, among them Francesco and Antonio Galli-Bibiena. The theatre, which was near Via Margutta, was named after Antonio Alibert, the son of Queen Christina's secretary. Its architects were Francesco and Antonio Galli-Bibiena and later renovations were carried out by Ferdinando Fuga (1738), Giuseppe Valadier (1804) and Nicola Carnevali (1859). The first part of this work provides the history of the theatre, while the second part is a chronology of performances, with the works first performed in this theatre asterisked.

743 Il Teatro Argentina e il suo museo. (Teatro Argentina and its museum.) Edited by Luigi Squarzina. Rome: Officina edizioni, 1982. 101p.

This is the catalogue of the museum of Teatro Argentina, which was inaugurated on the 250th anniversary of the theatre. It traces the history of one of the most important theatres in Rome, where numerous works were premiered, among them Rossini's *Il Barbiere di Siviglia* (The Barber of Seville) (1816) and Verdi's *Rigoletto* (1851). It is richly illustrated with plans and photographs of the theatre, portraits of performers, composers, impresarios, title-pages of plays and opera libretti, and posters.

744 Il Teatro di Tordinona, poi di Apollo. (The Tordinona [later Apollo] theatre.)
Alberto Cametti. Tivoli, Italy: Arti grafiche Aldo Chicca, 1938. 2 vols. 669p. bibliog. (Atti e Memorie della R. Accademia di S. Cecilia.)

The first volume of this publication is a detailed history of one of Rome's famous theatres. It was named after a tower in the Aurelian Wall, the Tor di Nona (which belonged to the Orsini family, Prefects of Annona), which was used as a prison between 1400 and 1657, the site of which the theatre occupied. The theatre, designed by Carlo Fontana, was built thanks to the efforts of Queen Christina and its first director was Giacomo d'Alibert, her secretary. Inaugurated in 1671, its fortunes over the following decades fluctuated according to the policies of reigning popes and it had the unusual fate of being demolished on the orders of one pope (Innocent XII in 1697, who hated theatrical entertainments) only to be rebuilt on the orders of another (Clement XII in 1733). In 1781, the theatre was totally destroyed by fire and a new theatre was built by Felice Giorgi and, renamed Apollo (though it continued to be known as Tordinona), it was inaugurated in 1795. The period between 1820 (when it was purchased by Prince Giovanni Torlonia) and its demolition in 1889 (necessitated by the construction of the Tiber embankments – the building was on the left bank by Ponte Sisto) was the theatre's heyday, with stagings of operas by Mercadante, Rossini, Donizetti, Bellini and the first performances of Verdi's *Il trovatore* (1853) and *Un ballo in maschera* (A masked ball) (1859). Giuseppe Gioachino Belli was an assiduous visitor and a huge number of the sonnets he wrote between 1831 and 1836 comment on performances and singers of the Tordinona. The second volume lists all the performances in the theatre from Francesco Cavalli and Alessandro Stradella's *Scipione Africano* (Scipio the African) in 1671 to Ambroise Thomas' *Hamlet* in 1888. Several entries not only discuss the performance and the circumstances of its creation (performers, stage designers, success or failure, etc.) but also provide useful bibliographical information about the printed libretto and summarize its plot. There are various indices – of operas and other music performances, ballets, choreographers, ballet dancers, composers, librettists, conductors, chorus masters, singers, stage designers, and impresarios.

745 Teatro nel Rinascimento: Roma, 1450-1550. (Theatre in the Renaissance: Rome, 1450-1550.)
Fabrizio Cruciani. Rome: Bulzoni, 1983. 719p. bibliog. (Biblioteca del Cinquecento, 22.)

A survey of festival representations and theatrical performances from the reign of Pius II (1458-64) to that of Paul III (1534-49). Each chapter contains a text introducing an event or performance followed by its description in contemporary accounts. It comprises a wide variety of festivals and spectacles – the *possesso* and other ceremonies inaugurating each pontificate; religious ceremonies and sacred representations (the translation of the head of St Andrew in 1462, the Passion performed on Good Friday in the Colosseum by the Arciconfraternità del Gonfalone from the 1490s onward); numerous carnival celebrations

Theatre

and other popular feasts at Agone (i.e. Piazza Navona) and Testaccio; triumphal entries and processions (Borso d'Este in 1471, Julius II in 1507 after the recapture of Bologna, Charles V in 1535, the triumphal 'classical' procession in honour of Paul II in 1466); festivals celebrating important weddings (Eleanor of Aragon's to Ercole I d'Este in 1473; Lucrezia Borgia's to Giovanni Sforza in 1493 and to Alfonso d'Este in 1502; Eleonora Gonzaga's to Francesco Maria della Rovere in 1510); and festivals celebrating individual events (the conquest of Granada by King Ferdinand in 1494). There are chapters tracing the evolution of theatrical performances from festival representations and the rediscovery of classical theatre, as well as descriptions of performances of the plays of Plautus and Terence by the Accademia dei Pomponiani (formed by Pomponio Leto) and the performance of Seneca's *Hippolytus* in 1486, performances of eclogues in the Farnesina in 1509 and 1510 and other theatrical representations during the last years of the pontificate of Julius II, and the first performance in Rome of Bibbiena's *Calandria* in 1514 in honour of Isabella d'Este Gonzaga (with stage designs by Baldassare Peruzzi who also provided, in 1531, the designs for the performance of Plautus's *Bacchides*). There is also a chapter on actors and jesters in the court of Leo X. There is a comprehensive index of the sources cited (listed in chronological order) and a full bibliography. The illustrations, however, are few and mediocre.

Cinema

746 Accattone, Mamma Roma, Ostia.
Pier Paolo Pasolini, introduction by Ugo Casiraghi. Milan, Italy: Garzanti, 1993. 628p. (Gli Elefanti.)

This volume brings together three screenplays by Pasolini set in the squalid *borgate* of Rome and the world of his novels *Ragazzi di vita* (The Ragazzi) (1955) and *Una vita violenta* (A violent life) (1959). Two of the films, *Accattone* (1961) and *Mamma Roma* (1962), were directed by Pasolini himself, and the third, *Ostia* (1970), by Sergio Citti, his linguistic adviser on Roman dialect. *Accattone*, the existential portrait of a pimp and petty thief, was Pasolini's first work as an independent film director and contains all the trademarks of his style – a cast of mostly non-professional actors, many of them his personal friends, uneven continuity, and deliberately slow pace. *Mamma Roma* is the story of a former prostitute (Anna Magnani) and her doomed attempts to provide a better life for her only son. *Ostia*, the tragicomic story of two brothers, revisits the world of the Roman *borgate* eight years later. The screenplays are accompanied by other texts by Pasolini related to the films – reflections on the films both before and after their premieres, diaries, and poems – and also articles on film-making and the work of other directors. There are also numerous stills from all three films.

747 Alberto Sordi.
Claudio G. Fava, with the assistance of Umberto Tani. Rome: Gremese, 1979. 260p. (Le Stelle Filanti.)

A biography and filmography of one of Italy's most popular comedians. Alberto Sordi was born in Trastevere in 1920. His first success as a film actor was in 1942 in *I tre Aquilotti* (The three pilots), a war drama. As the detailed and richly illustrated chronology in this volume shows, he had, by then, appeared in numerous variety shows, both as an actor and dancer, made recordings for children, and dubbed Oliver Hardy (the first in a long line of American actors he was to dub in the 1940s and 1950s). He continued to perform in theatres in Rome in the 1940s, when he also became popular as a radio personality. Sordi's greatest years were the 1950s and 1960s, the golden era of the *commedia all'italiana* (Comedy Italian-style), when his film credits included Fellini's *Lo sceicco bianco* (The white sheik) and *I Vitelloni* (The Young and the Passionate), his role as Emperor Nero in *Mio figlio Nerone* (Nero, my son) (in which Vittorio De Sica played Seneca, Brigitte Bardot Poppea and Gloria Swanson Agrippina), and a host of other comedies in which the characters he played combined high spirits and anarchy with pathos and melancholy. He appeared in some 150 films and directed another 20.

748 The belly of an architect.
Peter Greenaway. London, Boston: Faber & Faber, 1988. 191p.

The story of a middle-aged American architect who, with his younger wife, goes to Rome to organize an exhibition on the 18th-century visionary architect Étienne-Louis Boullée. The film, which makes spectacular use of Roman architecture, is divided into eight sections, each corresponding to a famous Roman architectural site – the Vittoriano, the Foro Italico, the Baths at the Villa Adriana, St Peter's, the Roman Forum, the Pantheon, Piazza del Popolo, and Piazza Navona.

749 Bicycle thieves: a film by Vittorio de Sica.
Translated by Simon Hartog. London: Lorrimer, 1967. 96p. (Modern Film Scripts, 14.)

One of the key films of Italian Neorealism, Vittorio De Sica's masterpiece is based on a novel by Luigi Bartolini, adapted chiefly by De Sica himself, Cesare Zavattini and Suso Cecchi d'Amico. The plot is the story of Antonio Ricci, a man whose work as a poster-sticker requires a bicycle to get around the city. When his bicycle is stolen, he begins searching for the thief in the streets of Rome, accompanied by his small son. Their search takes them through a variety of locations before their eventual confrontation with the culprit. Unable to prove his case, he is finally driven to steal a stranger's bicycle, only to be caught and publicly humiliated.

750 Cinecittà.
Federico Fellini, translated by Graham Fawcett. London: Studio Vista, 1989. 183p. filmography.

Though the core of this publication is Fellini's reminiscences of the studio, accompanied by illustrations from the making of his films, it, nevertheless, also includes a chronology of the Cinecittà studios from 1936, when Mussolini laid the foundation stone, and its opening the following year, to the era of the spaghetti western in the late 1960s and the crisis of the 1970s. There is also an article describing the studios and their workers, a filmography from 1937 to 1987, and numerous illustrations from the heyday of the studio.

751 Cinecittà anni trenta. (Cinecittà in the 1930s.)
Francesco Savio, edited by Tullio Kezich. Rome: Bulzoni, 1979. 3 vols. 1216p. (Studi Cinematografici, 6-8.)

A collection of 116 interviews between Francesco Savio and actors, film directors, scriptwriters, producers, and set designers working in the Cinecittà studios in Rome between 1930 and 1943. Some 720 films were produced in the studios during this period. They included fascist propaganda films, war films, swashbuckling adventures, escapist comedies and romantic dramas – the so-called *telefoni bianchi* (white telephones) – and the first neorealist films.

752 La dolce vita.
Federico Fellini. Milan, Italy: Garzanti, 1981. 219p. (I Garzanti, Cinema.)

Fellini's portrayal of 'decadent' Rome in the pre-swinging Sixties caused a scandal when it was released in 1960. It is a series of episodes in the life of Marcello (Marcello Mastroianni), a Roman reporter. Though overlong and already showing signs of Fellini's self-indulgence that was to become more irritating in his later output, the film has several remarkable and justly famous sequences – the statue of Christ flying over Rome hanging from a helicopter, Anita Ekberg in the Trevi Fountain, the monster washed out by the sea. The film also gave the world the word 'paparazzo' (it is the name of Marcello's photographer friend). This volume includes the original screenplay, written by Fellini, Ennio Flaiano and Tullio Pinelli, which differs substantially from the final version, together with a dossier of comments and reactions to the film and some fifty stills from the film.

753   La dolce vita: il film di Federico Fellini. (*La dolce vita*: the film of Federico Fellini.)
Edited by Gianfranco Angelucci, texts by Federico Fellini and Gian Luigi Rondi.   Rome: Editalia, 1989. 317p.

A sumptuous picture book containing 498 stills from the film and its making. In his introductory text, Fellini reminisces about Anita Ekberg's 'superhuman' and 'phosphorescent' beauty, and the difficulties of filming certain sequences in the streets of Rome which led to the decision to reconstruct Via Veneto in a Cinecittà studio. Gian Luigi Rondi discusses the film's profound pessimism, its juxtaposition of the sacred and the profane, and its anti-hero.

754   Fellini on Fellini.
Edited by Costanzo Costantini.   London; Boston: Faber & Faber, 1994. 223p.

This is a collection of extracts from interviews with Fellini about his life and work, published shortly after the director's death in 1993. The arrangement is chronological, beginning with his early years in Rimini, his arrival in Rome and at Cinecittà, his meeting with Giulietta Masina (his future wife), his early collaboration with Roberto Rossellini and, thereafter, his own films. Contributions by Fellini's collaborators (for example, Anita Ekberg and Pier Paolo Pasolini) are also included, sometimes providing amusingly different versions of events to Fellini's. There is also a complete filmography with full credits and plot summaries.

755   Fellini Satyricon.
Federico Fellini, edited by Dario Zanelli.   Bologna, Italy: Cappelli, 1969. 303p. (Dal Soggetto al Film, 38.)

Fellini's version of Petronius's *Satyricon* forms the second part of his Roman trilogy. The plot follows the adventures of its three young heroes, Encolpio, Gitone and Ascilto, and suggests similarities between ancient Roman decadence and the present. This edition includes an outline of the plot, the screenplay with full annotations about changes during the shooting and editing of the film, and a long essay by Zanelli which includes long extracts from Fellini interviews with Alberto Moravia, Peter Nichols and others. There are also 104 photographs, some in colour.

756   Una giornata particolare: soggetto e sceneggiatura. (A special day: subject and screenplay.)
Ruggero Maccari, Ettore Scola, with the collaboration of Maurizio Costanzo.   Milan, Italy: Longanesi & Co., 1977. 143p. (La Ginestra, 161.)

Ettore Scola's *Una gioranta particolare* (1977) takes place in a Rome apartment block on the day of Hitler's visit to Rome, on 6 May 1938. It is the story of a poignant brief encounter between two outcasts – Antonietta, a frustrated housewife (Sophia Loren) and Gabriele, a homosexual radio reporter (Marcello Mastroianni). The relationship between the two protagonists develops against the background of the preparations for the Führer's visit, with crowds pouring into the Via dell'Impero (now Via dei Fori imperiali) to see the parade, the enthusiastic coverage of the event on the radio, the end of the celebration and the return home of Antonietta's husband and children. Antonietta sees Gabriele being arrested by two police agents and returns resignedly to the marital bed. Scola described his film as a 'tragic comedy'. It is an ironic reflection on Fascist rhetoric and its ideal of virility and woman as angel of the hearth. The contrast between the public and the private is emphasized through the use of documentary footage, while the predominantly black-and-white photography with occasional symbolic colour highlights both evokes the period and reflects the greyness of the characters' lives. *La famiglia* (The family) (1987) is another Scola film with a Roman setting, this time a flat in which eighty years of a middle-class family's history unfold.

757 La Magnani: il romanzo di una vita. (La Magnani: the novel of a life.)
Patrizia Carrano.   Milan, Italy: Rizzoli, 1982. 274p.

In the final sequence of Fellini's *Roma*, the camera follows a solitary woman (Anna Magnani) returning home late at night. The unseen interviewer (Fellini) attempts to elicit an interview/statement calling her 'a she-wolf, a whore and a vestal virgin, aristocratic and threadbare, gloomy and clownish – I could go on until tomorrow morning...' before the *portone* is shut with a half-rebuking 'go home Federí'. This memorable and moving tribute, filmed shortly before Magnani's death in 1973, encapsulates all the qualities of the actress, who was the epitome of Roman womanhood. This biography examines Magnani's life and her varied career, both in the theatre (where she memorably collaborated with Totò in the 1940s) and the cinema. She developed her earthy persona in the films she made in the 1930s and 1940s by, among others, Goffredo Alessandrini (her husband) and Vittorio de Sica, but her most memorable interpretations are those in Rossellini's *Roma città aperta* (Rome, Open City) (1945), Visconti's *Bellissima* (1951), and Pasolini's *Mamma Roma* (1962).

758 Le notti di Cabiria di Federico Fellini. (The nights of Cabiria by Federico Fellini.)
Edited by Lino Del Fra.   Bologna, Italy: Cappelli, 1965. 239p. (Dal Soggetto al Film.)

Fellini's 1957 film about the life of a warm-hearted and dauntless Roman prostitute (played by Giulietta Masina) who is exploited and nearly murdered by her lovers is poised between Neorealism and the private fantasies and themes that would dominate the director's later work. This is the most Pasolinian of Fellini's films (Pasolini, in fact, acted as language advisor to Fellini and in an article included in this edition he describes preparatory research to establish authentic locations and characters for the film, including a car ride with the director in search of a legendary prostitute, nick-named 'la Bomba atomica', who was used as the model for one of the characters in the film) in both setting – the Roman *borgate* of Pasolini's novels – and the characteristic and poignant clash between two worlds, that of the city's outskirts and its centre (in this case Cabiria's night in Via Veneto, where she encounters the film actor). This edition gives the screenplay of the film (including sequences left out of the final version), together with 111 photographs from the film and its making. It also includes articles on the genesis of the film, its music (by Nino Rota), its producers, and reflections by Masina on her role.

759 *Roma* di Federico Fellini. (Federico Fellini's *Rome*.)
Edited by Bernardino Zapponi.   Bologna, Italy: Cappelli, 1972. 374p.

The third part of Fellini's Roman trilogy is an affectionate portrait of the city, with alternating episodes set in the 1930s and in the present. The former trace a young boy's first impressions of the Eternal City in his provincial town, his arrival as a young man at Stazione Termini, his life and experiences in Rome (the boarding house, a visit to the brothel, an open-air trattoria). The contemporary episodes have no single focus or 'plot' but show various aspects of life in the modern city (the digging of an underground tunnel and the fading away of the ancient Roman frescoes when exposed to the modern air, a traffic jam on the autostrada). Memorable set-pieces include an unruly vaudeville performance in the 1930s, an ecclesiastical fashion show (filmed in the Palazzo Doria Pamphilj), and the final nocturnal motorbike ride through the city. This edition of the official screenplay gives both the original text, written by Fellini and Zapponi, and the version finally filmed. It includes an introductory essay by Zapponi, an essay by Luca Canali on the trilogy, several photographs (some in colour) and artwork by Fellini.

760 Lo sceicco bianco. (The white sheik.)
Federico Fellini, introductory note by Oreste del Buono.   Milan, Italy: Garzanti, 1980. 150p. (I Garzanti Cinema.)

This is the screenplay of Fellini's first film as solo director, written by Fellini himself, Tullio Pinelli and Ennio Flaiano, who were both to become his regular collaborators. A commercial failure at its release in 1952, it has now assumed the status of a minor classic. It is the story of Ivan and Wanda who come to Rome on a Holy Year for their honeymoon, to visit Ivan's middle-class relations and be blessed by the Pope. Wanda, an avid reader of *fotoromanzi* (photo romances) and a fan of the 'White Sheik', the hero of one of them, immediately sets out to find her idol, and joins him on location outside Rome. Various comic episodes ensue as Ivan looks for his wife everywhere in Rome and attempts to hide her escape from his strait-laced relatives and as Wanda discovers that the world of *fotoromanzi* bears no resemblance to real life. The couple are reunited after Wanda's suicide attempt and somehow manage to get to S. Peter's just in time for the papal blessing, after which they are ready to begin their life together, sadder but wiser. The introductory note includes reminiscences by Fellini on the circumstances of the filming, the choice of Alberto Sordi as the eponymous 'hero' and the lukewarm reception of the film at the Venice Film Festival. There is also an interview with Alberto Sordi.

761 The War trilogy: Open City, Paisan [sic], Germany, year zero.
Roberto Rossellini, edited and with an introduction by Stefano Roncoroni, translated from the Italian by Judith Green.   New York, London: Garland Publishing, 1985. 489p. (Cinema Classics.)

These are English translations of the screenplays of Rossellini's immensely influential films. *Roma città aperta* (Rome, Open City) was the first film to draw attention, with its raw, newsreel-like depiction of war-ravaged Rome, on neorealism as a new style. It is partly based on true events – it was originally planned as a short documentary about the heroic sacrifice of Don Morosini (Don Pedro in the film), a priest shot by the Germans in 1944 – and, apart from Anna Magnani (the vibrant Pina who, alas, is killed halfway through the film) and Aldo Fabrizi (Don Pedro), the cast was non-professional. The plot relates the hunting down, capture and torture of a Communist resistance leader and his friends by the Gestapo. It was shot in Roman locations shortly after the entry of the Allies and the sense of oppression is palpable in the film right from the opening sequence, when the camera pans from the Pincian Hill at dawn, over the rooftops of Rome, into the balcony of an apartment where a fearful servant looks through the shutters at a German Red Cross truck, and a house-search team of soldiers knocks violently at the door. The screenplay is accompanied by several stills from the film, of an even grainier quality than the original.

Folklore

762 Leggende e racconti popolari di Roma. (Roman legends and popular tales.)
Cecilia Gatto Trocchi.   Rome: Newton Compton, 1982. 343p.
(Quest'Italia, 28.)

A collection of legends and popular myths of Rome, some of which involve real life characters (Beatrice Cenci, Lucrezia Borgia), or legendary figures like Pope Joan. The collection is based on hundreds of interviews the editor carried out in various *rioni* of Rome, on recordings in the Discoteca di Stato and on texts by Roman dialect writers such as G. Zanazzo and M. Menghini. The texts are divided into the following: popular religious legends; ghost stories; legends some of which involve real-life persons (Artemisia Gentileschi, Pope Sylvester II); stories from the Roman Ghetto; fables; and tales of witchcraft. The texts are accompanied by popular woodcuts, topographical prints, and portraits.

763 La Papessa Giovanna: Roma e papato tra storia e leggenda. (Pope Joan: Rome and the papacy between history and legend.)
Cesare D'Onofrio.   Rome: Romana società editrice, 1979. 286p. bibliog.

An examination of one of the most extraordinary legends of the history of Rome, that of a woman who, dressed as man, rose through the ecclesiastical ranks and, becoming pope in 855, reigned for two-and-a-half years before her secret was revealed when she gave birth, during a procession from St Peter's to the Lateran. She died immediately afterwards (perhaps stoned to death) and was buried with her baby in the place of the incident, a narrow street (Vicus Papisse) between the Colosseum and S. Clemente. This study looks at the development of the myth and its different versions and embellishments from the 9th to the 16th century – including its appearance in 14th-century guides to Rome, Boccaccio's account in his *De mulieribus claris*, and various Lutheran attacks. It also examines the abundant iconography of the subject in illuminated manuscripts, popular woodcuts and sculptures. The implications and symbolism of the legend are also investigated, together with the concept of 'Mater Ecclesia' ('Mother Church'). The study also investigates two related popular beliefs – that subsequent papal processions deliberately avoided the Vicus Papisse and that the function of the two pierced porphyry chairs (the *sedie stercorarie*) in the Lateran was their use in a special ceremony after the election of a pope to verify his gender – and attempts to provide a historically sound explanation about them. Other recent accounts of the legend in English include Peter Stanford, *The She-Pope: a quest for the truth behind the mystery of Pope Joan* (London: Heinemann, 1998); and Rosemary and Darroll Pardoe, *The female Pope: the first complete documentation of the facts behind the legend* (Wellingborough, England: Crucible, 1988). The legend has also inspired the novel *Papissa Ioanna* by the Greek writer Emmanuel Roïdēs (1835-1904), first published in 1886. The work, which earned its author notoriety and led to his excommunication, has been adapted and translated into English by Lawrence Durrell (Lawrence Durrell, *Pope Joan* (New York: The Overlook Press, 1960). See also Donna Woolfolk Cross, *Pope Joan* (London: Quartet Books, 1997).

Food

764   Apicius cookery and dining in Imperial Rome.
Joseph Dommers Vehling, introduction by Frederick Starr.   New York:
Dover Publications, 1977. 301p. bibliog.

'Apicius' is the proverbial name of several Roman food connoisseurs and *De Re Coquinaria*
(On Cookery) is a compilation of Roman and Greek cookery probably compiled during the 1st
century AD, although the earliest surviving text dates from the 4th century. The work is divided
into ten chapters and was intended as a practical treatise for use by professional cooks. This was
the first English translation of the text, originally published in 1926. It includes a critical
introduction and surveys various theories about the authenticity of the book and the identity of
its authors and their sources. It also has a bibliography of Apician manuscripts and printed
editions, a dictionary of culinary terms and an index. The translation of the text is accompanied
by notes and comments, but the text is difficult to read because of the decision to print the
translation in capital letters.

765   L'arte del convito nella Roma antica. (The art of banqueting in Ancient
Rome.)
Eugenia Salza Prina Ricotti.   Rome: 'L'erma' di Bretschneider, 1983.
313p. (Studia Archaeologica, 35.)

This monograph examines descriptions of food and banqueting in Rome from earliest
times to the 1st century AD, particularly in the work of eight writers: Cato *the Censor*,
Varro, Cicero, Horace, Petronius Arbiter, Martial, Juvenal, and Apicius. It also looks at
banqueting representations in classical art and contains numerous illustrations of food in
art (for example, mosaics of *asarotos oikos*, i.e. depictions of food on the floors of
banqueting halls), kitchen utensils, domestic architecture, etc. Ninety recipes are given,
taken from the writings of the above writers. Rules and hours of Roman banquets and
other customs related to eating are described in an introductory chapter, as are the
ingredients and condiments used in Roman cuisine.

766 La cucina romana. (Roman cooking.)
Ada Boni. Rome: Newton Compton, 1983. 253p. (Quest'Italia, 48.)

In her short introduction to this book, Ada Boni laments the loss of genuine Roman cookery traditions, which began with the post-1870 influx into the new capital of people from other parts of Italy who brought with them their own culinary traditions. Her collection of 225 classic recipes (divided into nine sections) includes forty-three soups, fifty-eight meat dishes, twenty-nine dishes with *erbaggi e legumi* (green vegetables and pulses) and thirty-two desserts. The work is preceded by an affectionate portrait of the author, the *doyenne* of Italian writers on food.

767 La cucina romana e del Lazio. (Roman and Lazio cooking.)
Livio Jannattoni. Rome: Newton & Compton, 1998. 736p.
(Quest'Italia, 260.)

In his introductory essay the author celebrates Roman cookery traditions which, he feels, are threatened by modern-day standardization. He also conducts a wide-ranging historical survey of Roman cookery and folklore related to food. Topics examined include: food in Ancient Rome (including the influence of Apicius on later writers); tales of gluttony in the Middle Ages; Renaissance treatises on food (Bartolomeo Platina, the great humanist and first Prefect of the Vatican Library is one of the many distinguished writers who contributed to this genre) and cookery manuals; street cries (some 240 different types were depicted in 16th-century prints) and descriptions of food markets in Rome; travellers' comments on food (from Montaigne to Des Brosses and numerous 19th-century writers); food and wine in hundreds of sonnets by Giuseppe Gioachino Belli; and, finally, food-related nicknames of the inhabitants of Rome's *rioni*. There are hundreds of recipes, divided into thirty chapters, embellished by numerous illustrations and extracts from other works.

768 Diane Seed's Roman kitchen: 100 seasonal recipes from the heart of Italy.
Diane Seed, illustrated by Marlene McLoughlin. London: Rosendale Press, 1998. 142p.

In her introductory note the author, who has lived in Rome for over twenty-five years, evokes the changing seasons and their produce. She also gives a brief survey of food in Rome, from antiquity to the present, pointing out contrasts in eating habits and customs as, for example, between the Republic, when laws existed to curb extravagant meals, and the Empire, with its extravagant banquets; or between the diet of the poor, consisting largely of bread, pulses and garlic, and the notorious gluttony of some popes and cardinals. Though she warns against the threat to Roman culinary traditions from convenience food she is not averse to changes in Roman cooking brought about by the use of new ingredients which have affected it in a more positive way, resulting in lighter dishes co-existing with the more robust traditional ones. Accordingly, while many of the recipes included in this book are traditional Roman dishes dating back to classical times, others have been adopted from other regions of Italy. There is a glossary and a 'Guide to Roman food' which includes advice on traditional restaurants in Rome, and speciality shops (bread, fish, meat, wine, cakes, ice cream, and *salumerie* [delicatessens]).

769 The Roman cookery of Apicius.
Translated and adapted for the modern kitchen by John Edwards.
London: Rider, 1984. 351p. bibliog.

This edition provides a translation of Apicius' cookery manual with adapted and tested versions of 360 recipes. The original, un-adapted recipes appear on boxed-in pages with identifying numbers in the margin. These numbers also appear in the margin by the modern recipe. The introduction describes Roman eating habits and cooking utensils and points out the importance of seasonings and sauces in Roman cookery (Apicius often uses ten to twelve condiments in the preparation of his dishes), especially pepper and lovage. It also singles out some rare or uncommon seasonings such as fish-pickle, laser (or silphium), rue, colewort, and elecampane. Roman cooking wines, including boiled wines used to flavour, colour and sweeten dishes, are also described. There are three appendices containing a list of the values and measures used by Apicius, a list of substitutes for hard to find ingredients, and directions for making boiled wine, wine sauce and fish-pickle.

770   **I vini italiani regione per regione.** (Italian wines region by region.)
      Edited by Lucio Pugliese, technical consultant Giuseppe Morrocchi.
      Florence, Italy: Lucio Pugliese, 1983. 223p.

This wine guide includes fifty-five wines produced in the Lazio region. Seventeen of these have a detailed entry while the rest appear in a list. Each entry gives a description of the wine (type of grape used, characteristics), information about the area of its production, and serving suggestions (temperature, types of food it should accompany).

Sport and Games

771 **The British Olympic Association Official Report of the Olympic Games 1960: XVIIth Olympiad, Rome August 25-September 11, 1960.**
Edited by Phil Pilley. [London]: World Sports, 1960.

The seventeenth Olympiad was, at the time, the biggest in the history of the Olympic movement. It involved eighty-four nations and nearly 6,000 competitors, who were addressed by Pope John XXII at a huge gathering in St Peter's Square. Various venues were used: the Stadio Olimpico, the Palazzo dello sport, the Stadio del nuoto, as well as prestigious locations such as the Terme di Caracalla and the Basilica di Massenzio. The organization and the facilities provided were much praised. This report provides a record of the Games with articles on all the events and listings of the results, a table indicating the number of titles won by the representatives of each country and photographs of all the winners as well as other picture features.

772 **I giochi a Roma di strada e d'osteria.** (Street and tavern games in Rome.)
Giorgio Roberti. Rome: Newton Compton, 1995. 448p. (Quest'Italia, 215.)

A collection of some 500 games played by children in Rome in the 19th century and the first half of the 20th century. They are divided into various categories and listed alphabetically within each category: cradle and early childhood games; games of skill, memory, strength, and imagination; racing, hiding and blindfolding games; ball games, hopping, skipping, jumping and dancing, throwing and catching; gambling and betting, practical jokes. An appendix lists tongue-twisters, enigmas, proverbs and sayings inspired by the games. There are two indexes, in Romanesco (the Roman dialect) and in Italian, and numerous illustrations.

Libraries, Archives and Learning

773 La Biblioteca Angelica. (The Biblioteca Angelica.)
Paola Munafò and Nicoletta Muratore.   Rome: Istituto poligrafico dello
stato, 1989. 84p. bibliog.

The Biblioteca Angelica is one of the oldest libraries in Europe and the first public library in Rome. It opened to the public on 23 October 1614 and was formed with the collection that Angelo Rocca, the Bishop of Tagaste, donated to the convent of S. Agostino. This monograph gives a chronological account of the library's history in five chapters. Chapters one and two focus on Angelo Rocca's collection and the foundation of the library. Chapters three and four look at 17th- and 18th-century bequests, especially those of Cardinal Lucas Holstenius (1661), Cardinal Enrico Noris (1704), and the purchase, in 1762, of Cardinal Domenico Passionei's library. The last two collections made the Angelica the major depository of Jansenist and anti-Jesuit literature. Chapter five covers the modern period, which saw the acquisition of 200 codices from the collection of Prince Massimo, and 954 opera libretti from the collection of Marchese Santangelo. In 1940, the library of the Arcadian Academy (40,000 volumes) was incorporated. The library's collections of material on Roman history and culture were considerably enlarged during Francesco Barberi's directorship (1944-52) and by the acquisition of the archive of Domenico Gnoli, a mine of information on turn-of-the-century Rome. The Angelica became a state library in 1884.

774 La Biblioteca Casanatense di Roma. (The Casanatense Library in
Rome.)
Vincenzo De Gregorio.   Naples, Italy: Edizioni scientifiche italiane,
1993. 360p. bibliog. (Pubblicazioni dell'Università degli Studi di Salerno,
Sezione di Studi Filologici, Letterari e Artistici, 23.)

The library of Cardinal Girolamo Casanate (1620-1700) was bequeathed to the Dominican church of S. Maria sopra Minerva in 1698 and opened to the public in 1701. It contained 25,000 volumes. Its present holdings include 250,000 volumes and 100,000 pamphlets, 2,000 incunables and 6,000 manuscripts. The library has rich collections of prints, opera libretti and music manuscripts (including items by Palestrina, Monteverdi and Paganini), and a notable collection of scientific instruments. This catalogue reproduces 234 of the library's greatest treasures with representative examples of all its areas of strength. It includes 87 manuscripts, 24 incunables and rare books, 48 prints, 9 music manuscripts, 17 Baroque stage designs, 15 scientific instruments, 14 books on science, 14 fine bindings, 3 periodicals, and 3 edicts and proclamations. See also *La Biblioteca Casanatense* (The Casanatense Library), presented by Carlo Pietrangeli (Florence, Italy: Nardini, 1993. 331p. [Le Grandi Biblioteche d'Italia]).

775 La Biblioteca nazionale centrale 'Vittorio Emanuele II' di Roma: cronistoria di un trasferimento, 1953-1975. (The Biblioteca nazionale centrale 'Vittorio Emanuele II' of Rome: the chronicle of a move, 1953-1975.)
Edited by Osvaldo Avallone (et al.). Rome: Fratelli Palombi, 1988. 75p. bibliog. (Quaderni dell'Ufficio Centrale per i Beni Librari e gli Istituti Culturali, no. 1, 1988.)

An account of the move of the Biblioteca nazionale from Via del Collegio Romano to its present home in the Castro Pretorio area. Since its foundation in 1876 the library had occupied a wing of the Collegio Romano, which soon proved to be too small to satisfy the requirements of a rapidly expanding library. The need to move the collections to a more spacious, purpose-built home had been voiced periodically during the first half of the century and new locations were proposed (one of which was next to the Pantheon!) but it was only after the crisis of 1953, when the library remained closed for some six months after structural faults were discovered in the building and some of the collections had to be outhoused to avoid the possibility of floors collapsing, that the problem was given emergency treatment. Various proposals for a different site were studied over the next few years and some of the operations of the library had to be carried out in other libraries such as the Vallicelliana and the Angelica, while the Vittoriano was used for the storage of parts of the collections. After a variety of sites had been considered it was decided, in 1958, to use the extensive area then used as barracks in the Castro Pretorio (also called Macao) area because of its proximity to the university and other cultural institutes. This study also looks at the winning project, the construction of the new building, the move of the collections, and the inauguration of the new library in 1975. There are numerous photographs showing both the reading areas and the unsatisfactory conditions in the book stacks of the Collegio Romano, and also the modern building and its spacious surroundings.

776 La Biblioteca nazionale Vittorio Emanuele al Collegio Romano. (The Vittorio Emanuele National Library at the Collegio Romano.)
Virginia Carini Dainotti. Florence, Italy: Leo S. Olschki, 1956- . 217p. (Collana di Monografie delle Biblioteche d'Italia, 2.)

The library owes its existence to the efforts of Ruggero Bonghi, Minister of Education when Rome became the capital of Italy, who wanted a great national library in Rome along the lines of other similar institutions abroad. The library was inaugurated in 1876 and occupied a wing of the Collegio Romano, and its original nucleus from the Jesuit collections was soon enriched as a result of the suppression of religious corporations in 1873. This volume (the first in a projected two-volume work) begins with a discussion of the cultural background, in the 1860s, in which the idea about a central national library was discussed. This is followed by an account of the establishment of the library, a description of its foundation collections, and an examination of its difficult first years, which were beset by scandals and ended with the appointment in 1880 of a parliamentary commission presided over by A. Baccelli which investigated its operations. The second volume, which was intended to cover the history of the library and its collections from 1882 to the present, has not been published.

777 **La Biblioteca Universitaria Alessandrina.** (The Biblioteca
Universitaria Alessandrina.)
Carola Ferrari, Antonietta Pintor.   Rome: Fratelli Palombi, 1960.
47p. (Guide delle Biblioteche del Lazio e dell'Umbria.)
A brief history of the university library named after Pope Alexander VII, its founder, and
a guide to its collections, catalogues and services. The library was originally housed in a
building adjacent to S. Ivo alla Sapienza until its move, in 1935, to the purpose-built
Palazzo del Rettorato in the Città universitaria.

778 **La Bibliothèque du Vatican au XV siècle.** (The Vatican Library in the
fifteenth century.)
Eugène Müntz and Paul Fabre.   Amsterdam, the Netherlands: Gérard
Th. van Heusden, 1970. 388p., [40]p. (Bibliothèques des Écoles
Françaises d'Athènes et de Rome, 48.)
A collection of documents showing the development of the Vatican Library and its collections
between the pontificate of Pope Martin V and that of Alexander VI. The library was essentially
the creation of the great humanist popes – in 1443, under Eugenius IV, it had 340 volumes, only
two of which were in Greek; by the death of Sixtus IV in 1484, their number had increased to
c. 3,650, 1,000 of them in Greek. The collection includes the inventories of the Greek and Latin
libraries of Nicholas V.

779 **Codice diplomatico di Roma e della regione romana.** (Public
documents of Rome and its region.)
Rome: Società romana di storia patria, 1981-89.
This a monographic series of catalogues of public documents in monastery and other collections
in Rome and its region. The collections covered are those of the Monastero di SS Cosma e
Damiano in Mica Aurea, the old archive of S. Andrea 'De Aquariciariis', the notarial register
of Lorenzo Staglai, the earliest documents in the convent of S. Sisto in Rome, the parchments
of Sezze, and the notarial register of Pietro di Nicola Astalli.

780 **I Corsini a Roma e le origini della Biblioteca Corsiniana.** (The
Corsini in Rome and the origins of Biblioteca Corsiniana.)
Panfilia Orzi Smeriglio.   In: *Atti dell'Accademia nazionale dei Lincei,
anno 355 (1958)*. *Memorie della Classe di scienze morali, storiche e
filologiche* (Proceedings of the Accademia nazionale dei Lincei, 355th
year [1958]. Papers of the Section of Moral Philosophy, History and
Philology), series 8, vol. 8, fasc. 4, p. 291-331.   Rome: Accademia
nazionale dei Lincei, 1958.
The Corsini family came from Florence, its origins going back to the 13th century and counting
among its members bankers, diplomats, statesmen, and priests. A branch of the family moved
to Rome on the accession to the papal throne of a fellow Florentine, Maffeo Barberini (Pope
Urban VIII). This study traces the family's history and the formation of its library, making use
of archival material, notably the *Liber Instrumentorum* which contains copies of all the notarial
acts concerning the Library and the documents, stating the sums allocated for its maintenance.
It also looks at the family's various residences in Rome, first the palazzo in Piazza Fiammetta,
and later the palazzo in the Lungara constructed by Ferdinando Fuga on the site of Palazzo

Riario. In the 19th century, the family ceded the Palazzo to the Accademia dei Lincei, and it later donated its library to the Academy.

781 **The culture of the High Renaissance: ancients and moderns in sixteenth-century Rome.**
Ingrid D. Rowland. Cambridge, England: Cambridge University Press, 1998. 398p. bibliog.

A wide-ranging study of Rome between 1480 and 1520 which looks at the culture and society that created the High Renaissance. Three characters figure prominently in the narrative, exemplifying different strains of Roman society – Angelo Colocci (humanist, publisher), Tommaso 'Fedro' Inghirami (papal librarian and orator), and Agostino Chigi (the wealthy merchant and art patron). Its cast of characters is, however, much wider. It includes, in fact, most of the prominent figures in Rome during this period, including the popes and their families, humanists, artists, and printers. It discusses the Roman Academy and the curial administration and examines all the major commissions of Raphael and Michelangelo.

782 **Esotismo in Roma barocca: studi sul padre Kircher.** (Exoticism in Baroque Rome: studies on Father Kircher.)
Valerio Rivosecchi. Rome: Bulzoni, 1982. 165p. (Biblioteca di Storia dell'Arte, 12.)

The Jesuit Athanasius Kircher (1602-80) was one of the most learned men in 17th-century Rome. He taught mathematics, physics and Oriental languages at the Collegio Romano, was fluent in twenty-four languages, and his interests ranged from archaeology to numerology. He was particularly interested in the study of Egyptian hieroglyphs and, after the erection of the obelisk in Piazza Navona during Innocent X's pontificate, he published a treatise on the monument (*Obeliscus Pamphilius*) and an interpretation of its inscriptions. His Museo Kircheriano was a mixture of Egyptian artefacts, scientific instruments, portraits of famous contemporaries and curiosities from all over the world. After 1870, the collections of the museum were incorporated into those of other Roman museums. This volume examines Kircher's studies of Egyptian antiquities and hieroglyphs; his *China illustrata* (1667, 1668, 1670)), an encyclopaedic and richly-illustrated work on China, India and other Far Eastern countries; and his collaboration with Bernini, first in the re-erection of the obelisk in Piazza Navona and the Four Rivers Fountain (1648-51), and later in the sculptural group in front of S. Maria sopra Minerva. The last chapter describes the Museo Kircheriano, which is seen here not only as a reflection of the variety of interests of its creator but also of the complexity of the culture of 17th-century Rome. There is also an essay and a bibliography of works on the cultural relations between Italy and the Far East in the 17th century. The texts are accompanied by some 200 plates. See also Joscelyn Godwin, *Athanasius Kircher: a Renaissance man and the quest for lost knowledge* (London: Thames & Hudson, 1979. 96p. bibliog.).

783 **Guida delle biblioteche dei pontifici istituti di studi superiori in Roma.**
(Guide to the libraries of the papal institutes of higher studies in Rome.)
Edited by Silvano Danieli and Giuseppe Tabarelli. Rome: Gruppo biblioteche ecclesiastiche, 1992. 92p.

This guide is divided into three groupings: the libraries of G.B.E. (Gruppo Biblioteche Ecclesiastiche romane), those of U.R.B.E. (Unione Romana Biblioteche Ecclesiastiche) and, finally, libraries of other religious institutes. In the first two categories, each entry includes a brief history and description of the collection, a bibliography of works about the library, opening hours and conditions of use, and information about the library's catalogues and its holdings. The entries for the libraries in the last category are briefer, limited only to addresses and subject coverage. There is also a separate subject index.

784 Histoire de l'Académie de France à Rome. (History of the French Academy in Rome.)
Henry Lapauze.   Paris: Librairie Plon, 1924. 2 vols. (530p., 595p.)

A detailed history of the French Academy in Rome from its foundation by Louis XIV in 1666 to 1910. It traces the changes of home the Academy has had during its long history. In the 17th century it originally occupied Palazzo Caffarelli, later moving to the more spacious Palazzo Capranica. In 1725 it moved into the Palazzo Mancini on the Corso, where it remained until its move in 1803 to the Villa Medici, the prestigious building it still occupies. Most chapters cover events and developments occurring during a single directorship. The length of directorships varied – Charles Natoire served for a record twenty-four years, from 1751 to 1775 – until, in the 19th century, the term was fixed at five years. The majority of its directors were artists, a number of them former *pensionnaires* at the Academy. Distinguished directors included Charles Errard (1666-72), Pierre Guérin (1823-28), Horace Vernet (1829-34), Ingres (1835-40), Hébert (1867-72 and 1885-90), and Carolus-Duran (1905-10).

785 Indici e sussidi bibliografici della Biblioteca. (Indices and bibliographical aids of the Library.)
Rome: Accademia nazionale dei Lincei, 1962- .

A series of monographic studies on the collections of the library of the Accademia nazionale dei Lincei. Most volumes are catalogues of specific parts of the collection (periodicals and academic acts; Arabic, Persian and Ethiopian manuscripts; the music collection; items related to Galileo) while others focus on subjects or figures related to the Academy (for example, the correspondence between G. G. Bottari and P. F. Foggini), or commemorate an anniversary (for example, the 7th centenary of Dante's birth).

786 La 'libraria' di Mattia Casanate. (The library of Mattia Casanate.)
Marina Panetta.   Rome: Bulzoni, 1988. 246p. (Il Bibliotecario. Nuova Serie, Saggi, 2.)

The library of Cardinal Girolamo Casanate (1620-1700), bequeathed to the Dominican convent of S. Maria sopra Minerva, contained over 20,000 items collected by the Cardinal himself but also from the library of Mattia Casanate, his father. In the present arrangement of the library it is difficult to establish which volumes were in the foundation collection and, within that, which were in the library of Mattia Casanate. The discovery of an inventory of the latter has made possible this catalogue of 1,639 items consisting of 17 manuscripts, 5 incunables and 1,617 16th- and 17th-century printed books. The introduction includes a biographical sketch of Mattia Casanate (*c.* 1580-1651) – an Aragonese diplomat and Regent in the court of Naples, who died a broken man after his dismissal in 1651 – and analyses the nine categories into which the inventory is divided, enumerating notable titles and editions in each category. The library has works in Spanish, Latin and Italian and is rich in civil and canon law, religion, Bibles, liturgies, Greek and Latin patristic literature, church history, humanist literature, geography and discovery, and alchemy and science.

787 **Lutyens in Italy: the building of the British School at Rome.**
Hugh Petter, with a foreword by Colin Amery. London: British School
at Rome, 1992. 55p. (British School at Rome Archive, 3.)
This study traces the history of the building of the British School at Rome in Valle Giulia.
Originally constructed by Sir Edwin Lutyens as the English Pavilion at the International
Exhibition in 1911, its design was an adaptation of the upper order of the west front of St Paul's
Cathedral. The success of the pavilion led to the donation of the site and the building of a
permanent home for the British School at Rome, which had hitherto been housed at a leased
wing of the Palazzo Odescalchi. The work discusses the importance of the commission to
Lutyens's career and traces the various phases of the construction of the building. It also
examines the establishment of a Rome scholarship, on the lines of the French *Prix de Rome*,
under the supervision of the director of the British School, with the building as a residential
and working centre for Rome scholars. There are numerous contemporary photographs,
architectural plans and portraits.

788 **Un pontificato e una città: Sisto IV, 1471-1484.** (A pontificate and a
city: Sixtus IV, 1471-1484.)
Edited by Massimo Miglio (et al.). Vatican City: Scuola vaticana di
paleografia, diplomatica e archivistica, 1986. 841p. (Littera Antiqua, 5.)
The proceedings of a conference organized in 1986 by the Scuola vaticana di paleografia,
diplomatica e archivistica. The thirty papers (in Italian, French or English) examine a wide
variety of subjects related to the social and cultural life during the reign of Sixtus IV. Subjects
examined include: the role of Rome in Italy; the Vatican Library (its changes of location and the
re-arrangement of its collections between 1471 and 1481, its early inventories) and other centres
of learning such as the Augustinian library at S. Maria del Popolo and the Dominican library at
S. Maria sopra Minerva; the patronage of Sixtus IV; humanism; society and social unrest (the
Porcari family; the death of Lorenzo Oddone Colonna); the relationship between the Jewish and
Christian communities; epigraphy; funerary monuments; book production; learning and the
Studium Urbis. The volume also includes an analysis (by various authors) of the population,
commercial life and social life of the *rione* Parione.

789 **The popes and the revival of learning.**
John Linus Paschang. Washington, DC: The Catholic University of
America Press, 1927. 146p.
The aim of this study is to determine the relationship between the papacy and the Renaissance
of learning in the period beginning with the reign of Pope Martin V in 1417 and ending with
the Sack of Rome in 1527 during the reign of Clement VII. It considers relations between the
respective popes and the prominent scholars of the time, their attitudes towards the Vatican
Library and the collecting of manuscripts, and their interest in the *Studium Urbis* and other
schools of learning. It concludes that papal patronage was crucial to the success of the
Renaissance and that in Rome scholars congregated or dispersed according to the disposition of
the reigning pope, the city becoming the meeting place for humanists and scholars during the
pontificates of Nicholas V, Sixtus IV and Leo X. The popes were instrumental in the survival
of classical texts which they bought, had copied (and later printed) and translated at the Vatican.

790   Praise and blame in Renaissance Rome: rhetoric, doctrine, and
       reform in the sacred orators of the Papal Court, *c.* 1450-1521.
       John W. O'Malley.   Durham, North Carolina: Duke University Press,
       1979. 288p.

A study of the style and content of Renaissance oratory composed in Italy in the 15th and early
16th century. It focuses on some 160 sermons (the sermons *Coram papa inter missarum
solemnia*) delivered before the pope during the sacred liturgies in the Sistine Chapel and St
Peter's between *c.* 1450 and 1521, of which it provides a detailed analysis. (An appendix
contains a short title-finding list of all the strictly liturgical orations at the Papal Court during
this period.) It also examines the adoption in these sermons of the *genus demonstrativum*
(epideictic genre) of classical rhetoric, which distributed 'praise and blame'. The work is an
important contribution to the study of the religious sensibilities of the period and to the
description of the nature of Renaissance humanism. For a study of oratory in the second half of
the 16th century see Frederick J. McGinness, *Right thinking and sacred oratory in Counter-
Reformation Rome* (Princeton, New Jersey: Princeton University Press, 1995. 349p.).

791   Renaissance humanism in papal Rome: humanists and churchmen
       on the eve of the Reformation.
       John D'Amico.   Baltimore, Maryland; London: The Johns Hopkins
       University Press, 1983. 349p. (The Johns Hopkins University Studies in
       Historical and Political Science, 101st series [1983].)

Based on unpublished manuscript sources from the Vatican Library, this study examines Rome
as a centre of Italian humanism. Part one examines the social and political context and
establishes that Roman humanism was closely related to the functions of the Roman curia, as
expertise in classical Latin was used for the administrative needs of the Renaissance papacy.
The nature of this curial humanism is examined together with that of Pomponio Leto's Roman
Academy, which cultivated expertise in poetry and oratory. Part two examines the idiom of
Roman humanism, the much satirized ciceronianism, which the author shows to be much more
than a mere preoccupation with style, an authoritative language that was an amalgam of
classical Latin and Christian theology and morality. It uses as examples the religious writings
of Paolo Cortesi (whose *De Cardinalatu* is a high point of Roman humanism), Adriano
Castellesi, and Raffaele Maffei.

792   The Renaissance in Rome.
       Charles L. Stinger.   Bloomington, Indiana: Indiana University Press,
       1998 (paperback edition). 444p. bibliog.

This is a comprehensive study of the intellectual and cultural history of the Renaissance in
Rome, from the return of Pope Eugenius IV to the city in 1443 to the Sack of Rome in 1527.
The wide-ranging discussion includes ceremonies, oratory, art and architecture and it focuses on
certain important themes such as the image of the city of Rome, the primacy of the Catholic
Church and the restoration of the Roman Empire. In the preface to this reissue of his work
(which was originally published in 1985), the author surveys recent research.

793 Roma e Lazio, 1930-1950: guida per le ricerche: fascismo, antifascismo, guerra, resistenza, dopoguerra. (Rome and Lazio, 1930-1950: a guide to research: Fascism, anti-Fascism, Resistance, the postwar period.) Edited by Antonio Parisella. Milan, Italy: FrancoAngeli, 1994. 559p. (Collana di Storia Contemporanea dell'Istituto Romano per la Storia d'Italia dal Fascismo alla Resistenza.)

A guide to printed and archival sources in Rome and Lazio on the period between 1930 and 1950. It is divided in three parts: the first gives fifty-nine locations where holdings of this material are to be found. These are in nine sections: state archives, the archives of the 'comuni' and the 'province', church archives, town hall archives, anti-fascist and partisan associations, state libraries, research institutes, army libraries and, finally, other institutions such as the Fondazione Marco Besso, the Museo storico della Liberazione in Roma, and the Comunità ebraica di Roma. The entry for each institution includes practical information and a short history of the collection. The second part is a bibliography and a catalogue of some 600 periodicals. Each entry is accompanied by the acronyms of libraries that hold the publication – twenty-two libraries are included in this section. The third part is a detailed chronology of the Resistance in Rome and Lazio from July 1943 to June 1944.

794 Rome in the Renaissance: the city and the myth. Edited by P. A. Ramsey. Binghamton, New York: Center for Medieval and Early Renaissance Studies, 1982. (Medieval & Renaissance Texts and Studies, 18.)

Twenty-nine papers read at a conference organized by the State University of New York at Binghamton in 1979 which examined the tensions and apparent conflicts in Renaissance Rome. They are divided into two sections, the first consisting of six plenary papers and the second of twenty-three special session papers out of some seventy read at the conference. Subjects discussed included: the physical evolution of the city and the political, social, and economic considerations that determined its development; the conflict inherent in the image of Renaissance Rome as the living embodiment of the ancient world but also the centre of the Catholic Church; the revival of the coronation of the Poet Laureate on the Campidoglio; the myths created by the Renaissance humanists and mythic inventions in Counter-Reformation painting; Martin V and the revival of the arts in Rome; Nicholas V and Rome; theatre in Renaissance Rome; the singers of the papal chapel and liturgical ceremonies in the early 16th century; Greek patristics and Christian antiquity in Renaissance Rome; Montaigne's and Joachim du Bellay's perceptions of Rome; Shakespeare's Roman plays; Ben Jonson and the English use of Roman history; Milton and classical Rome; Filippino Lippi's *Triumph of St Thomas Aquinas* in S. Maria sopra Minerva; Botticelli's *Temptation of Christ* in the Sistine Chapel; and the grain supply crisis and urban unrest of 1533-34.

795 Rome reborn: the Vatican Library and Renaissance culture. Edited by Anthony Grafton. Washington, DC: Library of Congress; New Haven, Connecticut; London: Yale Universiry Press, 1993. 349p. bibliog.

This is the catalogue of an exhibition held at the Library of Congress in 1993. The introduction by Leonard Boyle surveys the formation of the library and various stages in its development. It discusses the original library of Pope Nicholas V, which contained some 1,100 Latin and Greek codices, as well as his private library, the *Bibliotheca secreta*, which gave the Vatican library its ecumenical character. Nicholas wanted to build a library for the common use of the learned but the building had to wait for another twenty years, until Sixtus IV. The reign of Sixtus V, the 'third founder' of the library, saw the appointment of three *scriptores* representing the interests of the Latin, Greek, and Hebrew languages. The library today has some two million printed books and serials (including 8,000 incunabula), 75,000 manuscripts, 100,000 prints and drawings, and 330,000 Greek, Roman, and papal coins and medals. Boyle notes some of the most important acquisitions in the history of the library, which include: the Palatine Library from Heidelberg (in 1622, with 2,000 Latin and 430 Greek manuscripts, and 8,000 printed books), the Ottoboni library (3,000 Latin and 473 Greek manuscripts), the library and archives of the Sistine Chapel (in 1902, with 1,200 music manuscripts), and the Barberini library (in 1902, with 30,000 printed books, 11,000 Latin, 600 Greek, and 165 Oriental manuscripts). Since 1883, the library has been open to qualified researchers but Boyle is critical of its policy of producing elaborate catalogues rather than simple, straightforward inventories of its holdings when a large percentage of its manuscript collection has not been catalogued. The eight chapters of the catalogue examine various aspects of Renaissance culture, with examples from the collection – humanism, archaeology, ecclesiastical history, Egyptology, mathematics, astronomy, and geography; life sciences and medicine; music; Eastern churches and Western scholarship; East Asia. There are 216 colour plates of manuscripts and printed books from the collection. These are listed by *Fondo* (named and special collections) at the end of the catalogue.

796 **Scrittura, biblioteche e stampa a Roma nel Quattrocento.** (Writing, libraries and printing in Rome in the fifteenth century.)
Edited by C. Bianca (et al.). Vatican City: Scuola vaticana di paleografia, diplomatica e archivistica, 1980-83. 3 vols. (526p., 302p., 899p.). (Littera Antiqua, I, 1-3.)

Volumes one and three are the proceedings of the conferences held at the Vatican Library in 1979 and 1981. They contain twenty-one papers discussing humanism and printing in Rome in the 15th century, examining individual books and manuscripts, and considering notable 15th-century book collectors and their libraries. These include: Cardinal Bessarion, Bishop Domenico Lucari, Niccolò Cusano, Domenico Capranica, Jean Jouffroy, Cardinal Guillaume D'Estouteville, Marco Barbo, and Giordano Orsini. The second volume is an index of 1,828 Roman incunables published between 1467 and 1500, listed by publication date, with indexes of printers, authors, translators, recipients, and of anonymous works.

797 **Seventeenth-century Barberini documents and inventories of art.**
Marilyn Aronberg Lavin. New York: New York University Press, *c*. 1975. 756p.

This catalogue, based on the Barberini Archive in the Vatican Library, offers invaluable information about the activities of the family of Pope Urban VIII. The Archive covers the history of the family from the 13th to the 19th century but the present compilers chose to concentrate on the 17th century, the apogee of the family's power and wealth, when Francesco, Antonio and Taddeo Barberini, the three papal nephews, amassed huge fortunes, embarked on building campaigns and created one of the largest private art collections in Europe. The catalogue is in two sections: Documents (1-443), taken from household book-keeping records (which include orders, payments, receipts, entry and exit notices); and inventories, which record the contents of various family properties and include information about all types of works of art, their subject-matter, attribution and, occasionally, monetary value. Texts from some twenty inventories between 1608 and 1692/1704 were used, each preceded by a brief introduction naming the patron, the location described, and the purpose of the inventory. Inventories pertaining to paintings and sculpture are transcribed in full, with extracts from the much lengthier documents about decorative art. A 'Master Index' under artist and subject matter gives dates and dimensions and also other data, including, in some cases, present whereabouts.

798 A short history of the British School at Rome.
      T. P. Wiseman.   London: British School at Rome, 1990. 43p. bibliog.

The School was founded in 1901 to promote the study of Roman and Graeco-Roman archaeology and paleography and, more generally, Roman and Italian studies by assisting British students in Rome. It was originally housed at Palazzo Odescalchi until 1915 when it moved into the Sir Edwin Lutyens building based on his design for the British pavilion at the 1911 International Exhibition in Rome. From 1907 the School provided a base for students on travelling scholarships from the RIBA (Royal Institute of British Architects), the Royal College of Art and elsewhere, and from 1913 it provided scholarships for painting, sculpture and architecture and, later, for classical studies (1928) and medieval studies (1931). This short study gives an excellent account of the School's history and the often larger-than-life personalities of some of its directors (Thomas Ashby, director from 1906 to 1925, was a great archaeologist, scholar and collector but his brusqueness was a constant source of administrative problems, while Mrs E. Strong, his Assistant Director, possessed the social graces that he lacked and was the queen of the School until Ashby's marriage in 1924). The School's achievements in the fields of classical and medieval studies are also examined, together with the occasional tensions between archaeologists and artists. The names of the recipients of the School's various scholarships are given in two appendices.

799 Sixtus IV and men of letters.
      Egmont Lee.   Rome: Edizioni di storia e letteratura, 1978. 288p. (Temi e Testi, 26.)

A study of the intellectual climate in Rome during the reign of Pope Sixtus IV from 1471 to 1484. It includes a biographical sketch of Sixtus showing both his personal humility and his ruthless political actions (such as the plan in 1478 to overthrow the Medici from Florence) that foreshadow those of Alexander VI, highlighting his relationship with the projects and institutions he supported, in particular the University of Rome. It also examines: the history of other schools of learning, libraries, and hospitals (Ospedale di Santo Spirito); and Curial officials and the nature of their activities (the Curial officials were papal secretaries who, though involved in the intellectual life of their time, rarely had the opportunity or determination to pursue scholarly or literary work while holding a high position. Exceptions to this rule were Giovanni Andrea Bussi and Domizio Calderini, a popular professor at the *Studium Urbis*). Other notable secretaries included Leonardo Grifo, who exercised a strong influence on Sixtus on matters of patronage and carried out extensive correspondence with Francesco Filelfo, Platinus Platus and other intellectuals in Rome and elsewhere; Jacopo Gherardi and Sigismondo de' Conti, both distinguished historians, Gherardi writing a diary for the years 1479-84 and Sigismondo a history of his times (1475-1510) depicting events from a Roman viewpoint and giving a detailed picture of life at the Curia; Gaspar Blondus; and Andreas Trapezuntius. The author questions Sixtus's place among the great Renaissance patrons of arts and letters (such as Lorenzo de' Medici, Nicholas V and Pius II), establishing that bureaucratic competence rather than scholarly distinction was the prime criterion for employment in the Curia and, though the presence of intellectuals was sought, this was in order to add to the prestige of the papal court rather than out of interest in their work.

800   **Storia delle Accademie d'Italia.** (A history of Academies in Italy.)
Michele Maylender, preface by Luigi Rava.   Bologna, Italy: Licinio
Cappelli, 1926-30. 5 vols.

Literary academies played an important role in the study of classical literature, Italian language
and the development and diffusion of literary forms from the 16th to the 18th century. The most
famous was the *Accademia della Crusca* in Florence. In Rome, the most important academies
were the *Accademia dei Lincei*, founded in 1603 and counting Galileo Galilei among its earliest
members; the *Accademia degli Arcadi*, which had its origins in Queen Christina's *Accademia
reale* and was founded by Giovanni Mario Crescimbeni shortly after her death for the purpose
of reviving the study of poetry; and the *Accademia dei Belli Umori*, for the recitation of verses
and speeches. This essential reference work is arranged alphabetically under academy and each
volume has an index arranged by city – there is no general index. The entries for the more
important academies are monographic in length.

801   **Umanesimo a Roma nel Quattrocento.** (Humanism in Rome in the
fifteenth century.)
Edited by Paolo Brezzi and Maristella De Panizza Lorch.   Rome:
Istituto di studi romani, 1984. 352p.

Eighteen papers, in Italian or English, read at a conference held in New York in 1981. They are
divided into four sections: Rome in the 14th-century (which includes an overview of social,
political and economic conditions and an examination of aspects of book production and
circulation); Rome and the Papal Curia (with studies on humanism and the Curia, Poggio
Bracciolini, humanists and the *Studium Urbis* between 1473 and 1484, and two studies on
Lorenzo Valla's 'De voluptate' [On pleasure]); Rome and the visual arts (papal patronage under
the pontificates of Martin V, Eugenius IV and Nicholas V, ancient Roman monuments as
models and as topoi); and Rome and the humanists (a survey of humanist culture in Rome
as well as studies on Biòndo, Bruni and Annio da Viterbo).

Publishing

802 Gli annali tipografici di Eucario e Marcello Silber, 1501-1527. (The printing annals of Eucario and Marcello Silber, 1501-1527.)
Alberto Tinto.   Florence, Italy: Leo S. Olschki, 1968. 215p. (Biblioteca di Bibliografia Italiana, 55.)

The German printer Eucario Silber and his son Marcello were active in Rome from 1480 to 1527. The printing annals of the firm are divided into two categories. The first includes all the editions signed by them and also all those which, though their name does not appear in the publication, can nevertheless be identified as theirs. The second category contains all the editions signed by Giacomo Mazzocchi but printed by the presses of Silber. Little is known about Eucario Silber other than that he was a cleric from the diocese of Würzburg who, between 1480 and 1509, printed and sold books in his workshop on Campo de' Fiori. His publications included scientific works, classical literature and theology. 293 editions are known to have been printed by him between 1480 and 1500 and a further 66 between 1501 and 1509. Marcello continued the family business from 1510 to 1527. His output included official works of the Roman Curia as well as publications of a more popular nature (tourist guides, descriptions of battles, and religious tracts). The present catalogue includes Eucario Silber's publications from 1501 to 1509 (65 items), and those of Marcello Silber from c. 1510 to 1527 (274 items). There are 46 plates showing examples of their work. See also Fernanda Ascarelli, *Annali tipografici di Giacomo Mazzocchi* (Printing annals of Giacomo Mazzocchi) (Florence, Italy: Sansoni, 1961. 207p. bibliog. [Biblioteca Bibliografica Italica Diretta da Marino Parenti, 24]). It lists 167 works printed or published by Mazzocchi between 1505 and 1528.

803 Byzantium for Rome: the politics of nostalgia in Umbertian Italy, 1878-1900.
Richard Drake.   Chapel Hill, North Carolina: The University of North Carolina, 1980. 335p.

Drake traces the meteoric rise and fall of the pioneering publisher Angelo Sommaruga (1857-1941). Sommaruga's review *Cronaca bizantina* (1881-85) had among its editorial team Gabriele D'Annunzio, Edoardo Scarfoglio and Giulio Salvadori, a group of young idealists united by their common admiration of Giosuè Carducci. Other collaborators included Giovanni Verga (whose *Cavalleria rusticana* was first published in the review), Luigi Capuana, Matilde

Publishing

Serao, and Émile Zola. The success of the review enabled Sommaruga to begin publishing books (some 130 titles, mostly literature). His downfall was brought about when he was prosecuted by the government for allegations made in *Forche caudine*, an immensely popular political scandal sheet he also published, directed by P. Sbarbaro.

804 Catalogo delle edizioni romane di Antonio Blado Asolano ed eredi, 1516-1593. (Catalogue of the Roman editions of Antonio Blado from Asolo and his heirs, 1516-1593.)
Giuseppe Fumagalli, Giacomo Belli, Emerenziana Vaccaro Sofia.
Rome: Presso i principali librai, 1891-1961. 4 vols. bibliog.

The first two fascicles were edited by Giuseppe Fumagalli and Giacomo Belli and catalogued the holdings of the Biblioteca nazionale centrale Vittorio Emanuele II. The work of these two scholars was continued and completed by Emerenziana Vaccaro Sofia who published, in 1942 and 1961, the holdings of Blado editions in the following libraries in Rome: Alessandrina, Angelica, Casanatense, Corsiniana, Vallicelliana, the Archivio di stato di Roma, the Archivio segreto vaticano, and the Vatican Library. Blado was the most prolific 16th-century printer in Rome. He began publishing in 1516 and his workshop was situated on the Campo de' Fiori. His output was varied and included religion, music, medicine, law, classical literature and, from 1535, when he was appointed papal printer, numerous bulls, edicts, proclamations and other official documents. After his death in 1567 his heirs continued to run the family business until 1593. The catalogue contains 2,922 entries and the fourth volume provides a numerical index of locations with shelfmarks and also a general index.

805 Cronaca bizantina. (Byzantine chronicle.)
Edited by Vincenzo Chiarenza. Treviso, Italy: Canova, 1975. 260p. (Le Riviste dell'Italia Moderna e Contemporanea, 11.)

A collection of articles that appeared in *Cronaca bizantina*, the most famous review of the Umbertine period, the creation of Angelo Sommaruga. It was published between 1881 and 1885 and numbered among its collaborators some of the most famous writers of the time. Included here are articles by Giosuè Carducci, Luigi Capuana, Matilde Serao, Giovanni Verga, and Gabriele D'Annunzio. The review was short-lived as in March 1885 Sommaruga was arrested, sent to prison and later tried and found guilty of libel for articles published in *Forche caudine*, a political scandal-sheet he also owned. An attempt, in November 1885, to revive the review under the direction of D'Annunzio proved unsuccessful.

806 Indice delle stampe De' Rossi: contributo alla storia di una stamperia romana. (Index of the prints of De' Rossi: a study of the history of a Roman printing firm.)
Edited by Anna Grelle Iusco. Rome: Artemide edizioni, 1996. 608p. bibliog.

This is a critical edition of the 1735 catalogue/inventory of the most important print publishing shop in Rome. The firm had been active for more than a century and this was the last catalogue of its copperplates before the entire collection of Lorenzo Filippo De' Rossi was purchased, in 1738, by Pope Clement XII Corsini, leading to the establishment of the Calcografia camerale which, together with the Gabinetto delle stampe, formed, in 1975, the Istituto nazionale della grafica. The inventory is a barometer of 17th- and 18th-century print culture and commerce in Rome. This work examines the history of the shop and the role played by the De' Rossi family in the choice and diffusion of images. It includes a facsimile reprint of the 1735 catalogue with a synoptic table on facing pages giving references to mentions of each item in preceding and subsequent catalogues as well as its present inventory number in the Istituto nazionale della grafica. The Index includes: maps (notably the *Mercurio geografico*, a two-volume collection of 185 maps); battle scenes; antiquities of Rome (in volumes and on single sheets); maps and views of modern Rome; prints reproducing works by, among others, the Carracci, Correggio, Carlo Maratti, Federico Barocci, Domenichino, Primaticcio, Guido Reni, Michelangelo, Raphael, and Titian; sacred and profane subjects; architectural and ornamental works; portraits of twenty-six popes (from Nicholas III to Leo XI); a series of chronologies accompanied by portraits of popes, emperors, and kings; and a book of portraits of cardinals from the reign of Pope Paul V to 1735. There are copious notes for all items in the Index, and two useful appendices: a subject index to the *Mercurio geografico* and a subject index to the volume of portraits of cardinals, with full details of engravers and original artists.

807 Roma bizantina. (Byzantine Rome.)
Edited by Enrico Ghidetti. Milan, Italy: Longanesi & Co., 1979. 256p. (Immagini, 15.)

An anthology of texts from *Cronaca bizantina* but, unlike entry no. 804 where the texts selected were mainly short stories by some of the review's more famous collaborators, the choice here is mostly of articles published anonymously under one of the review's regular rubrics – 'Corriere di Roma', 'Sul Corso', 'Salotti romani', 'Blasone romano'– consisting of vignettes of contemporary Roman life and society. The introduction outlines the meteoric career of Angelo Sommaruga, the publisher of *Cronaca bizantina*. The texts are accompanied by numerous striking photographs of contemporary personalities, among them Prince Giovanni Torlonia, Prince Alessandro Ruspoli, the photographer Giuseppe Primoli, and various society beauties, as well as views of Rome.

808 La stampa in Italia nel Cinquecento. (Sixteenth-century printing in Italy.)
Edited by Marco Santoro. Rome: Bulzoni, 1992. 2 vols. 926p.

The proceedings of a conference organized by the Scuola speciale per archivisti e bibliotecari of the Università degli studi di Roma 'La Sapienza' and held at the Biblioteca nazionale centrale di Roma in 1989. There are thirty-nine articles dealing with various aspects of book publishing in 16th-century Italy. Though there are references to Rome in several of these articles, three of them concentrate on Roman book production. Jesus M. de Bujanda, in 'Il primo Indice romano' (The first Roman Index, 1559) (vol. 1, p. 49-70), examines the genesis, contents, and impact of the Roman Inquisition's first Index of Forbidden Books, the publication of which, in 1559, marked the real beginning of the Counter-Reformation in Rome. Valentino Romani, in 'Luoghi editoriali in Roma e nello Stato della Chiesa' (Publishing places in Rome and the Papal State) (vol. 1, p. 515-32), points out the widespread presence in Rome of non-Roman printers and booksellers and examines the institution of the book privilege which made Rome one of the poles of publishers' legal protection. Maria Cristina Misiti, in 'Antonio Salamanca: qualche chiarimento biografico alla luce di un' indagine sulla presenza spagnola a Roma nel '500' (Antonio Salamanca: some biographical clarifications in the context of an investigation of the Spanish presence in sixteenth-century Rome) (vol. 1, p. 545-63), looks at the presence of the Spanish community in the papal court and in the curial offices and also in various trades in the city. Antonio Salamanca was active as a bookseller, publisher and printer of Spanish literary texts noted for the quality of their engravings.

809 **Tipografi romani del Cinquecento: Guillery, Ginnasio mediceo, Calvo, Dorico, Cartolari.** (Roman sixteenth-century printers: Guillery, Ginnasio mediceo, Calvo, Dorico, Cartolari.) Francesco Barberi. Florence, Italy: Leo S. Olschki, 1983. 181p. (Biblioteconomia e Bibliografia: Saggi e Studi, 17.)

This volume brings together some of Francesco Barberi's writings on the output of four 16th-century Roman printers, previously published in the journal *La Bibliofilia* and elsewhere. The printers covered are: Stefano Guillery; Francesco Minizio Calvo; the Dorico; and Baldassarre Cartolari the Younger and Girolama Cartolari. This is a useful collection, although it omits the numerous illustrations that originally accompanied the journal articles. Moreover, the articles on Calvo and the Cartolari originally included analytical descriptions of their editions, replaced here by short title-lists in chronological order, which also accompany the articles on Guillery and the Dorico. The volume also includes a list of sixteen Roman imprints of the first half of the 16th century not included in F. Ascarelli's short title catalogue (see entry no. 854).

810 **Valerio Dorico: music printer in sixteenth-century Rome.** Suzanne G. Cusick. Ann Arbor, Michigan: UMI Research Press, 1981. 329p. bibliog. (Studies in Musicology, 43.)

Valerio Dorico, the publisher of the first editions of Palestrina's music, was the most important music printer in 16th-century Rome until the advent of Alessandro Gardano in 1583. He left a legacy of some 300 books and pamphlets. This study examines Dorico's role in the Roman music-printing milieu during his forty-year career. It begins with a general survey of printing in the city in the 16th century, followed by an examination of music printing, firstly multiple impression printing (expensive and laborious) and, from 1536, the single-impression printing invented by Pierre Attaingnant in 1528. It looks at the work of other music printers in Rome before 1527 – Andrea Antico, Giovanni Giacomo Pasoti, and Giacomo Giunta – and Antonio Blado and Antonio Barré, the other major music printers in the second half of the century. It finally focuses on the work of Dorico. A brief biographical sketch is followed by an examination of the mechanical, editorial and commercial aspects of Dorico's career as a music printer. He was responsible for over half the music output printed in Rome between 1550 and 1580; he was also the most versatile, his output comprising madrigals, polyphonic masses, and instrumental music. Composers whose works he printed include Orlando di Lasso, Palestrina, and Cristóbal de Morales. The study includes a bibliographical catalogue of Dorico's music output from 1526 to 1572. There is also an appendix giving the first lines of all pieces setting Italian texts printed by Dorico or his heirs.

Newspapers

811 Il Corriere laziale: giornale di informazione regionale. (The Lazio Post: a newspaper of regional information.)
Rome: Edilazio 92 Cooperativa, 1973- .
Published three times a week (Monday, Tuesday and Friday), this regional newspaper is noted for its extensive coverage of all types of sport – professional, amateur and youth. The Monday edition is dedicated to sport coverage, with reports on and results of all matches played in Lazio. The Tuesday edition, as well as sport, includes local news, politics, culture, and tourism. Finally, the Friday edition reviews the week's events and previews the weekend's sport. It can be viewed online at www.corrierelaziale.it .

812 Il Manifesto. (The Manifesto.)
Rome: Il Manifesto Cooperativa Editrice, 1971- .
A communist tabloid, published Tuesday to Sunday. It has a circulation of 84,913 and covers news, politics, economics, sport, the arts and entertainment. It can be viewed online at www.ilmanifesto.it .

813 Il Messaggero. (The Messenger.)
Rome: Società editrice il Messagero, 1878- .
Il Messaggero, founded in 1878, is the most popular daily Roman newspaper (it has a circulation of 250,000). It provides national and international news, articles on politics, economics and finance, culture, sport and entertainment. Its national edition has sections on *Roma città* and *Ostia, area metropolitana* covering issues of local interest. The paper also publishes editions for Lazio Nord, Rieti, Frosinone, Latina, Umbria, the Marche, Abruzzo, Civitavecchia and Littorale, each with its own regional news section. It has a substantial classified ads section on Thursdays and Sundays. It can be viewed online at www.ilmessaggero.it .

814 **Il "Messaggero" e la sua città: cento anni di storia.** (The "Messaggero" and its city: one hundred years of history.) Giuseppe Talamo. Florence, Italy: Felice le Monnier, 1979-91. 3 vols. (Quaderni di Storia diretti da Giovanni Spadolini.)

A history of the first one hundred years of one of Italy's oldest daily newspapers. *Il Messaggero* was founded by Luigi Cesana in 1878 and aimed to remain independent and become 'il giornale per tutti' ('the newspaper for all') – both by virtue of its low price and its publication of serialized novels, but also through its extensive coverage of local news, including famous trials, and debate of contemporary issues. In 1915, the paper was acquired by the company 'L'Editrice' (which was soon afterwards bought up by the Perrone family). The first volume of this work examines the paper's attitude, from its foundation until the First World War, to some important contemporary social issues – the role of parliamentary institutions, the 'social question' in the cities and the countryside, education, foreign policy and colonial expansion. The second volume covers the years between 1919 and 1946, during which the newspaper gradually lost its Roman character, becoming instead more 'national', in conformity with the requirements of the Fascist regime. The third volume discusses the post-war era up to the sale of the newspaper by the Perrone family in 1974, a period during which the paper's politics were those of the centre or centre-left parties.

815 **Il Tempo.** (Time.)
Rome: L'Editrice Romana, 1944- .

A daily broadsheet with a circulation of 84,913. It covers regional, national and international news, finance, politics, the arts, and sport.

816 **L'Unità.** (Unity.)
Rome: L'Arca Società Editrice, 1924- .

A tabloid-sized official newspaper of the Partito Democratico di Sinistra. It covers national and international news, finance, politics, and sport. It can be viewed online at www.unita.it .

Magazines

817 L'Evento Roma. (The event: Rome.)
Edited by Simonetta Bassi, Daniela Fiorelli, Maria Grazia Manni.
Rome: Comune di Roma, Ufficio Comunicazione, 1996- .
A bimonthly bilingual (in Italian and English) publication, giving information on exhibitions, art tours, music events, theatre, markets and fairs, and sport.

818 Roma c'è: il Manuale dela Settimana in Città. (Roma c'è: the manual of the week in the city.)
Rome: Villaggio Editoriale, 1994- .
This is a weekly guide published every Thursday. It has comprehensive listings for theatre, music, dance, film, museums and exhibitions, and nightlife. There is an English-language section.

819 Time Out Roma. (Time Out Rome.)
Rome: Rosabella, 1997- . weekly.
Published in the same format as the London publication (but without a 'lonely hearts' section), this weekly magazine has listings for art, cinema, dance, books, music (classical, rock, jazz, etc.), sport, theatre, television, gay and lesbian, and children, with numerous features and reviews. It is published every Thursday.

820 Wanted in Rome.
Rome: Società della Rotonda, 1985- . fortnightly.
This English-language magazine can be found on sale at many news-stands and international bookshops in Rome. As well as providing classified advertising, it publishes articles on cultural, political and social aspects of life in Rome. It also provides up-to-date listings of art, music, opera, dance, festivals, museum opening times, and news of local events organized by the international associations, schools and churches.

821 Where: Rome.
  Editor-in-Chief M. Angela Di Pietro.   Rome: Gary De Piante, 1995- .
  maps. monthly.
A free monthly publication in English, part of the Where International network. It contains features on cultural and other events, shopping, fashion, leisure and nightlife. There is an extensive section on restaurants, its listings being a mixture of advertisers as well as of establishments the editors judge worthy of attention. An 'Insider's guide to Rome' outlines the major sights and attractions and provides useful information on getting about the city.

Reviews and Periodicals

822 Capitolium Millennio: Rivista Bimestrale del Comune di Roma.
(Capitolium Millennium: a Bimonthly Review of the Comune of Rome.)
Rome: Fratelli Palombi, 1997- .

A relaunch, after a gap of twenty-one years, of *Capitolium*. Each issue concentrates on two or three subjects, which are discussed in several (usually five or six) articles by different contributors. Recent issues have included features on traffic and public transport, the colour of the buildings of Rome, the Esquiline as a changing quarter, and the Tiber. There are also book and exhibition reviews and editorials. The publication is richly illustrated in both colour and black and white.

823 Capitolium: Rassegna Mensile del Governorato di Roma.
(Capitolium: Monthly Review of the Governorate of Rome.)
Rome: Bestetti e Tumminelli, 1925-76. monthly.

Capitolium contained articles about all aspects of Rome, its history, and antiquities (their excavation and restoration), urban development (building projects, new streets, monuments, and fountains). It also reported on life in the city, important events, festivals and patriotic celebrations and commemorations, as well as on famous personalities. It also had a section about the administration of the city ('Cronache amministrative'). Between October 1935 and December 1936 *Capitolium* was replaced by a *Bollettino della Capitale*, which only provided information about municipal activities. From 1945 its subtitle changed to 'Rassegna Mensile del Comune di Roma'. Three general indexes, arranged by author and subject, were published in 1962 (for the years 1925-60), 1966 (for 1961-65) and 1976 (for 1966-76). These were compiled by Gaetana Scano and appeared as supplements to the review.

824 Catalogo dei periodici italiani. (Catalogue of Italian periodicals.)
Roberto Maini.   Milan, Italy: Editrice bibliografica, 1997 (latest edition).

This catalogue includes 13,760 current periodical titles. Each entry provides title and subtitle, starting date, frequency, print run, publisher and editor, and address. There is a place of publication index that lists 2,795 titles published in Lazio (2,550 in Rome). There is also a useful introductory survey of the periodical publishing industry in Italy, with numerous statistical charts.

825 Palatino: Rivista Romana di Cultura. (Palatine: Roman Review of Culture.)
Rome: Edizioni Palatino, 1957-68. quarterly.

This quarterly review of Roman literature, music, visual and performing arts, architecture and town planning was directed by Luigi Pallottino and its editorial board included Cesare D'Onofrio, Luigi Salerno, Manfredo Tafuri, and Enrico Crispolti. A typical issue would have two or three articles on each of the above subjects and also reviews of recent books, exhibitions, theatrical and musical performances.

826 Roma Moderna e Contemporanea: Rivista Interdisciplinare di Storia. (Modern and Contemporary Rome: an Interdisciplinary History Review.)
Directed by Giuseppe Talamo. Rome: Archivio Guido Izzi, 1993- . quarterly.

This includes articles on Rome and its history from the 15th to the 20th century. Each issue is divided into two sections: the first, and more extensive, section is dedicated to a special subject, discussed in five to six articles. To date, subjects have included: opera in Rome in the 17th and 18th century; history, literature and theatre in Rome in the 16th and 17th century; foreign visitors in Rome from the 16th to the 19th century; and architecture in Rome in the inter-war years. The second section includes articles on topics of current interest, reviews of recent publications and exhibitions as well as information about conferences and other cultural events.

827 L'Urbe: Rivista Romana. (L'Urbe: a Roman Review.)
Rome, 1927-88.

L'Urbe was founded in 1936 by Emma Amadei, Ceccarius, and Antonio Muñoz. It was directed by Muñoz between 1936-44 and 1947-59 (publication was suspended between 1944 and 1947). Ceccarius took over as director in 1960 to his death in 1972. A bibliography of his writings was published in the May-August 1972 issue of the review, pp. 60-76. The review published articles on the history, art, literature and folklore of Rome and included reviews of books and exhibitions about the city.

Encyclopaedias, Directories and Biographical Dictionaries

Encyclopaedias

828 Enciclopedia di Roma dalle origini all'anno Duemila. (Encyclopaedia of Rome from its origins to the year 2000.)
Edited by Caterina Napoleone.   Milan, Italy: Franco Maria Ricci, 1999. 1005p.

This is a lavishly produced encyclopaedia of the city and its people. It contains some 6,000 entries by 132 contributors. There are entries for historical events, monuments, works of art, newspapers and magazines, popular sayings, and hundreds of biographical entries for famous Romans – emperors, statesmen, artists and designers, scientists, actors, writers, as well as famous visitors to Rome. The volume includes 600 colour illustrations. There is also an introductory chapter, by Gianni Guadalupi, on the history of Rome.

829 Roma. (Rome.)
In: *Enciclopedia italiana di scienze, lettere ed arti.*   Rome: Istituto della Enciclopedia italiana fondata da Giovanni Treccani, 1936, vol. 29, p. 589-928.

This monographic entry is divided into the following sections: the name of the city; its physical geography; Ancient Rome; medieval Rome; Renaissance Rome; 17th- and 18th-century Rome; Rome from the end of the 18th century to 1870; Rome as the capital of Italy; and the idea of Rome. Each section is followed by a bibliography. The texts are accompanied by 107 plates.

830 Rome.
In: *The dictionary of art.*   London: Grove, 1996, vol. 26 (p. 747-925), vol. 27 (p. 1-116).

The entry for Rome in this dictionary provides a comprehensive examination of the city's history, urban development, architecture, and art. There are sections on: history (ancient and modern); urban development; art life and organization; centres of production (tapestry, marble inlay, furniture and design); buildings and monuments (divided into twenty-seven sub-headings

313

for individual sites, from Forum Romanum to Villa Albani); Accademia di S. Luca; and antiquarian revivals (spolia and re-use, sculpture gardens, descriptions). The heading for Ancient Rome follows that of Rome and covers both the city and the Roman Empire. It is divided into eleven sections, each with numerous subdivisions, as follows: introduction (history and geography, trade, patronage, religion, subject-matter); architecture; planning; sculpture; painting; mosaics; stucco; glass; metalwork; other arts (arms and armour, coins, furniture, ivory and bone, jewellery, lamps, leather, pottery, terracotta, textiles); and collections, museums, and exhibitions. Each section and sub-section is accompanied by a select bibliography compiled by the author of the article, reflecting the most important scholarship and international in scope. There is also an electronic version of the dictionary at http://www.groveart.com . Each article includes external image links, maps, charts and diagrams, and an index of related articles in the dictionary. The texts are also periodically updated.

Directories

831 Annuario regionale Lazio. (The Lazio regional yearbook.)
Rome: Guida Monaci, 1996 (latest edition).

The volume on Lazio is one of four volumes of *Annuari regionali* published by Guida Monaci. Like their parent publication, which has national coverage, each volume is divided into two sections – an index and a classified directory.

832 Duns 25,000: l'annuario delle maggiori società in Italia. (Duns 25,000: Italy's largest companies.)
Directed by Silvio Goglio.   Milan, Italy: Dun & Bradstreet, 2000. 20th ed. 1593p.

The companies are listed alphabetically and also by region. A total of 1,854 companies are listed for Lazio, of which 1,557 are in Rome.

833 Elenco ufficiale abbonati al telefono: rete di Roma. (Official list of telephone subscribers: Rome network.)
Turin: Pagine gialle, 1998 (latest edition). 2 vols. 3128p.

This is the Rome telephone directory, updated to 31 August 1998.

834 Guida degli archivi economici a Roma e nel Lazio. (A guide to the economic archives of Rome and Lazio.)
Edited by Maria Guercio.   Rome: Soprintendenza archivistica per il Lazio, 1987. 132p. (Ministero per i Beni Culturali e Ambientali. Quaderni della Rassegna degli Archivi di Stato, 54.)

The archives in this guide are divided into four categories: private operators, agencies that include state participation, public organizations, and municipal agencies. Each entry includes the address of the organization, its historical profile, and the contents of its archives (documentation, inventories, etc.). There are two appendices, the first giving information on the

Confederazione generale dell'indusria italiana (Confindustria) and the second a list of
companies that failed to provide information about their archives.

835   Guida Monaci.
Rome, Italy: Guida Monaci, 1870- . (latest edition 1998-99).

This annual directory started life as a commercial guide to Rome, later extending to Rome and
its province, Rome and Lazio, and finally the whole of Italy. It is in two volumes – an Index and
a Classified Directory. The Index is used to search for the information contained in the Classified
Directory; it contains an alphabetical listing of the various subject categories and indexes of
organizations and individuals. The Classified Directory is divided into an administrative and an
economy section. Though the information is not divided by geographical areas there are,
nevertheless, area subdivisions within each category (for example, Category 1211 covers the
Lazio Region, 1231 Provincial Administrations, 1235 Communal Administrations).

836   Kompass Italia: annuario generale dell'economia italiana. (Kompass
      Italy: general yearbook of the Italian economy.)
      Turin, Italy: Kompass Italia, [1962?]- . (latest edition 1999). 3 vols.

This business directory is in three volumes. Volumes one and two are arranged by sectors of
activity, with each sector subdivided into products and services. Volume three is arranged by
regions and provinces (from North to South) and contains detailed information on all the
companies mentioned in the other volumes. Each company's profile includes address,
telephone/fax/telex number, number of employees, turnover, and quality system certification.
The section for Latium (Lazio) is on p. 2035-2162 and that for the Province of Rome (Provincia
di Roma) on p. 2060-2156. The text is in Italian, English, French and German.

837   Pagine gialle Roma. (Rome yellow pages.)
      Turin, Italy: Pagine gialle, 1998 (latest edition). 2 vols. 2871p.

This edition of Rome's *Yellow Pages* is updated to 28 August 1998. It includes an index by
categories and a subject index divided into sixteen headings with sub-divisions.

Biographical dictionaries

838   Dizionario biografico degli italiani. (Biographical dictionary of the
      Italians.)
      Rome: Istituto dell'Enciclopedia Italiana, 1960- .

Volume 51 of this monumental, frustratingly slow to appear, but indispensable work was
published in 1998, reaching the name 'Gamba'.

Encyclopaedias, Directories and Biographical Dictionaries. Biographical dictionaries

839   Indice biografico italiano. (Italian biographical index.)
Edited by Tommaso Nappo.   Munich, Germany: K. G. Saur, 1997. (2nd cumulated and enlarged index). 7 vols.
This is an alphabetically arranged list of some 250,000 entries in the 1,700 microfiches of the accompanying *Archivio biografico italiano* and *Archivio biografico italiano, Nuova serie*. These were taken from 459 biographical reference works published between the 17th century and the middle of the 20th century.

840   La storia delle famiglie romane. (History of Roman families.)
Teodoro Amayden [Theodor Van Meyden], with notes and additions by Carlo Augusto Bertini.   Rome: Collegio Araldico (Istituto Araldico Romano), 1910. 2 vols. (463p., 255p.)
In his introductory note Bertini remarks on the scarcity of publications about Roman families, partly explained by the destruction of the Libro d'oro del Campidoglio during the 1848 revolution. A new volume commissioned by Pope Pius IX in 1853 and compiled by the Congregazione araldica capitolina only included families extant in 1853 and contained various inaccuracies, especially about coats-of-arms. Hence Bertini's decision to base this compilation on a more comprehensive work that included information on patrician families which, in several cases, had been extinct for centuries. This work is a codex in the Archivio Segreto Vaticano by Theodor Van Meyden (Teodoro Amayden), a Flemish lawyer working in Rome in the 17th century. The entries in this codex were copied from a manuscript in the Biblioteca Casanatense (no. 1335) but include additional material as a section of the original work was later removed from the manuscript in question (Fondo Barber. lat. n. 4902).

841   Who was who in the Roman world, 753 BC-AD 476.
Edited by Diana Bowder.   Oxford: Phaidon, 1980. 256p. maps.
A biographical reference work for the student and general reader of ancient Roman history and a collection of pictorial documentation consisting of portrait sculpture, coin portraits, maps, photographs of buildings constructed by, or associated with, individual persons (for example S. Maria Maggiore with Liberius, Bishop of Rome, who built the original Basilica Liberiana), and inscriptions. The dictionary includes all historical or cultural figures of importance. Most entries include a bibliographical reference to an ancient source or to a book for further reading. A chronological table and an outline history from 753 BC to the end of the Empire in the West in 476 AD are included. There is also a glossary and an index of persons mentioned but without an entry.

842   Who's who in Italy.
Edited by Giancarlo Colombo.   Bresso/Milan, Italy: Who's who in Italy, 1998 (latest edition). 3 vols.
Volumes one and two contain 8,500 concise personal profiles in the fields of politics, business, science, and the arts. Volume three contains Italian companies and institutions.

Bibliographies

General

843 Gli avvisi a stampa in Roma nel Cinquecento: bibliografia, antologia. (Printed proclamations in 16th-century Rome: a bibliography and anthology.)
Tullio Bulgarelli.   Rome: Istituto di studi romani, 1967. 227p.

The printed *avviso* was a special type of publication that developed during the 16th and 17th century, a precursor of the newspaper which supplanted it in the 18th century. *Avvisi* covered a variety of subject-matter – battles, conspiracies, festivals and processions, princely marriages, treaties, disasters and miraculous events – almost always concentrating on one particular event. The present work is a bibliography of 354 16th-century *avvisi* held by seven libraries in Rome (Biblioteca nazionale centrale di Roma, Biblioteca Angelica, Biblioteca Casanatense, Biblioteca Vallicelliana, Biblioteca Alessandrina, Biblioteca Vaticana, and Biblioteca Corsiniana). Most of these were printed in Rome and the selection was based on their value as first-hand accounts of particular events – discourses, poems, and lengthy philosophical and theological treatises were left out. The *avvisi* are listed by publication date, from 1526 to 1600. Each entry includes a transcription of the title-page or, in the absence of one, of other parts of the text containing dates, signatures and other useful bibliographical information. The publication also includes the full texts of twenty-two *avvisi*, their subjects ranging from descriptions of Christian triumphs against the infidel and executions of Protestants, to voyages to Peru and the death of Sir Francis Drake. There are thirty-two plates of title-pages.

844 The Baroque ceiling paintings in the churches of Rome, 1600-1750: a bibliography.
Robert England.   Hildesheim, Germany; New York: Georg Olms Verlag, 1979. 142p. (Studien zur Kunstgeschichte, Band 12.)

In his preface the author argues that, although there has been an explosion in Baroque studies since the Second World War, comparatively little work has been done on ceiling paintings. This he attributes to the dispersal of documentary information to various locations, which makes it difficult to access. This bibliography includes sections on contemporary guidebooks and lives of artists, iconography, and patrons, but the most substantial sections are those on individual painters and the churches.

845 **Bibliografia della festa barocca a Roma.** (Bibliography of Roman festivals of the Baroque era.)
Maurizio Fagiolo dell'Arco, edited by Rossella Pantanella. Rome: Antonio Pettini, 1994. 143p. (Biblioteca del Barocco, 1.)

A bibliography of some 600 works published between 1585 and 1721 related to Roman festivals. During the Baroque era, festivals were reflections of the policies of the papal and aristocratic families. The design and supervision of their costly ephemeral architectures and decorations involved the collaboration of the greatest architects, sculptors and painters, such as Bernini, Pietro da Cortona, Alessandro Algardi, Carlo Rainaldi, and Andrea Sacchi. The festivals covered include: ceremonies on the occasion of the election of a new pope (election, coronation, the procession of the *possesso*); religious festivals of the papal court (for example, canonizations, consecration of churches); solemn entries of foreign officials; *Quarantore* (the display of the Holy Sacrament in Jesuit churches during Carnival); secular ceremonies (coronations of sovereigns, royal births, victory celebrations); funeral ceremonies; Jubilee ceremonies; and ceremonies on the death of a pope. The libretto, published on these occasions, was extremely important as it commemorated the celebration and also elucidated the allegorical meaning of the decoration. Each entry includes indications of libraries (in Italy, Europe and the United States) which hold the work. Eighty-seven title-pages and frontispieces are illustrated.

846 **Bibliografia della Repubblica romana del 1798-1799.** (Bibliography of the Roman Republic of 1798-1799.)
Edited by Vittorio E. Giuntella. Rome: Istituto di studi romani, 1957. 238p.

This bibliography is in two parts, each divided into primary and secondary sources. Part one covers the French Revolution and the crisis of the temporal power of the church and is divided into ten subject areas: Europe and the Revolution, the French in Italy, Bonaparte and Italy, the generals of the Armée de Rome, the ministers of the Directory in Rome, Jacobin Italy, the Catholic Church and the revolution, the crisis of the temporal power of the church, Rome at the end of the 18th century, and the exile and death of Pius VI. Part two concentrates on the Roman Republic and is divided into fifteen subject headings: the Constitution, the Assembly, legislation, political writings, the polemics surrounding the republican oath and the legality of the appropriation of church property, the economic problem, French economic policies in Rome and the removal of works of art, life in Rome, the Departments, the military campaigns, the resurrection, other subjects, biographies, literary works inspired by the Roman Republic, and the iconography of the Republic. There are also two indices, of persons and place names, and of anonymous works.

847 **Bibliografia di Roma medievale e moderna.** (A bibliography of medieval and modern Rome.)
Francesco Cerroti, edited by Enrico Celani. Rome: Forzani, 1893. 603 columns.

The work of Francesco Cerroti, the librarian of the Corsiniana and Romana-Sarti libraries, was planned to be in four volumes. Having decided to leave out classical literature and archaeology, these were to cover: i) Church history; ii) topography; iii) art history and monuments; and iv) civil and municipal history, the geography of Rome, the Tiber and the

Campagna. Some 27,000 entries were compiled but Cerroti's untimely death in 1887 meant that only the first of the projected volumes was finally published. The bibliography contains 9,292 entries and includes monographs, articles, and manuscripts; it is divided into sections on church history; convents, monasteries, seminaries and confraternities; general biographies of the popes; biographies of individual popes; and the papal court and curia. Each entry includes author, title, imprint and, for manuscripts, the repository and shelfmark. Entries not seen by Cerroti or entered after his death are asterisked.

848 Bibliografia di teatri musicali italiani. (A bibliography of Italian lyric theatres.)
Alfredo Giovine.   Bari, Italy: Edizioni Fratelli Laterza, 1982. 67p.
(Biblioteca dell'Archivio delle Tradizioni Popolari Baresi.)
This bibliography includes thirty-five works, both monographs and periodical literature, on Roman theatres. Some are general works on theatrical life in Rome while others are about individual theatres, such as the Teatro Capranica, the Teatro dei Barberini or the Teatro di Tordinona.

849 Bibliografia di Tivoli. (A bibliography of Tivoli.)
Giuseppe Cascioli.   Tivoli, Italy: Società tiburtina di storia e d'arte, 1923. 146p. (Studi e Fonti per la Storia della Regione Tiburtina.)
In his introduction, the compiler points out some important i lei in the bibliography: writers of the Ancient Roman Republic and Empire (Strabo, Dionysius of Halicarnassus, Livy, Horace, Virgil, Statius), an extraordinarily large number of ancient inscriptions, works of the 12th and 13th century (after the town's recovery from the attacks of Totila), and the Renaissance. The bibliography is divided into two sections, the first listing manuscripts (in the Biblioteca Vaticana and other archives in Rome) and the second printed books.

850 Bibliografia generale di Roma. (General bibliography of Rome.)
Emilio Calvi.   Rome: Ermanno Loescher, 1906-12. 4 parts.
This bibliography of Rome from the Middle Ages to 1870 was planned to be in five volumes. It was intended to take up Cerroti's unfinished task of compiling an all-embracing bibliography of Rome. Volume one, which covers the Middle Ages (476-1499) and which was published in 1906 with a supplement and an *Appendix on the Catacombs and Churches of Rome* coming out in 1908, was completed. Volume two, part one, published in 1910, covers the 16th century (but does not include literature, art and topography), and volume five, part one, published in 1912, covers the Risorgimento up to 1846. Volumes three and four, which were intended to cover the 17th and 18th centuries, and the remaining parts of volumes two and five, were never published. The work, which includes both monographs and periodical literature, has a total of 11,282 entries (5,243 for the Middle Ages, 3,758 for the 16th century, and 2,281 for the Risorgimento).

851 Bibliografia romana. (Roman bibliography.)
Compiled by Laura Biancini (et al.).   In: *Roma ricerca e formazione*, anno 2 (1995-).
This annual bibliography includes monographs, periodical articles (of at least five pages), individual authors' contributions to collective works, and theses having as their subject Rome from the Middle Ages to the present. A number of different libraries in Rome contributed to this project, making use of a variety of sources. Nine different subject categories are used, each with numerous subdivisions. Not surprisingly for a city with such a rich artistic heritage, the greatest

number of entries is for visual arts. Four bibliographies have appeared to date, for the years 1994 to 1997, with a supplement for 1994-96, each containing *c.* 850 entries (though some titles appear in more than one subject category).

852 Bibliography of British and American travel in Italy to 1860.
R. S. Pine-Coffin.   Florence, Italy: Leo S. Olschki editore, 1974. 371p.
(Biblioteca di Bibliografia Italiana, 76.)

The introduction describes changing British attitudes to continental travel from the 16th to the mid-19th century. It also surveys the various stages of the journey – travel practicalities, routes by sea and land, established itineraries once in Italy (for example, Christmas and Easter in Rome), transport and lodgings, and the dangers of banditry. The travellers' reactions to the Italian social scene – the worldliness of the clergy, superstition, sumptuous ceremonials, public executions – are described, as are British reactions to art, music, theatre, opera, sport, and gardening. The bibliography is in three parts, the first containing first-hand accounts of Italy by British authors and English translations of foreign authors published in Great Britain, the second works by American authors, and the third travel literature (both contemporary sources and later works). Imaginative works in prose or verse, books of engravings (unless they contain substantial text), and works confined to particular interests (art, archaeology, religion, geology) are excluded. There are indexes of persons, anonymous titles, places, and publishers, printers and booksellers.

853 Biografie e bibliografie degli Accademici lincei. (Biographies and bibliographies of members of the Accademia dei Lincei.)
Edited by Roberto Ridolfi.   Rome: Accademia nazionale dei lincei, 1976. 1360p.

The proposal for a bio-bibliographical directory of the *Soci nazionali* (members) and the *Corrispondenti* (corresponding members) of the Accademia dei Lincei – one of the oldest and most famous academies in Italy – was made in 1969 and was intended to celebrate the centenary of the Academy's transformation into a national institution in 1870. The enormity of the undertaking (the Academy has 180 members and 180 corresponding members) and the need to edit the information provided by each member delayed its publication, however, hence the decision to extend the bibliography to 1973. The directory is divided into two sections: physical, mathematical and natural sciences (*scienze fisiche, matematiche e naturali*) on pp. 1-680; and historical and philological sciences (*scienze morali, storiche e filologiche*) on pp. 681-1319. Each entry includes a photograph of the Academician, a short biography and a chronological listing of his publications. There are over 20,000 bibliographical entries.

854 Le cinquecentine romane. (Sixteenth-century Roman imprints.)
Fernanda Ascarelli.   Milan, Italy: Editrice Etimar, 1972. 359p.

A short-title catalogue of *c.* 5,500 16th-century Roman imprints, mostly the holdings of fourteen libraries in Rome. Locations (which occasionally include other Italian and foreign libraries) are given for each entry. There is also an index of printers.

855 The Franklin H. Kissner collection of books on Rome, sold by order of the executors of the late Franklin H. Kissner.
London: Christie, Manson & Woods, Christie's South Kensington Ltd, 1990. 383p. bibliog.

Franklin H. Kissner (1909-88) had a lifelong devotion to Rome and was an avid collector of books and prints dealing with the art, history and literature of ancient, medieval and Baroque Rome. The sale of his library, which contained over 4,000 rare books, took place in London in three sessions between 3 and 5 October 1990. This catalogue provides full entries on the 1,129 lots and includes numerous illustrations from the works. Among the riches of the collection were a set of Lafreri's *Speculum Romanae magnificentiae* (1545-92), Piranesi's works, and an enormous number of early guidebooks.

856 Le guide di Roma: Materialen zu einer Geschichte der römischen Topographie. (Rome guides: materials for a history of the topography of Rome.)
Ludwig Schudt, Oskar Pollak. Vienna: Dr Benno Filser Verlag, 1930. 564p. (Quellenschriften zur Geschichte der Barock-Kunst in Rom.)

This bibliography, based on Oskar Pollak's card indexes, includes books concerned with Modern Rome and which have appeared since the invention of printing. It excludes medieval works and general works on Italy, even if the latter contain a substantial section on Rome. In his introduction, Schudt states that the bibliography is not aiming to be fully comprehensive but is intended as an overview and evaluation of the mass of material, and as a foundation for fuller works in the future. The arrangement is in seven main sections covering: guides, academic and topographical works, hagiological works, didactic works, foreign language guides, descriptions of Ancient Rome, and descriptions of individual churches, palaces, villas, squares, obelisks, fountains, and galleries. There is also a chronological index.

857 Guide e descrizioni di Roma dal XVI al XX secolo nella Biblioteca della Fondazione. (Guides and descriptions of Rome from the 16th to the 20th century in the library of the [Besso] Foundation.)
Edited by Gaetana Scano. Rome: Fondazione Marco Besso, 1992. 133p. (Collana della Fondazione Marco Besso, 19.)

This work includes 226 entries, ranging from the 16th century to the present. They are divided into two sequences: Ancient Rome (1-68) and Modern Rome (69-226). The arrangement within each sequence is chronological (facsimile reprints are entered under the date of the original publication). Each entry includes title-page information, bibliographical references and shelfmark. The name index includes authors, editors, translators, illustrators, and printers.

858 Italian civic pageantry in the High Renaissance: a descriptive bibliography of triumphal entries and selected other festivals for state occasions.
Bonner Mitchell. Florence, Italy: Leo S. Olschki, 1979. 186p. (Biblioteca di Bibliografia Italiana, 89.)

In his introduction the author discusses the importance of civic processions to the study of cultural history, pointing out that High Renaissance festivals are less well studied than those of later historical periods because of the comparative scarcity of surviving graphic material or music. There are, however, written accounts, including Latin inscriptions on *apparati* (ceremonial machinery), occasional verses and dramatic skits. The bibliography concentrates on festivals of a predominantly civic character, excluding those of a primarily sportive, religious or folkloric nature. It focuses on occasional and topical events such as investitures, marriages, and triumphal entries rather than annual celebrations. Ten festivals are listed for Rome, from the entry, in 1494, of Charles VIII of France (on his way to conquer the Kingdom of Naples), to the celebration for the election of Pope Julius III, a Roman pope, in 1550. Each individual festival is described in a summary that precedes the bibliographical references. These are divided into Sources (i.e. contemporary accounts) and Studies (post-1600 publications).

859 **La letteratura volgare e i dialetti di Roma e del Lazio: bibliografia di testi e degli studi.** (Vernacular literature and the dialects of Rome and Lazio: a bibliography of texts and studies.)
Paolo D'Achille, Claudio Giovanardi.   Rome: Bonacci, 1984- .

This is the first of a projected two-volume work which aims to provide a bibliography of works in the dialects of Rome and Lazio from the earliest times to the present. This volume covers the period up to 1550 and includes one of the earliest texts of Italian literature in the vernacular, the 9th-century Graffito in the Catacomb of Commodilla. It is divided into two parts: the first is a bibliography of texts in the vernacular and the second a bibliography of studies on the dialects of Lazio and their history and also of sociolinguistic studies. The second volume is planned to cover dialect texts written from *c.* 1550 to the present. The bibliography has 776 entries and includes both printed and manuscript texts. Entries include information on sources and, where appropriate, bibliographies. Part one is in two sections: the first covers Rome and is arranged by century with texts in Jewish-Italian dialects in an appendix. The second section is also arranged by century and is further subdivided into linguistic areas – southern Lazio (Cassino-Ciociara), Viterbo, Sabine area, and the central area (including the Province of Rome). Part two is in seven sections: Lazio; Rome (including Jewish-Italian dialect); Province of Rome; Province of Frosinone; Province of Latina; Province of Rieti; and Province of Viterbo. The arrangement within each section is as follows: bibliographies; general aspects (histories of language or literature); and special aspects (phonetics, morphology and syntax, dictionaries and etymology, personal and place names).

860 **Le livre à figures italien, depuis 1467 jusqu'à 1530: essai de sa bibliographie et de son histoire.** (The Italian illustrated book from 1467 to 1530: a bibliography and a history.)
Max Sander.   Milan, Italy: Ulrich Hoepli, 1942. 6 vols.

Volumes one to three contain a bibliography of 7,757 books, with 358 additional items. Volume four includes various indices and an essay giving a general history of the printing of illustrated books during this period, followed by sections discussing the special features of the book production of individual publishing centres in Italy. The section on Rome points out that book production in the city during the 15th century was almost entirely monopolized by German printers (for example, Pannarz & Sweynheym) who commissioned woodcuts from their compatriots, hence the prominence of the Gothic-German style in Roman imprints, tempered by Italian Renaissance influences. It also discusses special types of books such as the *Mirabilia Urbis Romæ* (popular pilgrims' guides to ancient and modern Rome), the *Indulgentiae* (lists of the indulgences given at each church in Rome), and books of portraits of saints. Volumes five and six contain 868 plates, Roman imprints being nos. 747-816. A supplement to this monumental work, with numerous additions and corrections, was compiled by Carlo Enrico Rava and published in 1969, also by Hoepli.

861 Die "Mirabilia Romae": untersuchungen zu ihrer überlieferung mit edition der deutschen und niederländischen texte. (The "Mirabilia Romae": studies in their transmission with an edition of the German and Dutch texts.) Nine Robijntje Miedema. Tübingen, Germany: Niemeyer, 1996. 589p. bibliog. (Münchener Texte und Untersuschungen zur Deutschen Literatur des Mittelalters, vol. 108.)

Four types of texts are usually described as *Mirabilia Romae* (The marvels of Rome) – *Historia et descriptio Urbis Romae* (History and description of the city of Rome), *Indulgentiae ecclesiarum urbis Romae* (Church indulgences of the city of Rome), *Stationes ecclesiarum urbis Romae* (Stations of the churches of the city of Rome), and the actual *Mirabilia Romae*. Only the last is a description of Rome, the others being guides for pilgrims. This study concentrates on the medieval German and Dutch translations of *Mirabilia Romae*, including the other three only with regard to their transmission. There are separate lists of Latin, German, and Dutch manuscript and printed editions of all four types of work as well as an overview of scholarly editions from the 19th century onwards. Later chapters concentrate more exclusively on the true *Mirabilia*, providing editions of three versions of the text: one is a 'short' version in German and Dutch, one a 'long' version in German (both versions are compared to the Latin original), and one from a manuscript in German only. Each version has a separate commentary. The last two chapters look at the designation of the *Mirabilia* (by genre) and its secondary reception in various types of literature (chronicles, travel literature, sermons, etc.).

862 Notiziario bibliografico di Roma e Suburbio, 1961-1980. (Bibliographical notices on Rome and its environs, 1961-1980.) Edited by Università di Roma I, Istituto di topografia antica. *Bullettino della Commissione Archeologica Comunale di Roma*, vol. lxxxix, no. 2 (1984), p. 305-476.

This comprehensive bibliography of Roman antiquities and archaeology is divided into two sections: Rome, and Suburbio & Roman Campagna. The entries for Rome are subdivided into: generalities (which include bibliographies, architecture and construction techniques); the history of the city, from its origins to the post-classical era; population and administration; monuments; and topography. Most entries are accompanied by an abstract.

863 Notiziario di scavi, scoperte, e studi intorno alle antichità di Roma e Campagna Romana, 1946-1960. (Notices on excavations, discoveries, and studies about the antiquities of Rome and the Roman Campagna, 1946-1960.) Edited by F. Castagnoli (et al.). *Bullettino della Commissione Archeologica Comunale di Roma*, vol. lxxxiii (1972-73), p. 1-156.

A comprehensive bibliography on the archaeology of Rome. It is in three sections: i) Rome (subdivided into generalities, monuments listed by type, and topography according to the Augustan regions); ii) Environs (Suburbio) and Roman Campagna; and iii) Ostia and Portus Romae. Most of the entries are accompanied by an abstract.

864 Roma bibliografica: cinque anni di bibliografia romana, 1989-1994.
(Bibliographic Rome: five years of Roman bibliography, 1989-1994).
Edited by Emilio Piccioni. Rome: Mortimer, 1995. 401p.

This is a supplement to the bibliography published in 1989, though it adopts a slightly different presentation. The subject headings have been reduced from fifty to thirty-one and are divided into four general chapters – Ancient Rome, Mediaeval and Renaissance Rome, Modern and Contemporary Rome, and *Varia* (eleven headings which range from folklore and tourist guides to museums, churches and the Vatican). It also covers works about the Etruscans and Lazio (which were not included in the earlier volume). There is an author and title index but, unfortunately, the subject index has been dropped.

865 Roma bibliografica: trent'anni di bibliografia romana, 1959-1988.
(Bibliographic Rome: thirty years of Roman bibliography, 1959-1988.)
Edited by Emilio Piccioni. Rome: Centro editoriale internazionale, 1989. 634p.

A bibliography of *c*. 9,000 monographs published between 1959 and 1988 having as their subject the city of Rome, ancient and modern. It includes Roman law and religion even though they are not limited to the city itself. Sources used were the catalogue of the Library of Congress and various national bibliographies (for foreign publications) and the *Bibliografia nazionale italiana* (for Italian publications). The entries are divided into fifty subject headings and are supplemented by author, title and subject indexes.

866 Rome: a bibliography from the invention of printing through 1899. Vol. 1. The guide books.
Sergio Rossetti. [Florence, Italy]: Leo S. Olschki, 2000. 306p.
(Biblioteca di Bibliografia Italiana, 157.)

This bibliography, which is planned to be in three volumes, will contain approximately 10,000 entries of works about Rome published from the beginning of printing to 1900. Its compilation involved a systematic examination of over 100 bibliographies and library catalogues, and the collaboration of numerous Roman libraries and antiquarian booksellers. The bibliography does not include: manuscripts; geographical charts and maps; journals, periodicals and abstracts from periodicals; engravings or woodcut illustrations without a title page; papal bulls and briefs, decrees, edicts, proclamations, indulgences, speeches, *motu propria,* leaflets, musical texts; orations and speeches of a purely religious nature (unless they concern directly the city of Rome); or works only indirectly associated with Rome (unless they contain chapters or illustrations of particular interest). The first volume of the bibliography is dedicated to guidebooks because of their great importance in the history of publications about Rome. It contains over 2,400 titles (among them 150 incunabula and over 1,000 titles not included in Schudt's catalogue) listed in chronological order. The entries include the acronyms of libraries with copies of the work in Rome and also information on holding libraries taken from the National Union Catalogue. The catalogue is preceded by an essay by Laura Biancini discussing the development of guidebooks during this period and the variety of their compilers.

867 Saggio di bibliografia ragionata delle piante icnografiche e prospettiche di Roma, dal 1551 al 1748. (An annotated bibliography of ground-plans and perspective maps of Rome, from 1551 to 1748.) Christian Huelsen. Florence, Italy: Leo S. Olschki, 1933. 122p.

This is a catalogue of twenty-eight maps with all their copies and variants. There is a chronological index of all the maps that can be dated and an index of proper names mentioned in the text.

868 Saggio di bibliografia romana. (Roman bibliography.) Ceccarius. Rome: Staderini, 1946-68. 12 vols. (Collana dei Romanisti.)

This Roman bibliography compiled by the noted *romanista* Ceccarius (Giuseppe Ceccarelli) began publication in 1943 as a supplement ('Largo ai romanisti') to the *Strenna dei romanisti* before it started appearing as a separate volume under this title. From volume four, its title changed into *Bibliografia romana* and from volume seven its publication came under the auspices of the Istituto di studi romani. Each volume is divided into subject areas (between 100 and 150) arranged alphabetically (from 'Accademie' to 'Vita religiosa'). Entries include monographs, and periodical and newspaper literature. Several entries are accompanied by bibliographical references, extracts from newspaper articles and other useful information. The last volume, published in 1967, covers the years 1956 and 1957. Ceccarius died in 1972 and this bibliography was his greatest achievement. Ceccarius's subject index cards of this bibliography were donated to the Biblioteca nazionale centrale 'Vittorio Emanuele II', together with 100,000 newspaper cuttings, over 3,000 monographs, and hundreds of periodical runs also donated to the library.

869 La stampa cattolica a Roma dal 1870 al 1915. (The Catholic press in Rome from 1870 to 1915.) Francesco Malgeri. Brescia, Italy: Morcelliana, 1965. 367p. (Biblioteca di Storia Contemporanea. Sez. 1. Il Movimento Cattolico in Italia e in Europa, 11.)

In his introductory note the compiler divides the period under consideration into four parts. The first of these, described as the 'heroic' era of the Catholic press, extends from 1870 to the death of Pope Pius IX in 1878. It was characterized by a proliferation of ferociously anti-liberal and intransigent newspapers which viewed the new political regime as the usurper of papal power and expected that a return to the pre-1870 status quo was imminent (hence the description of this period as 'the era of illusions'). *Romano di Roma*, *Voce della Verità*, *Frusta*, and *Lima* are typical exponents of this tendency. The second period saw the emergence of new, more conciliatory publications (*Le Moniteur de Rome*, *L'Aurora*, *Il Mattino*) reflecting the policies of the first years of Pope Leo XIII's pontificate. The third period saw the advent of Christian Democracy at the end of the century as an autonomous political force and, finally, the last ten years under consideration marked the decline of the old intransigent papers and the emergence of new tendencies favouring Catholic participation in political elections. The bibliography is not limited to political publications; it also includes religious and literary ones, as well as official bulletins of Catholic societies and associations. It omits, however, parish bulletins, publications of an exclusively religious nature and *L'Osservatore romano*. There are 105 entries arranged in strictly chronological order; their length varies depending on the importance of each publication, but they all provide a historical profile, lists of contributors, and a discussion of its political orientation and special features.

870 La stampa periodica romana dal 1900 al 1926 – scienze morali, storiche e filologiche. (Roman periodical publications from 1900 to 1926 – social sciences, history and literature.)
Olga Majolo Molinari, introduction by Fiorella Bartoncini. Rome: Istituto di studi romani, 1977. 2 vols. (1063p.) bibliog.

This bibliography continues the same compiler's work on 19th-century Roman periodicals. The period examined is the first quarter of the 20th century, up to the imposition of the fascist laws of 31 December 1925 (nos. 2307-09) that suppressed the freedom of the press. As the subtitle indicates, the subjects covered are humanities and social sciences, leaving out science and technical literature. Daily newspapers, reviews, bulletins and supplements are included. There are 726 titles, 592 of which have descriptive entries (the other 134 are references to entries in the earlier bibliography). Each entry is in two sections, the first giving bibliographical information (title, subtitle, dates, format, publisher, printer, owner, editor, frequency and price, holding libraries in Italy), and the second providing a historical profile of the publication, outlining its political, ideological, cultural and religious orientation, describing its contents and giving significant dates and events of its history. There are chronological, subject (grouping the periodicals in thirty-two categories), and name (with over 11,000 personal and institutional names) indexes, as well as a bibliography of 350 works about individual periodicals.

871 La stampa periodica romana dell'Ottocento. (Nineteenth-century Roman periodicals.)
Olga Majolo Molinari. Rome: Istituto di studi romani, 1963. 2 vols. 1188p. bibliog.

The introduction to this catalogue is a major study on 19th-century Roman periodical literature. It provides a detailed survey of newspapers and periodicals (both political and cultural) published before 1870, when there was a small number of publications in Rome, of a limited subject range and subject to censorship, and the proliferation of titles after 1870, catering for the interests of the much larger reading public of the new capital. The catalogue contains 1,703 entries. Each entry is in two sections, the first giving bibliographical information (title, subtitle, dates, format, publisher, printer, owner, editor, frequency and price, and holding libraries in Italy), and the second providing a historical profile of the publication, outlining its political, ideological, cultural and religious orientation, describing its contents and giving significant dates and events of its history. There are chronological, subject, and name (personal and institutional) indices. The chronological index begins with a newspaper that started in 1717. Unlike Majolo's volumes for the period 1900 to 1926 which exclude science, the present work includes all subjects.

872 La stampa periodica romana durante il fascismo, 1927-1943. (Roman periodicals of the Fascist era, 1927-1943.)
Edited by Filippo Mazzonis. Rome: Istituto nazionale di studi romani, 1998. 2 vols. 814p.

Chronologically this work is a continuation of the two bibliographies by Olga Majolo Molinari (see entry nos. 870 and 871), which covered the 19th and the first quarter of the 20th century. Its structure and contents, though, are different. Wanting to provide an all-embracing overview of daily and weekly publications in Rome during this period, it has a wider subject coverage including science and types of publications such as official publications, almanacs, *strenne* (gift books), and calendars, that were left out by Majolo Molinari. It consequently has a much larger number of entries (3,140 compared to the 726 for the period 1900-1926) containing summary information about each publication as opposed to the detailed descriptions and critical commentaries contained in the Majolo Molinari entries. There are, instead, thirteen long essays by different contributors, each dealing with a different subject or type of material – literature, art, science, law, politics, women's reviews, architecture and urbanism, education, official publications, cinema and theatre, agriculture, the armed forces and colonies, and trade unions. These occupy the first of the two volumes while the second is taken by the bibliography. Each entry contains: title, subtitle, author, run, format, number of pages, printer, notes, and holding libraries. There are separate indices to personal and institutional authors and a list of libraries with their acronyms.

873 **Viaggiatori italiani in Italia, 1700-1998.** (Italian travellers in Italy, 1700-1998.)
Luca Clerici.   Milan, Italy: Edizioni Sylvestre Bonnard, 1999. 405p.

This bibliography aims to dispel the cliché that Italians are no great travellers in their own country. It contains 1,828 works, which include several unpublished manuscripts, listed chronologically. Many entries are accompanied by an abstract providing bibliographical information about the work. There is also an author index which includes succinct biographies and a place index. 180 entries relate to Rome and a further 23 to its Province.

874 **Viaggiatori tedeschi in Italia, 1452-1870: saggio bibliografico.**
(German travellers in Italy, 1452-1870: a bibliographical essay.)
Lucia Tresoldi.   Rome: Bulzoni, 1975-77. 2 vols. bibliog.

This bibliography includes printed books by German writers or written in German which include descriptions of the journey to Italy from the middle of the 15th century to the unification of Italy. The works come from the collections of two libraries in Rome: the Biblioteca Hertziana and the Biblioteca dell'Istituto di archeologia e di storia dell'arte. As the compiler points out in the introduction, the journey to Italy was often a journey whose destination was Rome and it is, perhaps, for this reason that Roman library collections have extremely rich holdings of travel literature. The authors of the works are arranged chronologically by the date of their journey (not by the date of publication of the work) and each entry includes brief biographical notes related to the journey. Each century is introduced by a brief note discussing the reasons for undertaking the journey during the period in question and giving an overview of the descriptions. The bibliography contains 243 entries. There are numerous plates of frontispieces, title-pages, etc.

Library catalogues

875 **Biblioteca teatrale dal '500 al '700: la raccolta della Biblioteca Casanatense.** (A theatrical library between 1500 and 1800: the collection of the Biblioteca Casanatense.)
Laura Cairo, Piccarda Quilici.   Rome: Bulzoni, 1981. 2 vols. 785p.
(Il Bibliotecario, no. 5.)

When the Biblioteca Casanatense became a State library in 1884, its holdings of theatrical literature were grouped together and an inventory was prepared. The compilation of a special catalogue was also begun but was left unfinished while, in the meantime, the collection was enriched by new acquisitions. The compilers of this work re-catalogued the 1,500 items in the collection, to which they added another 1,500 which were kept in other parts of the library. The catalogue has 4,351 entries and covers all Italian imprints from 1500 to 1800. It includes all theatrical genres that flourished during the Renaissance and Baroque periods – comedies, tragedies, pastoral dramas, oratorios, cantatas, serenatas, and theatrical festivals. The main entries (arranged by title) are supplemented by the following indices: author, dedicatees and patrons, composers (including orchestra directors and chorus masters), stage designers (and also choreographers, costume designers, dance masters, actors, singers, impresarios), place of performance (followed by date of first performance if the place is not known), place of publication (under which are listed printers, publishers and booksellers) and, finally, a name index of printers, publishers, and booksellers.

876 **Catalogo collettivo dei periodici di archeologia e storia dell'arte.**
(Union catalogue of archaeology and art history periodicals.)
Edited by Rosalba Grosso and Antonella Aquilina. Rome: Biblioteca dell'Istituto nazionale di archeologia e storia dell'arte, 1992. 213p.

A union catalogue of current and retrospective periodical holdings in art and archaeology of the following libraries in Rome: Biblioteca dell'Istituto nazionale di archeologia e storia dell'arte, Bibliotheca Hertziana, Deutsches Archaeologisches Institut, and the Bibliothèque de l'École française. As well as serials, the catalogue also includes monographic series (for example, the various series published by the Accademia nazionale dei Lincei). There are 6,748 entries giving title and subsequent changes of title, place of publication, and library holdings.

877 **Catalogo dei periodici [della Biblioteca Casanatense].** (Periodicals catalogue [of the Biblioteca Casanatense].)
Alfredo Donato, Paola Urbani, introduction by Giuseppe Ricuperati.
Rome: Istituto poligrafico e zecca dello stato, 1988. 279p.

This catalogue is the result of a recent re-cataloguing of the periodical holdings of the Biblioteca Casanatense, which led to the recovery of *c*. 300 titles, some of them previously uncatalogued, others not easy to find in earlier catalogues as they were not entered under title. The library is extremely rich in 17th- and 18th-century scholarly journals, not only in Italian but also in French, German, Dutch and English. The main section of the catalogue contains the entries for general periodicals, with a separate listing for almanacs, prognostications, *strenne* (gift books), and *lunari* (almanacs). Each entry includes title and subsequent changes of title, place of publication, dates held by the library, and (for pre-19th-century publications) editors' names. There are author, date, subject, and place indices. The catalogue is embellished by numerous plates of title-pages.

878 **Catalogo dei periodici esistenti in biblioteche di Roma.** (Catalogue of periodicals in Roman libraries.)
Rome: Unione internazionale degli istituti di archeologia, storia e storia dell'arte in Roma, 1985. 3rd ed. 1438p.

A union catalogue of 17,418 periodical titles held in thirty-eight libraries in Rome. The names, acronyms, addresses, opening hours, conditions of use, and summer closures of participating institutions are given before the catalogue section. Each catalogue entry includes the title of the periodical, the acronyms of holding libraries and the extent of their runs.

879 **Catalogo delle edizioni di testi classici esistenti nelle biblioteche degli istituti stranieri di Roma.** (Catalogue of editions of classical texts held by the libraries of the foreign institutes in Rome.)
Rome: Unione internazionale degli istituti di archeologia, storia e storia dell'arte in Roma, 1969. 563p.

This union catalogue of editions of classical texts contains the holdings of eighteen libraries in Rome. It includes texts written up to the end of the patristic period, i.e. to the death of St John of Damascus in 749 (for the East) and St Isidore of Seville in 636 (for the West). It includes literary texts and also texts of a different nature (epigraphy, law) which have become part of the classical literary tradition. The catalogue provides bibliographical information taken from the title page of each item. Names of authors are given in their Latin forms. The sequence under each author is: complete works, single works in alphabetical order, fragments, and supposititious works. Different editions of the same work are arranged chronologically, by date of publication. The names of editors are given after the date of publication (or, if in a collection of texts, the abbreviated title of the publication) and are followed by the acronyms of the holding libraries. There is a list of abbreviations used for periodicals and collections of texts.

880 **I codici latini di Niccolò V: edizione degli inventari e identificazione dei manoscritti.** (The Latin codices of Nicholas V: an edition of the inventories and identification of the manuscripts.)
Antonio Manfredi. Vatican City: Biblioteca apostolica vaticana, 1994. 631p. (Studi e Testi, 359. Studi e Documenti sulla Formazione della Biblioteca Apostolica Vaticana, 1.)

This is the catalogue of 824 Latin codices in the Vatican library collected by Pope Nicholas V (1447-55). A bibliophile and a scholar, Nicholas V was one of the great humanist popes, and the introductory studies to this catalogue reassert the traditional view that he was the founder of the Vatican library against recent claims in favour of Sixtus IV (1471-84). During the eight years of his pontificate, Nicholas collected some 1,200 manuscripts which formed the basis of the library, later expanded by other popes, notably Sixtus IV who consolidated Nicholas's achievement and whose librarian, Bartolomeo Platina, reorganized the collections in the 1470s. The identification of the codices of Nicholas V included in this catalogue was based on inventories prepared after Nicholas's death and in the 16th century. Each catalogue entry includes a detailed description of the codex together with its description in previous inventories. There are numerous indices: names mentioned in the text, authors, *incipit*, provenance, and dated codices. The work also includes the inventory of the *Cubiculum* (with cross-references to their number in the catalogue proper), i.e. the fifty-six works that were kept in a small room for the private use of Nicholas V, later assimilated into the rest of the collections.

881 Guida alle raccolte fotografiche di Roma. (A guide to photographic collections in Rome.)
Rome: Unione internazionale degli istituti di archeologia, storia e storia dell'arte in Roma, 1980. 116p.

The ninety-one collections included in this guide are divided into eleven sections: the first three are those of various institutions in subdivisions of the Ministero per i beni culturali e ambientali – Biblioteche e archivi, Soprintendenze e musei, and independent institutes; the other eight sections are: Ministero della Difesa-Ministero dei Trasporti; the Università degli studi; Academies and cultural institutes; the Comune; Private collections; Foreign Institutes; Various other institutions; and Vatican City-Vatican Cultural Institutes-Religious organisations. Each entry contains practical information (admission, opening hours) and details about subject coverage, type of material (negative, positive, slides), numbers, arrangement and classification, and bibliography.

Indexes

There follow three separate indexes: authors (personal or corporate); titles; and subjects. Title entries are italicized and refer either to the main titles, or to other works cited in the annotations. The numbers refer to bibliographical entry rather than page number. Individual index entries are arranged in alphabetical sequence.

Index of Authors

Index of Titles

358

Index of Subjects

G

Gabinetto disegni e stampe degli Uffizi 170, 346
Gabinetto fotografico nazionale 166
Gabinetto nazionale delle stampe 605, 806
Gadda, C. E. 401, 416
Galassi Paluzzi, C. 3, 691
Galilei, A. 651, 701
Galilei, G. 378, 800
trial 378
Galleria Farnese see Palaces: Palazzo Farnese
Galli-Bibiena, A. 742
Galli-Bibiena, F. 588, 742
Galuppi, B. 742
Galzerani, G. 733
Games 772
Gardano, A. 810
Garden sculpture 367
Gardens 289, 338, 354-55, 367
Borghese 354, 662
Bosco Parrasio 741
of villas 354
Orti Farnesiani 355
Pincian 354
Villa d'Este 681
Gargiolli, G. 166
Garibaldi, G. 271-72
Gasparini, F. 742
Gates 8, 21, 156
Gauffier, L. 124
Gaulli, G. B. (il Baciccio) 492, 507, 522, 606, 696
Gautier, T. 98
Gell, W. 564
Genga, G. 664
Gentile da Fabriano 149, 701
Gentileschi, A. 472, 478
in fiction 472, 762

Gentileschi, O. 470, 472, 478, 606
Geology 16
Géricault, T. 569
German occupation 282, 285, 295
Gherardi, J. 799
German College see Collegio Germanico
Ghetto 8, 89, 109, 260, 280-81, 593
demolitions 289
legends 762
Mercatello 326
Ghéon, H. 87
Ghezzi, G. 510, 526
Ghezzi, P. L. 176, 510, 721
Ghezzi, S. 526
Ghirlandaio, D. 500, 562, 615
Ghirri, L. 11
Giardini family 539
Giardoni family 539
Giardoni, F. 599
Gibbon, E. 113, 219
Gifford, S. R. 101
Gigli, G. 261
Gill, C. 476
Gimignani, G. 455
Ginzburg, N. 401
Giobbe, N. 586
Giordano, L. 478
Giotto, 501, 511, 701
Giovanni da Udine 545
Giovannini, G. B. 618
Giovannoni, G. 342
Girandola 97
Giunta, G. 810
Giustiniani, V. 479, 481, 484, 508
collection of paintings and sculptures 509
Gladiators 148
Gluck, C. W. 736
Gnoli, D. 773
Goethe, J. C. 119

Goethe, J. W. 86, 95, 422, 471, 572, 602, 739, 741
Goethe-Nationalmuseum (Weimar) 119
Golden House of Nero see Domus Aurea
Goldoni, C. 739, 741
Goldschmidt, B. 238
Goncourt, E. de
Madame Gervaisais 120
Goncourt, J. de
Madame Gervaisais 120
Goudt, H. 467
Gounod, C. 110
Governorato 286
Gozzoli, B. 33, 149
Gracchus, Tiberius Sempronius 221
Gradwell, R. 324
Graeco-Roman controversy 587
Grahn, L. 733
Gramatica, E. 736
Grand Tour 95, 116, 497, 513, 565, 583
Granet, F.-M. 207, 573, 584
Graphia Aureae Urbis Romae 77, 111
Gray, R. 620
Gregorini, D. 654
Gregorius, Master 89
De Mirabilibus Urbis Romae 89, 102
Greek College in Rome see Collegio Pontifico Greco
Gregorovius, F. 6, 232, 277
Greuter, M. 31
Grifo, L. 799
Grimaldi, G. F. 129, 522
Grisi, C. 733
Grotesque ornament 187, 545, 564
Grottaferrata, Abbazia di 489

369

370

Villas 125, 338, 667, 670,
676, 688
Albani 123, 130, 141,
192, 354, 667
collections of ancient
sculpture 165
gardens 741
Aldobrandini 354, 680
Borghese 10, 513, 534,
586, 603, 662
Casina del Raffaello 577
Corsini ai Quattro Venti
355
D'Este 158, 367, 676, 681
Di Livia a Prima Porta
619
Doria-Pamphilj 355, 530
collections of
antiquities 129
Farnese (Caprarola) 494,
676
Farnesina 123, 354, 451,
499, 518, 682, 745
Hadrian's Villa 157-59,
171, 176, 340, 748
restoration 159
Lante 160, 493
Lante (Bagnaia) 676
Ludovisi 8, 145, 355
Casino dell'Aurora 577
Madama 493, 649, 651
Mattei 354-55, 564
Medici 104, 110, 118,
354, 466, 497, 577,
685-87, 712, 784
Mills 74, 629
Peretti Montalto 330, 619

Poniatowski 660
sale and redevelopment
286, 289, 351
Spada see Villas: Mattei
Viminal hill 187
Vinci, L. 742
Viola, G. B. 489
Virgil 167, 226
Aeneid 138
Visconti, E. Q. 113, 425
Visconti, L. 734, 757
Vite de' pittori, scultori e
architetti moderni 515,
702
Vitelli family 680
Viti, T. 519
Viviani, A. 671
Volpato, G. 176, 565, 574,
591
Vouet, S. 455, 478, 515,
606, 689
Vulpius, C. 422

W

Wagner, R. 229, 711, 736
Waldheim, K. 307
Walls 2, 8, 21, 156, 182,
465, 595, 661
Aurelian Wall 637, 661
Leonine Wall 661
Servian Wall 135, 661
Warfare, Renaissance 254
Weaver, W. 401
Webster, J.
The white devil 390
Weddings 247

West, B. 101
Wilfrid, Saint 322
Wilson, R. 2, 567, 575
Winckelmann, J. J. 130,
153, 159, 165
Wines 770
Wiseman, N. 324
Wittel, G. van 568, 588,
621
Wittkower, R. 442
Wladislaw of Poland,
Prince 26
Wölfflin, H. 561

Y

Yourcenar M.
Les memoires d'Hadrien
159

Z

Zanazzo, G. 762
Zavattini, C. 749
Zeno, A. 742
Zino, P. F. 316
Zola, É. 105, 110, 803
Rome 120, 414
Zolli, I. 206, 307
Zoological Gardens 10,
290
Zuccaro, F. 473, 506, 664,
668, 681, 696
Zuccaro, T. 473, 506, 552,
668
Zucchi, J. 466, 476, 685,
687

ALSO FROM CLIO PRESS

INTERNATIONAL ORGANIZATIONS SERIES

Each volume in the International Organizations Series is either devoted to one specific organization, or to a number of different organizations operating in a particular region, or engaged in a specific field of activity. The scope of the series is wide ranging and includes intergovernmental organizations, international non-governmental organizations, and national bodies dealing with international issues. The series is aimed mainly at the English-speaker and each volume provides a selective, annotated, critical bibliography of the organization, or organizations, concerned. The bibliographies cover books, articles, pamphlets, directories, databases and theses and, wherever possible, attention is focused on material about the organizations rather than on the organizations' own publications. Notwithstanding this, the most important official publications, and guides to those publications, will be included. The views expressed in individual volumes, however, are not necessarily those of the publishers.

VOLUMES IN THE SERIES

1 *European Communities*, John Paxton
2 *Arab Regional Organizations*, Frank A. Clements
3 *Comecon: The Rise and Fall of an International Socialist Organization*, Jenny Brine
4 *International Monetary Fund*, Anne C. M. Salda
5 *The Commonwealth*, Patricia M. Larby and Harry Hannam
6 *The French Secret Services*, Martyn Cornick and Peter Morris

7 *Organization of African Unity*, Gordon Harris
8 *North Atlantic Treaty Organization*, Phil Williams
9 *World Bank*, Anne C. M. Salda
10 *United Nations System*, Jospeh P. Baratta
11 *Organization of American States*, David Sheinin
12 *The British Secret Services*, Philip H. J. Davies
13 *The Israeli Secret Services*, Frank A. Clements